Related Books of Interest

A Practical Guide to Trusted Computing

by David Challener, Kent Yoder, Ryan Catherman,
David Safford, and Leendert Van Doorn
ISBN: 0-13-239842-7

Every year, computer security threats become more
severe. Software alone can no longer adequately
defend against them: what's needed is secure
hardware. The Trusted Platform Module (TPM)
makes that possible by providing a complete,
open industry standard for implementing trusted
computing hardware subsystems in PCs. Already
available from virtually every leading PC manufacturer, TPM gives software professionals powerful
new ways to protect their customers. Now, there's
a start-to-finish guide for every software professional and security specialist who wants to utilize
this breakthrough security technology.

Authored by innovators who helped create TPM
and implement its leading-edge products, this
practical book covers all facets of TPM technology: what it can achieve, how it works, and how
to write applications for it. The authors offer deep,
real-world insights into both TPM and the Trusted
Computing Group (TCG) Software Stack. Then, to
demonstrate how TPM can solve many of today's
most challenging security problems, they present
four start-to-finish case studies, each with extensive C-based code examples.

Understanding DB2
Learning Visually with Examples, Second Edition

by Raul F. Chong, Xiaomei Wang, Michael Dang,
and Dwaine R. Snow
ISBN: 0-13-158018-3

IBM® DB2® 9 and DB2 9.5 provide breakthrough
capabilities for providing Information on Demand,
implementing Web services and Service Oriented
Architecture, and streamlining information management. *Understanding DB2: Learning Visually
with Examples, Second Edition*, is the easiest way
to master the latest versions of DB2 and apply their
full power to your business challenges.

Written by four IBM DB2 experts, this book
introduces key concepts with dozens of examples
drawn from the authors' experience working
with DB2 in enterprise environments. Thoroughly
updated for DB2 9.5, it covers new innovations
ranging from manageability to performance and
XML support to API integration. Each concept is
presented with easy-to-understand screenshots,
diagrams, charts, and tables. This book is for
everyone who works with DB2: database administrators, system administrators, developers, and
consultants. With hundreds of well-designed review
questions and answers, it will also help professionals prepare for the IBM DB2 Certification Exams
730, 731, or 736.

 Listen to the author's podcast at:
ibmpressbooks.com/podcasts

Related Books of Interest

Implementing ITIL Configuration Management

by Larry Klosterboer
ISBN: 0-13-242593-9

The IT Infrastructure Library® (ITIL®) helps you make better technology choices, manages IT more effectively, and drives greater business value from all your IT investments. The core of ITIL is configuration management: the discipline of identifying, tracking, and controlling your IT environment's diverse components to gain accurate and timely information for better decision-making.

Now, there's a practical, start-to-finish guide to ITIL configuration management for every IT leader, manager, and practitioner. ITIL-certified architect and solutions provider Larry Klosterboer helps you establish a clear roadmap for success, customize standard processes to your unique needs, and avoid the pitfalls that stand in your way. You'll learn how to plan your implementation, deploy tools and processes, administer ongoing configuration management tasks, refine ITIL information, and leverage it for competitive advantage. Throughout, Klosterboer demystifies ITIL's jargon and illuminates each technique with real-world advice and examples.

 Listen to the author's podcast at:
ibmpressbooks.com/podcasts

RFID Sourcebook

by Sandip Lahiri
ISBN: 0-13-185137-3

Approaching crucial decisions about Radio Frequency Identification (RFID) technology? This book will help you make choices that maximize the business value of RFID technology and minimize its risks. IBM's Sandip Lahiri, an experienced RFID solution architect, presents up-to-the-minute insight for evaluating RFID; defining optimal strategies, blueprints, and timetables; and deploying systems that deliver what they promise.

Drawing on his experience, Lahiri offers candid assessments of RFID's potential advantages, its technical capabilities and limitations, and its business process implications. He identifies pitfalls that have tripped up early adopters, and shows how to overcome or work around them. This must-have resource can also act as a reference guide to any nontechnical person who wants to know about the technology.

From building business cases to testing tags, this book shares powerful insights into virtually every issue you're likely to face. Whatever your role in RFID strategy, planning, or execution, have Sandip Lahiri's experience and knowledge on your side: You'll dramatically improve your odds of success.

IBM Press™

Visit ibmpressbooks.com
for all product information

Related Books of Interest

Mainframe Basics for Security Professionals:
Getting Started with RACF

by Ori Pomerantz, Barbara Vander Weele,
Mark Nelson, and Tim Hahn
ISBN: 0-13-173856-9

For over 40 years, the IBM mainframe has been
the backbone of the world's largest enterprises.
If you're coming to the IBM System z® mainframe
platform from UNIX®, Linux®, or Windows®, you
need practical guidance on leveraging its unique
security capabilities. Now, IBM experts have written
the first authoritative book on mainframe security
specifically designed to build on your experience
in other environments.

The authors illuminate the mainframe's security
model and call special attention to z/OS®
security techniques that differ from UNIX, Linux,
and Windows. They thoroughly introduce IBM's
powerful Resource Access Control Facility
(RACF®) security subsystem and demonstrate
how mainframe security integrates into your
enterprise-wide IT security infrastructure. If you're
an experienced system administrator or security
professional, there's no faster way to extend
your expertise into "big iron" environments.

Lotus Notes Developer's Toolbox
Elliott
ISBN: 0-13-221448-2

IBM Rational Unified Process Reference and Certification Guide
Shuja, Krebs
ISBN: 0-13-156292-4

WebSphere Business Integration Primer
Iyengar, Jessani, Chilanti
ISBN: 0-13-224831-X

Understanding DB2 9 Security
Bond, See, Wong, Chan
ISBN: 0-13-134590-7

Mining the Talk
Spangler, Kreulen
ISBN: 0-13-233953-6

Service-Oriented Architecture (SOA) Compass
Bieberstein, Bose, Fiammante,
Jones, Shah
ISBN: 0-13-187002-5

Persistence in the Enterprise
Barcia, Hambrick, Brown,
Peterson, Bhogal
ISBN: 0-13-158756-0

Enterprise Master Data Management

Enterprise Master Data Management

An SOA Approach to Managing Core Information

Allen Dreibelbis   **Eberhard Hechler**
Ivan Milman   **Martin Oberhofer**
Paul van Run   **Dan Wolfson**

IBM Press
Pearson plc

Upper Saddle River, NJ • Boston • Indianapolis • San Francisco •
New York • Toronto • Montreal • London • Munich • Paris • Madrid •
Capetown • Sydney • Tokyo • Singapore • Mexico City

ibmpressbooks.com

IBM Press Program Managers: Tara Woodman, Ellice Uffer
Cover design: IBM Corporation
Associate Publisher: Greg Wiegand
Marketing Manager: Kourtnaye Sturgeon
Publicist: Heather Fox
Acquisitions Editor: Bernard Goodwin
Development Editor: Songlin Qin
Managing Editor: John Fuller
Designer: Alan Clements
Project Editors: LaraWysong, Elizabeth Ryan
Copy Editor: Bonnie Granat
Proofreader: Linda Begley
Compositor: International Typesetting and Composition
Manufacturing Buyer: Anna Popick

Published by Pearson plc
Publishing as IBM Press

IBM Press offers excellent discounts on this book when ordered in quantity for bulk purchases or special sales, which may include electronic versions and/or custom covers and content particular to your business, training goals, marketing focus, and branding interests. For more information, please contact:

U.S. Corporate and Government Sales
1-800-382-3419
corpsales@pearsontechgroup.com

For sales outside the U.S., please contact:

International Sales
international@pearsoned.com

This Book Is Safari Enabled

The Safari® Enabled icon on the cover of your favorite technology book means the book is available through Safari Bookshelf. When you buy this book, you get free access to the online edition for 45 days. Safari Bookshelf is an electronic reference library that lets you easily search thousands of technical books, find code samples, download chapters, and access technical information whenever and wherever you need it.

To gain 45-day Safari Enabled access to this book:

- Go to http://www.ibmpressbooks.com/safarienabled
- Complete the brief registration form
- Enter the coupon code 6YCG-LCUE-QIX3-64EQ-NIJ7

If you have difficulty registering on Safari Bookshelf or accessing the online edition, please e-mail customer-service@safaribooksonline.com.

Library of Congress Cataloging-in-Publication Data

Enterprise master data management: an SOA approach to managing core information/Allen Dreibelbis ... [et al.].   p. cm.

Includes bibliographical references and index.
ISBN 978-0-13-236625-0 (hardback: alk. paper)
1. Database management. 2. Web services. 3. Computer architecture. I. Dreibelbis, Allen.
QA76.9.D3E68 2008
004.2'2—dc22   2008015422

ISBN-13: 978-0-13-236625-0
ISBN-10: 0-13-236625-8

Text printed in the United States on recycled paper at Courier in Westford, Massachusetts.
Fourth printing, November 2012

To my wife, Nanci, and my children, Alexandra and Bennett,
for all their support.

A.D.

To my wife, Irina, and my sons, Lars and Alex,
for their support in my spending evenings and weekends on this book.

E.H.

To Janie, the Queen of my heart.

I.M.

To my ever-supporting wife, Kirsten, and my sons, Damian and Adrian.

M.O.

To my ladies: Lisa, Marcella, and Sophia

P.v.R.

To my family: My wife, Danelle, and my sons, Ben and Sam,
for their tolerance and support.

D.W.

Contents

Foreword

I meet with senior business and technical executives around the world, in both the public and private sectors, on a daily basis. CEOs, CFOs, CIOs, and line-of-business executives alike are all facing incredible pressures across all fronts. They need to create new shareholder value by improving both the top and bottom lines. They must improve customer service in the face of fast-moving global competition. They must mitigate risks inherent in basic business decision making and avoid fraudulent activities in their own operations. And, as if that isn't pressure enough, they must also deal with a plethora of regulatory requirements.

What they've come to find is that the availability of information provides them with some relief from these almost incessant pressures—the sense of relief that comes from unlocking information and letting it flow rapidly and easily to the people and processes that need it. Trusted information—complete, accurate, timely, insightful information—is delivered in the context of the task at hand.

Take, for instance, one leading electronics manufacturer. By providing unified, timely product master data, the company was able to speed product introduction cycles by weeks and improve the satisfaction of their distribution partners at the same time. An innovative retailer has created an "endless aisle" to drive up in-store sales—even when it doesn't have products on hand. This innovation is enabled with a unified view of product data that spans both the company's own inventory and that of its distributors. In the case of customer master data, a 360-degree view of clients helped one financial services company avoid the risk of offering more credit cards to clients who were already in default with their existing credit card accounts. Master customer data also helped one telecommunications company capture cross-sell opportunities across its landline, wireless, and long-distance services. The same project was the foundation for improved customer service in the company's call center and helped to reduce customer churn. The possibilities are endless.

Unlocking information and letting it flow rapidly and easily to the people and processes that need it is easier said than done. Over the past 20 years or more, the IT industry has focused on automating business tasks. The result of this effort is a highly complex information landscape; individual automation projects have led to disconnected silos of information. Little trusted information exists—there are multiple versions of the truth. Redundancy reigns—both logically and physically. Few common definitions of key data elements exist or are shared across the enterprise. No common processes for managing and ensuring the integrity of critical data domains exist. These facts define today's environment. They blind the business from the information it needs, add cost to the IT infrastructure, and slow the ability of the business to move forward with confidence.

Solving these problems is what Master Data Management and this book are all about.

As you'll learn, to successfully relieve today's business pressures, Master Data Management (MDM) has to address needs that exist in several distinct but related dimensions. Master Data Management must consider and possibly relate all kinds of Master Data. After all, product data likely relates to some customer data, and perhaps to account data, or perhaps to some other data domain. Unifying these views could lead to more effective customer service. Effective Master Data must also support multiple application styles. Master Data may need to feed an online, transactional ordering system, or perhaps a data warehouse needs Master Data to provide up-sell suggestions to a call center representative. Furthermore, decisions have to be made about how to architect the Master Data Management implementation.

The topic of Master Data Management may seem daunting, but it's really no more daunting than the industry's recent focus on Service-Oriented Architectures (SOA). As a matter of fact, the two topics, SOA and Master Data, are inextricably related. They are two sides of the same coin. A process is only as good as the information it processes, and similarly, information needs to be tied to the context of some process to be of any value. So we must step up to the Master Data challenge. By unlocking the silos of information created by the past 20 years of automation and providing a free flow of trusted information, we will put ourselves in a position to deliver significant value to our organizations.

I encourage you to take advantage of the opportunity this book provides to learn more about Master Data Management. You'll be learning skills you can use to relieve the pressure and deliver more value to your organization. Your time will be well spent. Enjoy the experience.

—Dr. Ambuj Goyal
General Manager, Information Management
of IBM Software Group

Foreword

How does one build a contemporary "super city" that is both technologically forward-looking and compatible with its environment? The challenge is even greater when we build a "super city" that is built on the foundation of an existing metropolis.

Clearly, architecture remains the key challenge in planning enterprise Master Data Management (MDM) infrastructure for the contemporary Global 5000-size enterprise. Experience-based blueprints and architecture patterns are invaluable in such an effort.

In our MDM research with very large-scale enterprises, analysts at the MDM Institute have seen multimillion dollar ($/€/£) projects fail due to poor MDM architectural planning. Such failures included economic failure caused by the inability to cost-effectively scale or political failure caused by the inability to integrate the twenty-first century corporate supply chain.

Inside this highly anticipated book, MDM practitioners will find architectural patterns presented as the nexus of seasoned enterprise architectural experience and early-adopter MDM operational experience. Moreover, the authors have shown their deep experience in delivering an essential guide for every MDM practitioner—from Enterprise Architect to MDM project leadership. This book provides a key technical foundation for understanding the fundamental MDM components and how they work together. As a bonus, the reader will benefit from clear extrapolations on how SOA implementations both benefit from and require MDM.

Enterprise Master Data Management: An SOA Approach to Managing Core Information provides a vital reference architecture for all serious enterprise MDM practitioners.

—Aaron Zornes
Founder and Chief Research Officer,
CDI-MDM Institute

Preface

What Is This Book About?

Master Data Management (MDM) refers to the disciplines, technologies, and solutions that are used to create and maintain consistent and accurate master data for all stakeholders across and beyond the enterprise. *Enterprise Master Data Management: An SOA Approach to Managing Core Information* explains key concepts of MDM, the business value of MDM, and how to architect an Enterprise Master Data Management Solution. The book is a comprehensive guide to architecting a Master Data Management Solution that includes a reference architecture, solution blueprints, architectural principles, and patterns and properties of MDM Systems. The book also describes the relationship between MDM and Service-Oriented Architectures, and the importance of data governance for managing master data. Figure 1 provides a summary of the book's chapters that are summarized in the following list.

> **Chapter 1:** "Introducing Master Data Management" describes the fundamental concepts of master data and MDM. We describe the key characteristics of a Master Data Management System and how the MDM System's ability to manage master data provides benefits to the enterprise. We also introduce the reader to multiple MDM methods and implementation styles.
>
> **Chapter 2:** "MDM as an SOA Enabler" describes the relationship between MDM and Service-Oriented Architectures. We demonstrate how MDM and SOA work together to help in the achievement of business and IT goals related to managing master data, and explain why we view MDM as an enabler for any SOA-style solution. The chapter includes topics such as SOA concepts, SOA principles, service granularity, service composability, and information services.
>
> **Chapter 3:** "MDM Reference Architecture" describes the functional characteristics of the Master Data Management Reference Architecture. We describe how to position and design a Master Data Management Solution within an enterprise. We describe

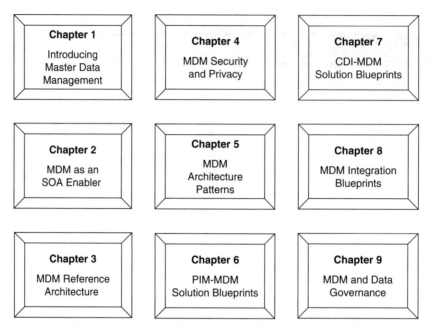

Figure 1 Chapter Summary.

the type of functionality required to deliver a Master Data Management Solution, identify the major architectural building blocks, and then demonstrate how those architectural building blocks collaborate in the delivery of MDM functionality.

Chapter 4: "MDM Security and Privacy" describes the role of security and privacy in an MDM architecture and deployment. We provide insight into developing an understanding of the value of and the risks to master data and then offer guidance for the tasks of selecting and applying the appropriate security controls. We then describe in depth the types of security services that provide the appropriate controls and how those services can apply to the implementation of an MDM Solution.

Chapter 5: "MDM Architecture Patterns" provides an overview of architecture patterns often encountered in MDM deployments. We describe in detail the architecture patterns that helped to shape the MDM Reference Architecture. The architecture patterns encountered were either new architecture patterns, variations of existing architecture patterns, or known architecture patterns that were applied in the area of Master Data Management.

Chapter 6: "PIM-MDM Solution Blueprints" introduces the concept of MDM Solution Blueprints; in this chapter, we explain the relationships between architecture patterns and business patterns for PIM-MDM solutions. The Solution Blueprints are based on the MDM Reference Architecture. Based on specific business requirements for product information management, we describe a variety of PIM-MDM Solution Blueprints for several industries and solution scenarios.

Chapter 7: "CDI-MDM Solution Blueprints" explains the relationships between architecture patterns and business patterns for CDI-MDM solutions. The Solution Blueprints are based on the MDM Reference Architecture. Based on specific business requirements for customer data integration, we describe a variety of CDI-MDM Solution Blueprints for several industries and solution scenarios.

Chapter 8: "MDM Integration Blueprints" provides further guidance on how to integrate an MDM System into an existing IT landscape. We provide guidance and describe sample integration scenarios, such as integrating the MDM System with a Data Warehouse and integrating an MDM System with an SAP application for the authoring of data.

Chapter 9: "MDM and Data Governance" explores the critical nature of data governance in Master Data Management, and how people, process, and technology work together to leverage master data as an enterprise asset. We explore the critical nature of data governance in Master Data Management and the direct and indirect roles that the architecture for the MDM Solution can play in enabling data governance.

Who Should Read This Book

Enterprise Master Data Management: An SOA Approach to Managing Core Information has content that should appeal to a diverse business and technical audience, ranging from the executive level to experienced MDM practitioners and especially those new to the topic of Master Data Management. Newcomers to the topic of MDM, and even SOA, will certainly benefit from the chapters that introduce MDM, that explain security and privacy, and that show how MDM complements the development of a SOA.

Readers with a strong technical background, such as Enterprise Architects, System Architects, and Information Architects, should enjoy reading the detailed content that provides technical guidance for implementing Master Data Management. Technical guidance covers a broad range of topics—implementation styles, methods of use, SOA, security and privacy, architecture patterns, and data governance—which are then all brought together into the Master Data Management Reference Architecture and a set of solution blueprints that span CDI-MDM, PIM-MDM, and MDM Integration Blueprints.

Executives trying to gain an understanding of Master Data Management, and even those who are already in the process of deciding how to proceed, will benefit from the content that introduces Master Data Management, data governance, and the solution blueprints.

What You Will Learn

This book is a comprehensive guide to understanding (1) the importance of Master Data Management, (2) the need for an MDM System, and (3) methods of architecting a Master Data Management Solution. We cover a wide range of topics in our discussions of the use of disciplines, technologies, and solutions to implement Master Data Management. Readers of this book have the opportunity to increase their knowledge about a broad range of topics related to MDM—from both a business and a technical perspective. Readers will learn the answers to the following questions about Master Data Management, which constitute its core concepts:

- What is Master Data Management, and why is there a need for managed master data?
- How can an MDM System provide a consistent understanding and trust of master data entities?
- What is the relationship between SOA and MDM, and how can MDM enable the implementation of a SOA solution?
- How can a security architecture to maintain the security and privacy of master data be implemented?
- What are the core architectural principles, properties, and patterns for MDM Systems?
- What data governance is critical for the management of master data?

In addition to learning MDM's core concepts, the reader will understand how they are incorporated into the design for a Master Data Management Solution. The MDM Reference Architecture provides the reader with a reference architecture that describes the functional characteristics of an MDM Solution implementation within an enterprise. MDM Integration Blueprints, PIM-MDM and CDI-MDM, and Solution Blueprints then provide the reader with knowledge of how to use the reference architecture and architecture patterns to implement a specific solution to solve a specific set of business problems.

How to Read This Book

There are several ways to read this book. The most obvious way to do it is to read it cover to cover to get a complete end-to-end picture of Enterprise Master Data Management. However, the authors organized the content in such a way that there are four basic reading paths through the book. Figure 2 depicts the following two reading paths:

- To **understand the key concepts of Enterprise Master Data Management**, we suggest reading Chapter 1, Introducing Master Data Management; Chapter 3, MDM Reference Architecture; and Chapter 9, MDM and Data Governance. This path should provide the reader with a clear understanding of Master Data Management, data governance, and how to implement MDM within the enterprise.
- To **understand the key concepts for designing Enterprise Master Data Management Architectures**, we suggest that the reader start with Chapter 1 in order to gain an understanding of the need for an MDM System, methods of such a system's use, and implementation styles. Chapter 2 describes the relationship between MDM and SOA, and how SOA principles can be applied to the design of the solution. Chapter 3 explains the MDM Reference Architecture—the foundation for any MDM deployment—from an architectural perspective. Chapter 4 details aspects of the MDM Reference Architecture that are related to MDM Security and Privacy.

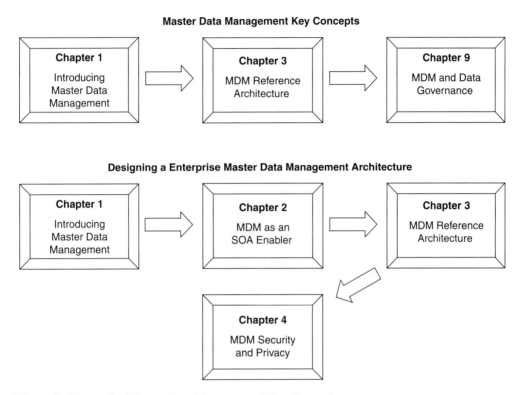

Figure 2   Enterprise Master Data Management Reading Paths.

Figure 3 shows the suggested reading paths for the reader who is interested in detailed knowledge about solution blueprints. In both paths, Chapter 8, MDM Integration Blueprints, is represented as an optional chapter by the use of a dashed arrow and would be of interest to those readers who desire further integration details. Based on the objectives of the reader, Chapter 9, MDM and Data Governance, should be considered for each of the suggested reading paths. The suggested reading paths are as follows:

- **PIM-MDM Solution Blueprints:** If the reader is investigating solutions for the Product master data domain, they are described in Chapter 6. Reading that chapter has prerequisites, though. The reader should be familiar with Chapters 1, 2, and 3. Because the solution architectures are based on the MDM Component Model, a sound understanding of the MDM Reference Architecture is necessary. Explaining certain aspects of a solution also requires an understanding of MDM Security and Privacy, which are described in Chapters 4 and 5. Chapter 5 also explains key areas of the solution architecture.
- **CDI-MDM Solution Blueprints:** Solutions focused on customer master data are described in Chapter 7, which has the same prerequisites as the PIM-MDM Solution Blueprints—namely, Chapters 1, 2, 3, 4, and 5.

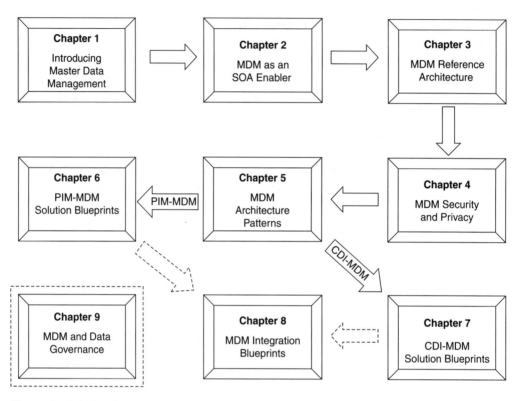

Figure 3   Solution Blueprint Reading Paths.

What Is Not Covered

This book covers many of the key business and technical aspects of Master Data Management and is a comprehensive guide to architecting a Master Data Management Solution, but it does not provide project planning management methodology or an MDM Solution Architecture based on software products. IT Architects will make design decisions and select software products capable of meeting the functional and nonfunctional requirements for a specific solution by considering the existing hardware and software infrastructure for the specific IT environment. Based on our experience, we have provided the reader with a comprehensive guide to designing an MDM Solution. We have also explained the criteria that the reader should use when selecting software for the MDM System. In Appendix B, Software and Solution Offerings for MDM Deployments, we offer a listing of Solution offerings and software products grouped according to the MDM Logical System Architecture. We also provide the reader with the links to relevant Web pages for the providers of those solution offerings.

There are organizational and IT aspects that should be considered as part of the implementation and deployment of an MDM Solution. The people who are developing a project plan and implementation strategy need to consider the priority of the business problems being addressed, technology gaps, and the current information management capabilities of the organization. We provide guidance throughout the book on how to address some of these aspects, but we have not dedicated any additional chapters to this set of topics. However, the reader will find in Appendix A, MDM User Roles, a summary of the types of user roles, responsibilities, and associated skill descriptions for the various types of roles that we have seen on MDM projects. The primary focus of our efforts has been on providing the reader with the information required for an understanding of the need for Master Data Management and with a comprehensive guide to designing an MDM Solution.

Conventions

Throughout this book, we mention a number of regulations that can influence how to configure, manage, and protect a Master Data Management environment. To help understand those relevant regulations and their scope, we have collected information about each regulation and provided a summary in Appendix C, Master Data Management and Regulations. We include a table that includes other information about each regulation, such as industries affected, master data domain, and Web site addresses where more information about the regulation is available. The book's text has frequent footnote references that direct the reader to Appendix C for further information.

We also refer to a number of industry and technical standards throughout the book and have chosen to include a description of those standards in Appendix D, Standards and Specifications. We do not use footnotes to direct the reader to Appendix D when a standard is mentioned, but we do encourage readers to refer to that appendix if they are unfamiliar with a particular standard. Appendix D contains a table that identifies the standard, provides a link to a Web site for further information, and presents brief notes about the standard.

Many of the chapters have references to additional sources of information that can provide further information about the subject being discussed. External references for each chapter are identified at the end of each chapter and referenced as footnotes. Each reference follows a format that includes the appropriate information relative to the reference, such as the author's name, title of the book or article, date of publication, publisher, ISBN number, and Web site.

Acknowledgments

The idea for this book was born during the 2006 IBM® Information on Demand Conference in Los Angeles. Early during the conference, Martin and Eberhard purchased the book *Service-Oriented Architecture (SOA) Compass* at the conference book store. After reading some of the chapters while still at the conference, Martin and Eberhard were inspired to write a book about Enterprise Master Data Management—a book that would provide IT Architects with a navigation guide in this complex area. Knowing that an undertaking of this magnitude requires an excellent team, the two reached out to Allen, Dan, Ivan, and Paul to get MDM expertise and thought leadership into the project from all areas of the IBM Software Group. Thus began the eighteen-month journey with authors collaborating across multiple continents and using their personal time to complete the effort.

While the book was in process, Harveer Singh from Tata Consultancy Services received an early copy of the manuscript and provided valuable, detailed feedback and deserves a special mention for his dedicated support. A special thank you is also due for Aaron Zornes from the CDI-MDM Institute for his feedback about the book and the foreword, which he generously provided. A thank you is also earned by Ambuj Goyal for providing a foreword to the book.

During the project, colleagues from IBM provided ideas for the book or reviewed various draft versions of the chapters and provided valuable feedback. The author team would like to express special thanks to Guenter Sauter for the valuable contributions and feedback he provided to enhance content in the book through his proofreading efforts. Martin owes a special thanks to Umair Akeel for the invaluable insight he provided for the PIM-RFID Solution Blueprint for Track & Trace and the latest news from the relevant standardization committees. Allen would like to acknowledge the efforts of all of his Information Platform and Solutions Acceleration Team colleagues and to all those in the IBM Software Group who have contributed to the development of the Master Data Management Reference Architecture. He would like to extend a special thank you to Oliver Claude, who in 2006 recognized the need for and value of developing a Master Data Management Reference Architecture. Ivan would like to express a special thank you to Sridhar Muppidi for his valuable assistance with reviewing and providing guidance for the SOA Security Architecture content in Chapter 4, MDM Security and Privacy, and to Heather Hinton for her insight into Information Risk Management in the same chapter.

The author team would also like to thank the following IBM colleagues for their contributions: Steve Adler, David Borean, Brian Byrne, Bryce Crapse, Brant Davidson, Mandy Chessell, David Corrigan, Ian Dallas, Tommy Eunice, Clive Hannah, Rachel Helm, Susan Kirk, Michael B. Moore, Dan Van Hammond, Daniel Whitacre, Don Whitecar, Ben Wilde, Anju Willard, and Wei Zheng.

In addition to the valuable feedback from the IBM technical community, the author team got a great deal of support and guidance from the IBM Information Management publishing department. Susan Visser introduced and guided the author team through the publication process. Eberhard and Martin, as non-native English speakers, owe Susan a special thanks for proofreading their chapters to improve the English. In addition, we would like to thank Tara Woodman, the IBM Press Program Manager. From the IBM legal department we are grateful to Elissa Wang, who guided the author team through the legal side for publishing a book.

Without a strong team from Pearson Publishing, the book would not have been possible. In particular, we would like to thank Bernard Goodwin, Michelle Housley, Songlin Qiu, Lara Wysong, and Bonnie Granat.

We have likely missed some names or possibly have not given everyone the credit they deserve—for this, we apologize. But to everyone listed and not listed who contributed to this book to make it better, thanks for all the help you have given to the authors. We hope that you will be as proud of this book as we are.

 **Allen Dreibelbis** has 30 years of experience in the IT Industry. He spent 16 years providing system integration and consulting services to public-sector clients while working for IBM. His expertise spans enterprise architecture, software development, complex systems integration, and Master Data Management. Allen currently is an Executive Architect in the IBM Software Group World-Wide Information Platform and Solutions Acceleration Team. He developed the Master Data Management Reference Architecture in 2006 while collaborating with colleagues across the IBM SWG Information Platform and Solutions organization and the IBM Information on Demand Center of Excellence. He provides customer briefings and training on the Master Data Management Reference Architecture and conducts architecture workshops for customers on implementing Master Data Management Solutions within their enterprises. Allen holds a B.S. in Computer Science from Pennsylvania State University.

Eberhard Hechler is a Senior Certified IT Architect (SCITA) and Executive IT Architect. He joined the IBM Böblingen Lab in Germany in 1983 as a junior programmer. Eberhard worked more than two years on an international assignment with the IBM Kingston Lab in New York, and he has worked on projects in software development, performance optimization and benchmarking, solution architecture and design, software product planning, management, technical consultancy, and technical alliance management. In 1992, Eberhard began to work with DB2® for MVS™, focusing on testing and performance measurements of new DB2 versions. Since 1999, his focus has been on Information Management and DB2 UDB on distributed platforms. He is currently the Technical Enablement Architect for IBM Information Platform & Solutions, working with System Integrators throughout Europe. Eberhard holds a M.S. in Mathematics (Diplom-Mathematiker) from Hamburg University.

Ivan Milman is a Senior Technical Staff Member at IBM, focusing on security and governance in the Information Management area within the IBM Software Group in Austin, Texas. Over the course of his career, Ivan has worked on a variety of distributed systems and security technology, including OS/2® Networking, DCE, IBM Global Sign-On, and Tivoli® Access Manager. Ivan has also represented IBM to standards bodies, including The Open Group and IETF. Prior to his current position, Ivan was the lead architect for the IBM Tivoli Access Manager family of security products. Ivan is a member of the IBM Security Architecture Board and the IBM Data Governance Council. Ivan is a Certified Information Systems Security Professional and a Master Inventor at IBM, and has been granted 12 U.S. patents.

Martin Oberhofer joined IBM in the IBM Silicon Valley Labs in the United States as a developer for database technology. After returning to Germany, he joined the IBM Böblingen Lab, from which he still works as a Technical Consultant and member of the World-Wide IBM Software Group Master Data Management Center of Excellence. His areas of expertise include database technologies, Java™ software development, MDM architecture, and IT systems integration. His special focus area is integrating MDM systems into the operational IT landscape by synchronizing and distributing master data with SAP application systems. He provides architecture workshops to customers and system integrators. He holds a M.S. in Mathematics from the University of Constance, Germany.

Paul van Run has almost 10 years experience in MDM and 15 years in IT. At DWL, he was part of the R&D leadership team developing DWL Customer, one of the first dedicated CDI products on the market. After the acquisition of DWL by IBM in 2005, he became a Senior Technical Staff Member, and he is responsible for the architecture of the IBM Master Data Management products: MDM Server (formerly WebSphere® Customer Center) and WebSphere Product Center, both market leaders in their segments. Before coming to DWL, Paul worked as a software developer in the insurance industry for an ING Group subsidiary in Canada. Paul holds a M.S. in Information Science from the Technical University of Eindhoven, the Netherlands, and a M.S. in Computer Science from the University of Waterloo, Canada.

Dan Wolfson is an IBM Distinguished Engineer and the chief architect and CTO for the Information Platform and Solutions segment of the IBM Information Management Division of the IBM Software Group. He is responsible for architecture and technical leadership across the rapidly growing areas of Information Integration, Master Data Management, and Industry Models. Dan's previous roles include CTO for Business Integration Software and chief architect for Information Integration Solutions.

Dan has more than 20 years of experience in research and commercial distributed computing, including transaction and object-oriented systems, software fault tolerance, messaging, information integration, business integration, metadata management, and database systems.

Chapter 1

Introducing Master Data Management

As companies struggle to become more agile by implementing information systems that support and facilitate changing business requirements, the management of core information, such as information about customers or products, becomes increasingly important. We call this information **master data**. In many companies, this master data is kept in many overlapping systems and is often of unknown quality. For many organizations, this situation constitutes a dilemma—it becomes increasingly difficult for organizations to implement change. Architectural approaches such as Service-Oriented Architecture (SOA) are difficult to implement when an organization does not have a common definition and management of its core information.

This chapter provides an introduction to master data and the characteristics of Master Data Management (MDM) systems. We start with a brief introduction of master data and explain why the management of master data is important to an enterprise. The second section will outline how different pressures have caused many organizations to lose control of their master data, resulting in a pool of partially redundant, sometimes unmanaged, data. Section three provides a more detailed description of the key dimensions of MDM solutions, describing the different domains of master data, the different ways in which master data management systems are used, and the different ways that MDM Systems can be implemented. The final section discusses how the management of master data can benefit an organization by providing a trusted foundation of authoritative data that can be used consistently across an enterprise and that can also evolve in a managed manner to meet changing business needs.

1.1   Introduction to Master Data Management

The management of key organizational data has always been important. Knowing who your customers are, what products and services you offer, and what the arrangements or accounts you have with your customers and suppliers is fundamental to the operation of most organizations. Whether your organization is a bank, a retailer, or a government agency, there is a core set of such data that is used across the enterprise. It is used to open new accounts, to introduce new products to the market, and to determine what products to offer customers. This data is called master data.

Master data is some of the most valuable information that a business owns. It represents core information about the business—such as customers, suppliers, products, and accounts—and the relationships between them. Each of these domains of master data represents information that is needed across different business processes, across organizational units, and between operational systems and decision support systems. In essence, master data defines an enterprise.

Master data captures the key things that all parts of an organization must agree on, both in meaning and usage. For example, it is important that all parts of an organization share an understanding of what defines a customer, which customers exist, where customers are located, and what products they have purchased or have been offered. A common understanding is useful both to prevent bad things from inadvertently happening—such as a bill getting posted to the wrong address—and to provide an opportunity for significant business benefits such as improving the ability to sell complementary products to customers. Master data is important in both operational and analytical environments. Many operational business processes touch master data—for example, introducing a new product to the market, signing up a new supplier, and adding a new phone service to a customer account. All of these processes touch many different application systems that must all share a core set of information about products, suppliers, and customers. For the business process to execute properly, this master data must be accurate and consistent. Analytical systems have similar requirements—master data often forms the key dimensions and hierarchies used for reporting and analysis of key business data. Increasingly, analytics are also being applied within operational business processes to better monitor and optimize business transactions. Trustworthy data is a fundamental ingredient of meaningful analytics.

Management of master data is not new. Most organizations have systems to store and retrieve the master data that is critical to their business. Unfortunately, many information systems have become increasingly complex in response to the pressures of growth, business changes, and technology changes. It has therefore become increasingly difficult for organizations to identify, maintain, and use an authoritative set of master data in a consistent way across the enterprise.

Many of the IT architectures[1] that were used to construct existing customer information files or master product databases were designed in support of a few, typically homegrown, applications. More often than not, these applications were themselves constructed in support of a particular line of business rather than for the enterprise as a whole. As the business changed over time, it may have been easier to create a new application and database to handle

---

1. The term Information Technology (IT) will be used to generically refer to the organization responsible for operating the computing environment in a large organization.

the new requirements than it was to modify all of the existing applications. For example, as the Internet arose as a powerful communications mechanism, companies wanting to enable customer self-service on the Web needed to either extend their existing systems or create new applications and databases to manage this new channel of communication. Because the Web introduced the need to maintain attributes such as e-mail addresses, login names and passwords that existing systems didn't support, many enterprises found it was easier to create new applications and databases to support the Internet channel than it was to extend existing systems. In other words, it was more expedient to build a new system and figure out how to synchronize it with existing systems than it was to extend the existing ones. Although not ideal, doing this may not be a problem if you only have a few simple information systems—but in a larger enterprise, especially one that has grown through multiple mergers and acquisitions, the situation can quickly become problematic. Information Technology (IT) systems, often easier to extend than to change, become increasingly complex with many point-to-point integrations and partially redundant information systems. For example, it is not unusual for a large financial institution to have more than 20 systems that maintain information about customers. Attempting to synchronize customer information across such a large number of systems can result in an unmanageable number of point-to-point integrations—a rat's nest of information flows.

The existence of these partially redundant data stores results in additional complexity throughout the systems architecture of an organization—not to mention additional IT costs. The definitions of what might appear to be common terms, such as "supplier" or "product," will likely be different within the different systems. The data itself may be inconsistent because of systems enforcing different rules for data validation and cleansing. It is therefore difficult for a business to achieve a complete and consistent understanding of master data that is spread across multiple systems if those systems lack the proper controls and integration.

This situation leads to several consequences. Perhaps the most fundamental issue is the quandary for users and applications—where should they go to find and use accurate data? Is there an authoritative source that can be trusted? Without an authoritative source of master data, business processes can become more complex to develop and implement when a complete and accurate view of master data is not available. Similarly, implementing decision support systems can also be tricky without well-known sources for trusted master data.

A second consequence is architectural brittleness—making a small change in one system can have a significant impact on many other systems. Analyzing the scope and cost of a potential change across a complex web of interconnected systems can be difficult. This difficulty is significant, because changes are frequently required to support new business requirements, to support mergers and acquisitions, and to integrate new applications. Indeed, this architectural brittleness significantly impacts the organization's ability to evolve and change according to market pressures. Supporting the growth of a business in terms of operational throughput or geographical distribution yields similar issues. Distributing master data through large clusters of computers requires careful design to manage the synchronization of the master data. The final issue is IT cost—redundant data requires redundant storage as well as the communications and computational infrastructure to maintain it.

The business consequences are perhaps even more significant. When master data is spread across multiple systems in an unmanaged way, there may be multiple competing views of master data: different customer lists, lists of suppliers or product definitions. Without a complete and authoritative set of master information, it is difficult for enterprises to optimize their relationships with customers and suppliers across different product lines; it is difficult to rapidly introduce new products to the market or to relate sales performance to product categories. For example, we have worked with large enterprises where customers in one business unit were suppliers in another—consolidating customers and suppliers into a common Master Data Repository allows the businesses to more effectively negotiate favorable contracts.

In an ideal world, there would be a single place where all common master data in an organization is stored and managed. The data would be accurate, consistent, and maintained in a coherent and secure manner. All updates would take place against this single copy of master data, and all of the different users of master data would interact with this single **authoritative source** of information. For customer data, such an arrangement means that all applications that use customer data would go to a single source; the data stored there would be the customer data used, for example, to open and close accounts across all lines of business, for provisioning accounts, and for all marketing and analysis.

A single source of master data represents three important capabilities: an authoritative source of information, the ability to use the information in a consistent way, and the ability to evolve the master data and the management of the master data to accommodate changing business needs. A suite of services can then be created around this master data that allows the data to be seamlessly integrated into business processes and analytical environments. Together, these three capabilities provide organizations with a powerful foundation for efficient business execution.

An authoritative source of master data can be trusted to be a high-quality collection of data that follows a well-defined and agreed-upon structure. The data has been standardized (e.g., all address information follows the same format). Duplicates have been rationalized. The currency of the information is maintained through continuous or periodic updates. The information is complete, secure, and accurate.

Authoritative master data exposed through reusable business services provides the organization with the flexibility to exploit master data in new ways by enabling applications to follow repeatable, defined patterns of usage for operating over this data. For example, in a banking environment, customer profile information maintained as part of the master customer data can be used consistently across all of the different ways that a customer may interact with the different parts of a business—the branch teller, the call center representative, and the Web—to ensure a smooth and consistent customer experience. Each of the supporting systems would use the same business service to retrieve customer information. As new opportunities to interact with the customer arise—for example, via a customer's cell phone—again, the same services could be once again reused, because both the data and their method of use have been agreed upon.

A critical element in this ideal world of master data is flexibility. As business requirements, regulations, and implementation technologies change, we often find that the definition and use of the master data needs to evolve along with it. Again, in our ideal world, this type of change would be a nondisruptive change to our environment. For example, if a retailer decides to open up stores in a new country, it should be easy to extend the definition of its products to accommodate additional information, such as new currencies and new regulatory requirements. At the same time, we don't want this simple data model change to break existing applications. The master data environment must thus support a smooth evolution of both the data structures as well as the services that manage the behavior of the master data. In addition to supporting evolution, the ideal system also supports the extension of the environment, for example, to add new domains of master data, and the linkages between them, in a nondisruptive manner.

The goal of **Master Data Management (MDM)** is to enable this ideal world. Through a combination of architecture, technology, and business processes, MDM provides an approach to incrementally reducing the amount of redundantly managed information and providing information consumers throughout an enterprise with authoritative master data. **MDM Systems** that focus exclusively on managing information about customers are often called **Customer Data Integration (CDI)** systems. MDM Systems that focus exclusively on managing the descriptions of products are called **Product Information Management (PIM)** systems. MDM Systems that enable multiple domains of master data, and that support multiple implementation styles and methods of use, are sometimes also called **Multi-Form MDM Systems.** The different technical characteristics of MDM Systems will be described in Section 1.3.

A Master Data Management strategy addresses a wide variety of business and technical concerns within an enterprise. It is often wise to address these concerns incrementally. Incremental deployment allows significant value to be provided as each phase of an MDM project expands the capabilities of the MDM System by integrating additional systems, extending the kinds of data managed, or providing new ways in which the master data may be used. The ideal MDM implementation represents a state of management that organizations may approach over time. An incremental approach allows benefits to be seen and measured throughout the many phases of an MDM implementation project. For these reasons, MDM projects are key strategic initiatives with measurable benefit to the entire enterprise.

MDM is a key facet of a broader enterprise information management strategy. MDM plays a key role within an information architecture as a provider and custodian of master data to the enterprise. This broader strategy must map from the business imperatives to the current and future IT environment. For example, the business need to cross-sell between different lines of business in a large organization may drive the need for MDM. Other drivers, such as the need to comply with Anti-Money Laundering regulations, require banks to apply a broader suite of technologies that are architected in such a way as to detect and respond to potentially fraudulent activities. These examples reveal the broader need to define an enterprise information management strategy and the architectures to support it.

This book provides a comprehensive guide to architecting MDM systems. It includes architectural principles, a reference architecture, patterns, and properties of MDM Systems. We have chosen to approach MDM from the perspective of Service-Oriented Architectures (SOA), and more specifically, from the viewpoint of treating information as a core set of business services within an enterprise architecture. This approach helps us to address the following three underlying principles—that an MDM System:

- Provides a consistent understanding and trust of master data entities
- Provides mechanisms for consistent use of master data across the organization
- Is designed to accommodate and manage change

Achieving these MDM goals requires MDM software that is capable of both managing master data and providing master data to a community of users and systems. These goals may also lead to organizational change to support the implementation of business practices that properly manage and exploit the master data.

We will explore these principles in further detail throughout this chapter, and they will be woven throughout the rest of the book as a set of underlying assumptions that define the nucleus of an MDM System. In the next sections, we spend more time on why MDM is an important aspect of an enterprise's information architecture. Section 1.3 introduces key technical characteristics of MDM systems, setting the stage for the deeper architectural discussions in subsequent chapters. The final section discusses the business benefits of an MDM system using the three principles described above.

1.2   Why an MDM System?

Master data has been around a long time, so why do we suddenly need MDM Systems to manage this kind of information? What makes this master data special? Why is it important? These are important questions—so within this section we look at how the information that is some of the most valuable information to an enterprise has become virtually unmanaged and often ungoverned. The fundamental purpose of an MDM System is to serve as the authoritative source for master data: An MDM System is a system that provides clean, consistent master data to the enterprise. If the business benefits of a managed master data environment are clear, then why is it that enterprises have unmanaged master data? Why do organizations have multiple, often inconsistent, repositories of data that should be maintained in common across the enterprise? For convenience, we call this data **Unmanaged Master Data.**

First, let's consider the distribution of unmanaged master data throughout a typical enterprise. Why are there multiple copies of master data? Are these copies redundant? This distribution may be viewed along any number of dimensions, including by line of business **(LOB)**, by organizational change—such as mergers and acquisitions, and by the introduction of packaged software.

1.2.1   A Cross-LOB Perspective

Lines of business (LOB) are the natural segmentations of responsibilities that form within an organization, especially where the organization carries a broad portfolio of products or services. By their nature, lines of business often have unique perspectives on core business

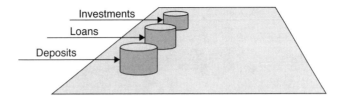

Figure 1.1 Lines of business often maintain their own business information.

information, such as products (the products that this LOB offers), customer (the type of customer information that is important), and account (the nature of an ongoing relationship with a customer based on one or more products). For example, a line of business within a financial institution that is focused on deposits will usually carry different product information than a line of business focusing on investments—see Figure 1.1. Similarly, the customer information that is important to a mortgage department is often different from the information that is important in the support of checking accounts. In reality, neighboring lines of business experience varying levels of cohesion—some lines of business share a great deal of business information, while others share a good deal less.

Within large organizations, lines of business frequently act as very different suborganizations, each funding and maintaining its own suites of applications and data. Even where similar, or indeed identical, applications such as Customer Relationship Management (CRM) or Campaign Management are in use, lines of business often install and manage their own instances of these solutions independently. For example, when multiple LOBs implement a software package like SAP, they often make unique customizations to the data models and look-up tables, which results in multiple independent implementations.

Typically, lines of business capture and maintain unique representations of core business information (customer, product, arrangement), each with their own unique slant on the usage and representation of that information. While regulatory requirements have a role in these differences, in many cases this issue is about control. A line of business sees this data as critical to its day-to-day operations and may not see value in sharing this data within the broader enterprise. All of these factors encourage lines of business to seek to control their own master data, and they sometimes act as barriers to the sharing of this business information.

1.2.2 A Cross-Channel Perspective

Each line of business may also have a number of distinct (distribution) channels to market. While these channels are often very similar, the resulting treatment of business information is often very different. For example, within a single line of business there are frequently entirely different solutions in place for attended channels (such as a branch office) and unattended channels (such as the Internet). These differences in customer interaction patterns across channels often drive a perception that the problem space differs sufficiently to merit an entirely different solution. In other cases, increased complexity is caused by evolution, with emerging channels adopting solutions that were simply not available when support for existing channels was defined.

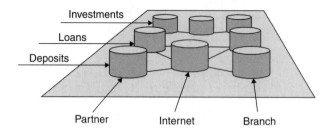

Figure 1.2 Channel variance further scatters business information.

There are, of course, valid differences in business information across channels—Internet-only product offers, in-branch deals, and so on. However, these variances are often best viewed as just that—minor differences of the business information rather than fundamentally different information.

The location of master data can also be influenced by the realization that core information[2] can be shared across lines of business, particularly where the adoption of a new channel acts as a catalyst driving a common view of master data across that channel but not across related channels. The result can be a unification of master data across lines of business for some channels but not for others. For example, many enterprises strive to provide a single point of entry for customer self-service over the Internet. Even if a customer has five different kinds of accounts at a bank (managed by five different systems), the organization will still want to present a unified view of that customer relationship through this channel. Indeed, one of the key business themes that we see across many industries is the desire to change the focus of the business from an account-centric one to a customer-centric one across the enterprise.

All of these factors add an additional dimension to the distribution of master data—the location of master data stores across lines of business, and distribution across channels, as shown in Figure 1.2.

1.2.3 A Cross-Business Subdomain Perspective

Different concerns across lines of business and channels often result in variation, not just in where and how business information is captured, but also in what information is required. In the case of customer data, the branch channel may seek to consider a much broader range of information (customer, contact preferences, contact and case history) than related channels such as partner networks, which may only be interested in a subset of this information. The result can be a fundamentally different scope of business information across channels or lines of business. Each channel and/or line of business may also distribute this information across solutions in different ways, adding further to the complexity of the distribution of customer information, as shown in Figure 1.3.

---

2. Regulatory requirements may, in some industries, limit the amount of data that can be shared across business segments.

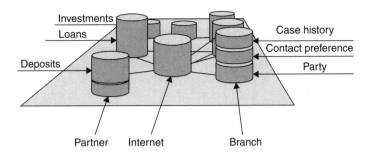

Figure 1.3 Variance in business information further fragments master data.

Additionally, different organization units may have different scopes of interest for product information. Financial controllers, for example, may wish to consider the profitability of different products, product groups, and services. This information is a different subset of product information than the information considered during the process of offering a product to a potential customer.

Variance of the business domain and the information needs of that domain drives further distribution of master data, because each line of business and each channel seeks to maintain its own unique perspective about the business information that best meets its needs.

1.2.4 A Cross-Application/Technology Perspective

An increasingly common reason for master data redundancy is the introduction of packaged applications and solutions (CRM, ERP, etc.). Typically, packaged systems are designed to manage their own master data. When multiple packaged applications are deployed in an environment, an interesting conundrum arises—each of the packaged applications will likely only store the information it needs for its own operations—so when you have two or more of them deployed in an environment, there is no common definition of the master data elements. For example, information about customers is normally needed by both an ERP system and a CRM system—because they each likely maintain unique customer attributes, neither represents a complete view of the customer information. As we describe in Chapters 3 and 5, a common pattern is to use the MDM System to support the complete representation of customer information through the aggregation or federation of customer data from multiple systems.

Integrating a packaged application system into an enterprise can be a difficult and costly endeavor, because the new system must be synchronized with existing sources of data, including master data. When packaged solutions contain multiple independent applications, they may need to synchronize master data within their own solutions as well as with the customer's environment. In an environment with many such applications, pair-wise synchronization can be complex and fragile. Using an MDM System as a common hub from which other systems are synchronized simplifies the number of connections and can improve the overall quality of master data and the manageability of the environment.

Finally, consider the effect of variance in the technical platform or application solution on the distribution of master data. Between lines of business or channels, many different representations of business information may evolve based on different platforms or applications. For example, if a customer has a well-tuned mainframe application already managing product data, extending that system to supply information to a new channel application may be perceived as too costly. Real or not, the perception is often that these platform differences are difficult to resolve, and often no attempt is made to integrate across different systems, which results in further distribution of unmanaged master data.

The result of all of these varying concerns is that master data is often widely scattered across the enterprise, with each channel, line of business, and solution stack evolving its own unique silo of master data. Where attempts to share business information do exist, they are usually ad hoc in nature and limited to a particular channel or product type. For example, it is not uncommon to find at least a couple of dozen stores of customer data in a financial institution.

1.2.5   Mergers and Acquisitions

Mergers and acquisitions serve to dramatically accelerate the replication of business information within an enterprise. Each party to a merger has its own distinct set of master data sources along the dimensions highlighted earlier—a sort of master data fingerprint. Without extensive effort to converge these data stores, the resulting merged organization will not be able to effectively leverage the combined assets (customers, products, etc.) of the new organization or be able to achieve economies of scale in the operation of the merged enterprise. For example, consider a case where organization A is to merge with organization B. Both organizations maintain LOB-specific stores of master data, as shown in Figure 1.4; however,

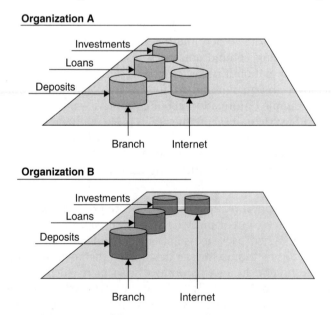

Figure 1.4   Two organizations with different patterns of data distribution.

both organizations consider themselves to have developed strong offerings for the Internet channel. Organization A shares information across lines of business within the Internet channel, while organization B has all but eliminated channel-specific perspectives on master data, and each line of business operates on the same data, regardless of the channel concerned.

Merging these organizations yields a very different picture, however. The result is a dramatic increase in line of business-specific solutions, because each organization brings to the table its own solution, in each line of business. Within a specific channel (e.g., Internet), the two contrasting approaches of sharing information across lines of business, and eliminating channel-specific variances do not align well, which results in further complexity, as shown in Figure 1.5, with one solution seeking to be a channel-specific source of truth for all lines of business, and another seeking to eliminate channel-specific management of business information.

Consolidation and modernization of existing systems often require a similar kind of convergence. For example, an organization may, after several years of geographic growth, realize that each region has independently created localized systems that contain partially replicated and overlapping sets of data, which has led to an incomplete and inconsistent view of its customers, suppliers, and products. Addressing these business problems can be viewed as a merger of the different geographically based organizations and systems.

In summary, there are many natural forces that have led many enterprises to have multiple copies of master data spread out across different lines of business, different communications channels, and different kinds of applications. As the number of unique copies of master data increases, synchronization via point-to-point connections becomes more complex, and the overall environment becomes more difficult to both manage and change. Indeed, when multiple systems manage the metadata, it is hard to achieve consistency of the information. For example, it is likely that many of the applications used to manage master data will have different rules for validating and standardizing the data—thus, even simple things like shipping address information for a customer may not be consistent.

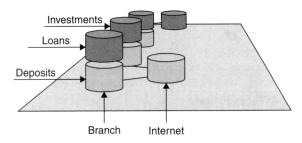

Figure 1.5   The resulting merger often suffers from the worst of all inputs.

1.3   What Is a Master Data Management System?

Master Data Management Systems provide authoritative data to an organization. But what kind of data? How do we work with the MDM System? How do we integrate the MDM System with the existing systems? These questions describe a solution space within which there are a wide variety of ways in which MDM Systems can be deployed and used according to the needs and goals of the enterprise.

In this section, we describe the three primary dimensions of this MDM solutions space. As shown in Figure 1.6, the three dimensions are the **domains of master data** that are managed, the **methods** by which the system is to be used, and the **styles of implementation** that are needed for a particular deployment. It is important to note that MDM implementations are typically not deployed in a "big bang" approach where all domains are managed across all methods of use. Organizations generally start with a limited scope that provides the highest return on investment in a relatively short time frame. As MDM implementations are rolled out over several phases, the space of the implementation may grow. Additional domains are added, the method of use may expand, or the implementation style may change to deliver additional business value. The term **Multiform MDM** is sometimes used to describe MDM Systems that support these three dimensions of MDM Systems. The following sections describe these dimensions in greater detail.

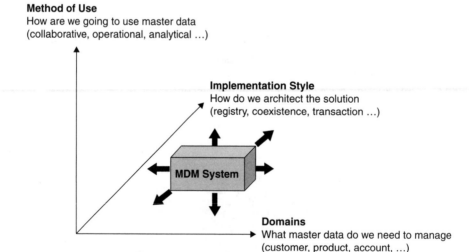

Figure 1.6   Dimensions of Master Data Management.

1.3.1 Master Data Domains

Master Data Management has emerged over the last few years from the recognition that the existing markets of Customer Data Integration (CDI) and Product Information Management (PIM) had key similarities as well as differences. CDI focuses on managing people and organizations—which we will collectively call **parties.** A CDI system can aggregate party information from many preexisting systems, manage the use of the party data, and distribute the information out to downstream systems such as billing systems, campaign management systems, or CRM systems.

PIM systems manage the definition and lifecycle of a finished good or service—collecting product information from multiple sources, getting agreement on the definition of products, and then publishing this information to Web sites, marketing systems, merchandizing systems, and so on. PIM systems are distinct from Product Lifecycle Management (PLM) systems, which focus on the design and development of products rather than the preparation of product information to support sales and distribution. There is a natural flow of information from a PLM system to a PIM system as a product transitions from engineering into marketing and sales.

CDI and PIM both represent a common pattern—that of aggregating data from existing systems, cleaning and augmenting that data, and then distributing that data to downstream systems. PIM and CDI systems differ in the most common ways in which the data is used after it has been loaded into the MDM System—we discuss the different methods of use in the following section. It is important to note that MDM Systems do more than just store and retrieve data—they incorporate business logic to reflect the proper management and handling of the master data. The rules for handling a product lifecycle are different than those for managing the lifecycle for a customer. The MDM System may also be configured to issue alerts when interesting things happen. For example, billing systems may need to get notified immediately when a customer address changes. This business logic can be customized for a particular deployment to reflect the needs of a particular industry as well as the unique characteristics of the implementing organization.

As CDI and PIM products have matured, it was also observed that while CDI systems focused on the customer, it was often convenient for such systems to include references to the products or accounts that a customer has. Similarly, PIM systems often need to store or reference the suppliers of the products or services. Supporting and using these cross-domain relationships has become a significant aspect of MDM Systems.

The kinds of information treated as master data varies from industry to industry and from one organization to another. An insurance company may wish to treat information about customers, policies, and accounts as master data, while a telecommunications company may be concerned with customers, accounts, location (of cell phone towers), and services. A manufacturer may be focused on managing suppliers, customers, distributors, and products. A government agency may want to focus only on citizens and non-citizens. In these examples, we see a lot of commonality as well as differences. In general, master data can be categorized according to the kinds of questions they address; three of the most common questions—"Who?," "What?," and "How?" are addressed by the **party, product,** and **account** domains of master data. Each of these domains represents a class of things—for example, the party domain can represent any kind of person or organization, including customers, suppliers, employees, citizens, distributors, and organizations. Each of these kinds of party shares a common set of attributes—such as the name of the party, where it is located (a party may have multiple locations such as home, work, vacation home, etc.), how to contact it, what kind of relationship the organization has with the party, and so forth. Similarly, the product domain can represent all kinds of things that you sell or use—from tangible consumer goods to service products such as mortgages, telephone services, or insurance policies. The account domain describes how a party is related to a product or service that the organization offers. What are the relations of the parties to this account, and who owns the account? Which accounts are used for which products? What are the terms and conditions associated with the products and the accounts? And how are products bundled?

Location information is often associated with one of the other domains. When we talk about where a product is sold, where a customer lives, and the address at which an insurance policy is in effect, we are referring to location information. Location information is tied to a product, a party, or an account—it does not have an independent existence. There are, of course, cases where location does exist independently, but those situations seem to be less common. Another interesting facet of location is that it can be described in many different ways (by postal address, by latitude and longitude, by geopolitical boundaries)—we need a particular context in order to define what we mean. A location can be a sales territory, a city, a campus with many buildings, a store, or even a spot on a shelf in an aisle within a store. For these reasons, we will treat location as a subordinate domain of master data.

Figure 1.7 shows how the three primary domains of party, product, and account overlap. These areas of overlap are particularly interesting, because they indicate fundamental

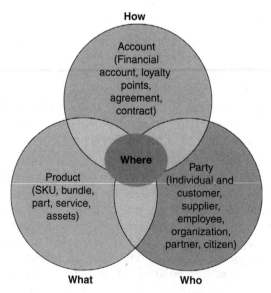

Figure 1.7 Domains of Master Data.

relationships between the domains. For example, when we define a product, we often need to specify the party that supplies that product and the location(s) in which the product may be sold. Explicitly capturing these relationships within the same environment allows us to address business questions that may be otherwise difficult to resolve. Building on the previous example, if we record the party that supplies a product as well as the parties that we sell products to, then we can determine which of our suppliers are also our customers. Understanding the full set of linkages that an organization has with a partner can be valuable in all aspects of working with that partner—from establishing mutually beneficial agreements to ensuring an appropriate level of support. Indeed, perhaps the key benefit of supporting multiple domains of master data within the same system is that it clarifies these cross-domain relationships.

Master data domains can be made specific to a particular industry through the application of industry standards or widely accepted industry models.[3] Typically, standards and models can be used to drive not just the definition of the data model within an MDM Solution but the services that work with the master data as well. In particular, use of standards and models aligns the services exposed by an MDM Solution with accepted industry-specific definitions, which reduces the cost of integration.

Gaining agreement on the definition of an MDM domain can be challenging when different stakeholders within an organization have different requirements or look at the same requirements from different points of view. If well-accepted industry models or standards exist, they can serve as a foundation for further customization, eliminating the need to laboriously gain agreement on every term or service definition. Table 1.1 provides a list of some of the standards and models that are available within a range of industries. Some of these standards and models could be used to guide the definition of data structures and access services for MDM domains.[4]

In summary, an MDM System supports one or more domains of master data. The domains provided are often industry-neutral but can be subsequently tailored (and/or mapped) to different industry standards or models. The domain definitions can be further customized during the design and implementation of an MDM Solution for a specific environment.

1.3.2   Methods of Use

As we look at the roles that master data plays within an organization, we find three key methods or patterns of use: **Collaborative Authoring**, **Operational**, and **Analytical**, shown in Figure 1.8. The simplest way to think about these methods of use is to consider who will be the primary consumers of the master data. Under the Collaborative Authoring[5] pattern,

---

3. Examples of industry models can be found in Appendix B.

4. The Solution Blueprints described in Chapters 6, 7, and 8 describe how several of these standards and models can be leveraged within an MDM Solution.

5. *Note:* We will sometimes just use the term Collaborative to mean Collaborative Authoring.

Table 1.1 Some Industry Standards and Models

Industry	Standard or Industry Model	Web Resource
Banking	IBM Information FrameWork (IFW)	www-306.ibm.com/software/data/ips/products/industrymodels/
	Interactive Financial eXchange (IFX)	www.ifxforum.org
Insurance	IBM Insurance Application Architecture (IAA)	www-306.ibm.com/software/data/ips/products/industrymodels/
	Association for Cooperative Operations Research and Development (ACORD)	www.acord.org
Telecoms	Shared Information/Data Model (SID)	www.tmforum.org
	IBM Telecommunications Data Warehouse	http://www-306.ibm.com/software/data/ips/products/industrymodels/telecomm.html
Retail	Association for Retail Technology Standards (ARTS)	www.nrf-arts.org
	IBM Retail Data Warehouse	http://www-306.ibm.com/software/data/ips/products/industrymodels/retail.html
Healthcare	Health Level 7 (HL7)	www.hl7.org

the MDM System coordinates a group of users and systems in order to reach agreement on a set of master data. Under the Operational pattern, the MDM System participates in the operational transactions and business processes of the enterprise, interacting with other application systems and people. Finally, under the Analytical pattern, the MDM System is a source of authoritative information for downstream analytical systems, and sometimes is a source of insight itself.

A particular element of master data such as a product or an account may be initially authored using a collaborative style, managed operationally through the operational style, and then published to other operational and analytical systems. Because MDM Systems may be optimized to one or more of the methods of use, more than one MDM System may be needed to support the full breadth of usage. Where multiple MDM Systems are used to support multiple usage patterns, careful attention to the integration, management, and governance of the combined system is required to ensure that the master data of the combined system is consistent and authoritative.

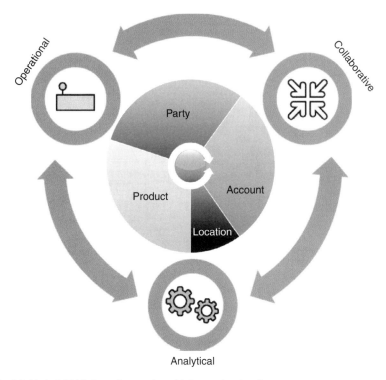

Figure 1.8   Multiple MDM domains and multiple methods of use.

It is important to note that the style of usage is completely independent from the domain of information managed. Although Product Information Management systems are often associated with a Collaborative Authoring style of use, and Customer Data Integration systems are often associated with an Operational usage style, this alignment is not necessary or exclusive. There are an increasing number of cases where organizations seek an operational usage of product information as well as a range of use cases for collaborative authoring of customer information.

1.3.2.1   Collaborative MDM

Collaborative MDM deals with the processes supporting collaborative authoring of master data, including the creation, definition, augmentation, and approval of master data. Collaborative MDM is about achieving agreement on a complex topic among a group of people. The process of getting to agreement is often encapsulated in a workflow that may incorporate both automated and manual tasks, both of which are supported by collaborative capabilities. Information about the master data being processed is passed from task to task within the workflow and is governed throughout its lifecycle.

As a consequence of the complexity of product development and management, PIM systems commonly support a collaborative style of usage. Perhaps the most common process

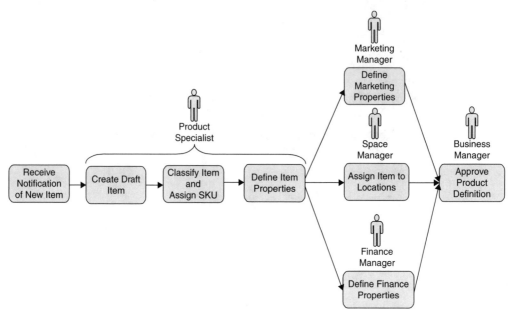

Figure 1.9 Simplified New Product Introduction process.

implemented by PIM systems is the process for introducing a new product to the market. An in-depth discussion on NPI can be found in Chapter 6. A typical NPI process is shown in Figure 1.9.

Here we can see that information about new products (or items) is received from one or more external sources and then incrementally extended, augmented, validated, and approved by a number of different end users with different user roles and responsibilities.[6]

The collaborative steps within a New Product Introduction process are used to define the kinds of properties that describe the product. A given product will be described by dozens, and often hundreds, of properties depending on how the product is classified and where it is sold. In the New Product Introduction process, product specialists, buyers, and other stakeholders describe all of the characteristics of the product that are necessary to bring it to market. These characteristics may include product specifications, marketing information, ingredients, safety information, recycling information, cost, and so on. Large retailers may have more than a million products that they sell, spanning categories from food to clothing to furniture to appliances. The kinds of properties that are relevant to a product depend on the kind of product it is. For clothing, examples include color, size, and material; for electronic appliances, examples might be specifications, color, warranty, and so on. The Collaborative MDM System helps users to capture all of the different relevant properties of the product,

---

6. Appendix A provides an in-depth discussion of the user roles in an MDM environment.

validate the properties, categorize the product, and coordinate the approval of the product. As buyers and product specialists come up with new ways to describe products, new properties are created to hold these new descriptions. In retail environments, the structure of the product information is constantly evolving.

Collaboration is a common pattern and can be found beyond the PIM domain. Indeed, we find that many of the tasks performed by a product specialist in the PIM environment are also performed in the management of Customer and Account information. A key role that spans all domains of master data is that of **data steward**. A data steward looks after the quality and management of the data. For example, when we believe that two or more party records in a data store may really refer to the same individual, data stewards may need to manually combine information from the party records together and then validate the proposed changes with supervisors. Similarly, where questions requiring human intervention arise about the accuracy of information, a request for attention may be made visible to all data stewards who are capable of handling the issue, which can result in a collaborative pattern to resolve data quality issues.

The Collaborative style of usage requires a core set of capabilities within the MDM environment. A combination of workflow, task management, and state management are needed to guide and coordinate the collaborative tasks and the master data being collaborating on. Workflow controls the execution of a sequence of tasks by people and automated processes. Task management prioritizes and displays pending work for individuals to perform, while state management helps us to model and then enforce the lifecycle of the master data.

Because many concurrent users and workflows may be executing in parallel, the integrity of the master data needs to be protected with a check-in/check-out or similar locking technique. To improve efficiency, master data records are often processed in batches within the same workflow, which results in the concept of a "workbasket" of master data records that is passed from task to task within the workflow. Tasks within a workflow may be automated actions (such as import, export, or data validation) or manual tasks that allow users to work directly with the master data. Typically, this workflow will involve business users and data stewards, a process that, in turn, has implications for the design of the UIs (user interfaces) for collaborative authoring of master data. User interfaces must be both efficient and comfortable to use, and must rely on a set of underlying services that create, query, update, and delete the master data itself, the relationships between the master data, and other related information, such as lookup tables. Tooling to support the flexible creation and customization of collaborative workflows and even user screens may also be provided.

Finally, a common set of services are typically also provided to enforce security and privacy, and to support administration, validation, and import/export of master data. These services are needed across all kinds of MDM Systems.

1.3.2.2   Operational MDM

In the Operational style of MDM, the MDM server acts as an Online-Transaction Processing (OLTP) system that responds to requests from multiple applications and users. Operational MDM

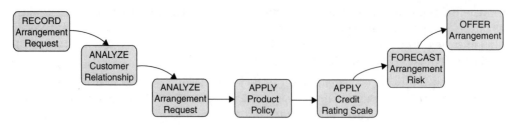

Figure 1.10   Example New Account Opening process.

focuses on providing stateless services in a high-performance environment. These stateless services can be invoked from an enterprise business process or directly from a business application or user interface. Operational MDM services are often designed to fit within a Service-Oriented Architecture as well as in traditional environments. Integration of an Operational MDM System with existing systems calls for the support of a wide variety of communications styles and protocols, including synchronous and asynchronous styles, global transactions, and one-way communications.

A good example of Operational MDM usage is a New Account Opening business process. In this process, a person or organization wants to open a new account—perhaps a bank account, a cable TV account, or any other kind of account. As shown in Figure 1.10, MDM services are invoked to check what information about the customer is already known and to determine if product policy is being complied with before an offer of a new account is made. If the customer isn't already known, then the new customer is added to the MDM System and a new account is created (presuming that the new customer meets the appropriate requirements). Each of the tasks within this workflow is implemented by a service, and many of these services are implemented by an Operational MDM System.

Operational MDM is also commonly used in the PIM domain. For retailers, after products have been defined, the approved product information may be published to an operational MDM System that then serves as a hub of MDM information that interacts with merchandising, distribution, or e-commerce applications. As such applications become more open and able to interact within an SOA environment, the need for such an operational MDM hub increases.

A wide range of capabilities is required for the Operational usage style. There can be hundreds of services that provide access and management of MDM data. Specific sets of services for each kind of MDM object managed provide for creation, reading, updating, and deletion of the MDM objects. Services are also provided to relate, group, and organize MDM objects. As with the Collaborative style of MDM, services are also needed for cleansing and validation of the data, for detection and processing of duplicates, and for managing the security and privacy of the information.

1.3.2.3 Analytical MDM

Analytical MDM is about the intersection between **Business Intelligence (BI)** and MDM. BI is a broad field that includes business reporting, data warehouses, data marts, data mining, scoring, and many other fields. To be useful, all forms of BI require meaningful, trusted data. Increasingly, analytical systems are also transitioning from purely decision support to more operational involvement. As BI systems have begun to take on this broader role, the relationship between MDM Systems and Analytical systems has also begun to change.

There are three primary intersections between MDM and BI.

- **MDM as a trusted data source:** A key role of an MDM System is to be a provider of clean and consistent data to BI systems.
- **Analytics on MDM data:** MDM Systems themselves may integrate reporting and analytics in support of providing insight over the data managed within the MDM System.
- **Analytics as a key function of an MDM System:** Specialized kinds of analytics, such as **identity resolution**, may be a key feature of some MDM Systems.

One of the common drivers for clean and consistent master data is the need to improve the quality of decision making. Using an MDM System to feed downstream BI systems is an important and common pattern. The data that drives a BI system must be of a high quality if the results of the analytical processing are to be trusted. For this reason, MDM Systems are often a key source of information to data warehouses, data marts, Online Analytical Processing (OLAP) cubes, and other BI structures. The common data models for data warehouses use what are called **star schemas** or **snowflake schemas** to represent the relationship between the facts to be analyzed and the dimensions by which the analysis is done.[7] For example, a business analyst in a retail environment would be interested in understanding the number or value of sales by product or perhaps by manufacturer. Here, the sales transaction data is stored in fact tables. Product and manufacturer represent dimensions of the analysis. We can observe that often master data domains align with dimensions within an analytical environment, which makes the MDM System a natural source of data for BI systems.

The insight gained from a data warehouse or OLAP cube may also be fed back into the MDM System. For example, in the travel and entertainment industry, some companies build analytical models that can project the likely net lifetime revenue potential of a customer. To build these projections, they will source the master data from an MDM System and transactional details from other systems. After the revenue potential is computed, the MDM System is updated to reflect this information, which may now be used as part of each customer's profile. Reservation systems can then use this profile to tailor offers specifically to each customer.[8]

Insight may also be derived from data maintained by the MDM System itself. An MDM System contains all of the information needed to report on key performance indicators such

---

7. An overview of Data Warehousing can be found in [1].
8. More details on MDM and Data Warehouse integration may be found in Chapters 5 and 8.

as the number of new customers per week, the number of new accounts per day, or the average time to introduce a new product. Reporting and dashboarding tools can operate directly over the master data to provide these kinds of domain-specific insights. Some MDM Systems also incorporate a combination of rules and event subsystems that allow interesting events to be detected and actions to be taken based on these events as they happen. For example, if a customer changes addresses five times in three months, that may trigger an alert that notifies event subscribers to contact the customer to validate his or her address on a periodic basis. Analytics may also be executed as an MDM transaction is taking place, using architected integration points that allow external functions to be invoked as part of an MDM service. A good example is the use of scoring functions to predict the likelihood of a customer canceling accounts at an institution. Such scoring functions can be developed by gaining a deep understanding of an issue, such as customer retention, through data mining and building a model of recurring customer retention patterns based on the combination of customer and transaction data maintained within a data warehouse. While it is time-consuming to develop and validate such a model, the scoring model that results can be efficiently executed as part of an MDM service. This kind of analytics is called **in-line analytics** or **operational analytics** and is an important new way in which MDM Systems can work together with BI systems to provide additional value to an enterprise.

The final kind of MDM analytics is where the MDM System provides some key analytic capabilities. One particular kind of insight that can be derived from the information within an MDM System is the discovery of both obvious and non-obvious relationships between the master entities managed. An obvious kind of relationship would be one that discovered households based on a set of rules around names, addresses, and other common information. A non-obvious kind of relationship might find relationships between people or organizations by looking for shared fragments of information, such as a common phone number, in an effort to determine that people may be roommates. Searching for non-obvious relationships may also require rules that look for combinations of potentially obfuscated information—for example, transposed Social Security numbers and phone numbers—to identify potential relationships where people may be trying to hide their identities. Identity resolution and relationship discovery are important for both looking for questionable dealings[9] and understanding a social network that a person is part of—and therefore are important for predicting the overall value of a person's influence.

The analytical style of usage encompasses a variety of capabilities. Populating external analytical environments such as data warehouses with data from an MDM System requires information integration tools to efficiently transfer and transform information from the MDM System into the star or snowflake schemas needed by the data warehouse. Integration with reporting tools is required in order to display key performance indicators and how they change over time. Rules, scoring, and event management are important capabilities for in-line analytics within the MDM environment.

---

9. More details on MDM-Analytical integration can be found in Chapters 3, 5, and 8. A blueprint describing the use of MDM in threat and fraud scenarios can be found in Chapter 7.

In practice, MDM usage will often cross the boundaries between collaborative, operational, and analytical usage. For example, collaborative MDM processes can be very useful in managing the augmentation of complex operational structures such as organizational hierarchies. On the other hand, there is valuable analytical information that can be gathered around the nature of the collaborative processes. An MDM implementation may start with the usage style that is most important to achieving their business need and then later extend the environment to incorporate additional styles to meet further requirements.

1.3.3 System of Record vs. System of Reference

The goal of an MDM System is to provide authoritative master data to an enterprise. Ideally, a single copy of key master data would be managed by an MDM System—all applications that needed master data would be serviced by this system, and all updates to master data would be made through the MDM System. The master data in the ideal MDM implementation can be considered a **system of record**. That is, the data managed by the MDM System is the best source of truth. If applications want to be sure that they are getting the most current and highest-quality information, then they consult this source of truth. Achieving this ideal MDM System can be difficult, at best, due to several confounding factors, such as:

- The complexity and investment in the existing IT environment
- Master data locked into packaged applications
- Requirements for performance, availability, and scalability in a complex and geographically distributed world
- Legal constraints that limit the movement of data across geopolitical boundaries

All of these factors contribute to the need for copies of master data—sometimes partial subsets, sometimes completely redundant replicas. These copies can be well-managed, integrated, and synchronized extensions of an MDM System. When the replica of the master data is known to be synchronized with the system of record—in a managed way that maintains the quality and integrity of the data within both the replica and the system of record—we can call this copy a **system of reference**. Although it is synchronized with the system of record, it may not always be completely current. Changes to the system of record are often batched together and then applied to the systems of reference on a periodic basis. In some cases, the copy may represent a special-purpose MDM implementation that has been specifically tuned to the needs of a particular style of usage. A system of reference is a source of authoritative master data because it is managed and synchronized with the system of record. It can therefore be used as a trusted source of master data by other applications and other systems.

An MDM system of reference is best used as a read-only source of information, with all of the updates going through the system of record. Figure 1.11 illustrates a simple environment where the system of record aggregates master information from multiple sources, is responsible for cleansing and managing the data, and then provides this data to both managed systems of reference as well as directly to other consumers of the managed information. We use the terms **Managed** and **Unmanaged** to define the scope of the overall MDM environment. In a managed environment, each source should only feed one system, and each consumer should receive information from only one system. Within the managed environment, we can track the movement of information between systems and audit the transactions that use the system.

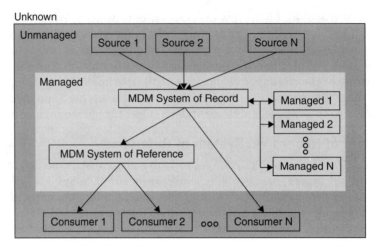

Figure 1.11   System of Record vs. System of Reference.

It is important to note that the system of record may, in fact, be made up of multiple phys-ical subsystems—but this arrangement should be transparent to all of the other systems and people that interact with it. For example, if legal requirements in a country dictate that per-sonal information may not leave the country, then different MDM Systems may be required. In this situation, the different MDM Systems can be logically brought together through the technique of **federation.**[10] The fact that there is more than one MDM System can be hidden from the consumers. Consumers issue requests to the MDM System as a whole and receive a response without having to know (or care) which particular system responded.

1.3.4   Consistency of Data

When data is replicated in an environment, questions of consistency among the replicas immediately arise. For example, as we discussed in the previous section, a system of refer-ence may not always be completely consistent with a system of record. It is useful to think about two basic approaches towards consistency. The first we can call **Absolute Consistency,** and the second we can call **Convergent Consistency.** In a distributed system with absolute consistency, information will be identical among all replicas at all times that the systems are available (for simplicity, let's ignore the case where a system is recovering after a failure). In a distributed environment, we commonly achieve absolute consistency by following a two-phase commit transaction protocol that is provided in most distributed databases, messag-ing systems, and transaction systems. The basic idea is that we can define a unit of work containing several actions that must either all complete or all fail. We can use this approach to write applications that update multiple databases and guarantee that either all of the

---

10. The technique of federation brings data from different systems at need. A discussion of federation at the database level can be found in [2].

updates worked or they all failed. We can also use this approach to concurrently update master data records in multiple repositories simultaneously, and with the two-phase commit transaction protocol, either all of these databases will be updated or none of them will be. In either case, all of the databases contain the same information and are therefore absolutely consistent. Two-phase commit can be costly from a performance, complexity, and availability point of view. For example, if we have three systems that all normally participate in a transaction, all three of the systems must be available for the transaction to complete successfully—in other words, if any one of the systems is not available, then none of the systems can be updated. So while two-phase commit is an important and widely used technique, it is not always the right approach. When we balance the needs for performance, availability, and consistency, we find that there are a range of options for each. Providing an absolute consistency can decrease performance and availability. There are many excellent books devoted to transaction processing that explore this topic further—see [3] as an example.

Convergent consistency is an alternative way to think about providing consistency across systems. The basic idea of convergent consistency is that if we have a distributed set of systems that we want to keep synchronized, whenever we apply an update to one system, that update gets forwarded to all of the other systems. There are a variety of ways to do this—we could do this as each change occurs (which can result in a lot of communications traffic), or we could accumulate a set of changes and process them a batch at a time. Passing along the changes as they happen allows the receiving systems to be only a few updates behind the system that was directly updated—but it can be costly in terms of resources. Processing a batch at a time means that the changes will be delayed in getting to the other systems, but fewer resources will be consumed. With either approach, if new updates stop arriving, all of the systems will eventually have the same data. That is, the information in the different systems converge, and all of the systems become consistent with one another. The benefit of following a convergent consistency strategy is that the systems can operate independently of each other so that processing of forwarded updates can happen at the convenience of the recipient. This fact means that we can achieve higher availability and potentially higher performance at the expense of consistency. The lag-time for changes to propagate across all of the systems can be tuned by increasing or decreasing the rate at which the changes are forwarded. One other consideration is that if new updates are being applied to multiple systems concurrently, significant care must be taken to prevent anomalous behaviors such as update conflicts.

Absolute and convergent consistency are both important strategies for managing replicated data across multiple systems. Absolute consistency is not always technically possible or pragmatic. Many systems do not expose interfaces that support two-phase commit. Convergent consistency can be quite pragmatic and can yield better performance and availability, but it also has its share of complexity. System architects implementing MDM Systems need to be well versed in these techniques to properly select the right combinations of techniques that will balance the requirements and constraints dictated by an implementation.

1.3.5 MDM Implementation Styles

MDM Systems are implemented to improve the quality of master data and to provide consistent, managed use of this information in what is often a complex and somewhat tangled environment. There are a variety of ways to support these requirements in ways that accommodate a range of methods of use (as described earlier) and implementation requirements. Implementation requirements can dictate:

- If the MDM System is to be used as a system of record or a system of reference
- If the system is to support operational environments, decision support environments, or both
- If it is important for the MDM System to push clean data back into existing systems
- If the system is to be part of an SOA fabric
- If geographic distribution is required

Different combinations of implementation and usage requirements have led to the evolution of a number of MDM implementation styles. Hybrid implementations that combine multiple implementation styles are common. Because some styles are simpler than others, organizations may start with a simpler implementation style that addresses the most urgent business needs and then subsequently address additional business needs by extending the implementation to enable additional styles.

In this section, we introduce four common implementation styles:[11]

- Consolidation Implementation Style
- Registry Implementation Style
- Coexistence Implementation Style
- Transactional Hub Implementation Style

As the styles progress from Consolidation Implementation Style to Transactional Hub Implementation Style, they provide increasing functionality and also tend to require more sophisticated deployments.

1.3.5.1 Consolidation Implementation Style

The **consolidation** implementation style brings together master data from a variety of existing systems, both databases and application systems, into a single managed MDM hub. Along the way, the data is transformed, cleansed, matched, and integrated in order to provide a complete **golden record** for one or more master data domains. This golden record serves as a trusted source to downstream systems for reporting and analytics, or as a system of reference to other operational applications. Changes to the data primarily come in from the systems that feed it; this is a read-only system. Figure 1.12 illustrates the basic consolidation style, with reads and writes going directly against the existing systems and the MDM System (in the middle) receiving updates from these existing systems. The integrated and cleansed information is then distributed to downstream systems (such as data warehouses) that use, but don't update, the master data.

There is a strong similarity between the consolidation implementation style and an operational data store (ODS). An ODS is also an aggregation point and staging area for analytical systems such as data warehouses—see [1,4] for more details. The distinction between them

---

11. A detailed discussion on the capabilities of these styles may be found in Chapter 3. Chapter 5 describes the implementation patterns associated with these implementation styles.

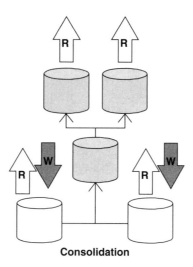

Consolidation

Figure 1.12   Consolidation Implementation Style.

lies in the set of platform capabilities that an MDM System offers, which go beyond the storage and management of data that an ODS provides. An operational data store is a database that is used in a particular way for a particular purpose, while an MDM System provides access, governance, and stewardship services to retrieve and manage the master data and to support data stewards as they investigate and resolve potential data quality issues.

Implementing the consolidation style is a natural early phase in the multiphase roll-out of an MDM System. A consolidation style MDM system serves as a valuable resource for analytical applications and at the same time provides a foundation for the coexistence and transactional hub implementation styles.

The drawbacks of the consolidation style mirror its advantages. Because it is fed by upstream systems, it does not always contain the most current information. If batch imports are performed only once a day, then the currency requirements for a decision support system would likely be met—but those for a downstream operational system may not be. Because the consolidation style represents a read-only system, all of the information about a master data object must already be present in the systems that feed the MDM System. Thus, if additional information needs to be collected to address new business needs, one or more of the existing source applications need to be changed as well as the MDM System—this lack of flexibility is addressed by the coexistence and transactional hub implementation styles.

1.3.5.2   Registry Implementation Style

The **registry** implementation style (as shown in Figure 1.13) can be useful for providing a read-only source of master data as a reference to downstream systems with a minimum of data redundancy. In the figure, the two outside systems are existing sources of master data. The MDM System in the middle holds the minimum amount of information required to

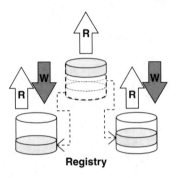

Figure 1.13 Registry Implementation Style.

uniquely identify a master data record; it also provides cross-references to detailed information that is managed within other systems and databases. The registry is able to clean and match just this identifying information and assumes that the source systems are able to adequately manage the quality of their own data. A registry style of MDM implementation serves as a read-only system of reference to other applications.

Queries against the registry style MDM System dynamically assemble the required information in two steps. First, the identifying information is looked up within the MDM System. Then, using that identity and the cross-reference information, relevant pieces of information are retrieved from other source systems. Figure 1.14 shows a simple example where the MDM System holds enough master data to uniquely identify a customer (in this case, the Name, TaxID, and Primary address information) and then provides cross-references to additional customer information stored in System A and System B. When a service request for

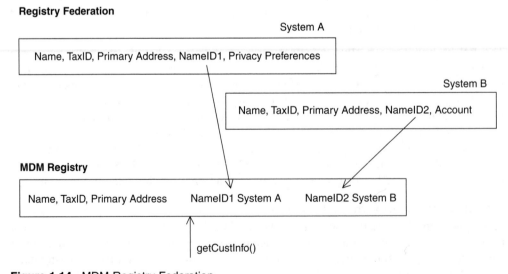

Figure 1.14 MDM Registry Federation.

customer information is received (*getCustInfo()*), the MDM System looks up the information that it keeps locally, as well as the cross-references, to return the additional information from Systems A and B. The MDM System brings together the information desired as it is needed—through federation. Federation can be done at the database layer or by dynamically invoking services to retrieve the needed data in each of the source systems.

Federation has several advantages. Because the majority of information remains in the source systems and is fetched when needed, the information returned is always current. This style of MDM System is therefore suitable to meet transactional inquiry needs in an operational environment. The registry implementation style can also be useful in complex organizational environments where one group may not be able to provide all of its data to another. The registry style can be relatively quick to implement, because responsibility for most of the data remains within the source systems.

There is, however, a corresponding set of issues with this implementation style. One fundamental issue is that a registry implementation is not useful in remediating quality issues that go beyond basic identity. A registry implementation can only manage the quality of the data that it holds—so while it can match and cleanse the core identifying data, it cannot, in itself, provide a completely standardized and cleansed view of the master data. Because the complexities of updating federated information lead most registry style implementations to be read-only, the cleansed identifying information is not typically sent back to the source systems. If the data in the sources systems is clean, the composite view served by the MDM System will also be clean. Thus, a registry implementation can act as an authoritative source of master data for the key identifying information that it maintains.

A registry implementation style is also more sensitive to the availability and performance of the existing systems. If one of the source systems slows down or fails, the MDM System will be directly affected. Similarly, the registry style also requires strong governance practices between the MDM System and the source systems, because a unilateral change in a source system could immediately cause problems for users of the MDM System. For example, in the scenario shown in Figure 1.14, suppose a change is made in the structure of the Privacy Preferences information in System A. If this change occurs without making corresponding changes in the MDM System, then a request such as *getCustInfo()* will likely cause the MDM system to fail with an internal error because of the assumptions it makes about the structure of the data it federates.

1.3.5.3   Coexistence Implementation Style

The coexistence style of MDM implementation involves master data that may be authored and stored in numerous locations and that includes a physically instantiated golden record in the MDM System that is synchronized with source systems. The golden record is constructed in the same manner as the consolidation style, typically through batch imports, and can be both queried and updated within the MDM System. Updates to the master data can be fed back to source systems as well as published to downstream systems. In a coexistence style, the MDM System can interact with other applications or users, as shown in Figure 1.15.

An MDM System implemented in the coexistence style is not a system of record, because it is not the single place where master data is authored and updated. It is a key participant in

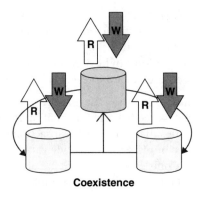

Coexistence

Figure 1.15 Coexistence Implementation Style.

a loosely distributed environment that can serve as an authoritative source of master data to other applications and systems. Because the master data is physically instantiated within the system, the quality of the data can be managed as the data is imported into the system. If the MDM System does a bidirectional synchronization with source systems, care must be taken to avoid update cycles where changes from one system conflict with changes from another—these cycles can be through a combination of automated and manual conflict detection and resolution.

The advantage of the coexistence style is that it can provide a full set of MDM capabilities without causing significant change in the existing environment. The disadvantage is that because it is not the only place where master data may be authored or changed, it is not always up to date. As with the consolidation style, the coexistence style is an excellent system of reference but is not a system of record.

1.3.5.4 Transactional Hub Implementation Style

A **transactional hub** implementation style is a centralized, complete set of master data for one or more domains (see Figure 1.16). It is a system of record, serving as the single version of truth

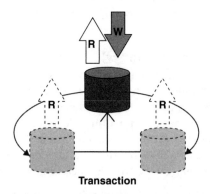

Transaction

Figure 1.16 Transactional Hub Implementation Style.

for the master data it manages. A transactional hub is part of the operational fabric of an IT environment, receiving and responding to requests in a timely manner. This style often evolves from the consolidation and coexistence implementations. The fundamental difference is the change from a system of reference to a system of record. As a system of record, updates to master data happen directly to this system using the services provided by the hub. As update transactions take place, the master data is cleansed, matched, and augmented in order to maintain the quality of the master data. After updates are accepted, the system distributes these changes to interested applications and users. Changes can be distributed as they happen via messaging, or the changes can be aggregated and distributed as a batch.

Sometimes data extensions are needed in the MDM System to accommodate information that is not already stored in the source systems. For example, in the product domain, a food retailer might find that consumers are interested in knowing the distance that food has traveled to a store (there is a growing interest in purchasing locally grown products). Rather than augment all of the source systems, the MDM System would be extended to support this new information and would become the only place where such information is managed.

Governance and security are key aspects of all MDM implementation styles. Access to the master data must be tightly controlled and audited. Auditing can be used to track both queries and changes to the data. Visibility of the information may be controlled to the attribute value level to ensure that the right people and applications are restricted to seeing the right information in the right context. Because a transactional hub implementation is a system of record, security and governance play an especially critical role in maintaining the integrity of the master data.

The benefits of a transactional hub implementation are significant. As the system of record, it is the repository of current, clean, authoritative master data providing both access and governance. Any of the methods of use can be implemented (collaborative, operational, and analytical) to meet the MDM needs of an organization. The primary difficulty in a transactional hub implementation is achieving the transition from system of reference to system of record. As a system of record, all updates should be funneled to the MDM System—this means that existing applications, business processes, and perhaps organizational structures may need to be altered to use the MDM System. Although potentially costly, the overall organization generally benefits as more comprehensive data governance policies are established to manage the master data.

The primary disadvantages of the transactional hub style are cost and complexity. The implementation of a transactional hub often means that existing systems and business processes have to be altered when the transactional hub becomes the single point of update within the environment. The transition to a transactional hub can be performed incrementally to minimize disruption. The significant benefits of a transactional hub implementation cause it to be the ultimate goal of many MDM projects.

The different implementation styles introduced in this section are complementary and additive. Table 1.2 provides an overview that compares the implementation styles and shows the individual benefits and drawbacks. Different MDM domains may be implemented with different styles within the same MDM System. As we have mentioned, it is common for an MDM deployment to start with one style, such as the consolidation style, achieve success with that

Table 1.2   MDM Implementation Styles

Style	Consolidation	Registry	Coexistence	Transactional Hub
What	Aggregate master data into a common repository for reporting and reference	Maintain thin system of record with links to more complete data spread across systems; useful for real-time reference	Manage single view of master data, synchronizing changes with other systems	Manage single view of master data, providing access via services
Benefits	Good for preparing data to feed downstream systems	Complete view is assembled as needed; fast to build	Assumes existing systems unchanged, yet provides read-write management	Support new and existing transactional applications; the system of record
Drawbacks	Read-only; not always current with operational systems	Read-mostly; may be more complex to manage	Not always consistent with other systems	May require changes to existing systems to exploit
Methods of use	Analytical	Operational	Collaborative, Operational, Analytical	Collaborative, Operational, Analytical
System of	Reference	Reference	Reference	Record

implementation by publishing authoritative master data to downstream systems, and then extend the system with a coexistence style. With the completion of the coexistence phase, the MDM System could then be used to support the master data needs of new applications while continuing to publish snapshots of master data to downstream systems. Over time, the existing systems could be altered to leverage the MDM System, which would become a system of record.

In an MDM System supporting multiple domains of master data such as customer, product, and supplier, we may find that the MDM System may appear as a consolidation style for one domain, a registry style for the second domain, and a transactional hub for the third domain.

1.3.6 Categorizing Data

There are many ways to characterize the different ways to store, manage, and use data. Because these characterizations can sometimes be confusing, we put forward a set of working definitions for five key categories of data that we discuss in this book. The five key kinds of data that we discuss in this section are:

- Metadata
- Reference Data
- Master Data
- Transaction Data
- Historical Data

Each of these categories of data has important roles to play within an enterprise's information architecture.

1.3.6.1 Metadata

The distinctions between metadata, master data, and reference data can be particularly confusing. In this book, we use the term **metadata** to refer to descriptive information that is useful for people or systems who seek to understand something. Metadata is a very broad topic—there are thousands of different kinds of metadata. It is beyond the scope of this book to provide an in-depth review of the topic; however, we can describe a few key characteristics.[12] Different kinds of metadata are defined and used pervasively throughout the software industry because it is useful to be able to have one kind of information describe another kind of information. A database catalog describes the data managed within a database, an XML schema[13] describes how an XML document that conforms to the schema should be structured, and a WSDL[14] file describes how a Web service is defined. Metadata is used in both runtimes and in tools. For example, a relational database uses metadata (the database catalog) to define the legal data types for a column of data, that is, to recognize if a column of information is a primary key and to indicate if values in a column of data can be null. Similarly, database tooling uses this same metadata to allow database administrators to author and manage these database structures.

In general, it is considered appropriate to hide the existence of metadata by making the creation, management, and use of metadata part of the systems and tools that need to use it. For example, many different tools and runtimes are involved in collecting data quality information. This metadata helps users determine how much they should trust the data and systems monitored. It is important that the collection and processing of this information be automated and transparent to users. If it is something that requires user involvement, then it is difficult to guarantee that the collection of the quality metadata has been done in an accurate and consistent manner. Similarly, most users should not have to explicitly recognize when they are using metadata—it should just be a natural part of their work environment.

Metadata is also stored and managed in a wide variety of ways—from files to specialized metadata repositories. Metadata repositories often provide additional benefits by allowing different kinds of metadata to be linked together to promote better understanding and to

---

12. While the topic of metadata management is very broad, one perspective can be found in [5].

13. XML Schema (XSD) is a standard that describes how XML may be structured. See [6] for a technical overview of XSD.

14. Web Service Description Language is a standard way to describe Web services. Chapter 2 will describe WSDL in more detail.

support impact analysis and data lineage across a range of different systems. For example, because there are many places where data quality information can be collected and exploited, it is useful to aggregate this information into a Metadata Repository where the information can be combined, related, and accessed by multiple tools and systems. An increasingly important new kind of metadata repository is a **Service Registry and Repository (SRR)**, which specializes in storing information about the services deployed in an SOA environment to support both the operation and management of a services infrastructure.

Because metadata is data that describes other kinds of information, there is metadata for each of the other kinds of data. For example, in the case of master data, the information model and services provided by an MDM System are described by a set of metadata that is used at both design and execution. Users of the MDM System rely on this metadata to accurately describe how to interpret and use the master data. When metadata plays such a critical role, governance of the metadata is important to users' confidence that the metadata accurately reflects the MDM System.[15]

1.3.6.2   Reference Data

Where metadata often describes the structure, origin, and meaning of things, **reference data** is focused on defining and distributing collections of common values. Reference data enables accurate and efficient processing of operational and analytical activities by enabling processes to use the same defined values of information for common abbreviations, for codes, and for validation. Reference data can be simple lists of common values to be used in lookups to ensure the consistent use of a code such as the abbreviation for a state, of product codes that uniquely identify a product, or of transaction codes that specify if a checking transaction is a deposit, withdrawal, or transfer. In all of these cases, the reference data represents an agreed-upon set of values that should be used throughout an organization.

Reference data is used throughout an IT system—including the processing of financial transactions, the analysis of data in a warehouse, and the management of the systems themselves. Wherever we want to guarantee a common value of a simple object, we are using reference data. When the values of reference data are able to change during the processing of long-running business processes, the management of reference data becomes particularly important. For example, when two companies merge, the stock symbol representing them may change, and so all in-flight transactions that referenced that stock symbol might fail unless the reference data is managed appropriately.

It is often the case that different applications have different values for the same object. For example, one application may refer to a state by its abbreviation, and another application may refer to it by its full name (e.g., TX and Texas). A reference data management system helps to translate from one set of values to another.

The management of reference data can happen in multiple places. Many applications have their own built-in management for reference data. Dedicated reference data management systems are sometimes used for specialized forms of reference data, and in particular for the

---

15. Chapter 9 describes governance in detail.

reference data used in financial investment transactions. Some MDM Systems can also be used to manage reference data in addition to master data.

1.3.6.3   Master Data

As we described earlier, master data represents the common business objects that need to be agreed on and shared throughout an enterprise. In previous sections, we described the domains of master data and the methods of use. Master data is most often managed within a specialized MDM System. An MDM System often uses both reference data and metadata in its processing. Reference data is used to ensure common and consistent values for attributes of master data such as a country name or a color. MDM Systems may either store metadata internally or leverage an external metadata repository to describe the structure of the information managed by an MDM System and the services it provides.

1.3.6.4   Transaction Data

The business transactions that run an organization produce transaction data. **Transaction data** is the fine-grained information that represents the details of any enterprise—in the commercial world this information includes sales transactions, inventory information, and invoices and bills. In noncommercial organizations, transaction data might represent passport applications, logistics, or court cases. Transaction data describes what is happening in an organization.

There is often a relationship between transaction data and master data. For example, if a person applies for a passport, the application and the processing of the application is transaction information that refers to the master data representing people. The master data contains citizenship status, existing passport details, and address information that is needed in the processing of the passport request. The processing of the passport itself is handled by other applications.

Transaction data is usually maintained in databases associated with the applications that drive the business and that may also be geographically and organizationally distributed. An organization can have a very large number of databases with transaction databases—each holding a large amount of data. Transaction data is commonly stored in relational databases according to schemas that have been optimized for the combination of query and update patterns required.

1.3.6.5   Historical Data

Historical data represents the accumulation of transaction and master data over time. It is used for both analytical processing and for regulatory compliance and auditing. Data integration tooling is typically used to extract transaction data from the existing application systems and load it into an ODS.[16] Along the way, it is often transformed to reorganize the data by subject, making it easier for the data to be subsequently loaded into a data warehouse for reporting and analysis. The ODS may be updated periodically or continuously.

The historical data loaded into the warehouse is used to gain insight into the functioning of the business. Many different kinds of analyses may be performed that can support a wide range of

---

16.   In some environments, transaction data may be directly loaded into a data warehouse or mart instead of, or along with, loading into an ODS. Please see [4] for more discussion.

Table 1.3   Key Data Characteristics

	What Kind of Information?	Examples	How Is It Used?	How Is It Managed?
Metadata	Descriptive information	XML schemas, database catalogs, WSDL descriptions Data lineage information Impact analysis Data Quality	Wide variety of uses in tooling and runtimes	Metadata repositories, by tools, within runtimes
Reference Data	Commonly used values	State codes, country codes, accounting codes	Consistent domain of values for common objects	Multiple strategies
Master Data	Key business objects used across an organization	Customer data Product definitions	Collaborative, Operational, and Analytical usages	Master Data Management System
Transactional Data	Detailed information about individual business transactions	Sales receipts, invoices, inventory data	Operational transactions in applications such as ERP or Point of Sales	Managed by application systems
Historical Data	Historical information about both business transactions and master data	Data warehouses, Data Marts, OLAP systems	Used for analysis, planning, and decision making	Managed by information integration and analytical tools

uses, including basic reporting, dashboards (which show key performance indicators for a specific part of the organization, and predictive analytics that can drive operational decisions).

Historical data is also required to conform to the wide variety of regulations and standards that organizations have to comply with. As described throughout many sections of this book,[17] the regulatory environment drives the need for the management of historical as well as master data.

Table 1.3 summarizes some of the key characteristics of these different kinds of information.

---

17. Including Section 1.4.2.2, Chapter 9, and Appendix C.

1.4 Business Benefits of Managed Master Data

In this section, we take a look at some benefits of using managed master data within an MDM System. We will categorize these benefits using the same three principles we discussed earlier, that is, that an MDM System:

- Provides a consistent understanding and trust of master data entities
- Provides mechanisms for consistent use of master data across the organization
- Is designed to accommodate and manage change

In Chapters 6–8, we focus on Solution Blueprints and discuss specific examples of the business benefits of MDM within particular industries and problem areas.

1.4.1 Consistent Understanding and Trust of Master Data Entities

One of the main objectives of MDM enablement of an enterprise is to improve the quality of the master data elements for the entire business. Here, we look at some different aspects of data quality and how MDM can help improve them. With higher quality in the data comes a more consistent understanding of master data entities. A broader discussion on data quality can be found in Chapter 9.

1.4.1.1 Accuracy

"Bad data costs money." High-quality data is required for sound operations, decision making, and planning. Data quality is high if the data correctly represents the real-life constructs to which it refers. A traditional development rule states that $1 spent in design costs $10 in development and $100 in support [7]. The same applies to data quality: Money and effort spent designing for higher data quality early on provides a good return on investment when compared to fixing data issues later on. Even this is a fraction of the cost of having to deal with data quality issues after they have caused business problems. In reality, the $100 measurement is probably not even close to covering the cost of bad data. It is estimated by the Data Warehousing Institute that bad data costs U.S. business over $600 billion a year [8]. The cost of bad data manifests itself in misplaced shipments, product returns, lost marketing opportunities, cost for immediate and near-term system repairs, loss of customer trust, loss of customers, and an adverse impact on sales and thus market share.

An MDM Solution needs to have the capabilities to increase the quality and thereby the trust in an enterprise's data compared to the previous state of unmanaged master data. Accuracy and completeness of master data, its consistency, its timeliness, its relevance, and its validity are the primary contributors to data quality. **Accuracy** of the data is defined as the degree of conformity that a stored piece of information has to its actual value. Because of the central positioning of master data within the enterprise, the accuracy of master data, in particular, plays a large role in determining the overall data quality. Data that can be validated while a customer service representative is on the phone with a client can be made more accurate than it was before by just updating a "validated-on-date" field. There is no change to the actual data, but it is now known to be accurate. Thus, knowing when the data has changed can be at least as important as the change itself. The accuracy of the data is also dependent on the context. Data that is sufficiently accurate in one context may not be accurate enough for another context. For example, a value for "age" may suffice for marketing purposes, whereas a legal document may require a date of birth.

Higher accuracy of data leads to greater efficiencies in business processes that use the data. Because of its high degree of reuse throughout the enterprise, this relationship is especially true for master data. Major improvements in data accuracy can be achieved through MDM functionality such as matching/de-duplication and structures data stewardship.

Matching and de-duplication refers to taking data from multiple source systems, multiple channels, or different interactions and matching them up with existing data in the MDM System. Before we begin the matching process, we first validate and standardize the data to improve the accuracy of the matching. Matching typically involves creating a candidate list of possible matches (also referred to as **bucketing**) based on the data already in the system and then comparing these candidates against the incoming record. By calculating a score for each comparison, the matches can be ranked. Typically, a threshold value indicates that certain records indeed match, and now these records can be collapsed together into a new combined record using a set of survivorship rules for each of the attributes of that record.

Data stewardship involves human interaction to determine match and no-match cases where automated processing cannot provide a guaranteed match. This process means manually assessing the possible matching and de-duplication and subsequently deciding on the survivorship of the individual attributes. Data stewardship and the management of data quality are discussed further in Chapter 9.

Data validation is a technique to improve the accuracy and precision of the data by using a set of rules to determine whether data is acceptable for a system. Examples are data formats, range validations, limit checks, and checksums on a data element, or cross-checks on multiple data elements. In an MDM context, there may be a validation rule to describe the format of a product identifier or to validate that a person can only have, at most, one legal name.

Because the master data in an MDM System often comes from multiple source systems, and because the validation rules across those source systems are seldom fully synchronized, the MDM System provides its own superset of data validation rules. Data validation can be enforced as part of an Extract, Transfer, Load (ETL) process (more on this later) when data is loaded into the MDM System. However, data validation also needs to be part of online transaction processing to validate data when MDM services are invoked. Centralizing data validation in an MDM System achieves a higher level of data validation for the enterprise as a whole.

1.4.1.2 Completeness
Completeness of master data is determined by the degree to which it contains all of the relevant entities, attributes, and values required to represent the real-life master constructs such as customers, products, or accounts. Typical questions asked in this regard would be whether all of the entities for a given master construct are present, including all of the

required attributes for these master data entities and their values. For example, in an MDM System managing customer information, are all of the required addresses (shipping, billing, or vacation) available? Do they contain the required attributes (address line city, postal/zip code) and are the values for these attributes provided?

Completeness is also dependent on business context—what is required in one context might be optional in another. For example, in the case of a life insurance customer, smoking status is a mandatory attribute, and the master data record for this customer would not be complete without a valid value for this mandatory attribute. The same customer record in the context of car insurance can be considered complete without this attribute. An MDM System servicing both verticals would need to be flexible enough to support this contextual distinction. MDM Systems typically have many different contributors of data within an enterprise. This enables an MDM System to maintain a more complete picture of the master data than any of the contributing systems on their own, because each keeps only a subset of the total data as required for their business purpose. In other cases, the MDM System might be the system where the collective data from the source systems is augmented with additional information not kept in any of the source systems.

1.4.1.3 Consistency

Borrowing from the general notion of **consistency** in formal logic, we can define master data to be consistent when data retrieved through two different locations, channels, applications, or services cannot contradict itself. In other words, at no time should the manner by which the data is accessed have an effect on the information it represents. In a consistent environment, the values for data should be the same.

This might seem obvious, but as we saw in the previous section, the initial scattering of unmanaged master data across the enterprise is often natural and more or less unavoidable. What is also unavoidable is that the quality of that master data differs from system to system. It is therefore entirely possible that these sources disagree on a particular aspect of a master data object. For example, what one system has stored as a billing address might be kept as a shipping address in the other. Similarly, the date of birth of a customer in one source system may be different from that in another. A billing system might have accurate account and address information but would not be the trusted source for date of birth or e-mail address, while an online self-service system would have more accurate e-mail information but not necessarily the best postal addresses.

Even when we only focus on a single system, there can be large variations in data quality due to variations in the level of data consistency. All of these types of inconsistencies need to be addressed by the MDM System, both at the time of deployment and throughout its lifecycle. Being centrally positioned within the enterprise, an MDM System is in a unique position to improve the consistency of master data for an entire enterprise. Consistency is also determined by the level of standardization, normalization, and validation that was performed on the data. Data standardization ensures that the data adheres to agreed-upon guidelines. For example, address standardization determines what an address should look like for a specific geography and gives a fixed format based on a postal code look-up. Many other elements, such as first and last names, can also be standardized. Standardization greatly improves the ability for computer systems to locate and manipulate data elements. Data normalization describes the organization of data elements in related subcomponents. This can be thought of in the traditional context of the database modeling technique of normalization but also on a much smaller scale, for example, parsing a personal name such as "MARIA LUZ RODRIGUEZ v. de LUNA" into the correct data structures.

As we saw earlier in Section 1.3.5, some MDM implementation styles are more prone than others to show some level of data inconsistency. In essence, as soon as master data appears in multiple places, there is a potential for data inconsistencies. This is true even if these sources are managed replicas. Replication technology is very good at being able to keep multiple copies synchronized—but there is often some amount of lag between copies as changes take place.

1.4.1.4 Timeliness

The timeliness of master data is another important factor determining its quality. Master data changes relatively slowly compared to other forms of business data. For example, we have observed that in financial institutions, customer data changes around three percent per day and that contract-related information can change eight percent per day. Address and phone numbers for individuals seem to change, on average, every 2.5 years. Product information in retail can change quickly as retailers introduce seasonal products into their catalogs.

These changes often take time to propagate through the enterprise and its systems. With this propagation comes a delay between the data being changed and the availability of this change to the data consumers—the longer the delay, the greater the potential loss in data quality.

A typical example of this is a traditional data warehouse where data is extracted from source systems, cleansed, de-duplicated, and transformed for use in an analytical context. Because many data warehouses are used for off-line decision support, it is common for them to be updated on a daily or sometimes weekly basis. Thus, the data is always somewhat out of date with respect to the operational systems that feed it. Such warehouses may not be suitable for operational usage. An MDM System may take on the task of maintaining this cleansed version of the master data on an ongoing basis, while serving as a source for the data warehouse. In this case, the MDM System is providing on-line access to this cleansed data.

Another factor in the timeliness of the data is its freshness. Captured data typically deteriorates by a certain rate because the real life constructs it represents change over time and not all these changes make it back into the captured data. For example, on average about 20% of all Americans change their address every year.

Timeliness thus affects both consistency and accuracy. Propagation delay impacts the consistency of the information across systems, whereas freshness is one indication of how accurate the data remains.

1.4.1.5 Relevance

Data **relevance** is a measure of the degree to which data satisfies the needs of the consumer. It measures how pertinent, connected, or applicable some information is to a given matter.

What is obvious from this definition is that relevance is also context-sensitive. Master data that is relevant in one context or to one user might be irrelevant in another context or to another user. If all relevant information is captured for the different consumers of the information, then the information can be considered to be complete.

For example, the physical dimensions of a grocery item in a product information system are relevant to someone in shipping but irrelevant to a translator who works on creating a Spanish version of the product catalog. In the description of completeness, we discussed the example of a smoker status and its relevance to different lines of business in an insurance company. Data relevance determines why and what we measure or collect. To ensure data relevance, the "noise" (unnecessary information) factor of the data needs to be reduced.

In the case of operational data, relevance is usually determined during the definition and requirements phase of an MDM project. For example, during this phase of an MDM implementation, a gap analysis can be used to determine which relevant data elements need to be added to an existing data model. If data from multiple source systems is combined in an MDM System, then the relevance of the data elements from a single system to the enterprise as a whole needs to be determined.

The MDM System does not necessarily need to contain the sum of all of the parts. Certain pieces of data might be irrelevant from an enterprise point of view. These additional data elements may continue to be maintained in the line-of-business systems. Relevance may also change over time. As business needs change, what is relevant today may change tomorrow. Accommodating these changes is a natural part of the evolution of an MDM System.

1.4.1.6 Trust

We can trust data when we know that it has met an appropriate set of standards for accuracy, cleanliness, consistency, and timeliness—that is, when we know that data stewards manage the data and that the data is protected from unauthorized or unmanaged updates. The more we know about the data, the more we understand the data itself and what is meaningful (and what is not), and the more we learn how to gauge our trust in the information. We can learn about the data and data quality using data profiling tools, and we can begin to understand the provenance or lineage of the data through a combination of automated and manual techniques.

We can aggregate master data from across the enterprise, clean it, reconcile it, and then manage it so that we control who is allowed to see it and who is allowed to change it. By actively managing master data in this way, we can assert our trust in this master data. When we believe that we can trust the data—that we manage and maintain a collection of trusted information—then we can be an authoritative source of that data for other users and applications.

1.4.2 Consistent Use of Master Data Across the Organization

It is not just the quality and consistency of the data that is important—it is also the consistent usage of that master data throughout the enterprise. MDM Systems offer a consistent, comprehensive view of master data across the organization. Typically, this unified view is not available before an MDM implementation takes place. In this pre-MDM situation, master data is typically spread out across multiple, autonomous line-of-business systems. These systems could be of a homogeneous or heterogeneous nature. An example of a homogeneous situation will be presented in Chapter 8, where we will see a solution blueprint using an MDM System to provide a consistent view of product data across SAP systems from multiple geographies. A heterogeneous example could be one where customer data is stored both in Siebel CRM and in a custom-built billing system. The benefits of using MDM in this situation come from the data quality improvements we saw earlier and from cost savings and efficiencies we will describe later, as well as from improved support for regulatory compliance.

1.4.2.1 Cost Savings and Efficiencies

Cost reduction and avoidance is another benefit of tackling MDM. There are many operational savings and efficiencies that can be achieved by implementing reusable services supporting key processes such as name and address change in CDI or product information changes in PIM. In an unmanaged master data environment, transactions like these typically need to be applied to every application that contains such data, often by manually re-keying information. Depending on the MDM implementation style in use, such processing can be drastically reduced by only updating the coexistence or operational MDM hub and automatically forwarding such changes to the interested applications, or by having these other applications consult the MDM System directly for this master data. This process can reduce the amount of effort required to propagate such changes through the enterprise and improves this propagation by ensuring all relevant systems are updated. This process also improves the quality of the propagation by ensuring that all the updates are the same and that no re-keying errors occur.

Other cost avoidance opportunities can be identified by focusing on the benefits of having an enterprise-wide view of the master data entities available in the MDM Solution. This enterprise view allows for the discovery of relationships between entities that were previously only distributed across multiple systems. In the case of CDI, we can therefore bring together all of the information about a party from across all of the different systems, including all of the addresses at which the client can be reached, all of the products the client owns (obtained from different lines of business), family relationships, or additional identifiers such as driving license or passport number. All of this information can be used to optimize dealings with the client and provide a better customer experience in dealing with the company—thereby increasing customer retention.

MDM can lead to a reduction in data storage costs and total cost of ownership of a solution by removing redundant copies of master data, although this benefit mainly occurs in a consolidation and transactional hub style of MDM. The data volumes occupied by master data in a typical enterprise are very significant and there can be substantial savings in storage costs. In a registry or coexistence style MDM implementation, the storage requirements typically increase, because all of the existing unmanaged master data copies are still maintained, together with the new data storage requirements for the MDM hub. Another caveat here is that in many cases an MDM System starts to store more master data than was originally available in unmanaged form. In essence, the master data in the MDM System is augmented with data previously not recorded in the enterprise. Data fields may need to be larger—for example, the ID field needs to be longer because more entities appear in a single system. Typical examples can be found in the area of privacy preferences or e-mail addresses that were previously not recorded in the older source systems.

Enterprise resources such as money, labor, advertising, and IT systems are typically scarce commodities that need to be applied in those areas where they can offer maximal return on investment. Unmanaged master data hinders this resource allocation because the information required to drive decisions is scattered among many systems. Questions such as "Who are my most valuable customers?," "Which are my best selling products?," and "Is there fraud—and if so, where?" require a managed set of master data.

In traditional operating environments, such decisions are based on information from a data warehouse, which often is the only location where data was available in cleansed, unduplicated form. Data warehouses, however, have inherent design characteristics to optimize them for analytics and reporting, and they are generally not designed to support operational transactions. In addition, this data often has a higher degree of latency and is therefore somewhat stale. Without MDM, a customer who just bought a high-end product over the Web and is calling in to the call center might not appear as a very valuable client to the customer service representative. Without managed master data, it is very difficult to get a complete view of such a customer or product and determine its value to the enterprise. Consequently, resources can't be optimally applied, and it is difficult to provide a higher level of service.

Supporting all channels with managed master data delivers common, consistent information that allows customer service representatives to give the same discount to a client on the phone as the one he or she just handled by mail or on the Web site. Managed master data allows for the product description in the printed catalog to match the one on the Web site and printed on the product. The consistency MDM offers leads to cost savings because it reduces the effort required to process this data at a channel level. This reduction in effort is a significant improvement over the effort required to keep consistency across channels in an unmanaged master data environment.

The overall picture that MDM creates of the master data is more complete than any of the pictures in the contributing systems, and it is therefore more useful for due diligence processes or to detect potential fraud. In fact, we can use MDM to proactively uncover fraud and to create alerts or take appropriate actions. After the master data is managed by an MDM system, we can determine relationships between master data entities that were not detectable before. For example, it is very valuable to detect that a new prospective client is co-located at an address of another customer with a very similar name who is on the bankruptcy list, or to figure out that the manager in charge of purchasing is married to one of your biggest vendors.

MDM allows for the streamlining and automation of business processes for greater efficiency. Furthermore, MDM centralizes the master data within the enterprise and enables the refactoring and reuse of key business processes around that master data. For example, CDI facilitates the development of enterprise-wide New Account Opening processes, and PIM enables the development of enterprise-wide New Product Introduction processes.

1.4.2.2 Regulatory Compliance

Many newspaper articles commence with "Since Enron and September 11, 2001" when discussing regulatory compliance, but regulatory bodies have been around for much longer than this. The original Anti-Money Laundering (AML) controls were implemented in the Bank Secrecy Act of 1970 [9] and have been amended up to the present. The Basel Committee first came together in 1975 as a result of the failure of Bankhaus Herstatt [10]. Since the two mentioned incidents, however, the pace and rigor of new regulations has increased significantly. In addition, it is very rare for one of these regulations to be withdrawn and disappear. Since 1981, over 100,000 regulations have been added in the United States [11]. Consequently, the number of regulations that a modern enterprise needs to adhere to is continually increasing, as are the expenses associated with compliance. According to a study by the Financial Executives Institute, companies should expect to spend an average of $3 million to comply with section 404 of the Sarbanes-Oxley Act (SOX) [12]. Forrester Research estimates the five-year cost of a Basel II implementation for the largest banks to be $150 million. Obviously, there are vast differences between all these regulations: by industry and by geography, and also by the strictness, penalties, and consequences of noncompliance. Some of the most well-known regulations are Basel II, Sarbanes-Oxley (SOX), the Patriot Act, Office of Foreign Assets Control (OFAC) watch lists,[18] Solvency II, "Do not call" compliance from the Federal Communications Commission (FCC), Anti-Money Laundering (AML), and HIPAA.[19]

Some of these regulations are global, while others are specific to North America or Europe, but most have equivalent regulations across all geographies. Obviously, implementing point solutions for each of these regulations separately is not viable, and enterprises have to look at approaching this situation in a more holistic manner. Fortunately, even though they have different policies, many regulations share common objectives that require that authoritative data is used in business processes and that proper controls over key data are in place. Organizations are therefore starting to establish regulatory frameworks instead of addressing each of these regulatory compliance initiatives with a dedicated point solution. This approach also better positions them to adapt to changes in regulation or the introduction of new regulations in the future. Achieving regulatory compliance initially does not add anything to a company's bottom line; it is a pure cost and used as a "penalty avoidance" measure. However, the solutions that are put in place to achieve compliance can be leveraged to drive many other advantages and differentiators in the market. Thus, as you can see in Figure 1.17, the more maturely compliance is handled, the more business value for the stakeholders can be derived from it.

---

18. Threat and fraud scenarios are discussed further in Chapters 4 and 7.
19. Health Insurance Portability and Accountability Act.

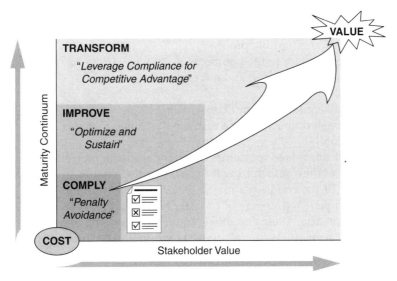

Figure 1.17 Maturation from risk mitigation and penalty avoidance to leveraging risk and compliance as a competitive advantage.

To illustrate the relationship between compliance and master data more concretely, we now describe a few of the high-impact regulatory policies.

- **CDI—Know Your Customer (KYC)**
  KYC is a compliance policy related to the Bank Secrecy Act and the USA Patriot Act and to international standards such as Solvency II and the International Accounting Standards. It requires financial institutions to diligently identify their clients and obtain certain relevant information required to enact financial business with them. One aspect of KYC is to verify that the customer is not on lists of known fraudsters, terrorists, or money launderers, such as the Office of Foreign Assets Control's (OFAC) Specially Designated Nationals list. Another is to obtain an investment profile from customers to identify their risk tolerance before selling them investment products. CDI systems are designed to store and maintain identifying pieces of information, such as driving licenses, passports, and Social Security Numbers on the parties in the system. Through the de-duplication functionality available in an MDM System, companies have a much better chance of correctly identifying two parties as being one and the same. CDI systems can store KYC party profile information like the questionnaire answers obtained for a financial profile of the client, and CDI systems can more easily check a company's entire list of customers, vendors, employees, and so on, against any of the known felon lists.
- **CDI—Privacy**
  Privacy is defined as a basic human right in the "Universal Declaration of Human Rights," and although data privacy legislation and regulation is not very strict in the United States, it is much more rigidly defined and enforced in Canada and especially in Europe. The European Commission's "Directive on the Protection of Personal

Data" states that anyone processing personal data must comply with the eight enforceable principles of good practice. These principles state that data must be:
- Fairly and lawfully processed
- Processed for limited purposes
- Adequate, relevant, and not excessive
- Accurate
- Not kept longer than necessary
- Processed in accordance with the data subject's rights
- Secure
- Not transferred to countries without adequate protection

Verification of these principles within an enterprise requires strict management and governance of the company's master data. This governance includes both the referential and persisted storage of the data as well as management of the processes handling this data. These and other requirements originating for data privacy legislation and regulations can be serviced by using MDM System features. Access to the data needs to be restricted to those who have the rights to administer it through user authorization and authentication, and data entitlements. Private data can not be kept indefinitely, and archiving and data deletion features need to be present. Preferences for do not mail, do not call, and do not e-mail need to be available within the MDM data models in order to comply, for example, with the "National Do Not Call Registry" in the United States. These kinds of data augmentations are often easier to implement in a centralized MDM System than in silo-based administrative systems.

- **CDI/Account, Credit Risk Mitigation**
Unfortunately, not everybody pays their bills. Credit risk is the risk of loss due to non-payment of a loan or other line of credit. Offering more credit to a particular client increases the credit risk for the company. Risk is offset against the potential gains that can be made on the loan. However, in many cases, companies cannot even clearly determine the credit risk of a particular customer they are exposed to because they do not have sufficiently cleansed and de-duplicated customer data. The same customer might exist in the system multiple times and carry credit on every instance, thereby increasing the creditor's risk. Using an MDM System to keep customer data clean and de-duplicated can help lower risk exposure for the company by providing a clear picture of the risk exposure of a particular client. Another common occurrence is that some of a company's vendors are also its clients. Realizing that these two parties are one and the same can increase a company's negotiation position when credit is drawn on one side of this relationship and offered on the other.

- **PIM and Regulatory Compliance**
Product information is also a heavily regulated asset. Packaging information, export and customs information, ingredients lists, warning labels, safety warnings, manuals, and many other types of product information all have to adhere to format, content, and language rules that are very industry- and geography-specific. Centrally storing this data in a PIM system helps the compliance process, but it is

the collaborative workflow processes around maintaining this data in a PIM system that enable proper control of product master data to ensure regulatory compliance.

- **PIM/RFID—Regulatory Compliance—Traceability in the Pharmaceutical Industry**
  The Prescription Drug Marketing Act (PDMA) of 1988 in the United States mandates that drug wholesalers that are not manufacturers or authorized distributors of a drug must provide a pedigree for every prescription drug they distribute. This regulation was created to prevent drug counterfeiters from entering illegal and potentially dangerous products into U.S. commerce. While the implementation of this regulation is still being contested in court and was postponed in 2006, several states have stepped up their individual pedigree legislation. Most noticeably, California has adopted a requirement that the drug's pedigree be available in electronic form. Electronic Product Codes (EPC) and Radio Frequency Identification (RFID) are two promising technologies that are being used in this area. By building applications around these technologies, individual shipment lots can be tracked to ensure their pedigree. Hooking this transactional data up to the product information stored in a PIM system allows for a full 360-degree view of a product, its detailed information, and its passage through the supply chain.[20]

- **Account Domain and Regulatory Compliance**
  Today, all financial institutions globally are required to monitor, investigate, and report transactions of a suspicious nature to their central banks. They must perform due diligence in establishing the customer's identity and the source and destination of the funds. The account domain of an MDM can be used to provide references to accounts that exist elsewhere, in other back-end administrative account systems, and how they are related to parties in the system. This information can be very useful in identifying possible cases of money laundering. Alternatively, the MDM System can be used as the system of record for account information, in which case the account exists and is managed solely within the MDM System. In this second case, the transactions that are being performed on such an account need to be monitored for possible fraudulent behavior.

1.4.3 Accommodate and Manage Change

In this section, we take a look at various aspects of managing and accommodating change within an organization, viewed from an MDM perspective.

1.4.3.1 Reducing Time to Market

Marketplaces are increasingly more volatile, competitive, and risky. For businesses to participate in these markets, they must be able to respond rapidly to directional, structural, and relationship changes within their chosen industries and market sectors. Reducing the time to market for their New Product Introduction is a critical objective in this pursuit. Time to market is defined as the amount of time it takes to bring a product from conception to a point where it is available for sale. Across industries, different phases in the product development

---

20. A detailed discussion on RFID Track and Trace can be found in Chapter 6.

process are identified as the start or end-point of the Time to Market process. In some indus-tries, the start is defined as the moment a concept is approved; in others, it is when the prod-uct development process is actually staffed. The definition of the end of the Time to Market measurement is also open to interpretation. In some industries, it may be defined as the handover from product engineering to manufacturing, or in other industries, it may be the moment the product is in the client's hands. Regardless of the scope of the process, what is important to a business is the relevant measurement of its Time to Market against that of its direct competitors. Getting to the market first is important for various reasons. It allows an enterprise more freedom in setting the product price, because no competitive products are available until the competition catches up. It may also allow an enterprise to obtain an early foothold and capture an initial market share before its competitors, allowing the organiza-tion to profile its brand as the industry leader in that area.

It is critical for a successful and optimal execution of the New Product Introduction that con-sistent, high-quality information about the product is available to all parties involved in the NPI process. Unmanaged, scattered master data about products leads to inconsistencies, inac-curacies, and therefore to delays in Time to Market for the product, providing opportunities to competitors to react and get to market first. MDM is a key enabler to the management of these collaborative workflows. By obtaining a consistent, cleansed, and accurate version of the prod-uct data in a PIM system, many NPI processes can be improved. Steps in the NPI product devel-opment process typically include checking, review, approval, and control of product structures. It is therefore critical to manage the related product information in the same man-ner and to provide a consistent implementation of the NPI process in the PIM MDM System.

1.4.3.2 Revenue Enhancement and Other New Opportunities

MDM provides a higher level of insight into master data, and this can be used to identify opportunities for revenue improvement. Increased insight into high-value customers through profiles, or account and interactions information, can be used to identify candidates for up-sell or cross-sell opportunities. Increased insight into master data around products can then be used to identify which up-sell and cross-sell opportunities[21] exist when selling a par-ticular product to that customer and which bundling opportunities can be leveraged.

Events relating to master data can be analyzed to identify revenue opportunities. For exam-ple, residence changes and other life events can alert sales to potentially changing customer needs. Without MDM, there is no enterprise-wide ability to recognize and communicate such events and thus no sales actions are taken, no e-mail campaigns are directed based on such events, and no outbound telephone calls or Web offers are made. All of these result in missed revenue opportunities.

1.4.3.3 Ability to Rapidly Innovate

Companies cannot grow through cost reduction and reengineering alone. Innovation is the key element in providing aggressive top-line growth and increasing bottom-line results (see [13] for details). Innovation is the successful implementation of creative ideas within an organization.

---

21.   A more detailed discussion on leveraging master data for cross-sell and up-sell can be found in Chapter 7.

Innovation begins with a creative idea by an individual or a team, and while the initial idea is a necessary input, it is not sufficient to guarantee innovation (see [14] for details). To achieve innovation, the implementation of the idea needs to be successful. It is in the implementation of those creative ideas where MDM can help an organization innovate. Innovation within an enterprise can take many different forms. Product, service, and process innovation are some of the more obvious types, but marketing innovation, business model innovation, organizational innovation, supply chain innovation, and financial innovations are other examples of innovations that can contribute to increased success. All of these innovations have dependencies on the master data available within the enterprise and the processes surrounding them.

1.4.3.4 Product or Service Innovation

If a company wants to introduce an innovation around a product or a service it offers, or if it wants to start offering a new product or service, an MDM System can help centrally manage the related changes that need to be made to the product master data. Where no MDM System exists, product data may be scattered across the enterprise. Integrating across these multiple copies and ensuring all copies are properly updated acts as an inhibitor to innovation.

A product innovation may require updates to the MDM System as well. For example, what was previously a valid value for a product attribute might now not be incorrect, requiring a change to data validation routines. Alternatively, the innovation might require additional attributes to be kept as part of the product information, requiring changes to the data structures and metadata information. In many ways, the advantages MDM can provide here are similar to the ones that offered streamlining of the new product introduction process, as we have seen earlier. Another usage of MDM for product innovation is product bundling. Many organizations have separate lines of business that manage their individual product lines, often backed by isolated IT systems geared specifically to supporting one particular type of product. A common example here would be a telecommunications company that sells landline and mobile subscriptions, cable or satellite TV, and high-speed Internet access. Such a company might want to provide product innovation by offering its clients bundled products with associated discounts. None of the existing administrative systems may be suited for this purpose—however, an MDM System managing a combination of customer, product, and account information would be a logical starting point to enable such a purpose. It can provide reference links to all of the administrative systems that manage the bundle components and oversee the terms and conditions of the bundle.

1.4.3.5 Process Innovation

SOA in general and MDM specifically are enablers of process change and innovation for the enterprise (we will go into more detail on the relationship between SOA and MDM in the next chapter). MDM delivers data management services to the enterprise that closely align with business tasks that manage master data. Therefore, the definitions of these services can be directly used in the conception and process modeling phase of a process innovation project. Additionally, the implementation of these services enables the enterprise to realize the process innovations much more quickly than was previously possible. Previously, process innovations would have resulted in extensive impact on the scattered master data elements in the enterprise. Where does the process retrieve its customer name and address information from?

Where can it find the related products sold to those customers? How are both of these source systems organized so the data can be retrieved effectively? All of these questions and this complexity would have to be dealt with each time an innovation in business process was considered. Because the implementation of the MDM System has already resolved these issues, it is now easier to change existing business processes and support process innovation.

1.4.3.6 Market Innovation

Marketing is focused on creating, winning, and retaining customers. Marketing innovations deal with the identification and development of new ways of achieving this. including new product designs or packaging, new product promotions, or new media messages and pricing. Successful marketing innovations depend heavily on the quality and timeliness of the market and enterprise data they use to do their analysis. This is where an MDM implementation can be very beneficial to these innovation initiatives. The MDM Customer Data Integration system contains the most accurate, up-to-date, and complete view of the current customers, vendors, and prospects. The MDM Product Information Management system contains the most complete view of the products available in the enterprise. Combined with data from other master data domains, this is a wealth of information vital to the marketing analysis and market innovations. The data warehouse is another typical source of data consulted for this purpose. Because cleansed data from the MDM System is an excellent data source for a data warehouse, its usage for marketing innovations is complementary to that of MDM.

1.4.3.7 Supply Chain Innovation

As communications and transportation have rapidly increased, opportunities for change in the supply chain have increased dramatically. The Internet has brought together suppliers and buyers that were previously unaware of each other and has opened world markets for even the smallest organizations. Internet advancements have also opened up the market for labor to be employed where it can be most economically sourced. All of these new possibilities offer opportunities for supply chain innovation. To implement these innovations, enterprises need to optimize their ability to switch between in-house and outsourced parts of their supply chain, cultivating the ability to quickly switch from one supplier to the next or from one distribution model to the next. When master data is not well managed, making such changes can lead to serious business errors. Well-defined and well-managed master data, combined with well run MDM processes, allows for quicker implementation of supply chain innovations. New sources of master data can be incorporated in the MDM infrastructure quickly, and because all of the data will go through the same data quality processes and the same MDM business processes, the overall stability of the corporate master data won't be affected negatively. It is also much easier to supply master data to new elements within the supply chain requesting it. Because of its hub architecture, the number of changes that need to be applied to application interactions is much smaller than in a traditional network infrastructure where unmanaged master data exists in many different systems. In Figure 1.18, the addition of a new distribution channel (A) leads to fewer changes (dotted arrows) in the enterprise application infrastructure when an MDM System is present.

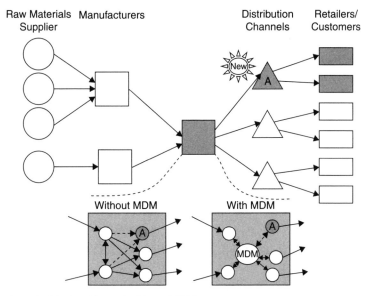

Figure 1.18 Supply Chain with and without MDM.

1.4.3.8 Accommodating Mergers and Acquisitions (M&A)

As we saw earlier, mergers and acquisitions are a common cause of the existence of unmanaged master data in an organization. The successful integration of data is heavily dependent on the data governance practices and the data quality standards of the participating organizations. If data governance is not practiced well within one of the participants, it is going to be very hard to identify the data sets that need to be consolidated. In many cases, much of the data is kept in places that IT is not even aware of, such as in spreadsheets or local databases. If the quality of the data is not adequate, the confidence in the data is low and consolidation is going to be problematic even when adopting an MDM strategy. More often than not, the anticipated cost of such a data consolidation effort is underestimated and partly to blame for a high number of failed mergers and acquisitions. The Boston Consulting Group estimated that more than half of the mergers and acquisitions between 1992 and 2006 actually lowered shareholder value.

1.4.3.9 Introduction of New Requirements

Business changes continuously, not just for the reasons described earlier, but often just to keep up with competitors and stay in business. In the change patterns described in this section, the role of an MDM System is to accommodate business change more easily and more rapidly within the enterprise, and to do so in a more controlled and governed manner.

First, let's consider changes to usage patterns and the user community. The user community that manages and retrieves master data changes over time. Common examples can be found in the many self-service Web sites where customers can change name, address, and phone number information online or through the integration of a vendor portal for a retailer.

These self-service and portal-based usages add whole new communities of end users to the enterprise. Using an MDM System, these new user communities can be integrated into the total user community by assigning them the appropriate security rights and privileges, providing them with suitable user interfaces, and managing the additional workload by scaling up the MDM System to an appropriate level.

Management of master data is governed by many business rules—rules that determine data validity, entity lifecycles, decision-making processes, event handling, matching, and merging. Over time these rules tend to change. Some rules are relaxed, others are tightened, others are corrected, and still more change because of external influences (e.g., regulatory or legislative changes). When using an MDM System, these business rules are encapsulated within services, so service consumers should not need to change their integration logic as rules change. Also, because business rules are componentized inside the MDM System, they are easy to change. Such changes require appropriate governance, as we will describe later in this book.

It is hard to predict future usage patterns of any IT system, and MDM is no exception. Thus, an MDM System must allow for new services to be built that address to new requirements without disturbing any of the existing integrations. It is important that the MDM System is able to quickly support such new services to reduce IT project implementation time. An MDM System typically contains tooling to create new service definitions augmenting the default set of services provided with the product license.

Few products change as frequently and dramatically as software products. In an enterprise context, there is a never-ending stream of new applications, new versions, new releases, and new fix packs of all of the software products being used with the organization. These must fit into the IT infrastructure with minimal interruption to the business. An MDM System can help accommodate some of these types of changes in a number of ways. First, an MDM System must respect backward compatibility. In other words, it must make sure that newer versions of the MDM software, with new and improved functionality, can be introduced without affecting existing integrations with the rest of the IT infrastructure. The new system must support the existing services, and the existing integrations and data, in order to not disrupt the business after upgrade. Secondly, MDM Systems typically run on a stack of other software products such as database management systems (DBMS), application servers, and message middleware. The MDM System isolates the end user of the services from the details of the underlying infrastructure. Clients of the system should not require software upgrades if an underlying stack component is upgraded. Thirdly, MDM Systems typically run on a variation of different hardware platforms. This enables the enterprise to select the platform most suitable for its needs. Infrastructure stack dependencies can become opportunities if the same MDM System can run on Microsoft®, Windows®, and IBM z/OS® Mainframes. Finally, the usage of SOA architecture (see Chapter 2) with service-based interfaces isolates the MDM users and client software from the details of the underlying implementation and related changes.

As we saw earlier in the discussion on mergers and acquisitions, MDM can play an important role in bringing data from the participating companies together into one managed location for master data. But adding additional sets of data is not only related to mergers and acquisitions. In many cases, enterprise MDM enablement is phased in by addressing only one subset of the applications and their data in the enterprise at a time. After an initial load involving a few enterprise systems, the rest is phased in iteratively over time. Even in relatively mature deployments, batch loads into the MDM Systems are fairly common. Facilitating quick and accurate migrations, creating initial or delta loads is an important capability of an MDM System, allowing the business to leverage the advantages of MDM more rapidly and to react efficiently to changing environments.

Conclusion

MDM is a broad subject that touches on many of the concepts of enterprise information architecture. MDM strives to untangle and simplify the complex systems that have evolved to manage core business information by logically consolidating this information into managed yet flexible MDM Systems. Acting as either a system of record or a system of reference, MDM Systems can provide authoritative data to all enterprise applications.

As we have described throughout the chapter, successful MDM Systems:

- Provide a consistent understanding and trust of master data entities
- Provide mechanisms for consistent use of master data across the organization
- Are designed to accommodate and manage change

These are the key principles of MDM that we will continue to detail throughout the remainder of the book.

The business drivers behind MDM are compelling—from regulatory compliance to improving the responsiveness of an organization to change. By providing authoritative information as a set of services, MDM is also a key enabler for broader enterprise strategies, such as SOA. The following chapter will dive into the details of SOA and the role of MDM Systems in an SOA environment.

References

1. Inmon, W. H. 2005. *Building the Data Warehouse*. New York: John Wiley & Sons.
2. Haas, Lin, and Roth. 2002. Data Integration through Database Federation. *IBM Systems Journal* 41(4):578–596.
3. Gray, J., and Reuter, A. 1993. *Transaction Processing: Concepts and Techniques*. San Mateo, CA: Morgan Kaufmann.
4. Inmon, W. H. 1999. *Building the Operational Data Store*. New York: John Wiley & Sons.
5. Inmon, W. H., O'Neil, B., and Frymann, L. 2007. *Business Metadata: Capturing Enterprise Knowledge*. San Mateo, CA: Morgan Kaufmann.
6. van der Vlist, E. (2002). *XML Schema*. Sebastapool, CA: O'Reilly Media.
7. Gilb, T. *Principles of Software Engineering Management (1988)*: Principles of Software Engineering Management, Addison-Wesley Professional.

8. Eckerson, W. W. 2002. *Data Quality and the Bottom Line, Achieving business success through a commitment to high quality data.* Retrieved 03/17/2008 from The Data Warehousing Institute at http://www.dw-institute.com/display.aspx?id=6045.

9. USA Comptroller of the Currency. *Bank Secrecy Act.* Retrieved 03/17/2008 from http://www.occ.treas.gov/handbook/bsa.pdf.

10. Bank for International Settlements. *History of the Basel Committee and its Membership.* Retrieved 03/17/2008 from http://www.bis.org/bcbs/history.pdf.

11. Lickel, C. W. 2007. Introduction. *IBM Systems Journal* 46(2).

12. Wayman, R. J. 2005. *The Trickle Down of SOX.* Retrieved 03/17/2008 from ResearchStock.com at http://www.researchstock.com/cgi-bin/rview.cgi?c=bulls&rsrc=RC-20050311-.

13. Davila, T., Epstein, M. J., and Shelton, R. 2006. *Making Innovation Work: How to Manage It, Measure It, and Profit from It.* Upper Saddle River, NJ: Wharton School Publishing.

14. Amabile, T., Conti, R., Coon, H., et al. 1996. Assessing the work environment for creativity. *Academy of Management Journal* 39(5): 1154–1184.

Chapter 2

MDM as an SOA Enabler

In this chapter, we discuss the relationship between Master Data Management (MDM) and a Service-Oriented Architecture (SOA). We demonstrate how MDM and SOA complement each other to achieve the business and IT goals related to managing master data. Furthermore, we explain why we view MDM as an enabler for any SOA-style solution. This chapter is targeted at Enterprise Architects, Solution Architects, Lead Architects, and Chief Technology Officers.

> *You will waste your investment in SOA unless you have enterprise information that SOA can exploit . . . .*
>
> Gartner Group, 2005[1]

2.1 Overview

Service-Oriented Architectures are about supporting flexibility and reusability in the enterprise through careful design and implementation of technical and business architectures.[1] Much has been written on this popular subject—both at the technical and non-technical levels. In this chapter, we focus on the critical relationship between Service-Oriented Architectures (SOA) and MDM, and how MDM will enable SOA-style deployments. But why is this relationship critical? Well, the Gartner quote that appears before the first paragraph of the chapter gives us a starting point for our discussion. From a technical point of view, an SOA promotes the definition and reuse of modular services that invoke core functions that may be used in many business processes. One such function might be to return the address of a customer, given some identifying information. This sounds simple—but where

---

1. Simply put, a business architecture describes how the business is put together. It describes the value chains, business process, organizational structure, information systems, governance models, and so on that are present in the enterprise.

does my service get the customer information from? If we do not have an MDM Solution in place, we will likely have many different places where this information resides—and it is unlikely that they will always agree. So do we try to check each one and look for a consensus? Do we choose one and hope it is correct? Does it matter if the service is being called from an e-Commerce application or from the billing system? Does each of the customer information sources structure the data in the same way? And what about the user of the service—how does a service consumer know which services he or she can trust to return clean and current data?

If we had an MDM Solution in place—in this particular example, we are considering a Customer Data Integration (CDI) MDM Solution—then the answer is clear; and in fact the MDM System itself would likely provide the service definitions and implementations for us to use. In establishing an MDM implementation, we set the policies on which information is authoritative, how it should be used, and how it may be exposed. MDM therefore plays a pivotal role in an SOA strategy; it enables an SOA-based solution.

In short, the core issue here is that SOA can give a very process-based focus on developing component-based architectures and the usage of component-based modeling to map components to process tasks. Data is not a focal point here anymore because a service orientation through an SOA has taken its place. However, when data is redundant and inconsistent, you will get conflicting results based on which system you use to provide the SOA service or component. Data quality has in fact become the "missing child." MDM alleviates this problem by providing services that access high-quality, consistent and de-duplicated master data. It puts the data back in SOA.

In Chapter 1 we described the three principles of a successful MDM System. Such a system:

- Provides a consistent understanding and trust of master data entities
- Provides mechanisms for consistent use of master data across the organization
- Is designed to accommodate and manage change

Each of these principles has a role in the discussion of MDM and SOA. The first and second principles say that we can trust that the MDM System is providing authoritative information that can be used by other services and processes; in an SOA environment, we provide this *information as a service* (see Section 2.3). Beyond having trust that the MDM System provides consistent, accurate, and complete master information, the first and second principles also relate to the need for being altogether able to retrieve valid master data records enterprise-wide. "Consistent use" also refers to reusability of the data and its related services and the ability to deliver information in the right context, at the right time, to an authorized user, process, or application.

The third principle is also important to SOA environments. One of the key benefits of SOA is to provide business flexibility to better accommodate change. To support this, we need to provide technical flexibility at all levels—from the business processes that coordinate business functions to the services that implement these functions and the underlying information that these functions act upon. Therefore, to fully support an SOA environment, an MDM System should be designed to accommodate and manage change.

In a common ROI (Return on Investment)-driven implementation approach, MDM and SOA are applied in those spots in the enterprise where they provide the most business and technical flexibility for business components. The components can then be leveraged to improve business competitiveness and react quickly to change as well as reduce IT inflexibilities.

It is vital to notice that change is not limited to the IT domain only: Change is above all a business requirement that is addressed through the service orientation of the entire enterprise: A service-oriented enterprise (SOE). In other words, an SOE maps and translates into a more technically oriented Services-Oriented Architecture. The key converging technologies driving service orientation for the enterprise are the usage of XML, Web Services, Business Process Management, and SOA. An SOE requires a change in how IT interacts with the business and incorporates changes in organizational structures, business, and governance processes to better enable service orientation. An MDM System enables this service orientation both from a technical and a business perspective in order to deliver bottom-line business benefits.

As we have seen in the introductory Chapter 1, the need for Master Data Management is driven by concrete business needs, such as providing 360-degree insight into the customer base; building and operating a single source-of-truth; optimizing key business processes, such as New Product Introduction (NPI), which works best with a service orientation across enterprises.[2] Because of this natural affinity of MDM to the service orientation of an enterprise and even across enterprises, we should view MDM as a very convincing business motivation—perhaps even the first real business motivation—to actually implement a Service-Oriented Architecture.

MDM Systems should be designed to both support and to exploit Service-Oriented Architectures.[3] In this chapter we take a deeper look at this relationship. We start with an introduction to SOA followed by a broader look at some of the key ideas and principles behind SOA and their relationship to MDM Systems. We then take a deeper look at the notion of Information as a Service and how this concept extends the basic principles of SOA. Finally, we look at how MDM as a Service fits into a Service-Oriented Architecture.

Although this is not a book on SOA, we consider it necessary to describe some basic SOA concepts and characteristics. While this will undoubtedly be a somewhat incomplete overview from an SOA point of view, it will allow us to put SOA and MDM into perspective.

2.2 Brief Introduction to SOA

Although there are many good books available on SOA (e.g., [2]), we include here a brief introduction into the topic. A key tenet of Service-Oriented Architecture is to align the technical architectures and IT environment with the business goals of the organization.

---

2. In Section 6.3 of Chapter 6, we provide much more detail about NPI.

3. However, we have come across customers who want to implement MDM without SOA, mostly because they have not been able to make a good business case for the latter yet.

There are many different views of what exactly an SOA is, mainly because there are many different perspectives through which to view it. For a business person, SOA can be seen as an architecture supporting a business strategy geared at business integration, higher quality, cost reduction, and agility. SOA in this interpretation involves a collection of standardized, self-contained business services that are available throughout the enterprise or to external parties and that can be used individually or in a composed manner. SOA in this case is about modeling the business processes, gaining insight from these models, and using it to increase quality, agility, and resilience of the business. This process furthers the attainment of the business goals and gives the business the ability to change its processes in response to changing business circumstances. It also ensures that those changes are reflected more quickly into the business' information systems. This view is essentially centered on the service orientation of the business itself. And as we have pointed out earlier in this chapter, it may very well be that this business view of the service orientation—the SOE—does not necessarily result in any concrete adjustments or changes in the IT environment.

To a developer, SOA can be viewed as a programming model, which is by definition an abstract conceptual view of the structure and operation of a computing system. For a developer, the SOA programming model consists of standards, tools, and technologies such as Web Services. SOA in this perspective is more centered on the implementation of SOA components.

In this book we focus on technical architecture, and we therefore use the definition most appropriate for a technical Enterprise Architect. For such an architect, an architecture can be defined as the fundamental organization of a system embodied in its components, their relationships to each other, and to the environment, and the principles guiding its design and evolution (as per IEEE Standard 1471-2000). Using this definition, we can define an SOA as follows:

> SOA is an integration architecture in which components are available through services. These services are available through platform-neutral interfaces and communication protocols. They encapsulate application functionality to be delivered to the service consumer. They are loosely coupled and based on a formal definition or contract.

In order to be useful and valuable for the enterprise, business services need to have a number of important characteristics:

- They need to be performed in a repeatable and sustainable manner. Repeatability and sustainability allow for the prolonged existence of the enterprise. A business cannot survive if its main business services cannot be repeatedly performed in the same manner.
- They need to adhere to the business' rules, guidelines, and principles in order to fit within the business' plans and goals. They also need to adhere to external rules, regulations, and laws.
- They can be decomposed in finer-grained business services or composed into business processes.
- They need to be managed, measured, and monitored to operate them, to ensure they perform within the norms, and to gauge their effectiveness.

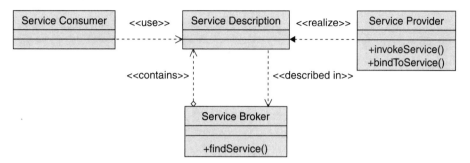

Figure 2.1 Conceptual Model of an SOA Architecture.

- They need to be agile, or adaptable, to allow the business to change and adapt to changing circumstances and markets, product innovations, or changing regulations.
- They need to be cost-efficient to ensure the business processes they are used for can be managed cost-effectively.
- They need to allow for integration both within the organization and with outside parties. These days, very few companies can operate as isolated entities and few even have isolated processes; an increasing number of tasks, or even complete processes, are outsourced.
- They need to provide a high level of quality in many ways, such as their availability, their speed of delivery, and the quality of their deliverables.

We can describe a conceptual model of an SOA architecture using four basic concepts. There is the **Service Provider** who realizes the service by providing an implementation for it, and who publishes a **Service Description**.[4] The **Service Consumer** can either use the Service Description directly or optionally find it using the Service Broker. It can then bind to and invoke the service from the Service Provider. The **Service Broker** component (also known as a Service Registry and Repository) is optional in this model. This component is a core repository and system of record for service definitions and policies. It is responsible for making (Web) service interfaces and implementation access information as well as metadata around policy enforcement available to potential requestors. Figure 2.1 is a depiction of the coherence of these four basic concepts.

2.2.1 SOA Enterprise Architecture

Before we discuss the relationship of SOA and MDM, let's try to understand the key characteristics of an SOA enterprise architecture. Figure 2.2 is a high-level depiction of a layered approach.

---

4. We use "service description," "service definition," and "service contract" interchangeably.

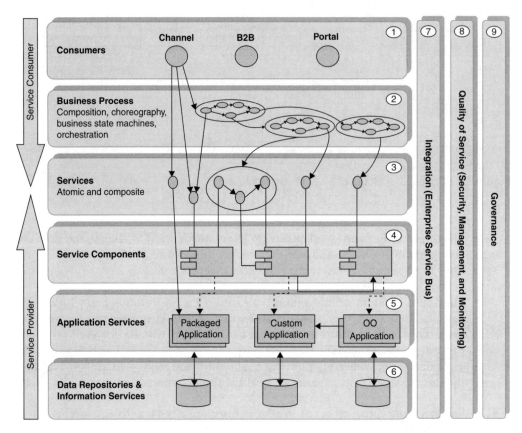

Figure 2.2 SOA Enterprise Architecture (the figure is an adaptation of similar figures from [4] and [5]).

We can describe the layers of an SOA Enterprise Architecture (for more details see [4] and [5]) as follows (the numbers in the descriptions are referenced in Figure 2.2):

> **Layer 1—Consumers:** This layer consists of User Interfaces (UI) and other end consumers of the services. These consumers can be part of many different channels, such as call centers, services kiosks, Web self-service, data stewardship functions, and business-to-business (B2B) integrations. SOA decouples the user interface from the service components, and this layer is often considered out of scope for SOA discussions. However, the mapping of user tasks in the UI to services in the SOA is an important component of the end-to-end SOA solution. Different users with dissimilar roles need access to diverse tasks and services. The presentation of similar data from identical services might need to be different based on the user's role and the user's device. We are also seeing a convergence of standards in this area, such as

Web Services for Remote Portlets (WSRP)[5] and other technologies, that seek to leverage Web Services at the application interface or presentation level.

Placement of Logic:

- No business logic should be present in the user interface layer. The UI should use the services available from the business process layer only.
- Should be limited to presentation only. No direct access to the data; access is available only through the services.

Layer 2—Business Process (Composition, Choreography,[6] Business State Machine,[7] and Orchestration[8]): Business processes in general, and specifically the service orientation of business processes, is key to building an enterprise SOA. The compositions and choreographies of services exposed in layer 3 are defined in this layer. Services are bundled into a flow through orchestration or choreography and thus act together as a single application. These applications support specific use cases and business processes. This layer allows for adequate composition and orchestration of services in the context of a given set of business scenarios with corresponding use cases. Here, visual flow composition tools can be used for the design of application flow.

Placement of Logic:

- Should be limited to workflow design and implementation that is defined by the business analyst.
- Business process should have no visibility or understanding of the underlying operational systems.

Layer 3—Services (atomic and composite): The services that the business chooses to fund and expose reside in this layer. They can be discovered, for example, by querying a registry, or be statically bound and then invoked. Services can be atomic, in which case they are self-contained and they do not invoke services themselves, or they can be aggregated into a composite service. This service exposure layer also provides for the mechanism to take enterprise-scale components, business unit-specific components, and in some cases project-specific components and externalize

---

5. Web Services for Remote Portlets (WSRP) is an OASIS-approved network protocol standard designed for communications with remote portlets.

6. Choreography describes externally observable interactions between services, peer-to-peer collaborations, by defining their observable behavior. Web Services Choreography Description Language (WS-CDL) is a language for describing multiparty contracts.

7. Business State Machine is an event-driven business application in which external operations trigger changes that guide the state machine from one discrete mode to another. Each mode is an individual state, and this mode determines what activities and operations can occur.

8. Orchestration relates to the execution of specific business processes. WS-BPEL is an OASIS standard and a language for defining processes that can be executed on an orchestration engine.

a subset of their interfaces in the form of service descriptions. Thus, the enterprise components provide service realization at runtime using the functionality provided by their interfaces. The interfaces get exported out as service descriptions in this layer, where they are exposed for use. They can exist in isolation or as a composite service.

Placement of Logic:

• Should be limited to discovery and allocation of the service request to the appropriate service component(s).
• Mostly technical rules, such as appending access control tokens, logging, error handling, and making routing and binding decisions.

Layer 4—Service Components: This is the layer of enterprise components that are responsible for realizing functionality and maintaining the Quality of Service (QoS) of the exposed services. These special components are a managed, governed set of enterprise assets that are funded at the enterprise or the business unit level. As enterprise-scale assets, they are responsible for ensuring conformance to Service Level Agreements (SLA) through the application of architectural best practices. This layer typically uses container-based technologies such as application servers to implement the components, workload management, high availability, and load balancing.

Placement of Logic:

• Predominantly, the rules needed to map a service request to a sequence of call(s) to operational systems.
• Includes the technical mapping, binding rules, and dependency rules for combining underlying operational capabilities into understandable service interfaces.

Layer 5—Application Services: This layer consists of legacy systems (existing custom-built applications), existing CRM, ERP, and other packaged applications and existing object-oriented system implementations. The composite layered architecture of an SOA can leverage existing systems and integrate them using service-oriented integration techniques. We can see the importance of legacy integration in Chapter 3 (on MDM Reference Architecture), in Chapter 5 (covering MDM architecture patterns), and specifically in Chapters 6, 7, and 8 (covering MDM Solution blueprints and MDM integration blueprints). Any MDM Solution needs to be able to integrate with legacy systems and needs to ensure master information synchronization between the MDM System and those legacy systems that contain master data of a chosen domain. In short, application services as part of an SOA enterprise architecture ensure the necessary integration with the MDM System.

Placement of Logic:

• Includes all of the business and technical rules already encapsulated into the existing application.
• Behavior in this layer is constrained by the application context boundaries.

Layer 6—Data Repositories & Information Services: This layer consists of the structured (analytical data, operational data, master data, metadata, etc.) and unstructured (documents, images, etc.) enterprise data managed by various data providers such as databases, data warehouses, directories, or file systems. This data is available directly by accessing the underlying data providers, but it can also be trapped in operational systems and therefore may only be available through their interfaces or UIs. The information services consist of data services, metadata services, content services, master data and information integration services, and analysis and discovery services. We discuss the information services that pertain to MDM in detail in Chapter 3, MDM Reference Architecture.

Placement of Logic:

- Includes all of the information services associated with Database Management, Content Management, Information Integration, Master Data Management, Analytics, Metadata Management, and Data Governance.
- Provides the Information-as-a-Service (IaaS) functionality (more on IaaS in Section 2.3).

Layer 7—Integration (Enterprise Service Bus): This layer enables the integration of services through the introduction of a reliable set of capabilities, such as intelligent routing, protocol mediation, and other transformation mechanisms, which is often described as the Enterprise Service Bus (ESB). On the other hand, an ESB provides a location-independent mechanism for integration.

Behavior:

- Replaces the many-to-many connectivity problems with a bus architecture. Every application connects to the bus. Changes in protocols now only impact one connection point.
- Handles the inter-application communication, that is, which messages need to go to which destinations.

Layer 8—Quality of Service (Security, Management, and Monitoring): This layer provides the capabilities required to provide a certain QoS, such as security, performance, and availability. This consists of integrated and background processes through sense-and-respond mechanisms and tools that monitor the health of SOA applications, including the standards implementations of WS-Management[9] and other relevant protocols and standards that implement QoS for an SOA.

Placement of Logic:

- Monitors the behavior of all of the other layers in the SOA to ensure QoS.
- Performs the monitor task in the SOA lifecycle (more on this task in Chapter 9).

---

9. WS-Management is a Web Services management standard defined by the Distributed Management Task Force (DMTF).

Layer 9—Governance: This layer represents the people, processes, and procedures required to maintain trust and control of the information services we establish. Details are provided on governance in Section 2.3.3 and Chapter 9, Master Data Management and Data Governance.

2.2.2   SOA Characteristics and Master Data Management

If we examine the definition of architecture again, we will recall that it is the fundamental organization of a system embodied in its components, their relationships to each other and to the environment, and the principles guiding its design and evolution. There are many excellent books on the topic of Service-Oriented Architectures, and we refer you to them if you want to dive deeper into specific SOA design principles, architectural aspects, or implementation methodologies. For details on SOA business value, planning, and the enterprise roadmap, see reference [2]. In the next section, we focus on a number of characteristics of SOA services and discuss their influence in an MDM environment.

- Service reuse
- Service granularity
- Service modularity and loose coupling
- Service composability
- Service componentization and encapsulation
- Compliance with standards (both common and industry-specific)
- Services identification and categorization
- Provisioning and delivery
- Monitoring and tracking

2.2.2.1   Reuse

Reuse refers to the use of existing software assets in building new software. Code reuse has been a software engineering goal from the early days of programming. Its target is to reduce the development time of a system, increase the reliability of the code by using code that's already been tested, which increases the maintainability of the code, and in general reduce the overall cost of developing software. In its earlier forms, reusable subroutines and procedures found their way into programming languages, and eventually entire reusable software libraries were created. With the advent of Object-Oriented Design and Programming (OOD & OOP), the focus shifted to creating reusable classes. Object-oriented principles of inheritance, encapsulation, abstraction, composition, and polymorphism all tried to make code more reusable. While there have been successes, especially in the areas of framework class libraries such as J2EE and .NET, reuse of business software at the class or object level remains very difficult, and initiatives in that area, such as the IBM San Francisco project, or Microsoft's Business Framework, have not been very successful.

Why is that? In order to create truly reusable business objects, there has to be an agreement on a single definition of an entity for an enterprise. In the case of a generic object such as a string or a hash table, there is very little additional context required to come to such a definition, but for many of the main business entities, such as customer, product, order, or account, there is much more context required, which makes defining entities a much harder task. The exact definition of an order to one business unit in an enterprise might be considerably different from that of another business unit. The definition of a customer for the commercial business side of an enterprise, where it refers to a company, is very different than the one for the private business side, where it refers to a person. When such a definition is used across multiple organizations within the same industry, or even across industries, this problem is magnified, and it is therefore much more complex to create such objects for general reuse.

In addition, when these components need to be integrated with those from other vendors, or those built in-house, the attached contexts need to be synchronized further, which complicates the integration. And even if agreement is reached, business change is inevitable, and business object definitions that hold true one day might be invalid the next day. Rapidly responding to business changes by adapting the involved information systems is a recurring IT challenge. But changing existing business object definitions used in many systems requires an enormous amount of rework. Lastly, even if such agreement can be reached, it is often difficult to convince the developers of an organization to actually make use of the available reusable business objects, and any enforcement of company requirements to use them takes considerable effort as well.

The element of reuse for an SOA architecture is the service itself. Service reuse is a big driver in SOA adoption, and survey results from, for example, the analyst firm Hurwitz & Associates [6] show that almost 90% of IT executives point to it as their number one priority here. When we map service reuse as an SOA guiding principle to a business requirement for a business task or service, we are mostly talking about IT cost reduction, as was the case with object reuse. However, in the case of services, reuse also leads to greater consistency. The more users use a service, the more consistently business processes within the enterprise can be performed.

As we saw earlier, rather than providing objects for developers to reuse, an SOA exposes reusable services that a developer can access. The internal structures are not exposed, and developers deal only with the service definition, the service contract. The underlying implementation can therefore be changed without affecting any of the consumers as long as the contract is preserved. The true value of SOA enablement becomes much more apparent after the services are being reused in many different business scenarios and when they do not need to be redesigned, rebuilt, or retested. Reuse of existing code assets should also lead to an increase in code quality. Moreover, the repeatability of the business processes is increased as well; the business processes can become more consistent through the reuse of services. This is something that is more unique to services reuse and not a direct result of object reuse. Reusing the entire business process instead of just the business objects allows for an entire new level of abstraction: that of business process modeling.

Reuse in SOA can be subdivided into two separate concerns. First, the reuse of existing IT infrastructure, such as legacy mainframe COBOL[10] applications and custom or packaged applications through their SOA enablement. The second is the reuse of the SOA services themselves.

---

10. COBOL (COmmon Business-Oriented Language) is one of the oldest and most widely used high-level programming languages still in active use, initially created in 1959. COBOL is targeted at business, finance, and administrative systems.

Reuse of existing legacy operational systems is often mandated. In many cases, it can be prohibitively expensive to attempt to replace all of the existing applications with newly created ones that were built according to an SOA. Therefore, existing applications may need to be SOA-enabled in order to integrate them into the SOA Enterprise Architecture. Many of the IT assets required to enable an on-demand[11] business already exist and have been supporting the business for years or even decades. Enabling these IT assets to participate in integrated business processes is key to improving business responsiveness. Enabling existing IT assets requires discovery, analysis, and enablement phases: Which applications are already available in the enterprise, which ones need to participate in the SOA ecosystem, and how can they technically be SOA-enabled? Several asset analyzer tools are available in the industry to help you find and identify COBOL copybooks,[12] CICS® regions,[13] and transactions, database assets, and message middleware queues and calls. After identifying such systems, an impact analysis of the effect of SOA enablement should be performed. Obviously, adding the load from an online Web system to a legacy application through an SOA enablement can have significant impact on the current performance of such a system. The actual SOA enablement of existing application is highly dependent on their technical architecture. It could, for example, exist in a proxy or wrapper routine that acts as a services interface between a COBOL application and an SOA infrastructure. Again, there are many products available to help with this phase, which is another indication of the importance of this type of reuse.

Let's now look at the second type of SOA reuse, which is reuse of the actual SOA services themselves, after they have been created. The business context that is required for the achievement of successful business object reuse is also a problem for business services reuse. Gartner Group mentions that only 20% of developed services are likely to be reused [7]. Yet some things do change when we compare service reuse within an SOA environment to business object reuse in a purely object-oriented environment. An SOA offers a developer reusable services as opposed to a reusable object class. For example, instead of a common customer business object, there are exposed services that allow for the creation, search of, inquiry into, maintenance of, and deletion of customer data. This eliminates some of the problems around reuse. There is less of a need to come to an agreement on a single definition of a business object. Instead, the services client needs to conform to the definition of the business entities that the services expose. If it is different from the one the client requires, then it must map its own view into the one exposed by the services. Because the services are the only way by which access can be gained to the underlying

---

11. On Demand Business: "An enterprise whose business processes—integrated end-to-end across the company and with key partners, suppliers and customers—can respond with speed to any customer demand, market opportunity or external threat." Sam Palmisano, CEO, IBM.

12. A Copybook is analogous to an "include file." It's a section of code that is copied into several different programs. It is most often used to define the layout of a physical data section, either for file input/output or as a work or communication area.

13. CICS (Customer Information Control System) is a transaction server that runs primarily on IBM mainframe systems. A CICS Region is a named collection of resources controlled by CICS as a unit. Such resources can include programs, queues, files, transactions, and so on.

data, enforcement of the reuse of existing services is easier. And as long as the existing externally visible services interfaces (the "contract") remains unchanged, the underlying implementation and business rules can change completely, which makes the entire architecture more agile.

The main driver for reuse remains, as it was in the object reuse case, a firm commitment to a service quality strategy for the enterprise. With top management support, strong commitment, and diligent effort, several companies are reporting significant savings from SOA-based reuse [8].

David Chappel mentions the following roadblocks to service reuse [7]:

- **Commitment:** As with object reuse, service reuse is hard to achieve without a corporate commitment to quality. Top management support, strong commitment, and diligent effort are required to achieve significant savings from SOA-based reuse.
- **Predicting the future:** How can one accurately predict which services are required in the future? Targeting existing needs is much less risky.
- **Variation in requirements:** There are often many variations in the exact definitions of what the different service consumers require. Some might need additional pieces of information, and some might not be allowed to see certain information.
- **Ownership:** There is not always a lot of incentive for the creator of a service to share it with others, both from a service as well as from an information asset point of view.

2.2.2.2 Master Data Management and Reuse

Master Data Management focuses on providing SOA services[14] for a clearly delineated set of objects in the enterprise: the master data. By limiting the scope in this manner, the effect of some of the roadblocks to reuse just discussed can be diminished, as follows:

- **Commitment:** MDM enablement is often positioned as an enterprise strategy. The whole premise of MDM is to elevate master data entities to a higher level within the corporation, away from the bounds of being locked into their proprietary, stovepipe,[15] applications. The business targets of an MDM implementation are often about obtaining a better view of an MDM entity, such as a customer or a product, across the organization. By elevating the adoption of an MDM implementation to this level, it is necessary to get a higher level of management commitment, and therefore usage of MDM services can be more easily enforced. The decision to pursue an MDM strategy is often more of a business decision than an IT decision. This fact brings with it more commitment from the business to promote reuse and

---

14. In practice, MDM can be implemented without services, but for the discussion on reuse, it is the SOA aspect we are focusing on.

15. A stovepipe application is typically a legacy information system in which the components (code, data, etc.) are so tightly bound together that they can no longer be upgraded or refactored. The application must be maintained until it can be replaced in its entirety. The application typically serves only one particular purpose or line of business.

service quality. With MDM, SOA enablement does not just represent a technology and architecture advancement—it also enables a whole new array of master data usage possibilities (more on executive sponsorship is presented in Chapter 9, Master Data Management and Data Governance).

- **Predicting the future:** When considering building an in-house MDM System from scratch, the future usage of the system is rather hard to foretell. In this respect, it suffers from the same hindrance to SOA reuse. Commercial MDM Systems available in the market differ in the way they provide SOA services. Some merely provide tooling to build MDM structures and services; others provide large sets of pre-built SOA services "out of the box." In the latter case, these services are built based on the requirements and experiences gathered from many different client implementations. This somewhat reduces the uncertainties around future use of the MDM System and the associated services. In addition, most commercial MDM Systems come with tooling to augment existing services within their frameworks, thus allowing for an easier adaptation to new business requirements. The critical factor in this process is the ability to augment a service without breaking the service contract with current service consumers, especially because any MDM Solution is to be viewed in the context of an evolutionary approach. MDM implementations often start with a single master data domain (e.g., only Product or only Customer), a limited set of services, and overall a limited scope of master data usage within the enterprise. Over time, many MDM implementations grow beyond their initial boundaries, and therefore it is important to be aware of potential changes early on and to proactively anticipate growth and adjustments over time. This plays an even bigger role in MDM than in traditional SOA implementations. To add to this complexity, multiple versions of MDM services may exist at one time, because requirements evolve at a dissimilar pace for different client systems. Using a strong commercial MDM product allows an enterprise to have some confidence that its initial MDM implementation can mature over time into a more comprehensive system.

- **Variation in requirements:** Even in an MDM implementation, different service consumers will have varying requirements around the MDM services they require. One of the biggest challenges is arriving at shared definitions for business objects, processes, and entities being enabled using MDM. Commercial MDM Systems typically offer frameworks and tooling to provide for additions and extensions of services and underlying entities, which makes the variation in requirements from the consumers more manageable. Alternatively, MDM services are often built with configurable behaviors, for example, a single inquiry service that can be invoked with various inquiry levels to return slightly different sets of data. This variation in requirements is also related to the master data domain: It could very well be that the initial scope of the MDM implementation is limited to a chosen master data domain that has to be widened to embrace additional master data domains in order to address the needs of other service consumers. Similar variations in requirements are related to the MDM methods of use and the MDM deployment or implementation style. In Chapter 5, MDM Architecture Patterns, we come back to these variations of requirements as they relate to MDM methods of use and MDM hub patterns.

- **Ownership:** In an MDM implementation, the services are often owned by an enterprise-wide IT organization. It governs the usage of these services, thereby reducing contentious issues around their ownership between different departments or business units. The issues now shift back to a data ownership question: Who owns a piece of data and who has access to it? Most commercial MDM Systems provide data visibility (security) and entitlement (ownership) functionality for their services, entities, and data. This enables different user communities to use the same services in order to access different data elements. All MDM deployment styles will consolidate the management of master data and naturally result in a stronger centralization of master data services. More on this topic is presented in Chapter 9, on Master Data Management and Data Governance.

MDM further enables the reuse of SOA by defining, delivering, and enforcing the quality of the most important enterprise entities: the master data. It is done by following the concepts of "Information on Demand," which are to deliver consistent, accurate information in the right context at the right time to an authorized user or application. By encapsulating data quality functionality in the services, we can ensure that any access to the data has to follow the same data quality rules. Incorporating metadata knowledge into this equation can further enhance the data quality notion. Metadata about the MDM service can tell us where the data came from, what its latency is, and how trustworthy it is. Higher quality guarantees lead to higher confidence in the data and the services, and this confidence, in turn, will be an important incentive to reuse the services.

2.2.2.3 Service Granularity

Granularity refers to relative size of the components that make up architecture. It relates to the level of detail that is considered in a particular piece of code. Finer granularity offers greater potential for parallelism and hence improved speed, but it also leads to greater overhead of synchronization and communication. In SOA, granularity refers to the granularity of the business services. Fine-grained services provide a small amount of business functionality, such as some basic data access, while coarse-grained services are constructed from finer-grained ones to meet a more complex business need. This construction typically includes program logic and business logic to manage the service composition. This pattern of decomposing coarse-grained services into finer-grained ones is sometimes referred to as a fractal pattern; the pattern keeps repeating itself at any level of detail.

There are several key areas to consider when determining the level of granularity of a service: Business Mapping, Performance, Transaction Scope, and Management and Governance. Let's discuss them in detail.

- **Business Mapping:** The SOA service granularity should resemble the business service granularity as described in the overall business design. The granularity should allow the SOA service to fulfill an entire business task and nothing more. Additions should only be made when absolutely necessary. This approach promotes reuse of the service because it matches the business thinking.
- **Performance:** Finer-grained services typically execute faster and contain less information, while coarse-grained services are the opposite; they generally take longer

than and deal with more information. Because we are dealing with remote invoca-
tions, network infrastructures, and overhead, in most SOA implementations this is
an important performance consideration. If the services are too fine-grained, too
much time is lost in network round trips, but if the granularity is too large, it could
harm concurrency in the system. Careful consideration must be given to this tradeoff
to determine the performance optimum.

• **Transaction Scope:** Services should be self-contained and should not require service state to be maintained in between calls. If the services are too fine-grained and
multiple calls are required to complete one business task, there is a potential for
inconsistencies in the event of system failures that occur before all of the calls are
completed. If the granularity is too coarse, substantial rework might be required if
one of its finer-grained services fails. Service calls should never perform more than
one transaction—for this same reason.

• **Management and Governance:** A proliferation of fine-grained services can lead to
increased costs of management and governance in addition to failing to achieve the
significant economies of scale associated with reuse of coarse-grained services that
provide more business value. We consider it important to harmonize fine-grained
services with business requirements.

2.2.2.4 Master Data Management and Service Granularity

Let's now try to map the preceding discussion on service granularity to our topic of Master
Data Management in an attempt to understand how MDM relates to the four key areas of
Business Mapping, Performance, Transaction Scope, and Management and Governance.
MDM influences the granularity of the services in various ways, and it therefore has an effect
on these key areas of consideration.

• **Business Mapping:** MDM Systems typically offer both fine-grained (singular) and
coarse-grained (composite) services. Using the Customer Data Integration (CDI)
MDM area as an example, a fine-grained service might be "addEmailAddress,"
which only adds an e-mail address to an existing customer record, while a coarse-
grained one might be "addCustomerWithMultipleContracts," which adds a customer with multiple names, addresses, identifications, contracts, and so on. It is up
to the service consumer to choose which service best fits its requirements. The service consumers can decide to go with one of the predefined services or decide to
build their own. If needed, new services can be custom-composed out of existing
fine- and coarse-grained ones, or existing services can be extended to best service
the consumers' needs. Providing coarse-grained services to the service consumer
reduces the efforts required for composition. Coarse-grained MDM services contain
all of the inter-service business logic and are optimized and pre-tested.

  Using another example from the Product Information Management (PIM) MDM
  area, a fine-grained service might be "addProductAtribute," which adds another
  attribute to an already existing product, while a coarse-grained service might be
  "categorizeProducts," which links a set of products to a product category in the
  MDM System.

As you can imagine, there are also fine-grained and coarse-grained services that address the linkage of the different master data domains. For example, a cross-domain, coarse-grained service that encompasses both CDI and PIM functionality might inquire about a client and the products he or she purchased. Determining the right balance between fine- and coarse-grained business services is the key to establishing a strong and adequate linkage to the business domain.

* **Performance:** Because of their centralized position within the enterprise, MDM Systems often need to be able to scale to very high usage and data volumes. When several applications use an MDM System to obtain their master data, a badly performing MDM application can quickly become a critical bottleneck for many enterprise processes. To ensure performance, both fine- and coarse-grained services need to be extensively tested and tuned to achieve nonfunctional performance requirements. Coarse-grained services tend to put more strain on concurrency and therefore require special attention during their design. Insert and updates, especially coarse-grained ones, normally perform slower than inquiries, but inquiries often constitute a larger percentage of the transaction mix. The transaction mix used for testing has a very significant impact on its outcome. Because service usage patterns vary widely between implementations, commercial MDM Solutions can require implementation-specific performance optimizations such as custom indexes or pluggable search queries. A key to delivering optimum performance is the use of the right balance of fine- and coarse-grained services in a deployment and the appropriate customization of the MDM Solution. That is, any vendor providing MDM Systems with a set of predefined fine and coarse-grained services needs to rely on the customization and the deployment, usually done by a System Integrator. A System Integrator will understand the customer requirements and will translate these needs in terms of transaction throughput, data volume, end-user response time, growth considerations, and other MDM Solution aspects, which will then result in a customized set of fine- and coarse-grained business services to be used for that particular implementation.

* **Transaction Scope:** In a stateless MDM System, no transactional information needs to be maintained between service calls. This significantly improves scalability of the system. Clustering of application server nodes as a means to achieve higher scalability is much less complicated and performs better without the need to maintain transactional state across the cluster. As we have seen earlier, when we discussed the transaction scope from a more general SOA point of view, the right balance of fine- and coarse-grained services is important to ensure completion of a required business task in a single service call. The transaction scope of an MDM service needs to encompass all of the data changes that are part of that operation. In many cases, however, the MDM service invocation can be part of a larger business process, and the transaction control function might not lie with the MDM System itself. An enterprise business process might span service calls across several systems, one of which could be the MDM System. In this case, the MDM service needs to participate in the larger transaction scope. If the entire business process completes successfully, all of its services, including the MDM ones, should commit their changes,

and if something goes wrong, they should all roll them back. An MDM System needs to allow for both situations, one where it is in charge of the transaction scope and one where it is but a participant.

- **Management and Governance:** MDM services often have to be available in their fine-grained form. These are usually services to maintain a relatively small part of an MDM entity, for example, updating an address for a customer. One reason for this centers around integration, for example, other systems have to be able to use fine-grained MDM services as part of their own business processes. In cases where an entire business flow, such as a "New Business Process (NBP)" or "New Product Introduction (NPI)," can be handled by an MDM System, the granularity of the services is more coarse-grained. As a consequence, an MDM System tends to have a fairly large set of services, both coarse- and fine-grained. Different consumers of the services tend to use different subsets of these coarse- and fine-grained services. While an initial MDM implementation might use only a limited set of services, this number tends to grow over time when more processes start to use the MDM data through the MDM services. This may also be influenced by adding additional master data domains and widening the scope to include additional MDM methods of use. Having all of the services related to MDM centralized in one location does allow for many advantages with regard to management and governance. It is easier to enforce a standardized set of granularity levels per master data entity and an associated naming standard. An example would be where every entity has the same set of "get," "update," "delete," and "search" services defined on it. Services such as security, data visibility and entitlements, auditing, and data quality can be managed centrally. Proliferation of services can be further reduced by, for example, offering inquiry levels for all of the inquiry services (the same inquiry service can return more or less information based on this predefined setting). In many cases, control of the MDM System is in the hands of a central enterprise architecture group, which helps to keep tighter control over the services that are being developed.

2.2.2.5 Modularity and Loose Coupling

Modularity is the property of a computer system that measures the extent to which that system is composed out of separate parts, called modules. Modularity in systems development allows for separation of concerns, the ability to do modular development, and other advantages. A system is considered more loosely coupled if the relationships between two random modules in that system occur through well-defined interfaces. A system is less loosely coupled if there are more direct relationships between modules of the system. A module has an interface describing the elements it provides and requires. This interface is used to hide the underlying implementation. Loose coupling is one of the key areas for SOA, because it guarantees the reusability of the services. Loose coupling in an SOA means that the client of the service is independent of the implementation of the service. The client does not need to know the details of the service implementation (which platform, which programming language) in order to communicate with it. And as long as the

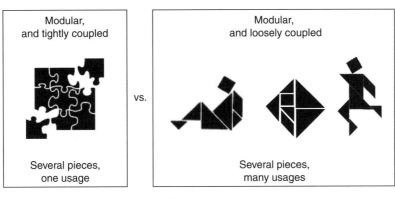

Figure 2.3 Tight coupling vs. loose coupling.

interface of the service remains the same, the consumer is shielded from any implementation changes.

Let's use a simple example to illustrate the earlier statements: A traditional analogy for modularity is that of a jigsaw puzzle [9] where modules are like the pieces of the puzzle; when they are fit together in the correct way, they offer a solution to a problem. A jigsaw puzzle is an example of tight coupling, where all of the modules fit together in only one predetermined way and the solution is a single, static result. This reflects the usage of modularity in traditional applications, where multiple modules delivered a single business process. A related analogy for a loosely coupled architecture like SOA would be a Tangram puzzle, where the puzzle pieces can be fit together in many different ways to construct a variety of end results. Figure 2.3 shows tight coupling vs. loose coupling.

This Tangram analogy is illustrative of the composition of loosely coupled SOA services. Loosely coupled, well-designed SOA services can be composed into multiple different business processes, in diverse ways. This brings many advantages, especially when combined with more effective reuse. New applications can be constructed more quickly by using existing modular SOA services. It also introduces additional complexities, because in the design, construction, and testing phases, multiple usages of the service need to be considered.

It is important to note that loose coupling can happen at a number of different levels. The commonly used example is that of consumers using service definitions and thereby only loosely coupling themselves to the service implementations.[16] It's important to note, though, that the same implementation can be used by multiple different service definitions and that a single service definition can be tied to multiple implementations. See Figure 2.4 for an example: Service A and Service B both provide services defined on implementation B, and Service A has two possible implementations, either A or B.

---

16. You can also read "component" where "implementation" is used here.

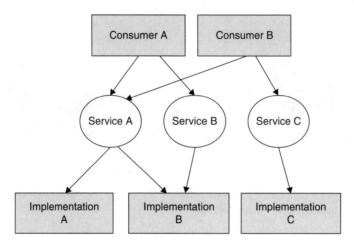

Figure 2.4   Loose coupling in a Service-Oriented Architecture.

2.2.2.6 Master Data Management Using Modularity and Loose Coupling

MDM Systems benefits from the usage of modularity and loose coupling in various ways.

- **Internal modularity and loose coupling within the MDM application:** As with any large system, a well-designed MDM System benefits from modularity in its own design. In the traditional sense, modularity improves the maintainability of the system, it helps manage its complexity, and it offers separation of concerns and other benefits in the development lifecycle. However, there is another specific advantage of modularity and loose coupling for an MDM System and that is its adaptability. By constructing various components of an MDM System in a modular way, the system can adapt more easily to changing requirements. By configuring a particular module differently or by replacing it with a different one, the system can be changed without impacting the base functionality. Practical examples here are the use of a business rules engine and associated business rules to modify the behavior of the MDM services, or the transparent use of an external data standardization tool by the MDM services to improve the data quality. Other examples of such pluggable and configurable components are data standardization rules, message adapters, matching engines, and scripting tools.

- **External modularity and loose coupling of the MDM Services:** By definition, SOA services are modularized, loosely coupled elements themselves, but there is a deeper level of modularity that is of interest here. In a well-designed MDM System, coarse-grained SOA services are compositions of modularized fine-grained ones. The fine-grained services in turn are reused in various coarse-grained ones because they are loosely coupled. This offers not only the advantages of code reuse but the advantages of reuse of the business logic defined at the finer-grained level. For example, a coarse-grained business service to add a customer might use a finer-grained service to add an e-mail address under the covers. Because of the internal modularity and reuse of the *addEmail* service, any business rules defined at that level are automatically applied at the composite coarse-grained, *addCustomer*, level. So if the fine-grained *addEmail* service is enhanced with data quality functionality to verify the correctness of the e-mail address, any composite coarse-grained services that use *addEmail* obtain the same improvement.

* **Modularity of the total MDM Solution:** An MDM System is often embedded into a larger business solution; it is not a solution on its own. It is therefore extremely important to be able to take the MDM puzzle piece (Tangram, not jigsaw) and fit it with all kinds of other puzzle pieces to construct your overall business solution. Many applications today have their own version of master data, and you want to decouple the consumer side from the provide side so you can exchange the provider without impacting the consumer and vice versa. This is important when you want to move from a legacy environment to a strategic architecture that leverages master data.

Modularity and loose coupling is tightly connected (pun intended) to the concept of composability, which we discuss next.

2.2.2.7 Composability

Composability is a system design principle that deals with assembling multiple self-contained components into new combinations. A system is highly composable if components can be selected and assembled in various combinations that yield new valid systems to satisfy specific user requirements. For an SOA system, this means that the SOA services need to be composable into higher-level services. This process is referred to as Service Orchestration and Choreography (see layer 2 of the SOA Enterprise Architecture in Section 2.2.1). The composite services are assembled as process services as defined in the business process layer of the logical SOA architecture. This is typically done by using a combination of workflow and state machine composition approaches using a language like Business Process Execution Language (BPEL).

The essential attributes that make a component, such as an SOA service, composable are:

* **Containment:** The component can be deployed independently, and while it can cooperate with other components, it is not dependent on those, and they can be replaced by others.
* **Statelessness:** Each request to the component is treated as an isolated transaction; there are no dependencies on earlier transactions.

Services need to be self-contained; within a single request, they need to fulfill all of the required steps to complete a business function. They should not be dependent on previous or subsequent service requests. For example, it would be considered bad design to create separate services to commit or roll back previous services. In addition, SOA services should not maintain state between requests. Maintaining state leads to the creation of interdependent services, lack of containment, and reduced isolation of concerns. Statelessness and self-containment go hand in hand; if a service does not maintain state, it is not capable of transferring such state to another service. It has to complete the business function on its own. Composability requires the service owner to publish an unambiguous contract for the service with clearly defined inputs and outputs. Collections of services can then be coordinated and assembled to form composite services.

2.2.2.8   Master Data Management and Composability

MDM does not differ much from a typical SOA application in this area. Good MDM design requires the same attention to self-containment and statelessness of the services to increase composability. In many cases, self-containment also relates to the fact that an MDM service should be able to be executed as a single unit of work. All of the database tasks a service performs either are all committed, or they are all rolled back. So the execution of the service has a predictable result (success or failure) and is not dependent on other previous, concurrent, or subsequent services. If this service is used in a composition, the transaction scope often has to change to the scope of the encompassing service. The success of the database updates of the finer-grained service is now dependent on the success of the composite service. Even in this case, it is recommended to ensure that the logic of the internal, finer-grained service is self contained. An obvious anti-pattern in this case would be the existence of specific commit or rollback services.

Statelessness of the services is also beneficial to an SOA-based system in order to handle larger volumes of service requests. Because there is no need for the transfer of state between subsequent calls, the application can be scaled up by providing more application server nodes that serve up the same service. Scalability that approaches a near linear progression is desired, to ensure that a system can scale efficiently. There are other aspects that influence scalability, like network bandwidth or hardware scalability, but the absence of service state is an important contributor.

It is important to note that the statelessness of the services is different from the statefulness of the MDM application. Of course, the MDM System itself needs to maintain state in order to store and retrieve master data. This state is basically maintained in the database, but there are other stateful application components as well, such as registries, application caches, and property files. When designing these components for an MDM System, we also have to be mindful of the consequences of maintaining state, which pose a different set of issues.

2.2.2.9   Componentization

Any large system as a whole consists of different parts or components. That is, looking at a system from a lower level yields a more detailed view and will naturally allow recognizing certain parts and components that the system is made of. The same is true for an SOA enterprise architecture: We are talking about modularization and gaining an understanding of the key parts of the architecture. The individual components will consist of a set of functions that have a certain affinity to each other. It's almost like grouping similar functions or services and "isolating" them in defined components, where these components will interact with each other. This is very much related to the earlier section on composability. Componentization has to do with the isolation of functions and design concerns. And in doing so, we are enabling composability.

2.2.2.10   Master Data Management and Componentization

In mapping componentization to MDM, we need to identify the key components of an MDM System. Later on, in Chapter 3, where we describe the MDM Reference Architecture (as well as in the blueprints presented in Chapters 6, 7, and 8), we dive into the architectural and solution aspects of MDM Systems. We will discuss then, on a more detailed level, the components of an MDM System. For the sake of the present discussion—trying to understand MDM in the context of SOA—we see specific architectural components. This is, of course, a simplification. However, looking at MDM at a high-level, we consistently recognize these components:

- **MDM services:** These are the fine- and coarse-grained services, which we discussed earlier. In essence, these are services to maintain master data as the "single source of truth," and services to support different MDM methods of use (operational, collaborative, and analytical).
- **Master Data Repository:** Depending on the MDM hub pattern (see Chapter 3 for details), this Master Data Repository is either fully materialized or contains a minimum of master data. In any case, this repository contains the instance master data from chosen master data domains (e.g., customer data), or it assembles the knowledge regarding how to assemble instance master data from different sources.
- **Information Integration Services:** This component encompasses important services used to build the MDM hub and to operate the MDM System. For instance, to build the MDM hub requires services to extract relevant data from legacy systems, to cleanse and transform the data, and to load the data into the MDM hub. Operating the MDM System requires ongoing information integration services such as information synchronization services.
- **Line of Business (LOB) Systems:** In any MDM Solution, we find a number of existing LOB systems, which the MDM System needs to work with. The boundaries of this collaboration could very well go beyond the enterprise to include collaboration with systems from other enterprises. Zooming into this collaborative infrastructure, we could even identify further subcomponents. These components play a strong role in the collaborative MDM method-of-use.
- **Third-Party Data Service Providers:** These components play a strong role in MDM Solutions. There will often be a number of external service providers that will be used to enrich master data from different domains. As an example, take a CDI-MDM hub of any bank, where customer data will be improved or validated through external data service providers, for instance, through credit rating companies such as Dun & Bradstreet (D&B).
- **Process Manager:** In the case of MDM Systems, there are many industry-agnostic, and industry-specific, business processes that require a well thought through orchestration of tasks that integrate usage of other components. MDM Systems consist of components that encompass these process models for further customization and optimization.
- **Connectivity and Interoperability Layer:** In general, there are many different ways to provide for connectivity and interoperability. In the case of SOA, this layer consists of an enterprise service bus, which provides different styles of integration. And specifically with regard to MDM, this layer provides the infrastructure that allows for the process- and application-focused information integration that is so essential for any MDM Solution.

You may very well have noticed that—in talking about MDM—we consider MDM services and Information Integration services as two important components of an MDM System, but there are other components as well. In Chapter 1, we discussed the various aspects of multiform MDM, and later, in Chapter 3, we elaborate on MDM hub patterns, which are very much related to MDM implementation styles. An interesting feature of MDM componentization is that these components can be consistently identified regardless of the various multiform MDM themes. In other words, regardless of the master data domain, the MDM method-of-use, and the MDM implementation style, these components are required to make up an MDM Solution. We also should like to point out that componentization in the MDM space is essential, because MDM is usually implemented enterprise-wide, meaning that it addresses a chosen master data domain in an enterprise-wide fashion with a need for collaboration and information synchronization with numerous other legacy systems. This can only be done based on a thorough understanding of key components of MDM Systems. As was stated previously, componentization goes hand in hand with composability. And in the MDM case, componentization provides a specific value regarding the evolutionary aspect of MDM Solutions. That is, componentization enables reuse of key components that are required to integrate other master data domains, or to implement additional MDM methods of use. It thus enables growth efficiently and with the right Total Cost of Ownership (TCO) in mind.

2.2.2.11 Compliance with Standards
Compliance with industry-accepted open computing standards to support interoperability is an essential aspect of the service orientation of an enterprise and of an SOA architecture. Proprietary system interfaces and APIs, programming models and access methods, communication protocols, and so forth, don't really have a big play here. As we mentioned earlier, much has been written on SOA; we therefore just mention a few of the key standards that are important in the SOA context. Some of the important standards are *Extensible Markup Language* (XML); *Web Service Description Language* (WSDL), an XML-based language for describing Web Services; *Simple Object Access Protocol* (SOAP), a network protocol to exchange data between systems; the *Java Message Service* (JMS) API messaging standard; Web Services specifications, such as WS-Security, WS-Addressing, and WS-Policy; the *Business Process Execution Language* (BPEL), an XML-based language to describe business processes. These standards are driven by numerous consortia (e.g., OASIS) and standards development organizations (e.g., ISO).

2.2.2.12 Master Data Management and Compliance with Standards
When we look at MDM from the perspective of whether there is compliance with technology standards, there isn't really any significant differentiating factor: Assuming that the MDM Solution is based on an SOA architecture, the earlier consideration on open technology standards applies as well. However, there is more to MDM, specifically in an industry context. Because of MDM's integrated, centralized position within an enterprise, an MDM System needs to be able to conform or adapt to industry-specific standards that are present. Of the MDM Systems available in the market, some are specialized for specific industry verticals, which allows them to target specific industry standards. Others are more generally

applicable and need to come with means to adapt them to the standards present in a particular industry vertical. In the retail industry, for instance, the *Global Data Synchronization* (GDS)[17] standard plays an important role. This is a standard that is part of the GS1 Global Data Synchronization Network (GDSN) set of standards, which is driven by the GS1 organization. In the insurance industry, the standards driven by ACORD play an important role. ACORD is a nonprofit association whose mission is to facilitate the development and use of standards for the insurance, reinsurance, and related financial services industries. Specifically, in the exchange of master information across enterprises (insurance companies, brokers, agents, distributors, and so forth), ACORD-based eForms management and exchange also has significant importance.

As we have stated previously, for any MDM Solution, electronic integration with business partners occurs in a very industry-specific manner that is based on common standards. SWIFT, EDI,[18] and RFID are just a few additional examples from the financial services sector, retail, and other industries. HIPAA and HL7 are common standards for healthcare.

2.2.2.13 Services Identification and Categorization

Services Identification is part of the service-oriented modeling and architecture process. It consists of a combination of top-down, bottom-up, and middle-out techniques of domain decomposition, existing asset analysis, and goal-service modeling to determine the required services in a particular enterprise situation [5]. After identifying the services, it is important to **classify or categorize** them into a service hierarchy. Classification is needed to determine the layering and composition of services, and to determine the interdependencies. A typical enterprise might have over 100 coarse-grained sets of services that in turn could be composites of finer-grained, lower level services that in turn could depend on particular data services, and so on. Obviously, such a huge set of available services requires classification to be available for reuse by business modelers or IT. Several different classification views, or taxonomies, of the services can exist in parallel to give different points of view. Commonly used ones classify services—by business category, process, area or function, level of complexity, or business entity. Composition and classification help alleviate the performance, maintenance, and governance problems associated with a proliferation of too many fine-grained SOA services. Coarse-grained services tend to provide more business value to the enterprise and allow for economies of scale[19] to be achieved. However, some number of fine-grained services are still required to provide for special consumer requirements such as creating custom composites.

---

17. In Section 6.3 in Chapter 6, we describe the *Global Data Synchronization Solution* Blueprint for Retail, and we describe GS1, GDSN, and GDS in much more detail.

18. EDI is used both to refer to a set of standards to structure electronic data exchange and to refer to the implementation and operation of systems and processes for creating, transmitting, and receiving EDI documents.

19. Economies of scale characterize a situation where an increase in scale leads to a decrease in the per unit cost. For coarse-grained services, their increased complexity is outweighed by their increased value.

2.2.2.14 Master Data Management and Services Identification and Categorization

MDM Services can typically be categorized by their usage type (collaborative, operational, or analytical) and their domain (customer, product, account). Within these categorizations, there can be additional subcategorizations of the services based on their business functionality (e.g., de-duplication, task management, lifecycle management, hierarchies). For example, in the case of an operational CDI Hub with Customer as its main domain, we can have services for demographic information, data stewardship, financial profiles, relationships, identifications, locations, contracts, and so on. In a multiform MDM Solution that supports multiple domains, there would typically also be cross-domain services that can be categorized in more than one domain category. The final categorization criteria is the composition level of the service: Is it a simple, single-task service or a richer composite with additional business logic and value that performs a more complicated business task?

2.2.2.15 Provisioning and Delivery

A key aspect of an SOA is provisioning and delivery, which has many different aspects. One of them is provisioning and delivery of the deployment environment in terms of providing the infrastructure for the SOA Enterprise Architect to actually deploy the anticipated solution. This deployment has to be executed according to defined Key Performance Indicators (KPI), administrative and operational policies and procedures, performance characteristics, and many other metrics. Another key aspect is the delivery of a service according to a set of specifications, such as a given Service Level Agreement (SLA). The provisioning and delivery of such a service requires a process to determine required resources, such as hardware, network, and memory.

In general, provisioning and delivery in the context of an SOA architecture ought to be viewed as a specific capability that is to be delivered under the umbrella of the management of resources, as one of the following three SOA management layers:

- **Business Service Management**, which provides for service-level planning, business-impact monitoring, and prioritization of event management.
- **Composite Application Management**,[20] which provides support for securing information about the SOA environment, flow content analysis, end-user response time monitoring for service requests, service problem diagnosis, and application trace that you can then pass back to your development environment.
- **Resource Management**, which enables orchestration, provisioning, infrastructure health monitoring, and event automation.

---

20. Composite Application, although not limited to the scope of SOA, in this context it is a term used to refer to an application built by combining existing services. Its functionality comes from different sources within the SOA, such as individual Web services or legacy systems with Web services wrappers.

2.2.2.16 Master Data Management and Provisioning and Delivery

What does this mean in the specific context of MDM? Let's examine the provisioning and delivery of the deployment environment, and of the actual services.

- **Provisioning and delivery of the deployment environment:** Analogous to general SOA-style solutions, delivering MDM Solutions requires a rather comprehensive deployment environment. MDM deployments come in all sorts and shapes, similar to what we would observe with typical SOA deployments. But even the largest businesses typically deliver and deploy MDM Solutions in a very phased, multiyear, multiproject approach. They typically start with a particular domain, MDM style, line of business, or geography and grow the solution out over time to a much wider scope. "Big Bang" MDM implementations are rare. Common contributing factors here are priorities, risk mitigation, availability of resources (funds, labor), and internal political factors and mandates within the enterprise. Such a phased approach requires a combination of a strong strategic vision and a series of directed tactical steps. The main focus needs to remain in order to achieve the ambitious and distinguishing characteristics of MDM Solutions—for instance, to maintain a single enterprise-wide "source-of-truth" for a master data domain. To be successful in this journey, the road traveled there needs to lead through a series of incremental steps, each delivering a ROI on its own, in order to maintain the project's momentum.
- **Provisioning and delivery of the services:** Provisioning and delivery of MDM business services, similar to general business services in an SOA, are to be performed in order to allow information provisioning in the context of specific business needs. In a typical first phase MDM deployment, only a subset of all of the available MDM services will be required: The scope of the project is limited and therefore so is the set of required services. This phased approach of MDM service availability brings certain maintenance and governance requirements. For instance, service implementations potentially need to be augmented in future deployment phases to serve additional needs from new consumers, but at the same time, current consumers of the services should not be impacted by future changes. Backward compatibility of the augmented services is a critical factor here. Commercial MDM Systems typically have provisions to accommodate for this need. Despite the typically phased approach, MDM is still an enterprise-wide concept, and it will therefore also require an enterprise provisioning and deployment strategy. Over time, many of the enterprise's systems will have to use MDM services to perform part of their business functions, or at least use them to inform the MDM System of certain changes. The services infrastructure of the MDM System has to be able to scale to these future demands.

2.2.2.17 Monitoring and Tracking

Comprehensive monitoring and tracking of the entire service landscape is vital for any SOA-style solution. Distributed systems increase the risk of failure by eliminating siloed systems and replacing them with sets of services available across a network. Such systems require comprehensive system-wide monitoring and tracking as well as operational visibility to guard against failures and downtime. Monitoring and tracking includes but is not limited to areas such as business impact monitoring; infrastructure health monitoring; monitoring performance of service request execution, including end-user response-time monitoring; SLA monitoring; database monitoring; monitoring the entire IT service environment; and so forth. Because we don't really intend to write a book on SOA, we do not dive into this any further. But the interested reader is of course encouraged to study the referenced literature for further details on this topic. The main point here is that SOA systems can consist of many components and be very complex. Such systems require extensive monitoring and tracking, and we now discuss if MDM adds any other requirements here.

2.2.2.18 Master Data Management and Monitoring and Tracking

In order to highlight some MDM-specific monitoring and tracking aspects, let's structure our discussion according to the following multiform MDM characteristics. At first glance, this discussion may sound a bit artificial. However, you will see that these characteristics will nicely facilitate the discussion and will highlight the distinctiveness of MDM when compared to SOA. These topics are not exclusive, meaning that a combination of the following monitoring and tracking characteristics may have to be considered:

- **Master data domain:** Always considering that the focus on a specific master data domain is to build and *maintain* a consistent, enterprise-wide single version-of-the-truth, monitoring and tracking—beyond what should be done for any conventional SOA solution—needs to encompass this requirement of maintaining consistency, completeness, accurateness, and currency of master data. This therefore requires a means to establish a baseline on data quality (e.g., using profiling), an ability to periodically track for improvements or degradations, and a means to act if problems are detected. This should all be governed by a set of data quality policies and processes.
- **MDM methods of use:** Just to repeat: We have operational, collaborative, and analytical MDM methods of use. Each of them have unique monitoring and tracking requirements when compared to conventional SOA solutions:
  - The operational method-of-use requires monitoring and tracking of all master data business services, far beyond performance, end-user response time, and other more conventional metrics. Monitoring of operational MDM business services needs to include the why, when, where, and how of changing master data. The reason for that is the strong linkage of the MDM System to the legacy infrastructure and the need for master data synchronization.
  - The collaborative method-of-use extends monitoring and tracking beyond enterprise boundaries and needs to factor in other systems and third-party service providers. It also brings additional monitoring and tracking requirements around the workflows required for the collaborative processes as well as the import and export requirements of collaboratively authored data.
  - The analytical method-of-use, which goes beyond the traditional BI and data warehousing schema to address, for example, KPI measurements, cross- and up-sell opportunities, and threat and fraud-related scenarios, needs to comprise use case-specific and even industry-specific monitoring capabilities. An example is the need to monitor the business impact and timeliness of identified and

returned records, individuals, or transactions that are linked to threat and fraud scenarios. Monitoring in analytical MDM needs to be responsive to changing business needs (e.g., additional threat scenarios).

- **MDM deployment styles:** Depending on the chosen deployment style (and related MDM hub pattern[21]), changes to master data can occur at different systems, and the MDM hub itself is only one of these systems; changes can also occur at any of the many existing legacy systems. Thus, monitoring and tracking need to be implemented according to these different styles. In essence, this is a specific flavor of MDM, which calls for a unique implementation of monitoring and tracking capabilities. An example: The MDM business service "addEmailAddress" could be submitted against the MDM hub, or against one or several of the legacy systems. Monitoring and tracking need to be sensitive about the variations of MDM business service execution that are linked to the various MDM deployment styles.

2.3 Information as a Service

2.3.1 Information as a Service, Introduction

Information is the key commodity upon which an enterprise runs. If the information stops flowing, the enterprise stops. If the information takes too long to flow from one part of an organization to another, then the business suffers. Information is stored, shared, analyzed, transformed, and consumed. Therefore, just as we seek to describe, implement, and consume discrete business services that may be reused in an SOA environment, we also need to consider how to describe, implement, and consume Information as a Service (IaaS). Without Information as a Service, processes are tightly coupled to the data. Such tightly coupled processes are brittle, and they do not adapt well to continuously changing business requirements. They also lead to:

- **Inconsistencies in the view and the packaging of the data:** Because each process creates its own custom access to data, the view of the data across those processes is inconsistent. For example, one process might get its customer data from a different place than another. The way the data is packaged typically also differs from process to process, which complicates integration efforts.
- **Inconsistencies in the rules applied to the data:** Because the rules are captured in stovepipe applications, they are tightly connected to the data, and they are not shared among processes. For example, data validation rules or the calculations involving that data can vary from process to process. This reduces the quality of the data.
- **Multiple points of maintenance:** There is duplication of logic across the applications that access the data. This creates multiple points of maintenance for the same logic. This is complex, error-prone, time-consuming, and expensive. For example, each process needs to use the same logic to standardize telephone numbers or verify a product ID.

---

21. For details on these MDM hub patterns, see Chapter 5.

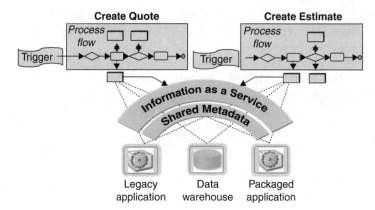

Figure 2.5 Information as a Service.

Without a foundation of usable information, your service-oriented architecture is just a loose confederation of abstract business processes. It's your business information that delivers the value to your SOA. Information as a service is about providing a new level of services that helps add value to information contained in data sources across an organization. By treating information as a service, organizations can improve the relevance and cost-effectiveness of their information, making information available to people, processes, and applications across the business and improving the operational impact that information can have in driving innovation.

2.3.2 Information as a Service, Concept

Figure 2.5 illustrates the concept of Information as a Service (IaaS). In this example, the CreateQuote and CreateEstimate process flows at the top both need access to data stored in a legacy application, a data warehouse, and a packaged application. Instead of building services that access these data sources directly, as shown by the dotted lines, Information as a Service provides an intermediate layer that abstracts the process flows from the manner in which the data is stored. The foundation for IaaS is the shared metadata repository.

Information Services provide facilities to create this layer of information virtualization. They can roughly be categorized into Analysis and Discovery Services,[22] Master Data Management Services, Information Integration Services,[23] Content Services, Data Services, and Metadata Services. We will not describe all of those in detail here, but we will focus on MDM in the context of IaaS in the next section, Section 2.4.

---

22. For example, query, search, reporting, mining, operational intelligence, embedded analytics, metrics.

23. For example, Extract Transform Load (ETL), Enterprise Application Integration (EAI), Enterprise Information Integration (EII).

2.3.3   Information as a Service, Characteristics

Using Information as a Service helps clients identify, access, manage, secure, and deliver information in real time regardless of the type of information or the platform on which it is stored. It ensures consistent packaging of data, consistent application of rules to the data, and centralized control and maintenance. To treat information as a service, one needs to agree on a number of characteristics of the information [10]:

- **Definition:** The structure and the semantics (the meaning) of the information needs to be well defined and commonly available. The heterogeneity of the information is transparent; the consumer does not need to understand the diversity of the data sources or formats. Understanding the structure and semantics of information exchanged by a service is the first step in being able to safely and effectively use the information service. We need to understand not only the format of the messages exchanged between the requestor of the service and the provider of the service, but also what the different elements of the message really mean, which is part of the metadata of the service. In an SOA environment, the structural information is typically described by a combination of the Web Services Definition Language (WSDL) and XML Schema Definition (XSD). However, to properly interpret the information being conveyed by a service, we often need more information—to know the relationship this entity has with others, or to know the domain of values that an attribute is allowed. In short, we need authoritative documentation that describes what the information is and how it should be used. This documentation could be written or could be managed by a metadata tool. These characteristics are not unique—they are important to most SOA services—but it is especially important to information services because the focus is on the proper use and understanding of the information.
- **Quality:** The quality of the information needs to be known, and the integrity of the data needs to be ensured for retrieval as well as update scenarios. The source of the information needs to be known, and so does its currency. This "information about the information" is what constitutes part of the metadata. After we understand the information service and what it means, we next need to establish the quality of the information to be served. Information quality is a very broad topic with an extensive literature. We recommend a couple of very good books (see [11] and [12]). Data quality aspects were discussed at length in Chapter 1.
- **Governance:** Changes to the service and the underlying information need to be governed in a uniform and consistent manner. Data Governance addresses the issue of how to maintain trust and control of the information services we establish. Through a combination of business processes, people, and technology, we need to define and implement policies that control access to information and information services. Authorized users need to be able to audit the execution of information services and to manage and coordinate changes to the information services and structures. Chapter 9, Master Data Management and Data Governance, is devoted to the topic of data governance.

2.4 MDM as a Service

Now that we have introduced the information as a service concept, in Section 2.3, we now apply this concept to the master data domain. MDM is a key component of the concept of Information as a Service. Just like IaaS, you can interpret MDM in this sense as an additional tier in a typical three-tiered architecture in which you have a presentation tier, a business logic tier, and a data tier. MDM provides an additional tier in between the business tier and the data tier. Data is provided to the business logic tier through MDM as a service. In providing this service, MDM improves the quality of the master data provided to the enterprise when compared to a situation where this data would have been accessed directly by the business logic.

As you will see, there is a lot of business value in doing so. In addition, granting access to master data through services allows seamless integration of master data in service orchestration to run business processes. Furthermore, encapsulation of master data into services allows consistent enforcement of duplicate prevention and data standardization, which, as a side effect, establishes trust in your master data.

2.4.1 MDM as an SOA Enabler

This discussion leads us back to the very important point about why you need MDM to enable SOA that we started this chapter with. Early on, SOA technology focused mainly on mapping service components to business processes, and on mapping business processes to business components. However, in many cases the quality of the data involved was ignored or merely an afterthought. Implementing services on top of distinct systems and repositories, each with their own levels of data quality and without cross-system de-duplication, leads to SOA systems with poor data quality characteristics. How can one, for example, implement a single-enterprise *getCustomer* SOA service if parts of the customer data are spread out over several systems with different levels of data consistency, and without proper data matching and de-duplication? Without MDM, applying an SOA can actually make matters regarding information worse instead of better, because low-quality data would now be exposed through untrusted services and thus consumed by even more consumers. Many SOA projects have failed because of this lack of data consistency across the enterprise.

MDM offers a new level of data quality that assists SOA enablement. Exactly those objects that occur frequently in the enterprise and are of high importance to many business processes—the core business entities—fall under the master data umbrella. The services offered by the MDM System ensure the quality[24] and timeliness of the master data and assist other SOA projects to achieve their enterprise objectives. The MDM services offer a consistent view of the master data within a context and with proper security, visibility, and entitlement constraints. MDM provides the technical foundation for master data use in an SOA-style architecture.

---

24. See Chapter 1 for a description of different data quality aspects.

2.4.2 MDM without SOA

It is possible to deliver MDM without services and without an SOA architecture. Instead of providing services to maintain and retrieve the master data, data extraction, transformation, and loading tools (ETL) could be used to build an MDM infrastructure. Data can be validated, standardized, cleansed, and de-duplicated while it is being loaded into an MDM data model. However, the ETL jobs to build such an infrastructure would quickly become fairly complicated in any approach to the same level of data quality as can be achieved by a set of well-designed MDM SOA services. In a rather simple scenario, such a non-SOA MDM Solution might work, but it would suffer from severe limitations caused by the lack of real-time SOA services. It would, for example, be very hard to integrate the operations that such a solution offers into larger processes in the way an SOA service could participate in a larger service. Capabilities such as instant updates with proper transactional (two-phased commit, XA compliant) control would not be available. Security, data visibility, and data entitlements would be hard to control if data access is done directly to the database, and so forth. In short, not only does MDM serve as an SOA enabler, it also requires SOA to reach its full potential.

2.4.3 MDM and Evolvability, Flexibility, and Adaptability

If the business ecosystem were static, every required system would have been built by now and IT staff would have been sent home a decade ago. Fortunately for those folks, the only constant in business is change. Everything changes: Consumer markets change, labor markets change, competitors change, technology changes, the geopolitical environment changes, law and regulations change, mergers and acquisitions happen, and so on, and all these influence the business environment. The rate of change has in fact been accelerating in recent years. An increasing number of companies need to outsource parts of their operations to stay competitive; they might need to reallocate parts of their business to other regions, share value chains with partner companies, and adapt to new rules and regulations. An enterprise that cannot adapt to such changes in a short enough time frame will be left behind and miss significant opportunities. But in many cases change can actually create opportunities as long as the business can adapt to them: New channels and markets can open up, cheaper manufacturing options become available, and new consumer needs arise. IT needs to support the business and adapt to these changes as well, and in other cases it needs to drive the change to move the business forward.

MDM plays a central role in enabling the ability to change and to evolve by centralizing the maintenance and governance of the master data. Changes to the business typically affect the master data elements of an enterprise. The impact of these changes on the master data can be determined more accurately in a managed model using MDM, and the number of touch points where changes need to be applied is reduced when MDM is used. In this way, an MDM System can improve the responsiveness to business changes by centrally changing the way master data is maintained. An example of this would be new requirements around privacy regulations. Enabling privacy information, to be held at a customer level, in all of the systems that maintain customer information in an unmanaged master data environment is cumbersome and, because of resulting synchronization requirements, also error-prone.

Using the MDM System to track such new privacy information at an enterprise level for customer master data reduces the impact of this extra requirement to the business significantly.

MDM extends beyond managing the master data solely for the purpose of enabling a decoupling of information from their original business process and applications. It also provides flexibility for changes to business processes, laws, and regulations. Master data that is no longer trapped within the confines of Line of Business, stovepipe applications can venture beyond the limitations of the business processes of that system. Additional business processes can be defined, and validations, augmentations, and changes can be applied. Therefore, the design of the MDM Solution architecture should be based upon service-oriented design principles and SOA concepts. Here, information is packaged as a service to business processes, so that consistent, manageable information is made available to business processes in a standardized way that enables reuse. Changes to the service implementations are hidden from clients through the use of SOA. The design of the MDM System should enable the composition and extension of these MDM services and schema in a way that provides stability moving forward. It should allow for the addition of new entities or attributes to the master data and for changes to their definition. It should enable the creation or composition of new services and allow for changes to be made to the behavior of the existing ones. The MDM System needs to enable the ability to rapidly respond to business-driven and legislated changes and provide the ability to improve business decisions and capabilities with up-to-date information at a global level.

An enterprise's business grows over time, and with growth come new requirements in the area of scalability of the MDM System. Typical areas of growth for an MDM System are:

- Connect to more application systems, with greater heterogeneity, downstream or upstream.[25] This can require additional adaptors, data flows, message queues, and so on.
- Support a larger user community, with additional types of users. Wider adoption of MDM usage within the enterprise leads, for example, to additional lines of business starting to use the system. A larger user community often requires additional user roles, additional authorization rules, and so on.
- Handle a larger data volume, possibly federated data across multiple databases.
- Keep more historical data or versioned data.
- Handle larger transaction volumes.
- Handle additional delivery channels: Web, self-service kiosk, IVR, mobile users.
- Include additional and more complex workflow flows.
- Deploy additional SOA services. Build more complex SOA services, for example, by building additional composite services.
- Handle more MDM domains (party, product, account, location, etc.).
- Support additional business processes, possibly through integration with business process software.
- Handle more data extensions and additions to the base domains.

---

25. *Downstream:* For example, exports or notifications originating from the MDM System. *Upstream:* For example, systems sending requests or changes to the MDM System.

- Handle increasingly complex business rules, such as those around de-duplication.
- Handle larger delta feeds via batch, such as daily updates from other systems.
- Handle increased reporting requirements.
- Handle more complex UIs, covering more user roles.
- Support multinational deployment.
- Higher service level requirements, increased up-time of the system.

Some of the infrastructure changes that can be made to support such growth are:

- Support more nodes in an application server cluster.
- Use partitioned databases.
- Change deployment topologies such as from UNIX®-based to mainframe-based.
- Deploy an ESB or other form of middleware.
- High-availability configurations.

Another way in which the MDM System needs to be able to evolve is in its technical architecture. Like business, technology constantly changes, and to increase the longevity of an MDM Solution and to lower its Total Cost of Ownership (TCO), it needs to be able to adapt to newer technologies. Many of the SOA principles we discussed earlier, like modularity, loose coupling, and componentization aid in this area. This technical evolvability needs to occur on these different levels:

1. An implementation of an MDM System for a specific enterprise or scenario needs to be able to migrate relatively smoothly to newer versions of the core MDM System software. This is not a trivial requirement. Configurations, extensions, and additions of a commercial MDM System are inevitable in a real-life enterprise situation. What is critical, though, is that those modifications survive an MDM System software upgrade without incurring large amounts of rework. This mandates the presence of frameworks, migration tools, metadata, and development tooling to support such upgrades.

2. The second form of technical evolvability is that of the underlying technology on which the MDM System is based. Specifications such as J2EE and Web Services evolve over time, and they do so at a much faster rate than the technologies that were used for enterprise predecessors such as COBOL or C++. Moreover, new promising technologies pop up constantly, and the MDM System software needs to maintain its technical currency. Its interaction points need to be able to handle new types of protocols and communication such as REST or RSS. Its underlying persistence mechanism needs to be abstracted so it can be replaced with improved technology. Its plug-in points, such as those for data standardization, need to be flexible enough to handle new technologies.

3. MDM software systems typically include a stack of supporting infrastructure components such as a database management system, message middleware, integration software, and an application server. None of these components are exclusively used by the MDM System but typically represent components of the enterprise architecture. They all evolve over time—newer hot fixes, fixpacks, and versions are released and new features are added to these products. To stay on a supported platform, the MDM System needs to stay in step with these changes. There are two major ways

to do this. The first, and simplest, way is to migrate the MDM product over to the new stack without any changes and to test it there. This typically only offers a minimal level of benefit to the end user. The second is to actually take advantage of new features offered in the new stack components, which will allow for new functionality based on new features in the underlying stack software. Obviously, the second approach is more complex and time-consuming, but it also provides more benefits.

In selecting or building an MDM Solution for an enterprise, one has to ensure that the system is both able to handle the present requirements and equipped to scale or transform in all of the required manners described here. This sounds easier than it is in reality. The pressures to deliver a tactical measure of immediate value and success from an MDM deployment in the short term sometimes overshadow the strategic, longer-term vision of a scalable, highly available, and extensible MDM architecture.

Conclusion

In this chapter, we introduced key concepts of Service-Oriented Architecture. We showed how MDM can enable consistent use of key business entities such as customer or product in SOA. Without MDM, applying SOA can make matters regarding information worse—not better—because low-quality data would be exposed through untrusted services and thus consumed by even more consumers. With this insight, you can see now how MDM provides the technical foundation for master data use in an SOA-style architecture. From an SOA standpoint, the service concept applied to information leads to the discovery of the concept of information as a service. Accessing master data is not directly done through database interfaces, as you will see in Chapter 3 when we explain the MDM Reference Architecture. Instead, access to master data uses services encapsulating a lot of functionality, such as duplicate checking or address standardization. Thus, master data access instantiates the information as a service concept—in other words, master data services are one type of information service. In the next chapter, we dive into the architectural details of the MDM Reference Architecture, which is followed by a more detailed discussion about MDM security and privacy, in Chapter 4.

References

1. Andrew White, Charles Abrams, Gartner Group 30, March 2005. *Service-Oriented Business Applications Require EIM Strategy*. ID Number G00124926.
2. N. Bieberstein, S. Bose, M. Fiammante, K. Jones, R. Shaw, April 2006. *Service Oriented Architecture (SOA) Compass—Business Value, Planning, and Enterprise Roadmap*. IBM Press, Pearson plc.
3. Lublinsky, B. Jan 2007. *Defining SOA as an architectural style*. Retrieved March 2008 from IBM developerWorks®: http://www.ibm.com/developerworks/library/ar-soastyle/index.html#resources.
4. Rob High, Jr., Stephen Kinder, Steve Graham, November 2005. *IBM's SOA Foundation, An Architectural Introduction and Overview, An IBM Whitepaper*. http://download.boulder.ibm.com/ibmdl/pub/software/dw/webservices/ws-soa-whitepaper.pdf.

5. Ali Arsanjani, November 9. *Service oriented modeling and architecture.* Retrieved March 2008 from IBM developerWorks: http://www-128.ibm.com/developerworks/webservices/library/ws-soa-design1/.

6. Carol Baroudi and Dr. Fern Halper, Hurwitz & Associates. Feb 27, 2007. *Executive Survey: SOA Implementation Satisfaction.* Retrieved March 2008 from cio.co.uk: http://www.cio.co.uk/cmsdata/whitepapers/4474/110206_Mindreef_Report[1][1].pdf.

7. David Chappell, *SOA and the Reality of Reuse.* Retrieved March 2008 from Opinari: http://www.davidchappell.com/HTML_email/Opinari_No16_8_06.html.

8. Joe McKendrick, *Ten companies where SOA made a difference in 2006.* Retrieved March 2008 from ZDNet: http://blogs.zdnet.com/service-oriented/?p=781.

9. Anthony Bradley, *SOA and Modularity, Net-Centricity, SOA, and Web 2.0.* Retrieved March 2008 from TypePad.com: http://ajbradley.typepad.com/soa_and_netcentricity/2006/08/soa_and_modular.html.

10. Martin Keen, Andrea Ames, Asit Dan, Robert A. Dickson, Simon Harris, Arthur Kaufmann, Ivan Milman, Guenter Sauter, Mahesh Viswanathan. *Case Study: Information as a Service SOA Scenario, IBM Redbook.* Retrieved March 2008 from IBM Red Books: http://www.redbooks.ibm.com/redpapers/pdfs/redp4382.pdf.

11. Larry P. English, 1999. *Improving Data Warehouse and Business Information Quality: Methods for Reducing Costs and Increasing Profits.* John Wiley & Sons.

12. Thomas C. Redman, PhD, 2001. *Data Quality: The Field Guide.* Digital Press.

Chapter 3

MDM Reference
Architecture

In this chapter, we describe the functional characteristics of the Master Data Management Reference Architecture (MDM RA). This chapter should help the reader better understand how to position and design a Master Data Management Solution within an enterprise. Our purpose here is to describe the type of functionality required to deliver a Master Data Management Solution, to identify the major architecture building blocks, and then to demonstrate how those architecture building blocks work together to deliver MDM functionality. For this purpose, this chapter is very much targeted at Enterprise Architects, Information Architects, Lead System Architects, and even Chief Technology Officers.

3.1 Definitions and Terms

In the previous chapters, we discussed many terms and definitions. But before we dive into the details about the MDM Reference Architecture, let's clarify what we mean by "architecture" and what we mean by the terms **MDM Reference Architecture**, **MDM Solution**, and **MDM System** in this chapter. The word "architecture" is widely used in many different domains, going far beyond the Information Technology (IT) domain. There are architectures for houses, landscapes, cities, automobiles, airplanes—the list is endless. And the word "architecture" may be interpreted and even defined a bit differently within each domain. For our specific purpose, we start with the following definition of an architecture used in ANSI/IEEE Std 1471-2000:[1]

> *The fundamental organization of a system embodied in its components, their relationships to each other and the environment, and the principles governing its design and evolution.*

---

1. IEEE Std 1471-2000 IEEE Recommended Practice for Architectural Description of Software-Intensive Systems–Description, http://standards.ieee.org/reading/ieee/std_public/description/se/1471-2000_desc .html.

While this ANSI/IEEE definition concentrates on design and evolution, we believe there are other aspects and characteristics that need to be considered by IT software architectures as well, such as guidelines and principles for implementation, operations, administration, and maintenance. Another essential attribute is the **description** of the architecture, how it is structured and described in a formal way, often by providing generic and detailed diagrams. Furthermore, a description about the architecture should provide a definition and an explanation of the architecture building blocks, the hierarchy of components contained with an architecture building block, and how those components can work together to deliver business or technical capabilities.

- Architecture building blocks are basically the IT components or technologies needed to support business processes and deliver functionality such as security, systems management, network management, hardware, and network support.
- Components are commonly defined to represent software functionality that has been logically grouped together to deliver a specific set of capabilities. Components are characterized by their responsibilities and a concept used by IT Architects to support modular design.

The architecture description should enable subsequent steps and tasks in building the overall system, such as developing other, more detailed architecture deliverables that build upon the deliverables that communicate the functional aspects of the logical architecture. For example, the operational architecture is derived from the logical architecture and describes the physical architecture of the solution based upon the actual hardware and network configuration, software product mapping, and placement of application components and data. "What is software architecture?" is an IBM developerWorks article[2] that is another great source about the topic of software architecture for reference by the reader.

Reference architectures are an abstraction of multiple solution architectures that have been designed and successfully deployed to address the same types of business problems. Reference architectures incorporate the knowledge, patterns, and best practices gained from those implementations into the reference architecture. There are reference architectures that are cross-industry and others that might be industry-specific. Reference architectures provide detailed architectural information in a common format such that solutions can be repeatedly designed and deployed in a consistent, high-quality, supportable fashion. Reference architectures describe the major foundational components such as architecture building blocks for an end-to-end solution architecture. Early in the analysis and design stage of a solution, it is common for IT Architects to search for reference architectures that can be used as input to design the solution architecture. They provide a framework for scope identification, gap assessment, and risk assessment to develop a roadmap to design and implement a solution. Reference architectures can reduce the associated costs and risk for developing a solution from scratch.

Throughout the book, we introduce important concepts about Master Data Management (MDM) such as MDM methods of use, implementation styles, data governance, security,

---

2. Eeles, P., *What is software architecture?*, IBM developerWorks, http://www.ibm.com/developerworks/rational/library/feb06/eeles/.

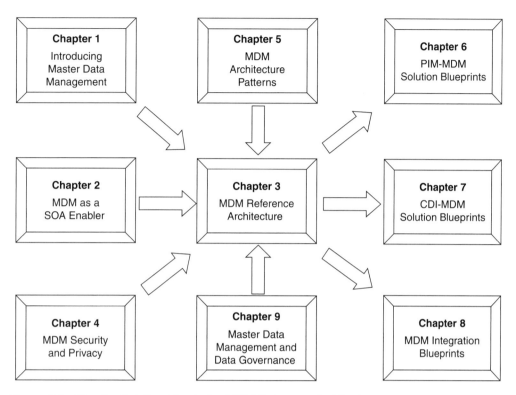

Figure 3.1 Chapter Relationships to the MDM Reference Architecture.

architecture patterns, and Service-Oriented Architecture. There is content throughout the book that assists the reader in understanding the business and technology concepts that were used as input for the development of the Master Data Management Reference Architecture (MDM RA). So the reader then might ask, what are the linkages between this chapter describing the technical architecture description of the MDM RA and other chapters in the book? Figure 3.1 and the following list briefly describe those linkages and how the MDM RA was used as input for development of business solution blueprints.

- **Chapter 1:** Introducing Master Data Management describes the core concepts about Master Data Management and master data that are fundamental for the basis of the MDM Reference Architecture. It describes the multiple Master Data Management methods of use and architectural implementation styles.
- **Chapter 2:** MDM as an SOA Enabler describes the relationship between Master Data Management and Service-Oriented Architectures. The chapter describes topics such as SOA concepts, SOA principles, service granularity, composability, and Information Services that support the motivation and implications for the design of the MDM Reference Architecture.
- **Chapter 4:** MDM Security and Privacy describes security and privacy concepts relevant for implementing a Master Data Management Solution.

- **Chapter 5:** MDM Architecture Patterns provides a set of MDM Architecture Patterns abstracted from analysis of multiple implementations of MDM Solutions.
- **Chapter 6:** PIM-MDM Solution Blueprints describes the business problem, business value, and the MDM RA as guidance to describe solution blueprints for Product Information Management Solutions.
- **Chapter 7:** CDI-MDM Solution Blueprints describe the business problem, business value, and the MDM RA as the basis to describe solution blueprints for Customer Information Management Solutions.
- **Chapter 8:** MDM Integration Blueprints provides further guidance on how to integrate an MDM System into an existing IT landscape and uses the MDM RA as guidance for those integration blueprints.
- **Chapter 9:** MDM and Data Governance explores the critical nature of data governance in Master Data Management, and how people, process, and technology work together to leverage master data as an enterprise asset. It describes concepts and further details about capabilities that the MDM RA should provide for data governance, such as data quality management.

The MDM RA is an industry-agnostic reference architecture that supports implementing the multiple methods of use for Master Data Management and multiple implementation styles, and enables the ability to design business solutions incorporating MDM capabilities. By industry-agnostic, we mean that the reference architecture incorporates the knowledge, best practices, and patterns discovered through review and analysis of how MDM was deployed in multiple Customer Data Integration and Product Information Management Solutions spanning multiple industry sectors. We have abstracted the knowledge and patterns from those implementations to develop the MDM RA as a way to describe how to implement a Master Data Management Solution within the enterprise.

This chapter describes the MDM Reference Architecture and how it enables high-quality MDM Solutions to be designed with well-defined architecture building blocks. It contains a set of technical diagrams and descriptions that describe the MDM RA at multiple levels, as described by the Conceptual Architecture, Logical Architecture, and Component Model as identified in Figure 3.2. The MDM Reference Architecture does not map software products and hardware onto the architecture building blocks but describes the functional aspects of the architecture as we move from the conceptual level to the logical level of the architecture. It defines a division of functionality that can then be mapped onto software and hardware components that will cooperatively implement Master Data Management functionality for a specific solution. The reader will notice throughout the chapter that the reference architecture is described in more detail in terms of services and how those services can work together to deliver Master Data Management functionality. Architecture principles and architecture decisions provide overarching guidance for designing and implementing a solution at all levels of the architecture.

We describe the reference architecture in terms of the Conceptual Architecture, Logical Architecture, and Component Model.

- **Conceptual Architecture:** At the conceptual level of the reference architecture, we start to translate the key concepts and capabilities into governing ideas and candidate

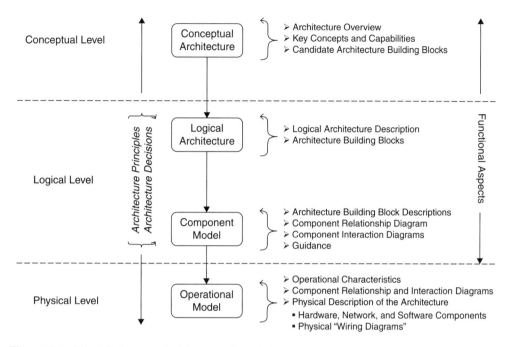

Figure 3.2 MDM Reference Architecture Description.

architecture building blocks for implementing an MDM Solution. The Conceptual Architecture includes an Architecture Overview Diagram and short description of those candidate architecture building blocks.

- **Logical Architecture:** The logical architecture is a lower-level decomposition of the Conceptual Architecture where through further analysis of the MDM methods of use, implementation styles, key capabilities, and candidate architecture building blocks, we start constructing the component model. Yet we describe the architecture in a way that can be understood by both business and IT professionals. We show, in the Logical Architecture Diagram, lower-level software components within key architecture building blocks and describe those components and their roles in the architecture.

- **Component Model:** The Component Model refers to the set of technical architecture diagrams and associated descriptions that provide lower-level specifications about the MDM Reference Architecture. The Component Model Section includes a technical description of the components and services within each architecture building block. The Component Relationship Diagram positions the MDM core set of architecture building blocks within a enterprise architecture by introducing new components that could be used to deliver an end-to-end Master Data Management Solution. Component interaction diagrams demonstrate how the components interact by showing the dynamic relationships between components to provide Master Data Management functionality.

When we use the term MDM System, we are referring to the collection of MDM Services defined within the Master Data Management Services architecture building block that delivers MDM functionality.[3] Implementing an MDM Solution may require implementing and deploying more than just the MDM System to deliver Master Data Management functionality. For example, the design of an MDM Solution may require integration with technologies that provide workflow services, presentation services such as a portal, and technologies that provide Enterprise Application Integration (EAI), Extract Transform and Load (ETL), and Enterprise Information Integration (EII) capabilities. Chapters 6 and 7 describe PIM-MDM and CDI-MDM Solution Blueprints using the MDM Reference Architecture as guidance to identify solution blueprints that solve specific business problems for various industries, such as consumer electronics, retail, healthcare, banking, and insurance.

For the development of the MDM Reference Architecture, we analyzed numerous CDI and PIM Master Data Management implementations to understand best practices and the types of architecture patterns applied for application and data integration. Chapter 5, MDM Architecture Patterns, describes these architecture patterns in detail and categorizes the patterns, as follows:

- **Process-Focused Application Integration:** These patterns are centered on the integration of the applications and transactions into the MDM Solution, and the necessary adjustments and improvements of chosen workflows and business processes.
- **Information-Focused Application Integration:** These patterns describe the aspects of building and materializing the MDM System, including the many different facets to synchronize master data among the MDM hub and the underlying legacy systems.
- **MDM Hub Patterns:** These patterns consider the different styles of MDM deployments, which will be described in terms of the materialization of master data, the impact on transactions, and the services aspects.

Patterns provide the knowledge and experience to develop architectures without sacrificing the quality and service expected to develop a solution. We applied these architecture patterns in the development of the reference architecture by following best practices regarding the construction, deployment, and operation of MDM implementations. Needless to say, it always makes sense to benefit from the lessons that others have learned while embarking down a new road.

3.2   Conceptual Architecture Overview

A Master Data Management Solution enables an enterprise to govern, maintain, use, and analyze complete, contextual, and accurate master data for all stakeholders, users, and applications, across and beyond the enterprise. The identification of stakeholders and users will be different based upon the industry sector and background of the reader. But for the purpose

---

3.   The MDM Services architecture building block is first described in the Conceptual Architecture section of this chapter and subsequently expanded upon in the MDM Logical Architecture and Component Model sections.

of this discussion, stakeholders consist of Line of Business (LOB) system users and data analysts within the enterprise, and stakeholders such as Trading Partners and Agents that have extended relationships with the enterprise. A key concept we have discussed about Master Data Management is that implementing an MDM Solution is more than maintaining a central authoritative repository of master data within the Enterprise. This chapter will provide the reader with further insight about how the design of an MDM Solution:

- Establishes the ability to generate operations to implement master data governance policies to manage and control the quality of master data
- Establishes data standards and provides for the cleansing of master data being used in current operations to improve data quality and improve consistency for use in operational environments across the enterprise
- Delivers business value by standardizing not only on a single version of the data, but standardizing the way that master data is used across an enterprise, treating master data as a unique corporate asset bridging structured as well as unstructured data
- Provides the authoritative source of master data for new and existing applications, and establishes guidelines for the lifecycle management of master data
- Provides high-value actionable services over the data, delivering business value by detecting and generating business operations derived from changes that occur to a master data entity during its lifecycle

In order to understand the types of capabilities desired for implementing Master Data Management, we need to briefly reflect on some of the primary concepts discussed about the ways that Master Data Management is implemented for managing and maintaining master data. Master Data Management can be a dramatic paradigm shift within an enterprise because it requires a proactive enterprise view of master data, and uses a combination of technologies and governance to manage and use master data across multiple master data domains. Managing master data throughout its lifecycle may ultimately require the ability to collaborate, define, and publish master data; operational capabilities to manage and maintain master data; and analytical capabilities to provide better insight and leverage embedded information. Master Data Management concepts are covered in great detail in Chapter 1, Introducing Master Data Management, where Master Data Management methods of use are introduced and how they apply to multiple master data domains is explained.

There are always business processes associated with maintaining master data, such as setting up new products to be sold, managing suppliers, managing vendors, or adding new customer accounts. The MDM System participates in the automation of such processes by either driving the entire process or by MDM services being requested by another system. The collaborative style of MDM provides the ability to author and maintain master data in one place that is typically maintained across many internal applications. The collaborative style requires the ability to manage and maintain the state of a master data entity as activities are performed as part of a collaborative process that controls the creation, management, and quality of that master data entity. As information about the master data entity is entered, validated, and approved, the MDM System supports the synchronization of master data with enterprise applications and data repositories within the enterprise and the exchange and synchronization of master data information with business partners.

The operational style of Master Data Management considers the MDM System as the authoritative source for master data, and the MDM System provides services that can be consumed by business systems as part of a business transaction. MDM services provide capabilities for business systems to control the creation, management, quality, and access of master data. For example, as part of a process to add a new customer, a business system could invoke an MDM service to validate if this customer is a new or an existing customer within the enterprise. This MDM service could cleanse and standardize the new customer information, perform matching logic to determine if the customer already exists within the enterprise, and return the results to the requesting business system as part of the same business transaction. The business system would then continue processing the business transaction with knowledge about whether this is a new customer or an existing customer within the enterprise. In the event that information about a master data entity is not stored within the MDM System, MDM services can be configured to maintain reference information about that master data entity across multiple enterprise business systems. For example, this cross-reference information can be used by a federated query service, portal, or enterprise service bus to retrieve both structured and unstructured content about a master data entity in order to provide a complete view of a person or product. Operational MDM would also support the synchronization of new master data with legacy systems, enterprise applications, and data repositories within the enterprise and with business partners.

Analytical MDM augments MDM operational services with in-line decision support analytics that can trigger business operations, and provides a Master Data Repository for analyzing accurate master data. In-line decision support analytics can be used to support regulatory compliance, perform conflict management, and detect threat and fraud, thus reducing the risk of increased costs and mitigating potential damage to an organization's reputation. In-line analytics is the analytical activity that can occur on a transactional basis with an understanding of how the master data is being used by the application consuming the MDM service. For example, an MDM service to open a bank account for a new customer could trigger identity or name analytics to screen the applicant against government and industry watch lists during the processing of that new account application. This analysis would support regulatory compliance requirements for verifying that the person is not on a list that prohibits financial institutions from conducting business with that person. Because the MDM System provides a database of clean, standardized master data without duplicates, analysis tools can also be used to accurately answer business questions such as how many customers have been added, how many cross-sell opportunities have been closed, and so on.

Lastly, the analytical style of MDM supports using master data from the MDM System as the clean, accurate source of master data to merge with transactional data while loading data into a Data Warehouse or other analytical structures and technologies. The MDM System contains clean master data and knowledge about master data domain relationships. As discussed in Chapter 5 with regard to the MDM Hub patterns, the amount of master data materialized in the MDM System may vary based upon the implementation style (transactional, registry, and coexistence) but will always maintain some amount of master data content that maps to the dimensional data used for a Data Warehouse. Using the MDM System as the source for clean dimensional data to transform and load transactional data into the Data

Warehouse will reduce CPU cycles for the integration, transformation, and loading of that data. Conversely, data derived from analysis of the data in the data warehouse, such as lifetime customer value and cross-sell and up-sell suggestions, could be important data to persist in the MDM System from a Data Warehouse feed. MDM services would then be available to provide operational access to this information of strategic value to the enterprise.

Designing and implementing an MDM Solution that will continue to deliver sustained value to the enterprise requires the ability to implement the multiple MDM methods of use across multiple master data domains to manage master data throughout its lifecycle. The desired end result should be an MDM System that will support the needs of the enterprise for many years while providing the flexibility to adapt to the use of new technologies, changing business processes and requirements, and the development of new applications. MDM enables companies to realize internal efficiencies by reducing the cost and complexity of business processes that use master data. As described in Chapter 2, MDM as an SOA Enabler, MDM services can be invoked to provide critical reusable information and business services that deliver information in the right context at the right time to any authorized user, application, or process. MDM and SOA complement each other to achieve the business and IT goals for effectively managing master data. MDM Systems provide business and information services such as:

- Services to access critical business information from the MDM data repository, which should provide the best source of consistent and accurate master information for the enterprise
- Common business services supporting consistent information-centric procedures such as adding a new customer or creating a new item across all applications within the enterprise and the extended enterprise
- Business services to make data actionable by detecting events and triggering operations for data governance or to integrate with business processes that may span multiple heterogeneous applications

3.2.1 Key Functional and Technical Capabilities

There is a common set of functional and technical capabilities that support the implementation of an MDM Solution that includes one or more master data domains and multiple MDM methods of use. This does not mean, though, that all of the capabilities identified to implement a Master Data Management Solution are necessarily implemented within the MDM System. IT Architects make architectural design decisions throughout the analysis and design process that support the allocation of requirements to software components within the existing IT environment and identify gaps that require new technologies. As requirements are allocated across existing technologies, then the remaining requirements can be used to identify features required for additional software components required to implement the complete MDM Solution and the MDM System itself. The IT Architect then continues to revise the design based upon the choice of available technologies to fill any gaps in the design. We have classified this common set of capabilities as Master Data Lifecycle Management, Data Quality Management, Master Data Harmonization, and Analysis and Insight Capabilities.

3.2.1.1 Master Data Lifecycle Management Capability

Master Data Lifecycle Management capability supports the definition, creation, access, and management of master data. Master data must be managed and leveraged effectively throughout its entire lifespan. The value of master data to the business changes during the various lifecycle stages of a master data entity, such as customer, product, or account. For example,

- Products may be manufactured and distributed by different manufactures and suppliers.
- Multiple vendors may be selected to provide common services as part of vendor optimization management.
- Customers may get married, have children, buy a house, buy a car, or become deceased.
- Customers open accounts, may have multiple accounts, and close accounts.

The MDM System should be able to provide the following types of Master Data Lifecycle Management capabilities across all three MDM methods of use and across multiple master data domains:

- Capability is needed to manage master data from the time it is first created in the MDM System until data retention is no longer required. This functionality understands the context of how master data is used within a business process and can detect events that trigger business operations.
- Capability should be available to group and define hierarchies between master data entities within the same master data domain. For example, the system should be able to identify the hierarchy of companies that roll up into a parent company as well as group accounts managed by an agent.
- Flexible mapping capability is necessary to manage complex relationships between master data domains such as product to vendor and customer to account and location. Master data domains have relationships that the MDM System needs to maintain for referential integrity and reporting accuracy.
- Functionality is desired to define master data hierarchies, relationships, and groupings either manually or automatically by receiving input from an external system about the legal relationships between companies and organizations and people and organizations, for example.
- Versioning capability is needed to understand how the state of a master data entity changes with the passage of time. This includes the ability to capture changes to the master data entity and any changes to established hierarchies and relationships, and the ability to query those point-in-time lifecycle changes. For example, mergers and acquisitions can change the hierarchical structure of a parent company and its subsidiaries, married couples may no longer be married, a retailer may change suppliers for a product and a product may be discontinued.
- Authoring capability may be needed to define, manage, customize, and extend different master data entities such as Product, Supplier, and Customer. This requires the ability to describe the master data entity such as the master data schema, attributes, and the ability to enter instance data for master data records. An example of

this capability would be to define the master data schema that would fully define a product item such as part number, product description, manufacturer specifications, dimensions, and supplier.

- Functionality should be considered to add new master data quickly, such as multi-channel attributes, privacy preferences, or events that can be made available across the enterprise and are not currently captured in enterprise applications. Multi-channel attributes could indicate the last date and time that a customer had contact with the enterprise, possibly through direct interaction with an agent, Customer Service Representative, telephony system, or the Internet, for example. Privacy preferences would indicate whether or not a customer's personal information can be shared across lines of business.

- There may be a desired capability to model multiple taxonomies such as product classifications from a Buyer Point of View and a Sales Point of View. Taxonomies provide a means of maintaining one copy of a master data record that can be viewed in multiple hierarchies as well as the ability to determine what attributes can be viewed for each hierarchy. For example, a Buyer may want to see products classified by supplier, and a Seller may want to view the same products by product category.

- Functionality is necessary to maintain data lineage to a source system for the location of master data associated with the master data entity in the MDM System. The MDM System may not contain all of the information about a master data entity within the MDM data repository but only the master data attributes that should be centrally maintained.

- Security capabilities such as those described in Chapter 4, MDM Security and Privacy, are required to manage the access, entitlement, and visibility of master data for security and privacy.

- Audit capabilities are needed to understand the "who," "what," "how," and "when" of changes that are made to master data over time. Audit capabilities not only help with problem resolution but also support regulatory compliance analysis and reporting for regulations such as those defined in Appendix C.

3.2.1.2 Data Quality Management Capability

Data Quality Management capabilities provide information integrity functionality to support the initial and incremental load of an MDM System and to maintain and manage high-quality, standardized master data in the MDM System. This category includes capabilities to automatically manage data quality as well as the ability to implement data governance policies for the management of data quality. As mentioned in Chapter 9, Master Data Management and Data Governance, master data governance plays a critical role in implementing Master Data Management. The MDM System should be able to support master data governance and provide Data Quality Management capabilities across all three MDM methods of use. Data Quality Management capabilities include:

- Data analysis and profiling capability is needed to understand the quality and structure of master data in the source systems and determine the rules necessary for data cleansing and the consolidation of master data from multiple master data records for the same master data entity. Data profiling capabilities also provide a means to establish a data quality baseline that can be used to assess improvements to the quality of master data across the enterprise.

- Capabilities are needed to improve the quality of master data through the use of consistent data standardization, data validation, and data cleansing logic. This requires the ability to define and enforce consistent data cleansing and validation rules and enforce standardization logic for data fields such as names and address.
- Data reconciliation capability should be available to automatically reconcile master data entities such as Customers and Products. This capability requires a combination of deterministic or probabilistic matching functionality with the ability to define survivorship rules for the merging of data from multiple records for the same master data entity. Deterministic matching logic uses a combination of algorithms and business rules to determine when two or more records match. Probabilistic matching algorithms weigh frequency and uniqueness of data and assign a score indicating the probability of a match.
- Data governance capabilities are required to manage the reconciliation of master data entities in the event of conflicts and to implement data governance policies for updates to critical master data. For example, Data Stewards should have the ability to manually reconcile conflicts through the collapse and splitting of master data records. The solution may also need to support policies that require a review and approval process for updates to critical master data elements that uniquely identify a master data entry.
- There should be the ability to measure the staleness of data and periodically refresh and revalidate the quality of master data persisted in the Master Data Repository. This is necessary in order to enforce information integrity and validate that the MDM System is achieving the goal for maintaining high-quality data as the authoritative source for the enterprise.

3.2.1.3 Master Data Harmonization Capabilities

Master Data Harmonization capabilities support the integration of Line of Business systems with the MDM System and the distribution of master data across the enterprise using application-to-application and data integration techniques. We want to emphasize that the MDM System itself may not perform the actual distribution of the master data to enterprise business systems or pull master data from the business systems, but that the overall MDM Solution architecture needs to provide capabilities for the MDM System to receive and to distribute master data updates across the enterprise. An MDM Solution should support the following types of Master Data Harmonization capabilities:

- Integration capabilities are required to improve the sharing, consolidation, and analysis of master data from business systems with the MDM System. For example, functionality should be available to receive master data updates from business systems through the use of synchronous and asynchronous techniques such as messaging, service invocation, batch, ETL, and FTP.
- The MDM System should be able to support EAI, ETL, and EII techniques to synchronize information from the MDM System with enterprise business systems and

to support a business process. The flexibility to use a combination of synchronous and asynchronous integration techniques will provide the ability to distribute master data updates in the "right time"[4] to support a business process, while avoiding disruption to the business. Coordinating the flow of master data from the MDM System with a business process can reduce the need for the duplicate data entry of master data updates into multiple business systems.

- Capability should be available to remove master data content from business systems based upon knowledge from the MDM System that a particular master data entity such as a customer is no longer an active customer within the enterprise, and all legal requirements have been met.
- Automatic or manual error-handling functionality should be available to manage the synchronization of master data across the enterprise in the case of failure. This is required in the event that a line of business system did not successfully receive and process the latest master data updates made available by the MDM System; hence, some action must be taken, either manually or automatically, to complete the harmonization activity.
- The MDM Solution may need to support a high-volume transaction environment for real-time processing and high availability. We include this capability statement as a reminder especially in the case of Operational MDM, where a business system may invoke MDM services as part of a business transaction. In such a case, the MDM System must be carefully designed for scalability and reliability, and must meet or exceed its agreed-upon performance and availability requirements. Generally speaking, though, for the design of any MDM Solution Architecture, the solution must be designed to support nonfunctional requirements such as reliability, availability, performance, and scalability.

3.2.1.4 Analysis and Insight Capabilities

The Analysis and Insight capabilities category simply identifies additional capabilities that specifically are associated with the multiple methods of use for MDM and span multiple capability categories. They identify how an MDM Solution can provide knowledge and insight to support business decisions, enable the ability to develop business solutions, and provide the complete view of a master data entity. We have learned through observing how organizations are implementing Master Data Management across multiple industry sectors that organizations are not just implementing an MDM System but using the MDM System to enable the development of business solutions such as those discussed in Chapter 1, Introducing Master Data Management, and Chapters 6 and 7, which discuss PIM-MDM and CDI-MDM Solution Blueprints. Some of these types of business solutions include the ability to know your customer, optimize the introduction of new products and services, and provide a single view of a person. Chapters 6 and 7 provide a detailed discussion about the types of users and capabilities required for implementing these types of business solutions.

---

4. "Right time" simply means to align the latency requirements for distributing updated master data in the right time to the dependencies of a business process for data currency.

The capabilities listed here identify fundamental capabilities that could support the multiple MDM methods of use.

- Analytic functionality may be required to discover insightful relationships, both obvious and non-obvious, that can support business decisions such as who belongs to the same household, understanding consumption patterns, and cross-sell and up-sell opportunities. Analytic capability could be implemented to support both inline analytic processing as part of a business transaction or as part of the background processing after completion of a business transaction.
- Analytic capability may be required to improve business decisions at the global level by providing up-to-date master data from regional organizations. For example, analytics functionality could assist the ability of a parent company to understand the relationships of when a corporate customer is a customer to one of its subsidiary companies and if that same corporate customer or a subsidiary of that company is a supplier to another Line of Business within the parent company. This information could be very useful in developing new business agreements between the two companies.
- Functionality should be available to access structured and unstructured information about a master data entity that is distributed over multiple data sources. An example would be the ability to create On-Demand a "Virtual Master Data Record" consisting of structured data about a person and possibly unstructured content such as a document image that can be retrieved from disparate data sources to deliver to an authorized requesting application, user, or process.
- Collaboration capabilities may be required to support the ability to manage the state of a process defined as a sequence of tasks performed by a person or automated by a system. The New Product Introduction process is an example of such a business process that would require collaboration functionality.
- Functionality should be available to configure event management services by defining the conditions for a business event and notification services to generate alerts. For example, if someone has reached an age that requires them to automatically start receiving annual distributions from their tax deferred savings account, a notification could be generated to a Customer Service Representative to contact this customer and make them aware of the consequences of not doing such.

These key functional and technical capabilities were used as input for developing the design of the MDM Reference Architecture and are closely linked to the component definitions identified in the architecture building blocks that work together to deliver a Master Data Management Solution.

3.3   MDM Conceptual Architecture

Now that we have described the Master Data Management key functional and technical capabilities, we describe the conceptual level of MDM Reference Architecture for the enterprise. At the conceptual level of the reference architecture, we start to translate the key concepts and capabilities into governing ideas and candidate architecture building blocks for implementing an MDM Solution that both a business person and IT professional can understand. This level describes the main conceptual elements and shows the relationships of those elements within the architecture. These elements include candidate subsystems, nodes, connections, data stores, users, and external systems. We have defined the following set of architecture drivers as a set of governing ideas based upon the analysis of the desired MDM key capabilities and methods of use for developing the MDM Reference Architecture at the conceptual level:

- It should provide a framework to manage and maintain master data as an "**authoritative source**" and securely deliver accurate, up-to-date master data across and beyond the enterprise to authorized users and systems using a combination of synchronous and asynchronous integration techniques.
- It should be a **scalable, highly available,** and **adaptive** architecture that is capable of supporting high performance for both real-time processing and high-volume batch processing. We define adaptive as the ability to easily extend and add MDM services and to extend the MDM Data model, yet providing the ability to support planned technology upgrade strategies.
- It should support the ability to **coordinate** and **manage** the **lifecycle of master data** across the enterprise.
- It should provide **accurate critical business information available as a service** that can be used in the context of a business process at the right time by any authorized user, application, or process.
- It should provide the ability to **cleanse data** being used operationally within a line of business system, and **improve the quality** and **consistency** of master data used within the operational environment.
- It should provide the need to make **master data active** by detecting events and generating operations to manage master data, implement data governance policies, and create business value.
- It should **enable** the ability to implement solutions such as those described in Chapters 6 and 7 for PIM-MDM and CDI-MDM Solution Blueprints for New Product Introduction, Track and Trace, Customer Care, and so on.

Master Data Management enables the ability to implement solutions that span many industry sectors, such as those identified in the Master Data Management Architecture Overview Diagram in Figure 3.3. The Master Data Management Reference Architecture for the enterprise represents the capabilities to implement a resilient, adaptive architecture to enable and ensure high-performance and sustained value for the enterprise. The reference architecture provides a framework of components that can manage the lifecycle of master data, manage the quality and integrity of the data, make master data actionable, and provides stateless services to control the consumption and distribution of data.

The enterprise consists of Line of Business systems that support the automation of business processes for business units within the enterprise and analytics capabilities such as those provided through the use of a Data Warehouse and OLAP technologies. Business systems may be a combination of custom-developed, legacy systems, and packaged applications such

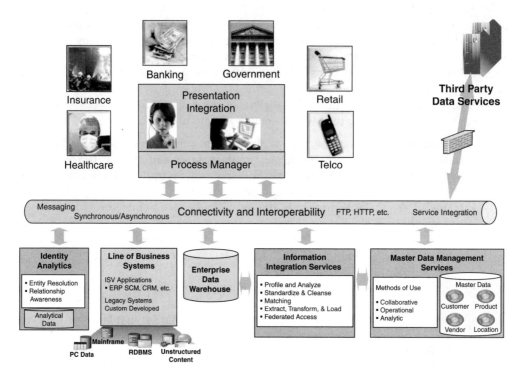

Figure 3.3 Master Data Management Architecture Overview Diagram.

as those that provide Enterprise Resource Planning, Customer Relationship Management, and Supply Chain Management functionality. Furthermore, these systems are typically implemented throughout the enterprise on heterogeneous platforms with multiple types of data stores containing structured and possibly unstructured data. Dependent upon the organization, various types of front-office and back-office users such as Customer Service Representatives, Case Workers, Analysts, and so on access their business systems through presentation integration services provided by the business system or through an enterprise portal.[5] While these users access their respective business systems to perform their work, those systems maintain and access master data either directly within the business system database or invoke Master Data Services to access and maintain master data within the MDM System. Business systems may invoke Information Integration Services or Master Data Management Services either directly or through the Connectivity and Interoperability Layer.

The key architecture building blocks represented in Figure 3.3 for the MDM Architecture Overview that interoperate to implement an MDM Solution include:

---

5. Enterprise portals provide a pre-integrated set of services that provide a common enterprise presentation infrastructure framework in lieu of supporting stand-alone user interface application logic for each application.

- Third-Party Data Service Providers like Dun and Bradstreet[6] and ACXIOM,[7] which may be accessed to support the enrichment of customer data about organizations and demographic information about people. In order to comply with government regulations, the U.S. Government also provides information from offices such as the Office of Foreign Assets Control that can be cross-referenced as part of a business process for screening applicants for financial services.
- The enterprise may use a Process Manager to choreograph and manage long-running processes that span multiple systems and involve human tasks. Industry-specific process models or custom-developed process models could be used to define the activities and tasks that would be automated by a Process Manager.
- The Connectivity and Interoperability Layer provides integration services for systems internal and external to the enterprise. This layer could encompass a variety of techniques such as batch processing, FTP, and messaging, or in the case of a Service-Oriented Architecture (SOA), could be an enterprise service bus that supports various styles of integration. Representation of this layer in the architecture does not preclude the ability for a Line of Business system to call a Master Data Management Service or Information Integration Service directly.
- Master Data Management Services maintain a Master Data Repository that contains instance master data from domains such as Customer, Account, Supplier, Product, and Location. As described in Chapter 5, the materialization of master data in the Master Data Repository will depend upon the MDM Architecture Patterns used to implement MDM functionality. Master Data Management Services provide data quality management, lifecycle management, event management, authoring, and hierarchy and relationship management services to maintain master data as the authoritative source of master data.
- Information Integration Services provide information services to support real-time interaction with MDM services, and support the initial and incremental load of large volumes of data to target systems such as the Enterprise Data Warehouse and Master Data Management System. They also provide profiling and analysis services to understand data that will be aggregated and merged for loading into a target database and services to standardize and cleanse information.
- Identity Analytics support the resolution of a person's true identity and relationship resolution services to determine both obvious and non-obvious relationships between people and organizations.

The MDM System should include a library of reusable common services consisting of both coarse-grained and fine-grained services to support information-centric master data procedures that business systems can consume as a service. The benefits and rationale for the use of SOA design principles are discussed extensively in Chapter 2. The MDM System provides

---

6. Dun and Bradstreet provides business information services about the structure of a business, such as parent and subsidiary relationships and location, and credit reports to businesses. The homepage for more information can be found in Appendix B, Software and Solution Offerings for MDM Deployments.

7. ACXIOM provides customer and information management solutions to businesses. The homepage for more information can be found in Appendix B, Software and Solution Offerings for MDM Deployments.

the enterprise with centralized control and maintenance for these information services, which deliver consistent packaging of the data and apply consistent business rules to the data. This ensures information quality and consistency for usage of master data in the right context at the right time for systems across the enterprise.

3.4 Architecture Principles

An architecture principle is a comprehensive and fundamental law, doctrine, or assumption that provides overarching guidance for development of the technical architecture for a solution. A good architecture principle will not be outdated by advancing technology and has objective reasons for advancing it instead of alternatives. Principles should include the defined motivation for the principle and the respective implications of this principle for the overall solution. Motivation statements highlight the value of the principle to the business and can be linked to strategic business initiatives. The implication statements provide an outline of the key tasks, resources, and potential costs to the business for implementing the principle. They also provide valuable inputs to future transition initiatives and planning activities. After they have been agreed upon and published, the architecture principles provide a framework that can be used to explain and justify why certain IT decisions are made, or need to be made.

We have identified a set of core architecture principles that are fundamental to the design and implementation of a Master Data Management Solution. Adopting these core architecture principles will influence the architectural style for the design and delivery of a Master Data Management Solution, ranging from the choice of integration techniques to the capabilities required of the MDM System. The associated motivation and implications for each principle could vary based upon the business initiatives driving the need to implement Master Data Management and IT strategy for a specific organization. Some of the architecture principles reference the need to utilize service-oriented architecture design principles and strategy for the implementation of the MDM Solution. The reader may want to reference Chapter 2, MDM as an SOA Enabler, for a further description of the rationale for using an SOA approach for implementing a Master Data Management Solution. The following core architecture principles were used as input to guide the overall design of the reference architecture:

- The Master Data Management Solution should provide the ability to **decouple** information from enterprise applications and processes to make it available as a **strategic asset** for use by the enterprise.
- The Master Data Management Solution should provide the enterprise with an **authoritative source** for master data that manages information integrity and **controls** the distribution of master data across the enterprise in a **standardized** way that enables reuse.
- The Master Data Management Solution should be based upon an **architectural framework** and **reusable services** that can leverage existing technologies within the enterprise.
- The Master Data Management Solution should be based upon industry-accepted **open computing standards** to support the use of multiple technologies and techniques for interoperability with systems in the enterprise and the extended enterprise.

- The Master Data Management Solution should provide the **flexibility** to accommodate changes to master data schema, business requirements, and regulations, and to support the addition of new master data.
- The Master Data Management Solution should be designed with the highest regard for **preserving the ownership of data,** the integrity, and the security of the data from the time it is entered into the system until retention of the data is no longer required.
- The Master Data Management Solution should provide the ability to **incrementally** implement a Master Data Management Solution so that a Master Data Management Solution can demonstrate "**immediate value.**"

The Master Data Management Solution should provide the ability to decouple information from enterprise applications and processes to make it available as a strategic asset for use by the enterprise. This is a fundamental concept for Information on Demand founded upon SOA principles to deliver information at the right time in the right context to the right authorized application, process, or user. An organization accumulates a vast amount of data through its normal day-to-day processing. The full business value of that data to the enterprise is not realized when acted upon only by a single system performing specific business logic for its particular scope. The principle considers the business motivation to get real value out of this vast amount of data in order to understand the significance and make it actionable. The business may also need to improve its ability to respond to business changes that could require the addition of new master data elements such as privacy preferences or to make changes to the definition or structure of existing master data. The motivation for this principle leads to some of the following design implications:

- Use SOA design principles to implement Master Data Management services to create and maintain consistent, complete, contextual, and accurate master data for use in existing and new applications. MDM services can be reused and composed to support business processes.
- Enable the collaborative sharing of information while protecting privacy and ensuring security.
- Provide the ability to detect scheduled events and business defined events to derive business insight and initiate operations such as those for master data lifecycle management.

The Master Data Management Solution should provide the enterprise with an authoritative source for master data that manages information integrity and controls the distribution of "trusted" master data across the enterprise in a standardized way that enables reuse. The primary motivation is to create an authoritative source of master data where the management of master data can be centralized to reduce data management costs and improve the accuracy and completeness of that data. This source of master data can then be used to maintain and support the secure delivery of accurate up-to-date master data such as customer and product data across the enterprise in a standardized way. The motivation for this design principle has the following architectural design implications:

- Provide **Master Data Management services** that can be consumed by business systems to access, manage, and control updates to master data information maintained in a centralized Master Data Repository. The business systems may also require the ability to create new services or customize existing services to consume MDM Services.

- Provide the ability to **distribute** "trusted" master data **updates** to systems that require the most recent master data in the "right-time" using synchronous or asynchronous application and information integration techniques.
- The design of the MDM Solution architecture should be capable of providing **high availability** and **continuous operations**.
- Implement **data governance policies** for the enterprise that provide for the **Data Stewardship** of master data to resolve issues of accuracy and completeness.
- Provide the ability to **harmonize core business information** across heterogeneous data sources, synchronize operationally, and ensure a consistent data view.

The Master Data Management Solution should be based upon an architectural framework and reusable services that can leverage existing technologies within the enterprise. This principle guides the architectural design decisions to leverage existing investments in technologies such as those that provide application integration capabilities to implement a Master Data Management Solution. The idea is to contain costs and improve the speed to deliver the MDM Solution benefits to the business. The principle is also a fundamental consideration for implementing a Service-Oriented Architecture where services can be consumed by an application or process without knowing the location and implementation details for that service. This provides a dynamically reconfigurable architectural style where a software technology could be replaced by a newer technology that provides the same capabilities at a lower cost of ownership and potentially includes additional capabilities. Some of the significant implications of this architecture principle are:

- Design of the MDM Solution architecture should be based upon **SOA Design principles** and concepts, such as the use of Web Services and the Simple Object Access Protocol (SOAP), as described in Chapter 2, MDM as an SOA Enabler.
- The Master Data Management Solution architecture and design approach should provide **flexibility** and be based upon a **well-defined** set of configurable components.
- The Master Data Management Solution should be based upon **industry-accepted open computing standards**[8] such as Web Services, JMS, and XML and should provide the ability to integrate technologies provided by multiple software vendors to implement Master Data Management and Information Integration functionality.

The Master Data Management Solution should be based upon industry-accepted open computing standards to support the use of multiple technologies and techniques for interoperability with systems within the enterprise and extended enterprise. This will guide development of the overall architecture to remain open and flexible so it can easily integrate with a variety of vendor software that may already exist within the enterprise and integrate with future unknown technologies. This provides for a best-of-breed software selection process to choose software technologies that meet the capabilities required to deliver an end-to-end solution. Ultimately, the motivation is to provide a resilient Master Data Management Solution infrastructure based upon software technologies, architecture patterns, and best

---

8. Industry-accepted open computing standards define interoperability specifications that promote the transfer of information between different computing environments and improve accessibility. The following Web site identifies a number of open standards organizations: http://www.openstandards. net/viewOSnet2C.jsp?showModuleName=Organizations.

practices that meets functional and nonfunctional requirements and mitigates implementation risks. This architectural principle can lead to the following implications for software selection and the choice of integration techniques to ensure access to master data within the MDM System as the enterprise continues to evolve with the addition of new applications over time:

- As part of the software selection process, emphasize the use of industry-accepted open computing standards to avoid software product interoperability challenges that could limit the selection of software products and restrict the use of new technologies required to enable new business processes.
- Utilize SOA design concepts to facilitate integration between the enterprise applications with the Master Data Management Solution.

The Master Data Management Solution should provide the flexibility to accommodate changes to master data schema, business requirements, and regulations, and should support the addition of new master data. Business units require the ability to quickly respond to business changes that may require the addition of new master data attributes, changes to existing master data, or changes to the behavior of a master data service. In addition to changing business requirements, a business requires the flexibility to rapidly respond to business-driven strategies such as mergers and acquisitions and to regulations such as those identified in Appendix C. Corporations that have business units geographically dispersed in today's global economy also need the ability to improve business decisions and capabilities with up-to-date information at a global level. The motivation for this design principle leads to the following implications.

- Design of the MDM Solution architecture should consider **service-oriented** design principles and concepts in order to provide a **secure, scalable, highly available and extensible** architecture.
- **Decouple information** from the business process and applications to provide the flexibility to support changes to business processes, laws, and regulations through the use of reusable information services and for changing master data schemas.
- Information is packaged as a service to business processes, so that **consistent, manageable** information is made available to business processes in a **standardized way** that enables reuse and maintainability.
- The MDM System software should provide the ability to easily extend the MDM Services and data model available out-of-the-box.

The Master Data Management Solution should be designed with the highest regard for preserving the ownership of data, the integrity, and the security of the data from the time it is entered into the system until retention of the data is no longer required. Chapter 9, MDM and Data Governance, and Chapter 4, MDM Security and Privacy, describe details about the core concepts applicable to the motivation for this architecture principle, such as the need for privacy and regulatory compliance. Data governance policies and processes should be enforced to support the management of critical master data information. Business units may also require the ability to understand the historical changes that have occurred to critical master data information throughout its lifecycle. This motivation leads to the following implications:

- A comprehensive Master Data Management Solution should build information integrity into its technology, processes, and people to manage and maintain quality master data as a product of the organization.

- A "Defense-in-Depth" security strategy and policies covering all layers of the architecture should provide for user authorization and accountability for access to master data.
- A data governance policy providing for Data Stewardship should be determined and agreed upon for updates to critical master data information that is common to multiple business units within the enterprise.
- The MDM System should provide the ability to maintain a historical record of updates to master data and the associated transactions that have accessed or changed master data within the MDM System.
- The MDM System should provide audit capabilities to understand who made changes and why the changes were made to master data, when the changes were made, and what changes were made to the master data.

The Master Data Management Solution design should provide the ability to incrementally implement a Master Data Management Solution so that a Master Data Management Solution can demonstrate immediate value. Master Data Management Solutions are driven by business initiatives such as those identified in Chapter 1, Introducing Master Data Management, and Chapters 6 and 7, which provide PIM-MDM and CDI-MDM Solution blueprint descriptions. The MDM System should enhance the ability of the business to respond to the changing demands on a business due to regulatory compliance and competitive pressures. Many commercial organizations cannot wait for a twelve- to eighteen-month delivery cycle of new functionality to address these issues. Government agencies such as those that provide social services are also being required to improve services for their citizens while receiving less money for those same programs. This motivation can lead to the following implications:

- Provide the ability to deliver the **benefits** of a Master Data Management Solution based upon a priority driven by specific **Key Performance Indicators** (KPIs) that can measure the business value.
- The Master Data Management Solution should be designed in a manner that provides for one or more of the components to be implemented incrementally to allow development and delivery of requirements in a **phased implementation.**
- The MDM Solution should provide capabilities to implement the various MDM methods of use (operational, collaborative, and analytical) for one or more master data domains and should maintain cross-domain relationships.
- A schedule should be developed for the delivery of each of the smaller projects planned to integrate with the MDM System that considers application pairs that share information with each other.

3.5 MDM Logical Architecture

As we move from the conceptual level of the architecture to the logical level, we continue to specify further details about the functional characteristics of the MDM Reference Architecture. The MDM Logical Architecture is intended for technical audiences or for business users with strong technical backgrounds. The technical design of the MDM Logical Architecture is guided by the architecture principles, identifies lower-level software components for the architecture building blocks, and describes the basic responsibilities for each of those software

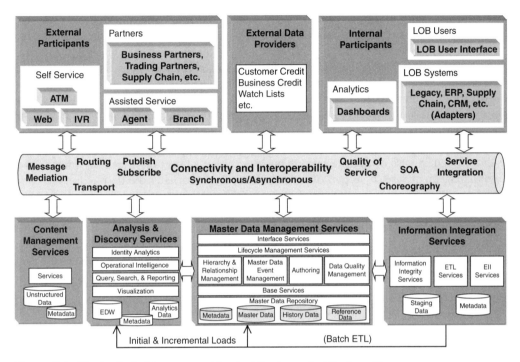

Figure 3.4 Master Data Management Logical Systems Architecture Diagram.

components without reference to software products. The software components are defined based upon overall analysis of the functionality required to support the MDM methods of use, implementation styles, and core MDM functional and technical capabilities.

The focus of the Master Data Management Logical Architecture, shown in Figure 3.4, is to communicate the responsibilities for the core architecture building blocks that provide Master Data Management functionality and integrate the MDM System with business systems across the enterprise. The Master Data Management Services and Information Integration Services architecture building blocks are fundamental to multiple master data domains such as Product, Customer, Supplier, Account, and Location. The MDM Logical Architecture is designed with the flexibility to provide the capabilities needed to support multiple implementation styles, as described in Chapter 1, Introducing Master Data Management, and multiple MDM Architecture Hub patterns to support:

- A transactional implementation style that may utilize Service-Oriented Architecture techniques to access Master Data Management Services as part of an application transaction
- A coexistence implementation style that utilizes techniques such as publish and subscribe to harmonize data across the enterprise
- A registry style that maintains a minimal amount of master data for each master data record and provides links to master data in the source systems

External participants may access and update master data through multiple delivery channels. Customers might access and update master data through business systems that provide self-service capabilities for shopping and online banking or through the use of telephony systems to access and update personal information. Supply Chain data from Suppliers, Trading Partners, and Business Partners participate in business-to-business transactions that involve the exchange of core master data entities such as Customer and Product data. Agents from multiple branch locations that conduct business on behalf of a company may access and update master data through a business system provided by that company or through a business-to-business transaction. Business system users update and query master data typically through the use of their respective business systems. Business systems request Master Data Management Services as part of a business transaction or after the transaction has completed based upon the MDM method of use and implementation style. The decision to invoke Master Data Management Services as part of a business transaction or after the system has completely processed the transaction is an implementation decision that should be based upon analysis of nonfunctional requirements such as performance and availability. Business systems and partner systems would request Master Data Management Services to access master data through capabilities provided in the Connectivity and Interoperability Layer.

Third-Party Data Service Providers such as Dun and Bradstreet, Acxiom, and Lexis Nexis[9] can be accessed for additional information about a person or organization to enrich master data maintained in the MDM System. Data from these organizations may be used to support the initial loading of master data into the MDM System or periodic updates, or may be used on a transactional basis based upon business requirements. Government agencies also provide watch lists required to support regulatory compliance, such as those described in Appendix C, Compliance, for the war against terror and anti-money laundering.

The Connectivity and Interoperability layer facilitates business-to-business communications with Trading and Business Partners, system-to-system communications within the enterprise, and communications to External Data Providers. Many IT organizations have realized the need to reduce the number of point-to-point interfaces between systems in order to reduce complexity and improve maintainability of the enterprise. They have implemented this layer using application integration techniques such as Enterprise Application Integration Hubs that support communications through the use of messaging, or have adopted the use of an enterprise service bus. Master Data Management and Information Integration Services provide information services that can be invoked and choreographed through this layer. The Connectivity and Interoperability Layer represents the enterprise service bus architectural construct or it can simply be thought of as a layer that provides choreography services, and synchronous and asynchronous integration capabilities such as message mediation and routing, publish and subscribe, FTP, and service-oriented integration through the use of Web Services. Service Integration represents the point that MDM and Information Integration Services can be requested directly from a business system, work flow engine, or portal.

---

9. More information about Dun and Bradstreet, Acxiom, and Lexis Nexis can be found in Appendix B, Software and Solutions Offering for MDM Deployment, Section B.3.

Just below the Connectivity and Interoperability layer in the center of Figure 3.4 resides the Master Data Management Services Architecture Building Bock. It consists of a set of Master Data Management Services that are grouped into the following software components:

- **Interface Services** support a consistent entry point to request MDM Services through techniques such as messaging, method calls, Web Services, and batch processing. The same MDM service should be invoked during batch processing that may be requested as part of a transaction in order to maintain and apply consistent business logic.
- **Lifecycle Management Services** manage the lifecycle of master data, provide CRUD (create, read, update, and delete) support for master data managed by the MDM System, and apply business logic based upon the context of that data. Data Quality Management Services are called by Lifecycle Management Services to enforce data quality rules and perform data cleansing, standardization, and reconciliation. Master Data Management Event Management Services are called to detect any actions that should be triggered based upon business rules or data governance policies.
- **Hierarchy and Relationship Management Services** manage master data hierarchies, groupings, and relationships that have been defined for master data. These services may also request Identity Analytics Services to discover relationships, such as those between people that are not obvious, and then store that information in the MDM System.
- **Master Data Management Event Management Services** are used to make information actionable and trigger operations based upon events detected within the data. Events can be defined to support data governance policies, such as managing changes to critical data, based upon business rules or time and date scheduled.
- **Authoring Services** provide services to author, approve, manage, customize, and extend the definition of master data as well as the ability to add or modify instance master data, such as Product, Vendor, and Supplier. These services support the MDM collaborative style of use and may be invoked as part of a collaborative workflow to complete the creation, updating, and approval of the information for definition or instance master data.
- **Data Quality Management Services** validate and enforce data quality rules, perform data standardization for both data values and structures, and perform data reconciliation. These services may request Information Integrity Services that are available from the Information Integration Services architecture building block.
- **Base services** are available to support security and privacy, search, audit logging, and workflow. Base services can be implemented to integrate with common enterprise components that support workflow, security, and audit logging.
- The **Master Data Repository** consists of master data, both instance and definition master data, metadata for the MDM System, and history data that records changes to master data. Master Data Management Services can also be used to maintain and control the distribution of Reference Data that should be maintained at the global level for an organization.

Information Integration Services provide Information Integrity Services, ETL services, and EII services for federated query access to structured and unstructured data distributed over disparate data sources. Information Integrity Services include data profiling, analysis, cleansing, data standardization, and matching services. Data profiling and analysis services are critical for understanding the quality of master data across enterprise systems, and for defining data validation, data cleansing, matching, and standardization logic required to improve master data quality and consistency. MDM Data Quality Management Services can request Information Integrity Services to standardize, cleanse, and match master data updates received by the MDM System from a business system. ETL services support the initial and incremental extract, transform, and load of data from one or more source systems to meet the needs of one or more targets, such as a Data Warehouse and MDM System. The initial and incremental ETL processing to load large volumes of data is represented in the MDM Logical System Architecture Diagram at the bottom of Figure 3.4. Synchronous and asynchronous communication techniques to support the transporting of low volumes of changed data could occur within the Connectivity and Interoperability Layer.

The Analysis and Discovery Services architecture building block contains an Identity Analytics component that provides analytical services that can determine the "true identity" of a person that might be trying to "hide" his or her identity. These services can also be used to discover non-obvious relationships between people, such as those that are part of the same household but have different names and address information, and between people and organizations. MDM Hierarchy and Relationship Management Services can request these services and then store the returned results in the MDM Data Repository. In order for Identity Analytics Services to effectively discover relationships and a person's true identity, it may be necessary to load and analyze data from external data sources along with data from within the enterprise. Information Integration Services can be used to load data into the Identity Analytics component.

The Analysis and Discovery Services architecture building block also contains additional components that enable businesses to adapt to changing market dynamics and everyday operational disruptions. The Operational Intelligence component consists of services that provide event-based analytic functionality, the ability to perform scenario analysis, and sense and respond capability. It may utilize information and process models as input to implement the analytics capabilities for these services. The Query, Search, and Reporting component provides services that support ad hoc queries, reporting services, and Online Analytical Processing (OLAP) capabilities for the reporting, analysis, and multidimensional modeling of business data. The Visualization component provides charting and graphing functionality, spatial dashboard reporting services such as for scorecard reporting, spatial analysis services, and rendering services for interaction with components that provide user presentation services.

The Content Management Services architecture building block provides services to capture, aggregate, and manage unstructured content in a variety of formats such as images, text documents, Web pages, spreadsheets, presentations, graphics, e-mail, video, and other multimedia. Content Management Services provide the ability to search, catalog, secure, manage, and store unstructured content and workflow services to support the creation, revision, approval, and publishing of content. Classification Services are used to identify new categories of content and create taxonomies for classifying enterprise content. Records Management Services manage the retention, access control and security, auditing and reporting, and ultimate disposition of business records. Storage Management Services provide for the policy-driven movement of content throughout the storage lifecycle and the ability to map content to the storage media type based on the overall value of the content and context of the business content. Master Data Management Services would reference content managed by Content Management Services and request these services to access unstructured content associated with master data, such as a Customer, Product, or Account. For example, an application could request an MDM Service to get product master data from the MDM Data Repository and then use the reference data returned from the MDM System to request a content management service to retrieve image data about the product.

The Master Data Management Reference Architecture is designed to support the multiple MDM methods of use for multiple master data domains, to maintain cross-domain relationships, and to provide the required functionality to maintain an "Authoritative Source" of master data for the enterprise. The architecture is structured to be scalable, highly available, and extensible, and will provide the flexibility to integrate technology from a variety of vendors and integrate with future unknown systems. It is based upon MDM Architecture Patterns, as described in Chapter 5, MDM Architecture Patterns, and provides the basis for developing industry solutions incorporating Master Data Management capabilities such as the PIM-MDM and CDI-MDM Solution Blueprints described in Chapters 6 and 7.

3.6   MDM Component Model

The MDM Component Model refers to the set of technical architecture diagrams and associated descriptions that provide lower-level details about the MDM Reference Architecture. We have provided this technical architecture content to communicate the role and responsibilities of the software components within the architecture building blocks that can interoperate to implement an MDM Solution. Sample services are identified for each of the software components to communicate the responsibilities of that architecture building block within the overall architecture. The order of the types of services identified in each of the figures is not meant to reflect a layering of the services within that architecture building block. Because the focus of our work is about Master Data Management, the technical architecture focuses on describing the core MDM architecture building blocks and their respective services. We do not provide descriptions about the components required to deliver presentation services, content management services, business process services, analysis and discovery services, and connectivity and interoperability services.

3.6.1   MDM Interface Services

MDM Interface Services provide a consistent entry point for requesting MDM Services and for MDM Services to interact with external IT components within the overall MDM Solution architecture. MDM Interface Services support multiple integration techniques to request an MDM Lifecycle Management Service, such as to create or access master data. MDM Interface Services should support industry-accepted open computing standards and provide for multiple styles of integration such as those described in Chapter 5, MDM Architecture Patterns. Real-time and batch interface services should be available to provide access to the same

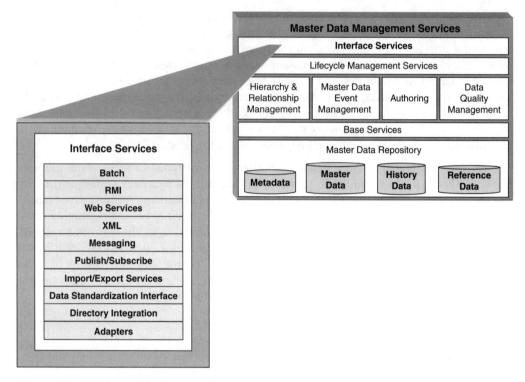

Figure 3.5 MDM Interface Services.

business service so that the same business logic will be applied consistently regardless of how it is invoked. Real-time integration between a business system and the MDM System should follow a standard request and response model. MDM Interface Services request MDM Security and Privacy Services to validate authorization to a service before calling an MDM Lifecycle Management Service.

Figure 3.5 identifies the various types of MDM Interface Services that may need to be available, which include:

- A Batch component to support receiving batch input from one or more business systems and to distribute master data updates via batch processing. For example, batch processing could request MDM Search Services to retrieve all of the latest master data updates since the last batch cycle and then load them into another business system or system that provides analysis and discovery capability.
- RMI Services that confirm authorization for an inbound MDM service request and then invokes that MDM service.
- A Web Services Interface that first confirms authorization for requesting an MDM service and then requests that MDM service.
- XML Services to provide the ability to parse inbound XML requests and construct outbound XML response messages.

- Messaging Services to get and deconstruct messages from a queue, confirm authorization for requesting an MDM service, and then invoke that MDM service.
- Publish and Subscribe Services that provide the MDM System with the ability to subscribe to messages published to a queue and post messages to a queue so that subscribing systems can retrieve master data updates from the MDM System.
- Import/Export Services that can import master data in a specific file format into the MDM System for processing and to export master data from the MDM System in a specific file format.
- Data Standardization Interface Services that request data standardization, data cleansing, and matching services from an external component such as the Information Integration Services architecture building block.
- Directory Integration Services that can request authentication and authorization services from an Enterprise Directory and Security Services component.
- Adapters should be available that can facilitate integration with External Data Providers such as Dun and Bradstreet, and possibly a Business Process Services component that supports the execution of a business process involving manual and system interactions.

3.6.2   MDM Lifecycle Management Services

MDM Lifecycle Management Services provide business and information services by master data domain to create, access, and manage master data[10] held within the Master Data Repository. Information and business services provide functionality based upon the context of the master data object and are usually invoked by a business system or as part of an enterprise business process that includes interactions with one or more business systems and users. These services support the enrichment of master data by maintaining data in the Master Data Repository, such as customer relationships, data received from external data sources, customer privacy preferences, and cross-channel interaction history, that provides additional knowledge about a master data object. Figure 3.6 identifies the types of services that this component could provide for the lifecycle management of master data. The actual types of lifecycle management services required for a master data domain would vary by master data domain.

Coarse-grained services are an aggregate of fine-grained services that are available at the function level for a master data domain. For example, an add customer coarse-grained service could consist of fine-grained services such as add name, add role, add home address, and add location data. Coarse-Grained and Fine-Grained Domain services can be composed to support business processes such as the opening of a new account for a new customer and to implement data governance capabilities. Lifecycle Management Services that update or add master data use MDM Data Quality Management Services to manage data quality, MDM Master Data Event Management Services to detect events, and MDM Hierarchy and Relationship Management Services to determine relationships and hierarchies with other

---

10.   Chapter 1, Introducing Master Data Management, provides an important overview of master data, cross-domain relationships, and the lifecycle of a master data entity.

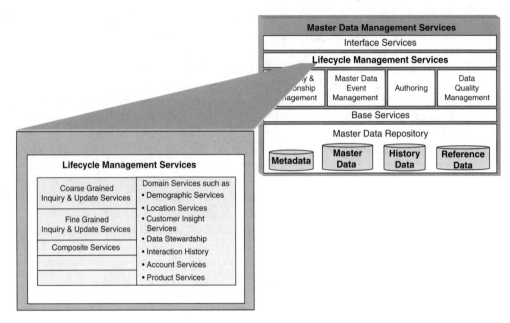

Figure 3.6 MDM Lifecycle Management Services.

master data entities. The following list provides descriptions for the sample MDM Lifecycle
Management Services identified in Figure 3.6:

- Demographic Services provide create, update, and delete capabilities for the Party
  Domain. The Party Domain, as described in Chapter 1, Introducing Master Data
  Management, includes master data covering party types such as individual customers, organization customers, employees, partners, citizens, and suppliers.
- Location Services could be available to maintain the home address, shipping
  address, billing address, and telephone contact information for a person or organization. For some industries, location could refer to buildings, plants, store, or even
  an aisle within that store.
- Customer Insight Services could provide business logic to determine when a customer meets certain criteria that might determine a cross-sell and up-sell opportunity for products or services by triggering a business operation based on a lifecycle
  event. For example, as a customer receives approval for a mortgage, this could present an opportunity to offer disability insurance.
- Data Stewardship Services should be available to analyze and evaluate the quality
  of master data within the MDM System and support the manual reconciliation of
  conflicts, groupings, and relationships.
- Interaction History Services can identify customer interactions that have occurred
  across business units through various communication channels such as interactions with a Customer Service Representative, mailings, telephony system, and Web
  self-service.

- Account Services provide services for the Account Domain. This master data domain includes master data account details such as financial accounts, loyalty points, agreements, and contracts.
- Product Services provide create, update, and delete capabilities for the Product Domain. The Product Domain includes master data covering product item details such as SKU, product description, product specifications, product dimensions, packaging dimensions, manufacturer, and product bundles.

3.6.3 MDM Data Quality Management Services

MDM Data Quality Management Services are called by MDM Lifecycle Management Services to manage data quality, standardize data, determine duplicate master data entities, and maintain cross-reference information. With the exception of the Conflict Resolution and Collapse and Split Services, which support Data Stewardship functionality, these MDM Data Quality Management Services are not typically exposed to external applications. They are used to establish the use of consistent data standards and quality rules for maintaining master data in the Master Data Repository. They also maintain cross-reference linkage to both structured master data maintained in business systems and unstructured content associated with master data maintained in content management systems. In the insurance industry, for example, the MDM System could maintain the linkage between a customer, multiple insurance policies stored across multiple business systems, and the actual signed policies that might reside in one or more content management systems.

As seen in Figure 3.7, the MDM Data Quality Management software component has been further decomposed into subcomponents with sample services to further describe the capabilities of this component within the MDM System. The Data Validation and Cleansing Services component provides services to define and enforce data validation, data standardization, and data cleansing rules for master data. These rules determine if data is acceptable to the MDM System, such as date formats, range validation, maximum and minimum values, and checksums on a data element or on multiple data elements. For example, rules could be defined at the data field level to validate, cleanse, and standardize date formats, account codes, postal code information, telephone numbers, and so on. Standardization Services could parse a text field into tokens such as title, first name, middle initial, and surname for name standardization. The External Data Validation Service provides functionality to request data validation, cleansing, standardization, and matching services from an enterprise component that provides Information Integrity Services as a service or from an External Data Provider.

Although it is normal for software components to have some sort of exception processing capabilities, we felt it necessary to call specific attention to this capability for this software component. For example, a company might want to process and receive credit for a financial transaction that has a minor data quality problem that does not affect accountability for the transaction. Based upon the type of data validation error, the MDM Lifecycle Management service in combination with the exception processing logic could take the following type of action:

- Continue processing the master data update.
- Flag the updated entry.

- Return the results for the business system to process the transaction.
- Notify a Data Steward to take manual action to verify and reconcile the data quality issue in both the source system and the business system.

The Reconciliation Services component provides services for the detection of duplicate master data entities and management services that can be requested by Data Stewardship functionality to manually or automatically resolve conflicts. As we just mentioned, the Data Quality Management Component should have the ability to request Information Integrity Services from an external component that performs data cleansing, standardizing, and matching. In the event that the enterprise does not already have a component that provides Information Integrity Services, the MDM System may need a combination of deterministic or probabilistic matching services to provide matching logic to identify duplicate master data entities. The major point here is that the MDM System should have the flexibility to utilize the best matching logic available to avoid duplicate master data records being maintained within the MDM System.

Probabilistic Matching Services use a combination of a weighting scheme and statistical differences to formulate a score and/or a ranking to determine if multiple master data entities are the same. Fields are evaluated for degree-of-match and a weight is assigned that represents the "informational content" contributed by those field values. The weights are then

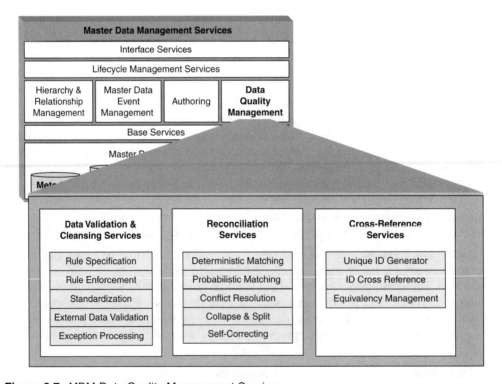

Figure 3.7 MDM Data Quality Management Services.

summed to derive a total score that measures the statistical probability of a match. Deterministic Matching Services use a combination of algorithms and business rules to determine when two or more records match. For example, multiple customer records may be considered equal if the Social Security Numbers are the same and the customers have the same driver's license number. This algorithm could catch common data entry errors such as typos, phonetic variations, and transpositions of the customer's name. Regardless of either type of matching technique, business rules can then be applied to determine a match and either automatically collapse the master data entries through the use of survivorship rules or require manual action by a Data Steward.

Conflict Resolution and Collapse and Split Services are used to implement Data Stewardship functionality to support the manual reconciliation of merging multiple master data records or splitting master data records into multiple records. This functionality is useful in the event that a match was automatically or manually performed incorrectly. These services would typically be called through a User Interface providing Data Stewardship functionality but could be invoked by another system. Self-Correcting Services would run periodically against the Master Data Management Repository to perform autonomous validation of the data quality. As part of any master data reconciliation activity, MDM Audit Logging Services should be requested by these Reconciliation Services to maintain a history and audit trail.

Cross-Reference Services maintain data lineage to the source system for a master data entity and enable the ability to provide the complete view of a master data construct such as a Customer or Product that has information contained in disparate systems. Unique ID Generator Services generate unique IDs for new master data entities such as Customer, Account, or Product as these entities are added to the Master Data Repository. External provided keys can also be used as the unique ID for that master data entity. ID Cross-Reference Services are used to maintain cross-reference linkage information such as an external reference key to both structured and unstructured data about that same master data entity maintained in multiple systems and External Data Providers. These services may also be invoked by systems that contain information about a master data entity that is not stored in the Master Data Repository but should be referenced by the MDM System. Equivalency Management Services manage cross-reference linkage information between master data entities that have a relationship, such as a customer to a product at a location. These services can then be requested by MDM Lifecycle Management Services to support an "intelligent query" to retrieve product data for a customer at all locations that are stored in multiple systems and not in the MDM System. In the event that a Data Steward is resolving a data quality problem using MDM Data Quality Management Collapse or Split Services to resolve a master data entity such as a customer, Equivalency Management services would manage these cross-reference linkages for the final outcome.

3.6.4 MDM Authoring Services

The MDM Collaborative method of use requires a core set of capabilities within the MDM environment. A combination of authoring services, workflow, task management, and state management are needed to guide and coordinate the collaborative tasks for the authoring of master data. Authoring Services provide user functionality for the authoring of master data and would typically be requested by presentation services that implement an MDM

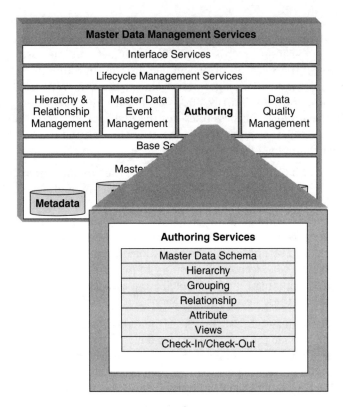

Figure 3.8 Master Data Management Authoring Services.

User Interface or a Data Stewardship User Interface. A user interface should be both efficient and easy to use, relying on a set of underlying services that create, query, update, and delete the master data itself, relationships between the master data, and other related information such as reference data. Figure 3.8 shows a set of services that might be needed to support the authoring of master data and to protect the integrity of the master data while multiple users create or update master data attributes simultaneously for the same entity.

Authoring Services are used to create and extend the definition of master data entities, create and update master data entities in the MDM System, and define master data hierarchies, relationships, and groupings. For example, a user interface for Category and Item Specialists could invoke Authoring Services to support the introduction of a new product such as described in the New Product Introduction scenario presented in Chapter 6, PIM-MDM Solution Blueprints. Authoring Services provide the following type of capability:

- Master Data Schema Services provide the ability to define the schema for master data entities such as the definition of a product, supplier, customer, or agreement.
- Hierarchy Services would be used to define and modify the hierarchy structures for linking the relationship of master data entities to each other, the parent entity, and the ultimate parent.

- Grouping Services are used to identify and manage a collection of master data entities with a common thread and associate miscellaneous values such as common
  contact information to a grouping. For example, a Sales employee might want to
  create a grouping that will link all their accounts together to assist with account
  management activities.
- Relationship Services are used to create and modify the definition of relationships
  between master data entities within the same master data domain and relationships
  between master data domains.
- Attribute Services are used to create or update master data values and to define the
  structure, default values, and data formats for master data attributes.
- Views are defined to support the querying of master data based upon multiple taxonomies. Views are represented in this component as a set of services that would
  provide capability to define multiple taxonomies for representing master data hierarchies and their relationships.

Check-In and Check-Out Services are used to maintain the state of changes being made to
master data attributes as part of a collaborative authoring process to define master data or
add the actual master data instance data. They enable concurrency while ensuring consistency by disallowing multiple updates to the same master data attributes at the same time.
Check-out services would prevent multiple users from attempting to change the same master data attribute values at the same time for the same master data record and would establish a synchronization point through the use of check-in services after a user has completed
his or her respective changes. For example, as part of the workflow for the introduction of
a new product,[11] a group of users could work on the technical attributes for an item description at the same time that another user could be working on the pricing attributes.

3.6.5 MDM Master Data Event Management Services

MDM Master Data Event Management Services derive intelligence from master data and
make information actionable by detecting events within the MDM System as part of an MDM
service request or driven by date and time. They can be configured to run prior to the request
of an MDM service or as part of the post-processing after the execution of an MDM service.
These services can be requested by MDM Lifecycle Management Services and trigger operations based upon event criteria defined by business rules, scheduled events, data governance,
and lifecycle management for master data. Figure 3.9 identifies the types of services that this
component would provide for the management of master data within the MDM System.

MDM Event Management Services provide the capability to define business rules for detecting events within the MDM System. Business rules define the conditions for an event, such
as changes to master data that may initiate a business process, relationships between master data entities, date and time conditions for an event, and the respective actions to be
taken for an occurrence of that event. For example, business rules can be defined to trigger
notifications for cross-sell and up-sell opportunities for customers that may experience a

---

11. Refer to Chapter 1, Introducing Master Data Management, and Chapter 6, PIM-MDM Solution
Blueprints, for a description of the process for introducing a new product.

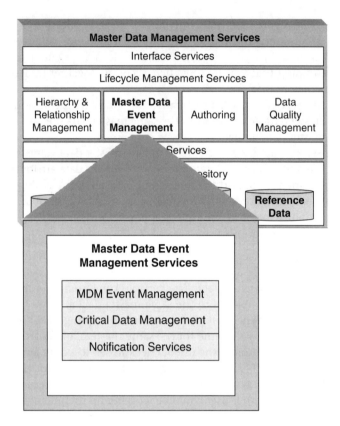

Figure 3.9 MDM Master Data Event Management Services.

life-changing event such as a birth of a baby, purchase of a house, or marriage. Date-driven events could be triggered to support a business process such as the removal or archival of information for a deceased customer after legal retention requirements have been satisfied.

Critical Data Management Services provide the ability to implement data governance policies such as those described in Chapter 9, MDM and Data Governance. Rules can be defined to determine the conditions for the management of master data that should require the involvement of a Data Steward. For example, a rule may define a data ownership policy for shipping address information such that only the owner of this data can make updates to this information. If a business system requests an MDM Lifecycle Management Service to update that master data record with new shipping address information, Critical Data Management Services will detect the conditions for this event. Critical Data Management Services would then use Notification Services to generate a notification to a Data Steward or send a notification to an external workflow engine to initiate a workflow process to verify and approve the updated shipping address information.

Notification Services provide the capability to notify a user or system that an event has been detected. Notification services can be configured to deliver an e-mail to a user for awareness about an event, or trigger an event detected by another system within the enterprise such as a workflow engine or event manager.

3.6.6 MDM Hierarchy and Relationship Management Services

MDM Hierarchy and Relationship Management Services establish and manage master data relationships, organize master data entities into hierarchies and groupings, and create multiple views of master data hierarchies. In addition to the services that focus on the organization and taxonomy of master data, the component also provides versioning capability to understand how the state of a master data entity changes and how that master data is organized with the passage of time. MDM Authoring Services are used to define hierarchies, relationships, and groupings for master data domains that are managed by this component.

As represented in Figure 3.10, MDM Hierarchy and Relationship Management Services may request Identity Analytics Services to discover obvious and non-obvious relationships such as those between people and organizations that can be used to establish master data hierarchies and relationships within the MDM System. Figure 3.10 presents a set of sample services that this component could provide for the management of hierarchies, groupings, and relationships between master data entities.

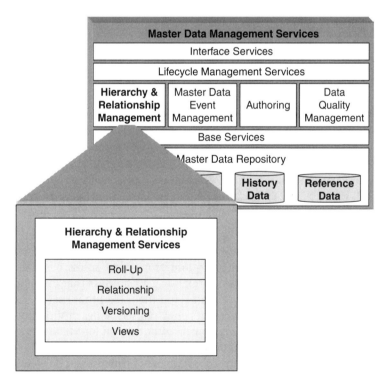

Figure 3.10   MDM Hierarchy and Relationship Management Services.

Hierarchies consist of master data entities that can logically be structured into parent–child relationships. For example, a corporate hierarchy defines the relationships between the ultimate parent company, domestic parents, and sub-companies of the parents, such as branches, subsidiaries, divisions, and headquarters. Another example would be products that are within the same product hierarchy but vary by model type. Roll-Up Services would provide organizational capability to query and view a hierarchy and manage the hierarchy as changes occur to master data for the entities within that hierarchical structure.

Relationship Services manage groupings that have been defined between master data entities within the same domain and relationships defined to create linkages across master data domains. For example, a typical cross-domain relationship would be customer to account and account to product, so that you can identify all of the products that a customer may have with an organization and the types of products and services being received. As updates occur to master data entities, these services would manage those relationships as well as provide query services to access related master data entities. Versioning Services provide functionality to capture and view the state of a master data entity, master data hierarchies, and relationships at a point in time for historical and regulatory compliance reasons. Versioning Services may provide this ability based upon a point in time established by an effective date.

Views are represented within the component to represent the ability to query master data stored in the Master Data Repository based upon multiple taxonomies. Querying master data would provide different results based upon the view associated with the role of the person performing the query. For example, a hierarchy may be defined to provide a structure that groups product master data into a particular catalog structure; thus, views could be created to view that hierarchy of products by product item within the hierarchy or to view all products in the catalog by manufacturer.

3.6.7 MDM Base Services

The Master Data Management Base Services component is further decomposed into four components identified in Figure 3.11 that provide a set of common services used within the Master Data Management Services architecture building block. With the exception of the Audit Logging Services component, these services may interact with external IT components through the MDM Interface Services component to implement security and privacy and workflow functionality.

Security and Privacy Services are invoked by MDM Interface Services to verify authorized access for users and groups to request MDM Lifecycle Management and MDM Search Services. Authorization Services implement both user- and group-level access controls to authorize access to MDM services and master data information. This implies that inbound requests for MDM services should contain both a user name and the role of that user or should identify a proxy service that requests MDM services on behalf of users. Rules of Visibility Services provide the ability to define and enforce fine-grained authorization for MDM services, including data-level entitlements to control access to data and the ability to update data. These services would control what master data elements or instances of elements can be viewed or updated by a user given the constraints. For example, not all users within the business should have the need to view customer Social Security Number or possibly contact information. MDM Security

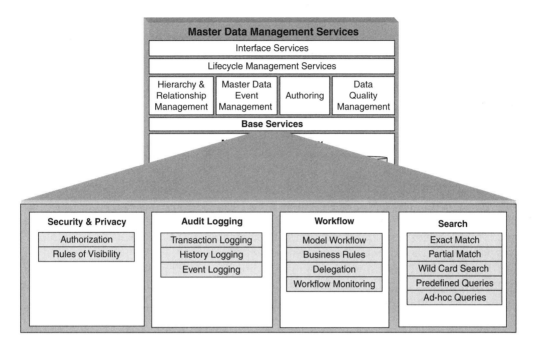

Figure 3.11   MDM Base Services.

and Privacy Services should have the ability to request External Security Services for authorization rights to an MDM service and to determine privacy preferences for access to data as described in Chapter 4, MDM Security and Privacy.

Audit Logging Services record transaction history, event history, and the changes that have been made to master data at that point in time. Transaction Logging Services log queries and requests issued by business applications requesting MDM services and provide accountability for tracing actions that could support legislative requirements and support analysis for problem determination. History Logging Services log the actual master data values that have been added or updated as part of an MDM service at that point in time for that transaction. Event Logging Services log events that have been detected and the respective action taken, such as generating a notification or initiating a workflow process.

Workflow Services provide the ability to model and manage a workflow for the associated user and system activities that support the authoring of master data, a business process, or a data governance process. These services may also delegate work to external providers such as an external workflow engine. Processes that require collaborative authoring, such as New Product Introduction, where one or more Category and Item Managers can author product data, would benefit from the use of MDM Workflow Services.[12] Model Workflow Services

12.   Chapter 6, PIM-MDM Solution Blueprints, provides a detailed New Product Introduction scenario for the consumer electronics industry that demonstrates the benefits of using MDM Workflow Services to fully define product data and a catalog hierarchy within the MDM System.

would be invoked through an MDM User Interface to define the associated activities and conditions for the flow of a business process. Model Workflow Services would define the user and system tasks that are performed within the MDM System and not the system and user activities that span multiple systems and are probably best coordinated by an external workflow engine. Business rules can be defined to support the workflow based upon successful completion of an activity and the maximum elapsed time between activities. For example, if the maximum amount of time elapsed for completion of an activity, a notification could be generated to call attention to the fact that there might be a problem.

Workflow Monitoring Services monitor the state of a process, control the execution of the sequence of tasks by people and automated processes, and perform state management and task management. Task management prioritizes and displays pending work for individuals to perform, while state management enforces the lifecycle of the master data. Because user and system tasks are completed within a process, these services detect completion of a task and initiate the next system activity or user tasks defined in the workflow. Delegation services provide for the ability to delegate assignment of a user activity or task to another user, but they still require the same activities to be completed. Workflow Services should have the ability to integrate with an enterprise workflow engine that supports monitoring workflow activities that span multiple systems and applications. For example, MDM Workflow Services could trigger a notification that would be detected by an enterprise workflow engine. The External workflow engine would then trigger and monitor user and system activities that occur outside of the MDM System and span multiple applications.

Search Services are requested by MDM Lifecycle Management Inquiry Services and MDM Data Quality Management Services, but they can also be requested by an application or user interface. Search Services support the ability to define and execute predefined queries in addition to performing ad hoc query requests such as those based upon wildcard search criteria using special characters. Search Services should be configurable in order to manage the number of records returned in the result set. They should be able to return a single record for the exact match of a query request, a results list for a partial match for some of the query criteria, and one or more records as a result of a wildcard search for a master data entity such as Customer, Product, Vendor, and Supplier. Search Services should be available to search both the Master Data Database as well as the MDM History Data Database.

3.6.8 MDM Master Data Repository

As seen in Figure 3.12, the Master Data Repository contains Instance Master Data, Definition Master Data, Reference Data, History Data, and Metadata. Definition Master Data is created through the use of Authoring Services and defines master data, and master data hierarchies and relationships. Definition Master Data identifies the master data schema, such as the attributes, attribute default values, and formats. Examples of Definition Master Data could be the definition of a Product, definition of a Supplier, or the definition of a Customer. Instance Master Data is the actual master data attribute values for the core business entities, such as information about a Customer, Supplier, Location, Organization, and Agreement. The Definition Master Data would define the Attributes, Relationships, and Hierarchies, and the Instance Master Data would contain the actual master data values, relationships, and hierarchies.

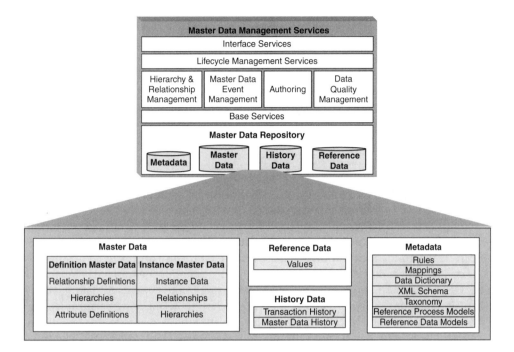

Figure 3.12 MDM Master Data Repository.

Audit Logging Services update the History Data in the Master Data Repository with point-in-time information about a transaction and the actual changes made to master data as a result of that transaction. The Master Data Repository also contains Reference Data values that could be maintained at the global level within an organization, such as currency codes, global country codes, and key performance indicators. Reference Data may also be defined to support the cleansing and validation of master data values by MDM Data Quality Management Services.

Metadata resides in the Master Data Repository that may have been created through the use of Authoring Services, and to support the configuration and administration of the MDM System for functionality such as data validation, data cleansing, deterministic matching criteria, and business and data governance rules. Mappings describe criteria such as system names and database table names to maintain cross-reference links between LOB source systems and the MDM System. Reference Process and Data Models represent the potential use of industry-specific or enterprise-specific models that can be used to support the implementation of workflow within the MDM System and to create or extend the master data model. The Data Dictionary represents the ability to create the semantic definition of terms for master data that would provide both the business and technical description of master data maintained in the Master Data Repository.

3.6.9   Information Integration Services

Information Integration Services provide Information Integrity Services, Extract, Transform, and Load (ETL) capability for loading and replicating data, and Enterprise Information Integration (EII) capability for federated query access to structured and unstructured data distributed across multiple data sources. Information Integration Services are instrumental for implementing a Master Data Management Solution and support many of the MDM Architecture Patterns described in Chapter 5. Figure 3.13 provides a further breakdown of the types of services within each of these components.

Information Integrity Services provide profiling, analysis, detection, cleansing, data standardization, and matching services. Information Integrity Services can be requested by MDM Data Quality Management Services, ETL processing, or from a business system as an information service to cleanse and standardize data, or match data records. Data Profiling and Analysis Services provide functionality to understand the quality of master data across enterprise systems from which data cleansing, matching, survivorship, and standardization rules can be determined for improving the overall data quality and consistency of master data. Data Profiling and Analysis Services are not only useful for the initial data analysis but can be used to establish an overall baseline for assessing improvements to data quality as a result of implementing Master Data Management. As the MDM System is implemented, these services can run periodically to assess the overall improvements to master data quality across the enterprise and be used for reporting improvements against Data Quality Key Performance Indicators.

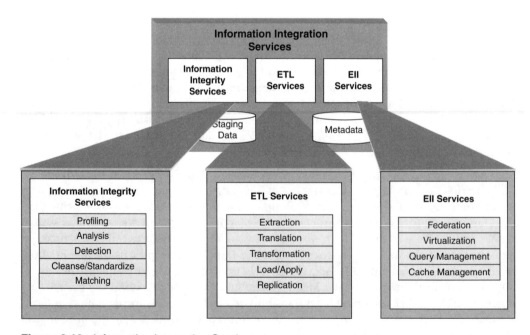

Figure 3.13   Information Integration Services.

Detection, Data Cleansing, Standardization, and Matching Services should be available as information services for real-time business transactions and to support batch processing for the loading and matching of records from multiple data sources into a target system. Detection Services provide the ability to detect user-defined conditions about data that require user action, business events, or to enforce a data governance policy. Detection Services would utilize a notification mechanism to send a notification to a user about a detected event. Data Standardization Services standardize data into an agreed-upon data structure and definition. This could be as simple as enforcing a specific date format or changing localized currency values from regional systems such as euros into dollars because the target system expects currency values to be in dollars. It could also be more complicated, requiring the parsing of a text field to standardize name format for a person or a product description. Data Cleansing Services provide functionality to "scrub" data such as:

- The ability to validate fields based upon simple validation rules such as known dimensions for a product or valid reference table codes
- Comparing data values against a range of values
- Populating missing required data fields with default values
- Accessing an external data source for information to look up for validation of a data field or to populate data fields

Matching services provide probabilistic matching capability to match and merge data records based upon survivorship rules and are used to eliminate the duplicate entry of master data entities such as Customers, Products, Suppliers, and Vendors into the MDM System. Matching Services are based upon configurable matching logic that can be tuned to a specific environment to match duplicate records, and to implement survivorship capability that determines how to remove duplicate entries and merge content from those duplicate records into a single consolidated record. In the event multiple records survive the matching logic but require a manual process to reconcile the final record, a notification can be generated to a Data Steward to manually review and reconcile the master data records.

ETL Services provide Extraction, Translation, and Transformation Services to extract data from one or more source systems and to translate and transform that data to load into a target database. Extract Services can be used to extract a copy of all of the data planned for the initial load or for the incremental load of a target system. Transformation Services provide data transformation capabilities that may enrich data according to rules and algorithms and can request Information Integrity Services for data cleansing and standardization, and matching of duplicate records. Translation Services are used to translate data formats from a source system to the target system data format. Replication Services are typically used to replicate data from the primary copy to a backup copy of the data without any data translation or transformation requirements, and usually as part of a batch process. Load/Apply Services should have the ability to load data directly into the target system database or request services from the target system to load records into the database. When ETL Services are used to load master data into an MDM System, cross-reference information for that master data entity is maintained to provide a reference to all of the source systems for this master data entity in order to establish data lineage.

The Metadata Repository contains metadata that is used by Information Integration Services for Information Integrity Services, ETL Services, and EII Services. It contains a description of the data from both a business perspective and from a technical perspective, such as the field length, format and data type, rules for data cleansing, data translation, and data transformation. The Staging Database provides a temporary working area that is used for the data profiling, analysis, cleansing, merging, and transformation of data.

Enterprise Information Integration (EII) Services provide information services to access structured and unstructured content contained in disparate data sources while retaining the autonomy and integrity of the data and content sources. EII Services enable applications to access and integrate diverse data and content sources as if they were a single resource. Virtualization Services make structured and unstructured database sources appear as if they were a single database, regardless of where the information resides. These services create integrated views of the data, making it possible to use standard SQL or standard Application Programming Interfaces (APIs) to access data sources and content. Federation Services provide the services that manage transaction consistency for maintaining the integrity of a query or update transaction being coordinated across multiple database systems. For example, in the case of a federated update, if one of the updates to a database failed, but a subset of the updates to the other databases completed successfully, all of those updates would be rolled back to their original state in order to maintain transaction consistency. The error processing for a federated query service could be handled differently, though, because no database updates are performed. In this case, the exception processing logic could return partial results to the requesting application but indicate that only partial query results were available. Cache Management and Query Management Services work together to cache and aggregate returned results and optimize query performance for locating and accessing distributed data.

3.6.10   Identity Analytic Services

The Identity Analytics component resides within the Analysis and Discovery Services architecture building block. Identity Analytics provide identity resolution capability for the unique identification of a person, and the capability to discover obvious and non-obvious relationships between people and organizations. Identity Analytics services can be requested by business systems and by MDM Data Quality Management Services to determine the identity of a person and to discover non-obvious and obvious relationships between master data entities. The Identity Analytics component may receive data from systems that support the analysis about people and organizations that should not be contained in the MDM System. Figure 3.14 provides a sample breakdown of the types of services provided by this component.

Identity Analytics Interface Services provide an entry point for systems to integrate with the Identity Analytics component. Visualization Services are requested by a user interface and provide functionality to view identity information, provide a graphical view of entity relationships, define and view event information, and to create and modify resolution rules. Visualization Services use Identity Management Services to view identity and relationship information, and to link and unlink records that require manual effort to properly associate

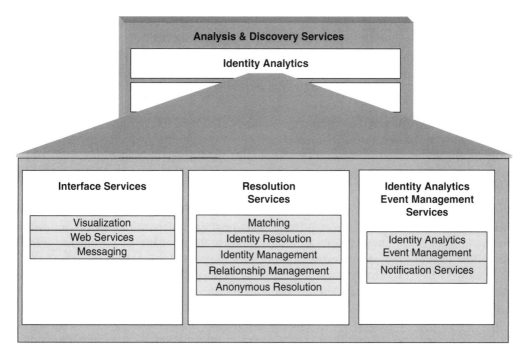

Figure 3.14 Identity Analytics Services.

records with the correct identity. When viewing the various degrees of separation between entities in a network, Visualization Services can be requested to support further analysis about the information that is used to link these entities together. Identity Analytics Interface Services support the use of Messaging and Web Services for integration with other systems. Query requests and data can be sent to Identity Analytics through the use of these services. A query request will receive results at the time it is submitted to Identity Analytics if the query request can be satisfied. In the event that there are no results for a query, the Identity Analytics component can continue to process the query as new data is received until results can be returned for that query or the query becomes inactive.

The Resolution Services component contains a set of services that uniquely resolve a person's identity and relationships through configurable matching services and perform identity management. These services will run on a perpetual basis as new data is loaded into the Identity Analytics component. The Identity Analytics database contains all of the data about a person or organization that has been collected over time. This is done because data that has been collected in the past may become relevant in the future to determine a person's identity or relationships. Matching Services execute rules defined to determine if the same column within multiple records is a potential match. Matching Services provide full attribution capabilities so that if multiple records exist about a person in the Identity Analytics database, they will all be used as part of the perpetual analysis to discover relationships and resolve identities. Matching rules can be defined to exclude known default values for columns such as dummy Social Security Numbers or telephone numbers, or to define a range of values that might be considered a match for values within a column. Identity Resolution Services use confidence evaluation criteria to compile the scoring results from the matching logic and to establish a confidence score based upon the results. The result of finalizing a match of multiple person records generates a unique ID for that person's known identity at that point in time.

Identity Management Services are used to manage identity and relationship information. They are used to process query requests about a person's identity and relationships, and to manage cross-reference information that maintains the lineage of each data record associated with that identity to the originating source systems. They provide the capability to group all associated records together that support a relationship or an identity, and the ability to link and unlink records that have been improperly assigned.

Relationship Management Services provide functionality to determine obvious and non-obvious relationships about people and organizations. Relationship Management Services determine relationships about people and organizations based upon rules that are defined to identify "what is meant by a relationship." For example, obvious relationships could be defined by rules that automatically associate people through marriage or by living at the same address. Non-obvious relationships would be defined by rules that discover relationships through various degrees of separation about people and organizations that may not be obvious but could be inferred by common pieces of information, such as telephone numbers, address information, loyalty card numbers, bank account numbers, and credit card numbers. These common pieces of information would be used to establish a "network" of related people and organizations that are associated through a common thread that links them all together.

Anonymous Resolution Services play a critical role for implementing Identity Analytics for solutions that must comply with government privacy legislation. Anonymous Resolution Services protect the privacy of personal information by not storing or displaying data in cleartext and by implementing matching logic "anonymously." A mechanism such as hashing could be used to provide this privacy protection. The hashing capability, though, must not only provide the ability to "hide the data" but must maintain the capability to match the information about a person, such as Social Security Number, name, and passport number, against information about people already contained in the Identity Analytics database.

Identity Analytics Event Management Services manage the ability to define, detect, and log events and to generate notifications based upon the results of identity and relationship resolution services. For example, a rule could be defined to generate an alert based upon the condition that someone might be trying to misrepresent his or her identity or if a non-obvious relationship has been detected that requires further investigation. Resolution Services perpetually run while new data from external and internal data sources are loaded into the Identity Analytics database. Notification Services are used within the Identity Analytics component for creating awareness of an event and for sending the results of queries that remain active in the system. Notification Services provide services to generate alerts to a user, to a system, or to an external component that provides enterprise event notification services to generate alerts or initiate a workflow process.

3.7 Component Relationship Diagram

In the preceding section, we described the technical architecture for the core MDM System architecture building blocks and their respective software components, responsibilities, and services. Those technical descriptions are used as the basis for the Enterprise Master Data Management Component Relationship and subsequent component interaction diagrams. In this section, we introduce and describe the MDM Component Relationship Diagram, which positions the MDM core set of architecture building blocks within an overall e-business architecture framework. The MDM Component Relationship Diagram provides us with the ability to show the hierarchy of components and the static relationships between the components. Component interaction diagrams are then used in the following section to document the dynamic relationships between components to implement Master Data Management functionality for the multiple MDM methods of use (operational, collaborative, and analytical).

The MDM Component Relationship Diagram in Figure 3.15 shows the static component relationships for implementing an MDM Solution within an enterprise using integration

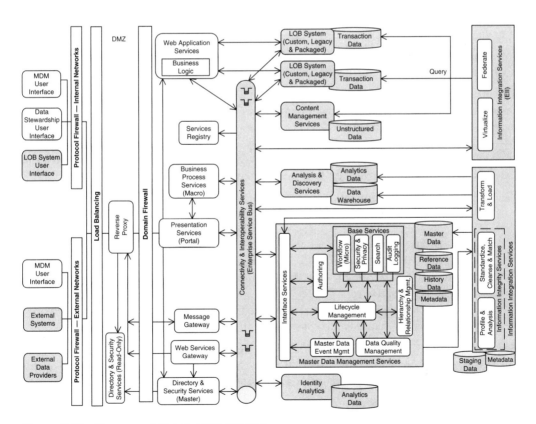

Figure 3.15 Component Relationship Diagram.

techniques such as Enterprise Application Integration, ETL, and Enterprise Information Integration. Note that the diagram does not include all of the components that would be required for a complete end-to-end solution, such as infrastructure management components for backup and recovery, audit logging, and network management. We have included components in the Component Relationship Diagram that demonstrate the viability of the overall MDM Reference Architecture and how MDM and Information Integration services can interact with business systems and users to implement Master Data Management functionality. The IT components that were not previously described in the MDM Logical Architecture section are not shaded, and are primarily to the left of the Connectivity and Interoperability Layer in Figure 3.15.

In Figure 3.15, we show a representative Demilitarized Zone (DMZ) providing controlled access to the enterprise IT systems for users from internal networks and access to External Systems and External Data Providers through external networks. In today's world of globalization, self-service applications, and mobile employees, users can access enterprise systems through multiple channels using a combination of public and private networks. The Data Stewardship User Interface represents a user interface component that provides Data Stewardship functionality. The MDM User Interface component represents a component that internal users, customers, agents, business partners, and so on can use to maintain master data that they are authorized to manage through a user interface. The LOB System User Interface component represents a user interface component that business users would use to interact with a business system. The actual implementation for any of these user interface components could be implemented as a thin client, such as a Web browser-based user interface.

The network architecture and implementation of a DMZ can be implemented in many different ways, but each variation has the same set of objectives to provide secure, authorized access to the controlled and trusted security zones of the enterprise. For example, an alternative DMZ implementation might have a proxy server supporting access from within the intranet and another proxy server to support access with external networks to and from external systems. The following types of components reside within the DMZ:

- The Firewall components are used to control access from a less-trusted network to a more-trusted network, regardless of how they are implemented. The Firewall components offer a series of services, including packet filtering and redirects.
- The Reverse Proxy component provides management of IP traffic, leveraging caching and security functionality. The Reverse Proxy component provides encrypted connections to the Presentation Services components, thus providing proxy, monitored access.
- The Load Balancing component is used to improve network and server performance by distributing requests for a system among several systems of the same type.

Because the MDM Component Relationship Diagram introduces new components (not shaded) that were not previously discussed in the MDM Component Model section of this chapter, we are providing a brief description of those components.

- The Presentation Services component provides the underlying mechanism for creating highly customizable portals for individual users. Some enterprise portals provide a pre-integrated set of services that can implement a common enterprise presentation infrastructure framework in lieu of supporting stand-alone user interface application logic for each application.

- The Business Process Services component is responsible for choreographing complex, long-running business processes that may include a combination of user interactions and integration between multiple systems to complete an end-to-end workflow.
- The Directory and Security Services component provides the Lightweight Directory Access Protocol (LDAP) based directory that houses user ids, passwords, and security policies, including rules and access control lists. Chapter 4, MDM Security and Privacy, describes the types of security services, such as Identity Services, Authentication Services, and Authorization Services, that could be provided by this component.
- The Web Application Services component is an application server that is typically designed to host both presentation and business logic. The purpose of this component is to provide central functionality, the J2EE runtime environment, and services for developing and supporting e-Business application logic.
- The Service Registry component is a Service Registry and Repository that acts as a service broker for service definitions and policies as described in Chapter 2, MDM as an SOA Enabler.
- The Query, Search, and Reporting component provides services that support report generation and management, ad hoc query services, On-Line Analytical Processing (OLAP), and contextual search services.
- The Web Services Gateway component routes authorized Web Service requests to the appropriate SOAP RPC Proxy.
- The Message Gateway component supports the use of messaging to communicate to and from the enterprise business systems with external data providers.

The MDM Component Relationship Diagram is not a physical description of an architecture that would represent each of the physical components and their connectivity, such as server and storage units, the network topology including IP addresses, routers and switches, software and so on. An IT Architect would determine the physical model for the actual hardware the network topology and software topology after mapping software products to a component model and after careful analysis of nonfunctional requirements such as workload volumes, availability, security, performance, reliability, and continuity-of-operations. This physical model is sometimes referred to as the operational model and would be the basis to show how the architecture supports scalability, performance, security, and high-availability requirements.

3.8   Master Data Management Component Interaction Diagrams

We have provided Master Data Management Component Interaction Diagrams as a further means to communicate the functional aspects of the Master Data Management Reference Architecture. Up until this point, we have described in detail the technical architecture of the MDM Component Model, but we have not demonstrated the dynamic interactions between components. The MDM Component Interaction Diagrams demonstrate the dynamic collaboration between software components based upon scenarios that represent the multiple MDM methods of use and deployment of an MDM Solution. They demonstrate the use of MDM Architecture Patterns for information-focused and process-focused application integration and MDM Hub patterns that are incorporated into the MDM Reference Architecture. Each scenario describes a detailed walkthrough of the MDM Component Model, describing the interactions between components to deliver Master Data Management functionality.

Table 3.1 lists the scenarios and identifies the MDM method of use, implementation style, and MDM Architecture patterns[13] relevant to the scenario for each MDM Component Interaction Diagram. The table is not meant to imply that the scenario only applies to a single MDM method of use or implementation style, or that only certain MDM Architecture Patterns can be applied. It is only a summary table to assist in understanding the context for each of the MDM Component Interaction Diagrams. For example, the Information Focused Application Integration Initial Load Pattern would apply to every scenario, because all of the scenarios are dependent upon master data already existing within the MDM System.

The component interaction diagrams show the most significant interactions between components to achieve the desired results for that scenario. Multiple integration techniques may be used to integrate enterprise systems with the MDM System. IT Architects make architecture decisions based upon functional and nonfunctional requirements, the use of architecture patterns, and best practices to determine the best way to engineer a solution. Those architecture decisions provide the justification for decisions that will guide the development process. Before we walk through the scenarios and component interaction diagrams, we provide some general guidance that should be considered for the development and deployment of an MDM Solution into an existing IT environment. The architecture decisions derived from the guidance identified in the following list could influence the techniques we choose to show for process and information integration of business systems with the MDM System.

- The existing IT environment, standards, and technologies supporting the various Line of Business systems and MDM System should always be taken into consideration for determining the use of synchronous or asynchronous communication techniques. Systems interact with the MDM System by requesting MDM services through the MDM Interface Services component. If a business system enlists an MDM Service as part of a global transaction, the technologies supporting the global transaction will need to support XA protocols such as WS-Atomic Transaction if the service is invoked as a Web Service or JMS if invoked through messaging. A global transaction can enlist one or more services as part of the same unit of work. A XA transaction manager would coordinate transactional work across multiple resource managers and drive the two-phase commit and recovery protocol for ensuring transaction consistency for the global transaction.

---

13. Please see Chapter 5, MDM Architecture Patterns for more details about all of the MDM architecture patterns mentioned in Table 3.1.

Table 3.1   MDM Component Interaction Diagram Scenario Summary

Scenario	MDM Method of Use	Implementation Style	MDM Architecture Patterns
Collaborative Authoring	Collaborative	Coexistence	Processed-Focused Application Integration (Publish/Subscribe) Coexistence MDM Hub
Transactional Interception for update of master data	Operational	Transactional	Process-Focused Application Integration (Messaging and Publish/Subscribe) Transactional MDM Hub
Federated Query	Operational	Registry and Coexistence	Process-Focused Application Integration (ESB) Registry MDM Hub or Coexistence MDM Hub
Information Synchronization	Operational	Coexistence	Information-Focused Application Integration (Information Synchronization) Process-Focused Application Integration (Messaging) Coexistence MDM Hub
Distribution of Updates via Batch Processing	Operational	Coexistence	Processed-Focused Application Integration (Messaging) Coexistence MDM Hub
Data Governance	Operational	Coexistence	Process-Focused Application Integration (Messaging and Publish/Subscribe) Transactional MDM Hub
Incremental Updates to a Data Warehouse	Analytical	Coexistence	Enterprise System Deployment BW Integration Process-Focused Application Integration (Messaging) Coexistence MDM Hub

- Existing enterprise architecture policies should guide the architectural decisions for application to application and data integration. Architecture policies sometimes determine when MDM services should be called directly by another system or if the service request should be brokered by a mechanism such as an enterprise service bus. An enterprise architecture policy might also provide guidance based upon non-functional requirements such as performance, reliability, and availability for when to use synchronous and asynchronous communications techniques for application integration.

- When enterprise common services are available, such as directory and security services and workflow, enterprise architecture policies may influence how to configure and implement MDM Base Services such as:
  - MDM Security and Privacy Services may need to integrate with external security services for authentication, authorization, and privacy.
  - MDM Event Management Services may need to integrate with an enterprise event management system to generate notifications and alerts.
  - MDM Workflow services may need to integrate with an enterprise workflow engine that supports human and system workflow activities spanning multiple systems and organizations.

- Data latency requirements for data harmonization and business process requirements that determine the flow of data should be considered for deciding the proper technique for distributing master data updates from the MDM System. The key is to make sure that accurate master data is available in the "right time" for use by an authorized user, application, or business process. Information focused and process focused application integration patterns should be reviewed to assist in making design decisions based upon best practices.

- If a business system completes a business transaction that adds master data to its database before calling the MDM System, that business system may require reconciliation logic to process any results received from the MDM System. For example, if the originating business system creates a new customer number for an existing customer and then calls an MDM service that determines that this is an existing customer, that business system may need to reconcile its customer data for that person after receiving the MDM service response.

When master data is distributed across the enterprise, there is additional functionality that the IT Architect should consider implementing to manage the distribution of those updates from the MDM System. We have not described this functionality in the MDM Component Interaction Diagrams. For example, all business systems that receive master data updates from the MDM System may require logic to avoid sending those same updates back to the MDM System and creating a "closed loop." Functionality should also be considered to track the successful distribution, receipt, and processing of those updates to all target systems, considering techniques such as:

- Log the completion status and transaction details for each business system to a common log file or message queue used for the reporting and analysis of distribution activity.

- Generate a notification to a Data Steward for master data updates that were not processed successfully by a business system or as part of a process to update a system that provides Analysis and Discovery Services.

The sample scenarios also do not demonstrate the usage of Information Integrity Profile and Analysis Services used to understand the quality of data and to assist in defining rules to validate, cleanse, transform, and match data. These same services can provide valuable support as part of a Data Governance Program. These services could first be used to establish the data quality baseline prior to implementing Master Data Management and then used on a regular basis to assess the overall improvements to the quality of master data as a result of a Master Data Management initiative.

3.8.1 MDM Collaborative Authoring Scenario

The purpose of the MDM Collaborative Authoring Scenario is to demonstrate the MDM Collaborative method of use where users are entering product data into an MDM System that maintains a Product Item Master. Product data would coexist in business systems, but the MDM System is used to support the centralized authoring, maintaining, and publishing of that product master data to multiple business systems. The product master data may consist of details such as product description, specification, product model, packaging dimensions, manufacturer name, manufacturer shipping address, and billing address. As actual product item information is imported or entered directly into the MDM System, the MDM System would manage the state of that product data as it is created, categorized, approved, and published. Chapter 6, PIM-MDM Solution Blueprints, describes this type of scenario from an industry perspective for New Product Introduction.

This scenario assumes that a business process is defined that requires an update, review, and approval process where multiple users collaborate to add item attributes, and then a final approval occurs before that data is added to the item master. Because the MDM System and LOB System User Interfaces are presented through an enterprise portal in this scenario, the workflow that supports the review and approval process is choreographed within the Business Process Services component. It is not uncommon for portal technologies to interact with Business Process Services directly to manage tasks associated with a business process modeled in the Business Process Services component. Workflow services are implemented within the MDM System to control the MDM System activities to check for duplicate records, update the final approved product information, and publish the new product data to subscribing LOB systems.

The scenario begins with a user accessing a portal from a Web browser. After a user is authenticated by the portal, the user receives a screen with functionality available to create new product item information. The Business Process Server component interacts with the Presentation Services component to present user task lists with open activities requiring attention. As a user selects an open task for new item data, a portlet calls MDM Authoring Services to check out the item, add additional attributes, and then check in the item for further editing and review. This cycle would continue for all LOB users until it is completed with the final approval committing the new item to the database. For simplicity's sake, the

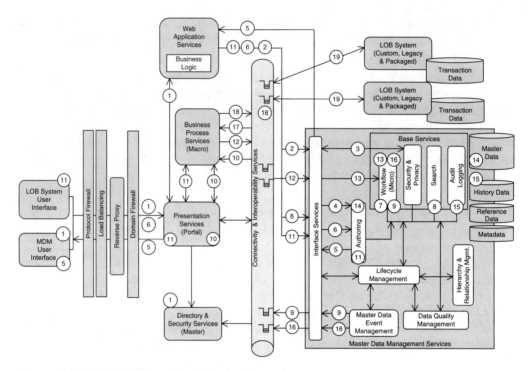

Figure 3.16 MDM Collaborative Authoring Scenario.

scenario only shows one workflow step for the multiple LOB users to complete the entry of the remaining item attributes.

The Process Focused Application Integration Publish and Subscription pattern is used to demonstrate one method for distributing the new product information to the LOB systems. This provides the ability for each of the subscribing systems to retrieve the information and update its database based upon its own quality of service requirements. It eliminates the need to develop point-to-point interfaces that would deliver the data in a specific format to each system. The data can now be published in one format and subsequently converted to the specific input format for each of the subscribing systems through message mediation services.

Figure 3.16 shows a step-by-step technical walkthrough of the scenario that is described in the following list.

> **1.** A user signs onto the portal through an MDM User Interface component that is Web-based. The portal requests authentication and authorization services from the Directory and Security Services component. The user is authenticated, and Presentation Services return an HTML page to the MDM User Interface client component. The user selects a portlet to create a new product item.

2. Presentation Services invoke a portlet on the Web Application Services component that issues a service call to the Authoring Create Item Service.

3. MDM Interface Services receive the service request, parse the message, and invoke MDM Security and Privacy Services to verify user authorization for the service.

4. MDM Interface Services receive the user authorization response and invoke the MDM Authoring Create Item Service.

5. The MDM Authoring Create Item Service returns a response based upon user authorized capabilities through MDM Interface Services. Presentation Services then render a form to the MDM Client User Interface to enter product item data. The user enters the product item data and submits the product item data.

6. Presentation Services send the item data via a service request to an Authoring Validate Item Service. MDM Interface Services receive the request and invoke the MDM Authoring Validate Item Service. The MDM Authoring Validate Item Service performs data validation, and after the data is validated, the item data is placed in a temporary work space for items awaiting approval.

7. MDM Workflow Services automatically initiate the next activity in the process, which is to verify that the item is unique, and if so, to start the review and approval cycle.

8. MDM Search Services are invoked to query the Master Data Repository to determine if this new item already exists in the Product Item Master. MDM Search Services determine that this is a unique item.

9. MDM Workflow Services trigger the next activity in the process to complete the entry of data, review, and approve the new product data. MDM Workflow Services request MDM Event Management Services to generate and send a notification message to start the approval cycle.

10. The Business Process Services component detects the notification message and initiates the process for multiple business users to enter additional product information, review, and approve the new product item.

11. Business users receive notifications based upon the workflow process to complete the entry of the new product item data. As users complete their respective tasks to enter additional product data attributes, MDM Authoring Attribute Services are requested by Presentation Services to add and update attributes. MDM Authoring Check-in and Check-Out Services are requested by the MDM Authoring Attribute Services to maintain and manage updates to the "gold copy" of the product item record. The Business Process Services component will interact with Presentation Services to monitor completion of each step in the process.

12. After all of the data is entered for the product item, there is a final review and the "golden record" is approved. Business Process Services sends a message with the approved product item information to a message queue.

13. MDM Interface Services detect the message and invoke MDM Workflow Services, which invoke the MDM Authoring Approved Add Item Service.

14. The MDM Authoring Approved Add Item Service commits the data to the Master Data Repository. After the data is stored successfully, the service calls MDM Audit Logging Services.

15. MDM Audit Logging Services update the MDM History Database with transaction information collected from the temporary work space and cleans up the work space.

16. After the item data is successfully updated in the MDM System, the MDM Workflow Services initiate an MDM Event Management Service to construct a message and post the message to a queue with the new product item information.

17. The Business Process Services component controls the distribution of the new product information to LOB systems. It receives the notification message from the MDM System to initiate the publishing process for the new product information.

18. Business Process Services publish the new product item message to message queues monitored by business systems. The Connectivity and Interoperability Layer translates the message to the specific format required for each subscribing system.

19. The business systems that subscribe to product item updates retrieve the messages and process the update.

Another version of this scenario could have MDM User Interface Services requesting MDM Authoring Services directly, without the use of a portal to provide presentation services. In this version, the entire business process could then be modeled in the MDM Workflow Services component, which would coordinate the workflow process for adding, reviewing, approving, and publishing the new product item data.

3.8.2 MDM Operational Scenario—Transactional Interception for Updates

The purpose of this scenario is to demonstrate the MDM Operational method of use and coexistence implementation style where a business system invokes an MDM Lifecycle Management Update Service as part of a global transaction to process updates to master data. The scenario starts with a user updating customer information through a business system user interface that is rendered through a portal. After the user completes entering the data, the business system enlists the MDM service as part of the same global unit of work to perform data quality management and to determine any additional knowledge, such as customer insight from the master data being created or updated.[14] The business system is considered the owner of the global transaction and enlists the MDM service through a Web Service using the XA WS-Atomic Transaction protocol. The business system commits the returned results to its database after it applies any additional business logic to the results returned from the MDM System.

A publish and subscription technique is used to distribute the updated master data to business systems within the enterprise. This technique provides the ability for each of the subscribing systems to retrieve the information and update its database based upon its

---

14. The Transaction Interception Pattern described in Chapter 5 provides further details about the pattern that applies to this scenario.

own quality of service requirements, such as immediately or on a scheduled basis. Business systems that receive a new master data entity that is unique to their system may not want to add the new master data entity immediately to their database until it is associated with a business transaction. The implementation logic would be driven by business requirements, the flow of data to support a business process, and the desire to avoid the redundant entry of data into a business system.

The result of this scenario is that both the business system and the MDM System will now have the same master data entity stored in both of their respective databases. It may not necessarily be the same data format, but the values will be consistent. The MDM System will have the core set of master data that is maintained in the MDM System, and the business system will contain master data and specific information about that business transaction. An IT Architect will need to determine how to handle a situation when the master data values returned the MDM system to the originating business have been enhanced due to data quality management. For example, the user entering the data could be prompted to verify and accept the returned results from the MDM System before completing the business transaction. Other alternatives could be for the originating business system to simply store the original data along with the unique ID provided by the MDM System, or to store the cleansed and standardized data and associate the original entry data with the cleansed record for accountability.

Figure 3.17 shows a step-by-step technical walkthrough of the scenario, which is described in the following list.

1. A user enters customer information into a business system user interface rendered through a portal. After entry of the data, the user submits the data for processing.

2. The Web Application Services component enlists the MDM Lifecycle Management Update Service via a Web Service request.

3. MDM Interface Services receive the Web Service request, parse the XML message, and invoke MDM Security and Privacy Services to verify user authorization for the requested MDM service.

4. MDM Interface Services confirm authorization and invoke the MDM Lifecycle Management Update Service, which invokes MDM Data Quality Management Services.

5. MDM Data Quality Management Services enforce data validation rules and request Information Integrity Data Cleansing and Standardization services to cleanse and standardize the data.

6. The MDM Lifecycle Management Update Service invokes MDM Search Services to query the Master Data Repository to verify that the update is to an existing master data entity. MDM Search Services locate an existing master data entity and confirm that this is an update request to an existing master data entity.

7. The MDM Lifecycle Management Update Service invokes Master Data Event Management Services to detect any conditions that could trigger an event.

8. Master Data Event Management Services determine that the requested update does not meet any conditions that require triggering an event.

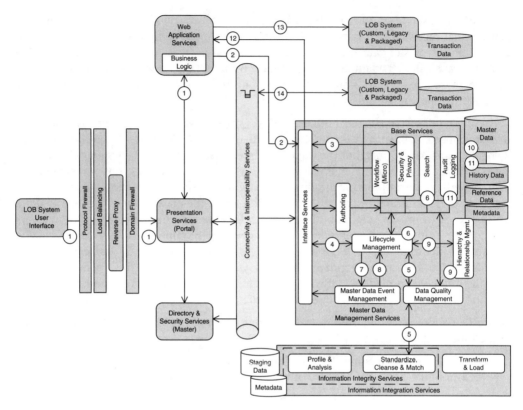

Figure 3.17   Operational Scenario—Transaction Interception for Updates.

9. The MDM Lifecycle Management Update Service is configured to request MDM Hierarchy and Relationship Management Services to determine and create any hierarchies, groupings, or relationships.

10. The MDM Lifecycle Management Update Service updates the Master Data Repository.

11. MDM Audit Logging Services update the MDM History Database with information about the transaction and the master data values that were updated.

12. The MDM Lifecycle Management Update Service requests MDM Interface Services to construct a response message. MDM Interface Services returns the response with any updated master data, hierarchy, grouping, and relationship information. MDM interface services are also called to publish the updated master data to a message queue for subscribing systems to retrieve.

13. The originating business system receives the response, and populates its transaction database using the master data contained in the reply message. (**Note:** The logic may want to notify a Data Steward about changes to the original transaction data if quality errors were detected or if any original data was changed.)

14. Business systems that subscribe to master data updates, retrieve the message and process the master data update based upon data governance policies defined for the management and distribution of master data.

If a business system is requesting MDM System services as part of a real-time user transaction, the MDM System should be designed for high availability, serviceability, and responsiveness. At a minimum, the MDM System must meet or exceed the availability requirements during the planned hours of operation for the business systems enlisting MDM services. The MDM System should be designed for reliability to support continuity of operations so that unplanned hardware and software maintenance can be completed during the normal hours of operation. In the case of unplanned maintenance, there may be some degradation to performance based on the nature of the problem, but processing can still occur. The hardware and software decision criteria for planning the deployment of an MDM System for the Operational MDM method of use is not unlike the planning required to engineer any solution delivering real-time support to a user community. We mention it here as a reminder for the importance of these considerations when implementing Operational MDM.

3.8.3   MDM Operational Scenario—Federated Query

The purpose of this scenario is to demonstrate the MDM Operational method of use where a user wants to retrieve structured and unstructured data about a person that is distributed across multiple systems. This scenario is representative of multiple implementation styles for MDM. It certainly is applicable to the registry implementation style where minimal data is persisted in the MDM System and the MDM System is used to maintain cross-reference linkages to master data contained in multiple systems. The scenario also applies to the coexistence implementation style where the MDM System could provide linkages to unstructured content maintained in a Content Management System and data that is not contained in the MDM System. The concept is that the user or application issuing the query request does not need to know the location of all the data being retrieved to support the query request. The MDM System can be used to support the request to query and dynamically aggregate data from multiple systems into a virtual person or product record to satisfy the query request.

A portal renders a business system user interface and provides query functionality for person data. The scenario starts with a user selecting a portlet that launches a query screen and the user entering query criteria about a person. A portlet invokes the respective MDM Lifecycle Management Inquiry Party Service that will return the query results to the user. The scenario assumes that user authentication services have already been performed by the portal as part of a Single Sign-On process that provides access to authorized applications and query functionality. We also assume that, if a user is authorized to request the MDM Lifecycle Inquiry Party Service, that user has authorized access to the structured and unstructured content accessed by the MDM Lifecycle Management Inquiry Party Service. Cross-reference information linking the MDM System master data entities to the business system entries is created and maintained when loading the MDM System and as part of the normal processing when MDM Lifecycle Management Services are requested to add and update master data.

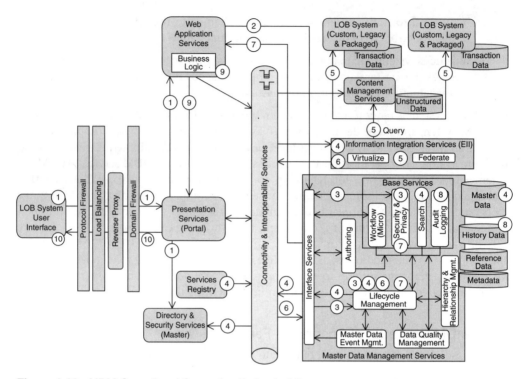

Figure 3.18 MDM Operational Scenario—Federated Query.

Figure 3.18 shows a step-by-step technical walkthrough of the scenario that is described in the following list.

1. After the user has signed onto the portal, Presentation Services retrieve user credentials from Directory and Security Services and present an HTML page with an authorized portlet to query person data. The user selects the portlet, enters the query criteria, and clicks on a submit button that submits a query request to an MDM Lifecycle Management Inquiry Party Service.

2. The Web Application Services component enlists the MDM Lifecycle Management Inquiry Service via a Web Service request.

3. MDM Interface Services receive the request, parse the message, and invoke MDM Security and Privacy Services to verify user authorization for the service. MDM Interface Services confirm authorization and invoke the MDM Lifecycle Management Inquiry Service.

4. The MDM Lifecycle Management Inquiry Service invokes an MDM Search Service to query the Master Data Repository to retrieve cross-reference linkage information and then constructs an EII Federated Query Service request. MDM Interface Services invoke the EII Federated Query Service as a Web Service. The ESB verifies authorization, accesses the Service Registry component to identify the service and policy details for calling the service, and invokes the EII Federated Query Service.

5. EII Virtualize and Federate Services connect to the multiple data sources and query the data either directly from the source system database or through a query service provided by the source system. The technique is based upon the interface mechanisms provided by the source systems for query access to data. Content Management Services provide access services to retrieve unstructured data such as digital images, documents, and so on.

6. The results are returned from the EII Federated Query Service through the MDM Interface Service to the MDM Lifecycle Management Inquiry Party Service to apply any further business logic.

7. The MDM Lifecycle Management Inquiry Party Service calls the MDM Security and Privacy Service as part of the post-processing to filter the query results based upon the rules of visibility. The filtered results are returned through MDM Interface Services to the portlet that requested the MDM Lifecycle Management Inquiry Service.

8. MDM Audit and Logging Services log the MDM Lifecycle Management Inquiry Party transaction details to the MDM History Database.

9. Web Application Services receives the query results containing structured and unstructured data and applies any additional business logic.

10. Presentation Services send the results via HTTP to the user who initiated the query request and the Web browser renders the HTML page with the query results.

When implementing a federated query, performance considerations must be analyzed to determine if it is feasible to perform the query as a real-time request or if the query should be submitted as an asynchronous request. If the availability of the data sources or infrastructure cannot support a real-time query, a "fire and forget" approach could be implemented where the user is notified when the query results are available to view. An IT Architect could also choose to implement federated query capability by having the EII Federated Query Service first call the MDM System for the cross-reference information and use that information to construct the federated query request. An IT Architect needs to understand the use case, the nonfunctional requirements for security and responsiveness, and the capabilities of the selected software technologies to consider engineering this capability.

3.8.4   MDM Coexistence Scenario—Information Synchronization

This scenario demonstrates how to replicate master data updates from a source by using information synchronization techniques to replicate the changed master data to the MDM System for processing and distribution. The MDM System maintains its role as the authoritative source of master data for the enterprise, and master data coexists in multiple systems across the enterprise. This scenario starts with the originating system updating master data to its database through user interaction or execution of a business transaction. We start the technical walkthrough at the point of the change data capture process to push master data updates to the MDM System. Only the master data information that is maintained by the MDM System is pushed to the MDM System for processing. There may be a subset of master data information that is used only by the business system and not managed by the MDM System.

The originating system for the updates will receive and process changes to the master data returned from the MDM System after MDM Data Quality Management Services have standardized, cleansed, and checked the MDM Data Repository for duplicate master data entities. The originating system must have business logic implemented for receiving those updates in order to not return those same updates back to the MDM System, and must determine how to process any new changes to the master data. For legal or technical reasons, the originating system may not want to override the original data that was entered and may want to simply store the unique ID information returned from the MDM System as a reference. Based upon business requirements and data governance policies, the MDM System could notify a Data Steward about a data quality issue with this data, especially if the MDM System detects that a duplicate master data entity, such as a person, already exists in the originating business system.

"Change Data Capture" techniques are used to monitor database events that insert, update, or delete master data in the source system database. ETL Services are then used to perform any transformation logic to create the respective MDM service request. The MDM System processes the update and publishes the results to a queue for subscribing systems to retrieve and process. We show message queuing used in the scenario to replicate master data updates to the MDM System for reliability purposes. Notice in the scenario that the ETL service does not update master data directly in the MDM Data Repository. Making updates directly to the MDM Data Repository could circumvent business and data governance logic implemented within the MDM System. Figure 3.19 shows a step-by-step technical walkthrough of the scenario that is described in the following list.

1. Changes to master data in a business system database are detected and captured through "Change Data Capture" techniques that use database logs, stored procedures, and so on. "Change Data Capture" processing detects an update to master data, constructs a message with the changed master data, and posts the message to queue.

2. Information Integration ETL Transformation Services detect a message on a message queue for processing. Data Transformation Services get the message and transform the data into an MDM service request format.

3. Information Integration ETL Transformation and Load Services post a message to a message queue to request an MDM Lifecycle Management Update Service.

4. MDM Interface Services detect the message, parse the message, and invoke MDM Security and Privacy Services to verify authorization to the service.

5. MDM Interface Services confirm authorization and invoke the MDM Lifecycle Management Update Service. The MDM Lifecycle Management Update Service invokes MDM Data Quality Management Services.

6. MDM Data Quality Management Services enforce data quality rules and invoke Information Integrity Services to cleanse and standardize data, and then return the results.

7. The MDM Lifecycle Management Update Service requests MDM Search Services to query the Master Data Repository to verify if this is a new master data entity or an update to an existing master data entity. The search results confirm that this is an update to an existing master data entity.

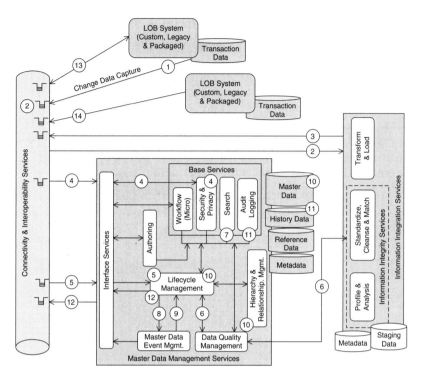

Figure 3.19 MDM Coexistence Scenario–Information Synchronization.

8. The MDM Lifecycle Management Update Service is configured to invoke Master Data Event Management Services to detect any conditions that could trigger an event based upon a business rule or data governance policy.

9. Master Data Event Management Services determine that the requested update does not meet any of the conditions for triggering an event.

10. The MDM Lifecycle Management Update Service is configured to request MDM Hierarchy and Relationship Management Services to detect and create any hierarchies, groupings, or relationships that have been defined. The service then updates the Master Data Repository.

11. MDM Audit Logging Services update the MDM History Database with information about the transaction and the master data values that were updated.

12. The MDM Lifecycle Management Update Service returns its results to the MDM Interface Services, which construct a response message and post the message to a queue. Business systems subscribe to messages posted to this queue.

13. The originating business system retrieves the message and determines that the original data remains unchanged and takes no further action.

14. Business systems that subscribe to updates retrieve the message and process the master data update based upon data governance policies for the management and distribution of master data.

3.8.5 MDM Scenario—Distribution of Updates via Batch Processing

One of the key concepts for all of these scenarios is that the distribution of updated master data should be implemented by use of an information or application integration technique that distributes updated master data in the "right time" to a business system. This scenario describes how batch processing can be used to distribute updates from the MDM System to business systems that do not require the latest master data updates throughout the day. For example, it may be satisfactory to distribute updated master data to a back-office system as part of the end-of-day processing when batch processing cycles are typically scheduled. Because some systems may require the latest updates throughout the day, master data updates are processed by the MDM System throughout the day.

We start the scenario after the originating business system updates master data in its database through user interaction or execution of a business transaction. The business system uses messaging to push the updated master data to the MDM System. Master data coexists in multiple systems across the enterprise, and the MDM System maintains the authoritative source of master data for the enterprise. The scenario shows one or more business systems using a batch process to receive the latest updates from the MDM System. The batch processing schedule could vary by each business system and could run more than once throughout the day. The scenario is simply showing another method for distributing updated master data from the MDM System. It is assumed that the batch processes are authorized to invoke the MDM Lifecycle Management Inquiry Services necessary to request updates to master data from the MDM System.

Another version of this scenario could use Information Integration ETL Services and batch processing to move updated master data from multiple business systems to the MDM System. In this case, the batch input process could use Information Integration Services to cleanse, standardize, match, and consolidate multiple master data records, invoking the same Information Integrity Services that are invoked by MDM Data Quality Management Services. The same MDM Lifecycle Management Update Services would be requested regardless of the method of invocation that provides for consistent MDM business and information logic to be applied for synchronous and asynchronous processing. Figure 3.20 shows a step-by-step technical walkthrough of the scenario that is described in the following list.

1. Master data is updated within a business system either through user interaction or through application integration with another system. The business system constructs a message with the changed data and posts the message to a queue for the MDM System.

2. MDM Interface Services detect the message on the queue, parse the message, and invoke MDM Security and Privacy Services to verify user authorization for the service.

3. MDM Interface Services confirm authorization and invoke the MDM Lifecycle Management Update Service. The MDM Lifecycle Management Update Service invokes MDM Data Quality Management Services.

4. MDM Data Quality Management Services enforce data quality rules and request Information Integrity Services to cleanse and standardize the data, and then return the results.

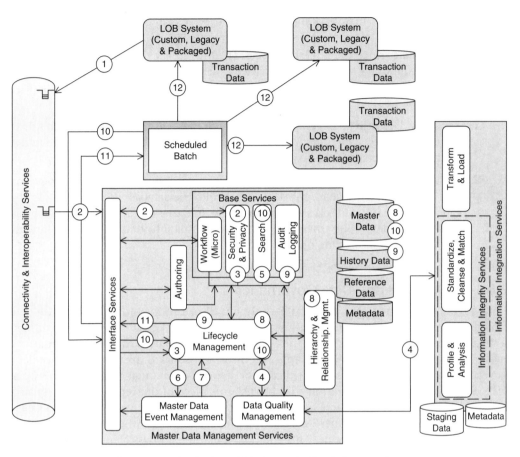

Figure 3.20   MDM Scenario–Distribution of Updates via Batch Processing.

5. The MDM Lifecycle Management Update Service requests MDM Search Services to query the Master Data Repository to verify that the update is to an existing master data entity. The search results confirm that this is an update to an existing master data entity.

6. The MDM Lifecycle Management Update Service is configured to invoke Master Data Event Management Services to detect any conditions that could trigger an event.

7. Master Data Event Management Services determine that the requested update does not meet any conditions that require triggering an event.

8. The MDM Lifecycle Management Update Service is configured to request MDM Hierarchy and Relationship Management Services to detect and create any hierarchies, groupings, or relationships that have been defined. The service then updates the Master Data Repository.

9. MDM Audit Logging Services update the MDM History Database with information about the transaction and the master data values that were updated.

10. A Scheduled Batch process runs for each business system and requests an MDM Lifecycle Management Query Service to query the Master Data Repository for the latest updates since the last batch cycle. The MDM Lifecycle Management Inquiry Service requests an MDM Search Service to query all master data updates that have occurred since the last time the query was executed. The MDM Search Service returns the results to the MDM Lifecycle Management Inquiry Service.

11. The MDM Lifecycle Management Inquiry Service returns the query results to MDM Interface Services, which then translate the results into the output format required by the batch process for that system.

12. Each batch job processes the returned results according to the business logic for that system and either loads the data directly into the database or through an application interface that invokes application logic. In either case, there should be business logic to determine when to add new master data to that system and how to handle updates to existing master data.

3.8.6 MDM Scenario—Data Governance

Data governance for master data should apply for all of the MDM methods of use and would apply to each of the component interaction scenarios. We have chosen to highlight a specific scenario to emphasize how the MDM System can be used to manage changes to master data that requires review and approval by a Data Steward. In this scenario, a data governance policy for changes to "critical data" requires a manual review process by a Data Steward from the organization that "owns" this piece of master data. This scenario could represent a situation where a Customer Service Representative (CSR) updates customer information in a Customer Relationship Management (CRM) system while speaking to the customer on the phone. This could be a mailing address change, for example, which could impact the shipment and delivery of orders in process for that customer from another business unit. We start the scenario after the originating CRM system updates master data in its database and then publishes the update to the MDM System for processing.

The Data Stewardship User Interface and the LOB System User Interfaces are all rendered through an enterprise portal. The change to the master data is first reviewed and must be approved by the "owner" of that data in order for the MDM System to continue processing the update request. Additional Line of Business Data Stewards are notified through Business Process Services about the update so that they can review and agree to accept the update into each of their respective systems.

A publish and subscription technique is used to distribute the new master data to other systems. This provides the ability for each of the subscribing systems to retrieve the information and update its database based upon its own quality of service requirements. The originating business system that pushed the update to the MDM System will receive and process the master data from the MDM System after it has been cleansed, standardized, and approved by a Data Steward. The originating business system must have business logic to not return updated master data back to the MDM System and business logic to support

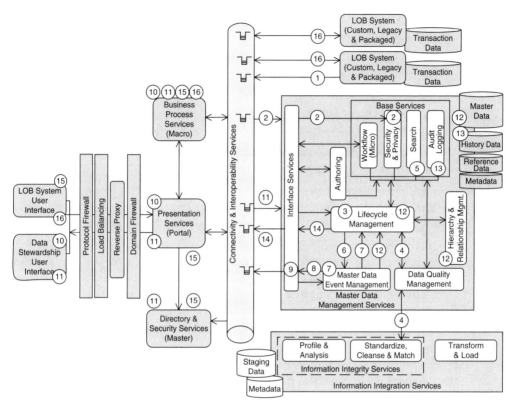

Figure 3.21　MDM Scenario—Data Governance.

processing of the returned results from the MDM System. Figure 3.21 shows a step-by-step technical walkthrough of the scenario that is described in the following list.

1. Master data is updated within a business system. The business system constructs a message with the changed data and posts the message to a message queue that is monitored by MDM Interface Services.

2. MDM Interface Services detect the message, parse the message, and invoke Security and Privacy Services to verify authorization for the MDM service.

3. MDM Interface Services confirm authorization and invoke the MDM Lifecycle Management Update Service. The MDM Lifecycle Management Update Service invokes MDM Data Quality Management Services.

4. MDM Data Quality Management Services enforce data quality rules and request Information Integrity Services to cleanse and standardize the data, and then return the results.

5. The results are returned to the MDM Lifecycle Management Update Service, which then requests MDM Search Services to query the Master Data Repository for the master data entity. MDM Search Services locate an existing master data entity and confirm that this is an update request to an existing master data entity.

6. The MDM Lifecycle Management Update Service is configured to invoke the Master Data Event Management Services.

7. Master Data Event Management Services determine that the updated master data is managed by a data governance policy. The MDM Lifecycle Management Update Service places the update into a temporary status awaiting further approval.

8. The Master Data Event Management Notification Services construct a notification message and request MDM Interface Services to send the notification to a Data Steward.

9. MDM Interface Services post the notification message to a message queue with information about the master data update.

10. Business Process Services detect the notification and initiate a data governance process. The Data Steward receives a notification message on his or her personalized portal home page, and selects a button on the home page to display the updated master data.

11. The portal verifies the user's authorization to review and approve or reject the update. The portal displays a page with the master data content for the Data Steward to approve or reject. The Data Steward approves the update. Business Process Services then send a message to an MDM Lifecycle Management Update Service to complete the processing of the master data update that was pending approval.

12. The MDM Lifecycle Management Update Service is configured to request MDM Hierarchy and Relationship Management Services to detect and create any hierarchies, groupings, or relationships that may have been defined. The update service then updates the Master Data Repository.

13. MDM Audit Logging Services update the MDM History Database with information about the transaction and the master data values that were updated.

14. The MDM Lifecycle Management Update Service requests MDM Interface Services to construct and post a message to a queue containing the updated master data. Business systems receive and process the update into their system only after each review and approval process is completed by the Data Steward for that line of business.

15. Business Process Services notify each Data Steward about the approved change. Each Data Steward receives a notification message on his or her personalized portal home page and selects a portlet that displays the updated master data. The portal verifies the user's authorization to approve or reject the update. The portal displays a page with the master data content for the Data Steward to approve or reject.

16. As each Data Steward reviews and approves the update, Business Process Services invoke a business system service to retrieve the message from the queue and process the update according to the Data Steward's decision to accept or reject the update.

3.8.7 MDM Scenario—Incremental Updates to a Data Warehouse

The analytical style of MDM supports the use of master data from the MDM System as the accurate, clean source of master data for the loading of transactional data from business systems into a Data Warehouse. We show in this scenario one approach for using master data from the MDM System as part of the incremental update process for a Data Warehouse. The

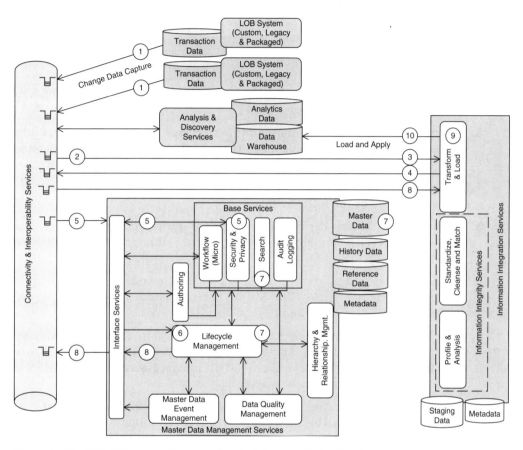

Figure 3.22   MDM Scenario–Incremental Updates to a Data Warehouse.

same scenario could be revised to support the initial loading of a Data Warehouse, but due to the amount of data being loaded, it requires additional steps for staging all of the data to merge, transform, and load into the Data Warehouse.[15]

The volume of data captured between intervals when the ETL process runs should determine if a messaging approach can be used to feed the ETL process or if a batch process should be used to request the most recent master data updates from the MDM System. We assume that the ETL process runs at a frequency that captures a small volume of changes that support the use of messaging to feed the ETL process. Figure 3.22 shows a step-by-step technical walkthrough of the scenario that is described in the following list.

---

15.   Chapter 5 MDM Architecture Patterns contains an Enterprise Deployment BW Pattern that can be referenced for more details about the use of the MDM System to support the loading of clean dimensional data into a Data Warehouse.

1. New and changed data is captured through "Change Data Capture" techniques that use database logs, stored procedures, database triggers, and so on. The "Change Data Capture" process constructs a message with updated data and posts the message to a message queue.

2. Information Integration Data Transformation Services run on a scheduled basis to retrieve messages from the queue.

3. Information Integration Data Transformation Services retrieve the messages, sort through the updates to determine what master data information is needed from the MDM System, and transform the data into an MDM Service request message format.

4. Information Integration Data Transformation Services post a message to a message queue monitored by the MDM System.

5. MDM Interface Services detect a message on the queue, parse the message, and invoke MDM Security and Privacy Services to verify authorization for the service request.

6. MDM Interface Services confirm authorization and invoke an MDM Lifecycle Management Inquiry Service. The MDM Lifecycle Management Inquiry Service invokes an MDM Search Service.

7. The MDM Search Service queries the Master Data Repository and returns the query results to the MDM Lifecycle Management Inquiry Service. The MDM Lifecycle Management Inquiry Service requests MDM Interface Services to construct a response message with the query results.

8. MDM Interface Services create a message with the query results and post that message to a queue monitored by Information Integration Data Transformation Services.

9. Information Integration Data Transformation Services use the returned results from the MDM System as the accurate source for the transformation and enriching of the business transaction data.

10. Information Integration Load Services load the records into the Data Warehouse to complete the incremental load process.

Conclusion

The Master Data Management Reference Architecture should be referenced as input for developing an MDM Solution for the enterprise. The MDM RA is designed to support the evolution of an MDM Solution to implement one or more MDM methods of use and accommodate multiple master data domains. Designing an architecture evolves through multiple stages of elaboration and specification, taking into account system distribution; nonfunctional requirements such as performance, reliability, and high availability; the use of specific products; the choice of middleware; and other technologies. One of the key drivers for the design of the MDM Reference Architecture is that it should be a scalable, highly available, adaptive and capable of supporting high performance. The implementation of an MDM Solution will always need to consider the existing IT environment, IT standards, enterprise architecture policies, and choice of software for the MDM System and for implementing Information Integration Services such as Information Integrity, ETL, and EII.

It is important to consider the long-term MDM strategy when selecting software for your MDM System. Designing and implementing an MDM System that will continue to deliver sustained business value to the enterprise requires the ability to support the multiple MDM methods of use for the management of master data throughout its lifecycle. In Appendix B, Software and Solution Offerings for MDM Deployments, we identify an overview of software products from relevant software vendors that can be considered for implementing master data solutions. Some of the more advanced MDM products support all of the MDM methods of use required in today's complex business and support multiple master data domains. These mature products also provide intelligent data management by recognizing critical data changes to the information that can trigger strategic enterprise processes and data governance. Finally, MDM products vary in their ability to support master data domains. Coverage may range from specializing in a single domain such as customer or product to maintaining relationships across multiple master data domains. Those that span multiple domains help to harness not only the value of the domain but also the value in the relationships between domains.

One of the desired outcomes for any MDM Solution is to support the needs of the enterprise for many years by providing the flexibility to adapt to the use of new technologies, changing business processes and requirements, legislative changes, and the development of new applications. The selected MDM software should provide the ability to easily include additional new master data domains and attributes, and to implement multiple MDM methods of use as the MDM Solution evolves over time. Criteria for selection of the MDM software should include both its ability to meet current requirements and its flexibility to easily extend to meet the needs of the future. Our experience in selecting Master Data Management software to support the concept of a Party, as defined in Chapter 1, leads to the following observations:

- Start with a robust data model to provide a solid foundation for a low-risk implementation that can drive an early win for the organization.
- A robust data model usually results in relatively few data model extensions or additions being required.
- If additions or extensions are required, it is important to select a software product that provides capabilities to reduce the level of effort to make changes to the data model and ensure consistency in the implementation of the associated services.

Because of the unique requirements of data models developed to implement Product Information Management Solutions, the software selection criteria should focus on the authoring capabilities of the MDM product to model, manage, and create product information. Product information is typically stored in a hierarchical structure. Data modeling capability should provide for reuse of data objects such as catalogs, items, hierarchies, product specifications, attributes, views, and localization. Catalog hierarchies are used to model item taxonomies, which are tree-like arrangements of categories and subcategories. There are typically two types of hierarchies—category and organization. Items, catalogs, and hierarchies all have attributes. Inheritance provides for the reuse of the same product information across items or categories. Ideally, the product should have attribute level inheritance to maximize the reuse of attributes to define multiple catalogs, items, and hierarchies. Authoring services should also provide localization capabilities to reuse attribute information that has been converted to a particular language to support users across multiple geographies in today's global economy.

From a best-practice perspective, there can be substantial value in selecting an ETL tool that can provide reusable Information Integration Services to support both the initial loading of the MDM System and subsequent use by all systems. Using configurable software that externalizes rules and interfaces provides the flexibility needed to implement an MDM Solution that drives business value to your organization while imposing the necessary constraints that maintain data quality and integrity. The MDM System, in combination with Information Integrity Services, should provide the following:

- The ability to use code tables to normalize data and align data cleansing options with organizational needs and processes
- Externalization of data cleansing, standardization, and matching rules to ensure flexibility in the implementation
- Data validation at the attribute level performed as a common service so that reusable information services can be consistently used across the organization

Implementing high-availability techniques would be specific to the software technologies selected for implementing the MDM Solution architecture. Planning for high availability involves the identification and elimination of "single points of failure" that could prevent the MDM System or Information Integration Services from being available or impact communications between the business systems and the MDM System. When designing how to implement an MDM System within the enterprise, design points for the physical architecture should consider unplanned outages due to hardware and/or software failures and should provide the ability to perform system maintenance without requiring a scheduled system outage. Designing for high availability requires implementing redundant conceptual nodes within the architecture and using hardware and software technologies that provide high-availability features such as RAID,[16] clustering with load balancing, dynamic switching, and hot failover capabilities.

High availability can be achieved by loosely coupling application and system to system communications through the use of asynchronous messaging and by avoiding the implementation of point-to-point communications between systems or between applications. Asynchronous communications provide a mechanism to safely quiesce a system component

---

16. RAID refers to a redundant array of independent drives that support a storage scheme using multiple hard drives to replicate data among the drive-through techniques such as data mirroring.

without the loss of transaction data communicated between components, thus making it possible to replace or perform application and software product upgrades and maintain continuity of operations. Although all of the system functionality may not be available during the outage of any one component, critical business functionality can be designed to remain active while less critical functions are down for maintenance. Scalability is achieved through the concept of implementing well-defined components that can be individually or collectively adjusted to meet variable demands by adding additional servers (scale-out) or by increasing the processing capability of a server (scale-up). Because messaging services or middleware can also be used to queue requests until an application is ready to process them, the application can control the rate at which it processes the requests so as not to become overloaded by too many simultaneous requests.

Best practices for high availability also employ the use of load balancing techniques, workload distribution, and the clustering of multiple servers. Hardware or software is responsible for making the set of servers appear to be a single server, balancing workload requests across available servers, and directing new requests to the least-busy server. Clustering technology with load balancing also provides the ability to increase capacity by adding more servers without taking the system down. Selection of the type of load balancing technology should consider if session data for a user must be maintained to support processing subsequent requests. If the application server is processing transactions that require multiple steps, then session data about previous user interactions needs to be carried forward to future interactions. In the event that session data must be maintained, techniques such as sticky ports or the use of a central data store containing session data and accessible by each server could be used.

Software selection criteria for the MDM System should also include the ability of the software to scale to meet the long-term needs for the organization. The ability of a software product to scale is usually assessed through the implementation of a proof-of-concept and through discussions with customer references provided from the vendor. However, planning for the implementation and deployment activities of an MDM Solution should always follow good system engineering practices. The risks of not understanding how the software will perform and scale as requirements increase over time can have negative effects on the overall value the MDM Solution can provide to the business. The performance of a system usually has three aspects that must be provided for when delivering an MDM System:

- Response time, both online and batch
- Transaction throughput, for example, the number of transactions per second, or records processed per time period (minute, hour, day, month, etc.)
- Capacity, for example, processor, memory, network, storage

Every MDM project will have its own unique set of challenges and risks that need to be considered for the selection of software and the implementation strategy. The Master Data Management Reference Architecture provides the basis for developing an MDM Solution for the enterprise that is based upon architecture patterns and best practices. Selecting the right software to meet both the tactical and long-term strategic business objectives is critical for achieving both the immediate and long-term business value of an MDM Solution.

References

When developing the MDM Component Interaction Diagrams, we referenced the publications listed here. These publications will provide the reader with additional guidance and implementation details that support the application-to-application communication techniques used in the component interaction scenarios, and they provide further insight about the structure of the MDM Component Relationship Diagram.

1. Endrei, M., Ang, J., Arsanjani, A., Chua, S., et al., 2004. *Patterns: Service-Oriented Architecture and Web Services*, New York: International Technical Support Organization, IBM Redbooks® SG24-6303-00. ISBN: 073845317X.
2. Adams, J., Koushik, S. 2001. *Patterns for e-business—A Strategy for Reuse*. Texas: IBM Press ISBN: 1931182027.
3. Bond, J., et al., Patterns 2005. *Integrating Enterprise Service Buses in a Service Oriented Architecture*. New York: International Technical Support Organization, IBM Redbooks SG24-6773-00. ISBN: 0738492930.
4. Hohpe, G., Woolf, B. 2006. *Enterprise Integration Patterns. Designing, Building, and Deploying Messaging Solutions*. Boston: Addison-Wesley, The Addison-Wesley Signature Series, ©2004 by Pearson Education, Inc., 8th printing. ISBN: 0321200683.
5. Moore, B., Aguilera, T., Bryniarski, L., et al., 2001. *User-to-Business Pattern Using WebSphere Personalization*. New York: International Technical Support Organization, IBM Redbooks GG24-6213-00. ISBN: 0738419656.

Chapter 4

MDM Security
and Privacy

This chapter explains the role of security and privacy in an MDM Solution. The key to securing an MDM environment is to first understand the value of and the risks to the master data, which will serve as a guide to selecting and applying the appropriate security controls. Privacy in MDM is an orthogonal concern to security—where security is focused on controlling access to master data, privacy is focused on the appropriate use of personal data based on regulation and the explicit consent of the party. Note that for this chapter we assume some basic understanding of computer security technology, especially cryptography. A good primer on this subject can be found here [1].

4.1 Introduction

As we described in Chapter 1, MDM increases the value of information—unfortunately, for that very reason, it also increases the potential damage to the organization (and its customers and partners) if that master data is lost, disclosed, or improperly modified. High-value centralized core business information is now a new target of opportunity for corrupt insiders (those people who work for your organization who misuse their legitimate access to internal systems) and opportunistic outsiders (e.g., hackers). We now discuss some characteristics of master data management that, if not properly addressed, can make master data more vulnerable to attack.

With MDM, previously scattered high-value information is now available in one place. Prior to deploying MDM, master data was scattered around the enterprise. An example of this in the customer domain (though it is also true in other domains) is shown in Figure 4.1. Each application is its own isolated silo containing a part of the master data for the customer domain.

Typically, each application would have its own security mechanisms, user interface, programming interfaces, and repositories. For an attacker to gain access to all of the master data, he must successfully penetrate all of the different systems *and* determine the mapping/relationship

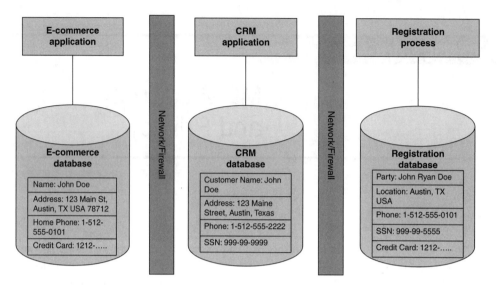

Figure 4.1 Typical Application Silos of Customer Master Data.

of all of this "uncorrelated" information. In other words, the bad guy has to actually do the job of integrating the master data across the silos! Further complicating the task of the rogue hacker or corrupted insider is the fact that these applications are often on different physical networks, separated by firewalls and rules that prevent access to the complete set of applications. Thus, the barriers that make it hard for attackers to reconstruct an enterprise's master data also make it difficult for legitimate employees to share and compile this master data. Of course, we aren't saying that these barriers can't also work to increase the risks to your systems. First, isolated application silos may not have implemented consistent and integrated levels of security controls. Based on security reviews conducted by the authors, it is not uncommon for line of business applications to have escaped a review for corporate security compliance, making them prime targets of opportunity for attackers. Second, if line of business applications do not have integrated auditing (securely recording key system events and who initiated them in a log called the **audit trail**), fraud or attacks against multiple lines of business may be hard to detect.

Master Data under an MDM regimen is the most valuable data in your organization. As discussed in previous chapters, master data entities really are the "crown jewels" of your organization. The domains of master data include:

- Sensitive customer information, potentially including personally identifiable information (PII) that can be used in identity theft, such as Social Security Number, date of birth, and credit card numbers and expiration dates.
- Information about vendors, suppliers, and contracts that are of utmost secrecy and sensitivity to the enterprise. These contracts may not only contain highly confidential information such as with whom an organization is doing business, but also the terms and conditions. This information is of great interest to industrial spies

working for competitors and to vendors who want to know what sorts of deals your organization will enter into.

- Unreleased details about new products and services that your organization is planning to offer, such as pricing, specifications, and marketing programs. Again, this is the sort of information that unscrupulous competitors would exploit to your disadvantage.
- Key financial data, including detailed account information, contracts, and purchasing information that is used to fulfill regulatory compliance mandates like Basel II and Sarbanes-Oxley (see Appendix C for more information on these regulations). Without strong controls over this master data, shareholders and customers may be at risk from insider fraud that manipulates the financial information to mislead the public on the true economic status of the business.

Such valuable data, stored in one logically centralized system, is already a very tempting target. But with master data management, the value of the data may further be increased by two common components identified in Chapter 3 as part of the MDM Reference Architecture:

- **Cleansing**—A key function of MDM is to ensure that the data is de-duplicated and accurate, so that the master data has the highest value to applications that consume the master data. Unfortunately, this also increases the value of the same master data to attackers.
- **Enrichment**—Organizations may choose to extend their master data by enriching it with data from third-party providers. Typical types of enrichment are credit ratings and organizational information. Often available only under stringent contract and for closely restricted purposes, this information can also be a boon to the bad guys.

Having enumerated some of the security concerns that *may* arise when deploying an MDM System we have an understanding of the "bad news." There are two pieces of good news that more than outweigh this bad news. First, by understanding the vulnerabilities, threats, and risks to your master data, you can begin the process of determining and applying the appropriate security controls to address those risks. Second, the logically centralized model of MDM, combined with well-established information security technologies, will provide a highly secure and compliant (in a regulatory sense) infrastructure for protecting master data. Just as centralized information can be seen to provide a new target of opportunity to the "bad guys," it also provides the "good guys" with a single simplified security process designed to meet the requirements of the enterprise and its data.

4.2 Information Risk Management for Master Data

Information Risk Management is a major component of an overall information security program that focuses on **mitigating** the risks to your information assets (see details in [2]). This means these risks also apply to master data, which is only one specific type of information asset. We introduce the concept of information risk management now and explain how it applies to master data management.

4.2.1 Information Risk Management Overview

Information Risk Management is the set of ongoing processes that identify and analyze the risks to your information assets, assess the costs and benefits of different approaches to mitigate the risks, and then implement (and monitor) the controls that mitigate the risks.

Mitigation in this case means reducing the risks to a level that your organization can live with. It is impossible to completely eliminate risk—all business operations carry some element of risk, such as customers that don't pay, authors that do not finish their books on schedule, and so on. With Information Risk Management, you are able to evaluate the risks to your information assets. This allows you to then balance how you address those risks against the ability to actually do business. Determining the level of risk your enterprise can live with is ultimately the responsibility of senior management, based on legal and regulatory requirements and the goals of the business weighed against the threats to the business operations.

Information Risk can be thought of as the business impact of loss events that (have the potential to) damage an information asset. The damage could be destruction, alteration, or disclosure of your information. The *risk* is the probability of a particular loss event occurring measured against the potential loss if that risk occurs. From a security point of view, the loss event is when a **threat** (like theft of information) occurs that exploits a particular **vulnerability** (like an insecure network).

The first part of Information Risk Management is an analysis of the risks to your information. The second part is the *selection* of the implementation, and the final step is actually deploying and monitoring of the controls you apply to address those risks.

4.2.1.1 Information Risk Analysis

Information Risk Analysis is the process where a cross-enterprise set of IT and business people lay out the landscape of the information assets and the risks to those assets, and then assess the cost and effectiveness of different approaches to reducing those risks.

The information risk analysis consists of:

- Identifying the information assets
- Assigning value to each asset
- Identifying each asset's vulnerabilities and associated threats
- Calculating the risk for the identified assets (the potential loss that would occur if an anticipated or unanticipated threat succeeded)
- Evaluating different countermeasures in terms of their costs and the reduction of risk they provide
- Recommending the appropriate countermeasures based on the risk level and spending acceptable to the organization

The output of the different parts of the analysis is rolled up into a report for senior management across the enterprise in both business and IT groups within the company. The goal of the risk analysis phase is to ensure that the different management teams understand the impact of threats to the information assets from a value and cost perspective. This impact includes both the cost to the business if something happens, and the cost to reduce that risk. The management team will then be focused in its decision making on selecting the best way

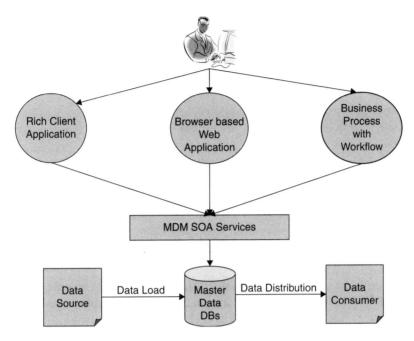

Figure 4.2 Simplified Deployment Model for an MDM implementation.

to mitigate the risks. The risk analysis should represent direct input into the overall security budget and into the security architecture and operations. For MDM, this analysis should also be factored into the costs (and benefits) of the MDM project.

The asset valuation and vulnerability and threat identification phase should look at all of the obvious IT assets—databases, applications, servers, metadata, business processes, and so on. Architecture and component diagrams (like Figure 4.2 or figures from the MDM Reference Architecture, in Chapter 3) are very helpful in developing a list of these assets. We discuss particular MDM assets in Section 4.2.2.1, introduce a simple methodology for asset valuation in Section 4.2.2.2, and identify MDM-specific vulnerabilities in Section 4.2.2.3.

The approaches to reduce risk fall into three categories:

- **Reduce/Mitigate:** With risk mitigation, you apply security controls to address a particular vulnerability. You may be concerned about an internal attacker using a tool that examines network traffic (*threat*) to obtain master data because the master data flows unencrypted over an internal network (*vulnerability*) and the malicious insider sells that information to identity thieves (*risk*). A recommended countermeasure might be to use the Secure Sockets Layer (SSL) to encrypt the traffic over the internal network. You can apply multiple security controls to reduce the risk—in the previous example you might also use firewalls to limit the systems that can access the network that carries master data. Whether or not you apply one or more controls depends on the costs (initial and ongoing) of implementing the different controls balanced against the reduction in risk.

- **Accept:** Accept the risk, based on the ability of your organization to absorb the potential losses.
- **Transfer:** Transfer the risk to another party by obtaining insurance or some other hedge against loss.

4.2.1.2 Different Types of IT Risks

When looking at risks related to IT, we are mostly concerned with the three categories of risks described here.

Operational risks are the first type of risks. These are risks from failures in your business processes, in your IT systems, and from the behavior of people. The latter category (people) can include external hackers as well as corrupt insiders. One operational risk is a **denial of service** (one that makes resources unavailable) attack that brings down your network, reducing your ability to do business and causing a loss of confidence in your organization. Note that other external events such as natural calamities, external network outages, and fires can introduce operational failures as well.

The second type of risk is related to **Regulatory and Compliance.** These are risks associated with failure to comply with laws and industry standards. If poor internal security allows corrupt members of senior management to change the information used for financial reporting, and these individuals are then caught and prosecuted for breaking the law, the ramifications may include jail time, fines, imposition of burdensome controls and reporting requirements, legal costs for defending the organization and working out settlements with shareholders or other affected parties, and loss of reputation leading to reduced business (this ties into reputational risk). Regulatory and Compliance risks can actually be mapped back into two ways of using data:

- **Using data to meet regulatory requirements in your business processes:** There are a number of regulations that mandate implementing certain processes and reports for compliance. Some of these (as mentioned in Chapter 1 and detailed in Appendix C) include Basel II and Sarbanes-Oxley (SOX) for financial risk management and financial reporting, and the Anti-Money Laundering Act. The focus of these requirements is on the soundness of the business processes that support the regulation, and the availability and quality of the information used to support the processes.
- **Adequately protecting sensitive data to meet regulatory requirements:** A number of standards and regulations have strict rules about how certain data is stored, transmitted, and used. The Payment Card Industry—Data Security Standard (PCI-DSS) and Health Insurance Portability and Accountability Act (HIPAA) fall into this category. PCI-DSS has specific procedures for handling credit card data, and HIPAA is very prescriptive about how a patient's health record and other sensitive data are made available to health-care providers and their partners.

Some regulations fall into both camps—SOX and Basel II also require certification of internal controls that protect the data. California Senate Bill 1386 (notification to consumers of data breaches) also requires using the same data that was breached in notifications (customer contact information). Appendix C has a list of regulations applicable to master data.

From an architectural perspective, it is more important to ensure that your MDM architecture is flexible enough to accommodate generic regulatory requirements than it is to focus on just complying with today's regulations. Regulatory requirements change over time and your enterprise may also enter new business areas that involve different regulations, so assessing compliance requirements and applying the appropriate controls will be an ongoing effort.

The third type of risks covers **Reputational Risks.** If an enterprise suffers a sustained *public* loss because of an operational or regulatory failure, customers, suppliers, and partners may lose faith in the ability of the enterprise to meet their business needs. Senior management will have to spend time and money communicating with customers and the press in an attempt to recapture external confidence in the enterprise—this may include bringing in new senior management as well as intense marketing and branding efforts.

Note that we are singling out information risk management as opposed to more general risk management. Financial institutions have to address financial risk management beyond IT risks, such as loan defaults or exposures due to currency devaluations. Most organizations also have to deal with strategic risks where the nature of the competitive environment changes in a way to threaten your core business (such as a competitor introducing a completely new product line). As discussed in Chapters 1 and 9, MDM can help with these other sorts of risk management by providing a clear, complete, and high-quality view of all of the relevant data for assessing financial risks, and by making it faster and easier to bring new products to new markets (as seen in the NPI solution blueprint described in Chapter 6, in Section 6.3) to cope with strategic risks. In this chapter, we are focused on threats and risks to the master data from an IT perspective only, but it should be kept in mind that MDM risk management, like MDM security and privacy, should be integrated into a larger enterprise risk management framework (a consolidated risk management system across IT and business that covers financial, operational, and IT risks).

4.2.1.3 Privacy Risks

Privacy risks cut across multiple risk categories—regulatory and reputational. Regulations and controls related to privacy have some distinct differences from the regulations and controls of other master data used by the organization. Privacy relates to an enterprise acting as a *custodian* of someone's PII—the PII is not owned by the enterprise but by the customer, employee, vendor, and so on. One difference from other types of risk is that many regulations (SB 1386, FACT Act) require the enterprise to take specific actions if PII is stolen—for other acts of theft, the organization may not be bound to take action (and may not do so to reduce reputational risk costs).

The rules of how PII is held, used, shared, and dealt with if stolen or missing are based on an agreement between the individual and the organization as well as on regulatory obligations. The agreement usually takes the form of a privacy policy, and if the organization offers multiple privacy policies, the user can choose one policy based on his or her privacy preferences. These privacy policies are driven by regulation, the needs of the business (including interaction with partners), and the desire to win customers and partners by showing them that the organization will not misuse their PII.

From a reputation standpoint, organizations can spend a lot of time and money trying to recover from a widespread breach of sensitive customer (or other parties such as employee) information that can be used for identity theft. Affected customers may bring lawsuits against the enterprise that "lost" their data, organizations may have to provide identity theft monitoring for those customers, and existing (and potential) customers will think long and hard about doing business with an organization that does not properly protect PII.

4.2.2   Information Risk Management for Master Data Management

Applying enterprise security best practices (proven security approaches based on the experience gained in numerous customer engagements) to a master data management environment allows us to simplify the risk analysis and control selection processes found in traditional information risk management. First, the identification phase of the risk analysis is relatively straightforward—identification of the master data should already be incorporated into the master data project. Second, the deployment architecture patterns for master data management can form the baseline for a threat and vulnerability assessment as well as a basis for selecting the appropriate security controls that can be directly mapped onto the architecture. Because master data is the foundation of a company's business, that fact alone should be enough to justify the investment required by extending enterprise security controls to master data.

Our simplified risk management approach for master data management restructures the risk analysis and control selection and implementation as follows:

- **Risk Analysis for MDM**
  - Identification of MDM assets and assignment of an estimated value to the master data using the ULAC methodology, as described in Section 4.2.2.2
  - High-level assessment of risks and threats to the master data
- **Security Control Selection and Implementation**
  - Identification of specific MDM vulnerabilities and associated threats based on the MDM deployment architecture and solution pattern
  - Recommendation of security controls based on services found in the enterprise security architecture (described in Section 4.4) that address the vulnerabilities and threats found in the identification phase

4.2.2.1   Identifying MDM Assets

The MDM assets can be partially cataloged by using a combination of the simplified deployment architecture shown in Figure 4.2, and more fully cataloged by using the MDM Reference Architecture in Chapter 3, in conjunction with the MDM solution blueprints in Chapters 6, 7, and 8.

MDM assets can be categorized as:

- **Sources of master data:** This category includes internal line of business sources for initial and delta loads of master data as well as any external sources used to enrich the master data.
- **Master data itself:** For the Registry Implementation Style of MDM, this category should include both the data stored in the Master Data Repository as well as the data

stored in the different registries. This category should also include the audit trail, history, metadata, and reference data stores.

- **Consumers of master data:** This category consists of the business applications that consume (and update) the master data directly via MDM Services, as well as downstream data warehouses, data marts, and other applications that are updated from the master data.
- **Other related assets:** This category includes other assets that have value (and can be compromised or destroyed), including backups and other metadata artifacts surrounding the master data. The metadata can include classification information on the master data, workflows, rules for data quality and data consistency, and ETL scripts/programs.

4.2.2.2   Estimating the Value and Potential Costs of Master Data

In Chapter 1, we talked about the different ways you can effectively use master data to generate value to your enterprise. In some circumstances, it is straightforward to compute a quantifiable number to represent the value of an asset, or the value realized by implementing a new initiative such as accurately identifying high-value customers. In other cases, the nature of the data itself makes it very difficult to derive a specific, quantifiable number to represent the value of master data. Data is a soft asset—it can be used and reused with minimal cost across multiple business processes. With master data management, it may be easier to derive a quantitative number for cost reduction than for business value, such as the reduction in personnel to deal with fixing data quality problems when data is scattered across multiple systems or the cost of maintaining the separate applications.

Any business case for master data management should have some quantified numbers on increased revenue and changes in costs in support of moving to master data management, and that information can be leveraged here. However, we now introduce a qualitative approach to looking at the value and risks to master data, an approach called the ULAC method (Use, Lose, Abuse, and Confuse). We can use ULAC to estimate value and costs by looking at our inventory of assets in light of the:

- **Value to your organization when you use master data effectively (see Chapter 1 for more examples)**
  - New business opportunities
  - Cross-sell/up-sell (see Chapter 7, Section 7.3, for more on this)
  - Operational efficiencies and agility (including compliance)
  - Elimination of redundant, incomplete, insecure partial stores of master data (in this case, we are reducing risk)
  - Faster time to market (see Chapter 6, Section 6.3, on New Product Introduction for an example)
- **Cost/Risk to master data if you _lose_ access to it. In this context, we are thinking about loss as data being unavailable for use, not theft of data.**
  - Business outage (data not available when needed). This is the cost to your organization for not being able to do business because your master data is unavailable.

This could be due to deliberate or accidental destruction and failure of backup media as well as network and application outages (again deliberate or inadvertent). Generally speaking, during long outages, customers (who can't order goods or services) and vendors (who can't get paid) lose confidence in the organization, which can have a long-term affect on business (this is part of what we call *reputational risk*), even if there is no direct immediate impact to the customers or vendors. Specific guidance on how to address business outages (often called high availability) is provided in Chapter 5.

- **Cost and risks if you *abuse* data. In this context, data is stolen, misused, or modified, which has an impact on customers, vendors, and partners.**
  - Data breaches (where information is stolen from the organization) of PII are the most frequently discussed risks in this category. Breaches can lead to operational, regulatory, and reputational risks. According to the Identity Theft Resource Center, 466 data breaches were publicly reported in the United States in 2007, potentially exposing over 127,000,000 identities to identity theft [3].
  - Failure to honor privacy preferences and follow privacy policies can also be a risk.
  - Allowing malicious insiders to manipulate sensitive data. As we have discussed, this can have severe financial, legal, and reputational costs.
  - Disclosing intellectual property to competitors. In the New Product Introduction business pattern, information about future products is kept inside of MDM. Leakage of this information can lead to strategic problems for the enterprise, because competitors can adjust their strategies accordingly.
- **Cost and risks if you confuse your data (data quality). We cover more on this in Chapter 9, but there are risks associated with not properly managing the quality of your data, such as:**
  - Bad business decisions based on bad data
  - Customer satisfaction problems
  - Regulatory risks if you do financial or statutory reporting based on inaccurate master data.

A typical approach to "scoring" these risks in your environment is to use a traffic light approach: red for critical risks, yellow for important risks, and green for risks that can be accepted. This yields a prioritized list to address in your deployment.

One of the primary benefits of MDM is that it explicitly helps reduce the costs and risks associated with data quality, so you would expect the "C" score (using ULAC) to be relatively low in an MDM deployment.

We can use the ULAC methodology to look at the JKE case study in Chapter 9, in Section 9.1. JKE is a large financial services, mortgage, and insurance provider that is looking to leverage master data across its business units. Applying ULAC to their environment, we see the results shown in Table 4.1.

Table 4.1 shows us the high value of the master data at JKE, and also shows where moving to MDM can enhance the value and reduce the costs of the current dispersed way that master data is handled at JKE.

Table 4.1   ULAC Matrix for JKE Case Study in Chapter 9

	Customer Master Data	Account Master Data	Contract Master Data
Use	High—JKE has identified a number of cross-sell and wallet share opportunities for using master data across JKE lines of business, offering value of up to $50M US.	High—JKE has identified a number of cross-sell and wallet share opportunities for using master data across JKE lines of business, offering value of up to $50M US.	Medium—This data is not as critical for the up-sell and cross-sell activities of JKE, though it is used in regular business transactions.
Lose	High—This would impact multiple lines of business at JKE. When moving to MDM, this would move to **Medium**—JKE is starting with a Registry style MDM, so there will be other paths to the data.	High—This would impact multiple lines of business at JKE. When moving to MDM, this would move to **Medium**—JKE is starting with a Registry style MDM, so there will be other paths to the data.	High—This would impact multiple lines of business at JKE. When moving to MDM, this would move to **Medium**—JKE is starting with a Registry style MDM, so there will be other paths to the data.
Abuse	High—JKE is in a highly regulated industry, faces a large number of retail customers, and manages a lot of money. Disclosure of sensitive customer information would be a huge problem. Moving to MDM helps reduce this risk because access is centralized, but with the Registry style MDM proposed by JKE, there is still direct access to the underlying master data outside of MDM.	High—JKE is in a highly regulated industry, faces a large number of retail customers, and manages a lot of money. Unauthorized manipulation of accounts can affect regulatory compliance, introduce reputational concerns, and increase JKE's liabilities. As with customer master data, MDM can help reduce but not completely drive down this risk in a Registry style implementation.	Medium—Risks to contract modification are a concern if an insider is collaborating with a customer on a fraud, which would also affect regulatory compliance initiatives.
Confuse	High—JKE has identified $20M worth of call center costs that can be reduced due to improved master data. Improving data quality is also important to the cross-sell and up-sell capabilities. Moving to MDM reduces this to **Low**.	High (non-MDM)/ Low (MDM)	High (non-MDM)/ Low (MDM)

4.2.2.3   Evaluate Threats and Vulnerabilities

The particular threats and vulnerabilities that apply to your particular MDM deployment depend on the MDM architecture, domains of master data, implementation styles, and solution blueprints you choose. In Section 4.3 and beyond, we discuss the different threats and vulnerabilities based on a simplified MDM deployment model—here, though, we look at some of the potential threats and threat actors to give a general idea of the weaknesses you should address.

Threat Actors are the individuals, groups, or systems that actually exploit vulnerabilities in your systems, facilities, or processes. We include groups because competitors or other adversaries may act in concert to pose a set of threats, including using compromised end-user systems to attack your IT resources.

External threat actors are typically **hackers** who are looking at vulnerabilities (sometimes called weaknesses) in your external systems to use to destroy, alter, or access your master data. They exploit weaknesses in Internet-facing services (Web servers that are not hardened against attacks like SQL Injection and cross-site scripting, networks that inadvertently expose internal traffic, etc.). They may combine these attacks with **social engineering** (obtaining a legitimate user's credentials through trickery like pretending to be a help desk person requesting the user's password) to gain unauthorized access to master data-consuming applications or to the master data itself.

Internal threat actors are the hardest to defend against, because they are already trusted to some extent in order to carry out their business roles. A set of inside threat actors includes:

- Less trusted users who obtain a trusted user's credentials: For example, a secretary may get access to the CEO's password, or a trader may get access to another trader's passwords [4]. The secretary may then execute a **privilege escalation** attack by assuming the identity of the CEO and accessing the master data with the CEO's higher degree of access to enable identity theft, fraud, and so on. The weakness exploited by the secretary is the weak authentication mechanism (password) for a highly privileged user like the CEO.
- Trusted insiders acting outside of their legitimate needs: Legitimate business users (see Appendix A for a full list of business users) such as data stewards and application resource owners may use their privileges to illicitly access master data. This includes accessing the master data outside of collaboration controlled workflow and going directly to MDM Services or the MDM repositories to obtain, modify, or destroy the master data. In this case, the trusted insider exploited the vulnerability of poor access control at the MDM Services or data layers. An interesting attack by data stewards and business customizers is actually changing the rules associated by the master data (to perhaps suppress an event that warns when a master data record was improperly accessed).
- Administrative users with a high degree of authority to access system resources: Operating Systems administrators can copy databases onto USB sticks, database administrators and backup administrators can often see all of the master data in the databases, and security administrators can give themselves (or a corrupt colleague) higher privileges to resources, access them, and then delete the audit trails and

other evidence. Network and application administrators also have enough authority to attack master data unless proper controls are put into place. Data integrators
(who create the feeds into master data from data sources) and developers (who can
look at test data, or create malicious applications that can destroy or disclose master data) should also be considered as potential threat agents.

A hybrid set of threat actors are third parties who are trusted to run some set of IT or business processes against your master data. These may be outsourced network hosting
providers, or in the case of master data, external data providers or data validation services.
In the case of providers, these services can inadvertently or deliberately provide false master
data. With validation services, your enterprise may be leaking sensitive master data to these
third parties.

4.3 Security Considerations in MDM

Now that we understand information risk management, threat actors, and vulnerabilities in
general, we investigate how these concepts apply in more detail in the context of the MDM
reference architecture. Because we assume the MDM reference architecture to be the baseline for an MDM Solution deployment—certainly adapted to current project requirements—
there are some key areas, which we now introduce, where security is crucial in all cases. First,
though we need to introduce a few terms (some of which will be defined in more detail later
in the chapter):

- **Policy:** A security or privacy policy describes the rules on how information should
  be protected. At a business level, the policy may be high-level and tied back to business and compliance objectives ("Agents can only see details about insurance policies for a customer when that agent wrote the policy.") At a technical level, policies
  are machine readable and more focused on specific enterprise resources so that the
  policies can be enforced by a policy enforcement point (defined later) in the
  enterprise.
- **Confidentiality:** Information is disclosed to only those authorized to see it.
  Encryption is a key (pun intended) mechanism that is used to provide confidentiality for data flowing across a network and **data at rest** (data that is sitting on a
  disk).
- **Integrity:** Integrity from a security viewpoint means ensuring that information
  cannot be modified by unauthorized users without detection. We describe this in
  more detail in Section 4.4.1.2.5.
- **Identity:** There is no simple definition for identity—in some senses, you know it
  when you see it. An identity is a software representation of a participant principal
  (person or system), representing the name of that principal (e.g., *jdoe*), any groups
  that principal may belong to (e.g., *department-101*), any roles the principal may
  have (e.g., *StockBroker*), and any relevant attributes of the principal (e.g., *Trading
  Limit=$1000*).
- **Authentication:** The process of verifying the identity of a person or system. There
  are two steps to this process: First, the person or system claims an identity, and second,

presents some verifiable proof of that identity through possession of something that can only belong to that user (such as a password or private key).

- **Authorization:** The process of granting access to a resource based on the identity of the requester, the type of access being requested, the resource, and the security policy of the component that is making the access check. The place in a component where security policy (especially authorization) is enforced is called the **Policy Enforcement Point (PEP).** We also refer to the component that actually evaluates the security policy to see if a particular request to a particular resource should be granted as the **Policy Decision Point (PDP).**

- **Audit:** As defined earlier, securely recording key system events and who initiated them in a chronological log is called an **audit trail.** Auditing is used to reconstruct who did what after the fact.

- **User Registry:** A repository of identity information: users, systems, groups, roles, and other attributes about users. Typically, this is an LDAP directory in an enterprise.

- **Identity provisioning:** A set of management services to simplify the creation and update of user information across user registries.

- **Identity token:** A secure representation of an identity that can be forwarded across components—usually these are digitally signed or encrypted when sent across a network.

- **Identity mapping:** The transformation of an identity token between one format (e.g., an ID and password) to another format.

- **Identity propagation:** The forwarding of an identity token between components. The combination of identity mapping and identity propagation enables **Single Sign-On** (where a user only authenticates once with a single identity but can seamlessly access multiple resources by having his or her identity securely mapped across the different resources).

- **Reverse Proxy:** A regular proxy acts on behalf of a client system. A reverse proxy acts on behalf of server systems, intercepting requests from clients and passing them on only if the requests are properly authenticated, authorized, and audited. Reverse proxies can also propagate and map identities between external domains and internal domains (as we see in Section 4.3.2).

4.3.1 Security in the Context of the MDM Reference Architecture

To guide our discussion, we are going to introduce an extended version of the simplified logical MDM deployment architecture introduced earlier in Figure 4.2.

The deployment model in Figure 4.3 has been scaled down from the reference architecture models in Chapter 3 to help illustrate the points at which security comes into play in an MDM deployment. In particular, we look at the interactions between components of the deployment architecture, the behavior of each individual component, and the interactions across multiple components in several end-to-end scenarios.

In most situations, there is a reverse proxy (HTTP or Web services gateway) in front of either a Web application service (typically a J2EE server) or service consumer such as a portal.

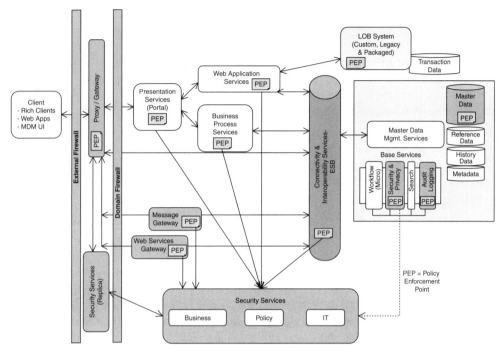

Figure 4.3 MDM Security Logical Architecture.

The Web application service/service consumer uses a set of MDM Services (either directly or through an ESB) to access the Master Data Repository. Data can be either loaded directly to this Master Data Repository or distributed out of this repository.

In a deployment like the one in Figure 4.3, security is enforced at various points (represented by PEP) within the architecture. Furthermore, different types of security will be enforced at the different components of the architecture. The reverse proxy may enforce confidentiality and integrity of information it sends and receives, as well as authentication and auditing of requests. The identity sent to the proxy may need to be propagated to the Web application services server, where the propagated identity needs to be accepted and additional security checks, such as authorization, may be enforced, as well as auditing of the activity. Further security enforcement may be performed by the other components within the architecture as well.

In the next few subsections, we take a look at some of the security considerations for MDM (based on an approach illustrated in [5]) and some potential elements of a proposed solution.

4.3.2 Identity Propagation, Mapping, and Provisioning

In this subsection we look at the challenges surrounding identity and elements of a proposed solution.

4.3.2.1 Challenges

Consider a use case where user John Doe is authenticated at the reverse proxy as *jdoe*. The proxy determines if the user is authorized to access the Web application service/portal server (for simplicity, we just assume the request goes to the Web application service for the rest of this discussion). If so, the request and identity is propagated to the Web application service. This identity, also known as an *authenticated identity,* is then used by the Web application service for its own authorization and auditing.

The Web application service then generates requests to MDM Services where a different identity may be required to access information required in the Master Data Repository. An identity mapping is required to transform *jdoe* into an identity suitable for the Master Data Repository (e.g., *W115403*). There are three different choices of identity mapping:

1. Map *jdoe* into John Doe's identity on the database. This requires a one-to-one mapping of user identities (from the Web application service to the database). This case is suitable when the database needs to perform authorization or auditing using John Doe's identity.

2. Map *jdoe* into an administrative or system identity on the database. This case is suitable when the database only requires a common administrative identity (perhaps the user's role, such as *StockBroker*) for authorization and auditing. The database does not need to know who the user is, but end-to-end auditing is somewhat problematic because the end user identity is not sent to the database—this may be a problem for regulatory compliance.

3. Map *jdoe* to a functional identity—that is, one used to represent the MDM Services layer (at this point, the authorization and audit is at the MDM Services layer). By providing a many-to-one mapping, this case simplifies the deployment topology but places more of the security controls at the MDM Services layer and also does not provide end-to-end auditing.

These cases introduce their own identity management concerns and may not adhere to some of the compliance requirements. Other than identity mapping, there is also an issue of identity token format. For example, *jdoe* may be represented as a Kerberos [6] ticket, whereas the *W115403* identity token may include a RACF® passticket (a one-time password used on z/OS [7]). Thus, there are two challenges: identity mapping and identity token translation.

We can further extend these challenges to the initial and ongoing loading of data into the Master Data Repository, and data distribution from the MDM System as well. Furthermore, there are typically many different user registries that exist in the environment (user registries are omitted from Figure 4.3 for simplicity but are shown in Figure 4.10). An organization might use RACF for the database, Microsoft Active Directory, Tivoli Directory Server, and potentially a number of other LDAP-compatible user registries as well to protect the application server, and so on. User identities created on these systems must be in accordance with policy and be up to date with changing user circumstances.

4.3.2.2 Elements of a Solution

To address the requirements of identity propagation, mapping, and provisioning, an ideal solution would need to include both business and technical aspects. From a business view, we need:

- **Trust Management:** In MDM, we often discuss trust of the master data—where trust means that the master data is accurate, consistent, well managed, and so on. One underlying aspect of trust in MDM is at the security level, where trust, generally speaking, relates to the confidence one organization places in another organization. From an information security perspective, trust is usually managed between groups and organizations by establishing an agreed-upon set of policies and using agreed-upon cryptographic keys to securely assert information shared between the organizations. Managing trust relationships between systems/businesses and reflecting the relationship in business transactions, system deployments, and service policies is fundamental to managing risk and security. At a finer level, trust also needs to be managed between components of the architecture (such as shared keys between two servers).
- **Identity and Access (Authorization) Management:** We need to understand and support the business aspects of management of identities both within an enterprise and across enterprises. From a business perspective, we need to be able to specify the people and systems that should be known to our organization, how these identities are logically grouped, policies on how they authenticate themselves to us, and policies about how these identities are revalidated or revoked. This also includes management of the authorization policies to resources based on identity information (groups the user belongs to, roles the user is in, organizational membership and other attributes) and resource information.

From a technical perspective, we need at least the following two capabilities to build a solution:

- **Identity and Authentication Services:** A common service to create user identities, to validate those identities, and to handle which user identity is passed to downstream systems and how those identities are passed to the downstream systems. One standard in this space is the OASIS Web Services Security *WS-Trust* [8], which defines a mechanism for taking security tokens and validating them, as well as issuing new and different security token exchange to validate and issue credentials within different **trust domains**. Trust domains refer to the scope of an identity—to use the example from earlier in this section, we have one trust domain between the client and the Web application service, and another trust domain between the Web application service and the MDM System. Along with Identity Services, we need a framework for provisioning identities in a consistent way based on business policies. *WS-Provisioning* and Service Provisioning Markup Language (*SPML*) [9] provide a standards-based framework for managing the provisioning and allocation of identity information and system resources within and between organizations.
- **Policy Management:** A mechanism is needed to create and manage security and privacy policies based on business drivers, and to distribute those policies in a consistent manner to all of the relevant components within logical deployment architecture. The policy service would have to support trust, identity, and access policies, both at a business level and a technical level. Having a policy infrastructure makes it possible to support a policy lifecycle, tie into corporate governance and compliance requirements, and increase the confidence that the correct policies are being created and enforced.

4.3.3 Authorization

In this subsection we look at the challenges surrounding authorization and elements of a proposed solution for MDM.

4.3.3.1 Challenges

Authorization is required from every component in the MDM deployment model, from very coarse-grained (application level) to very fine-grained (data level). The challenge with MDM is providing the appropriate level and type of authorization at the different components in the environment. For example, imagine a Web service in a financial institution deployed in the environment represented in Figure 4.3:

- The reverse proxy could implement service level authorization, for example, access to a Web service for insurance quoting.
- The Web application service could implement operation level authorization, for example, access to an operation that retrieves an individual's insurance history. A workflow service running on a Web application service could implement authorization controls dealing with who can initiate a workflow and who can execute individual steps within the workflow.
- The MDM Services may implement authorization to the master data, for example, access to master data specific to the geography of the user making the request, or the party in the Master Data Repository.
- The Master Data Repository may provide authorization based on specific data, for example, access to sensitive personal information of the particular individual, or ownership of a particular record.

This highlights a subset of the policy complexity in authorization: As the authorization gets finer-grained, so does the complexity in consistent policy management. Fine-grained authorization is a fundamental requirement of an MDM Solution—most business processes and regulations require only that the users can access the data related to their jobs. For example, the New Product Introduction (NPI) business pattern (described in Chapter 6 in Section 6.3 and illustrated in Figure 6.1) has a number of pattern level security touch points:

- There are roles for each individual who participates in NPI—and each role should only access the part of the master data required for that role (a category manager should not be able to change the price of a product, for example).
- There is an orderly workflow for NPI—the right master data should be updated only at the specified point in the workflow, and work should be routed only to users in the roles specified in NPI.

Finally, the very nature of master data introduces some other complexities:

- MDM data can be hierarchical—as seen in Figure 6.2 (with master data on electrical devices), master data can be put into hierarchies, and (from a policy perspective) authorization rules might need to propagate down the hierarchy.
- MDM data can have complex relationships. Besides hierarchies based on categories or locations, we can have relationships like householding (as described in Chapter 1) where a group of customers can be treated in a common fashion. Thus, authorization may be needed at the household level. There are also cross-domain relationships

(Customer is associated with multiple Accounts), and the authorization may need to handle situations (as arise in the insurance industry) where the customer core information is shared across the business, but only users who have particular need to access a particular account are granted access to it.

- Users of MDM data can also be tied into an organization or location hierarchy, have specific job roles, and specific attributes that should be examined as part of an authorization decision. Again, referring to Figure 6.2, we might have a rule where only Category Specialists (role) from Germany (location) can update the plug types for German appliances.

4.3.3.2 Elements of a Solution

Once again, we need to address both business and technical requirements for authorization in MDM. At a higher level of the business, we need Identity and Access Management services that let the business manage identities, roles, and groups inside the enterprise, and that link together identities and roles across organizational boundaries (which ties in the Trust Management Services). The new part needed at the business level is the management of authorization policies to MDM resources based on business and regulatory requirements.

At the underlying technical level, we need a standards-based approach to handle specifying, distributing, and enforcing authorization policies across all points in the MDM infrastructure (as shown in Figure 4.3). One standard in this space is eXtensible Access Control Markup Language (XACML)[10]. XACML contains both a common language for expressing access control policies to describe general access control requirements along with a request/response grammar that describes how to form a query to determine if a given action is allowed or not and how to interpret the result (this is the policy decision referred to in Section 4.3).

We also require a policy management mechanism like the one described in Section 4.3.2.2, specifically to handle authorization policies, and tie them into the other security policies (identity, authentication, and audit) as well as the higher-level business policies.

4.3.4 Audit

In this subsection, we look at the challenges surrounding securely keeping track of events across the MDM infrastructure, and the potential components of a solution to address those challenges. We start with the challenges, and then show how they can be addressed.

4.3.4.1 Challenges

For a complete picture of a transaction on master data, audit information must be gathered from every component along the transaction path. A record of critical events needs to be logged and to be available for real-time or later forensic review. These events can be security-specific, such as authentication of a service requester, authorization of a service request, mapping of an identity as a request crosses domains, and so on, or they can be of a more business-related nature, such as recording application access to master data.

There are a number of challenges in implementing consistent auditing:

- Audit trails are usually physically located on the server that generates the event. For example, looking at Figure 4.3, each of the different components, such as the reverse proxy, Web application service, MDM Services, and Master Data Repository, may write events to its own log file. This distribution of audit log information makes it difficult to later trace the events of a transaction end-to-end, because each individual log needs to be accessed and the different entries need to be correlated across the different logs. Additionally, different tools may be required to access this log information.

- The format of each individual audit log is often different on every component that generates an event. This is especially true when there is a heterogeneous mixture of middleware and applications. Real-time or forensic inspection of these logs becomes a difficult process of trying to understand the different log formats and collate related events.
- Implementing a consistent audit policy (deciding which events should be recorded under what circumstances) across the systems is also difficult. Just as each component typically has its own tools for querying the audit log, each one also has a different set of tools to manage the configuration of the audit policy. Ensuring a consistent level of auditing across the components may require a lot of manual configuration in this environment.

These factors show the difficulties that we face in consistently recording the correct events in the audit logs, which impacts our ability to verify the compliance of the end-to-end MDM environment with internal and regulatory policy.

4.3.4.2 Elements of a Solution

To address the requirements of auditing across the MDM environment, we need to address both business and technical concerns. At a business level, we need to be able to see if our organization is complying with our policies and to generate reports that illustrate how well (or poorly) we are doing relative to those policies. We could achieve this by looking at the actual behavior in the environment (captured in the audit logs) and comparing that to the defined security and privacy policies for the organization.

From a technical perspective, we need to be able to generate audit events across all of the relevant components, view all of the events in a consistent fashion, and allow real-time and post-processing of events for reporting. We also need technical mechanisms to support the business requirement of verifying that the actual events match the stated security and privacy policies. As with our other policies, we need to be able to use a policy infrastructure to create and manage audit policies across the MDM environment.

4.3.5 Data Protection

In this subsection, we look at the challenges surrounding data protection and elements of a proposed solution.

4.3.5.1 Challenges

As shown in Figure 4.3 and in the MDM Reference architecture, there are quite a large number of systems that "see" master data as the master data is routed from the repository to the consuming application. This makes it difficult to implement a consistent policy to protect the confidentiality and integrity of the master data as it moves across (and outside) the organization. Furthermore, the type of data protection can vary based on the components—if the master data goes through a message gateway (as seen in Figure 4.3), we may need protection for each individual message. If the connection is point to point (such as from the client to the reverse proxy), transport level security (protecting the link) may be sufficient. The data protection policy dictates what type of protection is required. In addition, data encryption may be used on the database to protect the database from vulnerabilities arising from administrator or physical access to the server hosting the database, or from backups of the master databases. This might be implemented by the native database encryption [11] available on a database. Because master data is highly trusted and valuable data, data protection of master data is a fundamental requirement.

4.3.5.2 Elements of a Solution

From a business perspective, we need to be able to specify security and privacy policies that describe at a business object level how master data should be protected from unauthorized disclosure and modification. At a technical level, these policies need to be translated to implement protection of the master data in transit and at rest. A common set of standards-based Confidentiality and Integrity Services should be used to handle the data protection issues consistently across all components.

The underlying technology for Confidentiality and Integrity Services is encryption. Building on top of that, the most common example of a secure transport service (to protect the data in transit) is SSL. SSL protects the entire data stream between two components at a protocol level below the application layer. SSL is normally the protocol used to protect traffic between a Web browser and Web server.

Protection can also be applied on a per-message basis, as described in the WS-Security specification [12]. The advantage of using WS-Security instead of SSL is that it can provide end-to-end message level security. This means that the messages are protected even if the message traverses through multiple services, or intermediaries. Additionally, WS-Security is independent of the transport layer protocol. It can be used for any SOAP binding, not just for SOAP over HTTP. In addition, confidentiality and integrity services are required for encrypting the data at rest in the database.

Similar to the previous cases, we need a mechanism to create policies based on business drivers and influencing factors (message protection, privacy rules) and to distribute them in a consistent manner to all of the relevant components within the logical deployment architecture. A policy infrastructure is important for keeping track of policy lifecycle management, adhering to governance and compliance requirements, and ensuring the enforcement of correct policies.

4.4 Logical SOA Security Architecture

We can extend the solution aspects from the examples shown to derive a general view of the enterprise logical security architecture built around an SOA model for security services [5]. As with MDM, we use an SOA model to provide a common, consistent set of interfaces across the enterprise, and that allows us to leverage new or existing security services transparently to the consumers of those services. In this architecture, we have three tiers of services, as shown in Figure 4.3:

- **Business Security Services:** These are the higher-level security aspects of the business that need to be specified for successful and secure operation of an enterprise. These are based on a number of influencing factors specific to the industry, such as regulations, business operations, competitive drivers, partnerships, and so on. Business Security Services drive security and privacy policies within an organization that need to be enforced at all relevant parts within the infrastructure. Business Security Services focus on the goals of the business from a security and privacy perspective.
- **Security Policy Management:** Security Policy Management is the link between Business and IT Security Services. It is the single place where the consistent actionable policies are defined and managed, and where those policies are transformed and distributed to the policy decision and enforcement points of the enterprise architecture. These actionable policies are derived from the Business Security layer and then passed down to the IT Security Services.
- **IT Security Services** are the underlying core technical components that deliver security functions as a service to the enterprise components. IT Security Services thus address the *how* of accomplishing the goals specified by the Business Security Services.

As we have seen before, there are multiple security enforcement points within an MDM environment. To correctly implement enterprise security and privacy, these enforcement points must consume a set of consistent, coordinated, business-driven policies distributed from the Security Policy Management services. Because master data management delivers the master data through a common set of shared services, the master data is shared, and the applicable policies to address changing needs, heterogeneous application platforms, and protocols (across organizations and vendors) are easily accommodated. Policies are distributed not only to different enforcement points but also to IT Security Services. These IT Security Services can be either available locally (within a browser) or can be leveraged by centralized services (the proxy taking advantage of external enterprise identity and authentication services, as shown in the policy enforcement point in Figure 4.3).

4.4.1 Capabilities of a Security Reference Model

Based on the security reference architecture we just introduced, we now provide insight into the various capabilities associated with each of these three layers. Within each layer, there are a various number of functions that are described throughout the Subsections 4.4.1.1 to 4.4.1.4.

4.4.1.1 Business Security Services

These services involve managing the security and privacy requirements of the organization. Business Security Services can be classified into six solution categories, as shown in Figure 4.4.

4.4.1.1.1 Compliance and Reporting

Compliance management measures the performance of the underlying business and IT systems relative to the measures established by the business controls and policies. The heart of

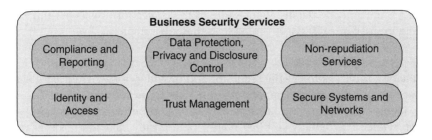

Figure 4.4 Business Security Services.

compliance management is reporting—using audit information and other information about system events to compare the actual behavior of the enterprise systems against the expected behavior based on the higher-level policies.

From a security and privacy perspective, audit records provide the basic data used by compliance management. The compliance function may be a manual process (with auditors inspecting audit trails), or an automated tool could be used to reconcile the business compliance requirements with the raw data extracted from the audit service.

There are multiple views of compliance that can be supported in this service. One is to use the audit data to assess the correctness of the implementation of the security elements of the MDM Solution against the solution design. A second set of compliance views could look for inconsistencies within a particular component, or multiple instances of that component. Finally, the security services themselves need to be reviewed for compliance.

4.4.1.1.2 Data Protection, Privacy, and Disclosure Control

Data protection management deals with protecting business information (in our case, master data) and provides the capabilities for data protection in transit and at rest. It includes policies for which data is to be protected and gives some context on how the data should be protected. Externalizing data handling rules from applications and IT systems can help to simplify the management of data protection.

Business policies are needed to define data protection policies for use in transit and at rest. Beyond the business services, governance and incident handling processes are needed in the event of misuse and for the handling of inappropriate use of data. Business policies are also needed to define sensitivity of data and apply the appropriate message protection and privacy policies.

In the context of information and business information privacy, the disclosure control capability helps reduce privacy compliance costs by automating manual procedures. The system builds trust by:

- Publishing a privacy policy for users to view and understand
- Managing user consent to privacy policies
- Capturing user preferences (such as opt-in to release of PII for certain purposes)
- Delivering detailed reports on access to sensitive information

In Section 4.6, we provide details about some of the drivers of privacy within MDM, and how the disclosure control services can address these requirements.

4.4.1.1.3 Non-Repudiation Services

Non-repudiation services protect the requestor and provider of data from false denials that data has been sent or received. Non-repudiation aims to prevent parties in a communication from falsely denying having taken part in that communication; for example, a non-repudiation service for digitally certified mail should ensure that the sender cannot deny sending the message, and that the receiver cannot deny receiving it.

The Non-Repudiation Services are implemented by cryptographic mechanisms that provide the following functions:

- Proof of origin of data (who sent it)
- Proof of submission of data (the sender sent the message)
- Proof of transport of data (the message was delivered across the network)
- Proof of delivery of data (the message was received)

The Non-Repudiation Service is different from the Confidentiality and Integrity Services, because it does not protect the data itself. Non-repudiation services are usually only deployed in environments where there are large risks if parties claim that they didn't send or receive a message (e.g., trading in financial instruments). Today, the digital signature mechanism is commonly the principal implementation of a non-repudiation service. Non-repudiation is not used very often in practice, so we will say little about it in the rest of this chapter.

4.4.1.1.4 Identity and Access Services

These are business processes for identity that include provisioning and de-provisioning of identities, and user self-care, that make it easy for users to manage their own identity information. It can also include processes and policies for approval of access to IT resources and business resources. In addition, policies for password management are also applicable.

Identity and access deals with identities both within an enterprise as well as across enterprises. It also includes management of access policies to resources based on identity information and resource information.

Identity lifecycle management is important. Identities need to be created, modified over time, and eventually deleted. Some important aspects are:

- **Identity feed:** Often the authoritative source of identity information for internal users is the HR (Human Resources) system. An identity feed from the HR system can indicate to the identity services that changes to the user population have occurred and that provisioning workflows need to be initiated. This is analogous to the initial and ongoing loads of data into an MDM System. If the users are external (such as customers updating or managing their own accounts), an MDM System can serve as the authoritative source of identity used by the identity management system.
- **Approvals:** Before accounts on end systems in the architecture are created or modified, approvals from the appropriate management and resource owners may be required. This can be automated.

- **Re-validation:** Access to systems may need to be approved at regular intervals. The system should collect the appropriate re-validation approvals.
- **User self-care:** Users of the system should be able to perform certain tasks without input from an administrator. For example, they may want to self-enroll to the system, or reset or change their password(s), and so on.
- **Delegated administration:** For approving requests for accounts, and other administrative functions, delegating the action to another user or users is an important function.

4.4.1.1.5 *Trust Management*

From a security perspective, Trust Management addresses trusted relationships between entities like organizations, enterprises, identities, security domains, and systems. These security trust relationships can be system-to-system, business-to-business, and so on.

The business aspect of Trust Management deals with two entities agreeing upon a set of rules to conduct business. These rules include trusted relationship management, liability management, and other legal and contractual aspects.

Business process and policies are required for establishing trusted relationships. These processes may include which legal process to follow and the process used for evaluating liability. This may also include the policies specific to resource access.

The technology aspect deals with managing the infrastructure that supports the capability for establishing trust by cryptographic methods. These include cryptographic key management (strength, key validation, and so on) protocols, attributes, and other technical considerations for establishing trust.

There are multiple ways of establishing trust relationships:

- **Tightly coupled trust relationship:** The trust may be explicit and simple, where consumer and provider are within a single trust domain and thus have the same trust source (such as using the same LDAP for a user registry).
- **Loosely coupled trust relationship:** Another approach where a consumer and target service may have separate trust zones and trusted relationship, or a trusted third-party security token service.

After these relationships are established, the trust management service must maintain them across the lifecycle, because the nature of the relationship may change (over time, external organizations may be considered more trusted) and the underlying cryptographic keys need to be maintained and changed on a regular basis.

4.4.1.1.6 *Secure Systems and Networks*

Business policies are required for intrusion detection (discovering when systems are under attack) and event management is required for ensuring secure systems and networks. Processes must be in place for handling alerts, for engaging the Computer Emergency Response Team (CERT), and for normal housekeeping of scheduled maintenance, patch management, and servicing.

This is a category of technologies and embedded systems that help protect infrastructure servers, systems, and networking resources from security threats. The desire is to protect the systems from external and internal threats such as hackers and malware (malicious software that can destroy or commandeer a computer without the owner's knowledge or consent).

Firewalls are used whenever there is a need to control the traffic between two networks. For example, a firewall is used at the connection of the perimeter of an organization and the Internet, and may provide simple protocol and port filtering, or more complex protocol inspection. Newer types of firewalls, such as XML firewalls, inspect XML and SOAP traffic and provide protection against higher-level protocol-specific attacks.

Operating system security involves the hardening of commercial operating systems so that they provide greater security controls. For example, one issue with UNIX operating systems is that the administrative user (root) has full control, including the ability to delete all security audit logs. In this case, operating system security software can control and securely log the access of root to applications and data, providing improved security, accountability, and separation of duties.

Intrusion detection (host and network) is concerned with detecting anomalies in the use of the operating systems or the network. This might be used, for example, to detect external or internal intrusions to these systems.

Malware detection is used to detect and delete any malware. This might be implemented at the border of the organization and the Internet, and also on individual host operating systems.

Patch management involves applying service patches to operating systems, application middleware, and databases and applications within the environment. These patches may contain security patches that remove vulnerabilities.

4.4.1.2 Information Technology (IT) Security Services

Consistent IT Security Services that can be used by different components of enterprise security runtime are required. For example, service consumers and providers, gateways, proxy servers, application servers, data servers, and operating systems all require access to the IT Security Services. This set of security services should be flexible and should allow for different mechanisms such as user registries or authorization engines to plug in.

The use of common IT Security Services enables a consistent security implementation. It also minimizes development and deployment costs for these security services and for the environment on which these security services are reused. Figure 4.5 shows the IT Security Services that are now discussed in more detail.

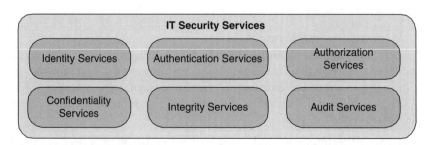

Figure 4.5 IT Security Services.

4.4.1.2.1 Identity Services

The Identity Services are an abstraction layer and framework that provide for managing, sharing, federating, and accessing identity information from a variety of authoritative identity sources. These services also manage relationships between identities and provision identity information to multiple identity systems. The components within the Identity Services include:

- **Identity Foundation:** This core component provides the uniform abstraction layer and administration facility needed to manage, store, and use the information about organizational entities (users, groups, roles), and to provide secure access to such information.

  Identities are stored in user registries, such as an LDAP directory. There may be a number of these in an organization, including a central user registry and separate user registries associated with individual systems. Synchronization of identity information across these user registries may also be required.
- **Identity Provisioning:** This component provisions and de-provisions identity information across multiple user repositories. Identity provisioning systems can implement provisioning policies to ensure that identity information across a wide range of user registries is consistent with that policy. Alternatively, request-based provisioning can be used to suit different business models. A combination of policy- and request-based provisioning may also be used.

  When these systems cross trust domains, such as organizational boundaries, federated provisioning provides the capabilities to provision attributes and other identity information across these boundaries. Standards-based federated provisioning protocols, such as SPML, are then the desired choice.
- **Identity Propagation:** This component can manage identity relationships and mapping to help propagate and transform identities across trust domains. This is necessary for service requests to traverse security domains and be able to flow identity context as part of an end-to-end transactional flow.

4.4.1.2.2 Authentication Services

The Authentication Services provide capabilities to authenticate users. These services may support multiple authentication mechanisms, such as user name/password, hardware token-based, or biometric-based. They may also support protocols such as Kerberos.

The Authentication Services also provide support for identity tokens and security tokens carried in messages, for example, Web services messages. Examples of these tokens are Security Assertion Markup Language (SAML)[13] assertions and user name tokens. The Authentication Services may call on a Security Token Service (STS) for validation of authentication credentials within security tokens or issue new security tokens with authentication credentials.

Authentication may be required at both the service consumer and service provider. Users may be requested to present authentication credentials at the service consumer to verify their identity to the environment. In this case, a security token may then be sent as part of the transaction flow from the service consumer to the service provider. The service provider authenticates the user based on this security token.

Alternatively, if the user has been authenticated at the service consumer, an authenticated identity may be presumed, where the service provider trusts that authentication has already taken place. The service provider then accepts the authenticated identity carried in the identity token, without requiring another authentication. The binding of a SAML-based identity token to a request is one means of asserting an already authenticated identity.

4.4.1.2.3 Authorization Services

Authorization follows authentication. That is, after a user or system has been authenticated, it is then possible to perform authorization. Authorization means making a decision about whether an authenticated identity is allowed to access a resource. An authorization decision is dependent on two key inputs:

- An authorization policy that describes the required security attributes of a user or system that will allow them to access a resource
- An authenticated user or system and his or her list of security attributes

To make an authorization decision, policies need to be in place. These policies are enforced by a Policy Enforcement Point (PEP) that relies on the decision made by a Policy Decision Point (PDP). An example of a PEP is the enterprise service bus, which would allow access to services based on the authorization decisions received from the relevant policy decision point.

Note: Access control is the ability to permit or deny (enforcement) the use of a resource by an entity. An authorization process is used to decide (decision) if an entity is allowed to have access to a resource.

Privacy authorization is used to indicate the runtime function of authorizing access to Personally Identifiable Information (PII) based on a privacy policy. Thus for privacy, the granularity of authorization (e.g., to PII in medical records) can vary, and management of these policies would likely involve users as well as administrators.

4.4.1.2.4 Confidentiality Services

Confidentiality is the security service for ensuring non-disclosure of sensitive information traveling through untrusted communication networks or at rest.

Information at rest includes security, user, and application information. For example, protection of cryptographic keys, passwords, and PII are all important. Beyond cryptography, additional confidentiality enablers include data and application isolation support provided in hardware, operating systems, and middleware.

Confidentiality Services commonly rely on cryptographic techniques such as encryption.

4.4.1.2.5 Integrity Services

Integrity is the security service for detecting unauthorized modification of data due to errors or malicious attack.

Organizations must allow for the use of data by authorized users and applications, as well as the transmission of data for remote processing. Data integrity facilities can indicate whether or not information has been altered.

Integrity Services commonly rely on cryptographic techniques such as message integrity codes, message authentication codes, and digital signatures.

4.4.1.2.6 Audit Services

Audit Services include maintaining detailed, secure logs of critical activities in a business environment. Such critical activities could be related to security, content management, business transactions, and so on. Examples of security-related critical activities that could be audited are login failures or successes, unauthorized or authorized access to protected resources, modification of security policy, noncompliance with a specified security policy, health of security servers, and so on.

An audit logging service provides mechanisms to submit, collect, persistently store, and report on audit data submitted as events. The events may be in a common format, such as Common Base Event (CBE).

Which events are audited and stored is defined in an audit policy. This policy should define which events are important, how long to keep the data, and whether to keep the audit data in a tamper-resistant form. Audit data should be collected for all of the security services.

4.4.1.3 Security Enablers

Security enablers are utilized by the IT Security Services to perform their task. Some examples include technologies such as:

- **Cryptography:** Providing symmetric-key cryptography, public-key cryptography, and one way hashing (or message digest) functions such as AES, Triple DES, RSA, and SHA-1. Implementations of high-level functions such as XML Encryption, XML Signature, SSL, TLS, and so on [1].
  Registries and Repositories: Used to store various user and system information.
  - **Directory:** An application that stores and organizes information about user, application, and network resources. This is typically the underlying repository for a user registry in an enterprise.
  - **Service Registry:** Service registry is a core repository and system of record for service definitions and policies.
  - **Configuration Management Database (CMDB):** A configuration management database is a repository of information related to all of the configuration items (CIs) of an information system. A CMDB helps an organization understand the relationships between these components and track their configuration.
- **Key Management:** This includes the generation, exchange, storage, safeguarding, and replacement of cryptographic keys.
- **Hardware Key Storage:** Related to key management, hardware key storage is used in conjunction with public key cryptography. Key stores may generate and hold private **cryptographic keys.** These can be smart cards (for end users).
- **Cryptographic Hardware:** These are used to implement cryptographic algorithms in hardware modules, usually for performance reasons. The hardware may also provide key storage function (described earlier).

- **Malware Protection:** Malware is software designed to damage or infiltrate a computer system. Examples are worms, trojan horses, spyware, viruses, and adware. Malware protection is used in a network to protect against these threats.
- **Isolation:** Isolation provides the protection from processes interfering with other processes' address space. For example, operating systems protect the address space of their processes, and virtualized environments provide isolation between different operating system environments.
- **Firewalls:** This is a hardware or software device that is configured to permit or deny traffic between two computer network zones. There are many different types of firewalls, including packet filters, stateful filters, and application inspection. They may also perform functions such as Network Address Translation (NAT).
- **Intrusion Detection:** This is a hardware or software device that is used to monitor the flow of network traffic, or access to operating systems.
- **Intrusion Prevention:** Related to intrusion detection, these hardware or software devices react to events that occur. For example, the firewall port may be closed during a denial of service attack.
- **Time:** Time is an important component when making access decisions. Security and identity tokens should be checked for freshness (that they are still within their valid lifetimes), and users with multiple incorrect password attempts should be locked out for some specified time. Time synchronization is important across a distributed environment, including between partner organizations. For example, security tokens exchanged, auditing, and forensics all require time synchronization between systems.
- **Security Event and Incident Management (SEIM):** Related to intrusion detection and prevention, SEIM involves processing of incoming events from various sources to detect security penetration attempts.

4.4.1.4 Policy Management

A policy-driven approach is fundamental to the success of enterprise security architecture. The goals established and driven by the business need to be implemented and enforced by the infrastructure. To achieve this, a complete policy management framework must be in place. There are three aspects to policy, the *abstraction level of policies, lifecycle management of policies,* and the *domains* that *policies* can be applied to:

- **Policy abstraction level:** Policy encompasses all aspects of the solution lifecycle, so there are different levels of abstraction—business policies, architectural policies, and operation policies.
- **Policy management lifecycle:** Policy management lifecycle helps guide the deployment of a policy-based information management system in an enterprise. This includes creation, transformation, enforcement, and monitoring of policies, and makes up all of the different stages of a closed-loop methodology.
- **Policy Domains:** Policy can be applied to multiple domains within an enterprise. Some of the domains include Business, Process, Service, Information, and Nonfunctional.

The three aspects discussed can be combined together in the form of a reference model for Policy, as shown in Figure 4.6.

Security is a part of the overall policy management and will be discussed in the next section.

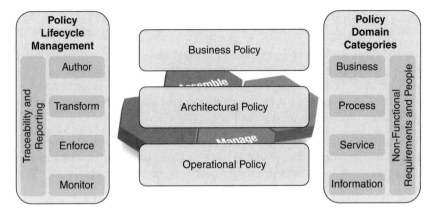

Figure 4.6 Reference Model for Policy Management.

4.4.1.5 Security Policy Management

Effective management of security policies requires a holistic approach that manages security policies throughout the lifecycle of applications. Policies in the context of SOA are the means by which processes and services express the conditions for their use and manage the behavior of the underlying infrastructure in order to secure access to information, provide availability and retention, enable audit, and so on.

Security policy management begins with authoring business policies that are refined to service-specific policies, such as security, performance indicators, metrics, trust policies, and so on. Policies in turn get enforced by the infrastructure when they are configured as requirements that the infrastructure should meet.

Policies are defined and managed centrally. When there is a Service Registry and Repository (SRR) in the environment, security policy management will obtain service definitions and metadata from an SRR and define policies based on that information.

After the effective policy is obtained, the policy is distributed to the PEPs. Policies are distributed in a common format from the security policy management to the enforcement points. Common formats include WS-Policy and XACML. Figure 4.7 highlights the Security Policy Management within the MDM Security Reference Model.

4.4.1.5.1 Policy Administration

Policy administration addresses policy lifecycle management, including creation, maintenance, change, and deletion. This allows business policies to be refined into service-specific policies

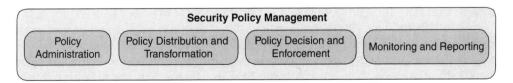

Figure 4.7 Components of Security Policy Management.

such as security, performance indicators, metrics, and trust policies. In turn, they are enforced by the infrastructure when configured as requirements that the infrastructure should meet.

After an application is deployed, application-related policies are administered to reflect changes that occur during the lifetime of the application. Changes to security policies include authorization policy changes (e.g., adding new roles that may access the resources), user management changes (e.g., users assigned to additional user groups), and changes to audit requirements or constraints such as integrity or confidentiality.

Underlying the policy management infrastructure is the ability to articulate policies in terms of metadata of the services. Policy metadata may include information about services, identities, or other contextual information such as strength of encryption.

4.4.1.5.2   Policy Distribution and Transformation

Certain requirements or constraints on the access to the service itself (including authentication, integrity, and confidentiality requirements) should be made known to a requesting client runtime. An organization may be capable of providing a range of options to serve a wide variety of client runtimes (e.g., browser clients, non-browser clients, PDA thin clients). In this case, policies may be published that declare the requirement for a requestor runtime to ensure message confidentiality and provide some evidence of the identity of the requesting user.

The security policies created need to be distributed to the enforcement and decision points within the infrastructure with the appropriate information. The policies may be defined centrally and then distributed to the enforcement points in a canonical format, for example, XACML, WS-Policy[14], or WS-SecurityPolicy[15]. The binding information to enforce the policies is also distributed appropriately. These policies are then transformed at the enforcement point to a local representation so that they can be enforced.

Standards such as WS-Policy and WS-SecurityPolicy provide descriptions of how service consumers and providers can specify their requirements and capabilities in a Web services world. Policy assertions can be defined for use within SOAP messages. Assertions can cover the authentication schemes (the required security tokens and the encryption algorithms), the transport protocol selection, the privacy policy, and information related to the quality of service.

The OASIS XACML provides a markup language to specify access control policies. It can be used as a generic format to store policies, although it also provides a request/response model (based on XML format) for enforcement and decision points. There may also be a policy that controls the transformation and distribution of the policies.

4.4.1.5.3   Policy Decision and Enforcement

Access to a resource is controlled by an appropriate resource manager, which is the logical policy enforcement point (PEP) corresponding to that resource. Administrators will update security policies through the resource managers, or administer policies through appropriate policy decision points (PDPs). In a typical deployment, you can find several enforcement points. Each of these enforcement points can have its own mechanisms to enforce security for the incoming requests.

The enforcements points rely on PDPs to make decisions. These PDPs contain the security policies defined in the infrastructure. The requirements and thus the policies are different, depending on the security domains and the application platforms.

One challenge of having multiple PEPs and PDPs in the infrastructure is that they are often administered by different entities. Providing integrated and centralized decision capabilities reduces the administrative tasks related to policy management.

4.4.1.5.4   Monitoring and Reporting

Closely linked to the decision and enforcement of these policies is the infrastructure to help monitor the behavior of system elements throughout the lifecycle of the business. When managing security policies, it is necessary to adhere to changing corporate business security policies and industry and government regulations, as well as compliance requirements. In addition to these reasons to change, another input factor is the discovery of vulnerabilities and new risks that may be identified through solution monitoring activities or through external notification of software vulnerabilities from CERT.

It is necessary to keep track of current policies, historic policies, and the assessment of compliance of lower-level policies against corporate policies. Traceability of policies from high-level business policies to enforced configurations and runtime requirements is necessary to verify what the runtime behavior is based on. This helps identify policy changes that occur and can help manage accountability of policy changes. Security policies need to be developed and deployed throughout the stages of the lifecycle of an application.

Changes to security policies must be tightly controlled; access to them should be traced and audit trails supplied so that the processes may be adequately monitored.

4.4.2   IBM SOA Security Reference Model

The IBM SOA Security Reference Model [5]—as shown in Figure 4.8—is derived from the list of capabilities previously discussed, and we use this reference model as a guide for MDM security. A reference model can help to address requirements and lead to a logical architecture, and then to a physical architecture, with products and technologies mapped to solve the problem at hand.

SOA security is applicable to all layers of an SOA model: across infrastructure, application, business services, and development services. It is applicable in serving the needs of a service consumer. Based on the capabilities discussed in the previous sections, the reference model can be viewed in terms of three layers of abstraction: Business Security Services, IT Security Services, and Security Policy Management. There are also Security Enablers for providing security functions to the IT Security Services.

4.5   Applying the Security Reference Model to MDM

We can now use the security reference model and the security architecture decision guidelines as a template to recommend how to apply the different business and IT Security Services, along with the security policy management and security enablers, to the MDM Reference Architecture (as described in Chapter 3). We start with understanding the

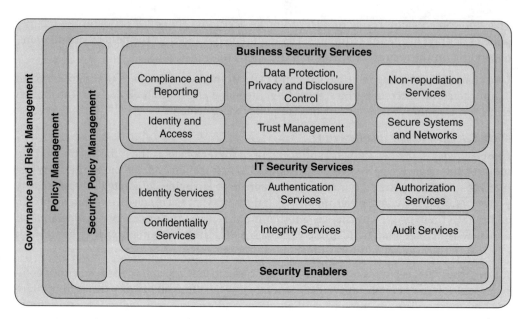

Figure 4.8   SOA Security Reference Model.

security-relevant changes to the application environment when introducing MDM (recapitulating some of the challenges noted in Section 4.3), and then explore the broader set of security service integration issues with regard to MDM.

4.5.1   Security Requirements

Prior to deploying MDM, the existing applications were developed with assumptions and constraints in mind about how they accessed master data, now additional requirements emerge due to the reference architecture described in Chapter 3, along with the MDM architecture patterns described in Chapter 5. The most common change is that applications will now go through a set of MDM Services to access the master data instead of accessing the individual application databases directly.

Beyond just moving to MDM, applications often undergo other significant changes, such that many of the original assumptions may no longer be true. So additional measures need to be taken to safeguard the information and protect the transactions. Here are a list of assumptions that need to be reevaluated when moving to master data:

- The application may have been developed for internal use only, but now having exposure as a Web service and access from multiple channels, there are no longer tight controls about where and how this information is being used. There may be a requirement to provide adequate measures to protect the information both in transit and at rest. Depending upon how and where this information is being accessed, either message level or transport level security can be applied.

- The underlying security mechanisms used to protect the existing application databases is often different from the techniques used to protect the master data repositories. For example, the Master Data Repository could use an LDAP directory as its user registry, and use XACML for authorization, while the application databases such as DB2 can use a mainframe identity and authorization provider like RACF. In such cases, there needs to be a mapping of security context and secure propagation of that context so that appropriate security controls are applied. We may also need to manage the same user identity between multiple identity stores (RACF, LDAP, Microsoft Active Directory, and so on). This is required for the life-cycle of the user. An identity provisioning solution is required.
- In the original architecture, auditing may have taken place only on the application. Every action taken by the user has been audited using the user's identity. The new architecture may have the requirement to audit information at multiple places for compliance reasons and drive the need for additional reports. For example, auditing along the entire request chain rather than just at the application may be required. There is a requirement for multiple authorization checks, because the existing underlying database may not know the context under which the information will be used. It is necessary to provide additional authorization capabilities at the services intermediary. For MDM, a financial application user may not be able to look at or update sensitive information such as Social Security Number or credit card, but a customer service representative may be able to do so. One technique for mitigation here is to group sensitive related attributes into *attribute groups* and specify policies against the attribute groups.
- It is necessary to provide the user with a seamless experience even when introducing intermediaries. For example, users should not need to input authentication details for the database if they are already authenticated at the service consumer. This requires that trust relationships be established along the request chain so that identity can be propagated.

The mediation between the line of business applications and the underlying master data, which is more flexible and dynamic, is implemented by the MDM Services. The MDM Services need to provide the ad hoc processing of messages that include security capabilities. Let's take a look at some more requirements to provide security mediation in MDM Services.

- There is a need to make sure the MDM Services are identity aware so that an identity can be propagated from the consumer to the provider in a seamless but secure fashion. This may require both identity mediation and token transformation along the MDM processing path.
- Authorization must be enforced in the MDM Services, especially where the authorization policy may depend on the contents of the information or the composition of a series of information. In other words, while it may be authorized for a user to access information A or information B, it may not be permitted for the user to access information A and B together at the same time. This is known as **separation of duty**. For example, an agent may be able to initiate the request to create an account, but a supervisor has to approve the action.

- **Confidentiality** and **integrity** of the transaction need to be maintained through the MDM transaction and into the database layer.

  Because the MDM *Services* and *data layers* are concentration points for information requests, they may need to be hardened to protect them from attack. This includes hardening the underlying operating system, databases, and network.

  It is important that MDM audit events be logged and be available for compliance, reporting, and the overall governance of the solution.

  The MDM Services layer has to access the underlying Master Data Repository, and in Registry style, needs to access back-end systems. We need to ensure that the credentials that are used here are (a) protected from theft, and (b) limited to the scope they need.

4.5.2 Business Security Services

The following Business Security Services define *what* the business requires when opening up its application functionality through the MDM scenario.

4.5.2.1 Compliance and Reporting

Because the original assumption of a closed environment no longer holds, the business needs to be sure that it is still compliant with regulatory and business policy. For example, the organization may need to implement a process to gather audit events from various points along the request path. These events are then available for compliance reporting. The business has to provide new reports to meet compliance requirements discussed earlier, such as the Sarbanes-Oxley Act (SOX) or Payment Card Industry Data Security Standard (PCI-DSS).

Business information about combinations of different databases that could constitute a compliance risk is required. Business guidelines need to be in place to ensure that composite information is not inadvertently created that allows greater access than was intended for particular consumer channels and groups of users.

4.5.2.2 Data Protection, Privacy, and Disclosure Control

The business needs to provide the classification of data being merged in this scenario. For example, parts of the data may be very sensitive for privacy or other business reasons and must be protected.

It may therefore become a business requirement to protect data in transit from unauthorized disclosure. Data then passes through the service intermediary and over untrusted networks. The business may need to have the data protected throughout the entire request path.

Procedures must be in place in this pattern, because the MDM Services are effectively a hub through which all data requests pass, and as such, they connect a variety of service consumers and data providers that may be both internal and external. These parties will have a variety of business requirements as they relate to data protection, privacy, and disclosure. It is important to ensure that those requirements are respected when service requests are mediated. For example, sensitive consumer data that has been encrypted at the message level must not inadvertently be sent to an external provider over an insecure channel after it has been decrypted at the MDM Services for processing.

4.5.2.3 Non-Repudiation Services

The business requirements surrounding non-repudiation must be defined. The business should list which transactions fall into this category. For example, the business may require all transactions of a particular type to have non-repudiation protection. The business may be satisfied with log file entries of events to be used as non-repudiation evidence. Alternatively, the business may require stronger mechanisms, such as digital signatures.

A combination of multiple non-repudiation records may be required to associate an incoming request with the events that occurred on a set of data providers. From the point of view of the service consumer, it is important evidence to record that the MDM Services has responded to the request. Again, non-repudiation is not typically implemented in production systems.

4.5.2.4 Identity and Access

The business needs to define the requirements surrounding user lifecycle management. For example, the business may prefer a policy-based approach to controlling user identity and access, especially because the business is no longer working under a closed access model. The definition of the authorization policy is the key input from the business. For example, the business may define that only certain partners can get access to information, and possibly under specific conditions.

While traversing the MDM Services it is important to maintain the user context. We need to be able to pass the identity of a user for a particular service request from the service consumer through the MDM Services and to the relevant data provider. The identity may need to be mapped and the token representing the user identity transformed as part of the request. A business decision also needs to be made as to whether such an identity mapping should be made on a one-to-one or many-to-one basis. This decision depends on the level of authorization and accountability that is required for the service request. The definition of authorization policy is particularly important in order to adequately control how services are orchestrated together. An organization needs to prevent data accidentally being combined in a way not intended or permitted for business reasons.

The definition of authorization policy is particularly important in order to adequately control how data elements are orchestrated together. An organization needs to prevent data accidentally being combined and used in a way not intended or permitted for business reasons.

4.5.2.5 Trust Management

When externalizing an application, the business must define which external parties are to be partners. For example, a set of partners for an insurance company may be able to access services for new insurance applications. The business needs to define the specifics of the relationship, such as information that has to be exchanged in order to establish trust and define the length and extent of the relationship.

We have to consider relationships between the service consumers and the MDM Services as well as between the MDM Services and the data providers. There have to be procedures in place to accommodate these multiple trust relationships so that MDM Services can maintain them. For example, the trust relationship with one data provider may be very different from that with another data provider.

4.5.2.6 Secure Systems and Networks

The business defines the requirements surrounding secure networks. If the data is sensitive, the business may mandate strong secure network technology be in place before the existing application can be opened up for access. For example, the business may mandate end-to-end protection of messages and a secure Internet-facing network infrastructure such as an IPsec VPN.

There are multiple protocols and transport mechanisms to consider as well as the fact that requests may traverse multiple network security zones and access different back-end systems that could be internal, or external and perhaps outsourced to a less trusted source. Procedures need to be in place to contend with and protect against malware and viruses being introduced at this concentration point in the architecture.

4.5.3 IT Security Services

In this section we introduce all relevant security services required by the MDM reference architecture as described in Chapter 3. For example, the Directory Services Master component shown in Figure 3.15 in Chapter 3 depicting the enterprise MDM component model will leverage authentication services that we introduce in Subsection 4.5.3.2.

4.5.3.1 Identity Services

Let's look at the two particular Identity Services—identity provisioning and identity propagation—as they apply to the MDM-based architecture. But first, let's look at the underlying identity foundation that supports identity provisioning and propagation.

4.5.3.1.1 Identity Foundation

It is typical that in most environments there will be a number of user registries and repositories, as we have previously discussed; this number is likely to be increased through the introduction of the MDM Services as data elements are combined. There will be an enterprise user repository containing identity information that is common to many applications and then a number of individual user repositories, typically one for each of the applications. The identity example of Joe Smith is spread across these repositories, with his identity being represented in many different forms in every one of them; for example, the identity could be *homejoe* at the service consumer, *jsmith* at the data provider, *joesmith* in the Master Data Repository, and *joey1234* in the mainframe.

Solutions need to cater to the need for some user repository synchronization. This is necessary when identity information needs to be kept up to date between these user repositories. For example, an update of a user home address at one data provider might need to be updated in other data provider repositories as well.

4.5.3.1.2 Identity Provisioning

To enable a policy-based approach to managing the identities across user repositories, an identity provisioning solution can be implemented. A central provisioning service creates, modifies, and deletes identity information across the user repositories. The advantage of an identity provisioning approach is that it allows the central definition of provisioning policies and a consistent implementation. In the federated provisioning case, where the provisioning needs to span administrative domains, open standards-based provisioning technology such as WS-Provisioning and SPML can be used.

4.5.3.1.3   Identity Propagation

This is an important aspect of this scenario, because as part of the request flow from service consumer to provider through the ESB, the user context needs to be maintained and the security of the identity information ensured. For example, consider a use case where a request is coming from an internal service consumer (such as a browser-based Web application) using an MDM Service to access master data, as shown in Figure 4.9. The request arrives carrying a username token that carries identity information for the user *homejoe*. The MDM Services calls the Security Token Service (STS) provided by a product like Tivoli Federated Identity Manager to exchange the security token format to one supported by the service provider. In this example, the username token is exchanged for a SAML token. In addition to changing token type, the Federated Identity Manager STS can map the incoming

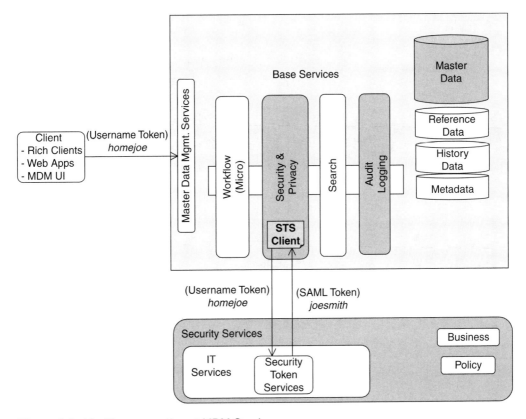

Figure 4.9   Identity propagation at MDM Services.

identity information to one suitable for the Master Data Repository, for example, the *home-joe* identity is mapped to the service provider identity of *joesmith*.

4.5.3.2   Authentication Services

There are several use cases for authentication. First, it is true to say that authentication often occurs at the boundary, especially for externally facing services. In general, the MDM is an intranet component and would rely on a proxy or gateway to perform the main authentication step and to receive a trusted form of the identity from it. However, there are cases where there can be a need for reauthentication or to provide authentication for requests originated from within the intranet.

The MDM Services may need to use the authentication service to authenticate the credentials supplied by the service consumer (one example of this is shown in Figure 4.10) before passing the service request on to the data provider. It is also likely that these credentials are in a different form than the back-end expects; again, this can be resolved by a WS-Trust Security Token Service (STS).

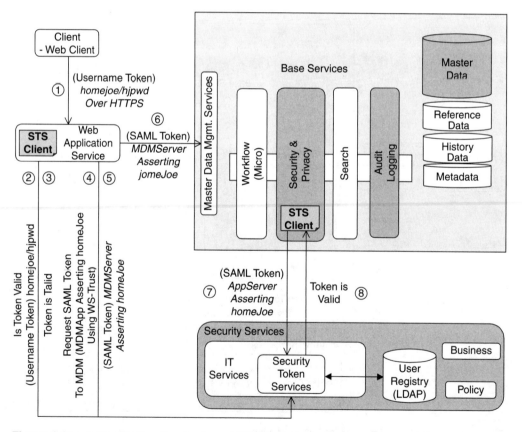

Figure 4.10   Authentication Service in an MDM Environment.

In Figure 4.10, we show a simplified transaction (no proxy or firewalls) that illustrates authentication, identity transformation, and identity propagation across an MDM transaction with the following steps:

1. The user initiates a connection to a Web application service and authenticates to the Web application service with the identity *homejoe* and password *hjpasswd* across a secure link.

2. The Web application service uses the STS to validate *homejoe/hjpasswd*.

3. The STS validates the identity against the user registry and informs the Web application service that *homejoe/hjpasswd* is valid.

4. The Web application wants to issue a transaction on the MDM System on behalf of the user. However, the MDM Services support only SAML tokens, so prior to making the Web services call, the Web application service requests a SAML token from the STS. The request is for a token indicating that the request comes from an intermediary (*MDMApp*) and that the intermediary is asserting that the original request comes from *homejoe*.

5. The STS verifies that the request comes from *MDMApp*, and that the policies of the STS allow it to issue a SAML token asserting the identity of *homejoe* for a request forwarded by *MDMApp*. The STS then issues the SAML token to the Web application service.

6. The Web application service makes the service call to MDM, passing in the SAML token.

7. The MDM Services invoke the Security and Privacy Services, which in turn call the STS to validate the received SAML token.

8. The STS validates the SAML token and informs the MDM security layer that the token is valid.

At this point, the MDM layer knows who made the request, but the request may not be allowed based on authorization policies (as we describe in the next section).

4.5.3.3 Authorization Services
The first application of the authorization services is shown in Figure 4.11. Requests that come in from the external service consumer must be authorized before being granted access to the master data. The MDM SOA Services Layer and the MDM SOA Services Implementation call out to the authorization services provided by external authorization providers to ensure these incoming requests are authorized. Any requests that are not authorized will be rejected.

There are four authorization service aspects within the scenario.

1. **Service Consumer:** For the portal and internal service consumers, authorization can be implemented to control what the user can see and do. In Figure 4.11, the Web application acts as the service consumer. For example, an Item Specialist might only be given menu choices appropriate to updating items—and not shown any menu choices for modifying a product hierarchy (because that is the responsibility

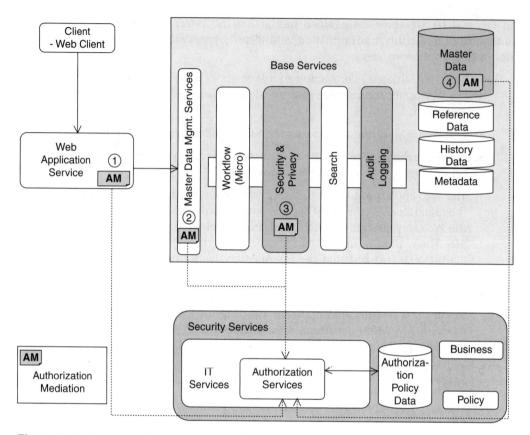

Figure 4.11   Multiple authorizations in an MDM architecture.

of Category Managers). This authorization can be externalized to the security service or alternatively implemented internally.

2. **MDM SOA Services Layer:** The authorization mediation of the MDM Services can
   call out to the authorization service to implement service-level authorization. This
   level of authorization controls who can call into a service operation.

3. **MDM Services Implementation:** In most cases, there will be finer-grained authorization at the internal MDM Services implementation level controlling what the
   user is allowed to do. Authorization can be externalized or performed within the
   MDM Services implementation. The MDM Services Implementation is the policy
   enforcement point for complex rules such as "Only the issuing insurance agent can
   update policy holder details" or "Updates to the English text description fields for
   electronic products can only be made by marketing managers based in the United
   States." The MDM Services layers and the MDM data must be properly designed to
   allow specification and enforcement of rules that are both role-based (like "marketing manager") and data-driven ("issuing insurance agent.")

In the MDM Reference Architecture in Chapter 3, we describe three internal authorization mechanisms that enforce MDM-relevant authorization policies:

- **Transactional Authorization:** This mechanism decides which transactions can be executed by a given role.
- **Rules of Visibility (RoV):** RoV determines which individual records can be accessed by a user based on the identity of the user, the contents of the record, and the rules. For example, we could have a rule that says an Agent (role) can only update customers where the agent is the agent of record (data).
- **Data Entitlements:** Data Entitlements enforce access to particular elements of an individual master data record. For example, marketing people may be able to see the address of customers but not their credit card numbers or Social Security Numbers.

4. **Master Data Repositories:** At this layer, requests are authorized to ensure that only trusted connections are allowed to directly access the master data. This is usually limited to requests from the MDM Services implementation (both query and update), MDM Data Sources (which may be limited to the domain of master data they can update), and MDM Data Consumers (which can only read master data). This level of authorization is most commonly implemented directly at the database layer, but an external authorization service may be used to push down database-specific authorization policy into the master data databases.

XACML is the emerging standard that may be leveraged to consolidate authorization management and enforcement.

4.5.3.4 Confidentiality Services

Data needs to be protected both at rest and in transit. A variety of cryptographic algorithms can be used to product data at rest. Techniques like database encryption should be leveraged to achieve this.

The MDM architecture adds many more network links between the user and data provider, and these should be protected. Protecting message content from being disclosed is the primary concern of this service. This is usually achieved by encrypting the message body, header, or any combination of these parts. Both SSL and WS-Security can be used to protect data in transit.

The decision whether to use SSL and/or WS-Security depends on the business drivers and the information that is being protected. Similarly, the decision whether to encrypt the individual databases or not is also based on business drivers.

Data from both service consumers and providers that are mediated through the MDM Services need to be protected from disclosure. This can be achieved by leveraging Confidentiality Services and choosing message-level security using WS-Security and/or transport-level security with SSL/TLS. Decisions about which method is appropriate depend upon the nature of the service being orchestrated and the business requirements. For example, if the MDM Services is expecting signed and encrypted messages from an external data provider, the service provider must be aware of this so that outbound messages are correctly prepared before sending. If the MDM Services then requires communication with one or more service providers to provide a response to the service consumer, MDM Services needs to be aware of message protection policies for interacting with those service providers.

Data protection, in reality, will be required wherever there is sensitive data, including passwords, cryptographic keys, configuration files, and so on.

4.5.3.5 Integrity Services

Protecting message content from being modified without detection, being sure of its origin and protecting against message replays are the primary concerns of these services. This is usually achieved by digitally signing the message body, header elements such as security token, or any combination of these parts in a WS-Security message. Many security tokens defined in WS-Security have the ability to include a data element such as a nonce to prevent reuse of a security token to protect against exploits that reuse a security token.

Integrity needs to be guaranteed over a series of transactions/mediations. Because we are traversing multiple links, information needs to be gathered from a variety of sources in order to build a complete picture of the integrity of a new offering. The MDM Services can leverage Integrity Services to safeguard the data from both service consumers and providers that are mediated through the MDM Services. A decision about which method is appropriate depends upon the nature of the service being orchestrated and the business requirements.

4.5.3.6 Audit Services

The Audit Services in the IT Security Services are in place to understand the operation of the security environment by collecting audit information and reporting on this information. When the user is directly connecting to a database, all information is collected at the database. For example, database- and application-specific logs may be created.

In the case of the MDM scenario, as shown in Figure 4.12, audit records are collected along the request path, at all points that are necessary. These can be processed and stored in a format ready for reporting. In the figure, a centralized audit service is used to collate, process, and report on the audit data. At a database layer, you may also introduce audit appliances that monitor database accesses at the network layer and consolidate database audit events into a consistent format inside the appliance.

We also need to consider a wider picture. Master data requests are being mediated through the MDM Services. This provides an opportunity to implement a comprehensive audit trail of all master data requests and activities that pass through the MDM Services. We may need to audit at the MDM Services because:

- Data providers may have weak or no audit facilities.
- Service consumers may need this audit information.

We may need to prove that there have been no abuses of separation-of-duty concerns. Because requests in this scenario traverse through the MDM Services, it provides an ideal audit point in the infrastructure.

4.5.4 Security Enablers

Typical Security Enablers used in MDM-based architecture include:

- **Cryptography:** Signing and encryption libraries such as XML Signature and XML Encryption enable higher-level message protection services that are a part of a WS-Security runtime.

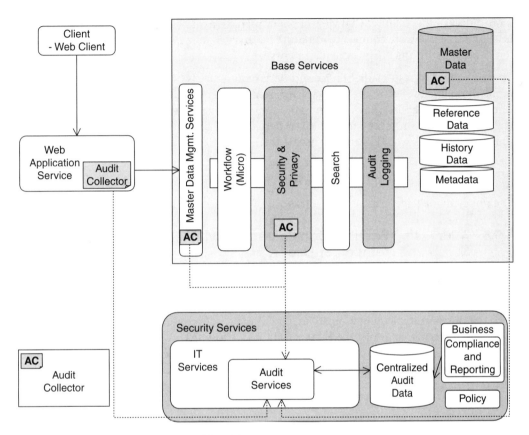

Figure 4.12   Audit services for MDM architecture.

- **Intrusion protection:** An intrusion detection service may be deployed on the Application Server to protect the server from malware and intrusion.
- **Directory:** As discussed earlier, a Directory Server is used as the directory for the intermediary that exposes the service.
- **Firewalls:** Firewalls provide network isolation of the databases and limit the traffic (origins and protocols) permitted to access the databases. Firewalls could also be used around the intermediary that exposes the service itself.
- **Key Management:** This includes the generation, exchange, storage, safeguarding, and replacement of cryptographic keys.
- **Malware protection:** An antivirus Server may be deployed on the Application Server to protect the server from malware.

4.5.5   Security Policy Management

Security Policy Management bridges business and IT Security Services, by providing infra-structure for creating business policies and distributing them to IT Security Services.

Before the introduction of MDM-based architecture, the various data providers were respon-sible for managing their own policies; their application policies were isolated and much more binary in their nature. That view of policy management needs to change in this scenario, because the services are composite in nature but may change in a much more dynamic fashion depending on the business requirements.

There is a need to respect the service interface requirements of these new services. Message protection policies specify the mechanisms, rules, and constraints about how a service consumer will use a service provider. The MDM Services is an intermediary; service consumers and data providers interact with the MDM Services and not with each other, so the message protection policies would need to describe the interactions between:

- Service consumer and MDM Services
- MDM Services and data provider

The policy management must deal with both of these interactions.

4.5.6 Addressing Security Considerations with MDM Implementation Styles and Methods of Use

From a component perspective in the MDM Logical Security Architecture, the different MDM Implementation Styles don't appear to differ much in how they are protected and how they consume the security services. However, there are a few security aspects that differ in practice with the different implementation styles. One thing that is common is that initial and ongoing loads of master data into the Master Data Repository from other sources require a high level of privilege for the processes that are doing the loads (because these processes could update all of the master data). The credentials used for these processes need to be well protected (perhaps stored in the cryptographic hardware described in Section 4.4.1.3), and the load processes should be subject to stringent audit and regular reviews for compliance.

4.5.6.1 Consolidation Style

Because Consolidation is primarily used for read access, the main concerns are disclosure of information and integrity of the information used for reporting. For integrity, the security measures described on the initial and ongoing loads should address those concerns. For disclosure of information, authorization policies that limit access to the master data to only authorized business users need to be created and then pushed down for enforcement to the MDM Security and Privacy Services.

4.5.6.2 Registry Style

Registry style MDM leaves the master data in the different underlying existing application repositories of master data. The Registry MDM System needs an identity and credentials to access to the underlying repositories. This can serve as a back door into the master data, so the identity and credentials should be protected similarly to how identities and credentials used to load master data are protected. Furthermore, applications may access both the MDM Registry and the underlying application repositories of master data. Without a coordinated Identity, Access, and Audit strategy, there may be inconsistencies in the way the master data is protected, so we recommend using the Business Security Services to ensure that there are no gaps that can be exploited when different people manage the underlying security across the different systems.

4.5.6.3 Coexistence Style

Coexistence Style MDM reduces the number of places where applications have to go to consume master data, which provides a corresponding simplification of the security management. On the other hand, because Coexistence style also pushes data into other application master data repositories, the consolidated hub also requires a set of identities and credentials similar to those in the Registry style. Furthermore, these identities and credentials are even more sensitive, because they are updating downstream systems, so they need to be placed under the same security measures as identities and credentials used to load data into an MDM System.

4.5.6.4 Transaction Style

Transaction Style MDM provides a single point of control for master data, so the management of the security is both easier and more critical (as we described in the introductory section of this chapter). The scale of the amount of data and number of users accessing it will likely be quite large, again making it mandatory to use the higher-level Business Security Services to drive security policy down to the MDM Security and Privacy Services (or to an externalized policy decision point for MDM). In particular, we should use the Identity Services to manage identities and assignments to roles (like the ones used in NPI, described in Chapter 6, in Section 6.3), and assign those roles and their accesses to the underlying master data, as we describe in Section 4.3.3.1.

4.5.6.5 Security Aspects of Methods of Use of MDM Data

As a result of discussing the different implementation styles, we have by implication discussed the security aspects of the **analytical** and **operational** methods of use. The **collaborative style** of MDM introduces a set of workflow security concerns:

- Ensuring that the steps of authored master data are routed in order to prevent checks and balances from being bypassed
- Ensuring that users are assigned to the proper roles in a workflow associated with the master data, to limit their access to only what they need
- Ensuring that there are controls in place to deal with users who have multiple conflicting roles (like managers who can approve employee travel expenses not being able to approve their own travel)

The underlying micro-workflow component in MDM must invoke the Security and Privacy Services to mitigate against these threats. Similarly, any external business process services must do the same. Attempted violations of policies in these areas should be audited and reported on.

4.6 Privacy

As we discussed in the section on risks, privacy is somewhat orthogonal to security, with the organization having custodial duties for the PII. MDM Systems that have Party data (customer and patient) are quite sensitive to privacy concerns and regulations. Key privacy regulations such as EU Directive 95/46/EC, HIPAA, and California Senate Bill 1386 are described in detail in Appendix C. The EU directive defines three participants in data privacy:

- Data subjects, the people whose personal information is being collected.
- Data collectors, the organization collecting, using, storing, and protecting PII. One person at the organization is given a specific privacy-responsible role, such as chief privacy officer.
- Data commissioners, the government officials responsible for supervising the execution of privacy regulations.

PII collected by organizations subject to EU regulations need to follow a set of principles to ensure the privacy, accuracy, and fair use of the PII:

- **Transparency:** The person whose sensitive personal data is being collected must be notified of the collection and processing of that information.
- **Legitimate Purpose:** The data collected must be used only for valid reasons (such as legal and contractual obligations, or other requests that have been agreed to by the data subject) and must be kept safe and secure.
- **Proportionality:** The amount and type of data collected should be minimized to only that which is needed for the particular purpose, and the data should be maintained only as long as needed and checked to make sure that it is valid and accurate.

In HIPAA, these principles are realized by the creation of explicit privacy policies that must be disclosed to and agreed upon by the patient, and by ensuring that sensitive patient information is kept to a minimum, disclosed only to those who need to know it, and protected from reasonably predictable threats. A solution like the Master Patient Index (MPI), described in Chapter 7, in Section 7.2, is very helpful to addressing HIPAA requirements, because sensitive patient master data can be migrated to a single authoritative source (the MDM System). The MPI solution can take advantage of the following security services described in this chapter, and in Chapter 3, to enforce the HIPAA security requirements:

- Transactional Authorization can be used to ensure only those medical staff in the proper roles can read or update the patient's master data.
- Rules of Visibility and Data Entitlements can be configured to limit the particular records and data elements that a particular user or role can see or update. For example, a clerk should not be able to read or update diagnostic information about a patient but should be able to read the patient's insurance information. Similarly, in theory, doctors in a clinic should only be able to read diagnostic information about their own patients. Often, this security policy is not enforced so that critical patient information can be accessed in an emergency.
- Audit is especially crucial given that fine-grained authorization (doctors accessing information only on their patients) may not always be enforced. Audit trails can then be used in the event of a breach (to see who violated the stated policy) or to show general compliance to policies.
- Confidentiality services should be used to protect the data at rest in the master data repositories and as it flows between the users and the data providers.

In most cases, use of the security services as described in the MPI scenario can address the full range of privacy requirements and regulations. However, one particular privacy concern is driven by user choice—privacy preferences. Customers, patients, employees, or other parties can inform the enterprise how and under what circumstances they should be contacted by your enterprise. Parties who wish to limit the contact initiated often opt out of notifications from the enterprise. These privacy preferences need to be stored in the MDM System and communicated to and honored by consuming applications.

Data-driven authorization may not be suitable for privacy preferences, because the authorization services may not be able to understand the intent and context of the enterprise user in consuming the master data—a legitimate user may be using the master data at cross-purposes from the stated privacy preferences. So it is up to the application to communicate the privacy preferences stored in the master data to the user and to let the combination of the user and application determine if the master data is being used consistently with the privacy preferences. In the Business Security Services, we describe a set of disclosure control services for this purpose, as well as for publishing privacy policies.

One of the more challenging problems in the proper handling of PII is ensuring that customer data is not exposed to software developers and testers. In order to properly test an MDM environment, developers and testers would prefer to use data that represents the real customer data used in a production environment rather than randomly generated data that may not have the same characteristics as production data. However, the controls over data in a test environment are necessarily more lax than those in production, and simply moving PII from production to development and test environments opens up the organization to breaches of PII. A simplistic approach to addressing this is to remove all identifying data from the test data set (as recommended by HIPAA). However, this makes the resulting test data practically useless.

A better technique to address this problem is known as **data de-identification** [16] (sometimes called **data masking**). Data masking uses a combination of statistical algorithms to transform live production data into a data set that maintains the demographic characteristics of the original data but can no longer be mapped back into the original sensitive PII. An example of masked data is shown in Table 4.2.

Table 4.2 Production Data Transformed into Masked Test Data

Record Fields	Original Data	Masked Data
Name	Ryan Keys	Lee Scott
Street Address	130 Longhorn Drive	4138 Bevo Boulevard
City	Austin	Austin
State	Texas	Texas
Postal Code	78712	78731
Sex	Male	Male
Social Security Number	911-32-9870	949-41-0453

In this example, the gender, city, and state demographics are preserved between production and test, but name, street address, postal code, and Social Security Number are changed to remove the identifying information that can be used for identity theft. The algorithms used in data masking can take names and map them into names that are similar in ethnicity, and map addresses to others that are geographically similar. Masked data can also be used for other purposes than testing, in particular, customer analysis, so it is critical to maintain the statistical similarity between the original data and the masked data. Additionally, data masking can also be used (as for HIPAA) to remove fields that are not required in test systems. Because MDM aggregates sensitive personal information across multiple business processes, we recommend using data masking for moving production data to test and when moving production data to other systems that need statistically related data for analysis but can use de-identified data.

Conclusion

Deploying security and privacy protections to an MDM environment is critical in order to reduce risks surrounding the deliberate or inadvertent disclosure, alteration, or destruction of master data, as well as to comply with regulations and industry standards surrounding control of sensitive financial and personal information found in master data. The first step in protecting your master data is to understand the potential risks to your master data by means of a risk management process. Next, use a deployment model of your master data environment to visualize where the vulnerabilities and threats associated with the risks can manifest themselves in your MDM deployment. Finally, you can use the enterprise security reference architecture and security services to apply the appropriate controls and common security technologies to address those risks.

References

1. Ferguson, N., and Schneier, B. 2003. *Practical Cryptography*. Indianapolis, IN: Wiley Publishing.
2. Harris, S. 2006. *Risk Management Guide*. Retrieved 03/20/2008 from techtarget.com: http://searchsecurity.techtarget.com/tip/1,289483,sid14_gci1158732,00.html#guide.
3. Identity Theft Resource Center. 2007. *Identity Theft Resource Center Breach Report 2007*. Retrieved 03/20/2008 from idtheftcenter.org: http://www.idtheftcenter.org/ITRC%20Breach%20Report%202007.pdf.
4. Brenner, B. 2008. *Societe Generale: A Cautionary Tale of Insider Threats*. Retrieved 03/20/2008 from techtarget.com: http://searchsecurity.techtarget.com/news/article/0,289142,sid14_gci1296774,00.html?track=NL-358&ad=617985&asrc=EM_NLN_2978300&uid=1456557.
5. Buecker, A., Ashley, P., Borrett, M., Lu, M., Muppidi, S., and Readshaw, N. 2007. *Understanding SOA Security Design and Implementation*, Retrieved 03/20/2008 from ibm.com: http://www.ibm.com/redbooks, publication SG24-7310-01.
6. Neumann, C., Yu, T., Hartman, S., and Raeburn, K. 2005. *The Kerberos Network Authentication Service (V5), IETF Request for Comments 4120*. Retrieved 03/20/2008 from ietf.org: http://www.ietf.org/rfc/rfc4120.txt.
7. IBM. 2007. *IBM z/OS Security Server RACF Administrator's Guide* (publication SA22-7683-11). Retrieved 03/20/2008 from ibm.com: http://publibz.boulder.ibm.com/epubs/pdf/ichza780.pdf.

8. Nadalin, A., Goodner, M., Gudgin, M., Barbir, A., and Granqvist, H., eds. 2007. *OASIS WS-Trust 1.3, OASIS Standard.* Retrieved 03/20/2008 from oasis-open.org: http://docs.oasis-open.org/ws-sx/ws-trust/200512/ws-trust-1.3-os.html.

9. Cole, G. 2006. *OASIS Service Provisioning Markup Language (SPML) Version 2.* Retrieved 03/20/2008 from oasis-open.org: http://www.oasis-open.org/committees/provision/docs/.

10. Anderson, A. ed. 2006. *OASIS XACML (eXtensible Access Control Markup Language) Version 2.0 specification.* Retrieved 03/20/2008 from oasis-open.org: http://www.oasis-open.org/committees/download.php/19135/access_control-xacml-2.0-core-spec-os-errata.zip.

11. Ben Natan, R. 2005. *Implementing Database Security and Auditing.* Burlington, MA: Elsevier Digital Press.

12. Nadalin, A. ed. 2004. *Web Services Security: SOAP Message Security 1.0.* Retrieved 03/20/2008 from oasis-open.org: http://www.oasis-open.org/committees/download.php/6367/oasis-200401-wss-soap-message-security-1.0.pdf.

13. Cantor, S., Kemp, J., Philpott, R., and Maler, E. 2005. *OASIS Security Assertion Markup Language (SAML) Version 2.0.* Retrieved 03/20/2008 from oasis-open.org: http://www.oasis-open.org/committees/download.php/11902/saml-2.0-os.zip.

14. Vedamuthu, A., Orchard, D., Hirsch, F., Hondo, M., Yendluri, P., Boubez, T., and Yalcinap, U. eds. 2007. *Web Services Policy 1.5—Primer.* Retrieved 03/20/2008 from w3.org: http://www.w3.org/TR/ws-policy-primer/.

15. Kaler, C., and Nadalin, A. eds. 2005. *Web Services Security Policy Language (WS-SecurityPolicy) version 1.1.* Retrieved 03/20/2008 from xmlsoap.org: http://specs.xmlsoap.org/ws/2005/07/security-policy/ws-securitypolicy.pdf.

16. Blakley, B. 2007. *Defusing the Personal Information Time Bomb.* Burton Group, White Paper.

Chapter 5

MDM Architecture Patterns

As outlined in the introduction of the MDM Reference Architecture (MDM RA) in Chapter 3, the analysis of many CDI and PIM solution implementations revealed two things. First, a set of best practices for designing the architecture for an MDM Solution was found. Second, a set of recurring architecture patterns was identified. The architecture patterns encountered were either new architecture patterns, variations of existing architecture patterns, or known architecture patterns applied in the area of Master Data Management. These patterns are the ones we call **MDM Architecture Patterns.** Thus, these architecture patterns shaped and influenced the MDM RA, as described in Chapter 3. The present chapter provides an overview of architecture patterns often encountered in MDM deployments. We describe in detail the architecture patterns that helped to shape the MDM RA. With an understanding of the MDM RA, it is easy to see how the pattern relates to one or more components in it. The MDM Architecture Patterns in this chapter show how to instantiate various components of the MDM RA for specific solutions. They encapsulate certain architecture capabilities, so that using these architecture patterns as best practices helps the reader to accelerate project deployment by making it easier and faster to develop comprehensive MDM Architecture Blueprints and industry-specific MDM Solutions. Architecture patterns provide a proven solution to a repeating problem in a given context. The MDM Blueprints coming up in Chapters 6, 7, and 8 are derived by using the MDM Architecture Patterns and the MDM RA as input. This chapter is targeted at Enterprise Architects, Information Architects, Lead Architects, and even Chief Technology Officers.

5.1   Introduction to Patterns

The success of an IT project often depends on the experience of the organization and personnel that have implemented similar projects in the past. In every implementation, we learn more about what works and what doesn't. As our experience grows, we hope that we make fewer (or at least different) mistakes, and using this experience, we can often do a better job of planning and designing new projects, improving their time to value, and decreasing risk. During implementation, we often have the opportunity to collect a variety of artifacts, such as project schedules, best practices, database designs, or code that may, with the proper attention, be saved for future reuse. If a series of similar projects are done and we can leverage our experience to abstract from individual implementations, we start to see the big picture: In a given context for a specific problem, we can use the same solution (and sometimes also the same methodology) to solve it. Considering solution architecture, we start to notice that in a given context for a specific problem, the same architectural building blocks—representing architecture patterns—are used. To capture a relevant subset or certain components of an architecture (e.g., a solution architecture or a reference architecture) will have the same impact: It ensures acceleration of architecture development and results in increased confidence in the correctness of an architecture. As Gamma, Helm, Johnson, and Vlissides put it in their book *Design Patterns: Elements of Reusable Object-Oriented Software* [1]."[1]

> [...] One thing expert designers know not to do is to solve every problem from first principles. Rather, they reuse solutions that have worked for them in the past. When they find a good solution, they use it again and again. Such experience is part of what makes them experts. [...]

But how do we ensure that architectural know-how from previous projects can be made available for subsequent projects? How do we capture, structure, and describe this know-how, and make it available for others? The key to answering these questions is the concept of patterns, specifically architecture patterns. Capturing these patterns is the first step toward reusing them. The value of these captured artifacts is the acceleration of future projects and risk mitigation by leveraging proven assets. Throughout this chapter, we focus on architecture patterns—with special attention on MDM Architecture Patterns in the scope of the MDM RA, described in Chapter 3. Thus, the patterns we discuss show the reader how to decompose the MDM RA to build an MDM Solution for a specific purpose.

This chapter is divided into three major areas. First, we introduce pattern terminology, in Section 5.2. To gain a common understanding, we discuss and clarify the terminology and illustrate it using a couple of examples. We will look at the term **patterns** in general and how we apply the concept of patterns to architectures and specifically, to MDM architectures.

The core of this chapter provides a pattern overview (Section 5.3) for assembling MDM Blueprints and MDM Solutions. Detailed descriptions of relevant MDM Architecture Patterns are included in Sections 5.4 to 5.7. These sections also contain the know-how regarding similarities and the different characteristics of MDM architectures. Importantly, these sections also present a structured approach for categorizing and describing MDM Architecture Patterns in such a way that they may be used both in new projects and for future phases of an on-going rollout. These MDM Architecture Patterns serve an important

---

1. The quote is from the introduction of the book. See the reference list at the end of this chapter for details.

purpose: to accelerate project deployment by making it easier and faster to develop comprehensive and even industry-specific MDM Solutions.

Finally, in Section 5.8, we discuss the composition of these MDM Architecture Patterns, how they contribute to the development of MDM Architecture Blueprints, and how these architecture blueprints serve as an architectural representation of various MDM Blueprints and MDM Solutions. Chapters 6, 7, and 8 are a continuation of this discussion, elaborating on several, very industry-specific MDM Blueprints, which are based on the MDM Architecture Patterns and also the MDM RA. In order to compose MDM Architecture Patterns to "build" an MDM Architecture Blueprint for an anticipated solution scenario, the right selection from all available patterns has to be made.

5.2 Terminology

Prior to diving into MDM Architecture Patterns, we clarify the key terminology, important concepts and coherences as they relate to patterns, the value of patterns, types of patterns, and what we actually mean by architecture patterns. This section on terminology serves as a foundation for the remainder of the chapter.

5.2.1 Definition of Pattern

Before we describe individual architecture patterns, we need to establish some common ground first by introducing relevant terms. Let's start with the term **pattern**: A pattern is a solution to a recurring problem in a given context. The problem for which the pattern provides a solution is usually difficult to solve, and the solution provided by the pattern is only valid in a certain context. For example, if the problem is to construct a home for a family, you might use the appropriate pattern to build a house. If the context "where to build the house" doesn't fit, the selected pattern might not be applicable. A common context for applying the house pattern is to have solid ground underneath—not considering this context and applying the house pattern in a swamp might have disastrous consequences. Thus, a pattern can be considered a template—if the context from which the pattern was derived changes a bit through a minor adaptation, the pattern can still be used. Important aspects of patterns are the system of forces and constraints, which can be viewed as reasons and characteristics as to why the problem the pattern tries to solve is difficult. The system of forces and constraints usually outlines how much the context can change before the pattern is no longer applicable.

A pattern can occur in domains such as house construction, business scenarios, methodology, or IT architecture. The situations where patterns can be found can be characterized by the relations that exist within a given context between problems and solutions. This **triangle** is illustrated in Figure 5.1.

For practical purposes, we assume the 80/20 rule for the applicability of patterns to a particular situation. That is, patterns fit 80% of the time in their given context out of the box, and 20% of the time they might require some minor adjustments to specific details in the recurring situations where they apply. Patterns—if they are supposed to be reusable assets in a

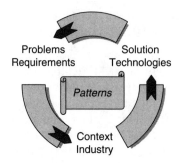

Figure 5.1 Patterns—Triangle of Problem, Context, and Solution.

practitioner community within a domain—need to be captured in reusable artifacts that differ depending on the domain. Patterns should be considered as a way to put artifacts into context: to describe a reusable solution to a recurring problem. These artifacts can be best practices, guidelines, services, blueprints, source code skeletons, and frameworks. For developers and architects in the IT domain, patterns captured in tools such as IBM Rational® Software Architect (RSA)[2] help to accelerate the development and deployment of IT solutions (for details see [2]). An IT Architect using tools with pattern support to define solution architectures can similarly reap benefits in the architecture domain comparable to the benefits the developer gets from using a tool in the software implementation domain. In summary, tools are an easy way to capture patterns in a consistent way for reuse.

5.2.2 Value of Patterns

Key advantages for using patterns include:[3]

- **Deployment Acceleration:** New projects don't have to start from scratch. Proven assets, components, and deliverables from previous projects can be used to accelerate deployment. Using pattern management tools will allow for additional productivity gains.
- **Improved Quality:** Project risks can be significantly reduced, and confidence is increased. By using pattern management tools, patterns will ensure the delivery of consistent quality of any output, such as architectures and solution blueprints. Even without pattern management tooling, patterns encourage more consistent decisions and thus improve quality.
- **Improved Business Flexibility:** If the IT architecture is built with appropriate patterns, the degree of decomposition and modularization is higher. It allows quicker adaptation of the IT infrastructure to changing business needs. Patterns will also

---

2. The IBM RSA is an advanced model-driven development tool that supports Model-Driven Development (MDD) with the Unified Modeling Language (UML) for creating well-architected applications and services.

3. More details on the benefits of patterns and pattern examples can be found in the following references: [3], [4], [5], [6], [7], [8], [9], and [10].

allow a closer and more consistent interlock with business artifacts such as business patterns and business architectures.

- **Cost Reduction:** The entire cost structure end to end will be improved by using patterns. This reasoning applies to all domains—business, architecture, development, test, deployment, and operational aspects. One reason is that faster development with consistent and compliant usage of patterns reduces errors.

- **Best Practices:** Patterns capture the best way to solve a specific recurring problem in a given context. They thus provide a productive way to improve solution development and deployment by capturing best practices and expertise from previous projects, which can be captured in tools and made available for reuse in other projects. It is also a way to govern proven approaches more effectively.

5.2.3 Types of Patterns

As we outlined, patterns exist in a variety of domains. We now show some of the different types of patterns that exist for a particular domain. For example, in the domain of e-business, IBM defines five types of patterns [3]:

- **Business Patterns:** Business patterns identify the primary business actors and describe the interactions between them in terms of different archetypal business interactions, such as:
  - **Service (a.k.a. user-to-business):** Users accessing transactions on a 24/7 basis.
  - **Collaboration (a.k.a. user-to-user):** Users working with one another to share data and information.
  - **Information Aggregation (a.k.a. user-to-data):** Data from multiple sources aggregated and presented across multiple channels.
  - **Extended Enterprise (a.k.a. business-to-business):** Integrating data and processes across enterprise boundaries.
- **Integration Patterns:** Integration patterns provide the "glue" to combine business patterns to form solutions. They characterize the business problem, business processes/rules, and existing environment to determine whether front-end or back-end integration is required:
  - **Front-end integration (a.k.a. access integration)** is focused on providing seamless and consistent access to business functions. Typical functions provided include single sign-on and personalization.
  - **Back-end integration (a.k.a. application integration)** is focused on connecting, interfacing, or integrating databases and other back-end systems. Typical integration can be based on function, type of integration, mode of integration, and topology.
- **Composite Patterns:** Composite patterns are previously identified combinations and selections of business and integration patterns for previously identified situations such as electronic commerce solutions, (public) enterprise portals, or enterprise intranet portals.
- **Application Patterns:** Each business and integration pattern can be implemented using one or more application patterns. An application pattern characterizes the

coarse-grained structure of the application—the main application components, the allocation of processing functions and the interactions between them, the degree of integration between them, and the placement of the data relative to the applications.

- **Runtime Patterns:** Application patterns can be implemented by runtime patterns, which demonstrate nonfunctional, service-level characteristics such as performance, capacity, scalability, and availability. They identify key resource constraints and best practices.

The list just presented represents only a sample of pattern types. As noted previously, this book will focus on MDM Architecture Patterns.

5.2.4 Architecture Patterns

To introduce the term **architecture pattern**, we must apply the concept of patterns to the architecture domain. An architecture pattern is a solution to a recurring problem in the architecture domain for a given context.

In a way, an architecture pattern is an architectural reusable building block or asset that describes a certain structural organization of functions, components, or even subsystems in a modular structure. It is done in such a way that these components or subsystems are specified in terms of their roles and responsibilities, the relationship between them, and their structure and guidelines of communicating with each other. Architecture patterns thus also drive the interrelationship between architecture building blocks.

At a **conceptual** level, Figure 5.2 is illustrating different architecture patterns. Again, this figure is very much a high-level abstraction, just to depict and illustrate different architecture patterns.

On the left side of Figure 5.2, we have illustrated a pattern that is hierarchical in nature. This pattern can, for example, be a hierarchical data model that is recurring in a specific application or industry context. Next to that, you can see an architecture pattern that is characterized by a central control of one instance (A1) over all others, accompanied by limited communication capabilities among the neighboring instances (e.g., A5–A4 and A5–A6). Next to this illustration is a depiction of a pattern that consists of two categories of instances (A1/A2/A3 and B1/B2/B3), where each instance in allowed to communicate with all other instances from the other category. Finally, the pattern on the right is a high-level illustration of an Enterprise Service Bus (ESB) that illustrates the role of the ESB in facilitating

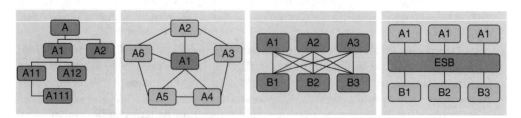

Figure 5.2 Architecture Patterns.

required communication among different service consumers (A1/A2/A3) and service providers (B1/B2/B3). Again, we are providing these abstract examples to further illustrate the term architecture pattern.

Composite architecture patterns (or **composite patterns**) are themselves patterns in that they name and document a recommended solution to a recurring and more complex and pervasive problem. A composite pattern can be described in terms of other patterns, even other composite patterns. The goal is to capture synergy between patterns and make it explicit—a task you would need to do otherwise yourself.

We have developed MDM Architecture Patterns for the domain of Master Data Management and have made them closely aligned with the MDM RA. Thus, MDM Architecture Patterns need to be seen in the light of the MDM RA.

Through implementation analysis, we discovered that existing architecture patterns, such as ESB and messaging patterns, can be applied while building MDM Solutions. In general, we are abstracting MDM Architecture Patterns from technologies and available products. However, we also found that traditional patterns such as federation, data consolidation, and data cleansing patterns appear in a variation due to the required support of the Information as a Service concept in the context of MDM deployments. Two examples of the new architecture patterns for the MDM domain are the **MDM Hub Patterns** or the **Transaction Interception** pattern (see Section 5.6.1).

One example of a set of architecture patterns are the IBM Patterns for e-business [3], which we have mentioned already. These patterns—well proven and successfully used many times in real projects—enable architects to accelerate the deployment of e-business solutions through the reuse of components and assets from proven successful deployments. These reusable components and assets are structured in a phased approach, where a given set of customer requirements is used as a starting point to guide you through the following layers or types of patterns, which we have mentioned: business patterns, integration patterns, composite patterns, application patterns, and runtime patterns. Product mappings, guidelines, and best practices further accelerate the design, development, implementation, deployment, and management of those e-business applications.[4]

The second example is a whole set of Service-Oriented Architecture (SOA) Runtime Patterns that describe interaction with an Enterprise Service Bus (ESB). Some of these patterns include:[5]

- Direct connection using a service bus runtime pattern
- ESB runtime pattern (which provides the highest-level view of the ESB)
- ESB gateway runtime pattern
- Business Service Choreography (BSC) runtime pattern
- ESB-BSC composite pattern
- Exposed ESB gateway runtime pattern
- Exposed ESB gateway-BSC composite pattern

---

4. For more details, also see [4].
5. Further details can be found in [9] and [11].

Many of these patterns can also be implemented with products that are listed in Section B.2 of Appendix B.

A final set of pattern examples is the Architectural Patterns Web site[6] of The Open Group, a vendor- and technology-neutral consortium. You can find a wealth of information regarding taxonomy and examples of architecture patterns there. As stated previously, these architecture patterns and compositions of these patterns can serve as a starting point for completion, refinement, adaptation, and further customization.

5.3 MDM Architecture Patterns Overview

The MDM RA presented in Chapter 3 is industry-agnostic and covers all MDM methods of use. Thus, the MDM RA can be considered a superset or an umbrella for MDM implementations that are further tailored for specific industries and customer requirements. On the technical side, functional and nonfunctional requirements drive the tailoring of a concrete solution, starting with the MDM RA. For example, there might be cases where you only need a subset of the functionality covered by the MDM RA. Adapting the MDM RA for a specific MDM Solution should be guided by best practices in a format known to architects. A concrete instantiation of the MDM RA should also take into account the various enterprise master data business and technical strategies, master data implementation approaches, and MDM methods of use. This instantiation should be captured in a set of documents that contain an MDM logical architecture, technical architecture, design templates, and MDM Architecture Patterns that are customized and applied to solve a class of customer problems. Specifically, the MDM Architecture Patterns will allow capturing experiences and will guarantee for appropriate reusability of architectural components and assets.

Master Data Management implementations are often done in a phased approach. Typically, the first phase is the master data integration that populates the MDM System with the initial data set. Subsequent phases integrate additional application systems that require access to master data at the MDM Hub. Because MDM is used to make certain business processes like New Product Introduction (NPI) more efficient, any MDM project requires a certain degree of business process adaptation or even a rather comprehensive business process reengineering on either all or at least a subset of chosen business processes. Thus, besides the new MDM Architecture Patterns, you will also need well-known architecture patterns from the Enterprise Information Integration (EII) domain as well as from the Enterprise Application Integration (EAI) domain.

To understand the business processes that will be impacted by the deployment of an MDM Solution is not the only challenge. Almost all MDM Solutions need to be deployed into an existing IT system landscape, where interfaces and collaboration need to be considered with Business Intelligence (BI) systems, packaged applications, or other Line-of-Business applications. These integration requirements may even go beyond the enterprise boundaries to

---

6. For more details, also see [12].

interface with systems of other enterprises. An example is the XML-based ACORD[7] exchange of data among insurance agencies and related enterprises to optimize claims processing. Another example is the Global Data Synchronization (GDS) process that allows efficient data exchange between retailers and their suppliers. Therefore, the set of MDM Architecture Patterns needs to take into account these integration requirements.

The following section presents details for these different MDM Architecture Patterns.

5.3.1 Types of Architecture Patterns for MDM

In essence, we see four types of architecture patterns for MDM. As can be seen in Figure 5.3, **MDM Hub Patterns** are in the center. One of the key capabilities of an MDM Hub is the materialization of master data in the Master Data Repository. The MDM Hub Patterns are directly related to the MDM implementation styles that were introduced in Chapter 1. Depending on the MDM style, you will deploy an MDM System with a specific set of capabilities—capabilities closely related to the architectural building blocks of the MDM RA. The MDM Hub Patterns have a strong affinity to the MDM services component of the MDM RA. This approach provides you with useful best practices that are needed to deploy the MDM RA.

For building an MDM System as well as for distributing data in the application landscape, a certain set of capabilities focused on information-related techniques is required. For example, for initially loading master data into the MDM repository of the MDM System, you will need patterns to extract, cleanse, transform, and load master data from various application silos into the MDM System. As we discussed in Chapter 1, this master data is most likely distributed in a highly heterogeneous data landscape. Depending on your IT environment and the underlying business requirements, federation and information synchronization techniques might be required to simply access and distribute your master data to application systems. This approach requires leveraging architecture patterns in the area of **information-focused application integration.**

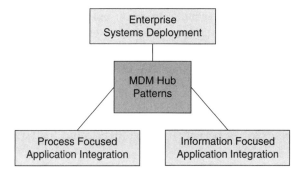

Figure 5.3 Types of Architecture Patterns for MDM.

---

7. Association for Cooperative Operations Research and Development (ACORD). For further details, see Appendix D.

A wide range of architecture patterns that describe how to integrate application systems, with a focus on the process and workflow capabilities, have been defined. This group of patterns is the type called **process-focused application integration** patterns. Because a lot of MDM deployments are in the context of SOA, the enterprise service bus concept is a core component in the MDM RA. However, to have an ESB component in the MDM RA doesn't necessarily mean that ESB technologies[8] are the only way to instantiate the ESB component. EAI techniques or a simple home-grown communication and interoperability layer are valid instantiations of the ESB concept as well. For implementing an ESB, there are a lot of ESB patterns covering ESB topologies as well as messaging patterns—both are covered in the literature already. Thus, we only point out relevant patterns that we have seen and provide references where the reader can find more. However, there is one new pattern—the **Transaction Interception** pattern—which is driven by specific requirements of Master Data Management deployments. We describe this pattern in full detail later in this chapter. The patterns in this category are application-agnostic. That is, they are not tailored for CRM, ERP, or other applications.

The fourth type of architecture patterns we see are **enterprise system deployment** patterns. Enterprise system deployment patterns are composite architecture patterns that collectively focus on the deployment of an MDM System and in particular the integration of the MDM System with various application systems such as data warehouse (DW), CRM, or ERP systems. The purpose of these architecture patterns is twofold:

- First, these patterns show how MDM Systems have dependencies on other systems in an IT landscape, for example, systems running analytical processing to resolve identities or analytical processes identifying the most valuable customers in the DW system. MDM Systems also complement other systems (again, an example is the data warehouse) by providing the master data for the dimension tables to such a system. MDM can thus simplify the provisioning of analytical systems, including the complex ETL[9] infrastructure.
- Second, these patterns show which type of application systems we often encountered, because they have certain affinities to one or multiple master data domains. For example, CRM applications are frequently encountered in the context of CDI-related master data projects.

The objective of these patterns is to show why these application systems benefit from a centralized MDM System and possible integration approaches. Furthermore, and even more important, we show here why these application systems cannot function as a replacement for MDM Systems. We should also mention that the MDM Architecture Patterns in this category are more coarse-grained than the architecture patterns in the first three categories.

---

8. For further details, see Section B.2 in Appendix B.

9. ETL is an abbreviation for extract-transform-load, a process used to extract data from application systems and move the data into data warehouses.

5.3.2 Architecture Pattern Overview

With the foregoing understanding of the basic types of patterns, we now take a look at which patterns belong in the toolset used by an IT Architect designing MDM Solutions. The architecture patterns are shown in Figure 5.4.

There is a logical order in which the patterns are presented. Because you need to have an MDM System before you can connect it to other systems, the patterns in the first major branch on the left in Figure 5.4 are the **MDM Hub Patterns.** As you will see, the type of MDM Hub significantly drives the selection of other integration patterns. The reason for this mechanism is because the MDM Hub Patterns bring together the method of use, implementation style, and the system type. It is from this correspondence that we see the MDM Hub Patterns in the center of all other types of MDM Architecture Patterns. In other words, the MDM Hub Patterns orchestrate the selection and usage of other MDM Architecture Patterns. An MDM System built and implemented with a certain MDM Hub Pattern will be called an **MDM Hub;** we use the term **Registry Hub** if the MDM System was built with the Registry Hub pattern, **Coexistence Hub** if the Coexistence Hub pattern was used, and **Transaction Hub** if the Transaction Hub pattern was used. In order to build the hub, you need to extract master data from various systems, cleanse, standardize, transform, and ultimately load it into the Master Data Repository of the MDM System (for more detail, see the Initial Load pattern). Even though this step needs to be performed prior to the existence of the MDM Hub, the selection of the hub type determines how the initial load has to be done. For example, a Registry Hub will have a thin layer of the master data attributes materialized, whereas

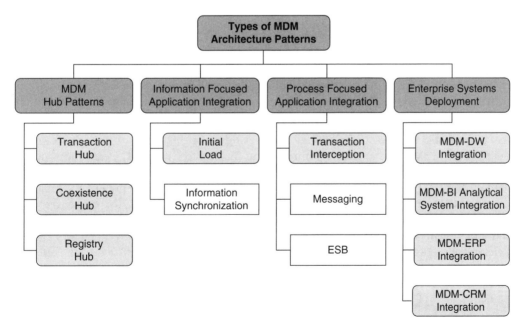

Figure 5.4 MDM Architecture Pattern Overview.

a Transaction Hub has the full master data model materialized. Thus, the amount and complexity of cleansing and transformation required will be quite different for these two hub types. In addition, the fact that the Initial Load pattern has building blocks known from the information integration services architecture building block is a reason for us to put this pattern into the second major branch. Because the Initial Load pattern is needed early on, we decided to discuss the information-focused application integration category prior to the process-focused application integration category. Finally, we put the MDM System in the context with other critical systems in the IT landscape and conclude the discussion of patterns with the enterprise system deployment category. During this discussion, we also provide a preview of the MDM Solution Blueprints that follow in Chapter 6.

Notice that these patterns in the four categories have either a dark-grey background in rectangles with rounded corners or a light-grey background in rectangles with normal corners. The difference between the two is that the dark-grey rectangles represent patterns that are MDM-specific. Examples are the MDM Hub Patterns and the **transaction interception** pattern—or variations of existing patterns where MDM changed the pattern and the architectural decision points significantly. The light-grey rectangles represent a pattern category, rather than an individual pattern, for which an IT Architect should have extensive knowledge in that pattern domain when building an MDM Solution. We name only relevant and known patterns and key characteristics from these architecture pattern areas, and we also provide relevant information about how we saw them applied in MDM implementations. For a complete pattern description, we point the reader to other sources.

As was previously stated, the MDM Architecture Patterns in this category bring together many concepts introduced earlier, such as the method of use, implementation styles, system type (system of reference versus system of record), and convergent versus absolute consistency. Furthermore, the MDM Hub Patterns are described in light of the MDM RA, and it is shown how they relate to the MDM RA. The **Registry Hub** pattern corresponds to the Registry implementation style, the **Coexistence Hub** pattern corresponds to the Coexistence implementation style and the **Transaction Hub** corresponds to the Transactional implementation style.

As you probably noticed, there are only three patterns in this category, though we introduced more MDM styles at the beginning of the chapter. In Chapter 1, we also introduced the Consolidation style. The reasoning behind this approach is that due to our experience with customers, these three MDM styles and the related MDM Hubs represent the majority of the MDM installations, providing the most business value for an enterprise. Implementing Master Data Management is a serious undertaking for any enterprise, and we think that, generally speaking, Consolidation style hubs (sometimes also called an External Reference hub) deployment do not offer sufficient business value compared to the effort it usually takes to build them. Thus, we consider this MDM style and the corresponding hub an exception to deploying an MDM System and do not elaborate on this style any further.

An IT Architect looking at them should have very good arguments about why the three types of MDM Hubs suggested earlier are not the right architectural choice. The detailed pattern descriptions coming up in this chapter provide the necessary details on these patterns and are provided to help you understand them from an architectural perspective. All of these hub patterns must be seen as archetypical instantiations of the Master Data Management Services component of the MDM RA.

In the second category, you see the **Initial Load** pattern. In many customer situations, this pattern is needed to load high-quality master data into the Master Data Repository of the MDM System. There are also customer situations in which a new business is created that does not rely on legacy data. In those cases, the Initial Load pattern has much less applicability. The business value of this pattern is that it provides the means to extract, cleanse, standardize, de-duplicate, transform, and load data into the MDM System, which is required to produce high-quality master data. However, depending on the MDM Hub, the instantiation of this pattern might look different; this coherence will be elaborated upon later in the chapter. After the MDM Hub is built, the master data needs to be accessible to a variety of application systems, such as packaged applications, legacy systems, and billing systems. There are other information integration patterns, such as data replication, that can be applied depending on the constraints in the project, such as timeliness, consistency, and so forth. We provide an overview of relevant patterns and their characteristics in an MDM context.

In the third category, we have a new pattern, the **Transaction Interception** pattern. The fundamental challenge addressed by this pattern is the need for business transaction synchronization. This need is especially important in situations where data replication cannot be applied to keep the master data consistent. The other two boxes in the overview are placeholders for a variety of messaging and ESB-related architecture patterns. We list the patterns from this architecture pattern group (Process-Focused Application Integration) that we have seen implemented when MDM Solutions were deployed, along with their relation to MDM Systems—for a detailed description we point the reader to appropriate resources. We know that there are other architecture patterns like the portal architecture pattern, which defines a solution for building enterprise portals. The portal pattern can be used as the MDM user interface for a variety of user roles, such as the operational data steward or an item specialist.[10] However, in this book, we don't provide an overview of portal-related architecture patterns.

In the fourth category, we collected the architecture patterns for enterprise system deployments. For example, here we show how MDM Systems and data warehouse (DW) systems provide more value than the sum of the parts if properly integrated. Also we show in more detail why certain application systems are not MDM Systems but how they benefit from each other when properly integrated with each other. Thus, many patterns discussed here address the fact that MDM is most often implemented in and must support an existing IT environment, even as it helps to transform and simplify that environment. The discussion here includes elaboration on the collaboration and interrelationship of the MDM System with other systems.

---

10. For details on MDM user roles, see Appendix A.

5.3.3 Attributes of Architecture Patterns

Before we start describing individual architecture patterns for MDM (in Section 5.4), we need to introduce the format that we are using for presenting them. Patterns have attributes that will help us to further characterize the various types of architecture patterns. Readers familiar with architecture pattern presentation will likely have seen most of the attributes elsewhere already (e.g., in [4], [5], and [6]). Some of the attributes are common for all architecture patterns, and some are specific for MDM Solutions, for example, methods of use.

For the discussion of the MDM Architecture Patterns, we propose the set of attributes shown in Figure 5.5.

Let's describe the various attributes in detail. The **name** of the pattern is the unique identifier of this pattern and is used whenever the pattern is discussed. Ideally, the name itself suggests the core function of the pattern. The **type** classifies the pattern according to its membership in the four pattern categories shown in Figure 5.4, and describes, if applicable, known subpatterns. The **methods of use** is an MDM-specific attribute. Valid values for this attribute are one or more entries from the following list:

- Collaborative Style
- Operational Style
- Analytical Style

For example, there are patterns such as the Transaction Hub pattern where all of the styles are applicable, and there are other Hub patterns where only one or two of the styles might be applicable. **System type** is also an MDM-specific attribute and applicable only for the MDM Hub Patterns. The system type can either be "system of reference" or "system of record." This "system type" attribute is most applicable for MDM Hub Patterns. For all other patterns, the value for this attribute will be "N/A," indicating "not applicable." The distinction between system of reference and system of record was given in the introduction of the three

Attribute	Description
Name	Unique identifier of the pattern
Type	Type and sub-type(s) of pattern
Methods of use	Links the pattern to the method(s) of use
System type	Applicable only to MDM hub patterns
Value proposition	Value provided by the pattern
Context	Description of the context of where the pattern plays
Problem statement	Key problems that are addressed by this pattern
Solution	Solution space that this pattern addresses
Forces	Reasons why the problem is difficult to solve
Relations	Other related MDM architecture pattern(s)

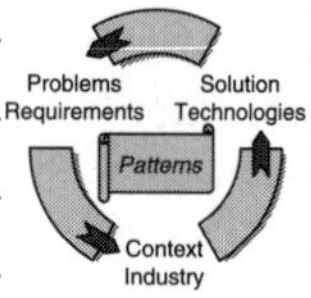

Figure 5.5 Attributes of Architecture Patterns.

implementation styles in Chapter 1. The attribute **value proposition** is used to describe which value the pattern provides. The value can be either on the business side or the technical side, or can be a combination thereof.

The **problem statement**, the **context**, and the **solution** are the key attributes of a pattern specification, as described earlier. It is the core set of information for all MDM Architecture Patterns, even if further customization of attributes needs to be done for a given project. The **context** attribute describes the usage context of the pattern in order to provide the information about when the pattern was successfully used before and can therefore be applied again. The context provides information about the assumptions of the deployment context of the pattern. As an example, you might find further information regarding deployment of the architecture pattern in an SOA-style architecture or in a non-SOA architecture, and how other environment-related aspects might affect the deployment of this pattern. For example, there is a specific set of assumptions regarding the integration and deployment context with **Global Registries** in the Retail Industry that needs to be captured in this context section.[11] Furthermore, the **context** section should provide MDM-specific background information, such as the specifics of the architecture pattern in the MDM context vs. another context (e.g., a traditional Business Intelligence context). A good example for this coherence is the Initial Load pattern, which is characterized with different assumptions in the MDM context vs. the BI/data warehousing context. We further elaborate on these aspects in Section 5.5.3. It is important to notice that the context attribute does characterize the **MDM-specifics** of the architecture pattern. The **problem statement** indicates which problem(s) the pattern tries to solve; it is the key motivation for the pattern. These pain points are recurring ones that serve as the key foundation for the pattern to be developed and used. The **solution** attribute provides a description on how the pattern addresses the issue(s) outlined in the problem statement. This aspect is, of course, not to be mixed up with the wider scope of a complete MDM Solution. The scope of the problem(s) and the given context determine the scope of the solution for this particular pattern. Depending on the granularity of the pattern, this solution scope can be rather small. The solution section may also contain some recommendations or guidelines for implementing the solution. Furthermore, there may be industry-specific or context-specific specializations of the solution that need to be described here as well. Later on, we will see that an MDM Architecture Pattern can be part of more complex and more coarse-grained MDM Solutions.

The **forces** attribute provides a description of why the problem is difficult to solve and what the constraints are for solving the problem. Thus, the context descriptions, as well as the constraints mentioned in the forces section, show the boundaries to an IT Architect when the pattern is applicable. It is a description of the relevant forces and constraints, and how they relate, collaborate, influence, and even compete with each other. Competing with each other in this context means that a certain set of forces cannot be appropriately addressed at the same time by a single pattern or even a set of patterns. As a consequence, certain compromises have to be done with regard to using this pattern and customizing it further in

---

11. Further details are presented in Chapter 6.

order to take into account the specific forces. This pattern attribute further characterizes the MDM environment and puts into perspective the different forces and constraints, and how these coherences are then reflected and transformed into an optimized MDM Architecture Pattern that best characterizes and addresses the **problem statement–context–solution** triangle. How do all these aspects relate specifically to MDM? Well, regarding MDM, we see the following categories of forces and constraints:

- **Legacy Environment:** The constraints and limitations due to the characteristics of the legacy systems create a wide range of forces. In Section 5.7, we discuss the complexity of the legacy environment and how this complexity influences a category of MDM Architecture Patterns.
- **Master Data Distribution Characteristics:** The complexity of master data in terms of its distribution throughout the enterprise, the diversity and inconsistency of existing master data records, and the relevance of at least part of the master data scope to almost all applications generates another set of forces and constraints.
- **Synchronization Aspects:** In the case of the Transaction and Coexistence Hub patterns, rather complex synchronization-related MDM Architecture Patterns will be used. Specifically, in the Coexistence Hub architecture patterns, bidirectional synchronization patterns need to be deployed. Aspects, such as timeliness of replication and synchronization tasks, the scope of replication, and the overlap of master data to be replicated among several systems in several directions, generate another set of forces and constraints.

There are additional categories of forces, such as scalability, reliability, extensibility, and maintainability. Although these categories apply to MDM, they are not as significant as the other categories, so we will not consider them in more detail in the remainder of this chapter. Relating these forces to each other and making conscious decisions regarding their priority will motivate the set of MDM Architecture Patterns that need to be built. These trade-offs will drive the adaptation of patterns in a concrete MDM implementation.

Finally, the **relations** attribute describes related patterns. If there are not any related patterns, the value will be "N/A" (indicating "not applicable"). This attribute lists patterns that are leveraged by this pattern or details why this pattern is related, but different from known patterns. This section also lists subtypes of this pattern. The relationship of patterns may be characterized by a certain level of dependency among a subset of patterns. This dependency can be related to the context of one pattern as it corresponds to the context of other patterns or subpatterns. Specifically, in the MDM area, there are alternative approaches to deploy an MDM Solution, for example, process-focused vs. information-focused application integration. Thus, some patterns may relate to each other as alternative patterns to build alternative architecture blueprints—but for the same problem(s). In other words, one pattern or set of patterns might be an alternative to another, based on the given context, the forces, and other circumstances and constraints of an MDM project.

We have completed the foundation and are ready to dive into the core architecture patterns for MDM Solutions: the MDM Hub Patterns.

5.4   MDM Hub Patterns

In this section, we describe the MDM Hub Patterns in detail. Implementing and deploying MDM is most often not a single deployment but introduced in a phased approach with multiple launches. Also, the scope of the solution usually evolves and grows in each iteration. Along with this evolution, the type of MDM Hub that is implemented may change. Over the last several years, we worked with customers who started their Master Data Management journey with a Registry Hub and over time expanded the capabilities of their MDM System until it became either a Coexistence Hub or even a Transaction Hub. Although there is no defined entry point in terms of which hub pattern to deploy first, we present the MDM Hub Patterns in the following order that starts from the MDM Hub with the least capabilities and finishes with the MDM Hub with all capabilities: Registry Hub $\rightarrow$ Coexistence Hub $\rightarrow$ Transaction Hub.

The list of patterns is shown in Figure 5.6. After describing the individual hub patterns in more detail, we present a summary in Section 5.4.4 that includes a comprehensive comparison of these patterns.

The description of each MDM Hub Pattern has two parts in the solution attribute of the pattern.

First, we describe how the MDM Hub Patterns relate to the MDM RA. This perspective allows us to understand the solution of the patterns by using components of the MDM RA.

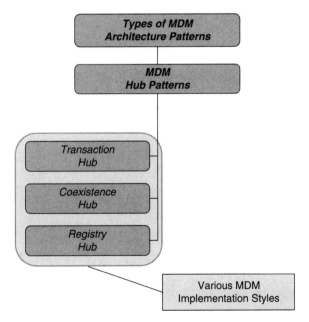

Figure 5.6   MDM Hub Patterns.

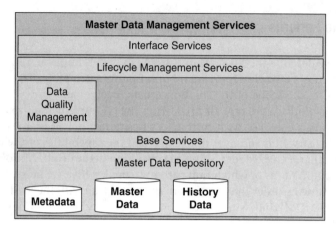

Figure 5.7 The Registry Hub Pattern in the Context of the MDM RA.

For example, using the Registry Hub pattern, relationship information is not usually material-ized in the MDM System, and thus relationship services are not provided by the MDM System. This describes in our perspective the general case, but we are aware that there are exceptions. For example, in the customer master data domain, we are aware of a Registry Hub deployment where about 30 attributes are materialized in the Registry Hub for uniqueness enforcement as are a few attributes for consistent access to relationship information. Thus, in terms of the MDM RA, the relationship services would be instantiated as well, which, as shown in Figure 5.7, is not part of what we consider a typical instantiation of this pattern. So when reading the pattern descriptions regarding the linkage to the MDM RA, keep in mind that these descriptions represent the general case and that exceptions may very well exist.

The second half of the pattern description presents how the pattern can be positioned in the context with other systems. In other words, this perspective focuses on how the MDM Hub works in the context of other IT systems—even beyond enterprise boundaries.

As was mentioned previously, in Section 5.4.4 we provide a comparison of all MDM Hub Patterns. In order to avoid redundancy in the pattern presentation, we extracted the key aspects of high availability and disaster recovery (HADR) as well as security of the MDM Hub Patterns in separate sections. Aspects related to HADR will be covered in Section 5.4.5, and security aspects will be covered in Section 5.4.6—both sections will follow the MDM Hub Pattern description.

5.4.1 Registry Hub Pattern

We now describe the Registry Hub pattern according to the most important pattern attrib-utes that we listed earlier. We begin with the more MDM-specific attributes, such as type and method of use. According to the triangle of patterns, we discuss this pattern in terms of its context, problem statement, and the solution. This subsection concludes with a description of forces that are relevant for this pattern and the relationship of this pattern to other MDM Architecture Patterns.

5.4.1.1   Type
This pattern belongs to the group of MDM Hub Patterns.

5.4.1.2   Method of Use
Although this pattern is mainly applicable to the operational style, it may also be applied to the collaborative and analytical methods of use. The reason why we see less applicability, for example, for the collaborative method of use is due to the strong need to support specific workflows and business processes, for example, New Product Introduction (NPI), which have a stronger need for a materialized Master Data Hub. But in this Registry Hub pattern, the Master Data is mainly stored in legacy systems, and can *only* be consistently viewed and derived through linkage to master data in these legacy systems. Thus, implementing new business processes or significantly improving existing business processes based on this MDM Hub Pattern may be clumsy and more difficult compared to the other two MDM Hub Patterns (Coexistence and Transaction Hub patterns).

5.4.1.3   System Type
This pattern represents a **system of reference**[12] for master data. The Registry Hub pattern is a system of reference type because we don't have a single copy of key master data that is managed by the MDM System. Instead, this pattern requires synchronization with other systems.

5.4.1.4   Value Proposition
The business value of applying the Registry Hub pattern is related to its relatively low deployment cost compared to the Coexistence or Transaction Hub patterns. It can also be deployed more rapidly as opposed to the other two hub patterns. The first reason for these two benefits is that only a thin layer of master data attributes is materialized in the Registry Hub. Usually, only the critical[13] attributes need to be materialized so that uniqueness of master data records can be enforced. Thus, the effort to initially load the records into the Registry Hub (including extracting, cleansing, standardizing, transforming, and loading) is lower than in the other hub patterns. Second, the Line of Business users continue to use their known application user interfaces for creating new master data records so that no user interface training is required. Third, the demand for high availability of the Registry Hub is usually not very high, thereby incurring less cost, because most of the creation and maintenance of the master data is done in the application system. If the MDM System of the Registry Hub pattern fails, the read-only view on all entities is unavailable. However, deploying a Registry Hub enables the business to assemble in near real-time or in real-time a complete and accurate view on a master data entity. For example, with a Registry Hub managing master data, a business can answer questions such as, "How many customers do we have?" This question may sound very trivial. Nevertheless,

---

12. A detailed description of both terms "system of reference" and "system of record" was given in Chapter 1.

13. Critical attributes are the subset of attributes on which the operations "compile candidate list" and "matching" are performed. For more details, see Chapter 9.

most companies without MDM Systems are usually not capable of answering it accurately[14] and in a timely manner.

On the technical side, the Registry Hub pattern provides the benefits of easier integration, particularly when compared to the Transaction Hub, partly because application systems usually do not need to be changed.

5.4.1.5   Context

The context of this pattern is usually the demand for an accurate and complete read-only 360-degree view of master data. This demand sometimes aligns with what can be contained in the scope of the first implementation project for an MDM System. Furthermore, it is assumed that master data is created and maintained in the original legacy application systems. The demand for capabilities from the analytical and collaborative style is usually also low or nonexistent. From the analytical side, this context might mean that for the deployment of the MDM System, integration with the data warehouse or other BI analytical systems is not required. If users do not need to collaborate a lot in the creation or maintenance of master data, this situation would indicate low collaborative style requirements. These requirements are more often found in the Customer and Account domains and less often in the Product and Service domains.

5.4.1.6   Problem Statement

Unmanaged master data in application silos limits the ability to access in (near) real-time a comprehensive view of master data such as a Customer (or any other master data domain). Duplicates can exist, which may cause inefficiencies in marketing and strategic planning stemming from the number of real Customers being unknown.

From a technical perspective, it is difficult—if not impossible—to establish in (near) real-time a comprehensive, unique, and accurate view of any master data domain. The reason for this conclusion is related to unmanaged master data, and the "unknown" in terms of which application source system contains which master data records.

5.4.1.7   Solution

We now illustrate key capabilities of the Registry Hub in the context of the MDM RA. From the MDM services component of the MDM RA, the following architectural building blocks are part of the Registry Hub pattern (see Figure 5.7). Architectural building blocks that are not part of the Master Data Management Services are less or even not applicable at all. Furthermore, architectural building blocks with limited functions are shown in light gray—for example, the data quality management building block. The same approach will be taken when presenting the other hub patterns.

---

14. On average, in the Customer master domain, we encountered 30%–40% duplicates when the Customer records were de-duplicated. An extreme example was a Customer with more than 1 million records initially, where after the de-duplication only 10% remained—in other words, only one out of ten records represented a real customer. This justifies from our perspective the claim that rarely, if ever, does a company know how many customers it has unless it implements an MDM Solution.

Let's now elaborate on how the Registry Hub Pattern is positioned in the context of the MDM RA. We will present the Registry Hub Pattern in terms of the key components of the MDM RA:

- **Interface Services:** From a technology standpoint, the Registry Hub pattern can support a variety of service bindings such as Java Messaging Services (JMS) or Web services depending on software selection.
- **Lifecycle Management Services:** Except for registering a new master data record, all interface service calls are read-only, thereby requiring a complete view for a master data entity. In other words, even these read-only queries assume a comprehensive view of the master data records. Because only a subset of the master data attributes is available, only a limited amount or no services can be invoked (e.g., master data quality or event management services).
- **Data Quality Management Services:** From this group, usually only the cross-reference services are part of the Registry Hub. An example is the unique ID generator service. Because the majority of the attributes are still managed and modified by the legacy applications and are not even stored in the MDM System, the low quality of the master data may not be improved through these services. That is, quality of the master data remains an issue to be dealt with in the legacy applications. Having made this statement, though, improving quality of master data can very well mean that master data quality will be improved in some or even all relevant legacy systems.
- **Base Services:** From this group of services, security, privacy, search, and audit logging capabilities are supported. Because the master data event management services are not present, there will be a reduced effort for event logging. Also the workflow capabilities are usually not enabled by the Registry Hub type deployment (even though the software bought for the MDM System might support it).
- **The Master Data Repository:** The critical master data attributes required for matching are usually the only attributes persisted in the Registry Hub. Often, comprehensive reference data is not managed by a Registry Hub deployment because there are only a few attributes in the Master Data Repository. A lookup table for titles is an example of reference data that can be managed by a Registry Hub. If auditing is enabled, history data might be captured as well. Depending on the business motivation, there may also be a need to materialize a specific subset of the master data in the repository. There are countless variations with regard to the degree of materialization of the master data.

When building the MDM System with the Registry Hub pattern, you will also need the Initial Load pattern. Thus, functions from the Information Integration Services group are required as well.

After examining the capabilities of the Registry Hub pattern in the context of the master data reference architecture, we now show how it works in the IT landscape. As can be seen in Figure 5.8, the Master Data Repository is part of the MDM System. However, there is limited materialization of master data in this new MDM repository.[15] The transactions changing master data are still executed against the operational systems. This pattern allows for an

---

15.   For example, there is a unique key for master records complemented by some linkage information.

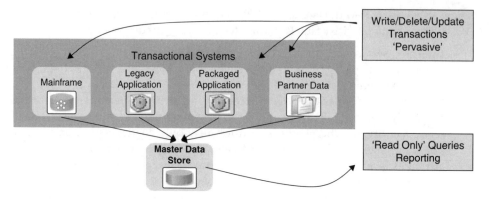

Figure 5.8 Registry MDM Hub—Illustration.

authoritative source to be used in read-only format for a thin master data slice. This hub pattern allows a deployment of an MDM System that is less complex compared to Coexistence and Transaction Hub deployments.

After this high-level overview, Figure 5.9 provides a more detailed illustration of the Registry Hub pattern. Initially, the application systems manage their local transactional and master data (1). The introduction of a Registry Hub requires two tasks. First, you need to extract,

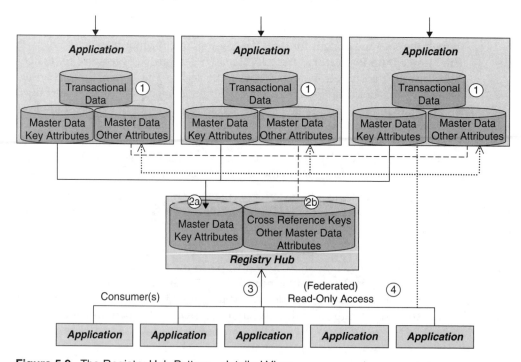

Figure 5.9 The Registry Hub Pattern—detailed View.

cleanse, and standardize the critical data attributes that are used to match and de-duplicate master data records. After matching and de-duplication is done, data of the critical attributes are stored in the data repository of the Registry Hub for uniqueness determination (2a). In addition, you need to store cross-referencing keys (2b). These keys indicate which application systems are the sources for a particular master data record. In a more comprehensive implementation, they also indicate which attributes are consumed or modified by which application. For example, there might be an attribute of a master data record that is only known by a single application.

After the Registry Hub is built, application systems consuming master data can access the thin slice of master data in the hub with read-only access (3). There are two ways to provide access to the master data attributes that are not stored in the Registry Hub. If the **Federation** pattern[16] is used, then the federation layer will query for the key attributes in the Registry Hub and the other master data attributes are queried from the source application systems. This coherence is shown with (4). In this case, the read access by the consumer applications invokes a federation service that might be registered in a service registry in an ESB. Another option is to build composite master data services in such a way that the composite service extracts the key attributes from the Registry Hub and the other master data attributes from the source application system. In this case, the federation approach would be implemented on the service interface of the MDM System itself. Note that all changes to master data can only be executed against the source application systems. This is an important characteristic of the Registry Hub pattern, and is the reason for its relatively straightforward implementation. The list of master data records registered in the Registry Hub is a superset of all master data records in the application systems.

5.4.1.8 Forces

On the business side, the problem is less difficult to solve compared to the other two MDM Hub Patterns. It still requires buy-in from various Line of Business owners, and—depending on the scope of the MDM project—some data governance capabilities need to be implemented within the enterprise. However, because of the scope and characteristics of the Registry Hub pattern, business-related forces are somewhat less challenging.

Technical challenges exist as well. Just think about how to implement an update on the Registry Hub. For example, if a master data record is created in an application system that only has a subset of the overall master data records locally, do you push this new record right away to the Registry Hub or do you do it in a nightly or weekly batch-oriented fashion? Regardless of the time interval that is applied to push the new record to the MDM System, cleansing and some degree of transformation is required. More importantly, you need to check whether or not the new master data record from the application system is a duplicate in the scope of the enterprise-wide set of records registered in the Register Hub. In case of a duplicate record, there are several options on how to address this scenario. First, compensation logic in the integration layer between the Registry Hub and the application layer might be used to remove the duplicate.

---

16. For implementation details using the information as service concept, see [17].

Alternatively, you can just add another alternate key to an existing record in the Registry Hub that indicates usage of this Customer record by another application. This approach makes the assembly of the view for a master data record more complicated: Information from various sources needs to be accessed, followed by a decision on which master data records from which source has to be provided to the requester. Multiple legacy systems may have overlapping and possibly conflicting information. Therefore, it may not be valid to pick a particular attribute from one source for all of the instances. In addition, data quality issues inherent in the source systems are not addressed in this pattern and may impact the quality of the aggregated information that is returned from the hub. As noted previously, it may very well be that master data quality issues in some or all legacy systems are addressed as part of the overall MDM project. This approach really depends on the business scope and motivation. Overall, deploying this hub type is easier compared to the other hub types, but the ongoing maintenance might be complicated and more costly. In any case, the Registry Hub will not provide a consistent, complete status due to the delay in new records being registered when coming in.

An MDM System deployed with the Registry Hub pattern usually lacks capabilities in the area of master data event management. For the product master data domain, business efficiency improvements in the area of cross- and up-sell cannot be gained effectively, because the master data is not yet actionable. Another constraint might be the inability to efficiently manage relationships and hierarchies. Because the Registry Hub has only a subset of the master data attributes, the capabilities to perform and enforce business rules and data quality constraints are restricted as well. For similar reasons, you cannot implement master data authoring effectively with this hub type.

5.4.1.9 Relations
Related architecture patterns are the Coexistence Hub and the Transaction Hub pattern, as well as the Initial Load pattern, on which this pattern has a dependency.

5.4.2 Coexistence Hub Pattern
Similar to the previous subsection, we now discuss the Coexistence Hub Pattern with regard to the defined MDM Architecture Pattern attributes.

5.4.2.1 Type
The Coexistence Hub pattern is an MDM Architecture Pattern that belongs to the MDM Hub Pattern group.

5.4.2.2 Method of Use
An MDM System built with the Coexistence Hub pattern can support analytical, collaborative, and operational usage styles. The required method of use really depends on the business motivation and the customer needs. It is also likely that the initial method of use (e.g., the operational usage style) will be complemented with another method of use (e.g., the collaborative usage style). In other words, multiple methods of use may exist concurrently. For example, new business processes may require adjustments to the MDM Solution with regard to supporting an additional method of use.

5.4.2.3 System Type

An MDM System built with this pattern is a **system of reference** type MDM Hub. According to the description on "system of reference" and "system of record" in Chapter 1, a system of reference refers to local copies of master data. These copies can sometimes be partial subsets and sometimes completely redundant replicas. However, this type requires management and synchronization with the system of record. And these aspects are exactly the case for the Coexistence Hub pattern: The master data is materialized in the Master Data Repository, but changes to master data may still occur—at least to some degree—at the legacy systems. Thus, synchronization of master data between some (or even all) legacy systems and the MDM Hub is required. In other words, the Coexistence Hub pattern requires synchronization of master data replicas with the system of record in a managed way that maintains the quality and integrity of the data within both the replica and the system of record.

5.4.2.4 Value Proposition

On the business side, an MDM System implemented with the MDM Architecture Pattern Coexistence Hub provides a single version of the truth with high-quality master data enabling informed business decisions. It is the foundation of effective master data lifecycle management. With the master data physically instantiated in such a centralized repository, it also enables improved business agility: If a new application has to be developed, it can subscribe to the MDM System to retrieve all relevant changes on master data. This approach also reduces the development cost of new applications.

On the technical side, it provides a single point of access to master data, hiding the complexity of a heterogeneous IT system landscape. Just think about the need to publish master data to a large number of consumers (e.g., Resellers in a retailer scenario). Instead of implementing a large number of point-to-point connections between each application source system and each consuming application system, the number of connections can be significantly reduced if all of the consuming application systems need only integration with the Coexistence Hub. We worked, for example, with a customer who used this approach to harmonize master data from more than 40 application systems in a central MDM System propagating changes in a nightly batch fashion to it. From the MDM System, using Global Data Synchronization,[17] the Product information was synchronized to a huge number of Resellers, significantly reducing costs by reducing a tremendous amount of point-to-point connections.

5.4.2.5 Context

The first characteristic of the deployment context of this pattern is when the creation and maintenance of the master data records is done to a certain degree within the applications. It can mean anything from having the entire master data authoring process driven by applications or almost all authoring done through the MDM System, except for maybe a single, small application.

The second characteristic is that there is at least one consumer of master data to which the MDM Hub actively publishes changes on master data.

---

17. See Section 6.4 for details on Global Data Synchronization (GDS).

The third characteristic is that the master data is fully instantiated in the MDM Hub, which means that the master data model is physically instantiated for all master data attributes. This characteristic is key to the Coexistence MDM Hub and enables the business to leverage a single source of truth for this specific master data domain.

The fourth characteristic is that master data can be stale within the MDM System. Because the master data authored in the application source systems only appears in the MDM System with a delay, the propagation to consuming application systems also will have a delay, indicating that the consuming applications need to be able to work with some degree of stale master data. The degree of staleness is something that needs to be adjusted to business needs. Due to this fact, the master data might not be actionable with the same efficiency as it would be if the Transaction Hub pattern had been selected.

The fifth characteristic is that the quality of the master data needs to be significantly improved before published to consuming application systems; examples include name and address standardization and de-duplication. Unlike the Registry MDM Hub, where master data quality improvements reside within the scope of the corresponding legacy systems, the quality of master data in the Coexistence MDM Hub is a key concern in the build and also the operational phase of the MDM Hub.

5.4.2.6 Problem Statement

The problem is that master data resides in application silos with a variety of data models. There is also a lack of consistency and completeness to the data. This implementation causes costly point-to-point integration between master data source application systems and master data consuming application systems, which in turn causes increased costs on the business side. The business requirements are also characterized by allowing some degree of staleness of the master data. Based on our experience, this implementation can actually be found in many business scenarios and use cases.

5.4.2.7 Solution

We start by describing the solution provided by the Coexistence Hub pattern in the context of the MDM RA. From the Master Data Management Services component, we see the following architectural building blocks, as shown in Figure 5.10, where the coloring in the figure is aligned with the description provided in Subsection 5.4.1.7.

- **Interface Services:** The Coexistence Hub pattern can support multiple technology bindings such as JMS or Web services for the Interface Services architectural building block, which then invoke the appropriate Lifecycle Management Service. The same MDM service should be invoked for batch processing that is consumed as part of a real-time transaction, in order to maintain and apply the same consistent business logic.
- **Lifecycle Management Services:** Because the Coexistence Hub pattern also supports the authoring of master data, the Lifecycle Management Services architectural building block can support CRUD (Create, Read, Update, and Delete) access for the master data domains managed by the MDM System and can apply business logic. Data Quality Management Services are called by Lifecycle Management Services

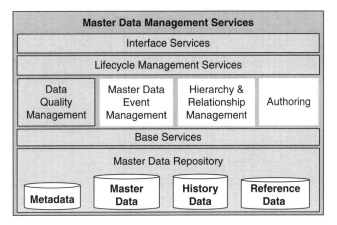

Figure 5.10   The Coexistence Hub Pattern in the Context of the MDM RA.

to enforce data quality rules and perform data cleansing, standardization, and reconciliation.

- **Data Quality Management Services:** This architectural building block is responsible for the delivery of the functions outlined in the MDM RA. It is important to mention that these master data quality management services will be leveraged not only as part of the MDM Hub build phase, but also throughout the operational phase. A new master data record (e.g., a new Customer record) needs to be verified in terms of duplication, completeness, accurateness, and so forth.

- **Master Data Event Management Services:** Services in this group might or might not be available, or they may only be available to a certain degree. For example, acting on a risk event[18] might only make sense if this information is available within a certain time window. Thus, if the staleness of the master data due to the delay in propagation of changes from source application systems to the MDM System is so significant that this time window is exceeded, triggering a risk event based on a business rule that might not make sense anymore.

- **Hierarchy and Relationship Management Services:** Again, the staleness of the data permitted in the Coexistence Hub determines whether or not it makes sense to, for example, implement Identity Analytics based on data from the Coexistence Hub. Thus, not all functions from this architectural building block might be available.

- **Authoring Services:** Assuming that at least some master data is authored through the MDM System, capabilities in this area have to exist. However, we worked with customers where all master data was authored in the application systems, and the MDM System, implemented with the Coexistence Hub pattern, was motivated to reduce the point-to-point connections between the enterprise and large number of suppliers. In this scenario, the hub was for harmonization purposes to publish master data not requiring any authoring capabilities.

---

18. See the solution blueprint in Section 7.4.

- **Base Services:** Security and privacy, search, and audit logging are needed whenever this pattern is deployed. Whether workflow capabilities are needed often depends on whether or not master data authoring in a collaborative fashion is required. Thus, these capabilities might not exist. Base services can be implemented to integrate with Enterprise Common Services that might exist for implementing, for example, a common security model with a security directory and audit logging.
- **The Master Data Repository:** The capabilities of this architectural building block are required. Note that the master data model is fully instantiated, and the master data is materialized within the MDM System. This is a key characteristic of the Coexistence Hub pattern.

Implementing the Coexistence Hub pattern depends on the Initial Load pattern, so most of the functions provided by the information integration services component have to exist as well when this pattern is applied.

Now that we have gained an understanding of the capabilities and characteristics of this pattern in the context of the MDM RA, we investigate how this pattern fits into an IT landscape. Figure 5.11 is a high-level depiction of this MDM Hub Pattern, where it can be seen that the MDM Hub is materialized. However, for some business processes, the change, read, update, and delete transactions may have to be done against the corresponding transactional systems. In other cases, all changes to master data will be performed against the MDM Hub. The MDM Hub, of course, can also be used to access master data and use it for master data reporting purposes. Although the master data is fully materialized, the MDM System is not the only one where changes to the master data will occur: Changes can occur at the MDM Hub system, which needs to be replicated down to the corresponding legacy systems. But changes to the master data may also occur—at least for some business processes or applications—at the legacy systems, where the changes to the master data then need to be replicated with the MDM Hub. Thus, we can also call this MDM Hub Pattern a hybrid pattern, because it may require bidirectional synchronization.

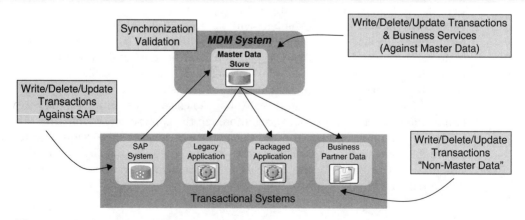

Figure 5.11 Coexistence MDM Hub—Illustration.

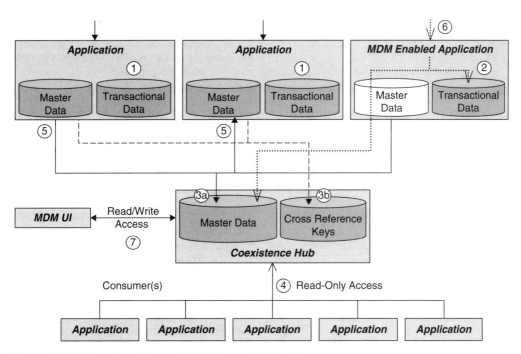

Figure 5.12 The Coexistence Hub Pattern—detailed View.

Let's now examine the details of the Coexistence Hub pattern, shown in Figure 5.12.

Before the Coexistence Hub pattern is deployed, the master data resides with low quality in the master data source application systems (1) and (2). Thus, when the Coexistence Hub is implemented, the master data is extracted, cleansed, standardized, de-duplicated, and loaded into the Master Data Repository in the Coexistence Hub (3a). Also, the cross-reference keys indicate which application(s) has a local copy of the master data records (3b). Notice that there is a difference in the Master Data Integration phase between (1) and (2). For (1), the local copy of the master data remains (you might want to reload the cleaned versions into the application systems). For (2), the application is changed and enabled for MDM. This approach means that the local copy of the master data can be, but does not have to be, removed (that is why the master data box is shown in white). This is also the reason why the Coexistence Hub will not have to maintain any cross-reference keys for this application (3b). The business services accessing the master data is reengineered (6) in such a way that the master data part of the business services is now invoking master data services of the Coexistence Hub. Thus, the master data will be modified at the MDM Hub, and only the transactional, non-master data portion remains in local persistency. Master data-consuming applications can now read all master data attributes from the MDM System. A federation with the source system is not required because the master data model is fully materialized. Operational data stewards, item specialists, or category managers[19] are able to perform read

19. For a description of these MDM user roles, see Appendix A.

and potentially also write operations on master data through an MDM user interface (7) against the Coexistence Hub. Finally, as outlined in Section 5.4.2.8, which describes the forces, decisions need to be made as to how data between source application systems and the Coexistence Hub are synchronized (5). For synchronization purposes, the information synchronization patterns can be used as described in Section 5.5.4.

5.4.2.8 Forces

We see several challenges when implementing this pattern. Let's assume you have two application systems named A and B, both with a need to author the same shared master data record Z. Furthermore, assume A triggers a delete of Z. At a later point in time, this delete is pushed to the Coexistence Hub, which deletes Z. Unless the MDM Hub has propagated the deletion of Z to all other depending systems, a subsequent update on Z submitted by B will fail. If the Coexistence Hub knows that the record Z is still in use by B, it can put the delete on hold until a delete request is also received from B. Alternatively, if the integration layer between your source application systems and the MDM System has a workflow component, and you filter out the delete requests submitted to the MDM System, you can deploy a workflow which we call **coordinated delete.** In essence, this workflow ensures that the delete request is submitted only to the MDM System if all source application systems no longer need the record Z. So the fundamental challenge you need to address is delete consistency on master data when using the Coexistence Hub pattern.

When using this pattern, another interesting question is whether or not you synchronize unidirectionally or bidirectionally between the application systems and the MDM System. Consider the following cases:

- **Standardization of Master Data:** If your MDM System standardizes incoming master data that is authored in the application system, do you write these changes on the data values back to the application system(s)? This step might be difficult, for example, if due to standardization on the MDM System, the value of a field now exceeds the maximum length of the corresponding field in the application system(s).
- **MDM Data Model Changes:** If the data model in the MDM System changes, for example, if a new field appears, do you push this change on the data model back to the relevant application system(s)? If the data model in one or even some of your application system changes, do you push these changes to the MDM System? The answer is most likely "yes."
- **Bidirectional Synchronization:** Let's assume you would like to synchronize both ways. Then you need to come up with a method or conventions avoiding circular, never-ending change propagation. Breaking the circular chain has to be done differently, depending on the technology chosen for the implementation.

In the context of change synchronization between application systems (be it systems that author master data or read-only consumer systems) and the MDM System, there is a question requiring an answer: How much consistency is required across the enterprise IT landscape? The data governance board[20] needs to decide how much staleness of master data in the MDM System is acceptable—in other words, how long it takes to propagate changes on

---

20. For details, see Chapter 9.

a master data record done in the application system to the MDM System (and vice versa). Thus, a decision has to be made about how much convergent consistency is enough or if absolute consistency[21] is required.

Another aspect is that the MDM System implemented with the Coexistence Hub pattern needs to publish changes to a large number of consumers. If this step requires the creation of large numbers of XML messages, this processing might consume significant memory and CPU cycles on the server hardware where your MDM System is running. Consequently, you might need to implement some sort of integration broker using well-known patterns from the ESB and messaging architecture pattern categories. The idea is basically that the MDM System sends only one message per change, and the integration broker transforms the changes to the various data models of the consumers and then dispatches the change to them using a message per consumer.

A challenge might also be to capture changes in your application system. If, for business transaction consistency reasons, you cannot apply the change data capture mechanism at the database level to track changes on master data authored by the application system, you might need to change the application in such a way that the application itself publishes all changes.

A constraint in using this pattern might be implied by the demand for accurate master data. For example, the more up-to-date the master data in the MDM System has to be, the more real-time your information integration processing needs to become.

5.4.2.9 Relations
The Coexistence Hub pattern requires the Initial Load pattern for constructing the MDM System. Often, the Transaction Interception pattern, which will be discussed in Section 5.6, is used. Other related architecture patterns are the Registry Hub and the Transaction Hub pattern. The Coexistence Hub pattern can be used for many MDM Solution Blueprints.

5.4.3 Transaction Hub Pattern
Similar to the two previous subsections, we now present the Transaction Hub pattern with regard to the defined MDM Architecture Pattern attributes.

5.4.3.1 Type
The Transaction Hub pattern belongs to the MDM Architecture Pattern group of MDM Hub Patterns.

5.4.3.2 Method of Use
An MDM System built with the Transaction Hub pattern can support the analytical, collaborative, and operational methods of use.

5.4.3.3 System Type
Building an MDM System using the Transaction Hub pattern is the only way to build a system of record type MDM Hub. If you recall the discussion on the system of record in Chapter 1, it will become clear throughout this section that this MDM Hub Pattern

---

21. For both terms, see Chapter 1.

addresses all required characteristics of a system of record type MDM Hub. Most importantly, this Transaction Hub pattern allows all consuming applications to consult the MDM
Hub as *the* single source of truth for a given master data domain.

5.4.3.4 Value Proposition

The value proposition of the Transaction Hub pattern is to deliver all of the business value
expected from an MDM System, as outlined in Chapter 1. We would like to provide a very
short summary of the value proposition:[22]

- Consistent understanding and trust in master data entities
- Cost savings and efficiencies
- Regulatory compliance
- Ability to easily integrate change required by new business demands

5.4.3.5 Context

The first characteristic of the deployment context of this pattern is that the creation and
maintenance of the master data records are done exclusively through the MDM System. The
second characteristic is that there is at least one consumer of master data to which the MDM
Hub actively publishes changes made to master data. The third characteristic is that the master data is fully instantiated in this implementation style, meaning the master data model is
physically instantiated for all master data attributes. If all application logic can be separated
from the local copies of master data, this separation will mean there remains only one
instance of master data per record. This is the one and only Master Data Repository of the
Transaction Hub. The fourth characteristic is that all master data has to be accurate at all
times within the MDM System. The fifth characteristic is that the data quality of the source
systems needs to be significantly improved before loading it into the MDM Hub. Examples
include name and address standardization and de-duplication of master data records.

5.4.3.6 Problem Statement

The problem is caused by the existence of master data in heterogeneous application silos
with a variety of data models, and lack of consistency, accurateness, and completeness.
These deficiencies cause costly point-to-point integration between master data source application systems and master data-consuming application systems. This problem is also the reason for increased costs on the business side. The business requires accurate master data at any
given point in time. Furthermore, the business relies on a single place for master data
authoring, such as an enterprise wide portal used by all users creating or changing master data.

5.4.3.7 Solution

We start by describing the solution provided by the Transaction Hub pattern in the context
of the MDM RA. From the Master Data Management Services component, we see the architectural building blocks shown in Figure 5.13. You will easily see that no architectural building block is missing and none is marked in light grey to indicate reduced functionality.
Thus, the Transaction Hub pattern requires full functionality in the Master Data Management

---

22. For a detailed discussion on the value proposition, refer again to Chapter 1.

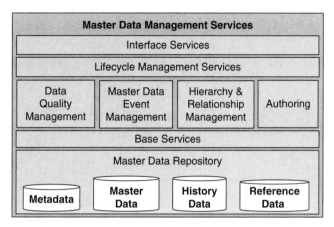

Figure 5.13   The Transaction Hub Pattern in the Context of the MDM RA.

Services component. It is the most sophisticated MDM Hub implementation and conveys the most comprehensive solution scope.

Because the master data is fully materialized, it should not be a surprise that implementing the MDM Transaction Hub pattern leverages the Initial Load pattern. When this pattern is applied, most of the functions provided by the information integration services component have to be used as well.

This MDM Hub Pattern can be used for any MDM Solution. Figure 5.14 is a high-level illustration that of course cannot portray all aspects of this pattern. However, we are trying to illustrate some of the key themes, such as the materialization of master data in the Master Data Repository. Beyond that, the figure also highlights that all of the transactions are executed against the MDM Hub. Of course, the situation shown in Figure 5.14 suggests an MDM

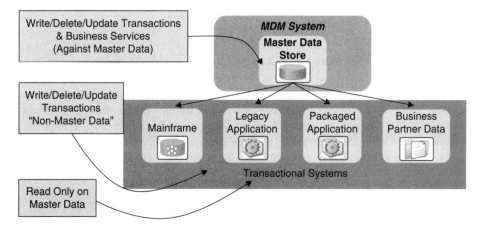

Figure 5.14   Transaction Hub Pattern—Illustration.

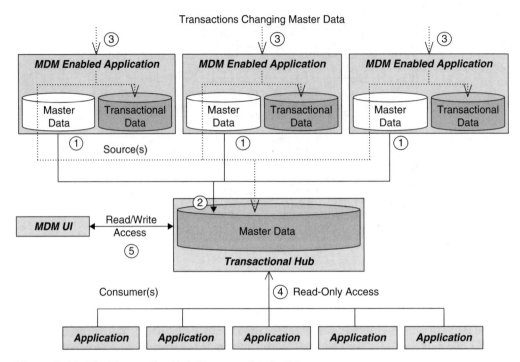

Figure 5.15   The Transaction Hub Pattern   detailed View.

Solution in an "ideal world." The key characteristics of this MDM Transaction Hub are the complete materialization of the master data in the Master Data Repository and the exclusive operational services to be executed against the MDM Hub. Variations of this pattern might be that there are still a few applications left, where master data is changed (source application systems), that are synchronized with the MDM System with synchronous information integration patterns leveraging two-phase commit operations.

Now that we understand the Transaction Hub pattern on a high level, let's look into some of the details, as shown in Figure 5.15. The figure depicts the MDM Transaction Hub pattern in an ideal state, not showing the synchronization details you might need to tackle if you cannot remove local copies of master data in the source application systems. Before the Transaction Hub is built, the master data resides in the source application systems (1). Using the Initial Load pattern, the master data is loaded with high quality into the Master Data Repository (2) of the Transaction Hub. In an ideal world, you would be able to remove the master data copies (1) in the source application systems—thus the boxes are shown in white.

Deploying the Transaction Hub requires changing business functions (3) in such a way that the master data changes are executed with the master data services of the MDM System and only the transactional part of the data involved in the business process is stored locally. These applications require read/write access to master data. Consuming applications can read all data from the Transaction Hub (4) because the master data model is fully materialized through an MDM UI (5) operational data steward or item specialists.[23] In a less ideal world, the local copy (1) of the master data might not be removed. As outlined in this section, information synchronization might be needed between the MDM Transaction Hub and the source application systems.

5.4.3.8 Forces

The most significant challenge for an IT Architect who intends to use this pattern is the following: Each and every application needs to be changed in such a way that whenever the application intends to create or update master data, this request is redirected to the MDM System. This change requires the interception of business transactions on the application level. The dedicated MDM Architecture Pattern that takes into account these forces is the **Transaction Interception** pattern described in Section 5.6.1. A detailed description of the problem and a solution can be found there. This interception of business transactions is usually a very intrusive act on the applications and thus costly to implement. Adding to the technical challenges, there may also be challenges from a budget and time perspective to contain this interception within certain boundaries.

5.4.3.9 Relations

Related architecture patterns are the Registry Hub and the Coexistence Hub pattern as well as the Initial Load pattern on which this pattern has a dependency. This figure also clearly shows the strong affinity to the process and information-focused application integration patterns.

5.4.4 MDM Hub Pattern Comparison

When implementing an MDM Solution using the Registry Hub, the Coexistence Hub, or the Transaction Hub pattern, one of the fundamental questions of the IT Architect is to decide what kind of master data integrity is required in order to address the business requirements. The master data integrity can be measured in the following three dimensions:[24]

- **Correctness:** With master data correctness (sometimes also called accuracy), a measure of correctness is meant to indicate how well master data describes real-world entities. Examples are correct names of Customers and Products, and accurate address information and Product descriptions. If you need to improve the correctness of your master data, you can use data cleansing techniques (see Section 5.5) such as data standardization, data enrichment, or de-duplication. De-duplication can be automated to a certain degree using deterministic or probabilistic matching algorithms,[25] or by operational data stewards.[26] For data validation, which verifies whether or not the data is correct, you can use integration with external data providers[27] or speak to individuals representing the Customer master data.

---

23. For details on these MDM user roles, see Appendix A.

24. We simplify here a bit in order to have a level of abstraction where it is easier to compare the three MDM Hub Patterns side by side; for a thorough discussion of master data integrity, see Chapter 1.

25. For details, see Chapter 9.

26. This MDM user role is described in Appendix A.

27. For some examples, see Section B.3 in Appendix B.

- **Completeness:** Master data completeness deals with the problem of whether or not you can access and work with all relevant attributes of a master data entity. An example is to have available all attributes that are relevant for a Product from a master data perspective. Another example is whether or not you have an enterprise-wide 360-degree view of Customer master data. Improving master data completeness can be done in a variety of ways. For example, you can use data aggregation techniques, as discussed in the Initial Load pattern (see Section 5.5.3). You can also use enrichment techniques by leveraging information from external data providers, or insight gained in analytical systems that can be integrated by using the Analytical System Integration pattern, as described in Section 5.7.3. Depending on the industry, true 360-degree Customer insight may require tight integration with other IT systems such as BI analytical systems.
- **Consistency:** Consistency describes whether or not master data is used across all IT systems in a consistent manner. In an environment where the MDM System is built with the Coexistence Hub pattern, other systems store master data as well, and the question is: Are all these copies consistent or are there differences? Whether all systems have the same Customer address (on which a call center representative using a CRM application might have performed an update due to a customer call) is an example. As introduced in Chapter 1, there is convergent consistency and absolute consistency. Measures to improve consistency are either data synchronization (architecture patterns for this aspect are discussed in Section 5.5) or business transaction synchronization (see the discussion of the Transaction Interception pattern in Section 5.6.1 for details).

We are now sufficiently prepared to effectively compare the MDM Hub Patterns side by side, as shown in Table 5.1.

As you can see from Table 5.1, depending on given business requirements, it is possible to select an MDM Hub Pattern that addresses these requirements.

We should also like to mention that there may be a natural evolution between these three different MDM Hub Patterns, which tends to begin with the Registry Hub pattern, which allows a certain degree of transactional integration of the MDM Hub with the legacy systems. The next evolutionary step is the Coexistence Hub pattern. This is the first step where the MDM Hub is fully materialized. The final evolutionary step leads to the Transaction Hub, where the hub serves not only as an authoritative source of master data, but where all master data services are executed against the MDM System.

Having said this, though, not every customer may begin this MDM journey with the Registry Hub pattern. We have worked with customers who started with a Coexistence Hub (often in the Product master data domain) and others who started with a Transaction Hub (often in the Customer master data domain in the financial services industry). In other words, there are several entry points and even different evolutionary and iterative growth paths. This MDM evolutionary growth is not only related to the MDM Hub Pattern, but also relates to the different methods of use and master data domains. It is from this correspondence of different influencing factors or dimensions that true multiform MDM deployments should be managed with a well-balanced growth strategy in mind.

Table 5.1   Comparison of MDM Hub Patterns

MDM Hub Pattern	Registry Hub	Coexistence Hub	Transaction Hub
Purpose	Central reference	Harmonization	Transactional access
System Type	System of reference	System of reference	System of record
Method of Use	(Analytical, collaborative), operational	Analytical, collaborative, operational	Analytical, collaborative, operational
Master Data	Stored in legacy systems, but can be consistently viewed and derived through linkage to master data in these legacy systems	Stored in MDM and legacy systems, where the MDM System serves as a base for a single source of truth	Stored in MDM and legacy systems, where the MDM System serves as a base for a single source of truth
Master Data Services	Master data creation and maintenance done in legacy systems	Master data creation and maintenance done in legacy systems and the MDM Hub as well	Master data creation and maintenance only done through MDM services provided by MDM System
Type of Access/ Transactions	Read only, where insert, update, and delete statements can only be performed against the legacy systems	Read only, where some of the insert, update, and delete statements will be performed against the MDM Hub, and some of these statements will be performed against the legacy systems	Read and write, where insert, update, and delete statements can be performed directly against the master data in the hub
Correctness	Only key attributes are materialized (cleansed, de-duplicated) in MDM System All other attributes remain unchanged (low quality) in legacy system	On initial load, all master data attributes are cleansed, standardized, and de-duplicated when materialized in MDM System On change, correctness delayed in MDM System due to potential delay in propagation	Given at all times, because access is through MDM services, which incorporate cleanse, standardize, and de-duplication routines

(continued)

Table 5.1 Comparison of MDM Hub Patterns (continued)

MDM Hub Pattern	Registry Hub	Coexistence Hub	Transaction Hub
Completeness	Only through reference to legacy system achieved by virtualization/federation	Complete, because fully materialized on initial load	Complete, because fully materialized on initial load
Consistency	No consistency: Master data remains inconsistent in legacy systems	Converging consistency: Multiple legacy and MDM System are updated; conflicts require resolution	Converging to absolute consistency: Transactions are invoked only through MDM services of MDM System and propagated to consuming applications (asynchronously or synchronously)

5.4.5 High Availability and Disaster Recovery

For an IT system, there are planned and unplanned outages. A planned outage is often a scheduled maintenance cycle required for updating a software component to the next version or for applying a critical security fix. An unplanned outage is a period of time when the system was expected to be available but wasn't. An example is a hardware failure or a software bug. To deal with both categories of outages, there are four important terms that are related to each other: high availability, continuous operations, disaster recovery, and fault tolerance.

High Availability of an IT system is a measure of its readiness for use. Reliability is an inherent characteristic of a component. Reliability is the probability that an IT system performs the intended function for a specified period under stated conditions. If the probability that an IT system performs as expected under stated conditions is low, the availability of such a system cannot be high. Thus, high availability of an IT system demands high reliability. **Continuous Operations** address the need to allow for scheduled maintenance tasks to be performed without any disruption to the overall IT systems operation. **Disaster Recovery** is a process that is required after a major business disruption caused by the occurrence of a disaster. Typical examples are flooding, fire, and earthquakes. **Fault Tolerance** is the ability of an IT system to continue to function as designed even though a fault has occurred.

Disaster recovery and fault tolerance are concepts that improve high availability. Continuous availability is the combination of high availability and continuous operations, thus addressing all categories of outages. As outlined earlier, Master Data Management is usually deployed on an enterprise scale. Thus, it represents a single point of failure, and an IT Architect designing an MDM System should carefully evaluate the key indicators shown in Figure 5.16.

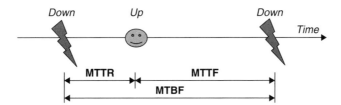

Figure 5.16 Availability of IT Systems.

In Figure 5.16, there are three key indicators related to availability of an IT system:

- **Mean Time To Recovery (MTTR):** This measure indicates how long it will take on average to recover if a system is not available after a disaster or an unplanned outage. In other words, how long can a business survive on average when a certain IT system is not ready for use?
- **Mean Time To Failure (MTTF):** This measure indicates how long on average a system can be used between two failure situations. Of course, this period should be as long as possible—particularly if you have a demand for high availability.
- **Mean Time Between Failure (MTBF):** This measure indicates how much time between two failures of an IT system passes. It is the sum of MTTR and MTTF.

What do these above statements mean for the high-availability requirement? If you have a strong demand for a highly available system, the MTTR and the number of occurrences where the IT system is down has to be as small as possible. An IT Architect needs to know two more formulas regarding availability:

- **Components involved in an IT System regarding Availability multiply:** If a system has three components and the availability of the individual components denoted with A1, A2, and A3, then the overall system has an availability A = A1 * A2 * A3, where A is smaller than A1, A2, and A3, indicating that the product is smaller than its factors. Generally speaking, the availability of a system is the product of the availability measures of its components.
- **Availability Improvements through Redundancy:** Assuming a system is duplicated using redundancy and load balancer techniques and we duplicate a system three times, and each copy is denoted with A1, A2, and A3, the overall availability of the system is computed by A = 1 − [(1 − A1) * (1 − A2) * (1 − A3)]. This formula can be easily extended for more than three redundant copies. If this route is taken to achieve high availability, the overall availability of a system is higher than each of its redundant components.

Let's now look at the MDM Hub Patterns. With regard to availability, the Registry Hub depends on the availability of the source systems. If the MDM System was built with the Registry Hub pattern, it needs to provide a consistent view on master data entities for a large number of source systems. The availability of the MDM Hub implemented with this pattern can decrease rapidly, according to the first formula presented. However, because the creation and maintenance of master data records is already done in the application source systems, this step might not represent a severe business disruption. The reason for this assessment is because only the read access to the enterprise view on all records might be disrupted for some time. Let's assume the software used for the MDM System has a relational database as persistency and the Master Data Management Services implemented as a J2EE application running on a J2EE application server. Making the MDM System highly available by making the J2EE application highly available with redundancy on the J2EE application server and database layer does not make sense beyond the availability of the source systems in this case.

The MDM System built with the MDM Architecture Pattern Transaction Hub manages all master data entities, and all operations on master data is performed through the master data services that are provided by it. The advantage of this system is that providing their master data service is no longer dependent on other source systems. Because fewer systems are involved for managing master data, this situation increases the availability according to the first formula presented. However, unlike an MDM System built with the Registry Hub pattern, all relevant business processes come to a sudden halt if an MDM System built with the Transaction Hub pattern fails due to a mission-critical business disruption. No create, read, update, or delete operation on master data is possible if the MDM System in this case is unavailable. Naturally, the continuous availability requirements for an MDM System built with the Transaction Hub pattern are significantly higher than the MDM deployments using the Registry Hub pattern. Thus, in this case we recommend having all components for an MDM System of this type usually redundant for failover as well as for planned outages for maintenance. For example, for software failures, vertical scaling techniques can be applied to achieve redundancy for J2EE application servers if the hardware servers are powerful enough in terms of CPU cycles, memory, and other resources. For hardware failures, horizontal scale-out techniques can be used by providing additional physical servers. Relational databases today also usually offer several different possibilities for making the database highly available and continuously operational. The specific feature selection depends on the concrete requirements, budget, and available hardware. For example, a hot standby with instant failover for a database server achieved with mirroring techniques on the physical storage level is available only with appropriate storage hardware.

The process of disaster recovery or recovery from an unplanned outage involves several components:

- **People:** For performing this process, users in the role of Problem Analyst, Resilience Engineer, IT Administrator, Database Administrator, and Security Administrator might be involved.[28] These users need to be educated on the disaster recovery process and regularly trained. Only if you have well-trained staff available to run the disaster recovery process in its most efficient manner will you possibly achieve minimal MTTR.
- **Software:** Performing disaster recovery requires support from technology. You need to select software products with appropriate features. You might need to implement appropriate backup processes using the right technology in order to be able to restore a database.
- **Hardware:** In case of a disaster, you might have the need to have a redundant IT Center with redundant server hardware in place to quickly perform disaster recovery.

In the end, it depends on your business requirements how much you need to invest on high availability and disaster recovery measures. From an MDM implementation style perspective,

---

28. All these user roles are described in detail in Appendix A.

generally speaking we usually see an increasing demand for continuous availability (including high availability and disaster recovery) capabilities from MDM Registry to Transaction Hub implementation styles.

5.4.6   Security

No matter which implementation style you choose for your MDM System—Registry Hub, Coexistence Hub, or Transaction Hub—you may have to deal with the following paradox: You improve the value of your master data by having a centralized way of accessing it and at the same time you are increasing the risk because there is now a centralized way of accessing *all* of it—this implementation means breaking into a single system is good enough to get access to all master data. The MDM System is a treasure box—it contains the most valuable business information an enterprise has, the gold nuggets that are your master data entities. These represent the lifeblood of a company—almost all critical business processes like manufacturing products or selling products and services contain Product or Customer master information, or both. Thus, for example, a CDI MDM Solution is a prime target for internal and external identity thieves—getting access to high-quality customer information in large quantities on an enterprise scale is tempting. Thus, we cannot stress the point enough that you should consider appropriate security measures, as outlined in Chapter 3. We are not repeating the details from that chapter here, but we strongly advise you to consult that chapter when selecting any of the MDM Hub Patterns for building your MDM System. In addition, in Section 6.5.5 in Chapter 6, you can find many security-related concepts introduced in Chapter 4 applied in the context of a concrete MDM Solution Blueprint. There you find a lot of information on how to apply security for concrete MDM Solutions.

5.5   Information-Focused Application Integration Patterns

Information Integration is a theme that has been well known in the IT industry for many years. Thus, not surprisingly, a lot of architecture patterns exist. For the scope of the discussion here, we intend to just summarize what is out there to establish common ground on the most relevant and well-known information integration patterns that have an affinity to Master Data Management, either for building the MDM Hub or for integrating the MDM System after it is built into the existing application landscape. After this initial step, in a second step we show how the Information as a Service concept introduced in Chapter 2 changed well-known information integration patterns such as the cleansing or the consolidation pattern. This step is particularly relevant if MDM is deployed in a larger SOA-style MDM Solution. Information integration patterns are applicable to data integration problems, such as data warehouse projects, system consolidation, or migration projects. The Information as a Service concept can be applied to many information integration patterns, and as we discussed in Chapter 2, the scope of the concept is not limited to traditional, well-known information integration topics.

5.5.1   Introduction of Relevant Information Integration Patterns

An overview of relevant information integration patterns can be seen in Figure 5.17. The information integration patterns are primarily linked to the information-focused application integration pattern category. Specifically, the Initial Load and the Information Synchronization

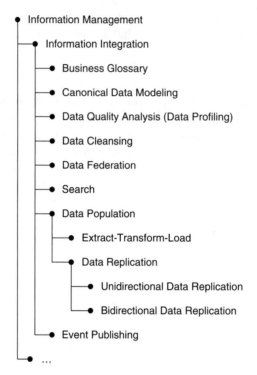

Figure 5.17   Overview of Information Integration Patterns.

patterns have a strong relationship with the information integration patterns. For example, the MDM Initial Load pattern has a close relationship to the Data Cleansing and the Data Population patterns (shown in Figure 5.17). The Information Synchronization pattern is related to the Data Replication and the Event Publishing patterns.

Even though the patterns in the category of information-focused application integration have strong relationships to the information integration patterns shown in Figure 5.17, there are also differences that are unique to MDM. For example, the Initial Load pattern coexists with the Information Synchronization pattern. The reason is that after the MDM Hub is built using the Coexistence Hub pattern, you might still load deltas authored in the application system using the infrastructure created with the Initial Load pattern parallel to bidirectional synchronizing of the master data with other application systems. Bidirectional replication is something which is rarely—if ever—applied in complex traditional data warehouse environments.

5.5.2   Effect of Information as a Service on Information Integration Patterns

In Chapter 2 we introduced the concept of Information as a Service, which has the ability to deliver information management functions as services in an SOA environment. This concept has undeniably also affected the peculiarity of traditional information integration patterns, such as data federation, data cleansing, and data population. For a comprehensive discussion on how the Information as a Service concept impacts information integration patterns such as the federation pattern, the data cleansing pattern, and the data population pattern, we refer the reader to [17], [18], and [19], and only highlight a few benefits here:

- **Real-time Master Data Qualification and Validation:** If you implement the data cleansing pattern as described in [19], you can move cleansing functions to the front-line application systems. Traditionally, the data cleansing pattern was used at the end of the data lifecycle, when data was loaded into the data warehouse where, for example, address standardization and verification were done. By applying the cleansing pattern with the Information as a Service concept, you can seamlessly integrate these functions into your MDM System or in your front-line application system, depending on where you author master data. Thus, if a customer is trying deliberately to provide a wrong address when speaking to a call center employee, the call center employee would immediately get a response from the application that, for example, an area code for a city does not exist. This approach enables real-time detection of low-quality data, which is prevented from entering the system.
- **Utilization of the Federation Pattern:** If you implement the Registry Hub pattern, using the federation pattern (as described in [17] with the Information as a Service concept applied to it) can be one way to interact with the MDM System. So the MDM System would provide the cross-reference keys for the lookup done using the federation pattern to retrieve the master data from the application systems.

The Information as a Service concept as applied to the patterns just mentioned can be implemented with products listed in Section B.4 in Appendix B.

5.5.3   Initial Load Pattern

Before we dive into the Initial Load pattern, we would like to elaborate a bit on Master Data Integration (MDI), a process used to build and initially populate an MDM System. It is a key component of any MDM Solution implementation. The process of Master Data Integration is condensed from the architectural perspective in the Initial Load pattern, which can be considered a variation and composition of known information integration patterns such as the data consolidation and the data cleansing pattern. Using the Initial Load pattern might look like using traditional ETL processes, as they are well known, for example, for loading data into data warehouses. And we recognize that there are many aspects where Master Data Integration and ETL processing are very similar, for example, in the extraction step of data from a variety of data sources.

Traditional DW and data mart ETL staging patterns are very much characterized by complex and sophisticated data transformation routines, which involve sophisticated data aggregation and grouping, consolidation, and preparation tasks. The primary purpose is to generate a consolidated view that serves specific, predefined reporting requirements. In essence, the data warehouse is built in a one-way fashion and mainly serves read-only reporting needs. In contrast to this objective, and as we have seen in Chapter 2, MDM Systems need to generate an application-independent, enterprise-wide view of the master data. Specific analytical reporting needs may still be derived from the BI systems. This difference also means that the MDM Initial Load pattern is lacking the complexity of the DW ETL staging patterns. Furthermore, the MDM Initial Load pattern needs to enable and coexist with the information synchronization patterns. And we see in this chapter that this approach requires bidirectional replication, which is not feasible in complex DW environments.

As a gross generalization, there are some aspects worth mentioning in comparison to traditional ETL processing.

The first interesting aspect is the load step. As you know, the access to master data is not on a database interface level anymore—it is through the master data services interface layer of the MDM System (see Chapter 3). Inserting a Customer record through a database interface is faster than an insert through the services interface of the MDM System (assuming proper coding on both interfaces). The reason for this difference is simple: The service creating a new Customer on the services interface layer performs additional tasks such as data integrity and business rule enforcement, duplicate checking, and events and notification processing. So if you need to load a huge number of Customer records through the services interface layer, this task will need more time than a load operation executed on the database interface layer for a persistency target. You might ask, "Why bother to load through the services interface of the MDM System in the first place?" The reason is simple: If you buy a piece of MDM software, you might not know all of the dependencies between attributes enforced by the services interface implicitly. Bypassing the services interface by loading directly to the tables in the database might cause your MDM System to not work correctly or to not work at all. Our recommendation[29] is to load master data through the services interface into the system whenever possible.

The second interesting aspect compared to traditional ETL is the availability of technology that supports the Information as a Service concept (see Chapter 2). As you can see, the traditional data cleansing pattern [19] and the data consolidation pattern [18], pieces of the ETL process, are already affected by SOA and the Information as a Service concept. We believe, in the context of Master Data Integration, this aspect can and should be taken to the next level: If you look at many cleansing tasks (name standardization, address standardization, de-duplication, etc.) performed in the context of loading data into a data warehouse, then these tasks were a cure for a problem caused much earlier in the data lifecycle—at the point when data entered your IT landscape through applications. In the past, applications could not easily integrate functions such as name and address standardization or address verification. With the ability to expose such functions as information services, they can now seamlessly be integrated into business processes. An example is a "create customer" process where the integrity services of your MDM System, as described in the MDM RA, reuses the cleansing tasks to ensure the master data quality does not degrade after the MDM build phase. If you use the MDM Transaction Interception pattern (see Section 5.6.1) to integrate an application system and an MDM System, another aspect

---

29. For every rule, there is an exception. We worked with a few customers where this recommendation could not be followed. In one case, significantly more than 30 million Customer records had to be loaded into the MDM production system, which, given the hardware resources on which the MDM system was deployed, was simply not possible. Because this was known upfront, a direct load through a database interface was implemented. However, due to this risky procedure, the phase for master data integration was significantly extended, mainly to test the procedure thoroughly to minimize—not exclude—the risk that the MDM system did not work afterwards. So if you deviate from the recommendation, we strongly advise extending the master data integration phase.

is that you might need the same transformations again when your MDM System is operational for a synchronous, real-time integration.[30] The key point here is that the data architect should analyze the entire IT landscape to verify whether or not cleansing and transformation routines built during the MDI phase can be leveraged for overall quality improvements or TCO reduction. This approach would simplify ETL processing for data warehouses and data marts by avoiding low-quality data in the system landscape from the beginning.

The third interesting aspect of MDI is the treatment of metadata. Without metadata, as described in Chapter 1, there is no way to establish trust in your master data. MDM and metadata management have some important affiliations. Implementing MDI with information services requires several things:

- **Information Services Description:** This description is metadata that needs to be stored somewhere (such as in the service registry) for subsequent discovery and usage purposes. Note that the services exposed through the services interfaces of the MDM System are information services themselves—in this case, master data information services (instead of a cleansing or information transformation services).
- **Metadata regarding Data Models:** The metadata describing the various discovered source data models and the known target data model of the MDM Hub has to be stored and managed somewhere. Developers designing and implementing transformations benefit from the availability of this metadata because it allows them to use graphical tools for defining mappings and reduces the development time.
- **Annotation of Metadata:** The target data model is the data model of the MDM System. The metadata describing the master data entities should be available with annotations to business analysts and business modelers who are in charge of changing business processes. New or changing business requirements can affect the data model for master data, too. Without the availability of this metadata in an easy-to-use and easy-to-understand form, you may encounter the first obstacle when your MDM Solution requires adaptation due to new business requirements.

The fourth difference is data governance. Establishing strong data governance procedures[31] is a critical success factor for deploying any MDM Solution. We believe the following areas are the key points relevant for the MDI phase:

- **Profiling and analyzing all source systems:** Before sizing the MDI phase, profiling of all systems potentially containing master data should be done. The data organization within an enterprise has then to decide on the convergence of the various data models from existing application systems to the MDM data model.
- **Management of changes against defined baseline:** As the final step of the MDI phase, the master data quality baseline should be profiled against the newly built MDM Hub. Based on this baseline and the business requirements, the data governance organization has to decide how and in which intervals the master data quality should be profiled again and compared against the agreed-upon baseline when

---

30. See Section 8.3 for an MDM Integration Blueprint where this is applied.
31. For details, see Chapter 9.

the MDM System was built. Procedures and methodologies should be defined as to what should be done in case the new master data quality measurements drop below the defined baseline.

- **Impact analysis based on new business requirements:** During the MDI phase, the data governance group has to define how data lineage tools can be used to perform impact analysis. This definition should be done based on the discovered data models and their stored metadata. The objective is to see immediately if business requirements mandate master data model adaptations and which transformation services (or other information services) and application systems are affected. Should you not be able to identify which information service is affected by a master data model change, you will not be able to effectively use an infrastructure based on them. Also, procedures have to be established to determine who is allowed to change the master data model, and what are the circumstances that permit such a change.

In our opinion, the end-to-end consideration as outlined earlier is a comprehensive approach to integrating master data for building MDM Solutions.

5.5.3.1 Type

The Initial Load pattern belongs in the information-focused integration pattern category. The Initial Load pattern is a composite pattern.

5.5.3.2 Method of Use

The pattern is not applicable for a specific method of use because its only purpose is the creation of the MDM System, whereas the method of use is determined by the way the master data is used after the system is built.

5.5.3.3 System Type

Because this pattern is not an MDM Hub Pattern, the value of the system type attribute is not applicable for this pattern.

5.5.3.4 Value Proposition

The value of this pattern is to load high-quality master data into the MDM System. This step is done after the data is extracted from application systems, cleansed, standardized, de-duplicated, and transformed. This MDM Architecture Pattern provides a set of structured assets that accelerate development of architectural deliverables that are applicable for the build phase of any MDM Hub. Subpatterns, areas of concerns, forces, constraints, and so forth are usable as a method to further customize and even refine a chosen subset of these architecture patterns for the needs of a concrete project.

5.5.3.5 Context

The deployment context of the Initial Load pattern is to reach out and access relevant master data, which is still captured in the heterogeneous legacy systems. These legacy systems do own, control, and "understand" the master data. Furthermore, the master data needs to be cleansed, enriched, and transformed prior to loading it into the Master Data Repository of the MDM System. In those cases where the MDM Hub is not fully materialized, for example, in the Registry MDM Hub pattern, the master data needs to be made available to the MDM Hub. It may sound like we are touching upon the traditional ETL staging processes that we are all familiar with from our data warehousing experience. Nevertheless, when we elaborate on the forces and constraints for these patterns, we further elaborate and provide additional reasons why the problem(s) the pattern tries to solve are a bit different from ETL. For example, not all data warehouses use a normalized data model. Within an MDM System, a fully normalized data model is a key technical feature for efficient data processing. Thus, the ETL processing needs adaptation to reflect these principal facts.

5.5.3.6 Problem Statement

The problem this pattern addresses is given by the issue to move master data from an unmanaged state into a managed state.[32] In order to accomplish this transition, master data needs to be extracted, cleansed, de-duplicated, transformed, and loaded into the Master Data Repository of the MDM System.

5.5.3.7 Solution

The MDM specifics of these architecture patterns are, furthermore, related to take into account the different MDM Hub Patterns. For example, in the build phase of the MDM hub, the master data needs to be transformed in such a way that, for example, transaction interception is enabled. That is, bidirectional replication and synchronization between the MDM Hub and the legacy operational systems need to be possible. From Figure 5.18 it can be seen that there are several information integration patterns used in the pattern composition to derive the Initial Load pattern. This list can very well be refined. Furthermore, the presented patterns need to be adjusted to the specific project characteristics and requirements. The solution should be viewed in accordance with the anticipated achievements of the pattern composition.

The following information integration patterns, illustrated in Figure 5.18, should be viewed as complementary and serve as input for initial load composition tasks in order to derive a customized, project-oriented MDM Hub build pattern.

Let's further describe the patterns used to compose the Initial Load pattern:

- **Profiling:** There are various profiling patterns, such as the Structural Profiling and the Semantic Profiling pattern. When the Initial Load pattern is deployed as part of the composition of this profiling pattern, profiling is done on all source systems to discover the data models in use as well as the state regarding data quality. Only if this basic analysis is done can accurate estimates as to how much effort is needed to perform Master Data Integration be determined in order to size the work of Data Integrators.[33]

---

32. Both of these terms were introduced in Chapter 1.
33. For details on this MDM user role, see Appendix A.

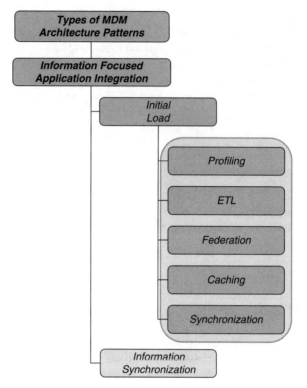

Figure 5.18   Patterns used in Pattern Composition for the Initial Load Pattern.

- **ETL:** This is a group of patterns to perform several tasks: First, the data has to be extracted from the source systems. Second, the data has to be cleansed. Third, the data has to be transformed from the source data model to the target data model (in the case of multiple sources with multiple source data models, it has to be transformed into a single target data model). Fourth, the data has to be loaded into the target system.
- **Federation:** Specifically, for the Registry MDM Hub Pattern, but to some degree even for the Coexistence Hub pattern, federation techniques will be used to allow for a single master data view because some legacy systems may still remain in control of *their* master data records. Thus, when populating the Master Data Repository using the Initial Load pattern, it must be taken into consideration how the federated access will be implemented to grant read-access. For example, these circumstances might affect the data model and consequently the transformation routines that are implemented with the Initial Load pattern. For granting federated access, there is the Federation pattern. However, in order to be able to deploy that effectively, a concrete instantiation of the Initial Load pattern has to take the federation requirements into consideration.

- **Caching:** The Caching pattern can be combined with the Federation pattern. It is useful to improve performance to access and retrieve the master data. This pattern is specifically applicable for the Registry Hub pattern.
- **Synchronization:** Based on the MDM Hub build process, delta changes happening in the source application systems might need to be captured while the bulk processing of the extracted master data records is performed. This task can easily run for several days. Thus, these deltas need to be captured and continuously added until the source application systems and the MDM System are synchronized. This task can be done with trickle feeds[34] into the MDM System.

From the earlier discussion of subpatterns, it seems obvious that there are important differences to the traditional BI/data warehousing ETL processes. We stress again that these patterns also need to address master data consolidation and migration, without necessarily building and *materializing* an MDM Hub. Most of these patterns are also used in cases of system migrations and consolidations, for example, when multiple ERP instances are consolidated into a single ERP instance. In this case, master data contained in the source ERP systems might be improved from a data quality perspective before the data is loaded into the new target ERP system. This improvement can be achieved by using these patterns without necessarily building and materializing an MDM Hub.

With respect to the MDM RA, the patterns mentioned earlier to compose and implement the Initial Load pattern are in the Information Integration Services component, as shown in Chapter 3.

Figure 5.19 depicts the scope of these patterns at a high level. This graphic illustrates clearly that the source of master data is included in the legacy transactional systems, be they mainframe operational systems, legacy, or packaged applications (e.g., ERP and CRM), or even industry-specific applications from Independent Software Vendors (ISVs).

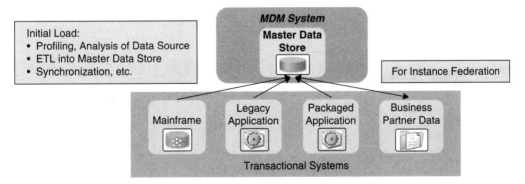

Figure 5.19   Initial Load Pattern—Illustration of Master Data Load from Transactional Systems.

---

34. Trickle feeds are used for similar reasons in the traditional data warehouse environment.

We cannot present here all possible compositions of the information integration patterns used to compose the Initial Load pattern. However, Figure 5.19 clearly illustrates the key themes of the Initial Load pattern: profiling, ETL, federation, and so forth. Furthermore, this Figure suggests a materialized master data store. However, this data store may not be needed under all circumstances: Specifically in architecturally less mature IT environments, we have very often been confronted with the need to "improve" the master data "situation." This can, for example, mean to consolidate operational data stores that store master data. It can also mean to improve the quality of master data within the distinct operational data store. All of these necessary tasks require the use of the Initial Load architecture pattern, specifically ETL subpatterns—but they need to be deployed in a specific and customized way. In these specific ETL scenarios, there is a focus on extraction, transformation, and quality improvement, followed by loading the data back into the existing operational data store. With this basic understanding, we can now dive into further details of the MDM Initial Load pattern, as shown in Figure 5.20.

In a first step (1), profiling is done on the source systems. Here, the Initial Load pattern implementation leverages profiling patterns, as mentioned before. In a second step, the data extraction (2) happens. Depending on whether or not this profiling task can be done at a database level, database replication technologies can be used to implement the data replication patterns. Otherwise, adapters to the application interfaces extracting the master data can be used. This is the reason why many comprehensive information integration software

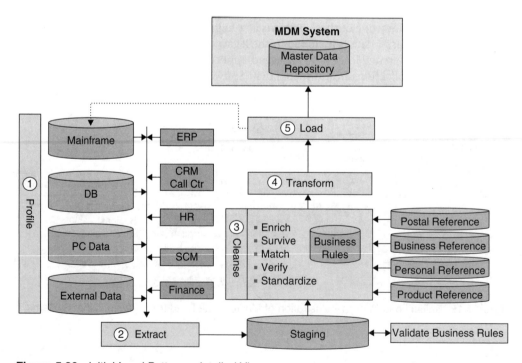

Figure 5.20   Initial Load Pattern—detailed View.

packages[35] provide these adapters in addition to database access and database replication technologies. For further processing, the extracted data is moved to a staging area. The next step is then the cleanse (3) step. For example, names, addresses, or Product descriptions are standardized. Address information might be verified against postal references. In this step, also de-duplication by implementing matching and survivorship rules is done.[36] In the cleanse step, enriching the master data with attributes from external resources is often done as well. For example, if a system for identity analytics is available, processing on the cleansed data can now be done to discover hidden relationships in Customer master data records. This hidden relationship information can be used to enrich the Customer master data. Other possibilities could be to include external resources providing credit scores for Customer master data. Then, the next step is to transform (4) the master data from the data model used in the staging area to the data model used in the Master Data Repository of the MDM System. Finally, the master data is loaded (5) into the MDM System and is thus materialized there. Note that the dotted line indicates that, for fulfilling master data consistency requirements throughout the IT landscape, the original low quality master data in the source systems needs to be replaced with the high-quality master data now available. This coherence is shown as an example for the mainframe data source through the dotted line. If this replacement is done, the transform from the staging area data model to the mainframe data model requires implementation in order to make this load step work.

5.5.3.8 Forces

The problem is hard to solve for a variety of reasons:

- **Profiling:** Here, the basic challenge is to map logical data models to physical data models. Let's explain this statement. There are applications that don't allow using data replication techniques. Data replication techniques might not always be able to respect the semantics encapsulated in business transactions spanning multiple database transactions across a broad variety of tables. The reason for this gap in the replication techniques is that they work at the row level. If you would use data replication techniques, consistency on the database is guaranteed. However, consistency from an application point of view might be violated. For example, the application submits the appropriate transactions to the database to take out a previously inserted record, and then the record that was extracted may be deleted. So these application systems often provide a business object interface. A business object is usually a hierarchically structured data object where individual attributes are drawn from multiple rows in multiple tables. The extraction of data to the staging area where cleansing happens, applicable also to extract master data, has to be done through this business object interface instead of directly accessing the database. Now if the profiling tool is working at the physical database level, the physical data model will be used to perform column analysis or cross-column analysis. Usually there is no or little documentation provided by the application vendor as to how

---

35. For examples, see Section B.4 in Appendix B.
36. For details on this data quality aspect and algorithms, see the data quality section of Chapter 9.

the logical data model is mapped to the physical data model. This mapping is often hidden in the application implementation. However, understanding the profiling results in the context of the logical data model is required because you need to know how the results relate to the fields extracted on the business object interface.

- **Harmonization of multiple Data Models:** Used by applications for the same master data entity. Even if there is only one data model that needs to be mapped to the MDM System, this mapping is not a simple task. As an example, consider mapping a Customer data model of an SAP ERP application to the Customer data model of the MDM CDI system.

- **Data Synchronization after the MDM System is operational:** This may sound trivial, but in these deployment scenarios, the data model of the MDM Hub needs to take into account the data structure of the master data model of those legacy systems. After the MDM System is loaded, information synchronization might require the same cleansing and transformation routines that were used by the Initial Load pattern. This requirement exists because the data model between the source application systems and the MDM System are still different. Thus, a data architect needs to think about the issue of how these cleansing and transformation routines can be designed so that you can leverage them for bulk processing and single record processing. Single record processing often needs to happen in real-time (particularly if these routines are used in the scope of the Transaction Interception pattern).

- **De-duplication:** The best candidate search and matching algorithms[37] will not be able to decide *all* cases of records that are looking similar. Thus, operational data stewards[38] need to work on the other cases to make decisions.

- **Load Window:** Because the master data must be loaded through the master data services interface into the MDM System, there may be an issue with the available window for the load task. The master data services need to apply a considerable amount of logic (e.g., data quality and business rule enforcement) to each new master data record to ensure a consistent state for when the MDM Hub starts to be used. This required logic, however, can cause longer load times for the same amount of data when compared to a load done at the database level.

Other forces and constraints are related to the problems and the context, which we have already discussed: An enterprise-wide MDM System can be materialized in an MDM Transaction Hub or built as an MDM Registry Hub. For an MDM Solution to take on an enterprise-wide scope, there is a need to be able to access literally all data sources in a potentially diverse and heterogeneous landscape with different relational database management systems and content sources from different vendors. Therefore, all of these patterns need to include special data access routines. For example, these access routines need to address the

---

37. See Chapter 9 for more details.
38. For a description of this MDM user role, see Appendix A.

needs for packaged ERP and CRM applications. Depending on the MDM Hub Pattern chosen, this consideration will have a significant impact on the Initial Load pattern.

Note that a DW system is not designed to be an MDM System, and the DW system is not intended to be tightly integrated into the operational environment. Another constraint for deploying the Initial Load pattern is the question on convergent versus absolute consistency on master data. What this context means, for example, in the context of a Coexistence or Transaction Hub, is that improving master data quality and loading it into the Master Data Repository is not good enough. After the master data is cleansed, there might be the requirement to replace the low-quality data in some application systems with the clean master data as well, making a big step toward convergent consistency. Unfortunately, the data model of the source system and the MDM System rarely match. Thus, the load step might need to be implemented multiple times: once for the MDM System and once for each source application system where the master data requires replacement to improve master data quality. This write back to the source application systems after the quality improvements are done is different than how ETL is traditionally done in the data warehousing environment. It might also be a required step in a master data harmonization strategy across the entire IT landscape.

5.5.3.9 Relations
The MDM Initial Load pattern is related to many information integration patterns that are listed in Figure 5.17. This relationship is because the Initial Load pattern uses many of them to accomplish its task. The Initial Load pattern can thus be considered a composite pattern that leverages basic patterns such as data replication or data cleansing.

5.5.4 Information Synchronization Patterns

This set of patterns is undeniably one of the most important MDM Architecture Patterns. Synchronizing master data from the MDM Hub "down" to the legacy systems and, vice versa, "up" to the MDM Hub is an essential aspect in any MDM Solution. Especially where either the Coexistence Hub pattern or the Transaction Hub pattern is deployed, these Information Synchronization patterns need to be leveraged and implemented.

5.5.4.1 Type
The patterns of this category belong to the type of information-focused integration patterns. Patterns such as the data replication pattern were introduced in Section 5.5.1.

5.5.4.2 Method of Use
The information synchronization patterns discussed in Section 5.5.4 can be used in the analytical, collaborative, and operational methods of use.

5.5.4.3 System Type
Because these patterns are not MDM Hub Patterns, this attribute is not applicable.

5.5.4.4 Value Proposition
The value proposition of the information synchronization patterns is that they help to implement convergent consistency or even absolute consistency of master data across the

IT landscape. These patterns are often encountered when an MDM System is built with the Coexistence or Transaction Hub pattern.

To achieve this synergistic view between the various architecture patterns, we should be guided by the understanding that quite a number of relevant patterns from different categories will actually have to adequately collaborate with each other. Gaining this understanding means that we have, for example, an operational MDM method of use, where the deployment is based on a Coexistence Hub. These patterns ensure proper synchronization between the MDM Hub and all relevant legacy systems. This synchronization can either be done in a unidirectional or a bidirectional way. Thus, they enable an MDM System to allow chosen transactions and master data services to be executed against the MDM Hub while still keeping master data in sync with the legacy environment. Beyond that, these architecture patterns also allow chosen transactions to be executed unchanged against legacy systems while still maintaining a single source of truth at the MDM Hub level. Through this rich assortment of information synchronization patterns, we gain the ability to complement any MDM Hub pattern and any MDM deployment with the required master information synchronization components. That is, we are now well positioned to plug in required information synchronization patterns in a given context.

5.5.4.5 Context

The context of using the information synchronization patterns can be industry-agnostic or industry-specific. An application system that consumes master data in read-only fashion and that cannot be separated from its local database must be served by unidirectional synchronization of master data changes from the MDM System via database replication techniques.

An industry-specific example is the retail and Product consumer goods market. There is a strong requirement to synchronize and retrieve at least part of the master data from public data pools (e.g., 1SYNC[39]), which needs to be addressed by these patterns as well. 1SYNC is a community of manufacturers and retailers that focuses primarily on supporting the community's data synchronization efforts.

Beyond that, the context is also characterized by the need to apply information synchronization for a heterogeneous set of applications, where many end users may continue to maintain master data through existing workflows and UIs to known business applications. Furthermore, data models in the different application domains need to be mapped to the data model of the MDM Hub. Finally, this information synchronization context requires the introduction of data governance methods.

5.5.4.6 Problem Statement

Synchronization is a process with a time dimension: It can be done in batch mode on demand, periodically (a batch run once every night), in near real-time or in real-time. There can very well be the need to maintain a single source of master data truth literally at any

---

39. 1SYNC and other relevant terms for Global Data Synchronization (GDS) are thoroughly discussed in Section 6.4. In that section, we will also dive into these industry-related aspects and will elaborate on, among other topics, GDS in the retail industry.

given point in time. This requirement would equate with the need to interlock or even combine transactional updates (e.g., done to a legacy ERP system) with the synchronization step. We continue to elaborate on this aspect when we discuss forces and constraints in more detail later. Another interesting challenge is naturally the bidirectional flavor of the information synchronization, especially for "overlapping" master data. The challenge here is to develop a master data replication strategy that is, for example, based on disjoining (meaning to eliminate the overlap) those parts of master data that get updated in different legacy systems or at the MDM Hub.

5.5.4.7   Solution

Given these problems and the discussed context, the solution space needs to address a rather broad scope of information synchronization aspects. And as can be seen in Figure 5.21, there are a number of subpatterns that are linked to this required solution space. These patterns are not completely disjointed they provide different views and highlight different aspects of

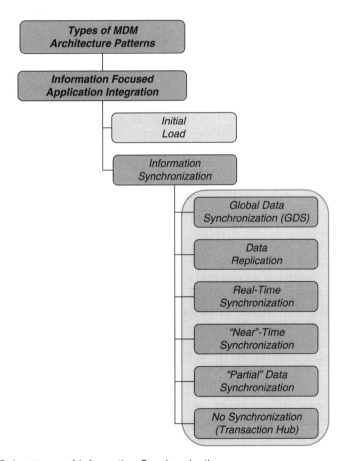

Figure 5.21   Subpatterns of Information Synchronization.

the required information synchronization solution scope. Depending on the MDM Solution requirements, there may even be a need to adequately compose several of these Information Synchronization subpatterns to work in concert.

The following list introduces the key subpatterns of the Information Synchronization pattern. Each of these subtypes can even be divided into further subpatterns. And as was stated previously, in a "real" MDM Solution, these MDM Architecture Patterns should be viewed as related to each other, where a particular MDM Solution may very well be leveraging multiple subpatterns.

- **Global Data Synchronization (GDS):** This is actually a set of patterns that is specifically tailored towards the needs of the retail industry, where standards-based exchange of master data is required. With regard to the master data scope, there may be a need to synchronize GDS-related attributes only.
- **Data Replication:** These data replication patterns are part of the traditional data replication pattern set shown in Section 5.5.1. They may be used for those synchronization needs where timeliness is not so critical. They have a strong affinity to traditional replication scenarios, where changed data from many decentralized data stores (e.g., from several distributed insurance agencies) need to be uploaded to a central store, for example, twice a day.
- **Real-Time Synchronization:** These patterns address the most sophisticated information synchronization scenarios, where synchronization steps need to be tightly interlocked and combined with the transactional updates. In other words, transactions against the MDM Hub should only be committed after synchronization of master data with the corresponding legacy operational systems is verified (just to illustrate one particular flavor of this pattern). Further customization is needed according to the specific MDM project needs.
- **"Near"-Time Synchronization:** Timeliness still plays a vital role for these patterns; however, these scenarios do not necessarily call for the stringent interlock of transactional updates with the synchronization step (like in the real-time synchronization pattern).
- **"Partial" Data Synchronization:** Not all master data needs to be synchronized with every legacy system. Some master data may not even be needed by certain applications. These patterns address the need to fully understand the distribution of master data in the legacy operational systems, and the need to link this master data placement to the required master information synchronization strategy.
- **No Synchronization (Transaction Hub):** To talk about "no" synchronization within a section that's entirely dedicated to information synchronization sounds like an interesting caveat. But there are deployment scenarios where all transactions, master data services, and even reporting requests are strictly directed against the MDM Hub. That is, all inserts, updates, deletes, and even all select statements against master data is directed against the MDM Hub. This implementation is a special flavor of the MDM Transaction Hub pattern. It transforms the MDM Hub into a true single source of truth, which is tightly integrated into the transactional, operational services, and reporting landscape. As a consequence, there is no need to replicate

and synchronize master data with the legacy operational systems. This approach is admittedly a very sophisticated MDM System—one that relies on an architecturally advanced and rather mature IT environment. It also comes with a rather significant cost that is related to the intensive process-focused application integration tasks.

Let's discuss various key aspects of these information synchronization patterns, such as **timeliness, direction, completeness,** and **consistency.** These dimensions drive the choice and adaptation of these information synchronization patterns for an MDM project implementation.

With the **timeliness** dimension, a range from on-demand replication (triggered by a user for a specific purpose) to real-time synchronization is covered. Real-time synchronization often uses two-phase commit and is used when absolute consistency for master data is needed. **Direction** means whether the data is synchronized unidirectionally or bidirectionally. **Completeness** means whether or not all master data attributes need to be synchronized with the source or consuming application. Let's assume for performance reasons the e-Commerce system has a local persistency where besides transactional data, relevant master data is also stored. The e-Commerce system uses master data read-only and maybe only a subset of the master data attributes relevant for the e-Commerce purpose. Thus, only a subset of the master data needs to be synchronized (unidirectional from the MDM System to the e-Commerce system, in this case). **Consistency** refers to whether you need convergent or absolute consistency for your master data.

Figure 5.22 shows different synchronization themes. Of course, it is almost impossible to include all different facets and patterns in just one graphic, but you can see the standards-based synchronization with external data pools, and the synchronization from the MDM Hub to the legacy operational systems. We invite and encourage the reader to customize a subset of these patterns according to the requirements of a specific MDM project.

5.5.4.8 Forces
The forces and constraints require a discussion on trade-offs and a thorough understanding of all advantages and disadvantages between information synchronization patterns (as part

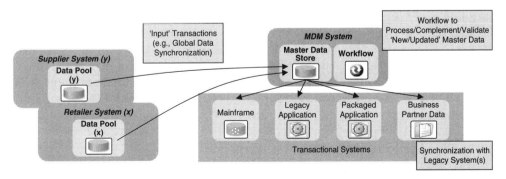

Figure 5.22 Information Synchronization—Illustration.

of the information-focused application integration) versus process-focused application integration patterns (such as the Transaction Interception pattern). Depending on the intricacies of the required business process reengineering and information synchronization tasks, a decision needs to be made with regard to privileges for a specific integration mechanism, which is then directly linked to choosing a certain set of architecture patterns. That is, most of the forces and constraints of these Information Synchronization architecture patterns are very much linked to the alternative approaches in implementing MDM Solutions. In a certain way, these forces and constraints will drive an appropriate selection of Information Synchronization subpatterns. For example, if the real-time synchronization is too expensive and complex to implement (given the specific context), other patterns (e.g., from the process-focused application integration category) should be chosen instead.

5.5.4.9 Relations

The information synchronization patterns have strong relations to the Coexistence Hub pattern and the Transaction Hub pattern and thus to any solution where either one of these MDM Hub Patterns is deployed. Having said this, the Registry Hub pattern may require some degree of synchronization as well. This synchronization depends on the degree of master data materialization. In practical terms, however, the requirements are less voluminous and sophisticated. In addition to it, the relation to any of the process-focused application integration patterns should be highlighted as well: As noted previously, there is a complementary nature between information synchronization and, for example, EAI techniques. Furthermore, we need to recognize—at least to some degree—a certain trade-off between these two categories of architecture patterns and integration methods. In other words, depending on the forces and constraints, the context and the problem space, the choice can either be in favor of one or the other categories of architecture patterns.

5.6 Process-Focused Application Integration Patterns

The patterns in this chapter address the need to integrate applications from a business process-focused perspective. If the master data authoring supposedly happens through the application user interface, then integration on a business process level rather than on the database replication level might be needed. Furthermore, distributing master data to consumers who require only read access, such as e-Commerce or printing systems, can be fed with master data using ESB or messaging patterns. That of course does not mean that an ESB can only be used in read-only scenarios. Thus, the overall theme of the patterns in this category of architecture patterns that are often beneficial for designing MDM Solutions is Enterprise Application Integration (EAI). This section thus introduces such patterns that appear in a variety of MDM Solution Blueprints. An overview of patterns in this category is given in Figure 5.23.

5.6.1 Transaction Interception Patterns

Let's now discuss the Transaction Interception patterns, which are no less important than the Information Synchronization patterns. And as we have done in the previous subsections, we again present the patterns with regard to its type, relevance to MDM methods of use, and so forth.

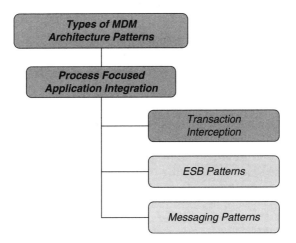

Figure 5.23   Overview of Process-Focused Application Integration Patterns.

5.6.1.1   Type
The Transaction Interception pattern belongs into the category of process-focused application integration patterns.

5.6.1.2   Method of Use
It is mostly applicable for the collaborative and operational method of use. For the analytical MDM method of use, this pattern is less applicable. The reason is that in the analytical case the operational systems may generate alerts and interface with the MDM System. However, the transactions themselves don't have to be necessarily intercepted. But this argument, of course, depends on the implementation details. There can be MDM deployments using the analytical method of use, where the MDM System is more tightly integrated with the operational systems, which then requires transaction interception as well.

5.6.1.3   System Type
Because this pattern is not an MDM Hub Pattern, this attribute is not applicable.

5.6.1.4   Value Proposition
The value of this pattern is to allow authoring of master data in the application system while still getting all of the benefits from the MDM System, like being the gatekeeper to prevent duplicates in the IT landscape. Thus, business transactions (also called business services or business functions)—not database transactions—need to be intercepted to synchronize the business function of creating a new Customer record with the MDM System *before* the application persists the new master data record locally.

5.6.1.5   Context
The context varies a lot with the underlying applications. While we know that there may be packaged applications, such as ERP or CRM systems, or certain ISV applications, where a split of transactions may not be meaningful or simply too complex or costly to implement, we—at least for this particular pattern—just consider those where the interception is

meaningful and needs to be considered. This pattern is often encountered if the Coexistence Hub or the Transaction Hub pattern is used. The more consistency is required and the more accurate (in other words the less stale) the master data in the MDM System has to be, the higher the probability that this pattern is used.

5.6.1.6 Problem Statement

The recurring problem that this pattern tries to address is the integration of the MDM System with legacy transactions. These transactions have to be adjusted in such a way that any update, delete, and insert statements against the master data are executed against the MDM System, where the non-master data part of the transactions may still be executed against the operational systems. Thus, the challenge is the necessary reengineering of the transactional landscape, which can be a costly undertaking.

5.6.1.7 Solution

The solution is based on the strategy to identify the update, insert, and delete portion of the chosen transactions. From a practical standpoint, there are many variations or subtypes possible. For example, assuming a very comprehensive Customer information hub, all or at least a significant subset of the business services (e.g., operational services) may be executed entirely against the MDM Hub—without any interception whatsoever. Furthermore, depending on the scope of a particular application, it may also be the case that certain portions or components of the applications will be submitted against the MDM Hub.

Figure 5.24 is an illustration of the transaction interception patterns, where the operational and transactional systems are shown at the bottom part, and the MDM System, including

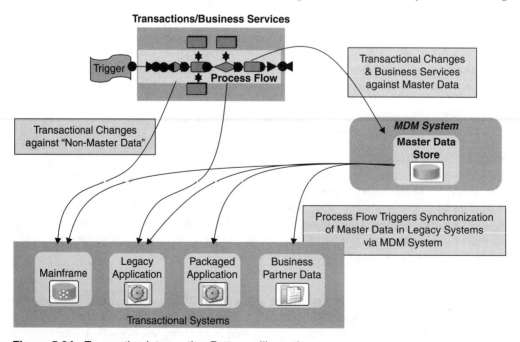

Figure 5.24 Transaction Interception Pattern—Illustration.

the master data store at the right side. This illustration assumes a Coexistence Hub or a Transaction Hub as the base for the deployment.

Figure 5.24 also shows the information synchronization from the MDM Hub to the transactional and operational systems. This synchronization, of course, is not part of the Transaction Interception pattern. With this basic understanding of the Transaction Interception pattern, we analyze it in more detail in Figure 5.25. In order to understand the impact of this pattern, we show a case with and also without the Transaction Interception pattern—the contrast, we believe, shows the value of this pattern in the most effective way.

For the remainder of this section, we use the term business service and transaction interchangeably. Notice that the term transaction in this context does not relate to a database transaction. Also, for the context of this discussion we assume the MDM System was built with either the Coexistence or the Transaction Hub pattern. We haven't seen a case where this pattern was used in the context of a Registry Hub yet. The reason is because, for this hub pattern, the master data remains with low quality in the application system anyway. Furthermore, only a small slice of master data is materialized in the MDM System. As a consequence, the benefit of this pattern for any consuming application is somewhat limited. From our perspective, this statement describes that the added value for this pattern in the context of the Registry Hub is fairly questionable.

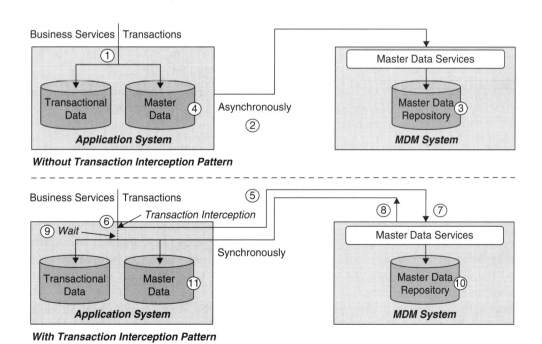

Figure 5.25 The Transaction Interception Pattern—detailed View.

Let's start with the case where the Transaction Interception pattern is not used. Explaining the same case, where the Transaction Interception pattern is used, will clearly show the benefits. The upper half of Figure 5.25 is a depiction of the case where this pattern is not used. If a business service (1) on a source application system does change transactional data, such as orders and master data, the business service completes and the transactional and master data is persisted locally. In a subsequent step, the master data change is propagated asynchronously (2) to the MDM System (e.g., using JMS messaging). When the JMS message arrives at the MDM System, a master data service is invoked. Assuming successful execution, this service triggers the appropriate update on the Master Data Repository as well (3). From a high-level perspective, everything seems to be consistent. But let's take a closer look at the scenario. The following is what really happened:

1. The application saved a master data change that is not consistent with all of the master data integrity rules enforced by the MDM System. This lack of consistency means the master data change was likely persisted with low data quality.

2. Assuming the master data change was an update of an existing record, depending on the delay of the propagation, there was a time window where the master data record in the MDM System and in the application system were not consistent—in other words, the MDM System would provide stale master data to other applications (which are not shown in the figure).

3. The application saved a master data record that might be a duplicate—in this case, the MDM System might have rejected the new master data record. Thus, compensation logic would be needed to take the master data change out of the local master data store of the application. This duplicate needs to be tracked and associated with the right master data record in the MDM System (assuming that there is a requirement to report revenue for a customer accurately).

Summarizing the above explanations, there are scenarios where these inconsistencies are not acceptable and the Transaction Interception pattern is the key to providing a solution that we now discuss in more detail.

Examining the lower half of Figure 5.25, a transaction is submitted through the application (5). Using the Transaction Interception pattern, this transaction is intercepted (6). In order to intercept the transaction, you must change the application code—it's a reengineering of the business service. The objective is to put the business service on hold (that's the wait time indicated with the dotted line at (9)) until the MDM System responds. Synchronously, the appropriate master data service is invoked (7), and the application system waits until the response (8) is back before the transaction continues to execute. Note that only the master data portion of the business service is sent to the MDM System. The processing of the transactional data portion is put on hold before committing it to the data store until the master data portion of the business service is checked by the MDM System. Using two-phase commit, the master data can then be synchronously committed to the Master Data Repository (10), and the replica of the master data can be committed in the application system (11). At the same time, the transactional data can be committed at the application side. The application receives consistent master data from the MDM System regarding all data integrity and business rules that are enforced by the MDM System. Effectively, the MDM System prevents the application from creating duplicates.

5.6.1.8 Forces

As a gross generalization, we need to take into consideration the characteristics of the applications and their corresponding transactions. This consideration is vital in order to decide on the transaction interception strategy and the applicability of this pattern for the legacy transaction landscape. Although it may be desirable to adjust and even completely reengineer certain applications, it may not be feasible to do so in all cases. As was already mentioned, some packaged applications may simply have to be executed unchanged, which means that no transaction interception is to be considered. Furthermore, it is important to notice that if the Transaction Interception pattern is implemented between an application system and an MDM System, all read operations on master data can be done locally. The reason is that the application is aware that the master data records in the local legacy database are consistent with the MDM System. Thus, there is no need to redirect the read operations for these records to the MDM System.

The MDM Hub contains a set of rules, guidelines, limitations, and constraints related to operations on the master data. And in order to keep changes consistent with this set of rules, these business transactions require interception to interact and verify with the MDM Hub that the planned changes are valid. Depending on the application, this interception might require simple notification, event connectivity towards the application, some application configuration changes, or more sophisticated code changes within the application itself.

The following list summarizes the most important forces and constraints for this pattern:

- Study the diverse characteristics of all applications.
- Determine a transaction interception strategy.
- Verify if convergent consistency is enough or if absolute consistency is required.
- Understand for which legacy application the Transaction Interception is applicable.
- Consider the set of rules, guidelines, limitations, and constraints related to operations on the master data as implied by data governance.

After taking a close look at the constraints and forces, we put the problem of the Transaction Interception into an enterprise-level view. An enterprise looking at a master data strategy needs to decide whether or not the master data services[40] are orchestrated locally through the MDM System or through a global workflow engine. The Transaction Interception pattern thus plays in the matrix of forces shown in Figure 5.26 in the lower right corner. Depending on where the master data transactions are orchestrated, the Transaction Interception pattern might be a requirement. This pattern comes at the cost of application reengineering, which might be a fairly easy or a rather complex task depending on the application.

---

40. We will use the term "master data transaction" synonymously.

Scope of Orchestration

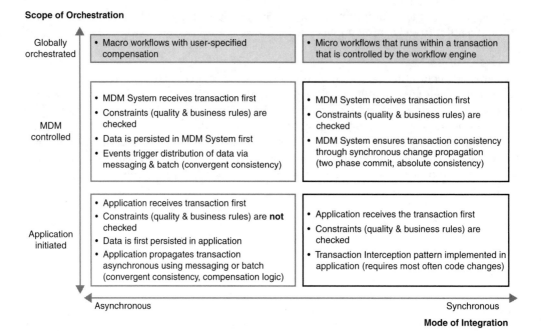

Figure 5.26 Local versus Global Orchestration of Master Data related Business Functions.

5.6.1.9 Relations

The pattern is often found in the context of the Coexistence Hub and the Transaction Hub pattern. From our perspective, it is less applicable in the context of the Registry Hub pattern. As we have seen in Section 5.4, the master data in the Registry Hub is viewed and derived through linkage to corresponding master data in legacy systems. That means selecting and gaining a single, true view of the master data involves going through the hub to access legacy data sources.

Because of the nature of this architecture pattern, it is applicable for many of the MDM Solution Blueprints presented in Chapters 6, 7, and 8.

5.6.2 ESB Pattern

This section will not follow the basic pattern outline structure; it will just summarize the applicability of ESB architecture patterns for building MDM Solutions.

In an SOA environment, the concept of an ESB is often used to loosely couple application systems. In many MDM implementations in an SOA context where we have been involved, some kind of ESB infrastructure was either in place or introduced along with the Master Data Management solution. The following are a few key points that explain why an ESB would be helpful when deploying an MDM Solution:

- Leverage messaging infrastructure to distribute master data updates to consuming applications
- Offload dispatching of an update to multiple consumers to external resources (ESB) reducing load on the MDM System

- Leverage ESB transformations to convert master data models while flowing back and forth between application systems and the MDM System
- Loosely couple the MDM System with the application systems

Because we focus on Master Data Management, we don't intend to elaborate on this ESB architecture pattern any further. However, we would like to point you to some great resources [11], [21], [22], [23], [24], [25], and [26] on ESB architecture patterns that help an IT Architect to integrate the MDM System more easily into an existing IT landscape. Fundamental capabilities of an ESB can be found in [11] and [27].

5.6.3   Messaging Pattern

Not every company has the need for a full-blown ESB infrastructure, nor does it always exist. However, you can use simple messaging infrastructure to push master data changes to application systems. Because ESB infrastructure relies on messaging, there is a close relation between ESB and messaging patterns. Often, ESB patterns focus more on topology aspects than on low-level messaging considerations. Themes that sometimes appear in the context of ESB patterns are presented as messaging patterns in other books. Because we focus on MDM, we provide only a summary of some key aspects and point the reader to appropriate resources for more detailed information. At a high level, we see two important patterns for messaging:

- Publish/Subscribe pattern
- Point-to-Point pattern

We elaborate on these two patterns in order to gain some basic understanding on messaging patterns available for the upcoming discussion on MDM Solution Blueprints. The Publish/Subscribe pattern is shown in Figure 5.27.

A producer generates a message and publishes the message on a topic. Subscribed consumers (2) receive the message from the topic. This concept is similar to subscribing to a newsletter. The newsletter would be the topic. Someone produces news and publishes the newsletter, and when this happens the consumers (who have subscribed to the newsletter) would get the news. The Publish/Subscribe pattern establishes a one-to-many relation between message

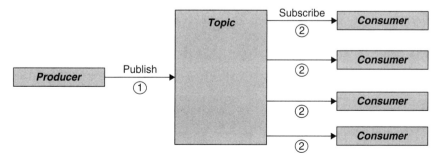

Figure 5.27   Publish/Subscribe Pattern.

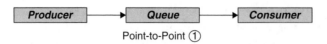
Point-to-Point ①

Figure 5.28 Point-to-Point Pattern.

producers and message subscribers. The Publish/Subscribe pattern is one way to offload the MDM System, as shown in the following case: Assume a set of master data-consuming applications that require read-only access to master data. For performance reasons, these applications access local repositories that should be updated when master data changes. In order to keep the load on the MDM System small, the MDM System can publish the changes using the Publish/Subscribe pattern. This approach means that a message containing the change needs to be produced only once and received by all consuming applications that subscribed to the topic where the master data changes are posted. This pattern can be implemented using Java Messaging Services (JMS).[41]

The Point-to-Point pattern can be implemented using JMS as well.[42] The pattern is shown in Figure 5.28. A message producer generates a message on a queue (1) where the message is received by the message consumer. The key difference between the Publish/Subscribe pattern and the Point-to-Point pattern is that the latter establishes a one-to-one relationship between message producer and message consumer. This relationship causes the MDM System to produce a message for each application that requires a master data update. This approach may not be a problem if there are only one or two applications that are notified about master data changes. However, with an increasing number of consuming applications, this approach might result in high resource consumption on the physical server(s) hosting the MDM System. In such a case, other mechanisms (such as the Publish/Subscribe pattern) would be more applicable.

Even though these patterns are different with regard to the relationship type they establish between message producer and message consumer, they also share some similarities regarding the messaging implementation. The following list is not complete:

- Messaging can be implemented in a transactional fashion.
- Messaging can be implemented asynchronously or synchronously.
- Message receipts can be acknowledged automatically or explicitly.

These are two messaging patterns that are presented at a high level of abstraction. There are many more messaging patterns available that are tailored towards very specific purposes.[43]

---

41. An overview and related resources are provided in [28].

42. For further details, see [29] and [30].

43. We recommend [31], a book that provides a wealth of messaging patterns used in concrete integration scenarios, to any IT Architect or Developer designing or implementing the integration between an MDM system and application systems using messaging infrastructure.

The Publish/Subscribe pattern and the Point-to-Point pattern can be often found with Coexistence Hub and Transaction Hub deployments, where master data-consuming applications need to be notified about master data changes.

5.7   Enterprise System Deployment Patterns

This section introduces enterprise system deployment patterns. Master Data Management solutions, similar to SOA solutions, are very seldom deployed on a green field. That is, existing application systems have master data, maybe inconsistent, maybe with low quality, maybe with duplicates—but master data exists in application systems. Introducing MDM Systems almost always means integration with application systems. Maybe there are only one or two, or maybe there are dozens that require integration. The authors have been engaged in a couple of customer situations where an MDM CDI solution had to be designed from scratch. Nevertheless, these are probably more exceptional opportunities.

The patterns shown in this section are useful for several reasons: They show which application systems are likely encountered and the benefit of integrating them with an MDM System. Furthermore, the patterns provide insight into key architectural decisions as to how this integration can be achieved. As can be seen from Figure 5.29, there are many systems that need to be taken into consideration when deploying an MDM System. Because diving into all of the different facets would be too time-consuming, we describe just two examples:

- MDM–Data Warehouse (DW) Integration Pattern
- MDM–BI Analytical Systems Integration Pattern

We strongly recommend that you customize and further develop these patterns for other systems that are relevant in your particular IT environment. The second example, BI Analytical Systems pattern, will be described in the following pattern section. So let's dive into the first example, which has been given the name MDM–DW Integration Pattern.

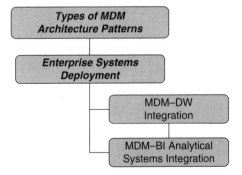

Figure 5.29   Enterprise Systems Deployment Patterns.

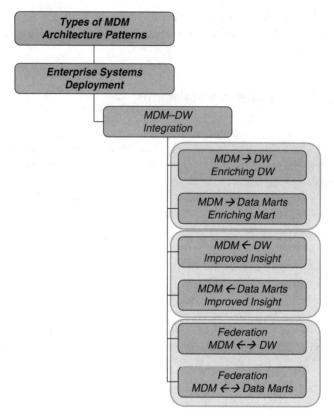

Figure 5.30 Subpatterns of the MDM-DW Integration Pattern.

5.7.1 MDM-DW Integration Pattern

The MDM-Data Warehouse (DW)[44] Integration pattern belongs to the category of enterprise system deployment patterns. We again present this pattern according to our previously used structure.

5.7.1.1 Type

As can be seen from Figure 5.30, there are many systems that need to be taken into consideration when deploying an MDM System. Data marts are often data replicas that are derived from a data warehouse system. Also note that the integration can be done with different collaborative approaches. A very natural approach is for the MDM System to serve as a base for the DW system(s). This approach allows for an acceleration of the DW build phase. Insight that is gained from the data warehouse can also be made available

---

44. Business Warehouse (BW) and Data Warehouse (DW) are used interchangeably throughout this chapter. Business Intelligence (BI) systems and decision support systems (DSS) are summarized under DW or BW systems as well.

to the MDM System, thus enriching the MDM Hub. This relationship will provide improved integration with the operational systems and allows for this insight to be leveraged by operational legacy systems—even in real time. Another important option is to use the Federation pattern to provide for enriched reporting that is based on a collaborative view across transactional data drawn from the data warehouse or data marts and master data from the MDM System. This pattern is not to be confused with the MDM–BI Analytical Integration Pattern, where a tight integration and synchronization with data from the BI analytical system with the MDM System can take place, as we discuss in the next section.

A couple of different cases are possible when using a federated approach for reporting, as indicated later, but these cases are not discussed in detail in this pattern.

5.7.1.2 Method of Use

This architecture pattern is linked to all three MDM methods of use. In this particular case, we need to explain what we mean by the term "linked": The relationship to data warehouses and data marts needs to be managed in the operational methods of use case, where updates against the MDM Hub need to be, for example, transformed according to the ETL staging processes and replicated to either one or even all DW and data marts. For collaborative MDM styles, where the collaboration between the MDM Hub and an external system takes place (e.g., public data pool), the possible linkage to a DW system depends on the scope and reporting needs that the DW or the relevant data marts need to address. Finally, in the case of the analytical MDM method of use, it depends very much on the overall system design. Beyond that, the objective and scope of the MDM System will also determine this relationship further. For example, if the MDM System serves the purpose of providing deep analytical insight into the client base, there can even be a two-way interlock with either one or several DW and data marts. As mentioned earlier, more information on this topic is provided in the following section.

5.7.1.3 System Type

Because it's not an MDM Hub Pattern, this attribute is not applicable.

5.7.1.4 Value Proposition

The MDM-DW Integration pattern enables and makes analytical insight from the DW system actionable. If, by using the DW system, the top customers are identified, a service representative can be enabled to act on this information. This enablement can be done by synchronizing this analytical insight into the MDM System to make it actionable. Thus, this approach supports one of the three flavors of analytical MD introduced in Chapter 1. Another benefit of this pattern is that the results derived in the DW system can be improved because high-quality master data is loaded into the DW system. Duplicate free Product Information is the foundation to accurately assess the revenue created by a Product. Thus, getting the duplicate free information from the MDM System (which supposedly was also used by the order entry system) into the DW system improves reporting results. As a side effect, the ETL processing for getting data into the DW system is simplified because the master data is already cleansed.

5.7.1.5 Context

The context is characterized by a legacy environment with a data warehouse and data marts that contain all or at least a subset of the master data. And depending on the master data domain that needs to be managed by the MDM System, this particular subset or domain of master data needs to be considered by this architecture pattern. For example, if the scope of the MDM System is limited to Product master data, those DW and data marts that contain only Customer data may not be impacted by the MDM System. In other words, this pattern can be applied when a DW system and an MDM System exist in the same IT landscape and should result in increased benefits to both systems. The objectives of this architecture pattern are clear: to describe the relationship to the warehousing environment and to enable accelerated MDM Solution deployment.

5.7.1.6 Problem Statement

The problem that this architecture pattern addresses is the interlock with the traditional DW and data mart systems, which exist in almost every IT customer environment. Master data stored in data warehouses and data marts may have been used in the build phase of the MDM System as a source of master data. However, in the operational environment, where insert, update, and delete statements are most likely submitted against the MDM Hub, data warehousing and data mart systems need to be updated again and kept in sync with the MDM Hub. Without high-quality master data, the DW system is unable to report how many new customers were gained over the last quarter or how much revenue was earned from a Product if the Products were not free of duplicates. In addition, this need for high-quality master data requires costly ETL processing whenever master data is loaded into the DW system. These costs can be reduced when the high-quality master data from the MDM System is leveraged.

Another problem is that analytical insight gained by the DW is not leveraged in the operational system landscape. This integration and usage of analytical insight for the operational environment can be done by the MDM System that has appropriate interfaces. However, if there is no integration between the MDM System and a DW system, this insight cannot be effectively used.

5.7.1.7 Solution

The solution is an architectural description of key characteristics of this interlock between the MDM Hub and the various data warehouses and data marts. It does not include, but is linked to, the Initial Load pattern and Information Synchronization patterns. The latter can be used to propagate changes between the systems. The MDM-DW Integration pattern needs to be further refined in order to accommodate the project-specific requirements.

In addition, there are many pattern variations or subpatterns, such as a relationship between the MDM System and the DW *only*, where further generation and updates of data marts will be done strictly by using the DW as the base. There may also be cases where some of the data marts can be updated directly from the MDM System. Of course, there can be a project-specific mixture or composition of these subpatterns. As was stated previously, another variation is a pattern where the reporting is based on federation of data from the MDM Hub and the DW. Furthermore, federation can also be done over the required parts of the MDM Hub and one or even several data marts. Again, pattern composition techniques

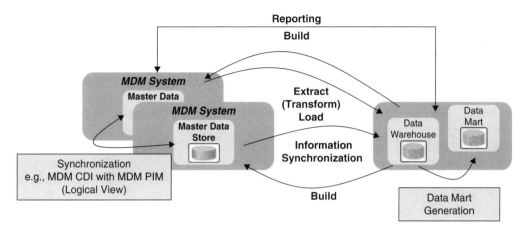

Figure 5.31 MDM-DW Integration Pattern—Illustration.

should be used to further respond to specific project requirements. These various subpatterns are illustrated in Figure 5.30.

Figure 5.31 is a high-level graphical representation of these patterns. On the left side, you can see the MDM System(s), and on the right side, you see a data warehouse and a data mart. This figure also illustrates the existence of several MDM Systems. This figure is not necessarily a physical representation based on concrete product and technology mapping but a logical representation to take into account the several master data domains and the different MDM methods of use. And again, at the logical and conceptual levels, synchronization between the various MDM hubs needs to be addressed.

This figure also illustrates the reporting aspects that we discussed earlier. Furthermore, the many aspects of the relationship are illustrated by the arrows that are connecting the MDM Hub(s) with the data warehouse and data mart: The DW system might contain master data used to build the MDM Systems; updates have to be "communicated" to the DW and data mart by using Information Synchronization patterns. In this case, it is assumed that the transformation steps are considerably less complex, because the master data is already prepared, cleansed, and improved.

5.7.1.8 Forces
Some of the forces that suggest usage of these patterns are related to the master data domain, the scope of the DW and the data marts, and the reporting needs. The master data domain may not necessarily overlap with the data in the warehousing systems. As an example, there may be cases where the MDM Hub is basically a CDI solution with the master data domain to be limited to customer-related data. The DW can be a classical reporting tool to address, for example, Basel II or Solvency II regulatory compliance requirements. In this case, at least from a pure data perspective, the overlap may be limited. Even in this case there is a relationship between the MDM System and the DW, which is more characterized by possibly enhancing the reporting capabilities (e.g., through federation), but there is no or a very limited update from the MDM Hub to the DW system. In those environments, the scope of the DW

and data marts does not interfere with the MDM System. As noted previously, the need to update the DW and the data marts will be addressed in the Initial Load and Information Synchronization patterns. As we have seen from the subpatterns, the forces and constraints for this architecture pattern are also related to the reporting needs: Depending on the scope and anticipated content of the reports, the data or part of the data in the MDM Hub can very well be leveraged to generate some reports. Even in those cases where the data in the MDM Hub (e.g., Customer data) is an essential component for almost all reports, an integration of the MDM Hub with some business warehouses and data marts may not make a lot of sense: The MDM Hub is essentially application- and services-independent, and is integrated into the transactional environment; the DW and data marts are optimized for specific application/ reporting needs, and are generally read-only. However, for every MDM project, utilization of these "relationship" patterns requires a thorough understanding and discussion of the relevant forces and constraints in order to further customize and adjust the patterns.

We should like to point out as well that existing DW systems may serve as a source to build the MDM Hub. With today's heterogeneous and diverse data landscape, it is more than likely that part of the master data is contained in the data warehousing systems. It will also be the case that—after an MDM System has been built—this MDM Hub will serve as a base for any new or updated DW system.

The advantage of these MDM Architecture Patterns is a structured approach to relate the MDM Hub(s) to the warehousing environment. This approach even includes a predefined set of alternative patterns that are motivated by the need to balance the various forces, constraints, and MDM project dynamics.

5.7.1.9   Relations

The MDM-DW Integration pattern is related to many patterns listed in Section 5.5.1, such as data replication patterns. However, these patterns also relate to some patterns of the "process-focused application integration" type. For example, changes from the MDM System can be propagated through messaging patterns to the data warehousing system. The MDM-DW Integration pattern is relevant for MDM Solutions where the business warehousing environment should be integrated. As mentioned before, these patterns are also in relation to the initial data load and information synchronization patterns. Furthermore, there is a strong relationship to the MDM Hub Patterns, which determine the scope of the MDM System and the MDM deployment style.

There is an MDM Integration Blueprint in Section 8.2 in Chapter 8 that shows how this pattern can be deployed.

5.7.2   MDM-BI Analytical System Integration Pattern

We would like to point out that the term "analytical system" should not be confused with business or data warehousing systems. Although the boundary may be a bit fuzzy, there is a distinction between a traditional reporting oriented DW and a more real-time oriented BI analytical system. In this section, we are elaborating on an enterprise system deployment pattern to address the integration of analytical systems such as fraud prevention systems, industry-specific analytical systems such as anti-money laundering (AML) systems, or identity analytics systems used to discover hidden relationships in the customer base. In Chapter 1 we provided some background information on these topics as strong motivation to build and integrate MDM Systems in the context of these analytical systems. Specifically, the need to provide analytical insight into the customer base is an underlying premise to provide regulatory compliance.

5.7.2.1   Type

This pattern, which we named the MDM-BI Analytical System Integration pattern, provides further insight into the relationship between the MDM and the analytical systems. It belongs to the type of enterprise systems deployment patterns. As you can see in Figure 5.32, there are many subpatterns—and the list is even incomplete: We have pointed out AML and identity analytics, which are just a few examples. Note that many analytics exist in the customer master data domain, which is usually addressed with CDI-related Master Data Management solutions. Thus, we used the abbreviations "CDI" indicating the customer MDM System where appropriate. Of course, we do not exclude the possibility of other analytical subpatterns in

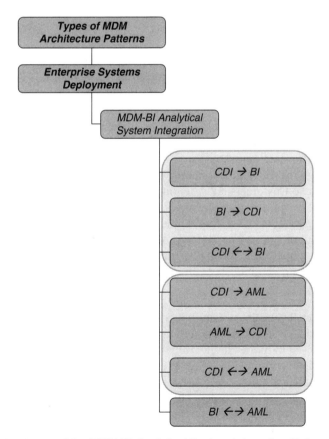

Figure 5.32   Subpatterns of the MDM-BI Analytical System Integration Pattern.

other master data domains such as Product, Account, or Location. There will also be a number of similar subpatterns that are more related to themes and standards in other industries.

5.7.2.2 Method of Use

This architecture pattern is linked to all three MDM methods of use. However, like in the previous section, we need to comment on this statement a bit further. Both the operational and collaborative MDM methods of use may require a much deeper analytical insight into the customer base. This insight can be provided through real-time or "near real-time" analysis of the transactional data, Customer data, or even a combination of both areas. A relationship and integration of the MDM System with an AML application is a good example for this case. The analytical MDM method of use has a strong affinity to BI analytical systems. However, we are separating an MDM System as a backend transactional system, which is deeply embedded into the operational environment, and a BI analytical system, which serves, for example, as a fraud discovery and prevention or as an AML alert generating engine.

5.7.2.3 System Type

Because it's not an MDM Hub Pattern, this attribute is not applicable.

5.7.2.4 Value Proposition

The value of this architecture pattern and the subpatterns are a well thought-out and structured approach to relate an MDM System to legacy analytical systems. It enables accelerated integration of these analytical systems with the MDM System. In Section 5.8, we describe how pattern composition will be used to eventually derive a more pervasive architecture blueprint. From an architectural perspective, we are considering the complementary nature of MDM and analytical systems. From a product and implementation point of view, the overall MDM Solution can very well include some analytical components. The following example illustrates this statement: Deep analytical insight into the Customer base, provided, for example, through real-time alert-generating components that discover non-obvious relationships between two Customers, may be implemented using identity analytics systems as an analytical MDM method of use. The analysis of transactional data, as stated previously, would then be implemented as a complementary application that collaborates with the MDM Hub. The pattern is a structural description of this relationship, including the different variations and subpatterns. Naturally, further refinement and adaptations need to be done—specifically in a given industry context.

5.7.2.5 Context

The context is given by business requirements demanding the integration of the MDM System with analytical systems. An example is where a bank might need to find out which Customers are involved in money laundering in order to comply with AML legal regulations. In this case, the MDM System would have the Customer data, and the AML analytical system would have analytical functions for the analysis and comparison of transactional data against given money spending profiles. The interfaces are multifold in terms of data and information to be routed in both directions. As you have seen in Figure 5.32, there are a number of subpatterns that further outline the possible solution space. And as stated earlier, we need to view this list of examples as an incomplete list. This list indeed needs to be further refined, specifically to account for individual industry-specific applications (e.g., to address fraud and other related themes):

- **CDI → BI Analytical Systems:** This sub-pattern means to leverage the MDM CDI Hub to enrich any identity analytics system. Access to a pervasive single source of truth and improved insight into the customer base will be made available to other identity analytics systems.
- **BI Analytical Systems → CDI:** Discovered, hidden relationships and other findings, alerts, or insight that are, for example, derived from transactional inconsistencies will be made available to the MDM CDI Hub to basically enrich the master data. Thus, the MDM Hub will develop into a more pervasive authoritative source of Customer truth by also capturing key findings from the transactional environment.
- **CDI ↔ BI Analytical Systems:** This, of course, is a combination of the earlier patterns, where a mutual enrichment of both systems is achieved. From an implementation perspective, there can be a collaboration of these systems, which is more based on a bidirectional dialog, or a tight integration of the corresponding functions with a single GUI.
- **CDI → AML:** In order to provide additional information regarding a single Customer or a set of Customers and to validate/qualify AML alerts, the MDM System will serve as a CDI service provider and transfers required Customer information to an AML application.
- **AML → CDI:** Vice versa, the AML application will route part of the content of the alerts to the MDM CDI system to further enrich the CDI system and to enable accumulation of relevant data in this single CDI source of Customer truth.
- **CDI ↔ AML:** This is essentially a combination or composition of the earlier patterns. However, we also need to consider a tighter integration, which—from an implementation and product perspective—may even result in, for example, an automated bidirectional dialog prior to generating a "money laundering" alert.
- **BI Analytical Systems ↔ AML:** Discovered hidden relationships from the identity analytics might be helpful for the AML analytical system or findings from the AML system might help to reveal another hidden relationship. So sometimes as a special case, in addition to integrating these systems with the MDM System, the analytical systems themselves require integration to further improve the results provided to the MDM System that are made actionable by the MDM System.

5.7.2.6 Problem Statement

The problem space that this pattern tries to address is the relationship between MDM and analytical systems with regard to the master and analytical data, functions, interfaces, and—most importantly—the information that needs to be derived through the collaborative and complementary nature of these systems. The advantage is to leverage the capabilities of both system domains in such a way that the information that is derived represents an overall enrichment. It is from this complementary nature that added value will be provided to the anticipated solution, which could never be derived by the individual systems separately.

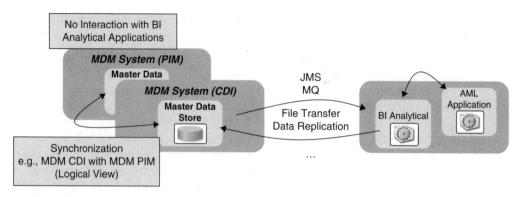

Figure 5.33   MDM-BI Analytical System Integration—Illustration.

5.7.2.7   Solution

Figure 5.33 is a conceptual graphical representation of the solution. Depending on the deployment scenario, there can be an MDM System (e.g., a PIM system), which does not relate in any way to the BI analytical domain. Depending on the software for the analytical side, there are different interfaces available.[45] Also, the software for the MDM System affects the integration options.[46] There might be JMS interfaces on both sides available, thus allowing communication between the two systems using JMS messaging. Maybe both sides can consume Microsoft Excel files, thereby allowing information to be exchanged via FTP file transfer. Data replication patterns, as shown in Section 5.5.1, might also be used to exchange data between the two systems. JMS file transfer and data replication are options shown later—but others exist depending on the software in use. Also note that the physical MDM System is separated into two logical systems: one for the Product and one for the Customer master data domain. Also note that the illustration shows integration between the CDI side of the MDM System and an identity analytics system. Depending on the business needs, collaboration between all involved systems may be different. For example, an Anti-Money Laundering (AML) application may very well interface directly with the CDI side (and even other components) of the MDM System.

5.7.2.8   Forces

The characteristics of the problem, context, and solution space are directly linked to illustrate the forces and constraints of this MDM Architecture Pattern. Depending on the master data domain (e.g., Customer data), and the scope of data that the analytical system acts on (e.g., transactional data), there can be significant overlap, or these data domains can be completely disjointed. The same statement applies to the functions or services of these systems: There can be significant overlap or they can be complementary in nature. For example: The MDM Hub may contain Customer-related business services *only*, where the analytical system may contain sophisticated algorithms to match a set of transactions from an identified

---

45. For a list of products for the analytical systems, see Section B.1 in Appendix B.
46. For software products for the MDM system, see Section B.5 in Appendix B.

person against a money-spending profile to actually discover inconsistencies in the money-spending behavior of that very person. The interfaces can be unidirectional (e.g., enrichment of an MDM CDI Hub through analytical and AML alerts), or bidirectional (e.g., complementing the BI Analytical Systems by the enrichment of analytical data through CDI Hub data and vice versa). The anticipated information is the key objective—the driving force—why collaboration between these MDM and analytical systems are desirable: for example, to gain true 360-degree Customer insight by combining analytical functions on customer **and** transactional data—in real-time fashion.

There is a multifaceted linkage and interface between the MDM and analytical systems. Depending on the needs and characteristics of this collaborative systems environment, this interlock can be more centered on JMS messaging and file transfer in either direction. It can also be, for example, based on a collaborative reporting strategy, where a federation layer interprets data from both system domains and generates meaningful business information. Figure 5.33 also highlights the role of an identity analytics system, which further analyzes entities (e.g., transactional or customer data) in collaboration with another analytical system (e.g., an AML or "fraud discovery" application). As noted earlier, there are several patterns to leverage this insight in conjunction with an MDM System.

5.7.2.9 Relations

This pattern is related to the information-focused application integration category. However, the strongest relation exists with almost all patterns of the process-focused application integration type. Although there clearly is a need to synchronize information, by far the biggest challenge still lies within the integration from a workflow and process centric view.

From an MDM Hub Pattern perspective, the strongest relation exists without any doubt to the Coexistence Hub and the Transaction Hub pattern. The Registry Hub has limited relation to this pattern because it provides simple linkage to corresponding master data in legacy systems. As we have stated at the beginning of this section, MDM Solutions where this pattern is likely encountered are limited to scenarios and use cases that are relevant to address fraud prevention, and specific industry themes, such as AML and deeper analytical insight into the customer base. Section 7.4 describes a solution blueprint where this pattern is leveraged.

5.7.3 MDM-CRM Integration and MDM-ERP Integration Pattern

We discuss these two patterns in parallel because they share many aspects. In fact, if you have CRM and ERP applications, you can then use Master Data Management to provide a good foundation for them simultaneously. A key reason why the integration of CRM and ERP applications with MDM Systems is discussed here is that we had to integrate CRM applications in numerous CDI projects and ERP systems in numerous PIM projects.

5.7.3.1 Type

Both patterns belong in the enterprise system deployment category.

5.7.3.2 Method of Use

Both patterns are applicable for analytical, collaborative, and operational methods of use.

5.7.3.3 System Type

This attribute is not applicable because these patterns do not describe an MDM Hub Pattern.

5.7.3.4 Value Proposition

These patterns enable the business value of Master Data Management for CRM and ERP applications. If integration is done as outlined, these applications can use managed master data and thus benefit from high-quality master data. An example is the duplicate prevention capability provided by the MDM System for the CRM and ERP application. Overall, the MDM-CRM Integration pattern and the MDM-ERP Integration pattern enable business value by delivering functions for which an MDM System was designed (and CRM and ERP were not) that are complementary to CRM and ERP systems. Let's start with the customer domain first. The top four reasons from a business value perspective to complement CRM and ERP systems with a CDI-MDM Solution for customer master data are:

- Companies need to improve customer visibility and insight due to an ever growing need for customer loyalty and retention. For example, customers might get frustrated if their bills continuously get sent to the wrong address and eventually motivate customers to switch to another company. A CDI-MDM Solution enables this improvement by:
  - Providing a single 360-degree master view of all Customer data across *all* applications in the enterprise.
  - Change propagation (e.g., propagation of address changes) to all consuming applications consistently. Thus, this information can be persisted enterprise-wide in all applications, thereby ensuring information is correct across all functions (billing, catalog, customer service, marketing).
- Companies have a need to increase selling effectiveness and to grow their revenue. A CDI-MDM Solution enables this improvement by providing consistent and correct customer information: A CDI-MDM Solution allows you to effectively manage a 360-degree view of your customers—through determining relationships and customer preferences supporting cross- and up-sell strategies for improved revenue streams.
- Companies need to reduce integration costs and for an enterprise-wide master data strategy, you should be positioned to take advantage of SOA and MDM in concert, as outlined in Chapter 2. This combination of SOA and MDM helps to reduce IT costs. State-of-the-art CDI-MDM software enables this cost reduction by:
  - Providing a comprehensive data model and a rich out-of-the-box, services-oriented approach that results in an MDM Solution that can be customized according to business requirements.
  - Having many interfaces for batch, near real-time, and real-time integration using interfaces such as JMS or Web services.
- Companies need to address requirements (e.g., AML) in such a way that existing investments can be leveraged and project risk on the IT side can be mitigated. A CDI-MDM Solution enables this mitigation by providing a unifying single view of Customer data across all applications, leveraging existing investments while taking action across the enterprise to maintain the single view.

Similarly, there are several important reasons from a business value perspective to complement an ERP system with a PIM-MDM Solution for Product master data. They are the following:

- Companies need to improve Product Master Data Management and quality in order to be able to reduce customer returns and costs and to increase productivity. A PIM-MDM Solution enables this improvement by:
  - Providing workflow infrastructure to centrally run processes for Product master data authoring centrally
  - Providing a central system designed for Product master data maintenance
- Allowing flexible data validation rules to improve the Product master data quality of Product Information added to the item or Product master catalog
- Reducing errors in downstream applications
- Companies need to overcome content limitations, which requires an agile, fully flexible Product master data model that covers thousands of attributes and the ability to distribute this Product Information in multiple sales channels. A PIM-MDM Solution enables this improvement by:
  - Providing a fully flexible and easy-to-extend Product master data model
  - Supporting any number of hierarchies of Products, such as merchandising hierarchies, Product type hierarchies, supplier hierarchies, reseller hierarchies, printing hierarchies, e-Commerce hierarchies, and location hierarchies
- Companies need the ability to enrich Product master information seamlessly due to an ever-growing need for business innovation and competitive differentiation. A PIM-MDM Solution enables this enrichment by:
  - Providing the appropriate infrastructure to enrich structured content for e-Commerce systems, Web sites, customer services, or business partner service departments
  - Providing the appropriate infrastructure to easily integrate with image and enterprise content management systems to support unstructured content such as images, warranties, and supplier agreements
- Companies need a framework for business processes to reduce time to market for new Products or to increase productivity with automated processes. A PIM-MDM Solution enables to establish this framework by:
  - Providing easy-to-use and easy-to-customize workflow infrastructure that enables more efficient implementations of processes like New Product Introduction[47]
  - Providing attribute-level security access privileges in the workflow infrastructure for editing and approval steps
  - Providing easy-to-configure workflow notifications and events
- Companies need to efficiently manage the dynamic nature of industry standards and legal regulations so as to comply with them while reducing costs. A PIM-MDM Solution enables this improvement, for example, with the ability to more easily accommodate changes in Global Product Codes (GPC) and Global Data Dictionary (GDD) standards.

---

47. For more details on this process, see Section 6.3.

The above statements give a good overview, from our perspective, as to why applying these patterns make sense.

5.7.3.5 Context

The MDM-CRM Integration pattern and the MDM-ERP Integration pattern can each be applied in three use cases.

5.7.3.5.1 Use Case Master Data Quality Improvement

In this scenario, the poor master data quality in either your ERP or CRM system needs to be improved in order to allow for business optimization. Thus, you would integrate the ERP or the CRM system as shown in Figure 5.34.

Key drivers are the removal of duplicates in order to enable actionable master data using the event infrastructure of the MDM System or master data standardization. For example, for a logistics company having standardized, verified, and clean address information available is paramount to running its business efficiently. This efficient business can be enabled by the introduction of an MDM System. Additional legacy applications can be connected to the MDM System later on as well in order to benefit from the standardized data.

5.7.3.5.2 Use Case System Harmonization

Here the use case would be to have multiple ERP instances or multiple CRM instances within the same enterprise, often from different software vendors. They might have duplicates (due to records being entered multiple times in various systems) or be inconsistent due to different customizations in lookup tables or due to running different versions of the application. In such a scenario, an MDM System can function as the harmonization infrastructure for these systems. Figure 5.35 shows the situation for harmonizing multiple ERP systems.

Figure 5.36 shows the situation for harmonizing multiple CRM systems. If you introduce an MDM System, other legacy applications can be connected to it as well.

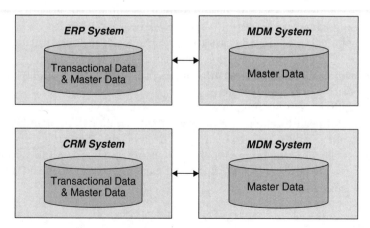

Figure 5.34 Integration of CRM with MDM or integration of ERP with MDM.

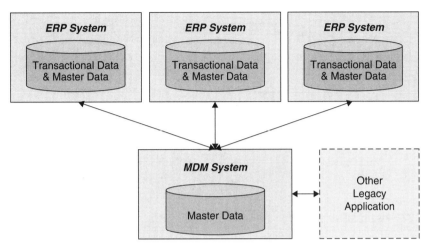

Figure 5.35 Harmonization of multiple ERP Systems using MDM.

5.7.3.5.3 Use Case MDM as the "Golden Middle"

If ERP and CRM systems are present, then the question is which one leads. Instead of declaring either one of them as the leading system, which often means there will be a lack of capability to efficiently enforce high-quality master data, we propose the use of an MDM System as the golden middle. For example, Customer information can be efficiently shared between two systems leveraging the MDM System. This concept is depicted in Figure 5.37, where the MDM System functions as the single source of truth.

For this use case, the MDM-CRM integration pattern, as well as the MDM-ERP integration pattern, is used for a combined solution.

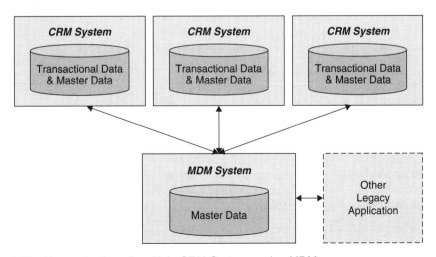

Figure 5.36 Harmonization of multiple CRM Systems using MDM.

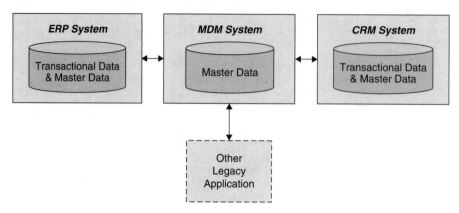

Figure 5.37 Using MDM as Bridge between ERP and CRM.

5.7.3.6   Problem Statement

Application systems are not designed for making master data actionable for the enterprise IT landscape. They do it only for the application purpose. For example, we have often encountered CRM applications focused on a department, channel, or country level. CRM applications usually need to integrate with non-CRM applications such as order entry processing or billing across departments or geographies. However, their main design objective was not Master Data Management and distribution, which often means a lack of interfaces designed to support a broad set of protocols and exchange formats. Furthermore, large enterprises may have the same application in each country or region of operation. We worked with customers who had dozens of ERP and CRM systems distributed globally. This situation means the customization of each of these systems (even though it's the same application) is different, thereby causing different lookup table settings and differently authored master data records. In addition, very often Product and Customer records are duplicated across these systems. Often, the business rules are also inconsistent. So for enterprises managing master data, quality becomes an issue. Assume the application can achieve the following (in many cases these applications were not designed for maintaining master data integrity):

- Extract, cleanse, de-duplicate
  - (+) Detect invalid values and duplicates
  - (–) Fixing dirty data after the fact is costly or even impossible
- Example online address validation and duplicate checks
  - (+) Can prevent creation of duplicates
  - (–) Information still restricted to the application silo

Then your application would be able to do some management of master data quality, which may not be sufficient. In order to manage master data on an enterprise scale, you need to manage master data centrally to achieve:

- (+) Prevention of duplicates
- (+) Integration of master data from all other applications
- (+) A 360-degree view of master data entities

Finally, if you have both ERP and CRM systems, which one leads with regard to master data entities?

5.7.3.7   Solution

The MDM-CRM Integration pattern and the MDM-ERP Integration pattern share the dependency on the Initial Load pattern and at least one of the MDM Hub Patterns. The Initial Load pattern is needed for initially populating the MDM System, and at least one MDM Hub Pattern is mandatory for the MDM Hub. Given our experience with customers, we have seen the following:

- **ERP Systems and MDM Hub Patterns:** In the context of ERP systems, we often encountered the implementation of MDM in the Product domain. In such a case, the MDM System was usually built using the Coexistence Hub or the Transaction Hub pattern. The reason for this linkage to certain MDM Hub Patterns is that the collaborative use cases where Line of Business users collaborate on authoring a Product require the full materialization of all attributes in the MDM System. Otherwise, keeping state in the workflow is difficult to implement.
- **CRM Systems and MDM Hub Patterns:** In the context of CRM systems, we have seen all three types of MDM Hub Patterns used. However, the Registry Hub pattern was used less often than either the Coexistence Hub pattern or the Transaction Hub pattern. The reason for this situation is that relationship management and the management of attributes related to privacy and preferences are often not covered when using the Registry Hub pattern, because the use of this pattern usually implies the prevention of duplicates in the MDM System.

The architecture patterns used for integrating the MDM System with an ERP or a CRM system depend on your business requirements and the decision on where you want to author master data.[48]

5.7.3.8   Forces

The problem described is difficult to solve if you need to synchronize your master data between the ERP and the MDM System or between the MDM and the CRM system.[49]

5.7.3.9   Relations

The MDM-CRM Integration and the MDM-ERP Integration patterns are related to the MDM Hub Patterns. As you certainly remember from the beginning of this chapter, an MDM Hub serves as the foundation and has an orchestration role in an MDM Solution. Because you need to populate the MDM System with master data initially, the Initial Load pattern is required as well. Finally, Information Synchronization and Transaction Interception patterns are required to completely address your MDM business requirements.

---

48. A comprehensive discussion on this topic can be found in Section 8.3.
49. For further details, see, for example, the SAP application integration blueprint in Section 8.3.

5.8   Pattern Selection and Pattern Composition

Although we have talked a great deal about MDM Architecture Patterns, any enterprise is eventually interested in MDM Solutions, and not only in architectures and technologies, best practices and methodologies, or products with functions and features. Therefore, we need to be concerned about the appropriate usage of these MDM patterns to develop MDM Architecture Blueprints, MDM Solution Blueprints, and—finally—to deploy comprehensive MDM Solutions. But what is an MDM Solution? This question sounds very simple, and the answer may be considered by many readers as rather trivial. Having said this, however, we would still like to give a suggestion regarding the key components of any MDM Solution.

In Chapter 1, we elaborated on the term MDM, and the motivation for an MDM Solution along with its key characteristics and components. An MDM Solution is comprised of those MDM components that need to be complemented mainly with an MDM strategy, a set of architectures, products and technologies, and best practices:

- **MDM Strategy:** Is a value-enabling combination of business and technical components. It needs to include the business participation, business motivation, and overall guidelines from the business. Part of this MDM strategy may even be captured within the MDM business architecture and a technical roadmap, which deliver value towards this MDM business architecture incrementally over time. Of course, this MDM strategy needs to be customized for a particular customer situation. An underlying premise is also the iterative approach in terms of adjusting the MDM strategy depending on changing business requirements.
- **Architecture:** Is a wide set of different but related architectures, such as a systems architecture, reference architecture, technical architecture, master information architecture, and so forth. In this chapter and in Chapter 3, we have seen the variety of different architectures that need to be considered in any MDM deployment. This architecture also includes a product- and component-mapping exercise to lay out the technology underpinning of the MDM Solution.
- **Products and Technologies:** This book is dealing with the topic of MDM in a pretty product- and technology-agnostic way. However, products and technologies are an essential ingredient of any MDM Solution. And, of course, IBM is well positioned to provide technical functionality in every aspect that is required to deliver an MDM Solution. It includes MDM-related products to address the entire Master Data Integration (MDI) scope of functions to actually build and operate master information hubs. The scope is considerably wider than what MDI technologies can deliver: It includes a set of Enterprise Application Integration (EAI) and Enterprise Information Integration (EII) technologies as well.
- **Best Practices:** The term **best practices** spans a wide area and is interpreted and looked at by different readers in different ways. As we have outlined, MDM Architecture Patterns (and other patterns as well) are derived from repeatedly executing similar tasks where patterns should then be captured in guidelines, best practices and services, blueprints and frameworks, and—desirably—in tools to accelerate usage and deployment. We would even go so far as to state that almost all MDM

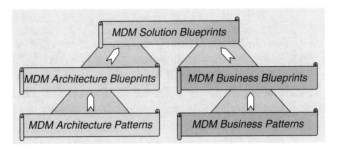

Figure 5.38   Affiliation and Flow of Patterns → Blueprints → Solutions.

Architecture Patterns are a special type of MDM best practices, where these best practices are required to address the entire MDM end-to-end scope, which includes integration, build, deployment, governance, and operational aspects of the MDM Solution. This point of view also factors in the need for best practices that are related to functional and also nonfunctional themes (e.g., performance optimization, migration and upgrades, and so forth). Furthermore, there is also a strong demand for master data best practices (e.g., to address master data categorization needs). Developing and leveraging these MDM best practices usually belongs in the domain expertise of any System Integrator. MDM best practices can, for example, be a collection of imperatives or guidelines on how to implement MDM Solutions in the most efficient way, yielding optimum systems performance (e.g., regarding real-time synchronization of master data). Another example of MDM best practices is a set of recommendations that link the usage of MDM Hub Patterns to specific categories of customer requirements. The scope of MDM best practices is naturally much wider than the scope of MDM Architecture Patterns.

Having explained MDM Solutions, let's now discuss the two remaining concepts or terms: MDM Architecture Blueprints and MDM Solution Blueprints. Figure 5.38 illustrates the relationship of these terms. It is a depiction of the affiliation and the flow from patterns to blueprints to solutions.[50]

An MDM Architecture Blueprint is based on a composition and customization of relevant architectural patterns (meaning to use only a subset from the available MDM pattern portfolio in an appropriate way). MDM Architecture Blueprints can be cross-industry or very industry-specific. They can also be limited to a specific master data domain or MDM method of use. This composition and customization exercise will yield an MDM Architecture Blueprint that serves as the architectural underpinning for an MDM Solution Blueprint. For such an MDM Solution Blueprint, there might be several MDM Architecture Blueprints that combine different domains or categories of MDM Architecture Patterns.

For example, an MDM Customer Data Integration (CDI) Solution Blueprint for a financial institution can be a combination of an MDM Architecture Blueprint, which is addressing all

---

50.   In Chapters 6, 7, and 8, we will elaborate on MDM Solution Blueprints even further.

operational aspects on the master data on one side, with an MDM Architecture Blueprint on the other side, which is addressing all master data integration or synchronization aspects. It is important to notice that an MDM Solution Blueprint is composed of one or multiple MDM Architecture Blueprint(s) as well as the corresponding MDM Business Blueprint(s). That is to say that an MDM Solution Blueprint has an architectural as well as a business representation or facet. Similar to architecture blueprints, the MDM Business Blueprints are composed of MDM Business Patterns. This synergistic correspondence between the business and the IT domains is an underlying premise that drives deployments of any MDM Solution.

Conclusion

In this chapter, we have elaborated on some rather ambitious and challenging MDM aspects that occasionally seem to have been somewhat on the theoretical side of things, and perhaps even a bit artificial. But these MDM Architecture Patterns have a very practical and down-to-earth meaning: They will support you through your various MDM architectural tasks and will help you in building MDM architectures leveraging proven architectural artifacts. The presented structure of the MDM Architecture Patterns and the special role of the MDM Hub Patterns as a means to facilitate and orchestrate the usage and composition of MDM patterns with all other types and subtypes can and should be applied to all architectural undertakings in the MDM space. It will accelerate the completion of your architectural tasks and will guarantee consistency among various architectures.

And still, you may have asked yourself about the applicability of these MDM Architecture Patterns to real-life MDM deployments: Why did we have to dig into the details of these different MDM Hub Patterns and the different subtypes of MDM Architecture Patterns? And even the key question regarding the linkage of various types and subtypes of MDM Architecture Patterns to real-life MDM Solutions or at least solution blueprints still needs to be answered. Well, the following chapters on MDM Solution Blueprints will illustrate this linkage. It will, furthermore, explain how the MDM RA, which we described in Chapter 3, and the MDM Architecture Patterns play in concert and contribute not only to our understanding of the structure of various MDM Solution Blueprints but also to our understanding of the value of patterns in accelerating design and deployment of MDM Solutions.

We would also like to highlight another final aspect regarding the value of these MDM Architecture Patterns: Deploying MDM Solutions isn't a "big-bang" approach, but an evolutionary undertaking. It comes in project phases, one phase after the other. There are different MDM entry points that depend on the MDM maturity level and set of customer requirements. But regardless of the initial set of requirements and the initial MDM Solution implementation, as time goes by, additional business and technical needs will surface. The initial MDM Solution will evolve into something different. It may grow and may have to encompass additional solution aspects: (1) additional domains of master data may have to be taken into consideration, (2) other methods of use may have to be implemented, (3) master data from other legacy systems may have to be integrated, (4) more sophisticated MDM Hub Patterns may be under investigation, and new business processes or improvements of existing business processes may have to be implemented—the list seems to be endless. This flexibility is the value of your MDM Architecture Patterns and your MDM RA. It allows for modular design and facilitates the evolutionary MDM Solution growth over time.

To summarize, MDM Architecture Patterns enable deployment acceleration, solution growth, structured thinking, and consistent implementations.

References

1. Gamma, E., Helms, R., Johnson, R., and Vlissides, R. 1995. *Design Patterns: Elements of Reusable Object-Oriented Software*. Reading, MA: Addison-Wesley.
2. *The IBM Rational Software Architect (RSA)*. Retrieved 2008 from http://www.306.ibm.com/software/awdtools/architect/swarchitect/.
3. IBM Patterns for e-business. *IBM developerWorks*. Retrieved 2008 from http://www.ibm.com/developerworks/patterns/.
4. Adams, J., and Koushik, S. 2001. *Patterns for e-business—A Strategy for Reuse*. Location: IBM Press.
5. Adams, J. et al. 2004. *Patterns: Implementing an SOA Using an Enterprise Service Bus*. IBM Redbooks, SG24–6346–00.
6. Altern, G. et al. 2004. *Patterns: Applying Pattern Approaches V2*. IBM Redbooks, ZG24–6710–00.
7. Ang, J. et al. 2004. *Patterns: Service Oriented Architecture and Web Service*. IBM Redbooks.
8. Bond, J. et al. 2005. *Patterns: Integrating Enterprise Service Buses in a Service Oriented Architecture*. IBM Redbooks, SG24–6773–00.
9. Buschmann, F. et al. 2001. *Pattern-Oriented Software Architecture, Volume 2, Patterns for Concurrent and Networked Objects*. New York: John Wiley & Sons.
10. Chessell, M. et al. 2005. *Patterns: Model-Driven Development Using IBM Rational Software Architect*. IBM Redbooks, SG24–7105–00.
11. Chappell, D. A. 2004. *Enterprise Service Bus—Theory in Practice*. Location: O'Reilly Media.
12. The Open Group (TOG). 2001. *Architectural Patterns website*. Retrieved 2008 from http://www.opengroup.org/architecture/togaf7-doc/arch/p4/patterns/patterns.htm.
13. Dreibelbis, A., Hechler, E., Mathews, B., Oberhofer, M., and Sauter, G. 2007. Information service patterns, Part 4: Master Data Management architecture patterns. *IBM developerWorks*. Retrieved 2008 from http://www.ibm.com/developerworks/db2/library/techarticle/dm-0703sauter/index.html.
14. Eeles, P. 2006. What is software architecture? *IBM developerWorks*. Retrieved 2008 from http://www.ibm.com/developerworks/rational/library/feb06/eeles/.
15. IBM. 2008. *IBM Industry Models*. Retrieved 2008 from http://www.ibm.com/software/data/ips/products/industrymodels/.
16. The Open Group (TOG). 2007. *The Open Group Architecture Framework (TOGAF™) Version 8.1.1 Enterprise Edition*. Retrieved 2008 from http://www.opengroup.org/togaf/.
17. Mathews, B., Lane, E., Sauter, G., and Selvage, M. 2007. Information service patterns, Part 1: Data federation pattern, *IBM developerWorks*. Retrieved 2008 from http://www.ibm.com/developerworks/webservices/library/ws-soa-infoserv1/.
18. Mathews, B., Ostic, E., and Sauter, G. 2006. Information service patterns, Part 3: Data consolidation pattern. *IBM developerWorks*. Retrieved December 05, 2006 from http://www.ibm.com/developerworks/webservices/library/ws-soa-infoserv2/.

19. Mathews, B., Ostic, E., and Sauter, G. 2007. Information service patterns, Part 3: Data cleansing pattern. *IBM developerWorks*. Retrieved April 06, 2007 from http://www.ibm.com/developerworks/ webservices/library/ws-soa-infoserv3/.

20. Altern, G. et al. 2004. *Patterns: Applying Pattern Approaches V2*. IBM Redbooks, ZG24–6710–00.

21. Adinolfi, O. et al. 2005. *Patterns: SOA with an Enterprise Service Bus in WebSphere Application Server V6*. IBM Redbooks, SG24–6494–00.

22. Bandaru, S. et al. 2007. *Connecting Enterprise Applications to WebSphere Enterprise Service Bus*. IBM Redbooks, SG24–7406–00.

23. Adams, J. et al. 2007. *Patterns: SOA Design Using WebSphere Message Broker and WebSphere ESB*. IBM Redbooks, SG24-7369–00.

24. Akiko, C. et al. 2007. *Connect WebSphere Service-Oriented Middleware to SAP*. IBM Redbooks, SG24–7220–00.

25. Ghandhe, M. et al. 2007. *Production Topologies for WebSphere Process Server and WebSphere ESB V6*. IBM Redbooks, SG24–7413–00.

26. Calcagno, L. et al. 2006. *Patterns: SOA Foundation Service Connectivity Scenario*. IBM Redbooks, SG24–7228–00.

27. Robinson, R. et al. 2004. Understand Enterprise Service Bus scenarios and solutions in Service-Oriented Architecture, Part 1, *IBM developerWorks*. Retrieved 2008 from http://www. 128.ibm.com/developerworks/library/ws-esbscen/.

28. Publish/Subscribe Messaging With JMS Topics and Using the Document Object Model. 2003. Retrieved 2008 from http://java.sun.com/developer/EJTechTips/2003/tt0415.html.

29. Wetherill, J. 2007. *Messaging Systems and the Java Message Service (JMS)*. Retrieved 2008 from http://java.sun.com/developer/technicalArticles/Networking/messaging/.

30. Mahmoud, Q. 2004. *Getting Started with Java Message Service (JMS)*. Retrieved 2008 from http://java.sun.com/developer/technicalArticles/Ecommerce/jms/.

31. Hohpe, G., Woolf, B. et al. 2004. *Enterprise Integration Patterns. Designing, Building, and Deploying Messaging Solutions*. Boston: Addison-Wesley.

Chapter 6

PIM-MDM Solution Blueprints

In this chapter we have two objectives: First, it introduces the concept of MDM Solution Blueprints which will explain the relationships between architecture patterns and business patterns. Second, this chapter explains a variety of PIM-MDM Solution Blueprints for several industries and solution scenarios based upon certain business requirements. MDM Solution Blueprints tailor the Master Data Management Reference Architecture (MDM RA) to specific industry solutions.

6.1 Introduction to Master Data Management Solutions Blueprints

Today, legal compliance in the banking industry increases in complexity with each additional law in the area of anti-money laundering, anti-terrorist financing, and traditional areas covered by Basel II and similar legislation. The electronic consumer device industry struggles to optimize its business processes and bring new products to market faster. It is difficult to orchestrate these processes across various Lines of Business with associated stovepipe-like IT organizations. The implementation of a self-service website is for many telecommunication companies a mandatory asset to compete in the market, but is, as you will see, a daunting task for many. Without efficiency improvements in the exchange of product information that reshapes the relationship between retailers and suppliers, the complexity in the involved IT infrastructure becomes a severe hindrance to business improvements. All cases mentioned earlier, and a lot more across all industries, share the same reality: Business optimization by improving existing or deploying new business processes currently requires a new approach in dealing with core business information entities like products and customers. Such an approach mandates the deployment of Master Data Management Solutions. However, there is no single way of deploying an MDM System that fits all needs.

While working with customers, we have observed that there is a certain affinity between business processes and requirements and certain architecture patterns previously described.

We capture this affinity as a *relation* between business patterns and MDM architecture patterns. Business patterns based on this relation drive the selection of architecture patterns to compose an MDM Solution Blueprint where the architectural side was given by an architectural blueprint and the business side was given by a business blueprint. In addition to the architecture patterns, the MDM RA, as presented in Chapter 3, is a major input for the Solution Blueprint architecture. Throughout this chapter, the discussion on the technical side will be motivated by sufficiently detailed considerations on the business side that drive the MDM Solution architecture.

We assume the reader is familiar with the MDM RA (Chapter 3) and the MDM Architecture Patterns (Chapter 5). Individual architectural building blocks from the Master Data Management services component described in the MDM RA are not repeated unless a specific function is very important. Applicable MDM Hub patterns are listed in the MDM Solution Blueprint description. Avoiding redundancy, security-related aspects for MDM Solution Blueprints are discussed only once in the context of the Solution Blueprint described in Section 6.5.5. For the security concepts, we assume the reader has also read Chapter 4, on MDM Security and Privacy.

6.2   Terms and Definitions

Before we start to explore MDM Solution Blueprints, a couple of basic terms and definitions should be clarified to obtain a common understanding. We rely on the introduction of the terms Product Information Management (PIM) and Customer Data Integration (CDI), which were defined in Chapter 1. In this chapter, the focus will be on MDM Solution Blueprints, with a focus on PIM as indicated by the chapter title, "PIM-MDM Solution Blueprints." In Chapter 7, the focus shifts to the Customer domain, as indicated by the chapter title, "CDI-MDM Solution Blueprints."

The first term is **Architecture Blueprint.** The MDM RA, as described in Chapter 3, is based upon the analysis of numerous MDM engagements spanning both PIM and CDI implementations. The level of abstraction applied is such that the MDM RA is industry- and solution-agnostic. The MDM Reference Architecture is the base model from which the Architecture Blueprints are derived. The adaptation of the MDM RA to obtain an Architecture Blueprint for a specific industry solution is based upon decisions concerning the choice of one or more architecture patterns for implementation. The terms *architecture pattern* and *architecture pattern composition* were defined in Chapter 5.

The selection of architecture patterns is driven by a business purpose. The business purpose drives architecture design, which should drive the choice of architecture patterns. The business architecture is thus input to the IT architecture design for which IT Architects also use reference architectures as input. You would use a motor vehicle reference architecture when you have the business need to build a car. Tailoring this motor vehicle reference architecture using architecture patterns like having wheels, a front and back windshield, doors, axles, seats, an engine, and more are composed in a specific way into the architectural blueprint of the car. The pattern selection in this example was driven by the purpose to build a car.

The patterns in this particular composition allow us to easily identify a car for what it is and also to distinguish it from a tractor. Both have several of the patterns in common, but a different composition and the addition of several other patterns make the difference between a car and a tractor Architecture Blueprint, which can both be derived from the motor vehicle reference architecture.

Similarly, when deploying an MDM System, the type of Architecture Blueprint chosen determines the architectural characteristics of the MDM Solution. Tailoring the MDM RA towards an Architecture Blueprint by using architecture patterns described in Chapter 5 is driven by a purpose such as optimizing the New Product Introduction process. In essence, the Architecture Blueprint captures the key architectural characteristics from the solution. Just as a car designer can accelerate the design by reusing an existing Architectural Blueprint to mitigate the project risks, IT Architects can benefit by leveraging Architecture Blueprints.

The composition of patterns to derive an Architectural Blueprint from a reference architecture is not arbitrary and also applies to the composition of architecture patterns to derive an **MDM Architecture Blueprint** from the MDM RA. The process of composition is governed by one or multiple purposes, namely, what problem the architectural blueprint supposedly solves. If the objective is to have a vehicle moved by a mechanical engine, for one or several persons where the passengers are not exposed to the elements, the likely outcome of the composition of the patterns presented is a car. It might have three[1] or four wheels, room for one, two, four, or more passengers, and different maximum speeds, but it can be recognized immediately as a car. If the objectives were different, with many of the same patterns, like wheels, axles, and so forth, the outcome could have been a bicycle or a truck. Conceptually similar, the composition of architecture patterns into MDM Solution Blueprints is not arbitrary.

The driving forces of the architecture selection process are **business patterns** and **business blueprints**,[2] the latter a composition of the aforementioned. They are the counterparts of architecture patterns and blueprints in the business domain. We only sketch the business context and relevant business patterns and blueprints in an informal way to sufficiently detail why certain architectural decisions were made. Another influencing factor of pattern selection is the current state of business and IT as well as the desired end state.

Finally, an **MDM Solution Blueprint** is the result of a composition of business blueprints and related MDM architecture blueprints. A good MDM Solution Blueprint describes what kind of business problems can be solved with it and what business benefits can be gained. It also outlines the business requirements for the IT part of the solution. Complementing the business blueprint and representing the architecture domain, the MDM Solution Blueprint shows the solution architecture underpinning for the given business context that actually solves the

---

1. There are several vehicles available in Germany where the front axle does not have two, but only one, wheel. These vehicles are usually limited in speed and only provide sufficient space for one or at most two passengers and are mainly used for driving around within a city.

2. The formal discussion of *business patterns* and *business blueprints* is outside the scope of this book. Some references to this domain were given in Chapter 5.

business problem. The solution architecture describes the key components of the overall solution and the relation between the involved systems as well as how they interact. In any concrete deployment situation, an MDM Solution Blueprint requires adaptation to reflect the functional and nonfunctional requirements of a particular customer situation. An IT Architect might need to refine an MDM Solution Blueprint due to constraints implied by the existing IT infrastructure in which the MDM Solution is deployed. Therefore, an MDM Solution Blueprint is not prescriptive—it is rather a proven accelerator asset that an IT Architect can leverage to mitigate risk and to design an MDM Solution faster.

The presentation of the MDM Solution Blueprints in this chapter is divided into the following subsections:

- **Business context:** The section provides the business context of the MDM Solution Blueprint, relevant business requirements, and indications for selecting relevant business patterns. If your business problem does not fit this description, the MDM Solution Blueprint is very likely not the right one for you. As you will see in Chapter 9, the organizational structure and political landscape affects the success of an MDM project as well. Also, political constraints (e.g., single-vendor strategy) influence technology choices and thus indirectly also affect the available architecture patterns.
- **Relevant business patterns:** The section mentions the key business patterns and their characteristics.
- **Relation between business patterns and MDM architecture patterns:** The section describes the relation(s) between business patterns and MDM architecture patterns. The relation(s) between business requirements given by business patterns and chosen architecture patterns should highlight why the latter were selected, in other words, which characteristics of the architecture pattern suit the business requirements particularly well. Because the MDM Hub patterns are closely related to the implementation styles, a linkage between the business requirements and the implementation styles is created by the MDM Hub patterns.
- **MDM Solution Blueprint overview:** The subsection shows the entire architecture of the Solution Blueprint and all relevant details.
- **Advantages:** The main advantages of the Solution Blueprint are listed here.
- **Alternatives and possible extensions:** Alternative Solution Blueprints and extensions to the MDM Solution Blueprint are provided in this section. For the discussion of required organizational transformations that introduce, for example, a data governance board, read Chapter 9, where we explain these aspects in detail.

6.3 New Product Introduction (NPI) Solution Blueprint for Consumer Electronics Industry

We start with the first MDM Solution Blueprint. The business driver for this Solution Blueprint is the New Product Introduction (NPI) process, which was introduced in Chapter 1. We introduce this business process now in more detail and then present a solution showing how Master Data Management helps to optimize this business process, which is not always implemented as efficiently as desired.

6.3.1   Business Context

In the consumer electronics market,[3] many devices are considered commodity devices with low profit margins. However, there is a customer segment that will buy a new device simply because it's a new technology gadget instead of having a real need for the product. These customers will wait in long lines just for the opportunity to buy the product—just consider as an example the launch of the iPhone by Apple Inc. in July 2007.

As soon as competitors offer a similar device, the price drops and thus the profit margin decreases. It is therefore very attractive for a consumer electronics company to optimize the business process of **New Product Introduction (NPI).** The optimization of the NPI business process maximizes the time and thus the duration where the device is sold with maximum profit margin while the company is the only one offering such a device in the market. It can easily be seen how this optimization benefits the bottom line of a consumer electronics company.

Maximizing the net profit is certainly a nice effect achieved by streamlining the NPI business process. However, there is another effect that can only be measured indirectly. If you are able to continually be the first company to deliver new technology gadgets to the market, customers will certainly start to perceive your company as the most innovative in the consumer electronics sector. Assuming that an image of innovation is part of your company's executive agenda, improved and faster delivery of consumer electronics devices by an improved NPI process supports this strategic goal. As we will see, a PIM system managing product master data is an excellent choice for supporting both the time to market and image objectives.

After this basic example showing some benefits of the NPI process, let's look at an industry-agnostic definition that also applies for the consumer electronics industry. The **New Product Introduction (NPI)** business process means the following:

> The capability of a company to design, develop, and manufacture products and services and bring them to market faster than their competitors is a key element of economic survival. For this capability, a comprehensive architecture bringing together the Lines of Business such as research, marketing, and manufacturing is a mandatory foundation.

A company implementing or improving the NPI process usually aims for improvement in a subset or all of the following business goals and objectives:

- Increase speed and efficiency in bringing products to market or to new markets.
- Improve internal and external collaboration.
- Increase the amount of new products and designs without increasing staff.
- Improve company revenue.

---

3.   We don't distinguish between consumer electronics manufacturing and consumer electronics retail.

- Increase project risk transparency and accountability for the company.
- Reduce product lifecycle costs.
- Prevent creation of duplicate product records that waste time and other resources.
- Enable product and operational innovation.
- Enable master data quality.
- Reduce integration complexity in order to share master data with suppliers/resellers.

If the optimization of the NPI process has such positive benefits, then why is it so hard to streamline? The business process New Product Introduction aligns product strategy and corporate strategy, end-to-end management of product concepts and ideas, and the gathering of requirements followed by product prototyping and authoring of product master data and documentation. As part of a New Product Introduction, product exchange with suppliers or resellers as part of a market ramp-up and/or product launch might be required as well.

First, consider the fact that before you can introduce a product into the market you need to *define* the product and then manufacture it. The *definition* of the product is given by many different attributes that can be grouped into several functional areas such as technical attributes, pricing attributes, and route to market attributes. Sometimes the definition is difficult if an agreement of relevant attributes is necessary across various Lines of Business. Here a data governance board (see Chapter 9) could help to solve the political issues. Adding, or editing, all of the attributes of a product is often called the *authoring* of product data and is part of the NPI process. Typically, this authoring process is referred to as a collaborative workflow, where users with different expertise collaborate. The collaborative authoring of master data is the key use case that drives the need for workflow capabilities for MDM Systems.

At the beginning of the NPI process, shown with a very simple example in Figure 6.1, an automated data validation step could exist if the NPI process is supported by a PIM system. Such an automated validation step could exist if, for example, a "product data skeleton" with raw product information is created automatically. An example is an external source such as product information on a part of the product delivered by a supplier. Note that when building the MDM System during the Master Data Integration phase, the automated data

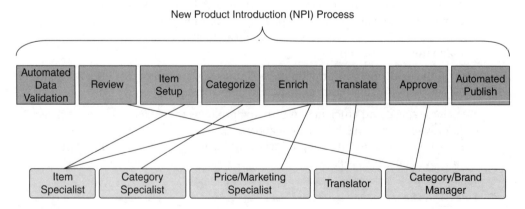

Figure 6.1 Simple version of the NPI process.

New Product Introduction (NPI) Process

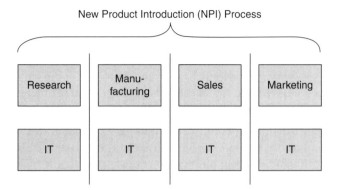

Figure 6.2   Line of Business and associated IT organized in a stovepipe-like fashion.

validation step may have been used already. Thus, during build and operation of the PIM-MDM System, the same data validation rules are used for consistency reasons. For the Master Data Integration itself, the Initial Load pattern is useful. At the end of the NPI process, usually after an approval step, the product information is commonly published to one or multiple channels through which the product is sold. Typical examples are printing solutions for catalog printing or e-Commerce platforms.

In an NPI process as sketched in Figure 6.1 users with different job roles collaborate. Examples of these types of users are Product Designers,[4] Pricing Managers, Sales Specialists, Marketing Experts, Item Specialists, and Category Managers. These users are often within different department units of a company, such as product research or sales, and the users may have different levels of knowledge about using IT systems. Consequently, for many companies today, the authoring of product master data may span multiple stovepipe-like organized IT islands, as shown in Figure 6.2, with heterogeneous computing environments. With an IT organization such as that shown in Figure 6.2, the simple-looking NPI process shown in Figure 6.1 is difficult to achieve across all stovepipes. Therefore, the NPI process is not as efficient as it could be today.

An IT environment such as that shown in Figure 6.2 makes it difficult to have a consistent, 360-degree view of product information while it is authored due to the different data models used by the different systems. In this fragmented environment, efforts to create consistent entry and validation processes for common attributes require the development of many point-to-point interfaces. Likewise, maintaining the state of a product as it is moved through a collaborative authoring cycle across a variety of systems is just as difficult if the IT environment is similar to that shown in Figure 6.2.

---

4.   Note that product designers often need to answer the question "build or buy?" for a new electronic subcomponent such as transistors or memory. The collection of available parts often consists of more than 100,000, reaching to a few million entries, which complicates the search in this huge set of products. Some of them differ only in a few attributes, such as voltage. So the PIM system intended to support this must have powerful search capabilities or needs to be enhanced with an appropriate search engine. See Subsection 6.3.6 for further details.

Overall, this silo approach creates many obstacles for the authoring of product master information, making it complicated. The result is the presence of many problems that can rarely be solved efficiently without implementing Master Data Management. Centralized product master data management also helps to identify duplicate products and avoid defining the same product multiple times when you already have a similar product or the same one. While working with customers, we have often found the same product defined differently in various systems, which can make, for example, revenue reporting at the product level very difficult.

After the base product definition is finished, there may be enough information to manufacture the products but not enough information about them to support selling the product. For example, if a company is doing business in several countries, it must also provide the product documentation in several languages. So even when everything is manufactured, the translation of the product information and the distribution of it into order entry systems and so on requires many weeks or even months for most companies today. Therefore, the translation of each attribute name and the attribute values used in the product documentation into various languages needs to be done efficiently. In such a scenario, Translators are part of the NPI process as well.

The translation process should be part of a managed product authoring workflow process and benefits from having all of the attributes in a central place with attribute-level security. This setup provides the technical foundation, so that only authorized users with the appropriate language skills can perform the translation of attributes into the languages in which they are proficient. Unfortunately, this technique for the optimization of translation requires certain critical technical capabilities that are missing in many companies. The translation part of the item information as well as the documentation is only one step in the NPI process.

Another aspect of global product information are the values for certain attributes that differ between countries or from region to region. Examples of such details that engineers need to consider are different voltages supplied by power grids and different outlets for power plugs. Unfortunately, the boundaries for these technical details are not always aligned with the language boundaries. For example, power voltage is the same in Germany, Austria, and Switzerland, but the type of power plugs supported varies. To minimize the translation effort, attribute inheritance capability by location (in Section B.5 of Appendix B, you can find a product with this capability) is a useful feature of the product information management system. This feature allows the classification of a product into a location hierarchy representing the locations where it is sold, where it can inherit all of the attributes from the parent level that should remain unchanged, and then overwrite (translate) location-specific values, thus reducing storage size and translation efforts. For the voltage and power outlets, this capability would mean that by establishing a base value for those technical attributes to be inherited through use of the attribute inheritance feature, they would only have to be overwritten for locations where a differentiation exists from the base value. Naturally, with such a feature, you then only need to translate those attributes where a differentiation exists, thereby minimizing these efforts. Figure 6.3 shows an example for this type of capability.

In Europe, German is spoken in Germany, Austria, and Switzerland. Thus, product attribute values of attributes such as "network voltage" and "plug types" should be translated only

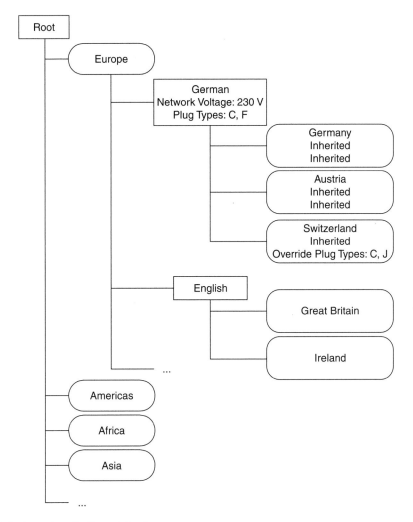

Figure 6.3 Location Attribute Inheritance.

where a difference exists. With "inherited" it is illustrated that the values for attributes from the parent node "German" was passed on to the child nodes "Germany," "Austria" and "Switzerland," indicating that the translator does not need to do the translation twice—doing it once for the parent node "German" is enough, thus reducing the work on master data maintenance and translation. In the case of the attributes "network voltage" and "plug types", the reduction of work means that the values for these attributes are the same as for the parent node, as indicated by "inherited" in the ellipses for Germany and Austria—leading to 230 V and types C and F, respectively for the child nodes.

Even though Switzerland shares the same network voltage as Austria and Germany, they support different plug types. Therefore, the node "Switzerland" inherits the value of 230 V for the network voltage attribute from the parent node "German," but overrides (indicated by the "override") the value and the translation for the plug type attribute supporting plug types C and J instead of C and F. So instead of maintaining network voltage and plug types each time for each of the three countries with an overall effort of having six attributes to maintain and translate, using the location attribute inheritance feature saves a lot of the work for attribute maintenance and translation. The same location attribute inheritance feature can be successfully applied for use cases such as micro-merchandising, where price information is inherited and overridden down to the individual store level. The micro-merchandising use case is valid for the NPI process as well if a product needs to be launched, for example, across the United States at the same time, with a lower price for a small town in Texas than the price for New York City.

So far, we have discussed only that value maintenance of attributes depending on location could benefit from a PIM system. If you are selling products worldwide, there might not only be attribute values dependent on location but also the existence of an attribute. For example, the VAT attribute representing a certain type of sales tax for Germany is not applicable across all countries. So the software product selected for the PIM system should have features that support the following: If a product is categorized in a certain node in a hierarchy, additional attributes for the product become available. So if in a location hierarchy a product is categorized under the node "Germany," this categorization would make an additional attribute "VAT" available. If the same product is also categorized under another node representing another country where a VAT doesn't exist, this attribute would not be available there.

In addition to translation, many systems need to have the new product information available (in the correct language) if a company uses multiple routes to market, such as selling in stores, through an e-Commerce website, and through retailers or resellers. Reasons could be due to differences for price attributes and or available product bundles sold in stores or through a retailer channel. The different routes to market are likely represented on the IT side by a variety of IT systems from different vendors with a broad set of open and proprietary interfaces. Also note that an e-Commerce system is a business-to-consumer[5] relation, whereas the route to market through retailers/resellers is a business-to-business[6] relation. If the retailer or reseller route to market exists, this channel expands the scenario from the Product master data domain by including relationships to the Vendor master data domain. In summary, the routes to market represent yet another complex dimension of the NPI process that makes streamlining it difficult without an appropriately built MDM System.

6.3.2 Relevant Business Patterns

As seen in the previous section, the current Solution Blueprint being discussed mandates optimizing the NPI business process. Depending on the routes to market, additional business

---

5. The abbreviation B2C will be used for business-to-consumer from here on.
6. The abbreviation B2B will be used for business-to-business from here on.

processes are required. Therefore, we need the following business patterns for this Solution Blueprint:

- NPI business process pattern (mandatory)
- B2C pattern[7]
- B2B pattern[8]

For the B2C pattern, we include an e-Commerce system in the blueprint. The B2B pattern could be instantiated if the consumer electronics manufacturer decides to exchange product information with retailers through the Global Data Synchronization Network (GDSN). The components for GDSN are described in the Solution Blueprint in Section 6.4.

6.3.3   Relation between Business Patterns and Architecture Patterns

The business patterns in Subsection 6.3.2 are related to the following MDM architecture patterns:

- Initial Load pattern
- Coexistence Hub or Transaction Hub pattern
- ESB patterns
- Messaging patterns

The Initial Load pattern is needed for building the MDM System because product information is often scattered in many application systems inconsistently. Extracting, cleansing, standardizing, transforming, and loading the product master information with high data quality can thus be achieved with the Initial Load pattern.

In the consumer electronics industry, defining master data in the Product domain requires flexible authoring capabilities, because only a small set of attributes may be shared among all products and a significantly larger group of the attributes are category-specific. A category is a group of products sharing similarities. An example is a category *"phones"* in which all phones are grouped. We worked with customers where several hundred categories are part of the production system. Only a small subset of those attributes was shared among all products, where the attributes in each category were then different by category. Often, products have many cross-sell relationships to other products or a product may be packaged in many different ways, resulting in many packaging relationships for a product. These relationships[9] need to be managed efficiently. Furthermore, the products are classified in several hierarchies reflecting semantics such as product type categories, sold-to relations (resellers), and bought-from relations (supplier). The requirements of flexible data modeling and effective relationship and hierarchy management are very well supported by an MDM System using the Coexistence Hub or the Transaction Hub pattern because they fully materialize the full set of master data attributes of the product data.

---

7. Business patterns and their value are discussed in [1] and [2]. The basic B2C pattern can be found in [3].

8. The basic B2B pattern can be found in [3].

9. The relationships mentioned in the examples can be modeled using multi-occurrence attributes.

Now imagine the situation where this complex product information is stored differently in a variety of application systems. If no harmonization of the product information is done enterprise-wide, a Registry Hub only linking data from various sources would not be an easy way to access the product information. It is difficult to implement workflows efficiently for processes like the NPI across multiple application systems that store product information differently because the Registry Hub would only store keys to the products, which are stored in different systems and in different formats elsewhere. For example, the review step depicted in Figure 6.3 cannot be performed efficiently by Category Managers today because incoming data is difficult to compare to existing products on an attribute-level due to different data repositories and processes. Attribute inheritance in hierarchies would also be complicated to implement with a Registry Hub. The lack of a central repository to review data causes creation of duplicate products, thereby causing costly cleanup processes, wrong orders, and flawed reporting. An implementation based on the Registry Hub pattern would not resolve this problem, because there is no harmonized data model.

As shown in the MDM RA, MDM Systems provide workflow and authoring services that include check-in/check-out functionality. Applying the Transaction Hub pattern, you can have one place for leveraging these services to incrementally add and publish attributes to other systems based on workflow steps so that the MDM System functions as the authoritative source for the item record. In Chapter 3, you also saw that these services are capable of maintaining state as the item proceeds from entry through enrichment and review to publication. Thus, leveraging the MDM System designed with the Transaction Hub pattern provides a central place to manage these workflows, which can be integrated with external workflow engines as needed for long-running processes or workflow tasks that span systems outside the MDM System. Therefore, applying the Transaction Hub pattern is a good architectural decision. Depending on your specific workflow requirements, the Coexistence Hub pattern might be possible as well.

For supporting the B2C pattern with the e-Commerce system, we suggest using ESB and messaging patterns integrating the MDM System. These patterns promote loose coupling of the MDM System and application systems consuming master data, thus increasing business flexibility and business agility.

The benefits of the solution built with these architecture patterns are described in Section 6.3.5.

6.3.4 MDM Solution Blueprint Overview

In Figure 6.4, you can see the Solution Blueprint based on an adapted version of the MDM Component Relationship Diagram presented in Chapter 3. There are three types of components:

- The mandatory components (1) to (7) in light grey are components either needed to build and run the MDM System (e.g., (7)), interact with it (e.g., (1) to (3)), or represent the MDM System (4). The core functions of these components were explained in the MDM RA. Key components for this MDM Solution Blueprint of the MDM System (4) are the Authoring, the Workflow, and the Hierarchy and Relationship Management components. As outlined in Section 6.3.2, the NPI process requires LOB users across various organizations to collaborate in workflows to author a new product. Therefore, the Authoring and the Workflow components should have the

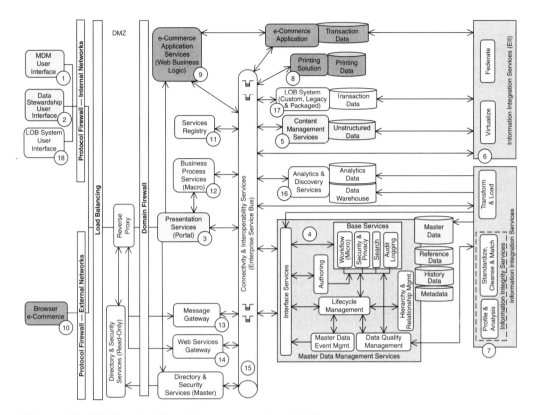

Figure 6.4   NPI Solution Blueprint—component model view.

special attention of an IT Architect designing a concrete solution of this type. Section 6.3.1 describes how important effective management of hierarchies is in reducing authoring efforts and supporting use cases such as micro-merchandising. Therefore, an IT Architect performing software selection for the MDM System should pay special attention to the features for the Hierarchy and Relationship Management component. The Information Integration Services component (7) provides most of the functions to implement the Initial Load pattern when building the MDM System. Furthermore, depending on the software selection for (4) and (7), it might also provide data integrity functions invoked by the Data Quality Management component after the MDM System has been deployed.

- The dark-grey components (8) to (10) are specific to this solution. An e-Commerce system (8) and a printing solution (9) for catalog and flyer generation are two channels through which information about new products can be launched to the market, which makes this set of components typical when implementing this MDM Solution Blueprint. Note that the browser (10) is usually the tool to request an e-Commerce website for enterprise and normal customers.
- The white components (11) to (18) are either optional components or components where integration might or might not be needed, depending on the existing IT infrastructure and the concrete functional and nonfunctional requirements for the MDM

Solution. In a Service-Oriented Architecture landscape, (11) represents the Service Registry and Repository. If it is present, master data services can be published to this repository. An enterprise-wide Business Process Services component (12) orchestrates business processes across IT systems. This component can orchestrate the NPI process, for example—details will be discussed in Section 6.3.4.1. The Message Gateway (13) and the Web Service Gateway (14) are optional components for secure access of backend systems. The Connectivity and Interoperability Services (15) can be implemented using a full-blown ESB product (examples can be found in Section B.2 of Appendix B) or simpler means. ESB or Messaging patterns used to implement this solution blueprint rely on the infrastructure provided by (15). Here, an IT Architect designing a concrete instance of this solution needs to consider what is already available for (15) in the IT infrastructure. An integration of the MDM System (4) with the analytical systems (16) or other LOB systems (17) such as billing might or might not be needed.

6.3.4.1 Workflow Orchestration

In an IT infrastructure, there are often several software products that provide workflow capabilities: Some examples are a centralized process server, a content management system, an e-Commerce platform, and the MDM System. Because the first three examples are all external to the MDM System, we limit our discussion in this scenario to the use of a Business Process Services component to demonstrate integration with the MDM System. Thus, a fundamental question for an IT Architect deploying this MDM Solution is where the NPI process should be orchestrated. Three choices are as follows (see Figure 6.3):

- Deploy the NPI process in the Business Process Services component (12).
- Deploy the NPI process in the Workflow component of the MDM System (4).
- Deploy the overall NPI process in the Business Process Services component (12), and deploy either an individual step or a subset of steps as micro-workflows on the Workflow component of the MDM System itself (4).

We first need to consider several things, such as the workflow capabilities of the MDM System itself or how many steps require interaction with the systems outside of the MDM System. Whether to use the MDM System Workflow Services or workflow services external to the MDM System requires looking at the capabilities of each component. The decision is also influenced by whether or not the presentation layer should interact with the MDM System and the content management (or an imaging system) directly or indirectly through the Business Process Services component.

We often encountered the following types of workflows in the context of this blueprint—however, not all of them were present in every situation:

- **New Product Introduction process:** The workflow represents the NPI process, as shown in Figure 6.1. Typical steps include the following:
  - Creation of attributes
  - Categorization of product in one or multiple hierarchies
  - Creation of price and marketing attributes
  - Creation of variations and product bundles
  - Creation of cross- and up-sell opportunity relationships

- Enrichment steps (e.g., pictures)
- Translation steps
- Approval steps before product can be published to other application systems
- **Product Maintenance process:** The workflow is used whenever a product has to be updated. Example steps are the following:
  - Change attribute values.
  - Create new variation or product bundle.
  - Re-categorize a product.
- **Discontinuance of product process:** The workflow is used to sunset a product for all applications. Example steps are the following:
  - Approval steps to remove the product from the MDM System.
  - Routing steps of products from the production catalog to the archive catalog.
- **New e-Commerce Product Enrichment process:**[10] The workflow can be encountered in two variations: Either it is a full-blown NPI process with the additional capabilities mentioned here, or it is executed only for the products used on the e-Commerce site after the NPI process is completed, adding more e-Commerce-specific attributes. In either case, these additional capabilities for e-Commerce-specific attributes might include a subset or all of the following items:
  - Categorization of products in e-Commerce product hierarchy (the e-Commerce product hierarchy might be an additional hierarchy that only exists because the e-Commerce system is used)
  - Creation of values for e-Commerce-specific attributes such as feature highlight lists and promotional content
  - Creation of the e-Commerce-specific cross- and up-sell relationships to other products[11]
  - Creation of e-Commerce-specific association of pictures, thumbnails, sound files, and other digital content stored in the content management or imaging systems
  - Approval steps for the initial release of products on the e-Commerce site
- **e-Commerce Product Maintenance process:** The workflow is for maintaining a product sold through the e-Commerce channel. Some example steps are:
  - Re-categorization of products in the e-Commerce product hierarchy
  - Update of values for e-Commerce-specific attributes, such as feature highlight lists and promotion content
  - Update of e-Commerce-specific cross- and up-sell relationships to other products
  - Update of the e-Commerce-specific association of pictures, thumbnails, sound files, and other digital content stored in content management or imaging systems
  - Approval steps for the release of the updated product on the e-Commerce site

---

10. Similar processes exist to support the printing component (8), which is just another channel with channel-specific requirements. An example of printing-specific attributes are headings. Specific workflow steps exist as well—an example is a preview step showing how the product appears on the page of a catalog.

11. In many cases, the development (or the finding) of these relationships is based on analytical results in the Data Warehouse (DW) system. In Section 8.2, you can find much more detail about why and how a DW and an MDM System can be integrated.

- **Discontinuance of product from e-Commerce process:** The workflow is used when a product is removed from the e-Commerce channel but not necessarily reaching the end of the lifecycle across all channels. Typical steps include the following:
  - Approval steps to remove the product from the e-Commerce site
  - Routing steps of products from the e-Commerce production catalog to the archive catalogs
- **Supplier/Vendor creation process:** The workflow is used to create a new supplier providing parts of a product or a new vendor who resells the product as well. Typical steps include the following:
  - Creation of supplier/vendor information
  - Classification of the supplier in a supplier hierarchy that can be used to establish a "supplied-by" relation
  - Classification of the vendor in a vendor hierarchy that can be used to establish a "sold-by" relation
  - Approval steps to add a new supplier or vendor

The IT Architect should examine the aforementioned processes regarding their requirements. Depending on interfaces, it might be possible to drive the NPI process from the Business Process Services component (12) and run micro-workflows representing a single step or a subset of steps of the NPI process within the MDM System. Simpler workflows such as the Product Maintenance process or the Supplier/Vendor Creation process, which are required in the context of this MDM Solution Blueprint, can likely run within the workflow component of the MDM System. They are less likely to require interaction with systems outside the MDM System.

6.3.4.2   Solution Blueprint Component Interaction Diagrams

In this section, we present two component interaction diagrams that show how the components presented in Figure 6.4 work together in typical use cases supported by the New Production Introduction Solution Blueprint. Each component interaction diagram uses only the required subset of the components. The first two flows are shown in the component interaction diagram in Figure 6.5.

The first flow covers the NPI process, and the base interaction of the components supporting the NPI process is explained.

1. The first step is optional and can be considered a pre-step. The idea is that some raw product information from a research or design department is loaded into the master data repository using an Information Integration Service (1) that includes some data validation or cleansing processing. The NPI process would not start with a product from scratch—it would instead use this product skeleton as input. However, this does not have to be the case. If the product research or design department is considered to be part of the NPI process, then employees from these departments would be the Line of Business users starting with step (2). If this is done, the MDM System might contain a lot of product descriptions that are not actually built. If that is the case, you need to define a procedure to remove or separate them from

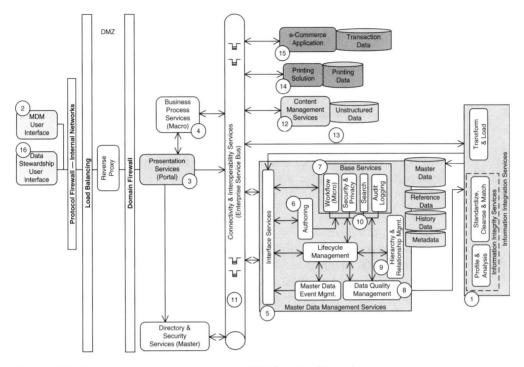

Figure 6.5   Authoring of master data for the NPI Solution Blueprint.

the production catalog by having a design and a production catalog in use. In this case, an approval step for products can be used to move them from the design to the production catalog.

2. Through an MDM User Interface (2), Line of Business users participate in the NPI process of authoring a new product. Examples for the Line of Business users are Category Managers and Item Specialists (more details on both MDM user roles can be found in Appendix A). For a consumer electronics manufacturer, an Item Specialist could author product features. For a consumer electronics retailer, a Category Manager could classify incoming products in the appropriate categories in hierarchies.

3. Using the MDM User Interface, presentation functionality deployed on the Presentation Services component (3) is invoked, which often can be provided through a portal.

4. Depending on which workflow infrastructure (see Section 6.3.4.1) orchestrates the NPI process, either the first user triggers the NPI hosted by the Business Process Services component (4) or it is triggered by the workflow component (7), which is part of the MDM System (5).

5. Depending on the individual tasks in one step, various components such as the Authoring component (6), the Data Quality Management component (8), or the

Hierarchy and Relationship Management component (9) are invoked. For example, in a step where a Category Manager classifies a product in a product hierarchy or a Supplier Hierarchy (establishing the "supplied-by" relation), the Hierarchy and Relationship Management component (9) will be invoked. In a case where an Item Specialist authors product attributes, data validation processing could be invoked and provided by the Data Quality Management component (8), which can be either built-in functions of the MDM System (5) or services provided and leveraged from the Information Integration Services component (1). The Data Quality Management component (8) could provide master data integrity functions for translation steps as well. If an item specialist defines relationships for setting up cross- and up-sell relations between products or if product bundles are defined, such a step would leverage relationship functions from the Hierarchy and Relationship Management component (9).

6. If unstructured information such as images or sound files are required, which is likely the case for an e-Commerce platform, an enrichment step would send inquiries to the Content Management Services component (12) to retrieve the appropriate Unique Resource Locators (URLs). The Interoperability and Connectivity component (11) will be used for this inquiry, which could be implemented using Web services or messaging.

7. After a final approval step, a new product can be distributed to systems such as a Printing Solution component (14) or an e-Commerce component (15), which require a local read-only copy of the master data. Depending on the interfaces of the MDM System (5) and the Interoperability and Connectivity component (11), distribution of the data can be accomplished by using messaging or ESB patterns. The Interoperability and Connectivity component (11) could leverage data transformations services (13) from the Information Integration Services component (1). Invocation of data transformation services might be necessary in order to map the data model from the MDM System to the data model of the consuming system.

The second flow shown in Figure 6.5 is related to tasks performed by an Operational Data Steward. A description of this MDM user role can be found in Appendix A.

1. An Operational Data Steward interacts with the MDM System (5) through a Data Stewardship User Interface (16). There can be functions that are part of the MDM User Interface (2) that are accessible only if a user with this role signs on. With portal infrastructure separation of function depending on user role can be done easily by using one set of portlets[12] dedicated to the Operational Data Steward and another set of portlets for the Line of Business user such as Item Specialists or Category Managers. Depending on the user role that signs in on the portal hosting the presentation services (3), only the permissible portlets associated for the user role are accessible.

2. The Data Stewardship User Interface (16) invokes presentation services (3).

12. JSR 168 is the standard by Sun Microsystems defining portlets.

3. Through the Interoperability and Connectivity component (11), services from the MDM System are invoked (5). Typical examples include services from the Data Quality Management component (8) for manual split or merge of master data entities.

Tasks performed by an Operational Data Steward are part of an overall Data Governance strategy, outlined in Chapter 9. Probabilistic or deterministic matching services are used to determine when a conflict has occurred and when the involvement of an Operational Data Steward to collapse or split a master data entity is required.

The next flow we see in the component interaction diagram in Figure 6.6 shows how an end user, such as a business customer or a regular customer, can access product master data through an e-Commerce platform. Through this flow we show how a customer (we don't distinguish in the walkthrough between the different customer types) can buy new products earlier due to the streamlined NPI process.

1. Through a browser (1), a customer interacts with the e-Commerce platform.

2. The presentation services (2) receive the browser requests and trigger the appropriate actions. These actions can be business process services (3) (like a process to perform online shopping) or e-Commerce Web application services (4).

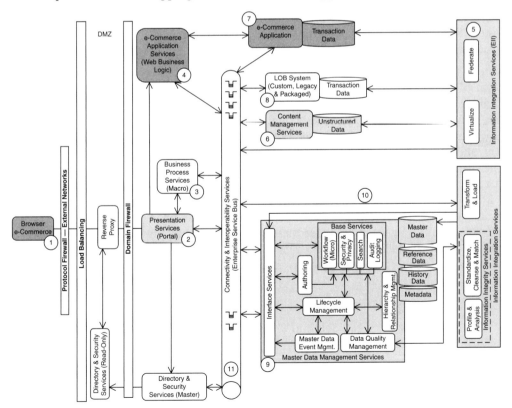

Figure 6.6 Accessing master data through the e-Commerce channel.

3. The e-Commerce Web application services component (4) could dynamically create a Web page through the use of a federation service provided by the Information Integration Services component (5). The federation service could retrieve graphics from the Content Management Services component (6) and product master data from the Backend e-Commerce Application component (7) database. Note that the read-only access to the master data in the local database of the Backend e-Commerce Application component (7) offloads the MDM System (9) from the read-access required by the e-Commerce platform.

4. If the online shopping process ends with a customer buying a product, the Backend e-Commerce application component (7) needs to trigger the billing process, which could run in another LOB System (8) such as a dedicated billing system.

5. The notification from the Backend e-Commerce application component with the appropriate data could then be sent to the billing system through the Interoperability and Connectivity component (11) using messaging or ESB patterns.

Note that if there are other LOB Systems (8) such as billing systems using master data, then these systems need to be kept in sync with the MDM System (9) with respect to master data. To accomplish this synchronization, transformation services (10) provided by the Information Integration Services component could be used to convert the data to the target system formats. Information synchronization patterns described in Chapter 5 can be used to accelerate the design of this type of approach.

Note that in the NPI Solution Blueprint we describe, the MDM System represents a single point of failure *enterprise-wide*. Thus, it is recommended to take special care planning for high availability and disaster recovery, as outlined in Section 5.4.5 of Chapter 5. However, this Solution Blueprint also represents significant advantages, because it optimizes the NPI process by providing the ability to edit and govern all of the product master data in one system and then finally publish the approved product data to all subscribing systems. Therefore, if something is wrong, you know exactly where to fix it. If your enterprise is operating in a decentralized fashion, then introducing this Solution Blueprint might require a business transformation to force a standard for authoring and maintaining product master data. The business transformation might delay the introduction of this solution due to political aspects in the organization hierarchies. Individual participants might consider the introduction of a centralized NPI process a loss of autonomy because they are forced to participate in a process governed at the enterprise level.

6.3.5 Advantages

On the business side, the NPI Solution Blueprint for consumer electronics can deliver the following results:

- Reduced time to market
- Optimization of the maximum profit margin time period
- Contribution to innovative company image
- Reduction of cost and time for translating product documentation and information

- Cost reduction in IT due to centralized PIM system for master data authoring
- Reduction of IT complexity for product master data distribution into downstream systems such as printing and e-Commerce, delivering lower TCO of overall system costs
- Consistent, high-quality product information as strategic business asset
- Reduction of integration complexity to share master data with suppliers/resellers

On the technical side, the NPI Solution Blueprint for consumer electronics can deliver these results:

- Consistent, high-quality product information in a single place in the PIM–MDM system, making integration work easier
- Consistent access to product information through service interface supporting SOAs
- Ability to easily implement and change workflows for authoring product information
- End-to-end audit ability for product information, allowing legal compliance
- Improved security with attribute-level granularity based on user roles
- Improved performance and scalability

As you can see from the list of benefits, this MDM Solution Blueprint enables business agility across various Lines of Business involved in authoring and management of product master data information.

6.3.6 Alternatives and Possible Extensions

Whenever retail products are being managed, there is an opportunity to improve supply chain efficiency by participating in the Global Data Synchronization Network (GDSN). Section 6.4 explains how participation in the GDSN can be done. Global Data Synchronization extends the concept of Publish/Subscribe across enterprises so that manufacturers can publish information efficiently to their trading partner retailers who have subscribed to a synchronization service for their products.

For complex search requirements, a PIM system might be enhanced with products[13] supporting full text or semantic search capabilities. The search engine would index the product information from the PIM system and the results would be displayed as part of the UI of an MDM System that is usually based on portal technology.

Another area of enhancement to improve the NPI process is to combine the PIM foundation with RFID technology (or more generally, item serialization technology). For details, read Section 6.5.

The apparel industry is another industry where the authoring of master data and streamlined, efficient product introduction into markets is crucial. For marketing in this industry, catalogs are often used for collections aimed for spring and summer or autumn and winter. Catalogs for specialized assortments of products (sporting apparel, underwear, shoes, etc.)

---

13. A product for this purpose can be found in Section B.1 of Appendix B.

exist as well. Creating these catalogs requires tight integration of unstructured master data (the images) and structured master data (attributes describing the product such as color and size) that is seamlessly consumable by catalog printing systems. Typically, the unstructured master data is persisted in content management or imaging systems, and the MDM System where the NPI workflow runs usually has a step to associate the resource identifiers of the unstructured with the structured product information. So if the catalog printing system processes a product, three different approaches of access may be used:

- **Enterprise Information Integration (EII):** Assuming the content management or imaging system has the unique identifier of the product persisted in addition to the graphics, a federation service representing a federated query could then be used to obtain the structured and unstructured master data information for a product.
- **Enterprise Application Integration (EAI):** In such a scenario, the printing system might subscribe to a queue where the PIM system publishes changes. After a notification is received due to the subscription, the printing system would then send a request to the content management system to obtain the unstructured information. If the MDM System publishes changes through messages onto an ESB, mediation flows within the ESB could be used to obtain the unstructured information from the content management system that is used to enrich these messages before they are finally sent to the printing system.
- **Batch:** It might be the case that there is not an ESB yet deployed, that the federation technology is missing, or that the EAI approach might not perform well enough due to the data volume. In any of these cases, a batch extract from the MDM System enriched with unstructured information from the content management system might be needed to provide the master data to the printing system efficiently.

With the MDM Solution Blueprint just presented, you can see how an MDM-based solution is a key business enabler to optimize the NPI process. We have shown which architecture patterns are needed to tailor the MDM RA for this MDM Solution Blueprint.

6.4 Global Data Synchronization Solution Blueprint for Retail

The Global Data Synchronization Solution Blueprint for Retail is driven by the need of larger retailers with hundreds or even thousands of suppliers to exchange product information efficiently. The Global Data Synchronization infrastructure, together with a PIM-MDM System, is the right infrastructure to effectively implement this type of solution.

6.4.1 Business Context

In the retail industry, major retailers deal with a large number of products—ranging from a few thousand to several million.[14] In addition, the same retailer works with hundreds or even thousands of suppliers that either provide parts of a product or complete products.

---

14. We worked with customers who have more than five million products in their PIM system.

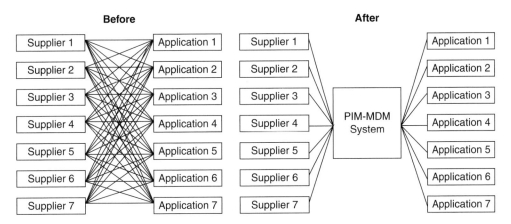

Figure 6.7 Situation before and after introduction of a PIM-MDM System.

Many of the products can have descriptions with a few hundred up to a few thousand attributes. On the one hand, depending on the supplier location, the product information received by the supplier might be in another language and created with different legal requirements. On the other hand, depending where the retailer intends to resell the products, the product master data may need to be localized to various languages and legal regulations. In addition to these considerations, as shown in Figure 6.7 on the left-hand side, you can see the current situation for a retailer before a PIM–MDM solution is introduced. Many applications from the retailer have point-to-point connections with each supplier. The applications have different interfaces requiring different formats so the exchange, and use, of product information between retailers and suppliers (or resellers) has become incredibly difficult due to the following:

- A very large number of point-to-point connections
- Various formats[15] (Microsoft Excel, text-based, EDI, handwritten for fax, e-mail, XML, proprietary)
- Various protocols (SMTP, FTP, JMS, SOAP/HTTP, proprietary)
- Different data models

Each retailer receives information in different formats from multiple suppliers. The IT infrastructure to support these multiple formats can become incredibly complex (see Figure 6.7). In the past, efforts were made with the introduction of EDI and formalization of B2B processes to integrate the supply chain. However, the master data exchange problem was not solved because (for a variety of reasons such as cost) EDI was not adapted across all systems by all participants. Suppliers usually do business with more than one retailer. As a consequence, the explosion of point-to-point connections, formats, and protocols is as much a problem for them as for retailers. Thus, they also benefit a lot from the solution described in the scope of this blueprint.

---

15. Even in 2007 some of the authors occasionally encountered formats like handwritten for fax used as "standard" in product information exchange while performing consultant work.

The situation regarding complexity with many point-to-point connections got worse because product information volume and complexity are growing due to the following:

- Decreasing lifetime of many products
- Increasing differentiation of products
- Rising demand from consumers[16] for more detailed product information
- Increasing number of special marketing campaigns[17]

Extending the current blueprint in Section 6.5, you can see how you can establish the ability to trace a product end-to-end through the supply chain.

Each supplier sends information to different retailers who each want the information in their own format. Thus, a supplier providing products to multiple retailers is also challenged in the same way by this increasing complexity.

To the right in Figure 6.7, we show a major part of the solution to this problem. A central PIM-MDM System providing a standardized interface to submit master data to the retailer as well as to provide product master data to applications consistently. The architecture suggested with the central PIM-MDM System reduces the IT complexity quite significantly by removing many point-to-point connections.

With the change as shown in Figure 6.7 on the right side, the following opportunity appears: With the centralized PIM-MDM System, the analytical method of use can be applied on the MDM System itself with the outcome of simplified enterprise-level reporting on product master data. An example would be how many new products were defined in a certain period and released to an e-Commerce system. Improved product category reporting is another benefit that can be realized on the centralized PIM-MDM System. Both operations are difficult, if not impossible, in a situation such as the one shown on the left in Figure 6.7.

A retailer has a higher throughput of products and marketing campaigns per year today than even only a few years ago. Given this background, many retailers have seen the need to take action, because costs and complexity are no longer containable. The world's largest retailers and suppliers came together in 2000 to establish a new process for exchanging product and trade partner information in an open, standardized way so that everyone could participate more easily. Another intention was to replace earlier proprietary systems.

The outcome of this event led to the standardization effort in what is now known as *Global Data Synchronization* (GDS) with *data pools* such as *1Sync* in the *Global Data Synchronization Network* (GDSN). A data pool is a repository storing production information that participates in the GDSN. *1Sync* is a data pool that replaced the former data pools *Transora* and *UCCNet* in August 2005. 1Sync is a subsidiary of GS1 US, the United States member organization of the GS1. GS1 is an international, non-profit organization that drives the development and administration of many e-Commerce standards, among them GDS and GDSN. *GDSN Inc.*, a

---

16. Common descriptions in this area are: fat content, gluten free, calorie content, etc.

17. Just consider the fact that Microsoft held special offerings together with major fast food chains and beverage distributors for the launch of Halo 3 in the second half of 2007. Examples are beverage bottles and cups with Halo 3 logos and pictures, which are supposedly available only for 6–12 weeks. For details, see [4].

subsidiary of GS1, is responsible for managing the GDSN. Any data pool that supposedly participates in the GDSN has to be certified by GDSN Inc. prior to participation. Within the GS1, since January 2002 a process called *Global Standard Management Process (GSMP)* has been used to establish the standards called *GS1 standards* (they are also known as EAN.UCC standards—thus these terms are interchangeable) and their implementation for the GS1 system. The effects of this effort reach out from the retail industry to other industries such as the beverage industry (see [6]).

The GDSN consists of two major components:

- The *GS1 Global Registry*
- An Internet-based connected network of interoperable data pools

The GS1 Global Registry is a directory where products and trading partners are registered for participation in the GDSN. It contains a very limited set of attributes in an *EAN.UCC*[18]-compliant style for products and trading partners that provides pointers to the source data pools where the full master data record is stored.

So what is GDS all about? The core of GDS is to streamline and harmonize the exchange of product and trading partner information between trading partners throughout the product lifecycle. The business benefits of implementing GDS are the following:

- Increased speed to market for new products
- Accurate, high-quality product information, reducing invoice inconsistencies
- Reduced number of out-of-stock situations
- Removal of *backdoor rejections*[19]
- Reduction of IT complexity on both sides, reducing TCO in IT
- Improved reusability of product information
- Reduction of product setup costs and error-corrections costs

At a high level, Figure 6.8 shows how GDS works. Suppliers publish their data into data pools and define who can access it. The *publication* process of master data means providing data to a data pool for further exchange with retailers. The full set of attributes is moved into the data pool and an EAN.UCC-compliant subset of these attributes is used to *register* the product in the GS1 Global Registry. A data pool in the context of GDSN is a repository containing supplier and product information that can be accessed electronically and is certified by GDSN Inc. prior to participation. From the supplier perspective, a data pool can be viewed as a *router* for product and supplier information on their behalf. Conversely from the perspective of the retailer, a data pool can be seen as an *aggregator* to which the retailer subscribes

---

18. *EAN.UCC* is the system of standards for enabling interoperability within the GDSN. EAN.UCC is administered by the GS1. Hence, the EAN.UCC standards are also known as GS1 standards. The EAN.UCC standards also get full support from the Global Commerce Initiative (CGI)—an organization that is dedicated to enhancing global commerce and improve consumer value in the supply chains. For more details, see [5].

19. A backdoor rejection is a situation where a distributor delivers products to a retailer and is rejected at the "back door," when supposedly offloading the trade items, because the retailer cannot book the arrived products into the IT systems because the product information is still missing.

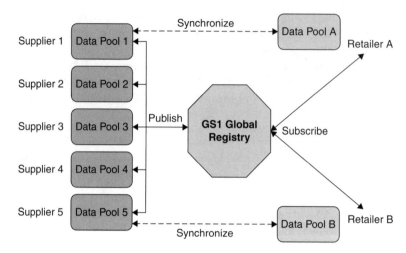

Figure 6.8 High-level overview of GDSN.

that provides an aggregated view of product and supplier information from more than one source.

A *subscription* by the retailer establishes a profile to obtain continuous updates on matching data for the retailer as the data recipient. The subscription is done on the retailer's home data pool and sent to the GS1 Global Registry. The subscription remains valid until deleted. In the case of Figure 6.8, retailer A placed a subscription to synchronize data from data pool 1 and retailer B placed a subscription to synchronize data from data pool 5. A subscription can be established by any combination of the following entities: Global Trade Identification Number (GTIN), Global Location Number (GLN), information provider, target market,[20] and Global Product Categorization (GPC). The only exception is that GTIN and GPC are mutually exclusive. Retailers using GDS often request product information using *GTIN* or by a category in general. A GTIN is given by a unique 14-digit number used to identify products. The first 13 digits represent the item reference number, and the last digit is the check digit. The process governing the assignment of GTIN numbers can be found in [7]. If retailers look for specific supplier information, they can do the same using the *GLN*. The GLN is a unique 13-digit number used to identify a trade location, where trade location is a broad term covering legal entity, trading partner, and locations. The first seven digits represent a company prefix, the next five digits represent the trade location, and the last digit is a check digit. Based on the subscriptions, the GDSN can then synchronize the data between the source data pool(s) of the suppliers and the target data pool(s) of the retailers.

---

20. A *target market* is a geographical region based on geographical boundaries sanctioned by the United Nations. The ISO-3166 code system defines the geographical regions as an ISO standard used by the GDSN.

The following is a list of data pools but is not a complete list:[21]

- 1SYNC (subsidiary of *GS1 US*)
- GenSync (used, for example, as the platform for Switzerland due to an agreement between GS1 Switzerland and Agentrics)
- Product Registry
- Parangon (used as GS1 France data pool)

The following is a partial list of well-known product hierarchies (also known as classifications):

- **UDEX classification:** According to [9], the proprietary UDEX classification will be aligned with the GPC classification so that information between the two can be exchanged more freely and easily. More information on UDEX can be found at [10].
- **UNSPSC classification:** Details on the UNSPSC classification can be found in [11]. Information on how UNSPSC and GPC are aligned is located in [12].
- **GPC classification:** You can read about details of the GPC classification in [13].

Unfortunately, there are two remaining pain points to consider when using GDS and GDSN. First, only a subset of the products is registered in the GDSN. Getting accurate numbers on the overall products registered in the GDSN is difficult, but to give you an idea, here are two numbers: According to [14], there are more than 300,000 products in the Product Registry 2.1, the data pool from Big Hammer Data. According to [6], in August 2005, 360,000 products were registered in the GDSN and growth to more than 750,000 is anticipated by the end of 2005.

Making the matter worse, only a subset of suppliers and retailers registered as users in the GDSN. According to the GS1 annual report 2005/2006 (see [15]), by the end of 2006 about 10,000 registered users, such as global, regional, and local retailers and suppliers, were subscribed to the GDSN.

GDS standards currently do not support every attribute that retailers need. Nonetheless, many companies have firm plans for GDS adoption or the implementation is already under way, which will increase the number of registered products over time. But for now, not all product and supplier records can be obtained through GDSN.

The second pain point is that even if a supplier provides entries for all products in the GDSN, a retailer obtaining these product records through the same supplier still needs to maintain a one-to-one connection with this supplier. Because everyone can subscribe to the GDSN, each attribute published there can be seen. Obviously, for competitive reasons among suppliers, attributes related to pricing are not published to the GDSN. There are standardization efforts under way to enhance the GDSN to support secure transmission with proper authentication mechanisms added to the infrastructure so that a supplier can control who can subscribe to sensitive attributes by having the ability to unambiguously identify the subscriber. Early pilots[22] are running to test these enhancements, but it will certainly take some time until these enhancements are widely adopted.

---

21. For complete lists of GDSN certified data pools, see [8].
22. See the GS1 annual report [15] for details.

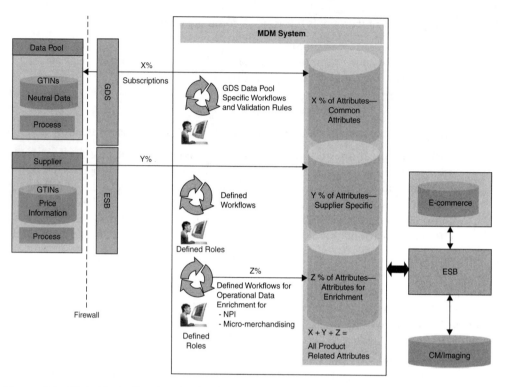

Figure 6.9   Global Data Synchronization Solution Blueprint for retail—high-level overview.

On the one hand, adopting GDSN enables you to participate in the GDSN now. You will also have the right infrastructure in place when the standardization that makes the one-to-one connections obsolete is complete.

On the other hand, a certain percentage X (see Figure 6.9) of product attributes for a product can be obtained through GDS, and another percentage Y (see Figure 6.9) of the same product will still be exchanged on a one-to-one basis between supplier and retailer. Due to this fact, we have a B2B pattern between supplier and retailer today.

Let's now consider the relationship between retailer and consumers. The buying behavior of consumers has changed over the last few years. Consumers demand an increasing amount of precise information about the products they buy. With the rise of the Internet, customers are looking for details and insight into products and services, especially if products become more complex and customers more sophisticated. Having enticing prices alone is no longer enough for establishing customer loyalty. In order to compete globally, a state-of-the-art e-Commerce website for retailers is often a very useful asset. The challenge is to have the latest, most accurate product information available there. The business benefits of this integration include improved revenue and profits, improved customer loyalty, and a reduced customer churn rate. We look at this B2C relation in the MDM Solution Blueprint architecture later.

6.4.2   Relevant Business Patterns

We have a business-to-consumer relation as outlined in the previous section due to the fact that a retailer runs an e-Commerce platform. We also have a business-to-business relation between retailer and suppliers. For addressing these business requirements, we have the following business patterns:

- B2B between retailer and supplier
- B2C between retailer and consumers through an e-Commerce website

These business patterns drive the selection of architecture patterns by simplifying the exchange of information between the retailer and the suppliers and by bringing products to consumers through online channels supported by e-Commerce platforms.

6.4.3   Relation between Business Patterns and Architecture Patterns

The B2B pattern between retailer and supplier mandates the use of the GDS architecture pattern, as described in Chapter 5, which is a subpattern of the Information Synchronization pattern. Because many attributes are received through the GDSN, the master data systems should be implemented by either using the Coexistence or the Transaction Hub architecture pattern. Using either of these two patterns allows the materialization of all product attributes in the MDM System for enterprise-wide enforcement of data integrity and business rules from a single place. Reasons why incoming master data from the GDSN should not be directly loaded into an ERP system can be found in Section 5.7.3 in Chapter 5.

Because the e-Commerce system is consuming master data for publishing, it will need read-only access to the master data. Thus, ESB or messaging patterns are useful for integrating the e-Commerce system with the MDM System, assuming the e-Commerce system has a local database that cannot be removed or directly bypassed. The Initial Load architecture pattern is needed for building the master data hub. So we need at least the following architecture patterns to comply with the requirements:

- Initial Load pattern
- Coexistence Hub or Transaction Hub pattern
- Global Data Synchronization pattern
- ESB and/or messaging patterns

The MDM Solution Blueprint overview shows where these patterns have been applied.

6.4.4   MDM Solution Blueprint Overview

A high-level overview of the GDS Solution Blueprint overview for retail is shown in Figure 6.9. In the top left corner, the depicted data pool is intended to show that the retailer is receiving product and supplier information from one or multiple data pools using the global data synchronization infrastructure and in accordance to the processes set forth by the global data synchronization community. However, pricing and other sensitive attributes are not yet exchanged through the GDSN. Therefore, the retailer needs to exchange these attributes with each supplier on a one-to-one basis, as depicted in Figure 6.9. The one-to-one connection uses some kind of ESB infrastructure that connects the supplier system with the sensitive information, such as price, as shown on the left-hand side. The supplier and the retailer each need to agree on the process, communication protocols, exchange format, security mechanism, and so on for this exchange to take place. For small suppliers, it could be that neither ESB nor GDSN is an affordable infrastructure. In this case, a supplier portal might be required where they upload all their product information. Here, a large retailer might need to compromise.

Note that both GDSN and suppliers are outside the company firewalls. In addition to the external data sources, internal users enrich the master data before it is finally ready for publishing to the consuming e-Commerce application. So for a single master data record, a certain percentage X of the attributes are retrieved through the GDSN, a certain percentage Y of the attributes are retrieved through direct exchange with each supplier, and a certain percentage Z of the attributes are then added or enriched by LOB users of the retailer. The enrichment of product information supports specific use cases such as micro-merchandising. Because the MDM System usually only persists relational data and links to unstructured data like images required by the e-Commerce site, the e-Commerce application consumes the relational master data from the MDM System. After this master data is received, it queries the content management or imaging repository system to retrieve the unstructured data based on the links to the images and other unstructured content from the content repository.

Involved in the process of putting the master data together are users with different roles, such as the GDS admin, who ensures that the GDS component runs smoothly. A GDS admin is also responsible for ensuring that data from the data pools is validated before the incoming data is added to the database of the MDM System where product specialists are performing the master data enrichment.

After this high-level overview, let's now take a look at Figure 6.10, which represents a component model view of the GDS Solution Blueprint for retail. The MDM System is initially built using the Initial Load pattern (see Section 5.5.3 in Chapter 5), and the architecture of the MDM System is either given by a Coexistence or a Transaction Hub pattern (see sections 5.4.2 and 5.4.3 in Chapter 5, where MDM Hub Patterns are discussed). Also note that components not relevant for the description of this blueprint from the MDM Component Model (presented in Chapter 3) are removed from the figure for reasons of simplicity.

There are three types of components:

- The mandatory components (1) to (6) in light-grey are components either needed to build or run the MDM System. Core functions of these components were explained in the MDM RA. Note that the Data Stewardship User Interface and the MDM User Interface have been merged into a single component for reasons of simplicity. The function of the Data Stewardship User Interface was shown in Section 6.3.4. Key components of the MDM System (3) are the Authoring, the

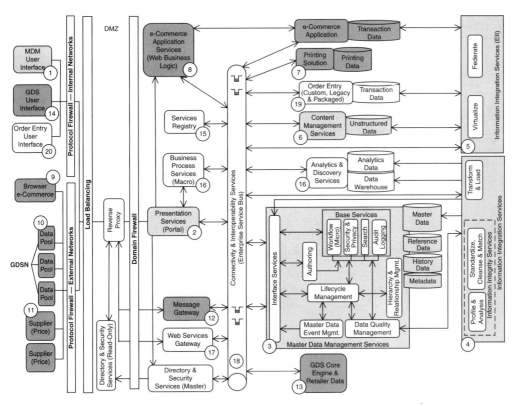

Figure 6.10 Global Data Synchronization Solution Blueprint for retail—component model overview based on MDM Reference Architecture component model.

Workflow, and the Hierarchy and Relationship Management components. As explained in Section 6.4.1, hierarchies such as GPC are a crucial piece of the GDSN. Thus, synchronizing master data through the GDSN needs powerful hierarchy management capabilities supporting such hierarchies. Superior workflow and authoring capabilities are an asset to the enrichment process for the Z% of attributes (see Figure 6.9) supporting use cases, such as micro-merchandising. An IT Architect performing software selection (for products, see Section B.5 in Appendix B) should thus pay special attention to features in these areas.

- The dark grey components (7) to (14) are components specific to this solution. An e-Commerce system (7) and a printing solution (8) for catalog and flyer generation are two channels through which information about new products can be launched to the market. Thus, this set of components is typical when implementing this MDM Solution Blueprint. Note that the browser (9) is usually the tool to request an e-Commerce website for enterprise and normal customers. The components (10) to (14) are the GDS-specific components. The external data sources (10) are data pools and the supplier systems (11). Usually (10) communicates with the GDS Core Engine component (13) through messaging infrastructure, thus mandating the Message Gateway component (12). The GDS User Interface (14) is used to administer the GDS infrastructure.

- The white components (15) to (20) are either optional components or components where integration might or might not be needed depending on the existing IT infrastructure and the concrete functional and nonfunctional requirements for the MDM Solution. The description of these components was provided in Section 6.3.4. The only difference is that (19) and (20) were a generic LOB system in Section 6.3.4, whereas we have an order entry LOB system in this case. The order entry system can be either custom-developed, legacy, or packaged software from an application vendor. In the scope of the discussion of this blueprint, please note that the e-Commerce platform is an example of a more generic Catalog Management system requirement.

Conceptually, we discuss five flows based on Figure 6.10 in two component interaction diagrams given with Figures 6.11 and 6.12. We describe these flows individually:

Flow 1: Administration of the GDS Core Engine using the GDS User Interface
Flow 2: Implementation of the Global Data Synchronization

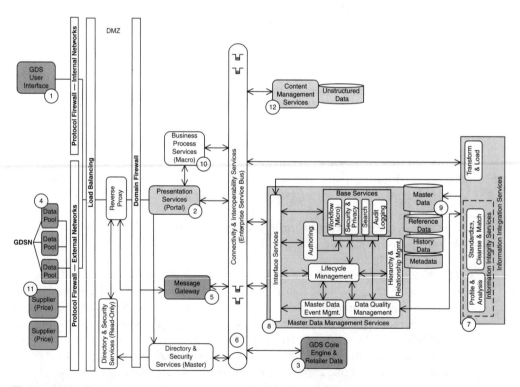

Figure 6.11 Component Interaction Diagram showing GDS flows of the MDM Solution Blueprint.

Flow 3: Integration between supplier and retailer to exchange sensitive attributes
Flow 4: Master data enrichment through the MDM UI with the flow
Flow 5: Customers buying products through the e-Commerce website using a browser

Flows 1–3 will be explained using Figure 6.11; Flows 4–5 will be explained using Figure 6.12. We start with Flow 1:

1. Through the GDS User Interface (1), the GDS Administrator performs the administration of the GDS Core Engine. An example of this administration is the creation and maintenance of subscriptions of data pools to synchronize product and trading partner (e.g., supplier) information. Many data pools require a provider supporting the AS2 standard for access, which means that a GDS Administrator needs to know about such standards as well.

2. The presentation services (2) receive a request from the GDS User Interface (1) and trigger the appropriate action. For administrative tasks, a service provided by the GDS Core Engine component (3) will be invoked for the data pool on the retailer side.

3. The GDS Core Engine Component (3) performs the requested administrative tasks, such as subscription management, user management, trading partner management, or monitoring.

Flow 2 is an implementation of the GDS architecture pattern (see the Information Synchronization pattern and the subpatterns discussion in Chapter 5). This flow is available only when the base configuration of the GDS Core Engine component (3) has been done.

1. When the subscription on a supplier data pool (4) is placed, product information is synchronized.

2. For security reasons, the messages with the production information pass through the Message Gateway component (5) to protect the company network.

3. The Connectivity and Interoperability component (6) routes the message to the GDS Core Engine component (3). If the Connectivity and Interoperability component (6) is implemented using a full blown ESB infrastructure, it might also provide message conversion capabilities, transforming the incoming XML message from AS2 to the format required by the GDS Core Engine. After the conversion, the Connectivity and Interoperability component (6) might also leverage JMS messaging, for example. If the Connectivity and Interoperability component (6) lacks this capability, transformation services from the Information Integration Services component (7) might be invoked for this task.

4. After the GDS Core Engine component (3) receives the new product information, it starts processing it by applying applicable business logic.

5. When the GDS Core Engine is done, it exports the product information to the Master Data Management Services component (8). One option is building a message with the product information as content, which is published to the Connectivity and Interoperability component (6). Depending on the master data format in this message, additional data model transformation to the master data model in the

MDM System is required. Implementing such a data model transformation can be done by either using conversion functions of the Connectivity and Interoperability component (6) or by using the Information Integration Services component (7).

6. When the MDM System (8) receives the product information, it processes and stores it in the Master Data Repository (9).

The third flow in Figure 6.11 is related to the small subset of attributes that cannot be synchronized through the GDSN yet, as explained in Section 6.4.1. There are numerous possible ways to implement this scenario, because the flow is a point-to-point connection. We sketch just two options:

- The supplier could upload price and other sensitive pieces of information through a supplier portal. In this case, employees of the supplier (11) would log in to a portal that invokes Presentation Services (2). Depending on the process for uploading the information from the supplier, the Business Process Services (10) could invoke Information Integration Services (7) to cleanse, harmonize, standardize, and transform the data to the master data model, which can be consumed by the MDM System (8). When the data validation is done, the Business Process Services (10) could then invoke the appropriate master data services from the MDM System (8), which persists the master data attributes in the Master Data Repository (9). If the information uploaded by the supplier contains unstructured information as well, then Content Management Services (12) could be invoked to save this information after the relational part is stored.
- Another option is to implement a Web service on the MDM System (8) that can be invoked by the supplier to upload the information. In this case, the Web Services Gateway (17) is necessary, shown as an optional component in Figure 6.10.

Figure 6.12 shows Flow 4 and Flow 5. At the beginning of Flow 4, the basic product information through GDS and sensitive information from suppliers, such as price, are loaded into the MDM System because Flow 2 and Flow 3 have completed.

1. Through an MDM User Interface (1), LOB users, such as Item Specialists, Category Managers, Translators, or Marketing Specialists, interact with the MDM System. The MDM User Interface (1) can be, for example, a browser through which the presentation services (2) hosted on a portal are invoked. The basic idea is that these users collaborate to author additional attributes or to enrich or translate existing ones to complete the product definition.

2. The MDM User Interface (1) invokes presentation services (2), which could be portlets running on a portal server. The presentation services then trigger the appropriate workflows for authoring the additional product attributes. In Section 6.3.4.1, options and decision points have been explained, where the business processes for authoring master data can be orchestrated. Also, examples of relevant workflows have been presented in that section. Possible places to orchestrate the authoring processes for various workflows, such as New e-Commerce Enrichment process or Product Maintenance process, are the Business Process Services component (4) or the Workflow component (5) of the MDM System (3). External hierarchies such as UDEX, GPC, or UNSPSC might not align

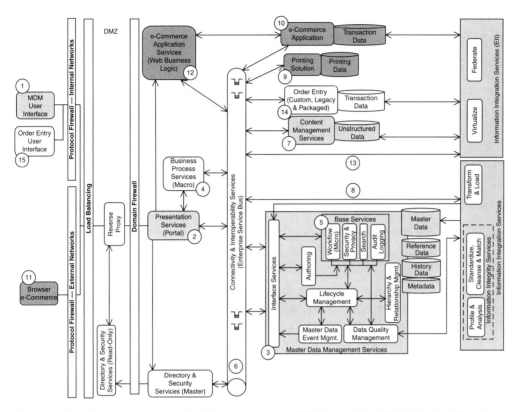

Figure 6.12 Component Interaction Diagram showing PIM flows of the MDM Solution Blueprint.

with either existing hierarchies that the retailer already has or new hierarchies the retailer needs. Thus, the authoring likely includes Category Managers performing additional classification of the incoming products in existing hierarchies or new hierarchies created by the retailer. The classification step invokes the Hierarchy and Relationship Management component of the MDM System (3).

3. Enriching product information for a consuming application such as an e-Commerce platform usually needs unstructured data such as images or sound files. For that purpose, content services provided by the Content Services component (7) are used as part of the authoring process.

4. When the authoring process is complete, usually after some kind of approval step, the product, which is now ready for use by other systems, can be distributed to the consuming applications, such as a printing solution (9) or an e-Commerce platform (10). Depending on the Connectivity and Interoperability component (6), integration can be done through the use of ESB and messaging patterns, which would mean, for example, that the MDM System (3) publishes the new product on a message queue. By implementing the Publish/Subscribe architecture pattern, the e-Commerce system could be notified using the event capability of the MDM System (3). It posts a message

on a topic queue indicating that a new product is ready for use in the e-Commerce system or that an existing product was updated. Alternatively, you could publish the change as the last step in the workflow, thereby not relying on the event infrastructure.

5. Required data transformations from the MDM System (3) to the consuming applications system in need of the product master data can be implemented either using functions from the Connectivity and Interoperability[23] component (6) or with the Information Integration Services component (8).

6. When the printing solution (9) or an e-Commerce platform (10) receives the message after the data transformation, it applies the new product (or the update on an existing product) to its local persistency—usually a relational database.

Flow 5 represents a customer interacting with the e-Commerce platform.

1. The customer, using a browser (11), invokes the presentation services (2).

2. The presentation services (2) invoke the e-Commerce Application Services (12) responsible for providing the necessary input for presenting products to the potential customer.

3. The e-Commerce Application Services (12) could then invoke federation services (13) provided by the Information Integration component. The federation services retrieve the structured product information from the database belonging to the backend part of the e-Commerce platform (10) and the unstructured product information from the Content Management Services (7). If this approach is taken, it offloads the MDM System (3) from the read-access to the product information required by the e-Commerce platform.

4. If a customer buys something, the e-Commerce Application component (10) in the backend would need to update the order entry system (14), where a LOB user involved in order entry processing could see the new order through the Order Entry User Interface (15). If an order entry system requires up-to-date product information as well, this requirement needs to be reflected in the master data synchronization processes. Examples of information synchronization patterns are explained in Chapter 5.

One of the assumptions made for the blueprint shown in Section 6.4.4 was that the e-Commerce system has a local database that cannot be removed, and that causes redundant copies of master data. We suggest that if project implementation costs allow it, and if the e-Commerce system is open enough to be changed, the master data should be directly read from the PIM–MDM system whenever needed. Furthermore, the copy of the master data local to the e-Commerce system should be removed. The suggested change to the e-Commerce system may require larger hardware sizing for the master data system to accommodate the increased load, which might not be desirable. However, from a security and performance manageability perspective, this enhancement could be seen as an advantage, because you do not need to worry about two database systems.

---

23. The component in this case must have the necessary capabilities usually provided by leading-edge ESB products. Examples can be found in Section B.2 of Appendix B.

6.4.5 Advantages

On the business side, the Solution Blueprint offers the following advantages:

- Simplified enterprise level reporting on product master data[24] using the analytical method of use in the MDM System itself
- Improved product category reporting using the analytical method of use in the MDM System itself
- Easier expansion of supplier base
- Support for micro-merchandising
- Reduced product introduction and product promotion lead times
- Reduction of catalog maintenance
- Elimination of cross-referencing tables between supplier and retailer product identifiers
- Error reduction in receiving shipments
- Reduction of backdoor rejections
- Increased customer satisfaction with consistent and timely data
- Contract compliance

Note that for suppliers, GDSN also offers a lot of the benefits mentioned earlier. One reason is that reduced backdoor rejections also reduce costs on the supplier side as repeated deliveries decrease. Suppliers also usually sell their products to more than one retailer. So the benefits of publishing product information once, information that can be consumed by all retailers they do business with, reduces IT complexity as well.

On the technical side, the Solution Blueprint offers the following advantages:

- Seamless adaptation to synchronize pricing information in the future, also through GDSN infrastructure, after standardization is complete.
- Provides evolutionary master data infrastructure that can easily accommodate master data model and business process changes.
- By using ESB patterns and messaging patterns such as Publish/Subscribe, consuming applications in addition to the e-Commerce system can be added to the system landscape without having the need to touch the PIM system. An example is a printing application added later.

6.4.6 Alternatives and Possible Extensions

For this MDM Solution Blueprint, possible extensions are the MDM Solution Blueprints presented in Section 6.3 and 6.5. Note that the GDSN and the EPCglobal network (see Section 6.5) start to collaborate more closely. Thus, if you are interested in a PIM-MDM Solution with GDSN, it is definitely worthwhile to check out the EPCglobal network as well for MDM enabled Track & Trace scenarios, which we describe in Section 6.5.

The e-Commerce system can also be integrated with the PIM-MDM System through other integration patterns besides the Publish/Subscribe pattern. State-of-the-art PIM systems support

---

24. The reporting on transactional data such as orders or bills is done in a data warehouse.

versioning and delta import/export. So another example for integrating the e-Commerce system with the PIM system is performing nightly delta batch extracts from the PIM-MDM System that are then applied to the e-Commerce system in batches.

A variation of this blueprint could be achieved for the automotive industry for parts management without the GDS components. The retail and the automotive industry share the characteristic that both work with many suppliers. Hierarchies, for automotive parts suppliers, into which parts are mapped establish conceptually the same "is supplied by"-relation as for products mapped into supplier hierarchies in retail. The parts can also be bundles of components with lots of relationships and attributes. For cars, there are also many categories of parts (such as wheels, axles, and seats). Concerning data modeling capabilities and category and hierarchy management capabilities, the requirements are therefore approximately on the same level. A supplier portal or an e-Commerce platform for the suppliers is also a very similar component. The car company offers deals for which a supplier can bid. The best bid is accepted, and thus bought. This online trading platform benefits from high quality master data as well.

6.5   PIM-RFID Solution Blueprint for Track & Trace

The MDM Solution Blueprint addresses the latest trends in the pharmaceutical industry where due to legal regulations each package of medicine needs to be tracked from the manufacturer to the location where it is dispensed to a patient. The traceability is significantly improved when leveraging the power of master data in this environment. The ability to track and trace items through the supply chain is a key IT capability applicable in other industries as well that has shaped this solution blueprint. Thus, we often use **Track & Trace** throughout this section to refer to this IT capability.

6.5.1   Business Context

We divided the business context discussion in several sections to address the various aspects.

6.5.1.1   Typical Supply Chain Management Problems

Out-of-stock situations are a problem for any store. Customers might become unhappy if products are unavailable and if they have to come again. They may stay away altogether if they experience such situations frequently, and even worse, might then visit a competitor store. From a business perspective, customer churn or lost business to a competitor must be avoided to keep the business running. Trying to pile up huge amounts of products on backroom shelves (increasing operational costs for the retailer) only partially solves the issue because retailers still need to check the shelves within the store to refill before an out-of-stock situation occurs. At least the time of the out-of-stock situation should be minimized if it cannot be avoided. With vigilant staff always checking the shelves in the store to avoid out-of-stock occurrences, a retailer might be able to solve the problem within the store. But how do retailers intend to ensure the replenishment of the backroom shelves? How do retailers know if the delivery truck from their usual distributor left in time? If the truck is not under way, for whatever reason, the store might need to call another distributor to get the required products in time.

From a distributor perspective, the situation is comparable to the situation of the store owner. If the warehouse is not refilled with deliveries from the manufacturers in time, nothing can be distributed. So very naturally the question arises as to how the supply chain from the manufacturer to the distributor, to the store, and then on to the shelf can be optimized. How do you employ Track & Trace end-to-end so that products are on the shelf in time to avoid out-of-stock situations?

Out-of-stock is only one business problem in this context; others include the following:

- **Automated receipt:** It is often too expensive to manually check a received order for completeness and create a manual receipt based on the items actually delivered. Creating an **automated receipt** based upon the actual delivered items solves the issue of inconsistency between what is actually delivered and what the IT system believes has been received.
- **Reduce shrinkage:** Shrinkage in the supply chain can occur mainly for two reasons: First, through theft; second, particularly applicable for perishable food and beverages like milk, by exceeding either the expiration date or by not complying with temperature requirements for storing the products (e.g., ice cream stored above 0 degrees Celsius melts and is no longer ice cream). Products that exceeded their expiration date or have perished must be thrown away, thus creating unnecessary waste and costs. A solution addressing the shrinkage problem would require mechanisms to detect theft while being constantly protected against tampering itself. Additionally, the solution requires capabilities to identify date and temperature and to trigger alerts if either the expiration date gets closer or the temperature hits critical lower or upper boundaries.
- **Backroom and shelf management:** To avoid out-of-stock situations, you need to know when you are about to run out of stock. Similarly, you need to know when a product requires replenishment on the shelves as well as in the backroom. Tracking these out-of-stock situations manually is expensive. Automating counts of the inventory and the ability to notify staff early enough to order replenishments, or even to automate the ordering of replenishments based on the automated counts, would significantly ease the management of product availability for a store.

Out-of-stock situations can also be a problem for a manufacturer; it can be very expensive in terms of labor wastage, loss of production capacity, and under-utilization of a plant. To make sure that material for every stage of the process is available, companies have tried to optimize the supply chain management and forecasting systems. In some cases, companies may still have to do more to avoid these situations. Such measures could be to change orders to alternative suppliers or to switch to faster (and possibly more expensive) transport carriers. The problems become even more difficult as the products themselves become more complex, which is the case in industries like the aerospace and automotive industries, where the subcomponents are fairly complex and are sourced from all parts of the world. Trying to make sure that a product can be assembled in a timely and cost-effective manner, therefore, requires a much deeper level of insight into the supply chain. In other words, how do you Track & Trace work-in-progress products between supplier and manufacturers so as to have advanced insight that can help you avoid out-of-stock situations?

6.5.1.2   Product Serialization

In the industry, solutions to the out-of-stock problem usually come in two types:

- Inventory Management (IM)
- Supply Chain Management (SCM)

These solutions tackle the problems just presented to a certain degree, but they are usually proprietary in nature. Assume one distributor uses SCM software from vendor A and another distributor uses SCM software from vendor B. If these two distributors belong to the same supply chain between manufacturer and store where the product is sold, the interoperability of the supply chain might be threatened. Even worse, this solution could be difficult to maintain if complex hand-written code is required whenever either one of the distributors upgrades the SCM software. For these reasons, all members in the supply chain would thus run an individually configured, isolated solution.

Track & Trace changes the game by taking the solution to the next level. The goal is to leave the four walls of the individual enterprise and bring together all players in the entire supply chain. A key concept here is the **serialized product movement**. Serialization means that the manufacturer assigns a **unique ID** to each instance of a product. The most important aspect here is that the serialization has to be **open standard** based on two layers:

- Data carrier layer (such as UHF Gen2—see [19])
- Data encoding for serialization—an **Electronic Product Code** (EPC)

Standardization on these two layers is the bare minimum to enable Track & Trace across the entire supply chain. Assume the manufacturer tags each product and stores serialization data on it. Tagging each item would be pointless if the next participant (a distributor) in the supply chain is unable to understand the transmission of the data due to the signal incompatibility with the reader devices (data carrier layer) or the serialization of the data due to an unknown data format (the way the data is encoded).

6.5.1.3   Brief Introduction of Radio Frequency Identification in the Context of SCM

Two common technologies for serialization are product barcodes and Radio Frequency Identification (RFID). Some hybrid technologies combine RFID with network interface support for Real-Time Location Services (RTLS) using, for example, the wireless network infrastructure for the determination of the location of very valuable or dangerous items. For the scope of the current discussion, we limit the architectural discussion to RFID-based serialization techniques. An important note to make is that EPC and RFID are not equal, which will become clear in our discussion.

RFID is usually used to generically refer to a set of technologies that allow the identification of tagged objects or people based on radio waves. RFID can be implemented in several ways. The most common one uses a unique identifier such as a serial number for product serialization, plus possible additional information on a microchip to which an antenna is attached. The microchip and the antenna together are known as an RFID transponder or RFID tag. For the context of our discussion, the difference between active and passive tags is not important. The antenna transmits the information stored on the microchip to a reader, thereby transforming the radio waves into electronic information consumable by other computing systems. RFID information is a type of sensor information. The radio waves can travel through most non-metallic materials, which allows them to be placed in protective plastic to make them weatherproof.

RFID is an old technology that has been around at least since the 1970s. There are three major reasons for the popularity of RFID in recent years:

Standardization of the data carrier layer: In particular, the recent introduction of standards (e.g., EPCglobal "GEN 2" standards—see [19]) and the certification of products against them allows for interoperability between tags and readers. This interoperability has helped to make it easy for the supply chain partners to work together.

Standardization of the data encoding layer: The data or unique tag identification that is encoded onto a data carrier, whether RFID or barcode, allows for various supply chain partners to clearly understand the content of the tag. Also, by relying on underlying global standards from bodies such as GS1, the value of the data is increased. One example here is SGTIN, a standard based on GTIN that adds serialization.

Price and Performance: Up to a few years ago, RFID tags were either too expensive or did not have sufficient performance for commercial use, even though with RFID technology many issues related to bar codes could be solved. In the past few years, however, advancement of the underlying technology and economies of scale in production have helped improve pricing and performance significantly.

RFID requires pervasive and enterprise computing, as shown in Figure 6.13. RFID readers are installed at various points in the supply chain, such as dock doors, conveyer belts, or handheld

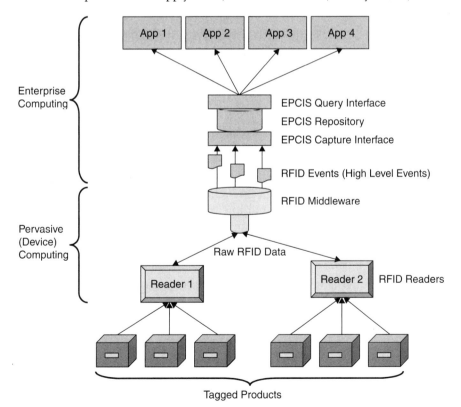

Figure 6.13 High-level overview of RFID system landscape.

reader devices that read the tagged items as they pass by. The raw RFID data is sent to the RFID middleware[25] by the readers, which do basic processing on the raw information. With regard to the RFID middleware, infrastructure is needed to distribute and update software on the RFID reader devices or to manage the RFID readers. However, these are aspects beyond the scope of our discussion. After the reader devices do their job, the raw RFID data and other sensor information is further processed and moved to the EPCIS system (see Section 6.5.1.4 for details), which consists of an EPCIS Capture Interface, the EPCIS repository itself, and the EPCIS Query Interface. The boundary from pervasive computing to enterprise computing is crossed when the raw RFID information is translated into EPCIS events. Enterprise applications such as SCM applications, data warehousing applications, and other internal or external applications can then further consume RFID information by querying the EPCIS system through the EPCIS Query Interface.

6.5.1.4 Brief Introduction of EPCIS

Standards relevant for RFID solutions are defined by an international organization called **EPCglobal**.[26] This organization defined a standard called **Electronic Product Code Information Service (EPCIS)**. EPCglobal also defined several other standards relevant to building RFID solutions, such as the Application Level Events (ALE) specification or the RFID device reader protocol specification (details can be found in [18] and [19]). As pointed out earlier, RFID represents only one way to implement product serialization. The goal of EPCIS is to enable applications in heterogeneous application environments to leverage EPC data with EPC-related data sharing services within and across enterprises. The goal can be divided into three objectives:

1. Store EPC event data efficiently.

2. Query EPC event data efficiently.

3. Share events with internal applications and trading partners securely.

The EPCIS standard specifies four types of XML events (Object, Aggregation, Quantity, and Transaction), and the attributes for each event can be extended as needed. Furthermore, you can define additional events for specific purposes if the base types are not sufficient. Also, events are accepted by the EPCIS Capture Interface and returned by the EPCIS Query Interface to consuming applications, as shown in Figure 6.13. The EPC events essentially answer four questions:

1. **WHAT:** Usually, the EPC number and other attributes, which can be product master data, belong here. Additionally, manufacturing data such as lot or expiration date and transactional data (invoice or shipment information) can be included as well.

---

25. See Section B.7 of Appendix B for an example.

26. The homepage is located at [16]. EPCglobal also provides an RFID Implementation Cookbook with a lot of useful information, which is available from [17].

2. **WHERE:** Location data, which can be either fixed (distribution center) or moving (position of moving truck). GLN numbers using global data synchronization can be leveraged here.

3. **WHEN:** A time stamp representing event time or record time is used to capture the time of an event.

4. **WHY:** The reason why an event occurred is a **business step**[27] such as shipping or receiving, or a change in product state (e.g., sellable or in transit) or **disposition**[28] (e.g., temperature).

If you think about a supply chain, the high-level system landscape, as shown in Figure 6.13, cannot be enough for tracking an item all the way through the supply chain, because that usually involves the item crossing multiple company boundaries—moving from manufacturer to distributor to retailer until it shows up in a store. That means at least some of the information in the EPCIS systems has to be exchanged between the involved players in the supply chain. EPCglobal, therefore, defined two types of EPCIS networks (and released drafts for standards that are at the time of writing not yet approved):

- **Point-to-point:** Here, two EPCIS systems are connected to each other with a point-to-point connection using a secure infrastructure.
- **Multipoint EPCglobal network:** In this setup, there is an Object Naming Service (ONS), conceptually similar to the DNS service used for the Internet, which is used by discovery services to look up a URL pointing to local computers where the information regarding the EPC is stored, based on an EPC number. The actual access to that information within the EPCglobal network is then managed at the local level through the EPCIS system; in other words, the company running the EPCIS system decides which trading partner has access to the information stored within the company's EPCIS system.

The details and relevant standards of how the multipoint EPCglobal network will come to fruition are currently being worked on as the logical next step for the standards body after the ratification of the underlying EPCIS and related standards.

6.5.1.5   Relation of GDSN Network and EPCglobal Network

As you recall from the previous blueprint on Global Data Synchronization, GTIN numbers are used for uniquely identifying products. Now, with EPC numbers and EPC networks, there are also unique global identification numbers. Figure 6.14 shows how they are related to each other.

---

27. A business step specifies the business context of an event, indicating the business process step that caused the event to be captured was taking place or what business process is being executed at this read point; an example would be "receiving."

28. A disposition specifies the business condition of the object at event time. The disposition is assumed to hold true until another event indicates a change of disposition. Thus, a disposition answers questions of the type, "What state was the product last seen in?" A possible answer could be "sold."

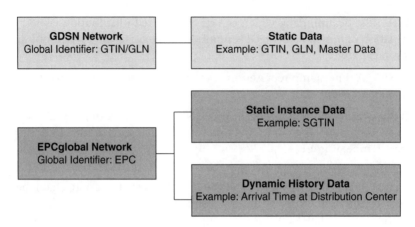

Figure 6.14   Relation of GDSN Network and EPCglobal Network.

The GDSN Network provides master data about a product or a trading partner with a unique identifier such as GTIN and GLN as well as attributes describing the facts, such as name, size, weight, and color for products, and name, address, and phone number for trading partner entities. The static information is shared by companies using the GDSN Network, where no information on specific instances of products is shared.

The EPCglobal Network has two types: Static instance data and dynamic history data. The instance data is static because after assignment, it can no longer be changed. It would not make sense to allow a change of a serial number if the serial number is intended to fulfill unique identification of this instance of a product. The serial number indicates that this item is, for example, the 4711th copy of an item of a certain type of product or the manufacturing date. The instance of a product shares the static information synchronized within the GDSN Network that is shared by all instances of a certain product, such as the same GTIN, but static instance data are attributes unique to that instance.

Dynamic history data is the set of EPCIS events for an EPC (for example, given by the SGTIN) for a product (for example, given by the GTIN) that shows the history of an instance of a product. The history is given by a set of EPCIS events such as arrival or departure time of this instance of a product from a distribution center or the complete history of all temperature measurements performed that show whether or not the temperature constraints were fulfilled at all times while the product was moved through the supply chain. For this verification, you might need to combine master data attributes with the history data by comparing each reading point with the lower and upper constraints for the temperature, which are part of the master data. Real-time access to the information of the EPCglobal Network allows tracking and tracing of an item through a supply chain end-to-end. GDSN and EPCglobal Network do not maintain overlapping information. Table 6.1 shows their differences.

Table 6.1   The Differences between GDSN and EPCglobal

Network	GDSN	EPCglobal Network
Use Case	Collaboration in e-Commerce	Supply chain visibility
Purpose	Guarantee information quality and easy exchange between trading partners	Track trade item movement throughout the entire supply chain
Primary Tasks	Data synchronization and GS1 system compliance to enable B2B e-Commerce through a foundation of collaborative transaction management	Recording of events and state changes within the supply chain to generate complete supply chain history providing full supply chain insight in real-time over the Internet
Information	Static information covering product and trading partner master data, where each product is identified through GTIN and each trading party is identified through a GLN	Dynamic information on item history such as movement and state change information where each item is identified using a EPC

Figure 6.15[29] presents the result of an RFID read for an EPCIS object event. Through analysis of it you will understand why bringing together the information from both data exchange networks is so powerful. On the left side, there is a lot of information—mainly numbers with no context. If you decode the numbers and put them into an initial context, as shown in the description column of Figure 6.15, the result is some basic information about the GTIN, the serial number, the GLN number, or when the event occurred. However, these important questions still remain unanswered:

- GTIN:
  - What product is identified by this GTIN?
  - What are units of measure for the product?
  - What are the critical lower and upper temperature limits for the product?
  - What are the relevant product categories in product classifications?
- GLN:
  - What is the GLN address?
  - Is it a store or a distribution center?
  - If it is a store, does it belong to a certain promotion area or campaign?

An MDM System connected to the GDSN network can provide answers to these questions. So if you intend to enrich RFID information for a deep understanding, integration of the

---

29. The authors took the freedom to convey an idea with this figure by using sample data instead of being necessarily compliant down to the last details of the relevant specifications.

Read Event	Description
20070808063342	Time event occurred - 08/08/07 06:33:42 GMT
20070808063349	Time event was recorded in EPCIS - 08/08/07 06:33:49 GMT
urn:epc:tag:sgtin-96:7.0614141.100734.333424	EPC # in Event - is GTIN # 061414100734 and Serial # 333424
OBSERVE	Action: observe which means existing tag is read here
urn:epcglobal:epcis:bizstep:fmcg: receiving	Business Step: Receiving
urn:epcglobal:epcis:disp:fmcg: sellable_available	Disposition: item is sellable and available
urn:epc:id:sgln:0652642.63421.742	Business Location ID - GLN # 065264263421 in backroom 742
<bizTransaction type = "urn:epcglobal:fmcg:biztransactiontype:PO> http://distributor.com/knr42"	Distributor PO # knr42

Figure 6.15 Example of RFID read event data and initial context data.

EPCIS system with a PIM-MDM System is required. The standard for the EPC is flexible enough to allow for different numbering schemes as identifiers; GTIN is one example.

In the case of the GTIN, as mentioned, the EPC would contain the GTIN, extended by the serial number representing the instance of the product uniquely identified by the SGTIN. With the GTIN obtained from the EPC as part of the SGTIN contained in a read event, you could then obtain all of the answers needed for the aforementioned questions from your PIM-MDM System, which can be connected to the GDSN network, as shown in the MDM Solution Blueprint in Section 6.4. Doing it this way allows exploitation of the complementary nature of the information of both networks for deep insight into EPC data.

The link between the product master data (products identified through a GTIN, for example) and the serialization needed for EPCglobal network is established by the EPC Tag Data Standard (see [20] for the specification), which provides:

• Encodings of an identity, together with additional information such as filter values rendered into a specific syntax
• A representation of a pure identity as a **Uniform Resource Identifier** (URI), which is commonly used in the information system layer

Figure 6.16 shows the process of creating an EPC-compliant encoding that is then stored physically on a tag, for example. A serialized GTIN (SGTIN) consisting of a company prefix, an item reference, and a serial number would use GTIN information in an encoding procedure when the serialization is created for an instance of a product. The encoding is then physically stored in a tag, for example.

With this example, we hope it is clear why bringing together EPC data and master data is so incredibly useful. We will show soon what the architecture for this solution blueprint could look like. Let's have a look now at another use case.

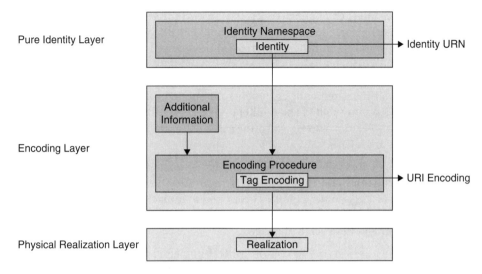

Figure 6.16   Illustration how the EPC Tag Data Standard process works.

6.5.1.6   Drug Pedigree Legislation

So far, we considered out-of-stock situations or other business issues driving optimizations in the SCM using RFID. A completely different driver for Track & Trace solutions stems from current and upcoming legal regulations such as the drug pedigree for reducing the amount of counterfeit goods and services. The vast majority of prescription drugs sold to consumers are safe. However, given the large number of players in the supply chain and different laws for the involved parties, opportunities exist to counterfeit or adulterate drugs, with potentially very dangerous effects for the consumer.

In the United States, first steps were made with legal regulations such as drug pedigree by federal and state lawmakers to combat counterfeit or adulterated drugs. As of June 30, 2007,[30] 23 states have enacted drug pedigree legislation, with Florida being the first state that had put such a law in effect, in July 2006. An additional 10 states have proposed drug pedigree legislation that is pending. Florida required pedigree only at a batch level, so no serialization was needed. For this reason, EPC wouldn't be required; however, we think pedigrees without serialization are not very useful, because as soon as the batch is opened, individual items can no longer be identified. California enacted a law requiring serialization; therefore, some form of EPC is required. Another difference between Florida and California is that Florida requires the tracing to start at the distributor, whereas in California tracing starts with the manufacturer.

These laws aim to establish a drug pedigree for all players in the supply chain, tracking the chain of custody from manufacturer to the point where the drug is received by a

---

30.   For further details, see [21].

consumer. In some states, drug pedigree legislation currently only covers pharmaceutical wholesalers and distributors, but it is expected that very likely doctors, drug manufacturers, pharmacies, hospitals, and others might soon be required to collect, certify, and store pedigrees for all drugs dispensed. If such a pedigree is available, the benefit for a consumer of a drug is the assurance that the drug is actually what it should be. Enforced drug pedigree legislation also offers tremendous benefits for the manufacturers of drugs. It is estimated[31] that by 2010 counterfeited and adulterated drugs worth an estimated US $75 billion will have been sold. For developing countries, this estimate means that one out of four medicine packages are fake.[32]

Besides the damage of lost sales due to counterfeited and adulterated drugs in the market, pharmaceutical companies also suffer indirectly regarding their brands. If counterfeited or adulterated drugs cause consumer illness or death and manufacturers or retailers are not able to prove that the drug was not manufactured by their enterprise, they might face lawsuits and their reputation will be severely damaged.

Pharmaceutical companies trying to comply with drug pedigree legislation are looking for electronic pedigree solutions, often referred to as **ePedigree solutions.** A relevant standard here is the Drug Pedigree Messaging Standard[33] (DPMS) from EPCglobal, released in 2007. At the time of writing, the industry is discussing the use of EPCIS, along with DPMS, as part of the overall ePedigree solution, but no agreement has yet been reached. We cannot predict what the outcome of the standardization discussion will be. So we would just like to mention that there are software vendors[34] offering ePedigree solutions aimed at complying with the drug pedigree legislation as well as with these ePedigree standards. At a high level, an ePedigree solution requires three capabilities:

1. **Product serialization:** One approach can be to use RFID tags included within or attached to a package of drugs by the manufacturer. These tags, when read, deliver unique information about the drug package as it moves through the supply chain. Other options are barcodes and other technologies.

2. **Data Capture:** While handling the drug, information regarding the products themselves, the movement within the enterprise, aggregation and disaggregation of the product also need to be captured by each participant involved in the supply chain. Each participant must also integrate other information, such as batch and lot numbers, expiration dates, and contact information of people responsible for shipping and receiving the product. All this information needs to be stored in a secure and tamper-resistant manner with the ability to report on it for audit purposes.

---

31. See the World Health Organization (WHO) fact sheet on counterfeited drugs [22] for further details.
32. For further details, see the WHO bulletin [23].
33. For the pedigree standard we refer to the EPC global specification located at [24].
34. Several products suitable for ePedigree solutions are listed in Section B.7 in Appendix B.

3. **Data Sharing:** To certify with the drug pedigree the chain of custody of the drug while it moved through the supply chain, information needs to be collected and exchanged with other participants. The IT environment—where all partners in the supply chain can exchange information, ensure data authentication, and contribute to the accuracy and certification of the pedigree—has to be secure.

The amount of data collected increases from the starting point of the supply chain to the end point, thus implying that the size of the pedigree grows in the same direction. The quality of an ePedigree solution could be improved when the attributes defining the drug are handled by a PIM-MDM System where all parties involved can synchronize the drug description with their local systems using the global data synchronization infrastructure. In this solution, the drug manufacturer synchronizes the relevant attributes describing the drug and how it should be handled to a global data pool where all subsequent participants in the supply chain can get the drug information. Attributes describing the drug could contain fields to provide information about special handling instructions such as the recommended temperature for storing the drug.

Regardless of the motivation—whether it is strictly a business consideration (avoiding out-of-stock situations) or the necessity of complying with a legal mandate, (the pedigree requirements)—the ability to Track & Trace products from manufacturer to the shelf within a store can be found in a solution that combines a PIM-MDM System, a RFID system, and EPCIS system. This combination is the reason why we named this solution blueprint the PIM-RFID Solution Blueprint for Track & Trace scenarios.

6.5.2 Relevant Business Patterns

As you saw in the previous section, we have several distinct business requirements driving business patterns. First, there is the business pattern on pedigree compliance. Second, there is the need for tracing a product from manufacturer through distributors all the way to the point where, for example, a product such as medicine is dispensed to a patient. Thus, we have a business-to-business relation that is captured in the B2B pattern. In order to get insight into the RFID data, master data, and transactional data, information integration is required. Overall, from a business pattern perspective, we have the following:

- **Pedigree Compliance:** The business pattern requires IT infrastructure enabling compliance with pedigree legal regulations.
- **B2B pattern:** Throughout the supply chain, from manufacturer to store owner, enterprises need to collaborate to achieve an ePedigree solution or to reduce shrinkage in the supply chain.
- **Information aggregation:** The user-to-data business pattern is relevant for any EPC-based solution. To find meaning in vast amounts of data created, for example, through RFID tags being read by RFID readers, you need to be able to somehow correlate the reads and aggregate them toward meaningful information. Along the way, you enrich it with data from other sources, such as GLNs from global data synchronization networks or information from master data systems. Without this aggregation, providing just raw RFID information to a user would make it difficult and time-consuming to see and understand the history of a drug through the supply chain.

6.5.3   Relation between Business Patterns and MDM Architecture Patterns

The business patterns from the previous section mandate at least the following MDM architecture patterns:

- **Initial Load pattern** to build the MDM System
- Either the **Coexistence** or the **Transaction Hub** architecture pattern is required for the PIM-RFID Solution Blueprint for Track & Trace scenarios. If product information needs to be exchanged efficiently between enterprise boundaries or provided to the EPCIS repository, then for performance reasons as well as consistency reasons, an MDM System built with the Registry Hub architecture pattern is not sufficient.
- The **GDS architecture pattern** (a subpattern of the Information Synchronization pattern explained in Chapter 5) is needed to provide GTIN and GLN information.

For the integration of supply chain management systems and enterprise resource planning systems, messaging patterns such as Publish/Subscribe might be needed as well. The EPCIS Query Interface as part of the standard supports standing queries that allow for an efficient implementation of this pattern. The same pattern might be used by the MDM client of the EPCIS system shown in Figure 6.16 to subscribe to changes from the MDM System.

6.5.4   MDM Solution Blueprint Overview

We now dive into the MDM Solution Blueprint, providing a high-level overview that shows required systems from a logical point of view. As described earlier, making this solution happen requires combining data from two networks, namely, the GDSN and the EPCglobal Network. As shown in Figure 6.17, the RFID data is generated by RFID readers such as dock door readers, conveyer belt readers, and handheld or shelf readers. The raw, incoming RFID data is processed by RFID middleware and then exposed to the EPCIS system through the ALE Interface.

The EPCIS system, consisting of the EPCIS Capture Interface, the EPCIS repository, and the EPCIS Query Interface, interacts with at least the following four types of systems:

1. **The MDM System:** The purpose of the interaction with the MDM System is that the MDM System contains the master data necessary for enriching the EPCIS information. The MDM System is connected to the GDSN network—so static information from the network relevant for the EPCIS system can be made available along with other relevant master information from the MDM System. Depending on the EPCIS software used, the MDM Client can be an interface able to consume master data in XML format, for persisting it into the EPCIS repository. If it is done in batch-oriented fashion, the MDM client likely receives the master data through direct interaction with the MDM System. If the MDM System sends out appropriate updates for the EPCIS system near real-time or in real time, it likely leverages ESB infrastructure. Due to these two options, we have two arrows in the figure connecting the MDM client directly and indirectly through the ESB with the MDM System. Storing for read-only access a subset of data in the EPCIS system is done for performance reasons and to support certain queries removing the need of federation.

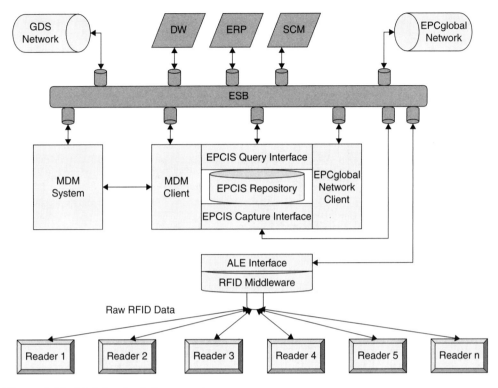

Figure 6.17   High-level solution overview.

2. **The EPCglobal Network Client and the EPCglobal Network:** The EPCglobal Network Client reaches out to the EPCglobal Network to perform:
   - ONS lookup by invoking an Object Naming Service (ONS)[35]
   - EPC Discovery Service
   - Remote EPC Information Service

3. **The previous or next EPCIS system in the supply chain:** To implement an ePedigree solution, the system may need to interact with the previous EPCIS system in the supply chain to retrieve additional data or with the next EPCIS system in the supply chain to make the pedigree available to the next system after the related item is under way to the next destination.

4. **Application systems:** Through the EPCIS Query Interface, application systems such as reporting systems (e.g., data warehouses), supply chain management systems, trading partner systems, and enterprise resource planning systems interact with the EPCIS system. An ePedigree application would integrate with an EPCIS system to create, for example, the pedigree for a drug.

---

35. At the time of writing, the ONS standard was final (see [25]), and the discovery-related standards were considered almost final.

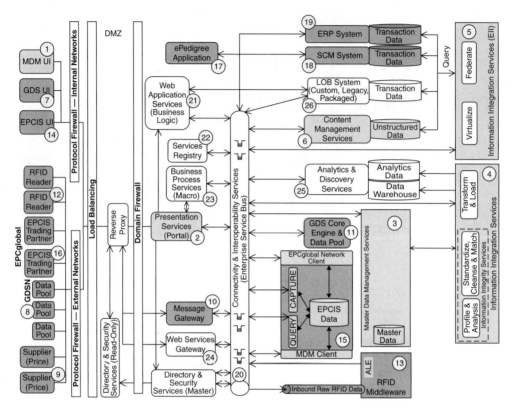

Figure 6.18   PIM-RFID Solution Blueprint for Track & Trace component model view.

After understanding the logical components, we now move from the high-level overview to a more detailed component model view. For a traditional Track & Trace scenario optimizing the supply chain, Figure 6.18 provides a detailed component model overview based on the Enterprise Master Data Component Relationship Model, as described in Chapter 3. Central pieces are the EPCIS system, the GDS Core Engine, the RFID middleware system, and the MDM System. In Figure 6.18, we have three types of components:

- The mandatory components (1) to (6) in light grey are components either needed to build or to run the MDM System. Core functions of these components were explained in the MDM RA, and their relevance for PIM-MDM Solutions was explained in Section 6.3.4.
- The dark grey components (7) to (19) are crucial in implementing this solution. For the GDS aspect of the solution, you need (7) to (11) (see Section 6.4). The components (12) to (19) are relevant for the Track & Trace aspect of this solution and cover RFID infrastructure, EPCIS infrastructure, and applications gaining the benefits of the Track & Trace deployment.

- The white components (20) to (26) are optional components and might or might not be there. A basic introduction to them has been given in Section 6.3 and 6.4 and in Chapter 3 as part of the introduction to the MDM RA.

Basically, the component model view shown in Figure 6.18 supports the following key flows through the IT infrastructure:

Flow 1: Master data entry through the GDSN into the MDM System (extensively described in Section 6.4)

Flow 2: Master data received from the suppliers (extensively described in Section 6.4)

Flow 3: Master data authoring/enrichment (extensively described in Section 6.3 and Section 6.4)

Flow 4: Master data entry from the MDM System into the EPCIS system

Flow 5: EPC/supply chain event from the readers through the RFID middleware into the EPCIS system

Flow 6: EPCIS event exchange between trading partners

Flow 7: Application systems querying the EPCIS system

Note that the first six flows together aggregate data to the level that a user working with an application such as SCM (18), ERP (19), or a data warehouse (25) for reporting and analytics can get deep insight of what happened with an item as it moved through the supply chain. These steps together represent the implementation of the information aggregation business pattern.

When the master data is available after the first three flows are completed, the initial load into the EPCIS repository can be done through Flow 4:

1. Through the EPCIS UI (14), the system can be configured and administrated. The configuration includes the definition of master data attributes. After the model for the master data that will be persisted locally in the EPCIS repository is created, two different integration approaches can be taken:
   - Initial batch load followed by periodic (e.g., nightly) delta batch updates
   - Initial batch load followed by near real-time or real-time updates using messaging infrastructure

2. In the first case, the MDM client (15) would trigger a workflow on the MDM System (3) through a service call generating a delta extract that is then processed by the MDM client and loaded into the EPCIS repository (15).

3. In the second case, after the initial load is done, the MDM client could subscribe to a queue on which the MDM System publishes changes using a Publish/Subscribe pattern.

Flow 5 describes how RFID data is captured and moved to the EPCIS system.

1. The first step is an RFID reader (12) reading an RFID tag from a tagged product.

2. The raw RFID information is sent using messages through the Message Gateway (10) to the RFID middleware (13).

3. The RFID middleware (13) processes the raw RFID data and removes duplicate reads. After the raw RFID data is processed, high-level events are published through the ALE interface (13). Through the ALE interface, the processed RFID data is then sent to the EPCIS capture interface (15). Between the ALE interface and the EPCIS capture interface a capture application could exist applying business rules.

4. The EPCIS capture interface persists the data in the EPCIS repository. The data is saved without changes, because the EPCIS capture interface cannot perform changes. Thus, changing the data, if needed, to enrich the data would be the job of the capture application that normally resides between the RFID middleware and the EPCIS system. The capture application would do this before the EPCIS capture interface receives the data.

Flow 6 describes the exchange of information through the EPCglobal network between trading partners, such as supplier and manufacturer.

1. Due to the subscription to the EPCIS system (16) of the trading partner owning the previous step in the supply chain, the EPCIS system receives appropriate EPCIS events from the EPCIS system of the trading partner through the EPCglobal Network client (15) and stores the EPCIS data in the EPCIS repository (15).

2. When the shipment is received, and the goods are processed and shipped to the next destination, all these steps are tracked and traced with RFID read operations done by the RFID readers (12) and processed by the RFID middleware (13), which provides the right events to the EPCIS capture interface (15) through the ALE interface (13).

3. Upon completion of these steps, when the goods are shipped to the next destination, the EPCIS system publishes an appropriate event consumed by the next trading partner (16) in the supply chain, which can query for additional information through the EPCIS query interface (15) if more information is needed.

Flow 7 shows the interaction of the application systems with the EPCIS system. Applications such as a data warehouse for reporting (25), an enterprise resource planning system (19), or the supply chain management system (18) can interact with the EPCIS system through the query interface (15). Also, some EPCIS software support alerts and notification infrastructure built on messaging technology. Alerting and notification capabilities enable the EPCIS system to publish alerts or messages to topic queues to which application systems can subscribe using messaging architecture patterns such as Publish/Subscribe. An ePedigree application (17) could query the EPCIS system for all relevant data through the EPCIS query interface (15) in order to produce a pedigree, for example, for a customer in a pharmacy or for a government regulator inquiring on a suspicious drug. A trading partner in the supply chain must be able to provide a pedigree based on an EPC that contains a certain national drug code (NDC). An NDC is not serialized—similar to a GTIN—thus you can consider NDC a kind of GTIN for drugs.

After this basic introduction to Track & Trace environments in the supply chain, we would like to provide some detailed insight about deploying such a Track & Trace solution, particularly if it is intended to be used for a situation such as Work in Progress visibility, where a manufacturer would like to use such an architecture to get deeper visibility into its upstream supply chain.

As any manufacturer of complex products such as those in the automotive and aerospace industry will tell you, they are effectively an assembler of a set of parts to create the final product; it is therefore vital for them to have supplies on time and at the right location. Mistakes and delays can be a serious problem, with global sourcing of the parts creating further problems. It is not enough for a manufacturer to attempt to increase overall production by just increasing the capacity of an individual plant; the supplier network might not always be able to provide the parts in time.

The Work In Progress (WIP) visibility solution for manufacturers relies on the basic EPCIS standard to allow their suppliers to share data with manufacturers, who are their customers, about where in the assembly process parts currently are. A point we cannot emphasize enough here is that the parts that are being produced by the suppliers themselves go through a series of steps as they are themselves very complex. By getting this visibility information in near real-time, the manufacturer has the ability to plan its internal operations much better and knows of a possible late shipment before it's too late and thus can take actions to address this issue.

Figure 6.19 shows a simple deployment model for a solution that will address the basic parts of the solution. As has already been discussed in the previous section, the EPCIS standard allows for capturing and sharing of serialized product movement information by individuals in the supply chain. The suppliers and manufacturers are able to communicate with each other, via direct point-to-point, or the EPCglobal network (in the future) using the EPCIS standard along with standard secure communication options, including HTTPS, AS2, or event point-to-point messaging through an inter-company ESB.

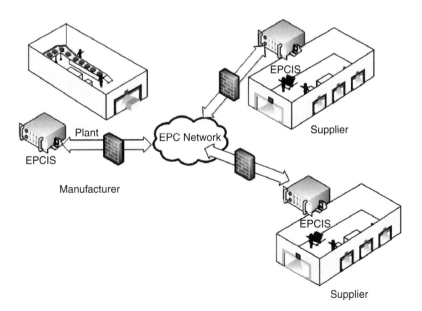

Figure 6.19   Simple deployment of an EPCIS solution.

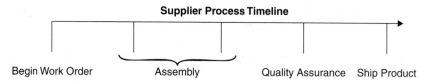

Figure 6.20 Supplier Process Timeline.

First, let's look at the most basic process for any supplier, regardless of how the details of the assembly steps may vary by industry. We focus on the most common steps (business steps) of beginning a work order, quality assurance (QA), and finally shipment of the order. Figure 6.20 shows this simple version of the supplier process time line.

We assume that the supplier and manufacturer will have to agree on the data encoding and data carrier for the products, because this agreement is the only way for the product serialization to be valuable. As the supplier gets an order from the customer via the preexisting order management system, the processing of building the product will begin—at this point, the serialized product will be commissioned and information about it can be shared with the manufacturer. The lifecycle of the EPC has begun—and subsequent processing steps, including assembly, QA, and shipment are captured by the Track & Trace solution and shared with the manufacturer. A simple version of the manufacturer process time line is shown in Figure 6.21.

After the product is received by the manufacturer, a number of business steps can follow, including storage in a warehouse or shipping it to another location. But at some point in time, the general business step of using the part in their assembly process will occur. Each of these events is captured as part of the Track & Trace solution and shared with the supplier.

After the data from the two trading partners starts to be effectively shared, it can be used to provide a significant amount of business value for each of them. A manufacturer can use this real-time information to ensure supplier compliance against their own work orders. Having more detailed knowledge of the supply chain means that delays are known long before the expected shipment is to be received, because the moment at which the shipment starts to slip is known immediately. The manufacturer can now choose to ensure that the following occurs:

- Labor resources and tasks are scheduled according to better inventory estimates.
- Requests can be made to expedite orders or do partial shipments.
- Alternative suppliers can be contacted.

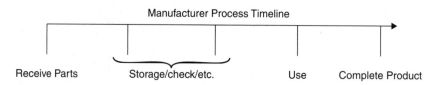

Figure 6.21 Manufacturer Process Timeline.

The supplier will also benefit by providing visibility to the manufacturer, because they are able to meet the demand better. Knowledge about the usage of a part provides demand signals that can help them adjust their own manufacturing capacity to ensure that they are not building parts that are just getting stockpiled with their customer.

6.5.5 Security Aspects of MDM Deployments

We use the Track & Trace Solution Blueprint as an example to show relevant areas where an IT Architect needs to address IT security aspects applicable for enterprise MDM Solution deployments. Many MDM security topics are the same for all MDM Solution Blueprints in Chapter 6 and Chapter 7—to avoid redundancy, we present the detailed areas for security only once in the context of this MDM Solution Blueprint. We choose this solution blueprint as an example because this solution blueprint has the full breadth of requirements from a security perspective. You can find a detailed discussion of MDM security in Chapter 4. The numbers throughout this section identify components shown in Figure 6.22. Figure 6.22 is identical to Figure 6.18. However, the coloring has been changed to highlight the security-related components. Also, the numbers in Figure 6.22 appear in the order of discussion of the various security aspects in this discussion.

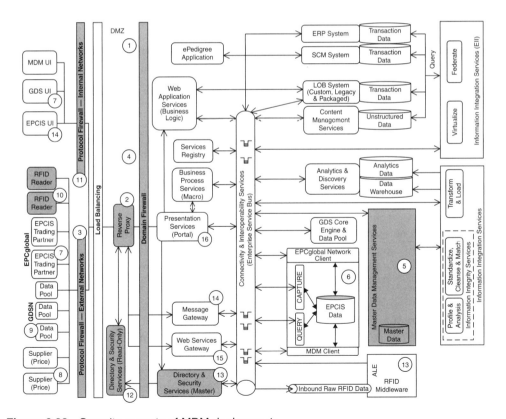

Figure 6.22 Security aspects of MDM deployments.

Because EPC tracking information (and potentially master data) from external partners will be created, queried, and updated in the EPCIS and other enterprise systems, only the internal systems need to be accessible to remote systems, and only to the extent needed for this solution. The solution employs the following standard enterprise security components and patterns to limit external access to the internal EPCIS and master data repositories to authorized externalized systems and users.

- **De-militarized Zone** (DMZ, see (1)) and **Reverse Proxy** (2): (At least) two firewalls (the external firewall (3) and the domain firewall (4)) are used to separate the external network from the internal network. In the external networks, components such as RFID readers or systems of trading partners (see (7) to (10)) are located. The internal network hosts the MDM System (5) and the EPCIS (6) system. The two firewalls protect the internal network from direct external access. Two firewalls are required for a DMZ, and it is not uncommon that in a customer environment the DMZ is deployed with multiple layers. The dual firewall configuration is called a De-militarized Zone (or DMZ). No direct access by external systems to the internal repositories is allowed. All access must go instead through a secured component known as a Reverse Proxy (RP), which is installed in the DMZ. The outer firewall is configured to send all traffic to the RP. The inner firewall is configured to accept only traffic from the RP. The Reverse Proxy thus provides a level of isolation by allowing only authorized connections to be passed through from the outer firewall to the internal firewall and thus back to the internal network. Furthermore, only the network protocols and network ports necessary to access the Remote Proxy are exposed by the external firewall. To ensure data confidentiality and integrity (in this case, protecting from network snooping and modification), only secure protocols, such as HTTP over Secure Sockets Layer (HTTPS) or SOAP over HTTPS, should be allowed to connect to the proxy and from the proxy to the internal network.

The Reverse Proxy is a system that sits in front of the EPCIS and MDM Systems (thus "reverse," because it is acting on the part of the servers) and mediates access to those systems from the external requesters (thus "proxy"). The Reverse Proxy minimizes the opportunity for attacks on the enterprise EPCIS and MDM Systems by ensuring that no outside system has direct access to them. All access from external actors must be mediated through the Reverse Proxy. Note that it is also a best practice to use internal firewalls (11) to further limit access to the various backend systems. In addition to the isolation we just discussed, the Reverse Proxy acts as a security mediator by enforcing the following controls:

- **Secure Communication:** As described in the DMZ section, the Reverse Proxy needs to use cryptographically secure mechanisms such as HTTPS or SOAP over HTTPS for any network transportation of sensitive information. Additionally, the Reverse Proxy may communicate with other backend services (such as the Directory Services) using the LDAP protocol over Secure Socket Layer (SSL) as part of the validation of the communication protocol or the identities associated with this protocol (for example, to validate that the SSL session belongs to a known EPICS partner and not to "hackers-are-us.com").

- **Authentication:** The Reverse Proxy authenticates all requests (whether for GUI access to manage product information or Web services requests to update item location information in the EPCIS) for protected information. In a typical environment, the authentication is based on validating a user identity and password against an enterprise LDAP Directory (shown as Directory Services (12) and (13) in Figure 6.22). Stronger forms of authentication, such as client certificates or multi-factor devices, can also be supported by the proxy—this is a security policy that is specified at the proxy. With these stronger forms of authentication, session maintenance techniques can be implemented so that not every request requires reauthentication if a secure session is used.
- **Authorization:** After the request is authenticated, the Reverse Proxy can annotate the request with the role and group membership of the user/requester. The Reverse Proxy will then make an authorization decision (based on access control rules) about whether or not to route the request on to the backend EPCIS and/or MDM Systems. The authorization can be coarse-grained ("Can partner X have any access to the EPCIS system?") or more fine-grained ("Can partner X access the 'Update Product' task in MDM?").
- **Identity Transformation and Propagation:** Security controls are also enforced at the target MDM and EPCIS systems. To enforce these controls, the target systems require the Reverse Proxy to deliver an authenticated identity. There are a number of known security patterns to authenticate an identity
  - Reverse Proxy using a Functional Identity to access the backend systems. In this case, the Reverse Proxy has its own authenticated identity, and all requests to the backend systems use that identity. Just using a Functional Identity is simple to set up, but vests a very high level of authority in the Reverse Proxy and makes fine-grained authorization and auditing impossible in target systems.
  - Using a Functional Identity and asserting an Initiator Identity. In this pattern, the Reverse Proxy still has its own authenticated identity but will also pass along the identity of the original requester to the backend system. For interactive applications, identity propagation can be done by simply passing an identity token in the HTTPS header.[36] For the EPCIS and MDM Systems to accept this token, a trust relationship must be established between the Reverse Proxy and the EPCIS systems. The trust can be established using a mutually authenticated SSL connection or by the Reverse Proxy authenticating with a functional identity and password over an SSL connection. In some cases, the initiator identity is automatically consumed within a Web Application container, so the backend system need not be aware that the identity was passed by a reverse Proxy. Certain security protocols (like Kerberos) have the characteristic that the Reverse Proxy can actually forward a token from the originator that can be directly consumed by the downstream systems. This protocol technique limits the potential of a Reverse Proxy to emulate any user, independent of whether or not that user is actually authenticated to the Reverse Proxy.

---

36. This is done by some products listed in Section B.6 in Appendix B.

- Identity transformation is another important task of the Reverse Proxy. When systems are exposed across the Internet, potentially millions of users may be allowed to access those systems. For some backend systems, representing all of those users in a user registry for authentication and authorization purposes is simply impossible—either the user registry cannot handle it or the tools to manage users in the user registry do not scale to that large a number. In this case, the Reverse Proxy has the ability to map a user identity into a role—for example, Item Specialist Judith Hall of JK Enterprises can be mapped to a generic identity of "Item Specialist," with an attribute of "Authentication Identity: Judith Hall/JK Enterprises" to ensure that end-to-end identity can be maintained in an audit trail.
- **Auditing:** The Reverse Proxy can be configured to log transactions. The auditing is based on an enterprise security policy and can be configured to support multiple use cases:
  - Logging based on the identity/role of the users (e.g., "Audit all actions by Judith Hall")
  - Logging based on the target system (e.g., "Audit all MDM transactions")
  - Logging based on the type of transaction ("Audit all updates to EPCIS")
  - Logging based on the details of the transaction ("Audit all updates to controlled pharmaceuticals"). This type of auditing may not be supported in the Reverse Proxy, because it requires deep introspection into the details of the transaction and may be more appropriate at the target system.
  - Auditing events can be collected and correlated at a central audit service (not shown in Figure 6.22) and can be reported at the central audit service.

After requests pass through the Reverse Proxy in the DMZ, in the case of Web services or message based requests, they reach the **Web Services Gateway** (14) or the **Message Gateway** (15), respectively. These components can use most of the same security services that are part of the Reverse Proxy (Authentication, Authorization, Identity Transformation and Propagation, Secure Communication, and Auditing). The main difference is that the Web Services Gateway and Message Gateway are inside the internal network and can only communicate to the outside network via the Reverse Proxy. Also, the Web Services and Message Gateways would use the internal Directory Services (12) for authentication and checking for user roles.

Within the internal network securing **applications** (e.g., Portal (16), MDM (5), EPCIS (6)) working with master data is the next step. These components also consume the same services as the two gateways, but differ in a few respects:

- **Authentication:** These services need to know how to consume a trusted identity produced by the Reverse Proxy (or they can delegate that to the application container).
- **Authorization:** At this level, the MDM and EPCIS systems have a deep knowledge of the transaction being requested and are better suited to perform fine-grained or data-driven authorization ("User Judith Hall in the Role of Pharmacy Manager queried location information for drugs that are not listed as controlled narcotics").

The MDM System (5) is responsible for managing the following security aspects:

- **Privileges:** Has the requester/role the necessary permission to read or modify a certain attribute? Has the requester/role the necessary privilege to invoke a certain service?
- **Audit:** All changes on master data need to be auditable on an attribute level. Depending on the country and industry, a full audit trail on employee or customer master data might need to be available for several years for compliance reasons.

For both aspects, and depending on the software chosen for the MDM System, integration with an identity management system such as LDAP may be required.

The security considerations listed so far apply to most enterprise system deployments. There are, however, some additional security concerns that are unique to the Track & Trace solution:

- **Authenticity of RFID events sent to the RFID middleware from RFID Readers (10):** If RFID readers are not authenticated to the RFID middleware and do not use secure communications to send events to the RFID middleware, there is a risk that a reader controlled by an attacker (or a network controlled by the attacker) can send out movement information that is not valid to the RFID middleware. For example, a malicious reader could send out an event that says a pallet of aspirin was shipped but suppress the fact that a shipment of Human Growth Hormone was stolen from the warehouse. There are two controls that can be put into place to mitigate this risk:
  - **Secure Communications:** The reader can send events over SSL, using the public key from a certificate of the middleware system. The public key can also be used for other forms of secure communications, such as secure messaging.
  - **Authentication:** The reader can have its own identity and authenticator used to communicate with the server. As with the Reverse Proxy, this authentication capability can be a user identity and password or a private key and certificate.
  - For both Authentication and Secure Communications, a provisioning action must take place to load the reader with the RFID Middleware certificate with the reader identity and authentication credentials. The load step may require an administrative identity and password on the reader to update this sensitive information.
- **Physical Security:** Cameras and guards should be used to augment the technical controls just presented, because some readers either do not implement the technical controls or they are easily subverted.
- **Unusual event detection:** If a complete end-to-end Track & Trace is implemented, the EPCIS system or RFID Middleware Solution may be able to detect events that should not occur (e.g., an outgoing shipment event from a reader in a distribution center when an equivalent inbound shipment event was never received).
- **Authenticity of RFID tags:** In order to prevent spoofing of RFID tags, you might need to implement tamper-proof RFID tags. They are more expensive, but if you need to exclude the risk that someone introduces duplicates of RFID tags by spoofing them into your environment, hiding theft or other criminal activities, tamper-proof RFID tags might be needed. A solution can be to use HF tags with chip IDs burnt in the silicon of the tag and then linking this to the EPC you record on the tag. The pair then becomes the single, unique tag that cannot be duplicated or otherwise spoofed.

If you are using the PIM-RFID Solution Blueprint for Track & Trace in the context of implementing an ePedigree solution, you also need to address the following security topics for the
pedigrees:

- You need to have certificates of the systems that sign the manifests.
- For signers, you must have secure storage of the private keys used to sign manifests.
- You must securely store the manifests and produce them as needed.
- You need to enforce that only known and authorized systems are allowed to gen-
  erate signatures for a pedigree. Enforcement might not be possible at signature
  time, but it could be detected when the event is sent to EPCIS.

We have now shown you how to apply the security aspects outlined in Chapter 4 to a specific
MDM Solution Blueprint. Recall that CDI-MDM Systems are prime targets for identity thieves
and a PIM-MDM System is a prime target for industry espionage. We cannot, therefore,
emphasize enough that you must take special care when you secure your MDM deployments.

6.5.6 Advantages

If you deploy the PIM-RFID Solution Blueprint for Track & Trace solutions, you are able to
reap the following business benefits, depending on your business:

- Improved insight into RFID data by enriching it with master data
- Compliance with legal regulations such as drug pedigree, using ePedigree solution
- Reduction of lost sales due to counterfeited or adulterated drugs
- Brand protection
- Improved backroom and shelf management, leading to the avoidance of out-of-
  stock situations
- Reduction of shrinkage due to theft, exceeding of expiration date, or perishing of goods
- Improved supply chain management with the introduction of the automated
  receipt, reducing costs and increasing reliability

On the technical side, the proposed solution architecture enables you to build an infrastructure with the following advantages:

- Ability to access latest master data from RFID software solution components
- Loosely coupled components due to SOA

With all these benefits, you can see why it makes sense to deploy the PIM-RFID Solution
Blueprint for Track & Trace for various business scenarios.

6.5.7 Alternatives and Possible Extensions

The New Product Introduction (NPI) process, as outlined in Section 6.3, can be improved if
combined with the Track & Trace Solution Blueprint.[37] For example, if new products are
introduced as part of special campaigns (e.g., for Christmas), then unless RFID and EPCIS
infrastructure is deployed, a company does not know if, or when, the products have arrived

---

37. A company that did this can be found in [26].

on the shelves in the targeted stores. As a consequence, the company does not know how many entities are in store, in the backroom, or sold. Integrating NPI and Track & Trace enables you to:

- Produce more instances of the product if it's sold more often and faster than anticipated.
- Launch additional marketing campaigns if the product doesn't sell as well as expected.
- Introduce the next new product after the previous product is sold out.
- Trigger alerts if products that are part of the NPI process are below previously agreed levels either in the backroom or on the shelf, to enforce compliance.

These benefits are just a few ways in which this MDM Solution Blueprint, together with the NPI Solution Blueprint, delivers additional value.

Conclusion

There are three key MDM Solution Blueprints in the Product domain that we have presented. Business optimization drives the selection of an enhanced NPI process using MDM. With the PIM-RFID Solution Blueprint for Track & Trace for an ePedigree, we showed you a solution driven by legal regulations (which also supports other business drivers, as explained). In Section 6.5.5, we showed relevant security aspects for MDM implementations using the PIM-RFID Solution Blueprint for Track & Trace.

In Chapter 7, we illustrate the business value of Master Data Management with MDM Solution Blueprints for the Customer master data domain.

References

1. *IBM developerworks patterns*. 2005. *IBM developerWorks*. Retrieved June 2007 from http://www.ibm.com/developerworks/patterns/.
2. Bloor, R., and Hanrahan, M. 2001. Bloor Research: Patterns of Experience—A Review of IBM's Patterns for e-business Initiative. *IBM developerWorks*. Retrieved June 2007 from http://www.ibm.com/developerworks/patterns/guidelines/bloor.pdf.
3. Endrei, M. et al. 2004. *Patterns. Service-Oriented Architecture and Web Services*. IBM Redbooks.
4. Microsoft Press Release on the Halo 3 launch. 2007. Retrieved September 2007 from http://www.microsoft.com/presspass/press/2007/aug07/08-09Halo3PreordersPR.mspx.
5. Global Commerce Initiative homepage. Retrieved March 2008 from http://www.gci-net.org.
6. "The impact of Global Data Synchronization on the Beer Industry. A guide for wholesalers & brewers," Edward Licul and Malia Hardin, IBM Software Group. ftp://ftp.software.ibm.com/software/integration/wpc/library/nbwaglobalsync.pdf.
7. *GTIN Allocation Rules*. Retrieved October 2007 from http://www.gs1.org/gtinrules/.
8. *Lists for GDSN certified data pools*. 2006 and 2008. Retrieved March 2008 from http://www.gs1.org/docs/gdsn/gdsn_certified_data_pools.pdf and http://www.gs1.org/docs/gdsn/gdsn_interoperability_report_0107.pdf.

  9. UDEX press release on UDEX alignment with GPC. 2004. Retrieved June 2007 from http://www.udex.com/cms/static/press_5.html.
 10. UDEX homepage. Retrieved July 2007 from http://www.udex.com/home.php.
 11. *UNSPSC classification.* 2008. Retrieved January 2008 from http://www.unspsc.org/.
 12. *UNSPSC alignment with GPC.* 2006. Retrieved July 2007 from http://www.gs1.org/docs/gpc/gpc_unspcs_integration_update.pdf.
 13. *GPC overview.* Retrieved August 2007 from http://www.gs1.org/productssolutions/gdsn/gpc/.
 14. Number of products in the Big Hammer Data pool. 2007. Retrieved October 2007 from http://www.bighammer.com/hdsupply/mktg_gdsn_faqs.html.
 15. *GS1 annual report 2005/2006.* Retrieved July 2007 from http://www.gs1.org/docs/publications/annual_report/2006/annual_report_2006.pdf.
 16. The EPCglobal homepage. Retrieved August 2007 from http://www.epcglobalinc.org/home.
 17. *EPCglobal provides an RFID Implementation Cookbook.* September 2006. Retrieved October 2007 from http://www.epcglobalinc.org/what/cookbook/.
 18. EPCglobal ALE specification. September 15, 2005 Retrieved October 2007 from http://www.epcglobalinc.org/standards/ale/ale_1_0-standard-20050915.pdf.
 19. EPCglobal website for details on RFID tag and RFID device reader standards. 2005. Retrieved January 2008 from http://www.epcglobalinc.org/standards.
 20. *EPC global tag encoding standards.* March 8, 2006. Retrieved October 2007 from http://www.epcglobalinc.org/standards/tds/tds_1_3_1-standard-20070928.pdf.
 21. The Shifting Sands of State Pedigree Laws. 2007. *Pharmaceutical Commerce.* Retrieved August 2007 from http://www.pharmaceuticalcommerce.com/frontEnd/main.php?idSeccion=576.
 22. World Health Organization (WHO) fact sheet on counterfeited drugs. 2006. Retrieved August 2007 from http://www.who.int/mediacentre/factsheets/fs275/en/.
 23. WHO launches taskforce to fight counterfeited drugs. 2006. *Bulletin of the World Health Organization,* September 2006, 84 (9). Retrieved August 2007 from http://www.who.int/bulletin/volumes/84/9/news.pdf.
 24. *EPCglobal pedigree standard specification.* January 5, 2007. Retrieved June 2007 from http://www.epcglobalinc.org/standards/pedigree/pedigree_1_0-standard-20070105.pdf.
 25. *EPCglobal Object Naming Service specification.* October 4, 2005. Retrieved June 2007 from http://www.epcglobalinc.org/standards/ons/ons_1_0-standard-20051004.pdf.
 26. David Sommer. 2007. *RFID Strategy—The RFID Revolution.* Retrieved February 2008 from http://www.industryweek.com/ReadArticle.aspx?ArticleID=13998.

Chapter 7

CDI-MDM Solution Blueprints

The core objective of this chapter is to introduce CDI-MDM Solution Blueprints for the Customer domain to complement the product master data-specific PIM-MDM Solution Blueprints described in the previous chapter.

This chapter is targeted towards an IT Architect audience and illustrates examples of CDI-MDM solutions in specific industry contexts that are based on the MDM Reference Architecture and MDM Architecture Patterns.

7.1 Introduction

In this chapter, we cover four CDI-MDM Solution Blueprints:

- The Master Patient Index Solution Blueprint for healthcare (see Section 7.2), which manages the sharing of patient data within the healthcare industry. The blueprint is a solution showing the operational method of use.
- The Cross- and Up-sell Solution Blueprint for banking and insurance (see Section 7.3) is another example for the operational method of use. In the context of this Solution Blueprint, we also show how to apply certain master data governance aspects such as ongoing master data quality profiling to detect degradation in master data quality.
- For fighting Theft and Fraud for banking and insurance, we show in Section 7.4 a CDI-MDM Solution Blueprint using the analytical and operational method of use.
- The last solution blueprint in this chapter applies multiple methods of use across multiple master data domains in the telecommunications industry.

We assume a reader of this chapter is familiar with the MDM Reference Architecture (Chapter 3) and the MDM Architecture Patterns (Chapter 5). Avoiding redundancy, security related aspects for MDM Solution Blueprints are only discussed once in the context of the Solution Blueprint described in Section 6.5.5 in Chapter 6. For the security concepts we assume the reader also read Chapter 4 on MDM Security and Privacy.

7.2 Master Patient Index Solution Blueprint for Healthcare

Before we investigate the business problems, let's clarify the players in the healthcare industry. There are **patients** demanding better and more healthcare services without an increase in cost. The services available are delivered through **healthcare providers** such as hospitals, pharmacies, and doctors. Finally, there are the **payers** for the services, the healthcare insurers. Healthcare insurers have relationships with patients and healthcare providers. These relationships are discussed in more detail later. The MDM Solution Blueprint discussion covers two areas: efficient management of patient information and efficient management of healthcare provider information. Thus, the solution can be applied to various problems in the healthcare industry. To explain the business problems, we took examples from the United States and from European countries such as Germany and Austria. Healthcare regulations and markets vary by country, so you need to adapt this MDM Solution Blueprint to the specifics of the country where it is deployed. The description of this MDM Solution Blueprint has a focus on healthcare providers. However, the other players can be affected as well because they might exchange patient information with healthcare providers deploying this solution.

7.2.1 Business Context

The healthcare industry grows at a fast pace and at the same time struggles with cost pressure, inefficiencies, and disgruntled customers—the patients. Healthcare is delivered to patients through discrete events of services: People get ill (when they need the services) and people recover (when they don't need the services anymore). This is a simplistic view—the authors are well aware that even if a person is not sick, the person might need prevention services to avoid illnesses; a basic example would be vaccines. In this flow of events, patient information needs to be shared between the patient, healthcare providers, and healthcare payers.

However, many healthcare providers such as hospitals struggle to share patient information effectively within internal departments, due to application silos, and with other providers or healthcare payers. Healthcare payers have comparable issues.

The difficulties in overcoming the current hurdles can be seen, for example, in Germany, where each German citizen should get an electronic health insurance card. In 2007, pilot programs were run and showed how difficult it is to establish easy, secure exchange of patient information where the patient can still control who can see what and when. The difficulty was mostly due to the proprietary nature and system incompatibilities of the existing IT landscape in the health insurer and health provider areas.

Since June 1, 2004, the European Health Insurance Card (EHIC) should have been available in all of the countries of the European Union (EU). In many of them, the EHIC has been introduced, but not all countries have been able to do so. The idea of EHIC is to simplify the process of receiving medical treatment in another country of the EU and to streamline bill-settling with the health insurance provider in the home country, in an effort to reduce costs. Pressure grows in the United States as well to introduce electronic health records.

Problems exist in other countries, too. In the United States, most health system purchases in hospitals are done on a departmental basis—neither considering interconnectivity nor interoperability and thus, for example, data sharing is difficult. When a doctor needs information, each department sends the data or hard copies via traditional means and no central system exists. Linking these systems together requires rationalization of data models, content, workflows, and security to prevent unauthorized viewing of patient data.

If a patient discloses patient information to the healthcare provider and the healthcare payers, these entities have custodial duties regarding the privacy of this sensitive information across all internal organizations involved (in addition to securing the IT systems processing it). The need to share patient information between healthcare providers and insurers must respect the privacy requirements of the patient (in many countries, patient privacy is protected by law). Ensuring privacy cannot be emphasized enough, and Section 4.7 in Chapter 4 describes key aspects of privacy, where compliance with such requirements is simplified if patient information is managed centrally with an MDM System.

Healthcare providers and healthcare insurers have been under tremendous pressure over the last several years to manage costs and provide effective patient care. There are many reasons for this.

When it comes to **member management**, that is, managing information about registered patients, the satisfaction rate among customers in many countries is usually low. Customers don't feel they get service and products tailored towards their needs. Healthcare providers are unable to respond because their customer information is duplicated across application silos with little consistency and cross-checking.

The most common cause of inconsistencies is duplicates in patient master data. Duplicates might be created, for example, in the emergency room in a hospital where third parties provide inaccurate identification information for an unconscious patient. Patient names also change due to marriage or divorce. Some people, like actors or musicians, might use aliases. And for these people, it is absolutely critical that their true name is protected. Similarly, this applies for people in witness protection plans—they also use alternate names. Also, many patients enter the patient care systems without names or any form of ID (an example is homeless people). Others will enter the hospital and deliberately hide their names. Furthermore, staff under time pressures who have a lot of patients waiting for admission might not perform a search with proper diligence and might create a duplicate. If there is more than one record for a patient, it creates a fragmented medical history.

External systems are another source of duplicates, where incoming patient records are not sufficiently checked and matched against the existing database. Sometimes matching fails due to the lack of standards (or lack of compliance with existing ones), or the patient record is incomplete or inconsistent. Insured patients are also more mobile today, both within the country and abroad. Legal regulations can interfere with the sharing of information, though. The bill from a doctor from another country, for example, likely has a different format than the bill from a doctor in the home country. In countries such as the United States, this is even a problem between states. In Europe, it is more common to work in another country and pay tax and health insurance in the country of origin. This mobility moves an existing fundamental problem more into the spotlight: Patients need to manage their own patient records and patient history. Thus, if a patient goes to a different doctor, the patient might know which other doctors have been visited and for what reason. Having a complete patient history that can be shared as the patient sees fit (for example, only a subset of the data) with specialized doctors is a problem today and becomes even more troublesome if you need to visit a doctor in another country.

Multiple records for the same patient in the system, with only partial patient history available, make a comprehensive view of a patient impossible. In the worst case, a doctor gets access only to incomplete patient history or to the wrong patient history because the patient could not be identified by the system unambiguously. As a result, the wrong treatment is possible, with dire consequences for the patient (negative impact on health condition) and the doctor (lawsuits, loss of doctor's license) alike. Today, patients also want access to their information through self-service Websites to check their bills or to change their address.

Finally, consider that even if matching detects potential duplicates requiring an Operational Data Steward to take care of them, this is a costly operation that should be avoided as much as possible.

Dialysis patients do not like the idea of going to the hospital every day or every second day to check the blood to see if the next dialysis is necessary. With the availability of a small handheld device capable of performing the blood test, the result can be transferred to the hospital. The handheld device would need for this a connection to a mobile phone (using Bluetooth for example), where a small application performs data transfer. If the blood test shows certain critical values, an alarm on the pager of a doctor notifies the doctor that an assessment is needed immediately, and a call to the patient to come to the hospital might follow. If there are no critical indications, the blood test result is added to the dialysis patient's record, where the doctor can review it later. The online health self-services require a consistent view of patient information across all systems as shown in this example.

In the business process area of **provider** and **partner management**, healthcare providers struggle to streamline processes with partners and insurers. Again, a lack of consistent treatment of provider and partner information by different applications causes an inability to see the full picture of a partner or a provider. Business optimization covering topics such as cost reduction or fostering relationships with premium partners and providers is almost impossible. Privacy is a big issue here as well when patient information is shared between healthcare providers and insurers. Sharing the fact that patient information is in a particular system could be a privacy concern in itself because it could impact a patient's health insurance premium. Features of analytical systems masking a patient record in such a way that it is anonymous are useful to prevent such a case. More details on solving privacy concerns can be found in Chapter 4.

Fraud, risk, and **compliance** mandate consistent access to patient information. Depending on the country, compliance with regulations (for details see Appendix C) such as the Sarbanes-Oxley Act (SOX), the Health Insurance Portability and Accountability Act (HIPAA), or PHI[1] might be required. To comply with the legal HIPAA requirement to match a claim with a National Provider Identifier (NPI) while processing the claim, consistent access to master data is required. The NPI is a ten-digit numeric identifier. The NPI is a HIPAA Administrative Simplification Standard. Details can be found on the homepage of the U.S. Department of Health and Human Services [1].

For the healthcare industry, there are several relevant standards and organizations:

- Logical Observation Identifiers, Names, and Codes (**LOINC**)
- **ACORD** refers to the ACORD XML Life, Annuity & Health Standards and the ACORD Life, Annuity & Health Data Model, which is used in the health industry (see [2] for details).
- Systematized Nomenclature of Medicine (**SNOMED**): SNOMED is a collection of medical terminology for pharmaceuticals, diseases, and so on that is organized systematically so that computers can work with it. A cardiologist might identify heart attack and myocardial infarction as the same thing, but for a computer system this is not obvious. The ambiguity problem of medical terms as shown by the example, is supposedly solved by SNOMED. More details can be found in [3].
- Integrating the Healthcare Enterprise (**IHE**, see [4]): IHE is an initiative by healthcare professionals and key players in the healthcare industry. The IHE defines the IHE Technical Frameworks such as the Cardiology Technical Framework.
- Open Healthcare Framework (**OHF**): OHF is an eclipse project aiming to simplify the usage of standards relevant for the healthcare industry by providing tools and frameworks. The OHF is, at the time of writing, in incubation; more information can be found at [5].
- Health Level 7 (**HL7**): HL7 is the most successful messaging standard in the healthcare industry that is used in the United States and other areas around the world. HL7 is an ANSI standard aiming to standardize the exchange of healthcare-specific information. The "7" in the name comes from the fact that "Health Level 7" refers to the topmost layer of the Open Systems Interconnection (OSI) protocol for the health environment. HL7 is often implemented using the Minimal Lower Layer Protocol (MLLP). More information on HL7 is available here [6].

Without consistent master information, fraud is also hard to combat and risks are not easy to mitigate. Applying standards makes it easier to share consistent patient information between healthcare provider and healthcare insurer. Thus, detection of members sharing the same member number or providers using the same tax identification number becomes easier.

---

1. PHI is the abbreviation for Protected Health Information, a federal law in the United States. It's also known as the HIPAA privacy rule. Under the PHI, all information that allows identifying a patient's name and address, as well as medications and health history, is covered. It affects all types of communication, such as verbal, paper, or electronic exchange of PHI information. PHI-protected information is not allowed to be considered in employment decisions.

These are two basic examples of misuse of the health system. In the United States, some healthcare providers are a significant source of fraud, causing increasing costs on the health insurer side and the patient side (indirectly, if the health insurer increases premiums for healthcare insurance contracts). The fraud is often caused by outpatient providers who over-charge, double charge, or create bills for patients they didn't see. Providing the capability to detect such healthcare provider fraud helps to mitigate this problem.

Claims management business processes are affected by poor member and provider man-agement as well as by inefficiencies in the business area of fraud detection. If you are not able to identify your member and the services the member is entitled to according to the subscribed health plan, then it is difficult to detect fraud. Similar reasoning applies for set-tling bills with providers and partners. Not being able to deal with fraud is costly—fraud is estimated to grow at a double-digit rate until 2012, causing tremendous financial loss to healthcare providers if not dealt with.

Medical management covering administration or disease management suffered over the last few years as well. Administrative costs are now rising, depending on the country, at an average rate of more than 10%. Premiums cannot be raised further—they have reached their market limits. It is expected that if the premiums do rise further, the number of people with-out health insurance will rise as well. In the United States in 2005, 16% percent of the population—that is, 47 million people—were already without health insurance. For details, see the report [7] from the National Coalition on Health Care. According to this report two reasons are:

> [...] Rapidly rising health insurance premiums are the main reason cited by all small firms for not offering coverage. Health insurance premiums are rising at extraordinary rates. Over the past five years the average annual increase in inflation has been 2.5 percent while health insurance premiums for small firms have escalated an average of 12 percent annually. [...]

> [...] Even if employees are offered coverage on the job, they can't always afford their por-tion of the premium. Employee spending for health insurance coverage (employee's share of family coverage) has increased 143 percent between 2000 and 2006. [...]

So if healthcare insurance premiums continue to rise, even more members will drop out of the health insurance system entirely, and this fosters a black market for medicines and health services. Other social costs are productivity loss due to illness or even higher treatment costs if an illness grows into something more serious because it wasn't treated early enough. So there is no way to balance the rise of administrative costs with increased premiums. The cost pressure needs to be solved with different measures. It also has to be taken into consideration that the increasing expected average life span has contributed to increased costs in some countries. Due to the scattered nature of master information on health insurance members, accurate demand for services or products cannot be predicted. The lack of predictability com-plicates the negotiation of appropriate contracts between payers and providers. Also, reach-ing the right customers through successful marketing is hard if a health insurer or a healthcare provider does not know, or respect, customer preferences or if insurers and providers do not have access to household information and other relevant attributes.

Business processes regarding **New Product Introduction,** covering products such as medicines and services (for example, a new drug or cancer therapy), became a focus area as well due to increased competition in the health market. If a provider can offer distinctive, high-quality services and products faster than the competition, it can obtain a competitive advantage.

From the six business areas explained, the MDM Solution Blueprint focuses on the first five. We exclude the New Product Introduction business area, which is covered in Section 6.3 in Chapter 6. Also, from a business perspective, the first five areas are currently causing the most problems, so we are focusing on those.

The following applications can be found within the healthcare industry in the business areas mentioned earlier:

- Electronic patient record (typically known as **eCard**): In 2005, the eCard was introduced by the federal government in Austria. The purpose of the eCard is threefold: It provides administrative electronic signatures for eGovernment applications, advanced electronic signatures for standard applications, and a social insurance signature as the entry card for healthcare services. Therefore, health insurance providers need to be able to process electronic patient records. For more details see [7].
- Bar-coded Medication Management (infrastructure to manage medicine identified through bar codes)
- Clinical Information Systems (systems used to provide medical care; an example would be an application providing guidance on certain procedures)
- Computer-Based Provider Order Entry (CPOE places order based on rules if medicine stock is below certain boundaries)
- Digital Picture Archiving System[2]
- Clinical Data Repository (could be a department-specific data store)
- Point-of-Care Decision Support (systems in various departments of a hospital to access patient information locally to make decisions)

To address the business demand, innovations in processes and IT help to transform healthcare to become more member-centric instead of transaction-centric, as it was in the past. Services and products need to be tailored towards customer needs, and service capabilities need to be aligned with this shift in the business model. A foundation for a 360-degree member view needs to be provided by an MDM System for patient information. The MDM System[3] functions as the *Master Patient Index* (MPI), giving this MDM Solution Blueprint its name. A Master Patient Index provides the following basic functions:

- Management of patient information.
- Authoritative source of patient information.

---

2. For example, if a dentist takes an x-ray, the picture can be streamed directly to a computer where the dentist can examine it. All these pictures need to be stored and associated with the patients to whom they belong. Therefore, the information from the Digital Picture Archiving Systems must be linked with the master patient information in the Master Patient Index system.

3. We will use MDM System and MPI system throughout this section interchangeably. The MPI system is also known as Enterprise Master Patient Index (EMPI).

- Operational data store providing real-time access to patient information.
- Automatic and manual data cleansing capabilities.
- Enforcement of privacy settings: Patients in many countries have the right to restrict access to their patient information record. Usually the patient has to explicitly grant a healthcare provider or healthcare insurer access to the patient history in whole or in part. This right is usually only disabled, for example, if an unconscious patient with a life-threatening condition is brought to the emergency room of a hospital. For providers and payers alike, it is mandatory to ensure that the privacy is guaranteed as asked for by the patient. Failure to do so might have, depending on the country, more or less dire legal consequences.
- Management of patient identities:
  - Cross-reference patient identities for system interoperability: Patient Index Cross-Referencing (PIX) is a process where different identifiers for the same patient from different health organizations are linked to a single master patient record in the Master Patient Index.
  - Patient identities can be used across the healthcare community.
- Management of patient relationships
  - Household relationships to support family health insurance plans
  - Relationships to healthcare providers
  - Relationships to healthcare payers

The MPI System delivers patient master data information to relevant applications just presented. With a Master Patient Index in place, a healthcare provider or hospital can improve patient service, differentiating itself in the market because it can tailor the offerings toward the patient's needs with a full understanding of the patient history and household relationships for family health insurance policies. With improved and streamlined services, cost reduction is possible. Also, with the newly gained ability to identify a patient accurately and have access to the full patient history, the quality of treatment a doctor can provide increases and chances for maltreatment are reduced—a benefit for both patients and doctors. A master data system for patient information also allows complying with legal regulations. Compliance with legal regulations (see Appendix C) is significantly streamlined with an MPI system in place.

7.2.2 Relevant Business Patterns

As we saw earlier, we have the following business patterns:

- The B2C business pattern: Healthcare providers interact with their members through a variety of touch points such as local offices, self-service websites, or mobile care infrastructure.
- The B2B business pattern: Health insurance companies interact with healthcare providers such as a hospital.
- The Information Aggregation business pattern: For a Line of Business user at a health insurance provider, information aggregation needs to exist to get access to member information where information about the member from a variety of sources is aggregated. Examples of information sources are records from the hospital, the dentist, the pharmacies, the family doctor, and the eye specialist.

7.2.3 Relation between Business Patterns and Architecture Patterns

Based on the business needs presented, we suggest implementing the following architecture patterns for this MDM Solution Blueprint:

- Initial Load pattern to build the MDM hub
- Transaction Hub architecture pattern, because patient information needs to be accessed in real-time
- ESB and messaging architecture patterns to feed patient information into downstream systems
- Transaction Interception pattern needed for synchronously accessing the MDM System to leverage capabilities such as duplicate prevention from application systems that might create patient master data

For pure cross-referencing of patient identifiers across the different business systems, an MDM System built using the Registry Hub or the Coexistence Hub pattern might suffice. On the one hand, if you intend to fulfill the operational real-time access requirement to patient information with consistent treatment of all relationships, then the Transaction Hub pattern is capable of delivering this functionality. On the other hand, based on some of the implementations of the MPI solution we know, the MDM System can be deployed using only the Registry Hub pattern. One reason usually is that healthcare providers like hospitals often only have limited IT skills in-house and thus the MDM Solution has to run with as little complexity and maintenance effort as possible. In these cases, less business value was accepted to keep the operational IT costs lower.

7.2.4 MDM Solution Blueprint Overview

The IT infrastructure of a healthcare provider such as a large hospital (or a network of hospitals that outsources IT) is the environment that we assume as the context for this MDM Solution Blueprint. We have three types of components for this MDM Solution Blueprint, as shown in Figure 7.1:

- The mandatory components (1) to (7) in light-grey are components needed to build and run the MDM System (e.g., (5)), interact with it (e.g., (3)), or represent the MDM System (4), which is the Master Patient Index (MPI) system. The core functions of these components were explained in the MDM Reference Architecture. Key components for this MDM Solution Blueprint of the MDM System (4) are the Hierarchy and Relationship Management component and the Data Quality Management component. The Hierarchy and Relationship Management component is important for managing relationships between family members and between patient and healthcare insurer. The Data Quality Management component is crucial for standardizing names and addresses and for preventing duplicates. Therefore, these components should have the special attention of an IT Architect designing a concrete solution of this type and performing software selection for the MDM System. The Information Integration Services component (5) provides most of the functions for implementing the Initial Load pattern when building the MDM System. Furthermore, depending on the software selection for (4) and (5), it might

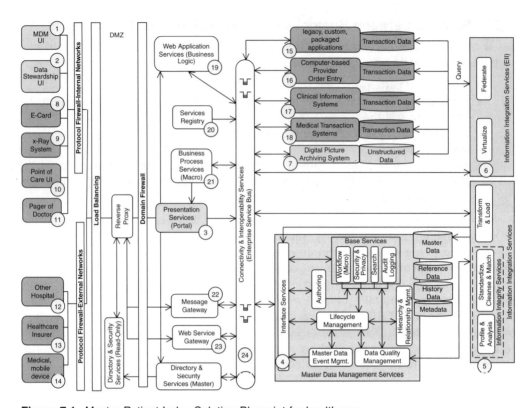

Figure 7.1 Master Patient Index Solution Blueprint for healthcare.

also provide data integrity functions invoked by the Data Quality Management component after the MDM System has been deployed. The components (1) to (7) are required for both healthcare providers and healthcare insurers.

• The dark-grey components (8) to (18) are components specific to this solution (healthcare providers such as large hospitals). Note that most of these components would not appear in the case of a healthcare insurer. There are systems such as Clinical Information Systems (17), Medical Transactions systems (18) that track what care has been provided, and Computer-based Provider Order Entry (16) or other legacy or pre-packaged application systems (15) for billing and other tasks. Because this infrastructure grew historically, each of these application systems might store the patient information with a different key. Besides all of these internal applications, external applications require some patient information as well. There might be another hospital (12) offering a specialized healthcare service not available in-house. If a patient needs such special treatment, it would be desirable if necessary patient information can be exchanged. Because healthcare insurers have a valid interest in paying only for real and insured patients, some minimum set of patient information needs to be exchanged here as well when the hospital sends a bill for settlement.

- The white components (19) to (24) are either optional components or components where integration might or might not be needed, depending on the existing IT infrastructure and the concrete functional and nonfunctional requirements for the MDM Solution. In an SOA landscape, (20) represents the Service Registry and Repository (SRR). If it is present, master data services can be published to this repository. An enterprise-wide Business Process Services component (21) orchestrates business processes across IT systems. The Message Gateway (22) and the Web Service Gateway (23) are optional components for secure access to backend systems by external systems. Security requirements and technology used to integrate the internal backend systems with the external systems define if none, one, or both of these components is required. The Connectivity and Interoperability Services (24) can be implemented using a full-blown ESB product (examples can be found in Section B.2 of Appendix B) or simpler means. ESB or Messaging patterns used to implement this solution blueprint rely on the infrastructure provided by (24). An IT Architect designing a concrete instance of this solution needs to consider what is already available for (24) in the IT infrastructure. An integration of the MDM System (4) with all legacy applications (15) might or might not be needed.

Let's start the explanation of this MDM Solution Blueprint with some observations regarding the data model that are important. There are other data related topics such as historical data, data lineage, and data validation that are outside the scope of the discussion presented here but likely relevant in a concrete production deployment. Different systems (omitting now the difference between internal and external systems) use different identifiers. Examples are:

- Social Security Number (SSN)
- Healthcare Insurance Number
- Passport number
- IHE/HL7 identifier, according to these standards
- Identifier (longitudinal health record) provided by the federal government unique for each citizen
- A generated (technical) key

The usage of such an identifier is an indication for the shift from the "transaction, medical incident" based perspective on patients towards a patient-centric view. Some governments plan to have valid identifiers for the entire life (so called "cradle to grave" identifiers).

An IT Architect has two choices: either selecting a unique, existing identifier as primary identifier or designing a new (and yet another) identifier that remains the same for the entire life of the patient (if such an identifier is not yet available). This is the traditional business or application key versus surrogate key data modeling discussion. A surrogate key is system-generated, unique system-wide, never reused, and cannot be changed by the application. The value of the surrogate key has no semantic meaning. Thus, using a surrogate key such as the longitudinal health record is recommended.

In any case, the data model needs to have the flexibility to accept an identifier as primary identifier (if it is a new one, it has to be generated using a certain algorithm ensuring uniqueness while initially building the MDM System that functions as an MPI system). Also, the data model needs to be able to accept any number of identifiers as "secondary" identifiers for cross-referencing purposes, one of the key business objectives for an MPI system.

Another area of the data model that is crucial is the relationship management. Basically, there are two types of relationships: person-to-person and person-to-organization. Examples for person-to-person relationships are:

- Person A and person B are spouses.
- Person A is a child of person B.
- Person A is the legal guardian of person B.
- Person A is the payer for the health insurance of person B.

We do not distinguish between unidirectional (e.g., is child of) and bidirectional (e.g., spouses) relationships here. We recommend using only MDM software capable of supporting both types, though. Relationship information is important as well in determining who is a patient's spouse, parent, legal guardian, personal physician, lawyer, and so on. For example, depending on the country, there might be legal regulations stating that in the intensive care unit only the spouse of a person or a direct family member has visitor rights. Or the hospital offers as special service that in the maternity unit only the father can visit the mother to provide a tranquil environment for better recovery after childbirth. Other examples of why managing family relationships is important is the ability to determine hereditary illnesses, knowing who to call in an emergency, or who is authorized to make treatment decisions in case of a minor.

In some countries, if a patient is in a irreversible coma or in a permanent vegetative state, connected to life-support devices for an extended period of time, and the doctors assess the likelihood of recovery to be close to zero, a spouse or court-appointed guardian has the right to decide to terminate treatment and life support. In such cases, in particular, you want to be sure that relationships are managed appropriately. In the first two examples, your customers (the patient and the relatives) might be unhappy if you wrongly turn them down or allow too many visitors in. In the last case, the decision is irreversible—certainty regarding the relationship status is essential here. Sometimes an MPI system must be able to record and store information about who is not allowed to see the patient record—due to a (family) relationship. Examples would be cases of spousal abuse or underage pregnancy.

Instances of person-to-organization relationship are the patient-to-health provider (e.g., hospital) and the patient-to-health insurer relationship. The latter relationship information is needed by the hospital to settle bills for the costs associated with medical treatment (if this relationship information is not available, the patient might be billed directly). The Master Patient Index system should thus have an appropriate relationship management infrastructure.

During admission into a hospital, a patient might be recorded with a different name than one that was used before (examples are nicknames, maiden names, naming children based on relationships that vary by culture, misspelling, alternative spelling, transliteration of foreign names). Thus, name standardization functions and duplicate prevention functions are essential for the MDM System. For example, *"Bob"*, *"Rob"*, *"robert"* should all find the first name *"Robert"* due to name standardization routines. Also, functions for address standardization should be implemented as well, because address attributes are often used by the matching algorithms for duplicate search. Duplicate prevention functions based on deterministic or probabilistic matching algorithms (see Chapters 3 and 9 for details) are critical for an MPI solution.

Because patient information is very sensitive information, only users with appropriate privileges should be able to see relevant parts of the patient record, which demands that appropriate security features are present in the MPI system. Patient data from patients with AIDS or cancer requires special protection from insurers in order to avoid misuse and inappropriate utilization on the insurer side. Insurers still need to see some of the patient data, but usually the patient needs to authorize the release depending on local privacy legislation. It cannot be stressed enough that an audit trail for all patient information is critical because this information is very sensitive. You need to be able to prove who saw what or who changed which piece of patient information and when.

Due to the heterogeneous system landscape in a healthcare environment, the systems are often connected using HL7 standard-based messaging infrastructure. If MDM software supports business service invocation at the interface services layer through JMS messages with certain XML structures as input and output format, you will need fast XML transformations from HL7 to the input XML format for the MDM System and from the output XML to the HL7 format. We suggest deploying powerful XML transformation software components as part of an enterprise service bus (24) supporting HIPAA, HL7, and other relevant standards for the healthcare industry. As best practice, we also recommend to deploy functions validating the messages. Message validation has to be done for several versions of HL7. When we wrote this book, HL7 versions 2.3.1, 2.5, and 3.0 were in use and required validation mechanisms because not every hand-coded conversion to the HL7 format for a message requesting a service is necessarily free of mistakes.

After this initial overview of some key components and aspects of the MPI solution, we now provide some example flows through the logical architecture overview of this MDM Solution Blueprint. We assume that the Connectivity and Interoperability component (24) in Figure 7.1 provides messaging infrastructure as part of an ESB software product. The five flows are based on the MDM Solution Blueprint component model shown in Figure 7.1 and presented in two component interaction diagrams (Figures 7.2 and 7.3). We describe these flows individually:

> **Flow 1:** Creation of a new patient record
> **Flow 2:** De-duplication of patient records initiated by an Operational Data Steward (for this MDM User Role, see Appendix A)
> **Flow 3:** Medical services for a patient treated in the hospital
> **Flow 4:** A patient using mobile medical treatment services
> **Flow 5:** Update of patient information on eCard when leaving the hospital

The first flow shown in Figure 7.2 starts when a patient comes to the hospital administration and checks in, based on the advice of a doctor (such as an orthopedic surgeon) who thinks that perhaps surgery (e.g., replacement of a knee joint) is necessary. A member of the hospital staff (a so-called ***admittance staff member***) would then use an MDM User Interface (1). The MDM User Interface (1) could be portal-based (2), leveraging Web application services

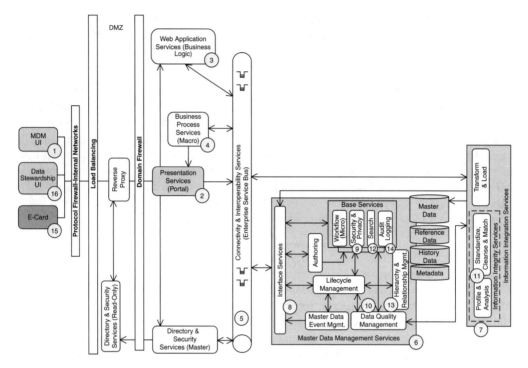

Figure 7.2 Component Interaction Diagram for the first two flows creating and collapsing a patient record.

(3) or business process services (4), or both. The admittance staff member would execute the following steps for admission of a patient:

1. Issue a **Patient Demographic Query (PDQ)** based on last name (e.g., Smith), date of birth (e.g., 07-23-1949), and gender (e.g., male) in order to retrieve the unique patient identifier. With the unique patient identifier, the patient record could be loaded. If a patient record is found, the admittance staff member could update it if needed (for example, new health insurance provider since the last visit or new last name due to marriage).

2. If there is no patient record found, the hospital employee decides to create a new patient record.

If a patient requires admission at a hospital, this usually triggers a so-called **Admission Demographic Transaction (ADT)**. The HL7 standard has several events of this type, for example, when an update on an existing patient record occurs, that would be an "A08" event, whereas the creation of a new patient record would be an "A01" event.

1. If a PDQ request is submitted (1) and all of the necessary application logic (provided by (3) and (4)) is completed, an inquiry is routed by the ESB (5) to the MDM System used as a Master Patient Index (6). While in the ESB, an XML transformation from HL7 to the XML input for (6) is occurring.

2. This transformation can be performed by the ESB (5) itself or by a transformation service provided by the Information Integration Services component (7).

3. The inquiry reaches the Interface Services Layer component (8).

4. Assuming the requester passes through authorization (9), the input data (here the name "Smith") would undergo name standardization (provided by (10) or (11)) and any other cleansing and standardization functions required.

5. Finally, the MDM System (6) would perform the search (12) and return the result (which on the way back is converted from the XML output from the MDM System to HL7 by (5) or (7)).

6. After the application logic consumed the HL7 message, it would display the result to the admittance staff member on the MDM User Interface (1), using the presentation services (2).

If the patient record was found for a subsequent update, additional functions like the relationship management functions (13) of the MPI system (6) might be invoked as well.

For the creation case of a new record, a similar path through the systems would be followed, with involvement of the Hierarchy and Relationship Management component (13) to create at a minimum the person-to-organization relationship between the patient and the healthcare insurer.

Whenever there is a creation or a change of sensitive patient information, many healthcare enterprises strive for compliance with the IHE standard Audit Trail and Node Authentication (ATNA). ATNA protects connections between systems sharing patient information.

ATNA compliance demands that the MPI system have a complete audit trail (14) on all transactions involving sensitive patient information. Also, the MPI system has to use certain procedures for node authentication for communications with other systems.

Note that the process will still look similar in the event that the patient has an eCard that stores the patient record. In this case, a patient eCard reader (15) would be used to read the patient demographic data (and history, if permitted). In this case, the application logic triggered by the MDM User Interface (1) would need to read this information from (15) and display it to the admittance staff member. A PDQ is still needed to find out whether or not the patient has been at the hospital before. If a previous visit occurred, the patient record can be loaded; otherwise, the record has to be created (which can leverage any information the patient is willing to share from the patient eCard). If the patient has been at the hospital before and an update is necessary, this could happen exactly the same way regarding the MDM System. However, regarding master data on the patient eCard, the choices that might be available are to update the card right away or upload the complete visit history (including, for example, name updates done at admission time) to the eCard at checkout time when the patient leaves the hospital.

The second flow shown in Figure 7.2 is triggered by an Operational Data Steward. If the MDM System marked two or more patient records as suspects (they have a certain degree of similarity but require human intervention to determine a match or non-match), an Operational Data Steward using a Data Stewardship User Interface (16) investigates whether or not the suspect records are the same or not. Through (16) an inquiry is sent to the MPI system

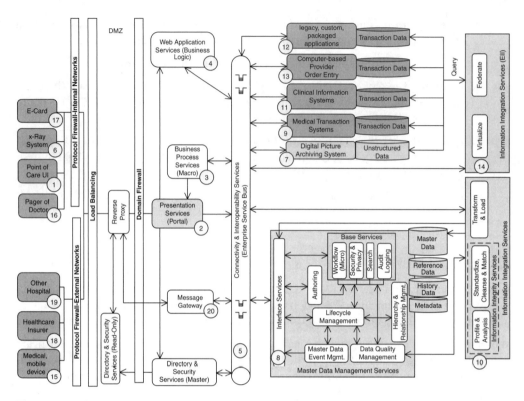

Figure 7.3 Component Interaction Diagram when patient receives medical treatment in hospital.

to retrieve the suspect records. After investigating and comparing them, the Operational Data Steward might trigger a collapse operation of two or more patient records into a single patient record. The change of master data due to the collapse has to be propagated to all systems that used at least one of the collapsed records. A messaging pattern such as a Publish/Subscribe architecture pattern could be one way to notify all dependant systems about the change.

The third flow shown in Figure 7.3 assumes the patient checked into the hospital. The doctor investigated the patient and decides that several medical services[4] are required for further diagnosis of the cause of the illness, including a blood test (for which blood was taken) and X-rays of the knee joint:

> **1.** The doctor will submit these transactions using a Point of Care application UI (1), which uses presentation services (2). The UI can run on a handheld device such as a personal digital assistant (PDA) or a Tablet PC the doctor carries along into the patient's room. The doctor can initiate the transactions also from a personal office after the examination performed on the patient is complete.

---

4. A request of a medical service is another type of transaction called "Order" and any finding or record as output of the medical service is called a "Result".

2. Business process services (3) and application logic (4) triggered by the input from the Point of Care UI (1) then initiate the appropriate next steps. A specialist in the X-ray department of the hospital receives a notification to the local instance of the Point of Care UI (1) through the ESB (5) to pick up the patient for X-ray investigations. Another nurse could be notified to deliver the blood of the patient to the hospital department responsible for blood tests.

3. A radiologist using another instance of the Point of Care UI (1) opens the patient record to look at the X-ray request. Then the X-ray is taken and each picture from the X-ray System (6) is annotated with information such as "view taken" before the radiographs are sent to the Digital Picture Archiving system (7). The application used by the radiologist department might store some pieces of the patient information (name, address, health insurer number) with a different local patient identifier. Thus, this application might have the need to be changed according to the Transaction Interception pattern. The Intercepting business function is needed to perform a cross-referencing request to the MPI system (8), known as **Patient Identifier Cross-referencing query (PIX)**. With this approach, the lookup of relevant local identifiers for the Digital Picture Archiving system (7) or the Medical Transaction system (9) is done to create requests to these systems with the right local identifier. Note that whenever a message is sent to the MPI system (6) message transformations from HL7 to the XML understood by (6) and back are required. The transformation services are either part of the built-in capabilities of (5) or are provided by the Information Integration Services (10).

4. After the medical service for X-ray investigation is finished, the radiologist completes the medical service by finishing it in the Point of Care UI (1). Upon completion, this initiates, through appropriate business process services (3) and application logic (4), the creation of transactional data in systems such as the Medical Transaction system (9), the Clinical Information systems (11), and any other application systems (12). If certain resources are depleted, the business process services (3) might invoke some replenishment services provided by the Computer-Based Provider Order Entry Services component (13). Similarly, the blood test medical service can be implemented.

5. After all results for all medical services ordered are available, the doctor who requested them could then use the Point of Care UI (1) again to load the patient record along with all results for analysis. Loading the patient record includes the retrieval of the radiographs from the Digital Picture Archiving system (7) and the result from the blood test either stored in the Clinical Information system (10) or in the Medical Transaction system (9). If the infrastructure is based on Web services and the federated access is needed, the Federation component (14) of the Information Integration Services component could be used. In this case, an information service performing this federation could be implemented based on standards such as WS-Federation [see 8]. In this case, we recommend reading this paper [9] on how this standard can be used, showing examples from the healthcare industry.

Federated access patterns can be deployed with other technologies too. The example presented was an example in the context of deploying this MDM Solution Blueprint in an SOA environment that uses Web services as technology for the service implementation.

Healthcare delivery to patients in a hospital is just one channel. Another channel is given by the fourth flow (see Figure 7.3), which is initiated by a patient from home.

1. In this example, a mobile medical device (15) for blood tests is used by a dialysis patient. After the blood test is taken, the patient uses the mobile medical device, perhaps in conjunction with a mobile phone, to transfer the results to the hospital. There, they are received by an appropriate system such as Medical Transaction system (9), Clinical Information system (11), or another application system (12).

2. The results are automatically analyzed, and if critical boundaries are exceeded, an alert is automatically sent to a pager of the doctor (16) who can respond immediately requesting, for example, that the patient comes to the hospital as soon as possible.

3. Otherwise, the doctor will see the results when browsing through the patient records as part of the daily check at the Point of Care UI (1).

The fifth flow (see Figure 7.3) starts after the patient leaves the hospital and the patient eCard might require an update[5] regarding the patient history.

1. In the administration facility of the hospital, an employee would use the MDM User Interface (1) after the patient inserted the patient eCard into a reader device (17).

2. Through (1), the staff member would trigger an update of the patient history.

3. Again, you can use federated access (14) to multiple data resources to get relational (e.g., Medical Transaction system (9)) and unstructured content (e.g., Digital Picture Archiving system (7) for the radiographs).

4. After all of the data for the patient history is retrieved, it would be stored on the patient's eCard (17).

Patient information might need to be exchanged with healthcare insurers (18) to settle bills or shared with other hospitals (19) that provide specialized medical services. If messaging infrastructure is used for the exchange, a Message Gateway (20) might be used for security reasons.

Healthcare providers such as hospitals, as well as the healthcare insurers, might aim for fraud elimination. In this case, analytical systems capable of anonymous identity resolution (see Chapter 3) might be needed. Section 7.4 shows how to integrate such systems.

---

5. Depending on the processes, some updates might have been applied earlier. Applying the missing deltas or performing a final check to see if all medical information created or changed while in the hospital is completely loaded onto the eCard is common.

7.2.5   Advantages

When the Master Patient Index Solution Blueprint is implemented, the business and technical advantages are:

- **Consistent patient information**
  - Fewer mistakes in patient information could save lives. An example would be to find the right patient record in an emergency room situation showing that the patient has a penicillin allergy.
  - Electronic patient record enables patients to decide who is allowed to see what and when. With a complete patient history at hand, medical errors can be reduced because the doctors' basis for medical decisions is significantly improved.
- **Tailored healthcare services and products**
  - Differentiation and thus competitive advantage through innovative products and services is enabled.
  - Patient and customer satisfaction increases (one of the key metrics of performance in many healthcare organizations).
  - Cost reduction on both sides through standards-based exchange of relevant information between healthcare payers and healthcare providers, removing costly point-to-point integrations with proprietary solutions from the past.
- **Reduction of administrative costs**
  - Loss due to fraud is reduced because it gets more complicated for patients to make illegal claims with healthcare insurers.
  - Healthcare insurers and healthcare providers can optimize their business relation. For example, healthcare insurers can foster relations with healthcare providers who deliver above-average results for patients, meaning that the treatment is on average done less expensively or with more lasting results. Computing these metrics require consistent patient information on both ends.
  - Premiums could decrease as the cost to insure decreases.

Overall, patients, healthcare providers, and healthcare insurers benefit from this MDM Solution Blueprint.

The success of applying this MDM Solution Blueprint depends to a certain degree on whether or not sufficient organizations participate in applying the relevant standards as well as the adoption rate. For example, in Germany during the pilot phase, some of the regions lacked success because not enough healthcare providers and healthcare insurers adopted the new technologies or were not able to adopt it fast enough. Depending on the country and healthcare system, not all benefits can be obtained by applying this MDM Solution Blueprint.

It might require a few years until everyone is used to the new technology (patients to eCards, healthcare providers and healthcare insurers adopting and complying with HL7 and other relevant standards) and therefore gaining the maximum benefits. Many software vendors do not have an end-to-end solution yet and focus on only one player in the healthcare value chain. Nonetheless, this MDM Solution Blueprint certainly provides some measurable benefits for an individual player. For example, a hospital is enabled to share patient information across all internal departments consistently, and patient treatment is improved if duplicates are removed, thus allowing doctors to see a more comprehensive patient history. For healthcare insurers, this MDM Solution Blueprint provides insight into their member base, allowing for medical management improvements that enable member-centric health plans with appropriate services and products and efficient marketing and member-relationship management.

7.2.6 Alternatives and Possible Extensions

In this blueprint, we focused on customer information. As outlined in Section 7.2, new product and service introduction is also something healthcare companies would like to improve. The Master Patient Index Solution Blueprint could be enriched by combining it with the New Product Introduction Solution Blueprint, as described in Section 6.3 of Chapter 6.

Another possible extension is the PIM-RFID solution for Track & Trace (see Section 6.5 in Chapter 6 for details), where healthcare providers such as hospitals and pharmacies use an ePedigree infrastructure (also explained in Section 6.5 in Chapter 6) to ensure dispensing to patients only medicine that was not adulterated or counterfeited.

Finally, proven models[6] for healthcare providers simplify the deployment of MPI solutions. Depending on the vendor, they might include not only a data model but also annotated glossaries for terms from business and technical perspectives that enable efficient, unambiguous communication between the two user groups, which will bridge a gap otherwise potentially causing misunderstandings.

7.3 Cross- and Up-Sell Solution Blueprint for Banking & Insurance

The MDM Solution Blueprint presented in this section is motivated by the need in the financial services industry for optimizing the revenue stream and thus, at the end of the day, improving the bottom line. The MDM Solution Blueprint described is based on implementations we did with several of the largest financial institutions in the world. The solution offers tremendous business value and is a proven solution deployed in large-scale implementations with more than 150 million customer records.

7.3.1 Business Context

In many countries, the banking industry is often fairly consolidated. Many of the larger banks cannot acquire more banks in their own country due to antitrust law enforcement. Thus, growth in their home market has to be organic. The first obvious approach is getting more customers—in such a market this means acquiring them from the competition, which is difficult. The second is to reduce the average customer churn rate by improved customer care, which is not easy either. The third is to expand the business with existing customers through improved cross- and up-sell deals. The last item also helps with the previous one

---

6. See Section B.1 in Appendix B for available accelerators using proven data models.

because the more products a customer has with a financial institution, the less likely it is that the customer leaves.

Cross-selling means to sell additional products or services to a customer. Sometimes cross-sell offers provide discounts on individual products if the customer purchases a bundle of products instead. For the company selling these bundles, the likelihood of losing a customer to a competitor often decreases with an increase of products sold to the same customer.

Up-selling is a term for the practice of suggesting higher-priced products or services to customers who consider a purchase. An example for an up-sell approach is trying to sell a faster computer than the one considered by the customer.

In some regions and countries of the world, the population is steady or declining. For example, Germany[7] is predicted to decline from an overall population of currently around 80 million people to 60 million people by 2050. Therefore, in light of this loss of customers due to the demographic outlook, banks in markets like these have the possibility of growing organically, by improving their sales into the existing customer base.

In the insurance sector, depending on the country or region, there are products such as family legal costs insurance. This type of insurance can only be sold once to an entire family. However, if only one member of a family is covered by a policy in this area, there is a cross- and up-sell opportunity to upgrade the legal costs insurance to a contract covering the whole family. The challenge here is to have the right relationship information at hand. Close to the concept of relationship information is the concept of roles. Let's assume a bank has a customer with a savings and a checking account. The same person is also the CEO of a medium-sized company and requires a number of financial products for the company. Obviously, for a successful cross- and up-sell strategy, you need to know which products belong to which of his roles for the right needs analysis.

In a market where merger and acquisitions took place, customer master data de-duplication can lead to cost savings and to cross- and up-sell opportunities when, for example, household information is properly established and managed after data cleansing. Making an acquisition into a successful takeover, like the Dresdner Bank acquisition of Allianz Insurance or cooperation between banks and insurance companies that significantly improve the bottom line, requires the ability to find and identify cross- and up-sell opportunities. In an acquisition, as well as in a cooperation case, having high-quality household and role information available is the key element to identifying these opportunities.

The examples given have two things in common—business growth is dependent on the ability to identify cross- and up-sell potentials, and the examples are all drawn from the finance industry. The issues discussed in this MDM Solution Blueprint are applicable in other industries as well.

Let's now examine what a cross- and up-sell strategy on the business side requires from the IT department. The basic piece of information required is clearly the customer master data record itself, which should be accurate, consistent, have standardized names and addresses,

---

7. For details on the demographic development in Germany for the next decades, see [10].

and be compliant with any other business and integrity rules required. In addition, the over-all set of customer records should be free of duplicates.[8] Otherwise, your company might spend efforts trying to sell the same natural person products twice with no real chance for success and potentially even annoying the client by sending advertisements multiple times for products already bought. Also, access to the customer information should be real-time across all channels. A call center employee as well as a bank clerk should be able to find and look up the right customer record quickly.

As you have seen with the third example presented, creating and maintaining household information is also very important for a successful cross- and up-sell strategy. One of the banks we worked with had a dedicated wealth management department that was very unhappy because of the following incident. The bank had an extremely wealthy customer living in the country where the bank had its headquarters. The customer had a grand-daughter who went to study in another country and had a credit card application declined at a local subsidiary of this bank. The vice president of the wealth management department got a call from the very angry grandfather. The vice president's concern was to avoid such cases in the future at all costs, because he did not want to lose his most valuable customers due to the lack of high-quality customer information. There was a business case for him for an enterprise-wide CDI solution able to deal with complex household information—the basis for avoiding cases like the one described. Such household information can be fairly complex if there is a need, for example, to manage three generations with many interconnections.

Let's examine now the concept of roles further. A traditional life insurance product allows for at least three roles:

1. The role of the party who is actually paying the premium, the owner or payee

2. The role of the party for which the insurance applies, the insured

3. The role of the beneficiary

The minimum number of natural persons required for such a contract is two, assuming the first two roles are the same party. With the given real-world example we showed how fast role networks can become more complex. Consider the following: Assuming that the three roles are mapped to three different persons and each of them has only this one relation to your business based on the role. Which one of them is your customer? Is it the person for whom the contract applies? Or is it the person who pays the premium? Or are all three "customers"? Assuming you would consider all three customers, would this still hold true if the payee specified in the preferences, "Please do not contact me at all with advertisements or other marketing material either online, by mail, by phone and so on"? So the point here is that based on roles there could be the need to approach customers differently regarding

---

8. While deploying CDI solutions, often up to 35% or more duplicates were found. You can easily see that business decisions and forecasts in the past on such poor customer information were not based on a good foundation.

cross- and up-sell initiatives. Although this is an insurance example, it can easily be generalized to other industries if you consider the different roles a party can play on a contract such as "subscriber," "member," "agent" or "lawyer".

With this last thought we enter the next area relevant for important cross- and up-selling: customer service. One crucial aspect of customer service and customer service satisfaction is the ability to comply with the detailed preference and privacy requirements across all lines of business in a company. If your call center employee calls a customer to offer a new product and the customer specified explicitly not to be called regarding new product offers, the chance of a successful sale are clearly significantly reduced. The customer might even be angered because the preferences were ignored and consider a switch to a competitor. Similar considerations apply for privacy wishes of customers. Recalling that a customer might have multiple roles, such as private person, CEO of a medium-sized company, and so on at the same time, for which a completely different set of preference and privacy rules might apply, you can easily see that the area of customer service can become fairly complex as well.

Let's consider another aspect: A couple decides to move in together in one of their apartments. Statistically, there is a certain probability that this couple might marry in the near or mid-term future. Statistics show that a marriage is often followed by a honeymoon trip or the acquisition of a house, requiring a mortgage. The scenario described is what we call a *life event* that shows that certain master data changes like a change of address might present cross- and up-sell opportunities.

We assume that each individual of the couple is a customer at the same bank. However, they do not have any products or services jointly. Thus, their relation is unknown for the bank. Now one of them is calling to notify the bank about a change of address but not mentioning a reason. However, when the call center representative entered the new address, a screen pops up stating that another customer is already living at that same address. Thus, the call center representative might ask immediately: "I notice another client of ours lives at this address. May I ask what your relationship is with this person?" Depending on the answer, the call center representative could then offer additional services like a small loan or ask the customer if an appointment with a financial advisor of the bank would be desired to obtain financial advice on the new life situation.

There are other types of relevant events such as *financial events*, *watch list events*, *risk events*, and so on. An example for a financial event would be a so called *fixed-term* or *time deposit*. If a bank consultant were notified automatically four weeks before a time deposit is due, he or she could talk to the customer about how the money should be invested next. With this proactive approach, it is more likely to generate new business than waiting until the due date, at which point the customer might transfer the money to another bank due to a lack of knowledge about the latest financial products available at the bank.

A watch list event should also be triggered if a match is found either during creation of a new customer or during the periodical comparison of customer records against watch lists. Processes regarding legal requirements in the area of anti-terror financing could potentially be started. Additionally, in this case an event should be triggered that might indicate to stop all cross- and up-selling activity, mitigating financial risks by reducing or at least not increasing business with such a customer. A risk event would be if the credit rating of a customer changes based on periodical checks with credit rating organizations like Equifax in the United States, Schufa in Germany, and so on. If the credit rating significantly improved, additional cross- and up-selling should be triggered. If it measurably dropped, all cross- and up-sell activity should be at least paused to mitigate potential financial losses with the customer. Note that risk events could also be created if a customer acquires more products from the same bank, such as adding a mortgage to the existing product portfolio.

Eventing infrastructure combined with *business rule engines* can be used to determine what should happen if certain events occur and thus provide a good way to identify and act on certain cross- and up-sell situations.

At the time of writing this book, one of the authors was performing consulting work with a very large company where the CIO invited three vendors to present their CDI offerings. One of the requirements this CIO spelled out explicitly was that the winning offering would need to have all customer attributes physically stored in the CDI hub database. The reason for this requirement was that monolithic application systems often compute a subset of these attributes within the application by reading multiple records and perhaps drawing data from a variety of sources. The disadvantage is that there is no single place where you can manage the data model because it is partially buried in application code and thus not manageable from a lifecycle consideration point of view. The CIO was pleased to see that a comprehensive data model physically persisted in the offering shown. The product is listed in Appendix B. Similar requirements were encountered many times before. A concrete, materialized data model provided by an MDM Systems offers a single place to manage all lifecycle aspects of the master data model. The materialized master data model is a key enabler for master data governance.

Summing up, from the business consideration we made, an IT solution for customer information should have at least the following abilities in order to adequately support a cross- and up-sell strategy:

- A comprehensive data model providing a 360-degree view of the customer, with the ability to adequately handle relationships, roles, preferences, privacy, and so on, where all attributes are materialized in the CDI system
- Name and address standardization:[9] It is hard to initiate a life event based on finding an address match if matching is impossible due to low-quality address data.
- Real-time transactional service interface in order to easily, consistently, and efficiently access customer information from all applications used by the bank or the customer through a website that provides fast access to it
- Duplicate check mechanism to prohibit duplicates from being entered into the system, with appropriate support for operational data stewards[10] to split and collapse operations on suspected duplicates

---

9. See the product Appendix B for data integrity tooling.
10. This user role is described in more detail in Appendix A.

- Event and business rules infrastructure
- Integration with external data providers such as watch lists and credit rating companies
- Not discussed explicitly, but also very crucial, particularly for this use case and this industry, is *scalability*.[11]

7.3.2 Relevant Business Patterns

Center stage in this MDM Solution Blueprint is the business pattern "Cross-sell and Up-sell," as exemplified in the previous section. It should be deployed for all possible customer touch points with the company, such as a website, a call center, or a local branch of the bank. Applying this business pattern across all channels drives related business patterns and leads to the following business pattern list:

- Cross- and Up-sell business pattern
- Business-to-Customer (B2C) pattern given by self-service on the website of the financial institution
- Business-to-Business (B2B) pattern

The B2C pattern is needed because online banking is common today where users can perform financial transactions and change some demographic information (e.g., their address). Also, there are some relevant instances of B2B patterns, for example, the cooperation between financial institutions and credit rating companies such as Dun & Bradstreet (USA) or Schufa (Germany). Another example is when banks resell insurance company products.

7.3.3 Relation between Business Patterns and Architecture Patterns

Based on the business patterns presented, and from the architecture patterns presented in Chapter 5, the following are required:

- Initial Load pattern
- Transaction Hub pattern
- MDM-CRM Integration pattern
- ESB and messaging patterns

The Initial Load pattern is a key element during Master Data Integration when the MDM System is built. The Initial Load pattern captures the key steps such as data model discovery, profiling, extraction, cleansing, standardization, transformation, and load of master data from a variety of sources into the MDM System. The Transaction Hub pattern is needed because many applications require real-time write access to the customer information, among them the online banking application, the call center application (often a CRM application), and the application that the bank clerk works with when customers show up at the

---

11. The largest companies in the financial industry we are aware of deployed CDI hubs managing significantly more than 100 million customer records. Just providing access to customer records in this magnitude is a challenge; doing this in real time is an even greater challenge. For scalability and performance results in this magnitude, see [12].

local branch. An MDM System deployed with the Registry Hub pattern or with the Coexistence Hub pattern will not be able to deliver this. The first one would require extensive lookup and transformations because it does not have a materialized data model, and the second one is often read-only.

Architecture patterns such as messaging patterns (e.g., Publish/Subscribe pattern) are needed, depending on the options available for integration of the internal and external systems that either consume (e.g., call center application) or enrich (e.g., external credit ratings) master data.

7.3.4 MDM Solution Blueprint Overview

For the cross- and up-sell MDM Solution Blueprint for banking and insurance, we propose the architecture shown in Figure 7.4 in the component model view, based on the enterprise MDM component model view presented in Chapter 3.

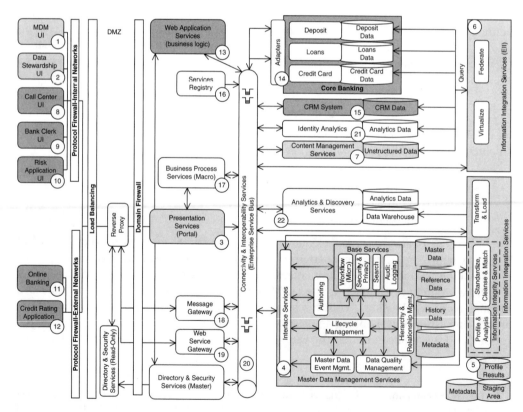

Figure 7.4 Component model of Cross- and Up-Sell Solution Blueprint for banking and insurance.

There are three types of components:

- The mandatory components (1) to (7) in light-grey are components needed to build and run the MDM System (e.g., (7)), interact with it (e.g., (3)), or represent the MDM System (4). The core functions of these components were explained in the MDM Reference Architecture. Key components of the MDM System (4) are the Master Data Event Management and the Hierarchy and Relationship Management component. The Master Data Event Management component triggers life events, risk events, or financial events. The Hierarchy and Relationship Management component is responsible for managing household information. For this reason, an IT Architect performing the software selection for the MDM System should pay special attention to the features for these components. The Information Integration Services component (5) provides most of the functions for implementing the Initial Load pattern when building the MDM System. Furthermore, depending on the software selection for (4) and (5), it might also provide data integrity functions such as address standardization and verification or name standardization invoked by the Data Quality Management component after the MDM System has been deployed. In the scope of this MDM Solution Blueprint, we describe a certain task of the data governance board—defining, measuring, and enforcing data quality metrics (for details, see Chapter 9). Therefore, the profiling and analysis services that are part of the Information Integration Services component (5) are a critical area requiring special attention during software selection.

- The dark-grey components (8) to (15) are specific for this solution. The core banking systems are represented through (14). Often, this is a CICS environment on z/OS mainframe. COBOL applications can also be encountered in this environment. Through adapters, these systems are connected to the Connectivity and Interoperability Services component (20). It is expected that during the next few years the adapter component will be updated to support new technologies such as Web services. The applications running in the core banking area run the crucial business functions such as deposit transactions, credit card transactions, and loan transactions. The MDM-CRM integration pattern, as described in Chapter 5, can be used to integrate the CRM system (15) with the MDM System (4).

- The white components (16) to (22) are either optional components or components where integration might or might not be needed, depending on the existing IT infrastructure and the concrete functional and nonfunctional requirements for the MDM Solution. In an SOA landscape, (16) represents the Service Registry and Repository. If it is present, master data services can be published to this repository. An enterprise-wide Business Process Services component (17) orchestrates business processes across the IT systems. The Message Gateway (18) and the Web Service Gateway (19) are optional components for secure access of backend systems. The Connectivity and Interoperability Services (20) can be implemented using a full-blown ESB product (examples can be found in Section B.2 of Appendix B) or simpler means. ESB or Messaging patterns used to implement this MDM Solution Blueprint rely on the infrastructure provided by (20). An IT Architect designing a concrete instance of this solution has to take into consideration what is already available for (20) in the IT infrastructure. The Identity Analytics component (21) is optional, depending on the requirements for determining the true identity of a customer. An integration of the MDM System (4) with the data warehouse system (22) might or might not be needed. If it is needed, see Section 8.2 in Chapter 8, which explains how to do this integration.

As shown in Figure 7.4, internal users such as Operational Data Stewards (2), Call Center Representatives (8), Bank Clerks (9), and Risk Officers (10) use the enterprise portal for their work. Based on the job role, the components shown in the portal will vary: All of them will share some portlets to work with customer information managed by the MDM System. This shared set of portlets for master data is summarized in the MDM User Interface (1). The Operational Data Steward may have specialized portlets for performing data governance-related tasks. The portlets are bundled in the Data Stewardship User Interface (2). The Call Center Representative might have additional portlets (captured as Call Center User Interface (3)), invoking some functions of the CRM system. The Bank Clerk might have specialized portlets for collaboration needs (e.g., calendar or e-mail) or other dedicated business functions, summarized as Bank Clerk User Interface (4). Similarly, the Risk Officer might have a dedicated set of portlets in a Risk Application User Interface (5). Customers of the bank use online banking through an Online Banking User Interface (11) hosted on a portal to change their address or to take care of their finances and perform appropriate financial transactions. Periodic or on-demand checks with credit rating services (12) require integration of another external component. These operations require access from outside the company or integration with external services.

We assume that due to the CRM application design, it cannot be modified in such a way that it no longer stores master data. Therefore, there will be some redundancy between the master data in the MDM System and the CRM system. Therefore, the CRM persistency and the Master Data Repository of the MDM System require synchronization.

The processes presented next are simplified versions of production processes and are used to show how the core components can interact and relate closer to the banking industry. Industry Models covering comprehensive process models for banking and insurance can be found in Section B.1 in Appendix B.

We look at these flows in several component interaction diagrams:

Flow 1: Customer signs up for a bank account at a local branch.

Flow 2: Customer changes address through an online banking application triggering a life event where a service representative calls.

Flow 3: A business rule in Lifecycle component triggers event where customer is called by service representative.

Flow 4: A business rule in Lifecycle component detects risk event, pushing an alert to a risk officer using the risk application UI.

Flow 5: A bank clerk creates a new customer. A search with some data fields returns customers living at the same address and a discussion with the new customer at the counter reveals that these are family members. Then the bank clerk is able to add the appropriate relationships right away. The MDM System updates the records of the other family members, adding the relationships automatically as well, which may then automatically trigger a life event.

Flow 6: The bank clerk creates new customer, where the new record is either a duplicate or a suspect and is collapsed by an Operational Data Steward using the Data Stewardship User Interface. The action performed by the Operational Data Steward is an example of the fact that keeping the master data quality high is important—sending marketing material multiple times to the same customer due to having multiple instances of this customer in the IT systems could cause customer churn. Customer churn eliminates any chance to cross- or up-sell.

Flow 7: This flow describes how to measure and enforce master data quality metrics.

The first flow starts when a new customer shows up in a local branch of the bank. Figure 7.5 shows the interaction of the components:

1. The Bank Clerk uses the MDM User Interface (1) to collect the customer information. This could be done through a browser invoking the presentation services (2) hosted on a portal.

2. The presentation services (2) trigger the business process "create new customer" provided by the Business Process Services component (3).

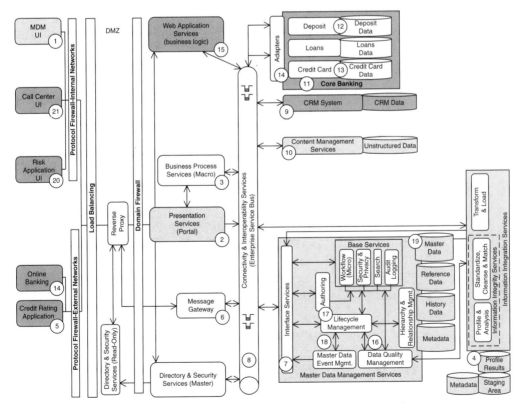

Figure 7.5 Component interaction diagram for the first four flows.

3. The Business Process Services component (3) invokes an information integration service from the Information Integration Services component (4), performing name standardization, address standardization, and verification. The information integration service is used to ensure the check credit service in the next step has the best possible information.

4. The Business Process Services component (3) invokes a check credit service from an external credit rating provider (5) based on the customer information provided. The Message Gateway (6) would be used if the invocation of the check credit service is based on messaging infrastructure.

5. Assuming the credit score retrieved was above minimum requirements, the Business Process Services component (3) invokes a create customer service from the MDM System (7).

6. As part of saving the new customer record, the MDM System (7) asynchronously publishes a message to a message queue to send the new customer record to the CRM system. A success result is returned to the Bank Clerk.

7. The Connectivity and Interoperability Services component (8) routes the message to the CRM system. Depending on the capabilities of the MDM System, the Information Integration Services component (4), and the Connectivity and Interoperability Services component (8), there are three options for transforming the data to the format expected by the CRM system:

   • The MDM System produces it in the right format. The advantage of this would be that neither the Information Integration Services component (4) nor the Connectivity and Interoperability Services component (8) need appropriate transformation capabilities in this case. The downside of this approach is that whenever the CRM data model changes, the MDM System needs modification. This tight coupling might not be desirable.

   • If the MDM System does not produce it in the right format, the second option is that the Connectivity and Interoperability Services component (8) invokes appropriate information integration services from the Information Integration Services component (4) to accomplish the required transformations.

   • The third option is usually available, if a full-blown ESB product is used for the Connectivity and Interoperability Services component (8), as offered by most of the products in Section B.2 of Appendix B, then the ESB could take care of the transformations.

8. The CRM system (9) receives the message and saves the new customer record locally.

9. The Bank Clerk takes a copy of an identification document (depends on the country and can be a driver's license or a passport, for example). A separate process takes care of associating this copy with the customer record and possibly storing a digital version in a content management system (10), updating the MDM System (7) with a link to it.

10. The Bank Clerk then enters all relevant information for a new bank account and a credit card triggering the appropriate updates. If the credit check service in step 4

returned a good result, there would be an opportunity to cross-sell additional products or offer a more expensive credit card with higher credit limits for the customer.

11. The presentation services (2) used in the previous step request the appropriate business services (3). The business services (3) trigger the creation of the account and credit card in the MDM System (7).

12. When the account and credit card is created in the MDM System, the MDM asynchronously publishes messages to update the deposit application (12) for a checking and savings account and the credit card application (13) for the credit card. Both applications are part of the core banking system (11). The Connectivity and Interoperability Services component (7) routes these messages to the adapters (14) that connect these applications to all other applications in the IT environment. A success message is returned to the Bank Clerk.

13. Now the customer can deposit (or withdraw) money that would trigger transactions processed by the core banking system (11).

Flow 2, also shown in Figure 7.5, starts with the customer using the online banking application (14):

1. The customer using a browser invokes the presentation services (2) that trigger the online Web application services (15).

2. The customer enters a change of address and submits it. The online Web application services (15), using their business logic, invoke a change address service from the MDM System (7) that is routed there by the Connectivity and Interoperability Services component (8).

3. The change address service executed by the MDM System invokes an address standardization and verification service in the Data Quality Management component (16). Depending on the capabilities of the MDM System, this can be a built-in function or provided by the Information Integration Services component (4) and invoked from there by Data Quality Management component (16).

4. A step in the change address service provided by the MDM System is due to deployed business rules in the Lifecycle Management component (17): Check whether or not another customer is living at the same address also. If this is the case, a *life event* has to be triggered by the Master Data Event Management component (18).

5. We assume that the address change triggered such a life event, which means at least one more customer lives at the same address. Thus, the Master Data Event Management component (18) triggers the creation of a message for the CRM system (9) indicating an alert should be sent to a Call Center Representative (in addition to the address update for the CRM system keeping the master data in the CRM system in sync with the MDM System). After all steps of the change address service are completed, the address change is saved in the Master Data Repository (19) of the MDM System (7). When returning the result of the address change through the presentation services (2) to the Online Banking User Interface (14), advertisement for additional, appropriate products could be added supporting cross-sell and up-sell strategies. Thus, if a customer changes something through the self-service Online Banking User Interface (14), triggering events applicable for cross- and up-sell offers could be exploited right away.

6. The place where the message triggered by the Master Data Event Management component (18) is transformed can vary—but is in principle within the same boundaries as outlined in step 7 in the first flow. Thus, that discussion is not repeated here.

7. After the CRM system receives the message regarding the address update and the alert, it saves the address change locally and creates an alert for the Call Center Representative.

8. When the Call Center Representative uses the Call Center User Interface (21) the next time, this alert appears in a "ToDo List" portlet indicating that the customer should be called to set up a meeting to discuss if the new situation might require additional financial advice or services. If a meeting is scheduled, the meeting details are sent to the CRM application (9) thus giving the financial institution a chance for seizing cross- or up-sell opportunities based on this life event.

Flow 3, shown in Figure 7.5, starts in the Lifecycle Management component (17) of the MDM System:

1. A business rule in the Lifecycle Management component (17), executed once a day, indicates that an alert should be triggered if a fixed-term deposit in the case of a bank or an endowment insurance[12] is due in three months. The idea is to notify a Call Center Representative to call the customer asking the customer for an appointment to discuss reinvestment options.

2. Similar to the second flow, the Lifecycle Management component (17) would interact with the Master Data Event Management component (18) if such *financial events* are detected, to send out the appropriate alerts to the CRM system (9).

3. As before, the place where the message triggered by the Master Data Event Management component (18) is transformed can vary—but is in principle within the same boundaries as outlined in step 7 in the first flow.

4. From the CRM system, the path would follow similar steps as in the case of the *life event,* which means that due to alerts the Call Center Representative would call the customer for an appointment.

The crucial point to observe is that the financial institution has a chance to talk to the customer before the money is invested elsewhere. The customer might also be pleased to be reminded that this event is coming up and thus may believe himself or herself to be in good hands because the financial service provider is offering advice on investments early on.

---

12. An endowment insurance is a special type of life insurance. Depending on the age, it can be typically signed for five, ten, fifteen, or twenty years. The difference from standard life insurance is that if the contract owner lives at the end of the agreed period, the contract owner gets the agreed money. If not, a beneficiary specified in the insurance gets the money.

Flow 4, also shown in Figure 7.5, starts in the Lifecycle Management component (17) of the MDM System. What we discuss now would be a very basic example for risk mitigation.

1. The bank or insurance company would run periodic checks on the credit rating of all customers, invoking external credit rating services (5).

2. The credit scores are submitted to the MDM System (7) as updates.

3. A business rule that is invoked as part of these updates in the Lifecycle Management component (17) checks if a credit score is below a minimum value.

4. In such a case, the Lifecycle Management component (17) would interact with the Master Data Event Management component (18) to trigger a *risk event.*

5. Similar to the life event and financial event described earlier, a message with the risk event alert would be sent to the Connectivity and Interoperability component (8) before the MDM System (7) saves the new credit rating as an update to an existing customer record. Regarding data transformation, similar reasoning as outlined in step 7 in Flow 1 applies.

6. As a result of the risk event notification, a Risk Officer would see an alert in a "ToDo list" when the Risk Application User Interface (20) is used the next time. The Risk Officer must then decide, based on the customer history and the current credit score, what needs to be done.

This example optimizes profit by mitigating losses through early warnings about customers potentially in trouble.

Flow 5, shown in Figure 7.6, highlights the importance of identifying and managing household and relationship information and starts when a customer shows up in the local branch of a bank.

1. The Bank Clerk uses a browser to invoke the presentation services (2) showing the MDM User Interface (1). Entering the basic information provided by the customer, the Bank Clerk submits a search.

2. Through the Connectivity and Interoperability Services component (3), the presentation services (2) invoke a search customer service of the MDM System (4), which is provided by the Search component (5).

3. The presentation services (2) renders the result of the search: The search customer service returns that the customer does not yet exist, but some other customers live at the same address who share the same last name.

4. The Bank Clerk can then ask if the customers found are relatives. The Bank Clerk enriches the customer information in the record currently under creation by adding household and relationship information.

5. After all relevant information is entered, the create customer business process is invoked from the Business Process Services component (6), as described in the first flow. Therefore, again, name and address information is standardized using information integration services (7). The credit scoring (8) is retrieved through the

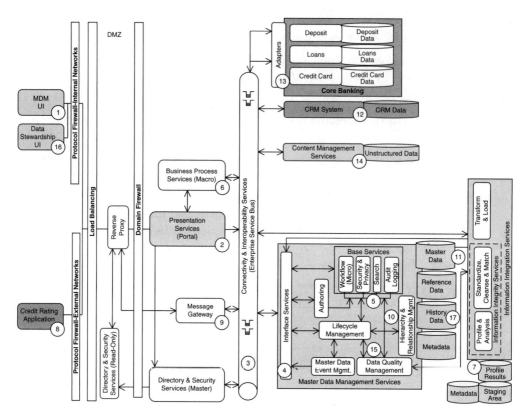

Figure 7.6 Component interaction diagram for flows five and six.

Message Gateway component (9) and then the master data service adding the customer is invoked. This time, the Hierarchy and Relationship Management component (10) would establish the relevant relationships of the new customer record. Note that for symmetric relationships such as *spouse-of*, having the relationship is enough for both parties in the relation. In an asymmetric relationship such as *parent-of*, between a parent and a child, when looking up the other party, the opposite relationship needs to be displayed. For a child in this case the *child-of* relationship information needs to be returned and for the parent of this child, the *parent-of* relationship has to be returned.

6. The MDM System (4) would save the new master data record in the Master Data Repository (11).

7. Asynchronously, the necessary updates are also sent to the consuming application systems such as the CRM system (12) and Core Banking Component (13). Regarding the data transformations, the same reasoning as outlined in step 7 in flow one are applicable. Also, the copy of the identification will be stored using a service from the Content Management Services component (14).

With the management of the relationships as outlined, it is ensured that when the related customer records are looked at later, the relationship information is there as well. Worth observing here is that as soon as the relationships are established, for the several customer records for which the relationships were established a more comprehensive view regarding cross- and up-sell opportunities becomes available as well as potentially unknown risks due to those relations.

Flow 6, shown in Figure 7.6, also starts when a Bank Clerk uses the MDM User Interface (1) to create a new customer. We reduce the explanation to the key steps of interest and leave out some intermediate steps already explained in previous flows.

1. The Bank Clerk enters the information for a new customer in the MDM User Interface and triggers the known customer creation process.

2. However, this time, the Data Quality Management component (15) of the MDM System (4) detects that the customer is, with regard to the critical data fields,[13] an exact match to an existing customer. Now there are two choices, depending on the software used for the MDM System (4): The first option would be to consider the create customer to be an update on an existing customer. In this case, if a value in the noncritical attributes provided to the master data service is different from what is stored, then this attribute would be updated on the existing record with the new value. The second option would be to return the existing customer with a notification that this customer already exists. Then the Bank Clerk can ask the customer at the desk if the record found is indeed the appropriate customer information and discuss what needs to be updated.

3. As an alternative to the previous step, consider the following case: The Data Quality Management component (15) of the MDM System (4) detects that the customer is, with regard to the critical data fields, similar to existing customers but not identical. Now two cases are possible:
   - The first case assumes the match score indicates high similarity with at least one customer; the record of the very similar customer could be returned and the new customer is not yet created. In this case, the Bank Clerk has the opportunity to talk to the customer still at the counter to find out if this very similar customer record does indeed belong to the customer. If yes, the customer data for the new customer could be disregarded and the record found could be used by updating the existing record. If the very similar record belongs to a different customer, the Bank Clerk can resubmit the customer information after setting a flag that is an indication for the MDM System that the customer record should be persisted without duplicate checking. Because the duplicate checking has been done, this would be a valid "override."
   - The second case assumes that no match score existed that indicated at least one customer record had high similarity. However, at least one customer record had

---

13. Critical data fields and different matching algorithms are explained in Chapter 9.

a lower match score, which indicated some similarity. In this case, the creation of the customer record would succeed—however, the Data Quality Management component (15) would mark the new and the existing record that has some similarity as suspects in a suspect table.

4. Later, assuming a suspect has been created, an Operational Data Steward using the Data Stewardship Interface (16) would see the two customer records marked as suspect. After careful analysis following relevant procedures provided by the data governance board on data quality (see Chapter 9), the Operational Data Steward might trigger the collapse of the two suspect customer records into a single record through the Data Stewardship Interface (16). The collapse operation is a master data service provided by the MDM System (4) using appropriate functions from the Data Quality Management component (15). As part of the collapse operation, several things happen: First, a survivor record is created in the Master Data Repository (11) of the MDM System (4), and the History Data (17) is updated accordingly. The survivor record has best-of-breed attributes from both original records as explicitly selected by the Operational Data Steward or as implicitly selected based on the collapse rules implemented by the MDM System. In the History Data, the time of the collapse is recorded as well as the information on which former records the new customer record is based. Finally, appropriate notifications to all dependant systems storing local copies of the master data (such as the previously mentioned CRM system (12)) have to be sent out to these systems to keep them in sync with the MDM System.

The last of the seven flows requires some preparation before it can be explained. As part of the Master Data Integration (MDI), several things had to be done (the relevant pattern is the Initial Load pattern described in Chapter 5). We present only a high-level description of each step:

1. The source data models of all systems from which master data was extracted had to be discovered. The data models have to be saved in a metadata repository.

2. The data quality in the source systems had to be **profiled.** Possible quality issues found are (and the list is not complete):
   • Duplicate records
   • Lack of standardization (e.g., customer name, address, product names, phone numbers)
   • Values in wrong columns (a phone number in a street field)
   • Violated semantics (a customer marked as child with an age of 37)
   • Anomalies in value distribution (an example would be 4711 times the same Social Security Number, where a value for a Social Security Number is expected only once)

3. The data governance board has to define the master data quality metrics based on business requirements for the MDM System as well as the **harmonization** process. Here, harmonization means how the master data as part of the MDI process is extracted, cleansed, standardized, de-duplicated, transformed, and finally loaded into the MDM System in such a way that the master data satisfies the master data quality metrics after this Initial Load. Examples for these metrics could be:

- Each Social Security Number appears only once.
- Phone numbers in the United States comply with (XXX-)YYY-ZZZZ, where XXX is the area code and YYY-ZZZZ is the phone number without area code.
- A customer marked as "child" in the profession column cannot have a value > 18 in the age column.

4. When the master data is loaded into the MDM System and before the MDM System is used in production, the profiling is done again to achieve two things:
   - Verify that the loaded data satisfies all master data quality metrics.
   - Establish the **master data quality baseline** of the MDM System, which is stored to be able to compare later on new measurements against the baseline and trigger alerts.

The two steps are needed to enable the following:

- Data lineage and impact analysis if a data model in any of the source systems is changed. Data lineage and impact analysis is impossible if the data models of the source system are not available in a metadata repository in such a way that the effect of changing a source data model attribute on the MDI infrastructure used for delta loads into the MDM System at a later time is traceable.
- After the MDM System has been built, it is difficult to know if the construction was successful regarding compliance with master data quality metrics without the baseline report of the master data quality. Furthermore, without a baseline, it is hard to find out if the master data quality improves or declines over time. Timely alerts on unexpected master data quality issues would also be impossible.

The next flow is part of the data governance processes on measuring and enforcing master data quality, as outlined in Chapter 9. It describes how periodically profiling the MDM System could be implemented and how alerting to Operational Data Stewards can be done if the profiling results indicate that certain master data quality metrics have been violated. The process is shown in Figure 7.7.

1. The Business Process Services component (1) periodically invokes the master data quality profiling process. The period length depends on business requirements.

2. Through the Connectivity and Interoperability Services component (2), a profiling service is called from the Information Integration Services component (3).

3. The profiling service (4) uses metadata regarding the master data quality metrics to enforce (5).

4. The profiling service (4) connects to the Master Data Repository (6) of the MDM System (7) and performs the profiling. Profiling often consists of column analysis to determine value distribution, cross-column analysis for semantic profiling, and cross-table analysis verifying, for example, that foreign key relationships are correct.

5. The profiling service (4) stores the result in the Profile Results database (8) upon completion. Then the profile service (4) compares the current profile result to the baseline on the master data quality. The baseline can be either the initial baseline or a new one if the data governance board raised or lowered the bar based on previous measurements reports and current business requirements.

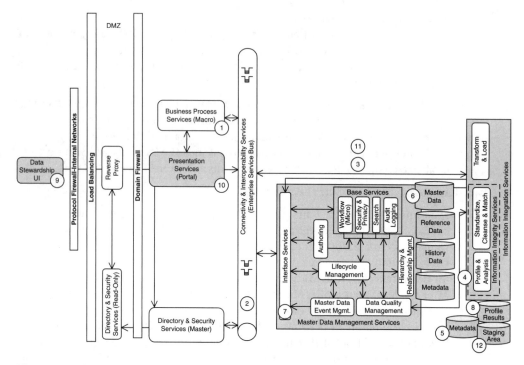

Figure 7.7 Component interaction diagram showing master data profiling and master data quality metrics enforcement.

6. When comparing the current profiling results with the baseline, the profiling service (4) detects that the master data quality degraded, an alert is created. The degradation could be caused by a change either in the ETL infrastructure loading deltas into the MDM System that was not expected or an external data provider used for enrichment suddenly delivering data with less quality.

7. Depending on the business policy, the alert could be an SMS to notify an Operational Data Steward for immediate action or an alert noticed by an Operational Data Steward when using the Data Stewardship User Interface (9) again.

8. The Operational Data Steward could then invoke presentation services (10) using services (11) from the Information Integration Services component to review the profiling results, analyze them as well as the root cause for the master data degradation, and then trigger appropriate actions.

Note that master data quality metrics change over time with changing business requirements, which require changes in the profiling infrastructure. These changes are governed by procedures of the data governance board. Also note that profiling creates a measurable IO load on the MDM System (7). Assuming the high-availability option of the database of the MDM System has a hot standby with read access, the profiling could be executed against the standby database. The profiling could also run in a window where the load of the MDM

System is low. Otherwise, the MDM System sizing with respect to IO throughput needs to be sufficiently large to allow the profiling IO load at the same time. Another option is to asynchronously publish any change on the MDM System (7) to a staging area (12). Then the profiling could run against this copy of the Master Data Repository (6) instead, thus reducing the IO load on the MDM System (6).

With these examples, we have provided an overview of how core components in this MDM Solution Blueprint are related to each other and how cross- and up-selling for bank and insurance companies could be improved. From a financial company perspective, if there is also an interest in fighting financial crime, this MDM Solution Blueprint is not comprehensive enough. Therefore, a more comprehensive blueprint is described in Section 7.4.

7.3.5   Advantages

This MDM Solution Blueprint provides a real-time foundation for customer master data for financial companies with the following business benefits:

- 360-degree view of a customer with full insight into household and other relationship information.
- Optimization of cross- and up-selling.
- Single place to secure customer master data.
- Improved customer loyalty and retention by ensured compliance with their privacy and preference settings across all touch points.
- Improved insight in customer base across all lines of business through high-quality de-duplicated customer master data.
- Reduced costs for marketing because marketing flyers are only sent to real opportunities for cross- or up-sells. (On a side note, consistent customer master data prevents sending multiple times the same flyer to the same customer due to duplicates or to the same household due to lack of household information—the latter might be caused by poor data quality for addresses—thus reducing costs further).

On the technical side, you enable service-oriented architecture with an MDM System, which provides customer master data along with relevant business services, that is flexible and easy to extend if new business requirements mandate a change in the data model or a master data business service. You also reduce operational costs by the takedown of silos of customer master data, thereby reducing the complexity of your IT infrastructure.

7.3.6   Alternatives and Possible Extensions

The MDM Solution Blueprint has a core focus on customer master data. It can be extended by including product master information (this would benefit the product development functions of a financial institution) and vendor master information (if an insurance company cooperates with banks or independent insurance agents by selling their insurance products, the banks and agents would thus be vendors for the insurance companies).

Managing customer data with this solution, a company is also well positioned for growth through an acquisition and merger strategy—if this is still possible for the financial institution. An MDM System built with the Transaction Hub pattern is a very good base into which customer information from an acquired company could be merged. Because an MDM System of this type distributes master data into all other required operational systems, the synergies of the acquisition materialize faster and more effectively because you can act right away on the cross- and up-sell potential of the newly acquired customer base.

Bringing products to market faster as well as more flexibility in establishing new product bundles is a new trend we observed while working with financial companies. Thus, the New Product Introduction Solution Blueprint presented in Chapter 6 might be a useful extension supporting the cross- and up-sell strategy of this MDM Solution Blueprint.

7.4   Fraud and Theft Solution Blueprint for Banking and Insurance

The Fraud and Theft Solution Blueprint for Banking and Insurance is mostly motivated by requirements for compliance with a variety of legal regulations. It combines the operational and analytical MDM methods of use. Also, due to the more acute threat of terrorism in recent years, many governments have created legal regulations aimed at preventing any financial transactions that support illegal activities. These new regulations typically require analytical capability to discover hidden relationships between people in which analytical insight gained in analytical systems needs to be leveraged by MDM Systems. Therefore, we use the MDM-BI Analytical System Integration pattern in the scope of this blueprint to show how these analytical systems and the MDM System can benefit from each other supporting these business requirements.

7.4.1   Business Context

Banks today are subject to fines if they are not able to comply with certain legal regulations such as the Anti-Money Laundering (AML) law. Depending on the countries the financial institution does business in, it might be affected by legal requirements from the following list, which is not intended to be complete:

- Sections 312 and 326 of the U.S. Patriot Act
- The Third European Money Laundering Directive
- Part 7 of the UK Proceeds of Crime Act 2002
- Title III of the International Money Laundering Abatement and Anti-Terrorist Financing Act
- Basel II (banks)
- Solvency 2 (insurers)
- MiFID (financial markets)

In addition, with the rise of the Internet, the options for criminals to commit fraud and theft by exploiting systems such as online banking, online auctions, and so on have broadened, and customers are expecting banks to take preventive measures.

For insurance companies, traditionally the question arises whether or not a claim is valid. So if in a supermarket a customer slips on a wet floor, it might be interesting to know if the supermarket employee reporting this case has a potential relationship with the customer. If so, the validity of the claim could be questioned. The MDM Solution Blueprint we discuss in this section is tailored toward addressing these business needs. Before we do so, let's look at the basics.

Money laundering is an attempt to disguise or conceal source, location, ownership, or nature of illegal money. The objective is to move money from one or many illegal sources originating from committed crimes in such a way that, as a result, the money is considered legal. Anti-money laundering (AML) processes are processes to detect and prevent successful money laundering, but they do not primarily target the crime that created the money.

Terrorist financing is the process where money from legal or illegal sources is used to finance activities indirectly or directly related to terrorism. Anti-Terrorist Financing (ATF), also known as Counter Terrorism Financing (CTF), is a process to detect these activities.

Comparing AML and ATF on a high-level, these are the differences:

- AML tries to detect the process to move money from an *illegal state* to a *legal state,* where the source of the money is a *crime committed in the past.*
- ATF tries to detect the movement of money in the opposite direction, from a legal state to an illegal state (and in some cases from illegal to illegal), for *crimes*—in this case terrorism—to be performed *in the future.* On a side note, ATF can be used on investigations of previously committed crimes.

AML and ATF are concerns for banks because they have the need to comply with legal regulations in these areas.

Another concern is theft and fraud for both banks and insurance companies—the difference is in the way the crime happens. The damage is done to the company itself, to the customers, or both. Financial crimes include:

- Credit and debit card fraud
- Check fraud
- New account fraud
- Successful identity theft used to steal through online banking, online auction, ATMs, and other systems
- Insider theft (e.g., insider knowledge exploitation by stockbrokers)
- Fraudulent insurance claims (see the supermarket example mentioned earlier)

Fighting fraud and theft requires processes to confirm identities and to detect irregular activities in financial transactions. If, on the same day using the same credit card, a book is bought in Munich, where the credit card holder lives, and a dinner is bought in Wellington, New Zealand, this would be suspicious. Another example would be the use of a credit card at an ATM. If the selected language is one where it is known that the owner lacks proficiency, this might indicate that the credit card is likely misused. The language proficiencies could be indirectly derived at least partially from exploiting citizenship or address information or by asking for it when a bank account is opened.

Obviously, the data model for customers needs to support this with additional fields if made explicit.

From a business perspective, for banks and insurance companies we can essentially see three major reasons why they might actively deal with the issues presented earlier:

- Economic consideration
- Regulatory motives
- Reputation

The first item is a very simple equation: If the economic damage done is larger than the costs to detect and prevent it, there is a business case for implementing the measures for detection and prevention. In this case, monetary assets are protected and secured. The measures to achieve protection and security are outlined in Chapter 4. Another option for mitigating the risk of financial losses is through insurance. Thus, due to an insurance policy, parts or the entire loss might be reimbursed.

The second item depends on the country where the company resides. If failure to comply with legal regulations means that you are not allowed to do business anymore or that you need to pay significant fines, external forces push financial service institutions into compliance. Institutions such as the Financial Service Authority (FSA) in the UK have the power to fine companies not complying with legal regulations. In the annual report of 2004/2005 (see [13]), the FSA lists banks lacking compliance with AML regulations that were fined in some cases. The list also includes companies and individuals fined for insider dealing or other criminal financial activities. In the annual report for 2002/2003 (see [14]), the FSA reports a 750,000£ fine for a bank that didn't comply with FSA rules in the anti-money laundering area. Furthermore, companies fined for lack of anti-fraud measures, failures in AML regulatory compliance, and other financial misconduct can also be found in the FSA annual report 2005/2006 (see [15]).

The third point means that you might lose customers due to a poor reputation based on more or less constantly appearing news articles that your financial institution was fined again for noncompliance with legal regulations or that criminals were again able to successfully commit credit card fraud and other crimes, or both. If criminals can access your customer information to perform fraud in any way, your customers won't trust that you can actually protect sensitive, private customer information. Your company's reputation is something that is hard to build but easy to lose. Losing a good reputation is the reputational risk as outlined in the MDM Security and Privacy chapter.

As we have seen, there are good reasons to implement measures to obtain compliance or prevent financial losses through crime. The first step to successfully address the crimes mentioned earlier would be **detection** and **prevention** processes. However, the IT environment of many banks is fragmented. Fragmentation can mean anything from a lack of consolidated, consistent customer information, which is buried in different silos and not integrated with analytical systems, to a lack of governance within the company, disallowing consistent and efficient implementation and lifecycle management of these processes. So the blueprint we discuss now is an example for an analytical MDM deployment addressing the business problems outlined.

7.4.2   Relevant Business Patterns

From the business perspective, we believe the following patterns apply:

- Compliance with legal regulations for AML, CTF, Basel II, and so on
- Information aggregation (external data providers, watch lists)
- B2B for including products from business partners

In order to achieve compliance for AML and CTF and to implement these business patterns successfully, a mix of methodology, technology, processes, and education is needed, as shown by the following high-level list:

1. Invest in a AML-CTF organization, which is responsible for designing comprehensive AML-CTF strategies, architecture blueprints, data quality monitoring procedures, and processes ensuring compliance.

2. Implement Know Your Customer (KYC)/Customer Due Diligence (CDD) processes covering effective relationship management based on risk assessment procedures, including customer closure and customer refusal procedures.

3. Implement automatic detection and prevention technologies, reporting technologies, and case management technologies.

4. Create and maintain staff AML-CTF awareness through training programs and measure their effectiveness and improvement until a behavioral change within the staff can be seen that shows that AML-CTF is considered important and its significance is reflected in work decisions.

The MDM Solution Blueprint that follows addresses the technology aspects of the first three items in the list just presented. As already mentioned, technology addresses only a subset of the business pattern—training staff on processes as indicated with the fourth point is out of scope of our discussion, because this is not a part of the technology infrastructure for the solution.

7.4.3   Relation between Business Patterns and Architecture Patterns

The business patterns require the following architecture patterns for this MDM Solution Blueprint:

- The Initial Load pattern
- The Transactional Hub pattern
- The MDM-BI Analytical System pattern

Optionally, the following patterns might be needed for system integration:

- The Transaction Interception pattern
- ESB and messaging patterns

For building the MDM System for customer and product information for this MDM Solution Blueprint, you need to implement the Initial Load pattern. As an additional step for the MDI phase, you might want to consider implementing a full watch list matching cycle before loading the cleansed and standardized customer information into the MDM System in order to know if there are already cases upon which you need to act.

If you need to prevent fraud cases through online banking or ATM machines, the access to customer information must be as fast as possible. From that perspective, only an MDM hub capable of providing real-time transactional access to customer and product information provides the infrastructure needed, which mandates using the Transaction Hub pattern. Only if read-only access to customer information is allowed through the ATM machine would a Coexistence Hub suffice.

For integration of the analytical processes with the MDM processes, you need the MDM-BI Analytical System Integration pattern. Recall, as discussed in Chapter 1 and Chapter 3, that there are three forms of analytical MDM:

- Analytics on MDM data itself
- Analytics to discover true identities and hidden relationships
- Analytics integration of business warehouse and MDM Systems

In the scope of this MDM Solution Blueprint, we focus to a certain degree on the first item (do the AML and CTF measures continuously reduce the number of money laundering and terrorist financing cases among new customers?). The second item is certainly center stage to implementing AML and CTF effectively. We do not cover the third item in the scope of this blueprint because that is covered in Section 8.2 in Chapter 8 with a dedicated MDM Integration Blueprint.

Further patterns like the Transaction Interception or ESB and messaging patterns such as the Publish/Subscribe pattern might be needed for further integration.

7.4.4 MDM Solution Blueprint Overview

For this MDM Solution Blueprint, we propose the architecture, shown in Figure 7.8, in the component model view, based on the enterprise MDM component model view presented in Chapter 3. There are three types of components:

- The mandatory components (1) to (7) in light-grey are components needed to build and run the MDM System (e.g., (5)), interact with it (e.g., (3)), or represent the MDM System (4) and have been described in the MDM Reference Architecture. For this blueprint, the Data Quality Management component of the MDM System (4) is very important to ensure high-quality master data—the key ingredient for better results in the analytical processing. It provides name and address standardization, address verification, and duplicate prevention. If these functions are not built in, this component leverages appropriate information integrity services from the Information Integration Services component (5). This component (5) also provides most of the functions to implement the Initial Load pattern when building the MDM System. The content management services (7) have multiple purposes:
  - They manage all of the unstructured data for the products, such as contracts or accounts and customers (images for products, copies of passport or driver's license for identification verification purpose, etc.). In the future, this might be biometric data.
  - They manage all of the scanned contracts from sold products as well as scanned paperwork of the case management infrastructure (19).

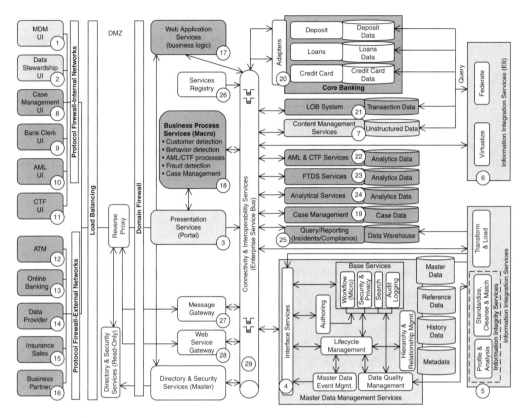

Figure 7.8 Fraud and crime control Solution Blueprint.

- The dark-grey components (8) to (25) are components specific to this solution. The core banking systems are represented through (20). Through adapters, these systems are connected to the Connectivity and Interoperability Services component (29). The applications of the core banking systems run the essentials of the banking business, such as deposit transactions, credit card transactions, and loan transactions.
- The component for enterprise-wide business process services (18) orchestrates all needed business processes. A full decomposition of all services is beyond the scope of our discussion. We just mention core areas needed for flows through the MDM Solution Blueprint. The interesting areas are:
  - Customer detection
  - Behavior detection
  - CTF processes
  - AML processes
  - Case management processes (orchestrating the services from the backend component for case management (19) and services from other components, as needed)
  - Fraud detection processes

These processes orchestrate individual services provided, for example, by the components (22) to (24). The AML & CTF Services component (22) covers at least the following services:

- AML rule engine services
- CTF rule engine services
- Behavior assessment services
- Risk assessment services
- Customer assessment services

The AML & CTF Services component also plays a crucial role in establishing compliance with relevant regulations in this area. The Fraud and Theft Detection Services (FTDS) component (23) covers at least the following services:

- Insider job detection (also known as staff malpractice; an example would be a stock trading agent performing insider jobs)
- Identity theft detection
- Fraud detection for all products sold (credit card, online banking, ATM, etc.)

The Analytical Services component (24) offers at least the following services:

- Identity resolution (might need cultural name variations and name standardization services)
- Relationship resolution
- Non-obvious relationship resolution
- Anonymous relationship resolution
- Watch list[14] matching

Note that the components (22) to (24) can also be divided into more fine-grained components and with a further decomposition of the individual service areas. However, for the scope of our discussion we believe this is detailed enough.

A lot of other applications of various types, such as CRM applications, are summarized in (21). For the discussion of this architecture blueprint, we will not focus on them.

The optional components (26) to (29), in white, have been explained in Section 7.3.4.

The authoring of product master information through an MDM User Interface (1) was discussed in the New Product Introduction Solution Blueprint in Section 6.3 in Chapter 6. The role of the Operational Data Steward using a Data Stewardship User Interface (2) was discussed in previous MDM Solution Blueprints described in Sections 7.2 and 7.3. We would only add here that the role might get some additional tasks related to data governance areas for the analytical MDM style. Examples would be the review of training material for staff related to AML and CTF to ensure appropriate content.

---

14. Here are two well-known examples: The European Union watch list is named "electronic-Consolidated Targeted Financial Sanctions List (e-CTFSL). For the United States, the Office of Foreign Assets Control (OFAC) of the Department of the Treasury manages a watch list. The homepage for more information on these external data providers can be found in Appendix B.

We would like to present the following flows through this solution:

Flow 1: Customer creation showing details specific to this solution
Flow 2: Insurance sales creating a new customer offline
Flow 3: Deployment of AML/CTF rules
Flow 4: Case Management of an incident
Flow 5: Ongoing analytical processing
Flow 6: Integration of external data providers

Let's start with flow 1, shown in Figure 7.9. A new customer visits a local branch of your bank. The bank clerk serving this customer would collect the client information and enter it through an MDM User Interface (1) that invokes presentation services (2). When the business logic in the application—residing in either (3) or (4)—initiates the creation of the new customer, there are two types of implementations possible:

- Using a composite MDM service of the MDM System (5)
- Orchestrating several information services using the Business Process Services component (3)

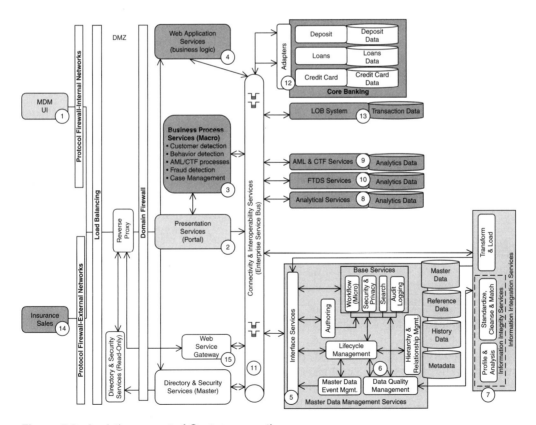

Figure 7.9 Analytics as part of Customer creation.

In the first case, while deploying the MDM System, a new composite MDM service is built. It should perform the following steps in this order:

1. Standardization services, for example, on name and address information, including creation of cultural variations of names and their background to improve the quality of the input data. Standardization can be achieved either through invoking data integrity services (6) built into the MDM System itself (1) or through data integrity services of the information integration services (7).

2. Analytical services (8) on the new customer information should be invoked, computing the identity resolution by using all information on names, including cultural variations. After that, relationship resolution as described in Chapter 3 should be done, including non-obvious relationship determination. Then, matching services performing matching against OFAC or e-CTFSL watch lists should be invoked.

3. Using the AML & CTF services (9) and the FTDS services (10), the potential new customer can be assessed regarding risk or involvement in fraud cases (perhaps as a witness in a discovered fraud case of another existing customer). Note that the information used by the AML and CTF services is now enriched due to the processing done in previous steps, thus improving the quality of results returned by the services. Due to this improvement on input data quality, alerts triggered by these systems are less likely to be false positives. A false positive is a case where someone was identified as supporting, for example, terrorists through financing them but this was suspected only because the input data was wrong or incomplete.

4. If a member or a relationship to someone on such a watch list is found, the composite create customer service should return this information to the bank clerk and not create a new customer. Alternatively, the customer record could be created with the flag indicating not to do business with this customer in order to prevent loss. With this information, the bank clerk should start with the procedure on customer refusal and the appropriate process of incident reporting.

5. If the analytical processes discover nothing, the composite create customer service could then create the new customer in the MDM System (5) and return the result on successful creation to the bank clerk through the presentation services (2).

When the customer is created, consuming applications of master data need to be notified. Thus, propagation to these systems (examples are (12) and (13)) through the Connectivity and Interoperability Services component (11) has to be initiated. ESB or messaging patterns could be used to implement this integration.

Using the composite MDM service is likely the better approach if your application does not have a lot of workflow capabilities itself, particularly if the logic is implemented in the scope of a Web application. In this context, the second option would be to deploy a create customer business process on the Business Process Services component (3). Then the enterprise-wide business process platform would drive the create customer process, invoking the services in the order just presented, with the difference that if all standardization and analytical services are done and nothing was detected, the standard create customer service from the MDM System would be used.

For the orchestration of these services, we assume in both cases that the enterprise architecture follows SOA principles and thus orchestrates loosely coupled services. In the example shown, most of them are information services, as introduced in Chapter 2.

The second flow is also shown in Figure 7.9 and starts when an insurance sales person visits customers at home with a business application running on a laptop to sign up a new customer using an Insurance Sales UI (14). Because the laptop might not be connected to the company network (lack of network connectivity), the customer is created *locally*.

The key observation is that this offline case means that data integrity enforcement such as duplicate prevention or business rule enforcement is *disabled* because the MDM System cannot be reached. The next time the sales person connects to the company network, the process of analysis of the potential new customer can be done very similarly to the process presented. If nothing is detected, the new customer will be added through the services interface of the MDM System (5) to the enterprise-wide authoritative source for customer information. The MDM service for customer creation could be invoked as a Web service if this is supported by the software selected. If the sales person has connectivity to the company network but is still outside (e.g., working from home), this could come in through a Web Services Gateway (15). However, the customer refusal process will be different because the sales person cannot directly speak with the customer.

The third flow shown in Figure 7.10 shows how to configure and deploy the analytical services using the AML Dashboard (1) for the AML and the CTF Dashboard (2) as examples for the corresponding component (3). There could be of course other user interfaces to configure the FTDS component (4) or the Analytical Services component (5). Core tasks include the rule engine configuration through the presentation layer (6). An example would be the configuration for suspicious financial transactions. A very simple rule could be that the same credit card cannot be used for payment in two locations in a time period smaller than the fastest plane to travel from the first to the second location.

Another example would be to track the language used at an ATM while performing cash withdrawal. Then it would be possible to determine the preferred language of a client by analyzing this data and save this insight in attributes of the MDM System (7). Alternatively, the client could be asked about his language preferences. Preferences could be obtained when the customer logs in the first time to the Online Banking application (8) and configures the preferences. Assuming it is known that a customer speaks German and English only and lives in Germany and the customer has a credit card, a rule for a suspicious transaction could be:

- Someone withdraws money at an ATM outside the home country using the credit card and selects a language other than German or English.

This withdrawal transaction could be an indication that someone stole the credit card from the customer and tried to withdraw money before the credit card is reported lost and blocked for money. If the customer would have used the German or English language menu for the ATM machine in the foreign country where another language is spoken, this would have been an indication that the customer is on vacation there using the known languages to get around and withdraw money. Another aspect of the dashboards (1) and (2) is reporting.

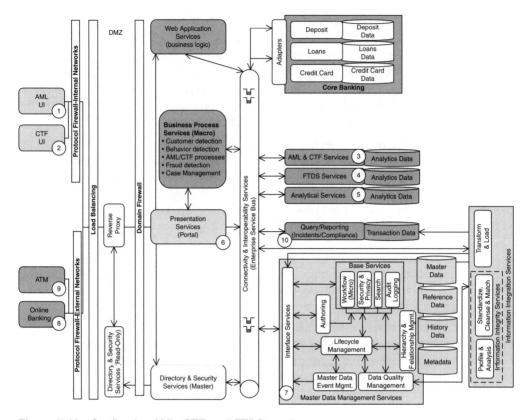

Figure 7.10 Configuring AML, CTF, and FTDS services.

For this, the presentation services (6) use reporting services (10). The reporting services allow the user to analyze:

- How many new customers signed up during the last quarter? For this, the MDM System (7) would be queried, thus being an instance of analytics of MDM data itself within the MDM System.
- How many incidents happened with the new customers during the last quarter querying the case management services? Is this ratio new customers/incidents better or worse compared to the previous quarter and thus an indication whether or not the employee training on AML and CTF is paying off?
- How many AML cases were detected?
- How many CTF cases were detected?
- How many fraud and theft cases were detected and what was the prevented damage?
- Is there a particular financial product or service more often attacked compared to other financial products?

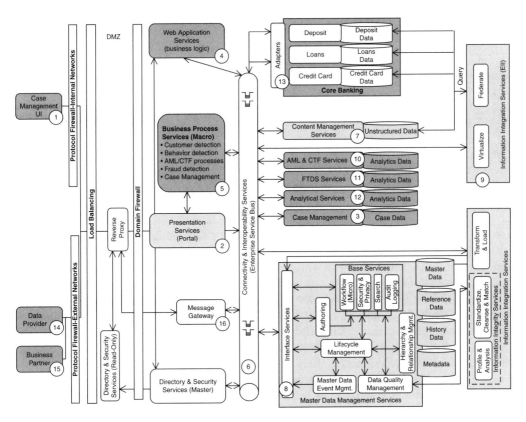

Figure 7.11 Incident Case Management and external system integration.

The fourth flow covers case management and is shown in Figure 7.11. Case Management is the process of handling an incident of a suspicious financial transaction or a watch list finding.

1. A Line of Business user involved in case management would use a Case Management User Interface (1), which leverages presentation services (2).

2. Depending on the case management application, the case management services (3) are either invoked through Web application business logic (4) or business process services (5), calling them through the Connectivity and Interoperability Services component (6).

3. If an incident occurred, a case is created and assigned so that it can be investigated, potentially escalated, and managed. A case often coordinates information from many sources, including the case management system (3), the content services (7), and the MDM System (8).

4. An implementation for loading all relevant information could be done by federation-based access using the information integration services (9) or through a

small workflow deployed on the Business Process Services component (5) orchestrating these services in order.

5. While working on the case, unstructured data such as scanned paperwork might be added to the case that needs to be persisted by the case management services (3), using the content services (7) for archiving purposes.

6. If a case requires escalation, appropriate business process services (5) enforce the right escalation order as part of the case management.

Over time there will be incidents due to ongoing analytical processing using the components (10) to (12). There are three reasons for this: First, over time as the customer uses either more financial services from your company or through the interaction history, you might collect additional information on the customer. This might allow the identification of this customer as a dangerous customer for your business, which enables you to act accordingly. Examples can be fraudulent attempts to sign up using a slightly different name and address or the customer appearing on a watch list. Second, for all financial transactions processed in (13), searches are running to find suspicious ones as defined through the applied rules for the components (10) and (11). A suspicious transaction might just cause a service representative of your company to call your customer ("Was the cash withdrawal in that foreign country performed by yourself or was your credit card stolen?") or immediate, more severe measures. The third reason could be that a non-obvious relationship between two customer records is only discovered later in (12). For example, due to a change of phone number, two customers share the same phone number. In any case, the analytical services and the MDM System require tight integration using the BI analytical system pattern. For example, you want to have all discovered relationships between your customers managed and stored in a single place, the MDM System. Thus, relevant analytical insight that belongs to the customer description should be stored in the MDM System as well.

The fifth flow exists if a bank resells insurance policies for insurance business partners, as shown in Figure 7.11. The business partner portal (15) is a way to enable business-to-business processes. Through this, a business partner can provide the product information on the insurance products that are part of a reselling agreement.

The sixth flow integrates external data providers (14) providing credit rating applications or watch lists. The exchange of information could use the Message Gateway (16) if the services are invoked using messaging.

7.4.5 Advantages

Deploying this MDM Solution Blueprint has the following benefits on the business side:

- Compliance with legislation such as AML, CTF, Basel II, and others
- Reduction of loss through fraud (external and insider)
- Protection of your company's reputation

On the technical side, you will gain the following advantages:

- Business agility through SOA-style deployment: If there is a change in legal regulations, due to the service decomposition into service components, new functions can be added rapidly.
- Centralized customer and product information, with an SOA-style service interface enabling master data service orchestration and composition supporting changing requirements on master data easily
- TCO reduction through complexity reduction in the integration layer
- TCO reduction through reduced storage costs for master data

The list of the benefits is intended for showing the most important ones and is not complete.

7.4.6 Alternatives and Possible Extensions

Using proven process and data models (see Appendix B) can speed up the deployment of this MDM Solution Blueprint. If the data model supports, for example, Basel II requirements, accelerated deployment of risk engines for calculation is possible.

In the gambling industry, finding hidden relationships between casino employees (e.g., card dealers) and customers (e.g., gamblers) requires many of the analytical processes on employee and customer master data. Thus, the MDM System and the analytical components presented in this MDM Solution Blueprint are the backbone for fighting fraud and theft in casinos. Because the casino industry is a multi-billion dollar industry and losses are largely due to fraudulent gambling, casino owners started to deploy analytical MDM Solutions to minimize these losses.

A variation of this Solution Blueprint is applicable for the public sector with two main drivers:

- Homeland security
- Citizen services

Most people hearing the term "homeland security" naturally just think about keeping the bad guys out. The flipside, letting the good guys in, is something easily overlooked. A government got bad press[15] in 2005 when by mistake legal citizens entitled to enter their home country were declined entry or held in detention. A key point here was that citizen information was incomplete, inconsistent, and scattered across multiple IT silos with no means to unambiguously resolve the identity of the citizen. But homeland security is more than just border control on people. It includes freight control and export and import control of weapons and/or other dangerous or restricted goods. Furthermore, it might include whether or not a foreign investor or a foreign company is allowed to buy a strategic company (e.g., in the defense industry) within the country. Finally, also crime committed by legal citizens is something the government is fighting against. So homeland security has an external and internal dimension. The crime-fighting departments are immigration, police, and secret

---

15. The report [16] should be read by decision makers in government institutions. It provides a very good overview of ten pitfalls and lessons learned in immigration processing. Many other reports on the case are listed in this report, too.

service departments and international organizations (e.g., Interpol) on federal, regional, and local government levels.

Governments in many countries provide services to their citizens where the following list certainly varies depending on country and is thus only intended as illustration:

- Pension services
- Tax services
- Social services (food stamps, child welfare, refugee support, unemployment, etc.)
- Veteran services
- Educational services

All these services are delivered through multiple channels. However, governments are challenged to effectively deliver these services for several reasons:

- Cost pressure on IT budgets
- Inefficiencies in IT (service redundancies, lack of integration between departments, etc.)
- Aging population (demanding the services longer)
- Citizens' demand on privacy protection and personalized services increase
- Fraudulent use of government services

To address the homeland security and the citizen services use case efficiently, a 360-degree view of the citizen is required to deliver citizen-centric services across all departments. In both cases, analytical services are needed to establish a citizen identity beyond a doubt to support use cases like allowing entitled citizens entry at the border and to prevent fraudulent use of citizen services. Some analytic services certainly change in this scenario for the public sector, for example, you are not checking for credit card theft anymore. You would instead deploy analytic services to discover misuse of social services or tax services (someone not providing information on all income sources trying to reduce tax payments). In the front end of the MDM Solution Blueprint, some other application user interfaces are needed for immigration officers or social service workers, but at the end of the day, many of the software technologies for standardizing names or for managing citizen information, using an MDM System in the backend, are identical or very similar.

7.5 Self-Service Website Solution Blueprint for Telco

So far we have focused on PIM or CDI-specific MDM Solution Blueprints. The Self-Service Website Solution Blueprint for the telecommunications industry spans multiple master data domains (Customer, Product, Location, Network Asset) and applies multiple methods of use. With this MDM Solution Blueprint, we show that business requirements can be mapped differently into master data models depending on technology and other constraints.

7.5.1 Business Context

The MDM Solution Blueprint shown in this section is particularly interesting because it shows a use case that provides all of the expected business results efficiently if an MDM

Solution covering the Product *and* Customer domain is deployed at the *same time*. This is different from the MDM Solution Blueprints discussed so far, which focused either on the customer or on the product but not on both domains simultaneously. In addition to these two well-known domains, two more will be covered as well, the Location domain and the Network Asset domain. The business motivation for the two different model approaches for the multi-domain master data model is as follows:

- The first one is based on the Product, Customer, and Location domains (see Section 7.5.1.1).
- The second one is based on the Product, Customer, Location, and Network Asset domains. For this second model approach, the Product and Location domain need to be modeled differently in order to appropriately align with the Network Asset Domain (see Section 7.5.1.2).

From our perspective, the business problem discussed here is not the only one where comprehensive MDM Solutions are required that cover multiple master data domains. However, we intend to use this one to demonstrate what can be achieved in a multi-domain approach.

7.5.1.1 Master Data Model Based On Product, Customer, and Location

As the title of this MDM Solution Blueprint indicates, the examples are drawn from the telecommunications industry. To get started, take a look at the offerings available in this industry today. In the category of phone subscriptions, there are plans available for landline, mobile, and Internet based. For Internet access, customers can choose from dial-up, DSL broadband, and satellite. For television, in addition to traditional TV based on satellite technology, digital TV is available as well on digital TV networks. For all these communication subscriptions, there is an abundance of devices available to customers. Providing an example only for phones, on the one hand you have simple landline devices that you can just use for making phone calls. On the other hand, devices from RIM or Nokia combine phone capabilities, Web browsing, and e-mail in a single device. Or compare a little cell phone sold into the consumer customer segment versus a PBX switch sold to business customers.

Beside these more technical choices, variations in financial attributes exist as well. Telecommunications companies also use billing plans to gain competitive advantages. For Internet access, *flat* fees can be limited by time, volume, or both (or none at all). For phone subscriptions, a monthly base fee plus fees based on actual use represent a traditional setup. Protecting teenagers from significant financial debts, a prepaid plan for their mobile might be applicable to limit the maximum amount they can spend for phone calls per month. Depending on the telecommunications provider, offerings with flat fees or reduced costs for calling a certain country or a certain set of countries might be available. Also, there are plans where calling at a certain *time* is cheaper (e.g., in the evening) or free of charge (e.g., weekend). Other phone companies offer plans where calling a certain number (e.g., mobile of spouse) is cheaper or free. Telecommunications providers also offer special plans for families or couples. Plans where *location* matters are available as well. In Germany, for example, some companies offer a *homezone*. This is an area around the home where the landline exists where mobile phones can be used at the same charges as the landline phone or at least with reduced charges.

The homezone area might vary in size depending on location or phone provider. The financial attributes of a plan can also be combinations of the items presented earlier. So you might have a plan where you can call a certain number free of charge at certain times (e.g., in the evening or on weekends). Summing up, the financial details of a telecommunications plan could differ based on at least calling time, calling number, location, volume versus time-based, and there are many more.

So what makes a product in this industry? A product can be a physical device or a service (the subscription) based on one or multiple types of communication (telephone, Internet, etc.) at certain locations or any combination thereof a business in this industry offers. In fact, a product is often now a bundle consisting of a service subscription that can only be bought in combination with a certain, predefined set of devices and also a predefined set of financial attributes. For example, a service subscription for a mobile phone use could allow the customer only to choose from eight different devices that are cheaper if bought together with this particular subscription. The service subscription itself could be only available with the option to choose a plan where all calls to landline numbers are free with a higher base price and calls to other mobile phones are charged with a certain rate per minute. The plan could have no base price at all, where calls to landline numbers and mobile phones are charged with certain rates per minute depending on the time of the day. The bundles are usually much more complex than the given example. A few hundred attributes describing a product that is a bundle, as shown, are not uncommon. Relationship management (e.g., which service is available for which device) is a crucial feature of the MDM System supporting flexible data modeling infrastructure.

Living in a house somewhere in a remote village in the Alps might certainly provide a beautiful view of the mountains with lots of hiking and climbing options. However, certain telecommunications networks like DSL and broadband might not be available at all or only with limited speed. Similarly, network coverage for mobile phones is not available everywhere or at increased costs when making calls from other countries. Availability of certain offerings thus depends on the *location* (either where you live or where you are). There might be different packages offered to different customers who live in different places (e.g., U.S. customer versus European customer with different plans and prices). Telecommunications providers therefore need to manage locations efficiently in order to be able to check quickly whether or not a certain product can be offered at a certain address. A complex rule engine needs to determine this. A location certainly requires attributes describing facts like bandwidth, type of available connectivity (broadband DSL, dial-up, etc.), and so on. The infrastructure for location also needs to be able to map postal addresses of a customer to network locations. Depending on the telecommunications service, network infrastructure must be assigned residing at a physical location different from the customer postal address, as shown by this DSL example:

In DSL broadband networks, telecommunications providers deploy devices with *ports* in the physical network layer. There is a one-to-one relation between households using DSL and these ports because for each household there is exactly one port assigned. As a result, if within a district of a city only a certain number of these ports are available, all your neighbors might have DSL, but you won't get it if there is no port available. Unless the telecommunications provider invests again in the physical network layer, deploying an

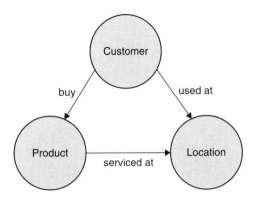

Figure 7.12   Triangle of master data domains for the telecommunications industry.

additional devices with these ports in your area, DSL is not available to you. If one of your neighbors in the area terminates the DSL subscription, that triggers a port release so a port becomes available.

Besides products and location, customer information has to be managed as well. Here, typical CDI requirements are common, so they are not repeated. Instead, we finish the discussion with a look at the following triangle of MDM master data domains, shown in Figure 7.12. A customer can buy a product (often a subscription and a device) that is serviced at a location. For a mobile phone, depending on the subscription type and the location where the service is used (home or foreign country), for each transaction charges might vary. So for creating the transactional, historical data (such as how many calls from where and for how long), call data records are read off a phone switch in real time and then perhaps loaded in a data warehouse. Using the phone number, a lookup could happen to pull the master data from the MDM System. Therefore, this system must be able to serve high-volume loads on short lookups of information.

7.5.1.2   Master Data Model Based on Product, Customer, Location, and Network Asset

The business situation remains the same as outlined earlier. However, the representation of the entities such as Customer or Product in the data model will change, and we will focus on this aspect. The Customer domain remains unchanged. Due to the new Network Asset master data domain, the Location and Product domain will change. Thus, we introduce the Network Asset domain first and show how this affects the other two. A network asset is a physical device (an asset) to which a telecommunications provider can deliver a service. Thus, we consider a network asset a service delivery point (either for an internal service routing network traffic or by providing a concrete service to a customer). A network asset might also record the transactions, such as to whom and when you made a call and how long that call was. For example, a network asset can be your landline phone receiver in your apartment where the telecommunications provider is able to deliver phone services to you. A network asset could be a wireless hotspot in your favorite café where you can use wireless

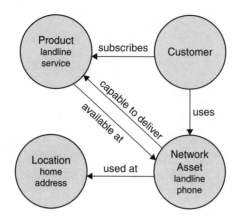

Figure 7.13   Customer, Product, Location, and Network Asset domain—simple example.

Internet access by a telecommunications provider. It could also be your mobile phone, which can deliver phone, Internet, music, and digital TV services to you, depending on the device. With this last example, you can already see how the Product domain is affected. Physical devices such as mobile phones or landline phones are no longer products by themselves. Products in this new model are only services (and the physical device is part of the service bundle). These services come in two types:

1. Subscribed services (like a landline phone subscription), which you have available as long as you pay the periodic fee (e.g., on a monthly basis).

2. On-demand services, like ordering a specific TV show to be streamed to a mobile device. These services are explicitly ordered on a case by case basis.

A location in this model is a description of where the service is used (the home address for the landline phone subscription) or a mobile phone used in the area of a UMTS[16] network capable of delivering digital TV to it. With this approach, the Location domain from the approach in Section 7.5.1.1 can be simplified. In Section 7.5.1.1, a complex rule engine needs to determine in near real time if a service can be delivered to a physical device. Often, a number of devices must be queried to determine if they can deliver the service. With the separation of location and network asset, you separate the concerns. Now take a look at Figures 7.13 and 7.14. In Figure 7.13, service capability and service availability are bundled in a single network asset. The opposite is true in Figure 7.14. Here, only two network assets together can complete the service delivery through a dynamic binding between them—in the example shown, it just depends on the fact whether or not the antenna (also known as a cell phone tower) and the mobile phone are close enough to each other. A secondary aspect

---

16. UMTS is the abbreviation for Universal Mobile Telecommunications System, an example of third-generation (3G) cell phone technologies.

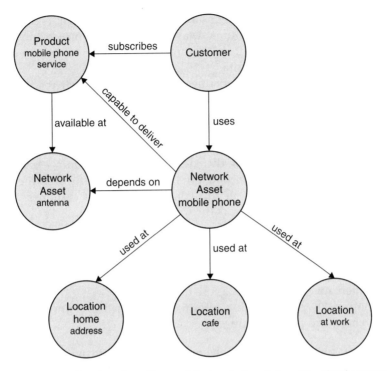

Figure 7.14   Customer, Product, Location and Network Asset domain—simple example.

is the location. As the location changes from home to work or to a café, the antenna-mobile phone binding might change.

7.5.1.3   Demand for Self-Service—Customer Perspective

In the telecommunications industry, customers demand an increasing amount of flexibility to apply changes to their purchased subscriptions. For example, the youngest child of a family moves out, so the family plan might not make sense anymore. Or the child gets old enough and demands a mobile phone, because the older ones have phones. The child should then be added to the family plan. Or in rural areas, DSL broadband becomes available and the bundle of landline phone with dial-up Internet can be upgraded to landline phone and DSL broadband. Whatever the reason, customers in many countries expect the ability to perform such changes, from anywhere at any time. One possible solution to satisfy this demand would be a Web self-service application.[17] In this particular use case, it should be able to allow for the following:

---

17.   The term "website" here is not meant to indicate a particular technology. It could be a JSR 168-compliant portlet implementation running on a portal server as well as traditional HTML websites running on a standard Web server such as Apache, or any of the new Web 2.0 technologies able to deliver the required functionality.

- A customer can review the current subscriptions. Even though "accurate" is claimed by Web sites of this type, a time delay anywhere from one to four weeks is not uncommon until the data from the order entry system is replicated to the data repository serving this Web site.
- Customers can review other offerings and *reliably* check whether or not they are available at the desired service addresses. As simple as it sounds, this is often a reason for frustration for telecommunications customers in Germany today, because the reliability of these checks outside major cities (where service availability is rarely a problem, making the checks almost obsolete) is not given.
- Customers can *reliably* modify the current purchased product selection by adding additional ones, changing existing ones, or removing parts from the existing purchased offerings. "Reliably" in this context means that customers can trust the transactions made, not receiving the wrong service later on.
- New customers can sign up and purchase products.
- Customers can terminate some or all subscriptions.
- Customers can change address (and the services should then be adapted accordingly by provisioning them, if possible, at the new address or immediately showing what alternatives are available at the new location).
- Customers can change billing information, household information, passwords, preferences, and privacy settings.

7.5.1.4 Demand for Self-Service—Telecommunications Provider Perspective

Sometimes the telecommunications providers have a strong interest in establishing a self-service channel as well. We worked with telecommunications providers that were under cost pressure for their call centers. Call center cost reduction by providing a self-service infrastructure can be a valid driver for the self-service website as well. Beside this very basic business driver, we also encountered the following:

- Relevant master data is scattered in many systems due to siloed lines of business (organically or as a result of mergers and acquisitions) and their respective IT solutions. Due to this, cross- and up-selling was difficult because a 360-degree view of customer data across all lines of business did not exist.
- Data consistency requirements across all systems as well as the current complexity in the IT landscape did not allow solving the problem. An integration layer in a portal could solve this issue across all lines of business (phone, Internet, digital TV, etc.), which should be available through the self-service website.
- Telecommunications providers observed significant customer churn because competitors could offer such a website.
- Customers were asking for such a self-service website to ease their interaction with the service provider and avoid the need to call the call center or to visit the local store.
- High rate of order adjustments (wrong product, wrong customer address, etc.) causing additional costs in order fulfillment.
- Reduction of unbilled services.
- New product introduction was taking too long.
- Optimize customer care: Modern phone networks allow the discovery of disconnect reasons. For example, based on usage patterns seen indirectly through the disconnect

reason code, you can detect that the network interface of the mobile phone is likely to fail soon. Thus, if you have your master data organized, you can improve your customer care by proactively letting your customers know that the mobile phone might break. Because the customer might think that the service offering is not very good if the connection is often lost, this might keep the customer from switching to a competitor.

Solving this problem was not easy, but in the following sections we show what a successful solution could look like.

7.5.2   Relevant Business Patterns

For a self-service website, the relevant business pattern is defined by an Account Access pattern (see [17]) composed of the Self-Service pattern and optionally the Information Integration pattern. Because business partners might provide network infrastructure or other services, the B2B pattern is used as well.

7.5.3   Relation between Business Patterns and Architecture Patterns

For this MDM Solution Blueprint, we need the following patterns:

- Initial Load pattern
- Transaction Hub pattern

Depending on the IT infrastructure and existing applications, the following patterns might be needed as well:

- Transaction Interception pattern
- ESB and messaging patterns

If master data is scattered, then the first step towards the self-service website is to build an MDM System by performing master data integration using the Initial Load pattern. The Transaction Hub pattern is required for two reasons:

- A self-service request updating master data needs access to the MDM services as well as workflows performing, for example, the necessary changes if a service type is upgraded. Transactional access enables fast read and write access to master data efficiently. The services interface with write access is a key characteristic of the Transaction Hub pattern. MDM Systems built with the Coexistence Hub pattern are not necessarily able to provide real-time transactional write access.
- The data model for customer, product and location must be reflected within the MDM System. If other systems store the attributes for a master data entry that needs to be read to retrieve all of the attributes by using the cross-referencing keys of the Registry Hub, then this might be too slow. First, the indirect lookup of the master data, and second, invoking data transformations to map the retrieved data to the website front-end due to a lack of an enterprise data model is just not fast enough under heavy load. Therefore, the Registry Hub pattern is not an option here. Furthermore, the Registry Hub would introduce a dependency on the availability of all of the contributing systems, which is not desirable in this context either.

We don't imply that the Transaction Hub pattern for customer, product, and location information is necessarily a single MDM System provided through a single product. Appropriate software might be chosen independently for PIM and CDI. It is important that they are architected using this MDM architecture pattern. If a decision is made to have separate CDI-MDM and PIM-MDM Systems, appropriate integration needs to be implemented as well. An IT Architect needs to strive for a balance, selecting the market leading technology perhaps in both areas against the cost of a more complex integration.

The Transaction Interception pattern, ESB, and messaging patterns such as the Publish/Subscribe pattern can be used to do the integration of the various application systems with the MDM System, depending on business requirements.

7.5.4 MDM Solution Blueprint Overview

A good starting point for an MDM implementation in the telecommunications industry is an overview of the **New Generation Operations System and Software** (NGOSS)[18] framework covering relevant business processes and data models such as the Shared Information and Data Model (SID). Due to the acceptance of NGOSS in the telecommunications industry, we advise an architect designing an MDM Solution for this industry to take a look at the relevant specifications. SID, for example, contains descriptions for entities such as product, customer, service, resource, or partner. On the process side, NGOSS has the **enhanced Telecom Operations Map** (eTOM), which is a business process model covering relevant processes for a service provider in the telecommunications industry. It includes, for example, process maps for a complete cycle of an order from sales to billing. The processing of an order is decomposed in subprocesses such as service availability for ordered service, service provisioning, service execution, and fulfillment.

The MDM Solution Blueprint is shown in Figure 7.15 and is based on the enterprise MDM component model presented in Chapter 3 as part of the MDM Reference Architecture. There are three groups of components.

- The components from (1) to (7) are shown in light-grey in Figure 7.15. These components are the key MDM components and have been described in Sections 7.2.4 and 7.3.4.
- The components from (8) to (19) are specific for this solution and are shown in dark-grey in Figure 7.15. The self-service website (10) is the key driver for the MDM System in this solution. Other relevant components are the customer care components ((8) for the UI, (15) for the backend system). The provisioning component (17) deploys a service subscription that could have been ordered through the self-service website (10).
- The white components (20) to (24) are optional components and might or might not exist, depending on the existing IT infrastructure and the concrete functional and nonfunctional requirements when this solution is deployed. The functions of these have been explained earlier in this chapter.

---

18. The NGOSS framework was developed by the TeleManagement Forum, an industry body driving standardization. For relevant links on the TeleManagement Forum, NGOSS, and SID, see [18], [19], and [20]. At the time of this writing, NGOSS version 6.1 was the latest one available.

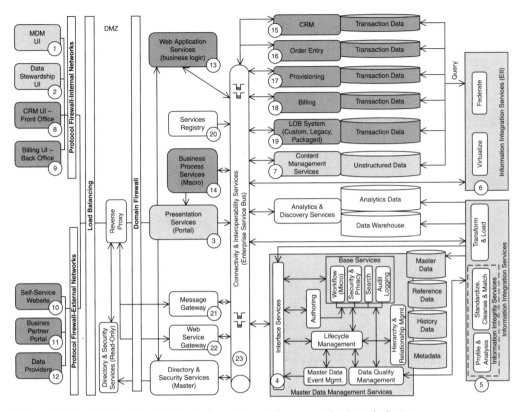

Figure 7.15 Self-Service Solution Blueprint for telecommunications industry.

The creation of product master data as well as the introduction of new products into the market has been explained in Section 6.3 in Chapter 6. Similarly, subject matter experts will author and maintain location master data related to things like cell phone towers. For this, the components (1), (3), (4), (5), and (7) are used. Depending on the workflow capabilities of the MDM System, the Business Process Services component (14) might have been used to orchestrate the collaborative authoring. An Operational Data Steward would reconcile, if needed, master data entities across all domains using a Data Stewardship User Interface (2). This process was explained in previous MDM Solution Blueprints.

In the context of this MDM Solution Blueprint, we describe the following three flows:

> **Flow 1:** Customer creation using the self-service website or the call center.
> **Flow 2:** The customer orders a product, and the process is shown with the provisioning.
> **Flow 3:** Integration with external systems.

The first flow is the customer registration using the self-service website, shown in Figure 7.16. The application logic used for the self-service website (1) is either some kind of eCommerce

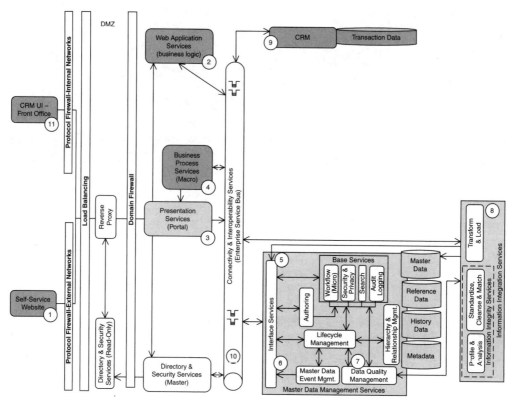

Figure 7.16 Customer creation using the Self-Service Web platform.

system provided to the presentation layer, like a portal (3) through Web application services (2) or through business process services on a process server (4).

1. A potential customer uses a browser to reach the self-service website (1) of the telecommunications company.

2. The new client registering enters the relevant information such as name, address, preferences, privacy, and billing master data and submits them using presentation services (3).

3. The Web application (2) or the business process services (4), depending on implementation of the self-service website, use master data services exposed by the MDM System (5) through the Interface Services Component (6) for the creation of the customer data.

4. The MDM System (5) performs several tasks, such as standardization of names and addresses or duplicate checks, as part of the creation service, by using either capabilities of the Data Quality Management component (7) or by leveraging data integrity services (8) from the Information Integration Services component.

5. The creation of this customer record has to be propagated to the CRM system (9) through the Connectivity and Interoperability Services component (10). The propagation is needed if the CRM system has a local database storing master data that cannot be removed through an Enterprise Application Integration (EAI) effort. ESB or messaging patterns can be leveraged for this part of the solution design.

Many telecommunications companies allow a customer registration through a call center as well. A Customer Care Representative uses the CRM User Interface for the front office (11) to invoke functions offered by the CRM system (9) for new customer registration. In order to achieve consistency, a customer created through this path should be the same as if it were created through the self-service website. Thus, the same create customer service of the MDM System (5) should be used. The IT Architect has two choices for integrating the CRM and the MDM System: asynchronous and synchronous integration on a service transaction level. Using asynchronous, message-based integration, key functions such as the duplicate prevention of the MDM System are disabled. The CRM application could save the new customer record locally even if the customer is a duplicate. Using synchronous integration with the Transaction Interception pattern, the CRM system would not save a new customer record locally unless the MDM System approved the record (and saved it in the scope of the same synchronous context). Thus, both systems are in sync, and the MDM System can deliver the business value desired such as de-duplication, name and address standardization, address verification, and centralized master data lifecycle management. For further details, see Section 8.3.2 in Chapter 8 and Section 5.6.1 in Chapter 5, which discusses the Transaction Interception pattern.

The second flow starts when the customer is registered and places a product order. The customer could order, for example, a phone service (consisting of a physical device and a service subscription). This flow is shown in Figure 7.17.

1. Before ordering, the customer likely browses through the available product offerings on the self-service website (1). On behalf of the presentation layer (2), either the Web application services (3) or the business process services (4) requests the product information.

2. One implementation choice is using a federation service (5) from the information integration services, which collects the structured data from the MDM System (6) and the unstructured data (such as images) from the content management system (7). As an alternative, this can be done in sequence. First, getting the structured data from the MDM System (6), and then, in a second step, retrieving the unstructured content using the service of the content management system (7) by using the product identifier. If the Web application services (3) are implemented using an eCommerce software with a local database to which the MDM System must publish master data to work, then (3) could get the required information locally.

3. After product selection is done, the customer can choose to perform an availability check to see if the service is available at the desired address. Through the presentation layer (2) and the business logic used either from (3) or (4), a check availability service from the provisioning system (8) can be invoked and the result returned to the user.

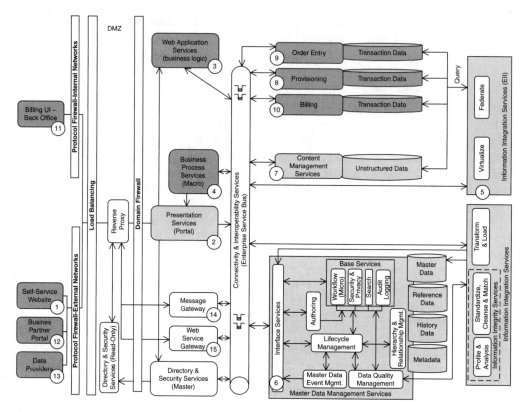

Figure 7.17 Customer creation using the Self-Service Web platform.

4. Assuming the service is available and the customer places the order, the order entry has to be processed. Thus, initiating the order entry processed by the order entry system (9) is the next step.

5. When the order processing starts, the order is decomposed into individual steps and services such as resource assignment or service deployment, which are invoked from the provisioning system (8).

6. After the order is created, the user receives feedback (1) that the order was placed successfully.

When the customer then uses the phone service, the service usage is tracked, and systems like the billing system (10) ensure order fulfillment and bill collection. If, for a technical reason, the provisioning of the service fails or the customer is not paying the bill, back office employees using a billing User Interface (11) can retrieve the customer information from the MDM System (6) and contact the customer. Depending on the business requirements, the integration of the systems involved could use integration patterns discussed in Chapter 5.

The third flow shown in Figure 7.17 is given by the fact that business partners might provide network infrastructure, phone devices, or other services to a telecommunications company. Thus, using a business partner portal (12), they need to be able to update their party information and all relevant master information (location of network infrastructure where a service can be deployed) using services of your MDM System (6) and content management system (7), in case unstructured master data has to be processed as well. External data providers (13) offering, for example, credit score services might require integration, too. Depending on available APIs and technology, the integration of these external systems could require a Message Gateway (14) or a Web Service Gateway (15).

7.5.5 Advantages

Deploying this MDM Solution Blueprint establishes the foundation for reducing customer churn. When customers can change, for example, their address easily, through a website instead of calling at least one customer care representative in each Line of Business, this contributes to customer satisfaction. With a customer-centric view, you are enabled to provide services tailored to customer segments and treat your individual customers better. You can efficiently design cross- and up-sell strategies because now you know your customer.

With a single place for product master data, authoring is streamlined and at reduced costs. With the streamlined authoring process, you can introduce products into the market faster because the relevant information can be pushed from one system with all relevant product master data to all dependent systems such as order entry, eCommerce, Portal, or billing systems.

Consistency of product and customer information reduces the number of incorrect orders, which in turn reduces the associated costs in order fulfillment.

With the self-service website, you can gain a competitive edge, tailoring your marketing campaigns based on your customer preferences and on the side delivering the flexibility of account management the customers are asking for.

You can reduce TCO significantly because you reduced data redundancy and integration complexity (less point-to-point connections between systems storing master data). Also, you can adapt your IT more easily to new business requirements by having the master data and the master data services in a single place.

7.5.6 Alternatives and Possible Extensions

A possible extension of the architecture of the MDM Solution Blueprint shown could be to include credit ratings[19] for customers from external data providers. Based on the credit ratings, you can implement additional business controls for customers, for example, providing better quality services to customers with good credit ratings.

Conclusion

As you have seen, Master Data Management offers business value in a variety of industries, either optimizing business processes such as cross- and up-sell scenarios or enabling compliance with legal regulations.

---

19. See Section B.3 in Appendix B for examples.

In the next chapter, we focus on MDM Integration Blueprints of MDM Systems with typical application systems, showing how MDM Systems can complement other systems such as business warehousing systems. We also highlight a major architectural decision point by showing the integration between MDM Systems and SAP applications.

References

1. U.S. Department of Health and Human Services provides information on the National Provider Identifier (NPI). Retrieved July 2007 from http://www.cms.hhs.gov/NationalProvIdentStand/.
2. ACORD homepage. Retrieved July 2007 from http://www.acord.org/standards/lifexml.aspx.
3. SNOMED standard. Retrieved October 2007 from http://www.ihtsdo.org/.
4. The IHE Technical Frameworks. Retrieved September 2007 from http://www.ihe.net/Technical_Framework/.
5. The Open Healthcare Framework. Retrieved August 2007 from http://www.eclipse.org/ohf/index.php.
6. The Health Level 7 standard. Retrieved August 2007 from http://www.hl7.org/.
7. The National Coalition on Health Care. Retrieved October 2007 from http://www.nchc.org/facts/coverage.shtml
8. eCard in Austria, July 6, 2007. Retrieved October 2008 from http://www.epractice.eu/cases/1976 and (in German): http://www.sozialversicherung.at/esvapps/page/page.jsp?p_pageid=110&p_menuid=65791&p_id=2.
9. WS-Federation standard. December 2006. Retrieved June 2007 from http://specs.xmlsoap.org/ws/2006/12/federation/.
10. Understanding WS-Federation, Marc Goodner, Maryann Hondo, Anthony Nadalin, Michael McIntosh, Don Schmidt, May 28, 2007. Retrieved June 2007 from http://msdn2.microsoft.com/en-us/library/bb498017.aspx#wsfedver1_topic8.
11. The article (in German) is named "Der demographische Wandel in Deutschland—ein Überblick". Retrieved September 2007 from http://www.bmi.bund.de/nn_122688/Internet/Content/Themen/Bevoelkerungsentwicklung/der__Wandel__in__Deutschland.html.
12. DWL Customer and IBM Performance and Scalability Results, Rick Bardine, John Byrd, Vince Russo, IBM Redbooks Paper, 2004. Retrieved November 2007 from http://www.redbooks.ibm.com/redpapers/pdfs/redp3885.pdf.
13. Financial Services Authority (FSA), Annual Report, 2004/2005. 2005. Retrieved July 2007 from http://www.fsa.gov.uk/pubs/annual/ar04_05/ar04_05.pdf.
14. Financial Services Authority (FSA), Annual Report, 2002/2003. 2003. Retrieved July 2007 from http://www.fsa.gov.uk/pubs/annual/ar02_03/ar02_03.pdf.
15. Financial Services Authority (FSA), Annual Report, 2005/2006. 2006. July 2007 from http://www.fsa.gov.uk/pubs/annual/ar05_06/ar05_06.pdf.
16. Report by the Commonwealth Ombudsman, Prof. John McMillan, under the Ombudsman Act 1976, REPORT NO. 11|2007, published August 2007, ISBN: 9780980387827, publisher: Commonwealth Ombudsman, Canberra Australia. Retrieved September 2007 from http://www.comb.gov.au/commonwealth/publish.nsf/AttachmentsByTitle/reports_2007_11/$FILE/report_2007_11.pdf, © Commonwealth of Australia 2007.

17. IBM developerworks patterns. Retrieved June 2007 from http://www.ibm.com/developerworks/patterns/account/index.html.
18. The TeleManagement Forum homepage. Retrieved July 2007 from http://www.tmforum.org/browse.aspx.
19. NGOSS. Retrieved October 2007 from http://www.tmforum.org/TechnicalPrograms/NGOSS/1911/Home.html.
20. SID. Retrieved October 2007 from http://www.tmforum.org/TechnicalPrograms/NGOSSSID/1684/Home.html.

Chapter 8

MDM Integration Blueprints

Master Data Management is never implemented as a greenfield deployment: There is always an existing IT landscape in which an MDM Solution needs to be integrated. The objective of this chapter is to provide guidance on how to integrate MDM Systems with other systems in the IT landscape, such as data warehouses (DW). We also show the impact of the architectural decision of authoring of master data in the application system or authoring it in the MDM System.

8.1   Introduction to MDM Integration Blueprints

In the previous two chapters, we focused on MDM Solution Blueprints addressing certain industry-specific solution requirements. In this chapter, we focus on a smaller scope of integration topics, which we call **MDM Integration Blueprints.** The MDM Integration Blueprints help to address some of the integration problems and to understand some the architectural decisions an IT Architect has to make when integrating an MDM System with other systems.

An MDM Integration Blueprint requires adaptation to reflect the functional and nonfunctional requirements of a particular customer situation. An IT Architect might need to refine an MDM Integration Blueprint due to constraints implied by the existing IT infrastructure in which the MDM Solution is deployed. Therefore, an MDM Integration Blueprint is not prescriptive. For an IT Architect, it is instead a proven accelerator asset that mitigates risk and enables rapid design of MDM Solutions.

In Section 8.2, we look at an MDM Integration Blueprint that combines an MDM System and a data warehouse system. This is an example where two systems can complement each other. Section 8.3 highlights a fundamental question that arises when an MDM System is introduced into an existing IT environment: Does the MDM Hub become the System of

Entry (SoE) for master data changes, or will entry still happen in the original applications? As you will see, the answer is complex and has tremendous implications. Moreover, this thorough analysis of the implications should be done before an MDM System is designed.

We assume the reader of this chapter is familiar with the MDM RA (Chapter 3) and the MDM Architecture Patterns (Chapter 5). For security concepts, we assume the reader also read Chapter 4 on MDM Security and Privacy and Section 6.5.5 in Chapter 6, where concrete examples in the context of an MDM Solution Blueprint were given.

8.2   Leveraging Data Warehouse (DW) Systems for MDM Integration Blueprint

Today, almost every medium-size to large-size company spends a great deal of money on costly data warehouse (DW, see [1]) and business intelligence (BI) systems. Analytical systems such as DW and BI have been introduced in Chapter 1. The companies need these systems for a variety of reasons, such as to determine quarterly or yearly revenue, to track trends in order entry, and to ascertain valuable customer segments based on which customers drive the most revenue or profits. Rarely, if ever, is insight computed in the data warehouse returned to the operational systems to help optimize business. However, there are good reasons to change this practice, and MDM Systems can provide a way to leverage the analytical insight gained from DW and BI[1] systems into operational systems. The Integration Blueprint will show how this can be done.

8.2.1   Business Context

Let's consider—for the sake of simplicity—the following basic CDI example to get started. We assume that the DW system was used to compute the following traditional customer segmentation based on revenue from previous sales:

- **Premium segment:** Representing customers with the highest revenue
- **Medium segment:** Representing customers with medium revenue
- **Low segment:** Representing customers with the lowest revenue

A bank would like to improve customer service and thereby profitability per customer without spending more on the call center or other service-related departments. How can this be done? If the costs for the call center and other service-related departments have to stay flat, then the overall time the service representatives can spend with the customer should not increase. One way to optimize service would be to enable the service representatives to know in which customer segment a customer belongs.

Policies can then be deployed so that a customer in the premium segment could receive more attention and more time while on the phone. Customers in the medium segment should receive more attention and only rarely should get more time, whereas customers in the third segment should be always kept to the minimum amount of time required to deal

---

1. From here on, we use these terms interchangeably.

with them without any special treatment. This way, customers from the medium and premium segment experience a more satisfying service experience. The result is an increase in their customer loyalty and the associated increased profitability per customer. There might be a slight risk of losing some customers in the low segment due to reduced service experience. However, this might have only a small impact on business. Note that the importance for customer segments can be different. If you do a lot of business with small transactions in a large customer base and only a small percentage of the sales with only a few customers are large transactions, the focus should be on the first group rather than the second to increase profitability.

Here are more examples of potential differentiated service opportunities:

- A telecommunications company could offer customers in the premium segment an upgrade on DSL bandwidth or free phone calls on the weekend.
- A car company could offer a navigation system free-of-charge for premium business customers.

The list could be continued with many more examples through all industries. The key point is this: If you efficiently want to leverage the analytical insight gained in the data warehousing environment to improve and optimize your business, you need to have it available whenever a customer record is accessed in the MDM System.

The computation of the customer segments just mentioned requires having all customer records in the DW system. When loading the data into the DW system, data from order entry, billing, and other systems has to be cleansed and transformed, which improves data quality. So the interesting question is: Why should you deploy a CDI-MDM System in the first place if you have good-quality customer information in the DW system? The reason we raise this question is because certain software vendors today position the BI or DW system as an MDM System. Then they point out that a warehousing system can efficiently do data warehousing and Master Data Management at the same time, concluding that an additional MDM System is not required.

Software vendors of DW solutions are not the only ones who position their software offerings now as MDM Solutions. Billing system software and other application software have occasionally been positioned as MDM Solutions, too. We believe this is due to the fact that companies are currently willing to spend money on solutions addressing master data issues. So analysis comparing the MDM System with the application system regarding purpose could be done for these as well, including considerations about how they complement each other. The reason why we picked the integration with DW systems was because we are seeing the highest business potential when insight from these systems is appropriately leveraged.

Before we lay down our point of view about whether a DW system can replace an MDM System or vice versa, we consider two things:

1. What are the characteristics of the MDM and data warehousing systems; in other words, for which task were they designed and optimized?

2. Could they complement each other, and if yes, how can this be done?

A data warehousing system is designed to efficiently compute insight to support certain business-relevant decisions. The characteristic workload on the database is Online Analytical Processing (OLAP, see [2]). Its design characteristics are:

- De-normalized,[2] star schema[3]-based data model
- A subset of the overall attributes, which represents historical, transactional data such as orders and invoices
- Can grow very large
- Users are typically Business Analysts, dashboard and scorecard portals, and forecasting systems
- Latency of data is high because it enters through an ETL process (though some efforts are made to reduce this with trickle feeds[4])
- Typical data access is via a complex query
- A DW is not designed for returning correct data to operational systems (even though the data is cleansed when the data warehousing system is built). The reason for this is simple: If a DW only receives updates in a nightly or weekly batch mode, the data is likely outdated. So even if the DW has the right interfaces (which it doesn't) for real-time distribution of data to operational systems, the distributed data could be outdated. A situation where an update from a DW would overwrite a new address with an old address because the new address has not been moved via batch to the DW is not desirable.
- Very rarely connected to front-end systems such as call-center applications
- Not designed to support authoring and maintenance of hierarchies like organization or product hierarchies[5]

An MDM System is designed for efficiently providing access to master data. The workload on the database in certain MDM domains, like Customer, is Online Transaction Processing (OLTP, see [7] and [8]). OLTP essentially requires support for real-time read and write operations in the database. Typical operations in an MDM environment are *create customer*, *change address*, or *lookup customer*. Its design characteristics are:

- Highly normalized data model.
- Compared to the warehouse system, data volume is small and only grows at the same rate as the business, for example, not faster than the business acquires new customers.

---

2. We are not going into the details defining the various levels of a "normalized data model." Simply put, data model normalization is a process to remove functional dependencies between attributes of data tables and anomalies on database operations. An example for a table that is not normalized is a table that allows insertion of the same customer twice with the same identifier living at two different addresses. This causes an anomaly because you cannot tell where the customer actually lives. The interested reader can find more details on data model normalization in [3], [4], and [5].

3. A simplified definition of a star schema for a data warehouse is a data model that has a fact table (e.g., for orders or invoices) and dimension tables (e.g., for customers or products). Details can be found in [6].

4. A very simple explanation of a trickle feed is a stream of ongoing delta updates for a DW from an operational system such as an order entry system.

5. This might seem like it is not a very severe limitation. But if you intend to improve your selling strategy with a given organization, it might not be sufficient to only know the individual from that organization; also knowing the level and the role of the individual within the enterprise organization is important. Managing this kind of information efficiently is a strength of MDM Systems but a weakness of DW systems. So the MDM System is strong on authoring and maintaining hierarchies, but DW systems are strong for reporting purposes on hierarchy objects.

- Users are call center representatives, sales staff, order entry systems, invoice systems, ERP systems, and other transactional systems.
- Typical data access is for real-time transactions or record lookup (call center representative looks up a customer record to change an address).
- Designed to return correct data to operational systems.
- Requires constant connectivity to front-end systems like call center applications or applications used by staff members in local branches.
- Designed for hierarchy support, including organization or product hierarchies.

Clearly, the systems are quite different regarding workload type and structure of the data model.

Despite these differences, there are also some similarities, mostly on the project implementation level. Both types of systems are built by the IT department but funded by other departments. Both are cross-organizational and, in the MDM case, often with an enterprise-wide scope. Organizations must agree upon a unified data model, security, and relevant business processes for the data, and should put in place Operational Data Stewards as members of a data governance board to govern the data.

Orders or invoices, two typical entities in a DW system, have an affinity to entities of the master data domain such as products and customers. An order describes which customer bought what products when, at which price, and with which set of conditions (discounts, shipping address, time of sales, etc.). Thus, customer and product information is usually in dimension tables in the warehousing star schema model, whereas orders or invoices are represented in the large fact tables. Before MDM Systems appeared, loading data into a DW system usually required de-duplication of the customer information with address and name standardization, and other cleansing and transformation tasks. The ETL work for master data for the dimensional tables of a DW is not needed anymore if it is drawn from the MDM System. Figure 8.1 shows how MDM and DW systems complement each other with respect to leveraging master data from the MDM System.

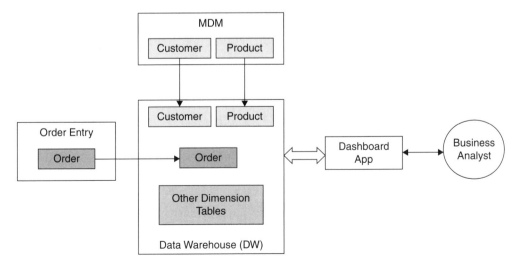

Figure 8.1 MDM and DW system complement each other.

Due to the design of the MDM System, master data enters the system if and only if all data integrity and business rules are fulfilled, meaning the master data is persisted with high quality. Furthermore, due to its design, the MDM System—as opposed to the DW system—can feed master data into the operational systems. Thus, orders, invoices, and so on are created with consistent, up-to-date master data from the MDM System. The result of this overall improvement of data quality is that the DW system can now also compute more accurate results.

As you recall, using the Customer domain as an example, the question was: Is there a need for an MDM System if the DW system has good-quality master data? And we believe the answer to this question is affirmative. As you can see with all of the architectural and design differences outlined earlier, you should not use a DW system for MDM or vice versa because neither one is capable of the task of the other. Instead, we propose maximizing the business benefits by combining the MDM System and the DW system in the most efficient way:

- Reduce the cost for ETL required for building DW systems by leveraging the MDM System.
- Feed certain analytical insights gained by the DW application back to the MDM System and thus leverage insight in the operational system environment, as explained at the beginning of this subsection.

Leveraging the analytical insight from the DW system through the MDM System is one of the three types of the analytical method of use of Master Data Management explained in Chapter 1. If the DW and the MDM System are integrated, the result will be the shift depicted in Figure 8.2.

On the left side, the application data from order entry or invoice systems was, at some time, moved to the DW system. Once there, any insight gained from DW was not moved back to the operational systems, as indicated with the unidirectional arrow from the applications to the DW system. The MDM System is not used in this situation to leverage DW insight.

Now, with the shift to the right side in Figure 8.2, the crucial point to observe is the bidirectional arrow between the MDM System and the DW system. The flow from MDM to DW is illustrative of master data being leveraged by the DW system. The flow from DW to MDM is motivated by the idea of leveraging analytical insight through the MDM System. The MDM

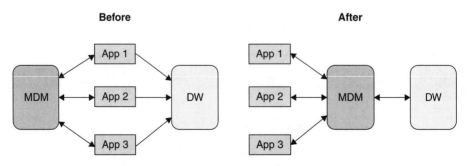

Figure 8.2 MDM and DW system—before and after integration.

System can feed this information back to all applications, thereby enabling service optimization per customer segment, as previously sketched. It is, of course, an option to implement only one of these two directions, but not implementing both reduces the value the bidirectional approach is able to deliver.

So far, the focus of the discussion was to make analytical insight from the warehousing environment actionable through the MDM System. The warehousing environment is also able to deliver better results if master data from an MDM Hub is used. For example, when a PIM solution is deployed, product information is standardized and de-duplicated. Thus, a PIM-MDM System is capable of providing high-quality product master data to the warehousing environment. Clean product master data improves revenue reports for a product. Thus, if the MDM System is the source for master data, reporting in the warehousing environment improves.

Summing up, these are the key reasons why MDM and DW Systems should be properly integrated:

- Improve reporting results in the DW with high-quality master data.
- Make insight from DW actionable for operational systems through the MDM System.

8.2.2   Relevant Business Patterns

For this Integration Blueprint, there is no single business pattern or set of business patterns available to describe all of the needs that make this Integration Blueprint useful. We think the many insights computed with DW systems and the broad variety of business optimization strategies based on the analytical knowledge derived are the reasons why this integration is useful. Also, this Integration Blueprint is not industry–specific, because data warehousing and MDM Systems can be found in any industry. So the only common ground for a sound business justification for this Integration Blueprint is the aim to more effectively use DW insight through the MDM Systems and the goal of reducing costs in building DW by leveraging the high-quality master data available through the MDM System.

8.2.3   Relation between Business Patterns and Architecture Patterns

The business requirements mandate at least these MDM architecture patterns:

- Initial Load pattern
- Transaction Hub or Coexistence Hub pattern
- MDM-DW Integration pattern

If you intend to leverage the MDM System to populate the dimension tables with master data in the DW system, you need to have a consistent data model for your master data within your MDM System. This excludes MDM Systems built with the Registry Hub pattern because such a hub has no centralized data model and does not enforce the same master data integrity and business rules enterprise-wide.

8.2.4 MDM Integration Blueprint Overview

In Figure 8.3, a high-level view of the Integration Blueprint is shown. Starting from the left, there are different types of front-end applications, such as a call center application (1), a local branch staff application (2), and an e-Commerce website (3) where customers can buy products. Because the focus of this Integration Blueprint is not the integration of these systems with the MDM System (4) and the order entry system (5), the (6) indicates that with appropriate EAI and EII techniques (see Chapter 5), this integration can be done either directly or indirectly by invoking the service interface of the MDM System or the interface of the order entry system.

For the sake of simplicity in the figure, only one backend system, such as an order entry system, is depicted. If there are more sources for the DW system (7), the consideration for the order entry system shown needs to be duplicated for each additional source system. The orders from the order entry system (5) are loaded into the data warehouse (7) through an extract-cleanse-transform-load process (8). Because the master data is clean, the cleanse step can be omitted (9). The transformation step in (9) might or might not be needed, depending on the data model for the dimension tables in the data warehouse and the data model of the MDM System.

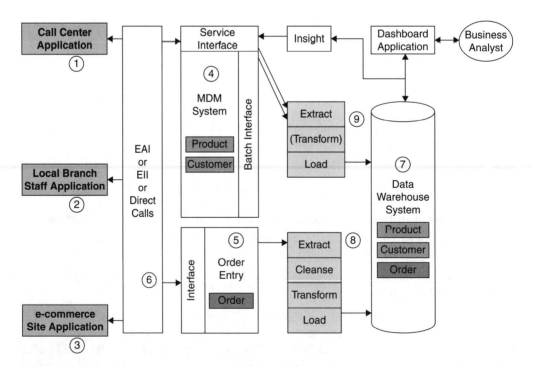

Figure 8.3 Leveraging DW systems for MDM Integration Blueprint.

8.2.4.1   Forces

The design of the integration between an MDM and DW systems has to consider many different aspects. From our perspective the IT Architect should consider at least the following ones:

- Did the DW system exist when the MDM System was built?
- If the answer to the first question is yes, is the DW system a source system for master data?
- If the answer to the previous question is yes, does the DW system need to be reloaded after the MDM System is built? The reason for this might be the fact that while building the MDM System, master data was cleansed, standardized, and deduplicated to a higher level of data quality than was used while the DW was built. It is possible that better reporting could be achieved if the cleansed master data is loaded into the data warehouse. However, a complete ETL cycle for the orders or invoices to link them to the right customer and products in the dimension tables is required if the dimension tables are reloaded with clean master data. Overall, this would essentially be a complete reload of the DW system—a tremendous undertaking, where business benefits and costs need to be validated carefully. One option could be that some MDM Systems have the flexibility in the data model to store any number of alternate keys, where an alternate key is the unique identifier of a master data record in another system. So if the DW system is a source system of master data when the MDM hub is built, the unique identifiers of the master data records from the warehouse could become alternate keys in the MDM System. Whatever mechanism you choose to implement the delta change movement from the MDM System to the DW system can then be leveraged to harmonize the master data dimension tables identified by the alternate key information to the latest values for any master data record in the MDM System. This would likely be one of the least intrusive ways to perform the integration in the warehousing infrastructure. On the other hand, if the ETL infrastructure is not documented and hand-coded, and the DW system exists on an outdated hardware and software stack that will require replacement in the near to mid-term future, the deployment of the MDM System together with the integration of the two systems as outlined in this blueprint could justify the rebuild of the data warehouse from scratch.
- Did the MDM System exist before the DW system was built?
- If the answer to the previous question is yes, is absolute or convergent consistency implemented between the MDM System and all other systems (except the DW) using master data? If absolute consistency is implemented, then you can have two separate streams of data to the warehouse: one from the MDM Hub for updating the dimension tables and another one from other systems like order entry to populate the fact tables. In the second stream from transactional systems such as order entry, the master data part does not require loading because due to accurate primary keys the links into the dimension tables work. In the case of convergent consistency, each time a delta load from an order entry system happens when a new order is created, the master data in the order requires update while moving the order to the warehouse. The scenario is described in detail in Section 3.8.7 in Chapter 3 in a component interaction diagram.

- What are the data quality requirements for master data in the data warehouse? The most critical one is timeliness, illustrated by the following question: Does the data warehouse require synchronous real-time updates on master data from the MDM System or is a monthly batch good enough?
- What are the data quality requirements for the analytical insight from the DW system that is returned to the MDM System? Again, timeliness is the most important one because the sooner the analytical insight can be leveraged through the MDM Hub, the more business value can be gained from it.
- What type of interfaces do the MDM and the DW system available for data exchange have?

With this list, we have illustrated that there is no one-size-fits-all approach for this integration. In the following sections, we look into some details.

8.2.4.2 Deployment Scenarios
There are several basic scenarios:

1. Initial Load of MDM System with master data from data warehousing system.

2. Initial Load of DW system with master data from MDM System and transactional data from order entry systems.

3. Delta feed of transactional updates into the data warehouse system with lookup of master data from the MDM System.

4. If absolute consistency with a Transaction Hub deployment is implemented, then two separate delta feeds could also be implemented: the first one sending updates from the MDM System to the DW system, and the second one sending delta updates on transactional data to the data warehouse.

5. Delta feeds from the MDM System to the data warehouse.

6. Sending analytical insight from the data warehouse to the MDM System.

The first scenario is captured in the Initial Load pattern for the MDM Hub and described in Chapter 5. The data warehouse would be just one of many sources of master data during the Master Data Integration phase. The second one is leveraging many of the same data integration techniques and is thus for redundancy reasons, also not covered here. The third item is explained in full detail in Section 3.8.7 in Chapter 3. The fourth scenario is a modification of scenario 3 and very similar to it, so we do not go into details. We focus, though, on the last two items and start with the fifth one.

Figure 8.4 shows how delta updates are moved from the MDM System to the data warehouse.

A new customer record is likely a master data change you need to reflect in the DW system. A change in the privacy preference attributes of a customer record might be a change not necessarily relevant for the data warehouse. Going through the component interaction diagram, we assume a change relevant for the data warehouse was requested by the Line of Business (1) system.

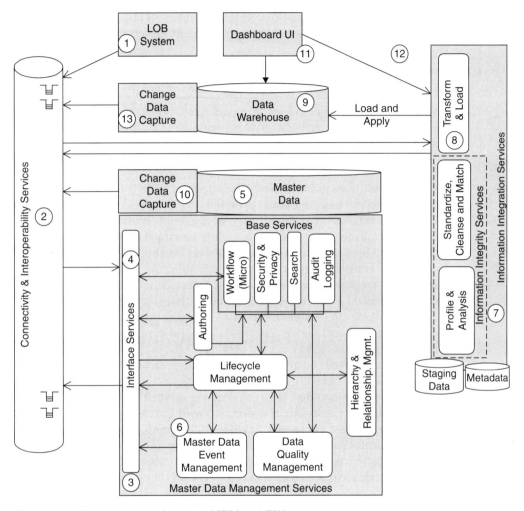

Figure 8.4 Delta exchange between MDM and DW.

1. A Line of Business (LOB) system (1) requests a master data change.

2. The Connectivity and Interoperability Services component (2) routes this request to the MDM System (3).

3. Through the Interface Services (4), this request is received and processed. Assuming the request was valid and all processing successful, the result will be saved in the Master Data Repository (5).

4. Assuming the MDM System (3) has a Master Data Event Management Component (6), one option for sending the delta change would be to post a message with the change asynchronously to the Connectivity and Interoperability Services component (2).

5. The Connectivity and Interoperability Services component (2) routes this request to the Information Integration Services component (7), which initiates a transform service (8).

6. After the transform service (8) converting the master data model to the model of the dimension tables is complete, the change is loaded into the data warehouse (9).

7. Upon completion of the master data change service request through the Connectivity and Interoperability Services component (2), the result is returned to the LOB System (1).

For the fourth step, alternative options are possible:

- Some MDM software products have two interfaces: One is the service-oriented, real-time interface used for normal operation, and the other is a batch interface for fast mass extracts[6] after the MDM System is built. With the batch interface, you could implement, for example, a nightly batch job moving all master data changes since the last job execution to the data warehouse.
- If the MDM System lacks appropriate notification mechanisms, Change Data Capture (10) mechanisms of database replication technologies can be used. They are either based on database triggers together with history tables or transactional log analysis. Both can be used to continuously extract the deltas as input for the required transform and load operations because the initial load of the dimension tables in the DW system has already occurred.
- Usually, the data model in any MDM System can be changed to a certain degree. Changing the data model is a viable way to introduce a change flag indicating that the record was modified, if this change is combined with a periodically running program that extracts all of the records with the change flag activated and then resetting the flag afterwards. The flag could require at least four states: The first one indicates record creation. The second one indicates modification. The third one indicates deletion, because MDM Systems usually only perform logical deletes. If the delete of a master data record is a physical delete, this approach is not viable for delta transfer. And the fourth one indicates that no change occurred. The program could be a stored procedure (SP) or user-defined function (UDF) running within the database of the MDM System or any external program, perhaps a piece of code executed periodically from the Information Integration Services component (7). Such a program would use transform services (8) and the load services (9).

The way you actually implement this delta update of the DW system certainly depends on the business requirements, such as the timeliness of the changes reflected in the warehousing system, failover constraints, and the availability of software and budget for the project.

The sixth scenario, moving analytical insight from DW to the MDM System, is also shown in Figure 8.4.

---

6. To populate the MDM Hub initially, some MDM software products also offer a batch interface for mass loading purposes.

A Business Analyst uses a Dashboard UI (11). The Business Analyst uses for analytical processing the data warehouse and based on the results would decide what kind of insight, if any, needs to be reflected back to the MDM System for business optimization. For example, consider a customer data model that contains the customer segment, customer importance, and customer potential. Naturally, if based on customer insight from the data warehouse, such as the identification of valuable customer segments, these would be the spot in the MDM System to reflect this insight. Customer segmentation can be done in other categories as well, such as demographics, geography, or buying behavior. Because the dashboard application interacts with the DW system on behalf of the Business Analyst by submitting inquiries and retrieving results, this is the right spot to trigger the updates to the MDM System with analytical insight.

So the Business Analyst would have the ability to initiate the sharing of relevant analytical insight from the data warehouse with the MDM System. The sharing could happen by requesting the appropriate information services (12) from the Information Integration Services component (7). If the Dashboard UI (11) is not extensible to integrate this, another, maybe portal-based, UI can be developed and used to initiate this. The information services would transform the data model from the warehouse model to the master data model if needed. Depending on the amount of data either through the master data services or through the batch interface of the Interface Services (4), the analytical insight is loaded into the MDM System (3).

Instead of the "on-demand" move of analytical insight initiated by the Business Analyst, periodic and ongoing feeds could be implemented as well. If there are jobs running periodically in the data warehouse generating this analytical insight and storing it in database tables in the DW system, Change Data Capture (13) can be applied to these tables. Thus, from these result tables of the analytical processing, relevant changes are moved automatically and on a continuous basis to the MDM System.

A downside of this Integration Blueprint is the disruption it causes in the existing ETL infrastructure for the DW system if the DW system existed at the time when the MDM System was deployed. As of today, many ETL processes are partially or in whole hand-coded, with little or no documentation on the cleansing and transformations done. Changing such an ETL infrastructure is a daunting task, and here, often the rule mandates, "Never touch a running system." Even with leading edge technology (see Section B.4 of Appendix B for examples) for data model discovery that is applied on the source, staging, and target systems, the change in the ETL infrastructure is not easy. From a positive perspective, however, it is also an opportunity to fix things that were architecturally right at the time the ETL processes for DW systems were conceived, when neither MDM Systems nor information services were available. There are better architectural choices available today, though.

Reusing information services such as a cleansing task whenever a business process such as an order entry was executed was not possible a few years ago. When ETL was done at that time, in order to load data into the business warehouse, data cleansing had to be applied to low-quality data that should not have entered the system in the first place. It this sense, it was a patch for a problem that could not be fixed at the right spot. With the paradigm shift to SOA, information services can be seamlessly invoked in business workflows to ensure that low-quality data is no longer entering the systems. They can also ensure that data consistency is guaranteed enterprise-wide, because the same service for the same task is reused through-out all IT systems in the enterprise. Using this state-of-the-art approach, reduction of the ETL complexity when populating the DW system, as well as a reduction of the load times caused by fewer cleansing and transformation tasks, decreases the Total Cost of Ownership (TCO) and improves business performance.

Not leveraging the high-quality master data for the master data dimension tables of the DW system would be a waste, because there is no source with better master data quality any-where in the IT. So adaptation of existing ETL processes to include the master data from the MDM System is feasible. Even though the disruption in existing ETL processing for DW is a result of the deployment of this MDM Integration Blueprint, it can also be seen as a further opportunity for business optimization.

8.2.5 Advantages

MDM and DW systems both provide specific business value to an enterprise in the areas they were designed for. The main advantage of deploying this Integration Blueprint is if it is deployed in such a way, as outlined in Section 8.2.4, that the MDM System and the DW system complement and leverage each other. The combination exceeds the sum of the parts regarding business value because new efficiencies and business optimization areas are unlocked; examples have been given in Section 8.2.1.

8.2.6 Alternatives and Possible Extensions

The approach described in Section 8.2.4 was made without making any assumptions on how the data model for the MDM System and the DW system came into existence, in other words, whether a Data Architect had to design them both from scratch or whether they were part of a software package. As an alternative to building the data models from scratch, and thus speeding up the deployment of these systems, we would like to make you aware of the fact that certain system integrators and software vendors provide complete process and data models (see Section B.1 of Appendix B for Examples) for these tasks. The models are com-prehensive and fit the 80/20 rule. Typically, for about 80% of the attributes you need, you can use the model, and for around 20%, you will need to apply minor changes.

The analytical method of use, as pointed out in Chapter 1, has three facets, namely, analyt-ics on master data itself, integration of analytics done in analytical systems into MDM Systems, as outlined in this Integration Blueprint, and analytics in the area of identity and relationship resolution and management. Only the second facet was covered in this Integration Blueprint. Naturally, though, for the first facet, the question arises in the context of this Integration Blueprint as to whether these analytics should continue to run within the MDM System or if they should be offloaded to the DW system. From a performance per-spective of the MDM System, it would certainly be beneficial to move these analytics to the DW system.

From the end user perspective, such as Business Analysts, this would make sense as well, because they know the UI and tools based on the DW system, and if these analytics con-tinue to run in the DW system, they could perform these tasks with familiar tools. In the likely event that the DW system existed before the MDM System was deployed, they might already have analytics on master data in the dimension tables, so they might even be able to continue with their analytics. In this case, the MDM System could improve the results, though, by providing higher-quality master data input for the dimension tables or allow for additional analytics on master data due to a possibly more comprehensive data model with greater support for hierarchies. So moving the analytics on master data itself from the MDM System to the DW system would be a natural extension of this Integration Blueprint.

The downside of moving the analytics on master data to the DW would be twofold: If the master data is moved to the DW only on a weekly or monthly basis, the reports would not be current (e.g., "How many new customers were acquired over the last week?" could not be answered immediately). Furthermore, the analytical insight on master data itself might be needed in the MDM System. Then a transfer has to be implemented for this, too.

Therefore, based on concrete functional and nonfunctional requirements, it has to be decided where analytics on master data should run.

8.3 SAP Application Integration Blueprint

Using SAP applications as an example, this MDM Integration Blueprint puts a fundamental architectural decision point into the spotlight: Where is the master data authored? We illustrate the consequences of this decision through an example using SAP applications and an MDM System as input systems for authoring master data. We look at this decision point from a variety of angles and show you the impact this answer has on the business side as well as on the technical side.

8.3.1 Introduction

Previously, we discussed various MDM Solution Blueprints by industry, master data domain, business process, or a combination of these. In this subsection, we focus on how the integration architecture will be affected by the answer to the following question: Is the master data authored and maintained through an application user interface (UI) or through the user interface of the MDM System, or both? In other words, what is the system of entry for master data? In order to grasp the complexity of the question, let's assume the following context as an example:

- The application and its relational database persistency cannot be separated, and some functions of the application not related to master data record maintenance are still required after the MDM System is deployed in the IT environment.
- The application is an SAP application.[7]
- The company is a medium-sized company where at least 500 Line of Business users use the application system to work with master data records.

The first item implies that even after all master data records were consolidated during a Master Data Integration phase in the database supporting the MDM System, the master data

---

7. Because SAP is among the leaders in the business application space, MDM Systems are very often required to integrate with SAP applications, justifying the relevance of this example.

records remain in the relational database local to the application. Furthermore, the application will read master data records from its local relational database due to the tight coupling between application and persistency. If the authoring of master data is done through the application UI, this data is stored in the local application database. Because a central MDM System is supposedly the authoritative source of master data, you need to keep the application system and the MDM System in sync.

The second item implies that you cannot use database replication technologies (either transactional log or trigger based) to keep the application database and the database of the MDM System in sync. The reason is the fact that the database replication technologies do not always respect the boundaries of SAP business transactions. As a result, database replication technologies work fine from a database transaction consistency point of view, but not from the SAP business transaction consistency point of view. Thus, the implementation of business transaction consistency between the MDM System and the SAP system is required where the exchange on the SAP side has to use SAP interfaces such as BAPI (Business Application Programming Interfaces) or IDOC (Intermediate Document).

The third item confronts you with the following business problems: If all 500 users supposedly start to work with the UI of the MDM System, then you need to train them on a new UI, which is costly. Avoiding these costs through the continuous use of the application UI comes at a considerable price because of the additional complexity in the integration architecture.

Now let's step back for a moment from the SAP example to get the big picture. Underlying this business problem from an architectural perspective is this more fundamental problem: Can you integrate at the UI level, or are you forced to integrate at the application level to avoid redundant and inconsistent data entry? The problem is illustrated in Figure 8.5. On the left side, the application UI (for example, portlets in an enterprise portal) has to use certain

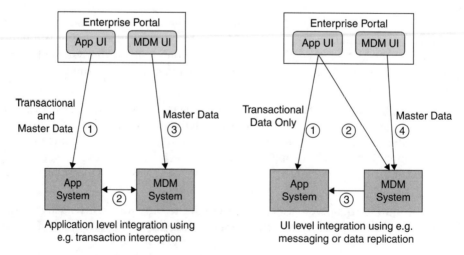

Figure 8.5 UI integration versus application integration.

application-specific functions. These functions mix master data changes with transactional data changes (1). Thus, at the UI level, there is no option to separate the areas of concern—application functions dedicated to working with transactional data and functions dealing with master data. Thus, the only way to integrate is either to intercept the application functions using the Transaction Interception pattern (see Chapter 5 for details on this pattern) or to asynchronously integrate the application system and the MDM System. Note that if MDM is deployed, some custom portlets might need to be added to support user roles such as the Operational Data Steward (for details on this user role see Appendix A) so that the Operational Data Steward might change master data as well (3).

In the right half of Figure 8.5, the situation is shown where "integration on the glass" and separation of concerns is possible. The application UI (in this example, portlets on an enterprise portal) can be reengineered in such a way that it invokes application functions touching (1) transactional data in the application system, and (2) master data services changing master data in the MDM System. Due to this change, the application UI stops using application functions touching master data. The MDM System propagates the master data changes to the application system using, for example, messaging or data replication techniques (3), depending on the application and MDM Systems interfaces. Again, some portlets might need to be added to the enterprise portal to allow for an Operational Data Steward to split or collapse[8] master data records.

In addition to the costs for user education, there are the costs for the MDM UI itself. Buying MDM software with a UI available out of the box has the advantage that no custom development costs occur for the UI as part of the MDM implementation project. The obvious disadvantage from a cost perspective is the fact that proprietary software does not allow you to easily and economically change the UI for your specific needs. Furthermore, such changes might only be possible to a limited degree. This might be a particular hurdle in the product master data domain, because changes in the data model during the product lifecycle and the associated business processes often vary more compared to the customer master data domain. Buying MDM software without a UI requires developing the UI for the MDM System as part of the MDM implementation project, with the associated costs. The advantage of this approach is the flexibility to tailor the UI—for example, JSR 168-compliant portlets running on a Portal Server—to the specific needs of your company. Today, enterprise portal frameworks have evolved to the degree that they can solve integration problems with an "integration on the glass" approach. The widespread use of industry-standard JSR 168-compliant portlets in combination with SOA-style architecture building blocks supported adaptation. Architecture patterns for "integration on the glass" exist as well (see [9] and [10]). The combination enables you to "integrate on the glass" applications through service composition invoking services. An example of this is shown in Figure 8.6.

First, note that with External Data Provider and Master Data Management Services, we refer to two architectural components of the MDM Reference Architecture, as described in Chapter 3. The example, of course, implicitly assumes that the process is simple enough that a workflow engine like a business process platform is not needed. Otherwise, there would be one layer of

---

8. Data governance enforced by Operational Data Stewards is discussed in detail in Chapter 9.

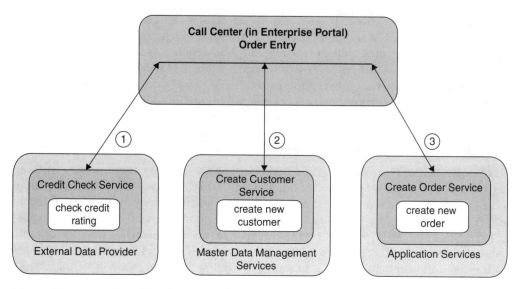

Figure 8.6 Integration at the "glass level."

indirection between the enterprise portal and the services shown in the figure due to a process layer between the presentation layer (enterprise portal) and the service providers (the three boxes at the bottom in Figure 8.6). The enterprise portal would—if a workflow engine driving the business process is needed—interact with the workflow engine, and the workflow engine would then invoke the services offered by the service providers appropriately. But—as shown in the example—we assume that this is not the case. If you can use "integration on the glass" you can, for example, model an order creation business process. If a new customer calls your call center representative, relevant steps are invoked from the user interface, in this case an enterprise portal. We assume the customer selected products and provided all relevant information to the call center representative who enters it and submits the order. Then the business process could be implemented in such a way that first a check credit rating service is invoked (1) verifying the customer credit rating is okay. In a next step, assuming this check credit rating service was successful, the new customer could be created in the MDM System using a master data service such as a create customer service (2). Again, if this step is successful, the order can be created in the application system using a create order service (3).

8.3.2 Forces

Underlying the discussion whether the SAP UI or the UI of the MDM System is used for authoring and maintaining master data is the more fundamental question of how to orchestrate and synchronize master data services[9] enterprise-wide. Recall that a master data problem is not a data problem; it is a problem caused by not using only one business service for a single task but using multiple and inconsistent implementations. The problem typically

---

9. Throughout Section 8.3, we use the terms "service" and "transaction" interchangeably. With transaction, we do not mean database transactions. "Transaction" is used as equivalent to a service on a business function level.

surfaces when siloed applications with business logic specific to their business process requirements work with master data that is scattered in numerous databases and content management systems throughout the enterprise. If enterprise-wide absolute consistency is required, in an ideal world each and every function, such as creating a customer, would invoke the create customer function from the MDM System. In a less ideal world, this might not be possible, because an application system cannot be changed to invoke the create customer function of the MDM System. Then, synchronization has to be implemented differently. Business requirements drive the following decisions:

- Between convergent and absolute consistency
- Where master data is authored (MDM System or application system)
- The timeliness of propagation of master data changes to application systems (synchronously or asynchronously)

The level of integration influences the business value of your MDM System. Figure 8.7 depicts the range of integration options. One dimension is the scope of orchestration, reaching

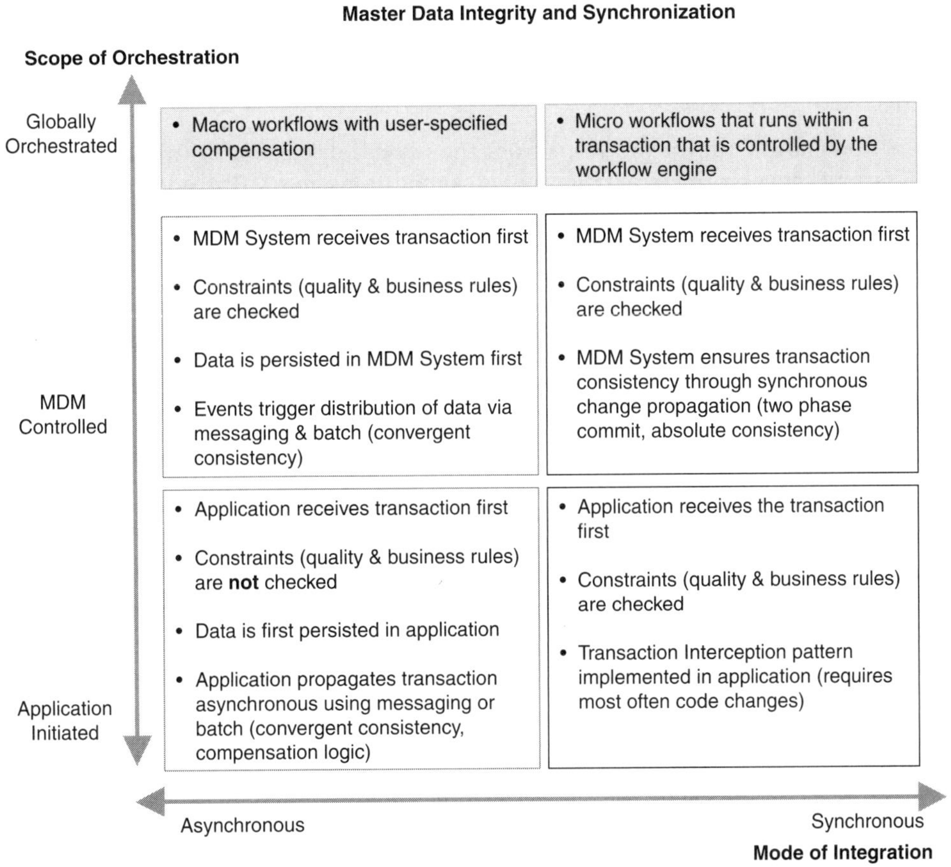

Master Data Integrity and Synchronization

Scope of Orchestration

	Asynchronous	Synchronous
Globally Orchestrated	• Macro workflows with user-specified compensation	• Micro workflows that runs within a transaction that is controlled by the workflow engine
MDM Controlled	• MDM System receives transaction first • Constraints (quality & business rules) are checked • Data is persisted in MDM System first • Events trigger distribution of data via messaging & batch (convergent consistency)	• MDM System receives transaction first • Constraints (quality & business rules) are checked • MDM System ensures transaction consistency through synchronous change propagation (two phase commit, absolute consistency)
Application Initiated	• Application receives transaction first • Constraints (quality & business rules) are **not** checked • Data is first persisted in application • Application propagates transaction asynchronous using messaging or batch (convergent consistency, compensation logic)	• Application receives the transaction first • Constraints (quality & business rules) are checked • Transaction Interception pattern implemented in application (requires most often code changes)

Mode of Integration

Figure 8.7   Dimensions of Integration.

from local application-initiated transactions to globally orchestrated transactions. This is the primary dimension.

The other dimension describes the mode of integration between application systems and the MDM System, which is either synchronous or asynchronous. This is the secondary dimension.

Let's consider in this general scope just two examples, briefly, to give you an idea of the concepts illustrated with Figure 8.7:

- An MDM System receives a master data service request to change master data. The change is asynchronously propagated to application systems consuming master data. This would be the case in the left column (asynchronous) and the second from the bottom (MDM controlled). In this scenario, all of the benefits from the MDM System, such as duplicate prevention, are enabled.
- The second case is an LOB application processing a master data change, which is asynchronously propagated to the MDM System. This would be the case in the lower left corner (asynchronous, application initiated). Many benefits of the MDM System are disabled (such as duplicate prevention), and costly integration logic pieces need to be implemented. An example would be the compensation logic required in the integration layer between application and MDM System removing a duplicate record from the application if the MDM System rejects a new customer record for this reason.

Figure 8.8 now narrows down the scope from the general discussion to the discussion of how this is applicable for the integration of SAP applications and MDM Systems. Basically, the scope of the orchestration is given by the system of entry, which is either the SAP UI or the MDM UI. The system of entry has the point of control regarding the transaction unless the ownership is handed over to a distributed transaction manager component (XA component) managing global transactions. For the scope of our discussion, we assume the system of entry is the point of transaction control. The mode of integration is either synchronous or

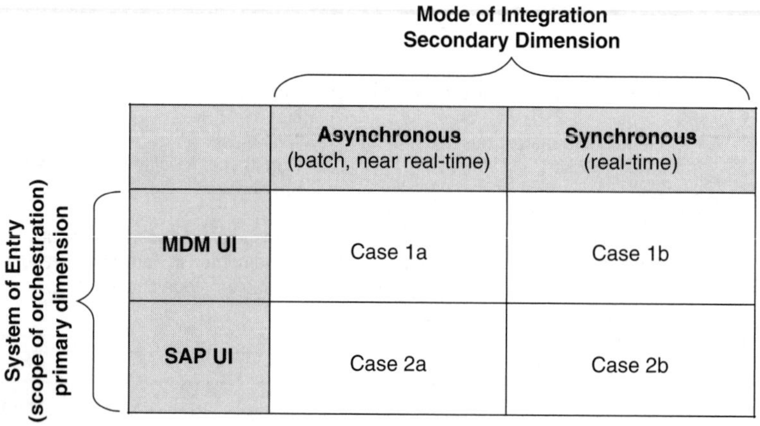

Figure 8.8 Cases of integration—MDM UI versus SAP UI.

Table 8.1   Forces Affecting Integration Architecture

Option	Applicable for MDM Hub Types	Mode	Consistency	Timeliness	Integration Complexity
1	Registry Hub, Coexistence Hub	asynchronous	not consistent/ convergent consistency	Batch	Lowest
2	Registry Hub, Coexistence Hub	asynchronous	not consistent/ convergent consistency	near real-time	Medium
3	Coexistence Hub	asynchronous	convergent consistency	near real-time	Medium
4	Transaction Hub	synchronous	absolute consistency	real-time	High

asynchronous (batch, near real-time), leading to the four cases in the 2×2 matrix shown in the figure. Because the system of entry is the primary dimension, the mode distinguishes only two cases in the scope of the same transaction control point. Thus, we have the system of entry being the MDM UI (Case 1) with the two sub-cases 1a and 1b, indicated by the mode. Also, we have the system of entry being the SAP UI (Case 2), with the two sub-cases 2a and 2b indicated by the mode.

The integration architecture for these four cases is different and is affected by several forces, as outlined in Table 8.1. The table illustrates the underlying forces for Figures 8.7 and 8.8 and also relates the forces to the applicable MDM Hub architecture patterns explained in Chapter 5. The integration complexity also depends to a certain degree on the type of MDM software used and the available APIs and interfaces it offers for the integration task. However, the complexity measure in this column reflects the difficulty of the integration as implied by the combination of the factors consistency, timeliness, and mode. Asynchronous integration using messaging is usually easier to implement than synchronous integration with real-time data model conversions and changes in the application system code. **Batch** in the timeliness column means everything less than near real-time, such as synchronization on a nightly basis or once every three hours, and so on.

Table 8.1 gives you an overview of the options. If you integrate your SAP application in the case of 2a in Figure 8.8 with your MDM System using option 1 from Table 8.1 by performing nightly batch processing, moving all changes from SAP to the MDM System, you are required to tackle the following problems:

- **Deletion of duplicates created by SAP Application:** Deletion of a master data record on SAP usually means setting the status of the record to inactive. It usually never means immediate physical deletion of the master data record from the local application persistency.

- **Compensation transactions for business transactions implemented in integration architecture:** Assume an SAP application created a duplicate of a customer master data record that already existed in the MDM System. Further assume that an order using the ID of this duplicate customer master data record was created within the SAP application. A compensation transaction would need to ensure that the correct customer master data record from the MDM System is applied to the SAP application and that the order with the wrong customer ID is corrected.
- **Transformation of the data model:** Depending on the software you applied during the MDI phase of the MDM implementation, you might be able to reuse the data model transformation jobs when performing an asynchronous batch processing after the MDM hub is built.
- **Transformation of code tables:** MDM software often has built-in code tables for country information, and so on. A code table usually has at least one column with a code number such as "3" and another column with an associated value such as "Germany". SAP applications exploit similar code table structures. However, on the SAP side for the country code table, the value "3" might be associated with the value "Canada". As a result code table conversion tables are needed where the MDM System code number is mapped to the right SAP code number for the corresponding table. A lookup or reverse lookup in such code conversion tables allows the appropriate mappings from the MDM System to SAP and vice versa.

Assuming the SAP UI is used for master data authoring in the case 2b of Figure 8.8, then choosing option 4 in Table 8.1 relieves you from the deletion of duplicates created by the SAP application and the need for compensation transactions. However, this option requires the ability to intercept SAP transactions and the ability to put them on hold until the MDM System responds back on the new or changed master data record. Putting the SAP transaction on hold needs to happen before SAP commits it through completion of the business transaction to the local persistency. Similar to option 1, you still need the transformation of the data model and the code tables with the additional requirement to be able to perform them in real-time. The two brief examples discussed were intended to just scratch the surface of the implications caused by the forces listed in Table 8.1. More details follow in the next sections.

8.3.3   Only Using SAP UI for Master Data Authoring and Maintenance

In this section, we describe the Cases 2a and 2b before showing that you can achieve even more by using the MDM UI as system of entry in the Cases 1a and 1b.

8.3.3.1   Business Context

We use an example that provides a context for the discussion of the architectural implications. A global manufacturer has business operations around the world. In each of the major geographies, dozens of business users work with several SAP systems processing product and vendor information in various languages across many countries. The product information also needs to be exchanged with a very large number of retailers and vendors that the manufacturer is working with. Due to the scattered, inaccurate, inefficient, inconsistent, and incomplete product information, accurate global reporting on brands and categories is impossible. The wasted resources associated with this inefficient product information exchange are becoming a major obstacle for the business. The inefficiencies were the reason that the company decided to deploy a central Master Data Management system for product and vendor information, with the following results:

- Reduced time and cost to deliver product information to retailers/resellers (the vendors)
- Improved efficiency of brand and category managers
- Reduced invoice deductions
- Reduced inefficiencies handling product information worth tens of millions of dollars per year

The benefits were achieved because the MDM System reduced the number of point-to-point connections between the SAP application systems and the systems from the resellers by decoupling them with a central MDM System, shown in Figure 8.9. The efficiency improvements for brand and category managers were achieved because for the first time there was a 360-degree view across all products and all hierarchies available with clean, de-duplicated master data.

However, the executive board of our example company decided that, rather than training the huge numbers of users to use a new system, the lines of business users should continue to author the product and vendor master data through the SAP UI, thus avoiding the training costs.

8.3.3.2   Solution Architecture

Figure 8.9 shows the solution architecture at a high level. On the left hand side in the figure are the SAP systems in the various geographies. The SAP user interfaces are used by the Line of Business users to enter master data. Due to the extensive customization possibilities of SAP systems such as SAP R/3 or SAP ERP, it is likely that the UI and processing of product information is done slightly differently in each of these systems. The data models of all of them differ from the data model used for products and vendors in the MDM System, which can be either designed using the Coexistence Hub or the Transaction Hub pattern. The Registry Hub pattern cannot be used here because any meaningful integration with the Global Data Synchronization Network (GDSN),[10] through which the product information is available for retailers, requires a harmonized and fully materialized data model in the MDM hub. Another reason the Registry Hub pattern is not appropriate here is that the system performance for category managers, brand managers, and analysts using a portal-based UI to access the product and vendor information would suffer too much due to the involved federation.

Because the data model of the SAP systems and the MDM Systems are different, master data harmonization is required using ETL infrastructure. The arrows from SAP systems through the EAI layer to the ETL component to the MDM hub represent asynchronous integration. Starting the discussion of this flow on the left, capturing the master data changes within the SAP systems can be done in a variety of ways—we list just two examples:

---

10. The GDSN has been explained in detail in Chapter 6.

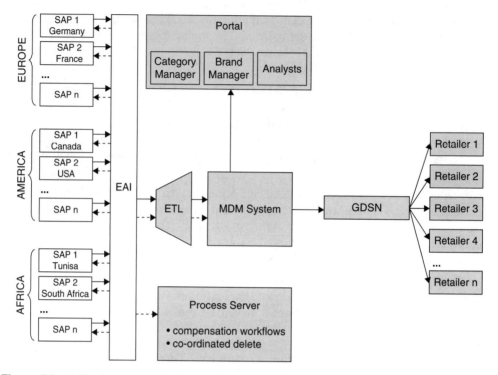

Figure 8.9   Authoring master data through SAP UI.

- **Change pointers and periodic jobs:** For example, in a SAP R/3 4.7 system, you could use the SAP built-in functions to enable change pointers on SAP business objects. A change pointer marks a master data entity as changed when a change occurred. Using the SAP built-in variant-mechanism and another SAP transaction, you can then set up a periodic job creating IDOCs[11] in the SAP IDOC outbox. The periodic job creates an IDOC for every master data object in SAP marked with the change pointer and removes the change pointer afterwards. From there, external programs such as enterprise SAP connectors, available from a variety of software vendors, can pick up the IDOCs containing the changes. You can schedule the periodic job daily, hourly, or every minute, depending on your requirements.
- **SAP connector or SAP adapters with change capture capability:** Available from software vendors, these SAP connectors and SAP adapters can be used as well to track changes on the SAP side and push them asynchronously through messaging infrastructure to the MDM System.

The implementation of the EAI layer depends on how master data changes are tracked in SAP and extracted. It could be a messaging infrastructure, if the SAP adapter has the capability

---

11. For example, IDOCs of the type MATMAS for materials can be used for products.

to write outputs to JMS message queues. Maybe the SAP adapter itself can be used directly by the ETL tooling. In this case, the EAI layer might not exist at all.

The ETL infrastructure, invoked either in batch mode periodically or asynchronously whenever a message with a new master data change arrives, would be responsible for performing the data standardizations, data model transformations, and code table conversions. Also, duplicate checking should be done to avoid the creation of duplicates by the different SAP systems. In essence, the ETL infrastructure needs to compensate for the fact that master data is not entered directly through a UI using a service interface of the MDM System itself.

Now there are a couple of issues—the list below provides the subset of the more urgent ones:

- SAP systems are not known for state-of-the-art, built-in duplicate checking. A single product can be entered multiple times into the same system by the same or different users with slightly different values for some of the attributes. The duplicates are only found during the duplicate checking in the ETL infrastructure—at that point, the duplicate product records are already persisted within SAP and potentially in use in some business processes. Similarly, product duplicates can be created in two more different SAP systems. This is detected, again, only by the ETL infrastructure—after the master data is persisted within the SAP systems originating the duplicates.
- A user of an SAP system decides that a product has reached the end of its lifecycle and marks it for "deletion."[12] However, in at least one other system (let's say a supply chain management system or an order entry system), the product is still in use. So the interesting question becomes: How do you ensure a master data record is not removed from the central master data system until it is no longer needed by any depending system?

For the first workflows with compensation logic for the SAP systems triggering appropriate updates on them, using SAP interfaces such as RFC,[13] BAPI, or IDOC is required. This is indicated with the dotted lines in Figure 8.9 pointing from the EAI box (very likely an ESB in this case) to the SAP systems. A Process Server could address the required workflow capabilities. The compensation logic might have the requirement to reflect de-duplication in the SAP systems. If there are different types of SAP applications systems or different versions of the same SAP application, performing a de-duplication step in the source SAP system might require multiple implementations depending on the specific SAP system.

The compensation logic might be fairly complex, depending on the business processes in which a product is already involved. You might not be able to perform an update of the master data record in certain business processes requiring a complete termination of the business process and a restart with the surviving master data record. An example might be an order entry process. In other cases, you might not be able to stop the business process (for

---

12. "Deletion" does not necessarily mean physical deletion. It could be setting a deactivation flag or marking it for archiving.

13. RFC is the SAP client/server programming model for Remote Function Calls and often used to integrate SAP systems among each other.

example, if the product is included in an order that was already partially delivered) if you need to comply with Sarbanes-Oxley or other legal requirements. Here, the key point is that certain legal requirements no longer allow change of master data in entities like orders. In such a case, the duplicate used for this order needs deactivation on the SAP side. On the MDM System, you need to relate this duplicate with the active master data record. Thus, by querying for a master data record, you would also now get at least two primary identifiers, one for the active and one for the deactivated duplicated record, which both need to be used to query an order entry system for all orders in order to get accurate revenue for the product. We conclude that allowing temporary duplicates makes reporting so much more complicated, and thus we recommend preventing duplicates whenever possible, as shown later.

The second case where a product reached the end of its lifecycle requires that the master data change is identified as a "delete" operation within the integration infrastructure. The MDM System needs to store alternate key identifiers[14] providing information regarding the primary key identifier that other systems use for this record locally. A workflow triggered by a master data change of type "delete" would query the MDM System for the alternate key and system information. Then, with each SAP system having a copy of the record, it is cross-checked whether or not the record is still in use. Only if all systems no longer need the record would the workflow trigger a "delete" operation on the MDM System, as indicated by the dotted line arrows from the EAI through the ETL into the MDM System in Figure 8.9.

8.3.3.3   Advantages

The solution architecture has the following advantages—the list is not intended to be complete:

- The integration is not very intrusive in the SAP systems.
- The performance of the master data services is not slowed due to global transactions.
- Line of Business users do not require training on a new user interface and can continue with their current processes to create, author, and maintain product information in their known SAP user interfaces.
- The exchange of product information with retailers is simplified due to the integration with the GDSN, where the manufacturer publishes the relevant product attributes. The former one-to-one connections between the manufacturer and each retailer could be replaced by this streamlined process, unlocking significant cost reductions in the IT infrastructure.
- The MDM System enables global reporting for brand and category managers, making them more productive.
- Product and vendor master information is immediately available to create orders or bills within the SAP applications.
- Minimal impact on existing SAP systems used in production.

---

14.   The cross-referencing information could be available in the integration infrastructure itself, but we recommend having it within the MDM System. This way, you can get all the information on a master record and determine where it is used from a single system at any time.

8.3.3.4   Disadvantages

The solution architecture has the following disadvantages—we provide only a subset for illustration:

- Duplicate product records can be detected only during the ETL processing, when the data is moved from the SAP systems to the central MDM System. Therefore the integration infrastructure needs to deal with compensating transactions on the SAP systems to remove duplicates. The reason for this is the asynchronous nature of the integration. Also, a user cannot see all products because access to the MDM System is missing and work efforts might be wasted due to duplicate product creation and maintenance. In essence, the business value of an MDM System as the gatekeeper to prevent duplicates, the enforcer of data integrity and business rules, and the enabler of a global comprehensive view is significantly reduced due to this asynchronous integration.
- Brand and category managers are not able to see up-to-date, accurate information due to the asynchronous nature of the integration. Also, they likely only have read access for reports on brands and categories if the Coexistence Hub pattern is used. And even if brand and category managers can change data (assuming the Transaction Hub pattern was used for the MDM System), these changes are not reflected in the SAP systems.
- Due to the fact that the data is entered through the SAP UI, the master data requires harmonization before it can be entered into the MDM hub using ETL infrastructure. Due to the asynchronous nature, de-duplication is required as well.
- The central MDM System can only enforce the weakest set of all data integrity rules across all SAP systems. As a consequence, the purpose of an MDM System (of having high-quality master data) is, to a certain degree, diminished. If the central MDM System enforced stricter data integrity and validation rules than at least one SAP system, the MDM System or the ETL processes would reject low-quality records, violating at least some integrity rules. Again compensation logic in the integration environment updating the SAP system from which the record originated must solve this issue.

8.3.3.5   Synchronous Integration Scenario

As you saw, the asynchronous integration is causing several severe disadvantages. Let's now take a look and determine if synchronous integration would remove all of them and what the price for that would be. This scenario requires the implementation of the Transaction Interception pattern described in Chapter 5. On the SAP side, several options are available for synchronous integration, depending on the SAP system and master data domain. All of them share the following characteristics:

- The SAP system has to be changed through additional extension code deployed inside the SAP system. The extension code is usually written in ABAP.[15] The changes in ABAP in a SAP System are more intrusive than an asynchronous integration.

---

15.   ABAP is short for "Advanced Business Application Programming," a programming language widely used for SAP applications.

- The SAP systems usually have different synchronous integration points to hook in this extension code.
- The extension code needs to interact synchronously with the MDM System. For synchronicity, the SAP business function creating or changing master data needs to be put on hold until the answer from the MDM System is back.
- Real-time data model transformations need to be invoked before the MDM System can be called to transform the SAP data model to the MDM data model. "Reverse" data model transformation has to be invoked when the result from the MDM System is back.
- In a create case, the MDM System might return a list of suspects looking similar to the new master data record submitted through SAP. The list has to be displayed to the SAP User to let the user decide if the new record was indeed a duplicate of one of the similar-looking existing records or if it is truly a new master data record.

For a reader with some knowledge of SAP, here are just a few options for implementing this synchronous integration:

- Web Services if the Web Application Server of SAP is available in Version 7 or newer.
- Business Transaction Events (in essence user exits).
- Business Add-ins (also known as BADI): For synchronous integration with software from other vendors, SAP provides two predefined extension points for synchronous address cleansing and standardization. A skilled ABAP programmer can extend this interface to transport the customer data model, for example.

Compared to the asynchronous mechanism (configuring change pointers and a periodic job on the SAP side, which requires only a couple of mouse clicks), the synchronous mechanisms require ABAP coding and deep intrusion in SAP business transactions. Project implementation costs could increase due to the coding efforts. So naturally the question comes up—was it worth it? Are the major disadvantages of the asynchronous integration resolved?

Let's start with the good news first:

- Category managers, brand managers, and analysts can see consistent information in a real-time synchronous integration. Accuracy of reporting and analysis work improves, and branding and categorization tasks are aided, making this user group much more productive.
- Line of Business users are more efficient: They don't waste as much time creating and working with duplicate master data, because the de-duplication is occurring at creation time. The amount of orders that need to be redone or changed is significantly reduced, thus improving the productivity of these users significantly.
- The MDM System can deliver most of its business value to SAP applications, such as enterprise-wide enforcement of data integrity and business rules, and gatekeeper functions, avoiding duplicates.

However, open points remain, such as:

- The business users working with the SAP systems still do not see all master data records.

- If the network connection between a SAP system and the MDM System fails in the synchronous case, you might need to allow the users of the SAP system to continue with their work. If you do so, this has some consequences, because resynchronization is required. First, you need to collect all of the master data changes (possibly in a file or database table) locally, on the SAP system itself. Second, you need to have a mechanism to move them, after the network is available again, as a "mini-batch" job to the MDM System that is doing all of the necessary work such as master data transformation and duplicate checking. Third, if duplicates are found, you need to implement compensation logic for the SAP system. If you have multiple SAP systems, you would need to implement that for each and every one of them. Having these multiple spots of maintenance is not a nice fact from an IT cost perspective. Also, duplicate checks performed while moving master data from other SAP systems into the MDM System are not as good because they cannot see master data records relevant for de-duplication, thus leading to less accurate results and potentially causing additional clean-up efforts.

So summing up, synchronous integration between the SAP application systems through which the master data is entered and maintained and the MDM System definitely increases the value derived from deploying the MDM System measurably. However, the solution still has some disadvantages. Let's see if they are solved with an MDM UI as entry point.

8.3.4 Only Using MDM UI for Master Data Authoring and Maintenance

8.3.4.1 Business Context

We reuse the business context outlined in Subsection 8.3.3.1 with the following modification: This time, the company decided to incur the cost for training all of the users on a new user interface, the MDM UI for master data creation and maintenance. The benefits gained through significant simplification of the IT environment by using the MDM System to decouple the internal application systems from the reseller systems remain. We focus the discussion on what benefits can be gained in the integration infrastructure between the SAP application systems and the MDM System.

8.3.4.2 Solution Architecture

If you look at the solution architecture in Figure 8.10, you will notice that the right-hand part of the architecture that enables efficient product master data distribution to the vendors (in this case retailers) remains unchanged. The interesting changes happened in the center and on the left. As you can see in the center top portion of the figure, all users are working with an MDM UI—likely based on enterprise portal technology—for master data creation and maintenance. The MDM System receives requests for master data creation and updates through the service interfaces and needs to reflect all these changes in the dependent SAP application systems.

As outlined in Chapter 3, which described the MDM Reference Architecture, event and notification mechanisms and business rule infrastructure capabilities are part of the MDM System. These notification capabilities provide the ability to trigger updates for external systems asynchronously through message middleware and interfaces such as JMS.

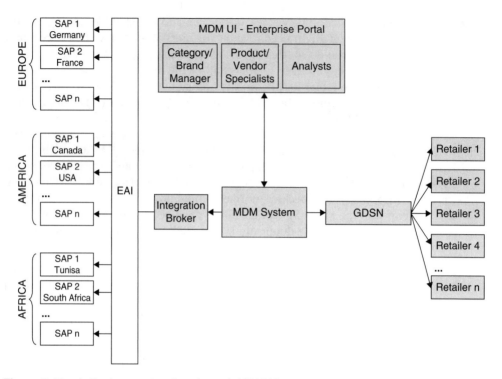

Figure 8.10   Authoring master data through MDM UI.

For performance reasons, if more than a few dependant systems need to be updated, we suggest implementing an integration broker. The integration broker receives a single notification through a JMS message from the MDM System about a master data change, with all relevant pieces of information, and dispatches this notification to all dependant systems that need the update. The integration broker also invokes, if necessary, appropriate data transformations to transform the master data record from the MDM System to the data model of the different SAP systems for consumption. The EAI layer depends again on the way the asynchronous integration is done—possible options include:

- **SAP connector or SAP adapter:** Such components are able to consume messages and create the needed IDOCs based on the context and then place them into the SAP inbox. SAP Systems can then consume these received IDOCs asynchronously. Readers familiar with SAP IDOC inbox know that the program placing an IDOC there only gets a confirmation from the SAP application that the IDOC was received. Because SAP applications always consume IDOCs through this interface asynchronously, if you need to take care of error handling, you need to periodically check with the SAP application system to see whether or not a specific IDOC was processed successfully until you receive confirmation that the IDOC was processed and persisted successfully. If the SAP application returns an error for processing an IDOC successfully, the integration broker clearly needs to implement polling and error handling mechanisms.

- **SAP BAPI interface and the SAP Java Connector:** If this combination is used, Java code deployed within the integration broker infrastructure would invoke the SAP BAPI interface through the SAP Java Connector, executing the necessary updates after completion of the data transformations. The BAPI interface uses synchronous RFC calls under the covers. So, technically, the BAPI interface is a synchronous API. Because the communication between the MDM System and the integration broker is asynchronous, for example, message-based, we consider the overall integration still asynchronous because the MDM System completed the service call without waiting for a synchronous feedback from the SAP systems.
- If **SAP Netweaver PI** is present in the IT environment in addition to the SAP application systems, the integration broker can also trigger updates of the SAP application systems through JMS or Web service calls based on SOAP/HTTP.

Another way of asynchronous integration would be using a periodic batch mechanism. This would likely apply in situations where the enterprise architecture does not follow the SOA paradigm. In this case, based on time stamps indicating when the master data record was modified for the last time, ETL infrastructure could extract all changes from the MDM System since the last batch run took place, transform the data to the SAP data models, and use SAP batch loading mechanisms to load the data into SAP. If the batch mechanism is used, the integration broker is likely not needed at all.

8.3.4.3 Advantages
Enabling master data creation and maintenance through an MDM UI leads to a number of benefits:

- The approach is not very intrusive on the MDM System.
- The master data services do not suffer from performance degradation because they do not need to wait until the SAP system confirmed the master data change.
- The duplicate record problem is significantly mitigated[16] because the duplicate checking occurs at creation time synchronously. Thus, workforce productivity is improved, and the cost of removing duplicates from the systems later is measurably decreased.
- The end users can see and work with all records. In the previous situation, with driving master data maintenance through the SAP user interface, you would not have been able to easily see master data records from other SAP application systems. This could have been the case even though you might have been entitled to see them, unless you would have enabled data replication between the SAP systems as well or from the MDM System to all SAP application systems.
- Changes from brand and category managers are visible to product specialists as well.
- Changes can be easily propagated to SAP using messaging infrastructure, keeping the integration costs low.

The approach also delivers the benefits for master data distribution to retailers.

---

16. There will always be a small set of suspect records where only an Operational Data Steward can decide whether or not two master data records match. Due to this, we decided to use this wording instead of claiming entire elimination.

8.3.4.4 Disadvantages

As nice as it would be to have all problems disappear with an MDM UI and an asynchronous integration with SAP applications, unfortunately, there are at least two disadvantages worth mentioning:

- All end users familiar with the SAP user interface need to be trained on the MDM UI. For large companies with dozens or hundreds of end users working with the SAP user interfaces, this is costly and time-consuming, and needs appropriate consideration when implementing the MDM project.
- Master data information created or changed is not immediately available within SAP applications for order creation, billing, or other business processes. For example, for a service employee in a call center where a vendor can place orders, not having the latest vendor information available might not be acceptable.

The second disadvantage mentioned points towards synchronous near real-time or real-time integration. We investigate in the next subsection if all issues can be resolved.

8.3.4.5 Synchronous Integration Scenario

From the previous subsection, the major open point is whether or not SAP application systems can be integrated synchronously. This question finally moves the extensibility, adaptability, and openness of your MDM System to center stage. As described in Chapters 1 and 4, extensibility, adaptability, and openness are key functional requirements of your MDM System supporting the evolutionary nature of MDM Systems. All master data services used where change propagation should happen to SAP synchronously need synchronous extension capabilities[17] for the integration we describe now. In essence, before the master data service commits, a synchronous call to the integration broker is made that dispatches it into a series of synchronous calls performing data transformations. It then uses an SAP interface such as SAP RFC[18] or SAP BAPI to reflect the change within the SAP applications synchronously. This would be a real-time synchronous integration with the side-effect that the MDM services perform slower because they need to wait for the SAP response. Removing this slowdown could be achieved with a near-real time approach that is not 100% synchronous end-to-end: First, call the integration broker from the MDM service asynchronously (meaning the service completes without waiting for feedback from the integration broker and therefore does not wait until SAP responds). In a second step, a synchronous processing between the integration broker and the SAP applications occurs. With this integration approach, you would eliminate the disadvantage that master data is not available to end users working with the SAP applications due to the delay caused by asynchronous integration.

It also delivers another advantage by resolving the issue where the integration broker cannot reach one or multiple SAP systems due to network failure: There is only one spot where master data changes that should be reflected in SAP application systems need to be collected. As a result, there is a single point of maintenance. Also, de-duplication checks can see the entire set of records in the IT environment because they are all in the MDM System already, which

---

17. A product with these capabilities is mentioned in Section B.5 in Appendix B.
18. Only the synchronous RFC mechanism is considered here. SAP BAPI API uses RFC under the covers.

was not the case when master data entry was performed through the SAP user interfaces. Also note that the synchronous integration with master data entry through an MDM user interface does not require deep intrusion into one or multiple SAP systems. Because the extensibility, adaptability, and openness of the MDM Systems is mandatory no matter what the integration architecture looks like, the deep embedding into the service interface for this integration approach is easier to accept than the deep embedding into an application system.

8.3.5   Comparison of the Four Integration Options

In this section, we compare the four options mentioned in Figure 8.8 in Table 8.2 on a high level. The first column provides the information about which case we discussed. The second column highlights whether or not the approach requires deep intrusion into the SAP systems or MDM System. The third column indicates if the integration approach impacts the performance of the master data services. The third column is applicable for only the cases 1a and 1b, because the services are unchanged in the Cases 2a and 2b. In the Case of 1b, the impact depends on how fast the responses from the SAP systems are back. However, in the product domain where you might have only a couple hundred to a few thousand changes a day, this might not be even noticeable. The integration complexity is an indication of how hard it is to build the integration considering UI components, synchronous communication, and compensation logic (if needed). The last column indicates how much business value offered by an MDM System is actually leveraged.

Table 8.2   Comparing the Four Discussed Integration Choices

Case	Intrusiveness on SAP/MDM	Performance Impact on MDM Services	Integration Complexity	Business Value of MDM System
1a—MDM UI async	Low	Low	Low	Full benefits
1b—MDM UI sync	Medium—some change of master data services required	Measurable	Medium	Full benefits
2a—SAP UI async	Low	Not applicable	High—due to compensation logic	Low, e.g., duplicate prevention disabled
2b—SAP UI sync	High—change of SAP functions required	Not applicable	High—code for synchronous reach out to MDM System and UI for suspect list	Almost full benefits

8.3.6 Simultaneous Use of MDM and SAP UI for Master Data Authoring and Maintenance

It is possible to allow master data changes through the SAP UI and the MDM UI at the same time through combination of the techniques outlined earlier. From the perspective of moving end users gradually over to the new MDM UI, this could be feasible. Another scenario could be in a first-phase implementation where the SAP UI is used and the MDM System deployed for master data harmonization. In the second phase, the MDM UI is introduced and the flow of master data reversed. Then there might be a short period of time where both user interfaces are used until the transition is complete.

Generally, we doubt that having both is a feasible approach after considering the following issues:

- Maintaining two integration architectures for both directions incurs increased IT costs.
- If the MDM UI is deployed, additional benefits are available to end users—thus it is questionable what the value of still using the application user interface for creating and maintaining master data would be.
- If the MDM UI development or adaptation is part of the MDM implementation project, why would you spend this money and still continue to use the application user interface?

Summing up, we think that having both user interfaces in use at the same time is a rare case that is justifiable only through exceptional circumstances and business requirements.

8.3.7 Summary

Now that we have seen the challenges when master data authoring and maintenance is allowed through the SAP UI, either asynchronously or synchronously, we conclude:

- The preferred option for deploying an MDM System is to allow master data authoring and maintenance only through the MDM UI.
- Allowing master data authoring and maintenance through the SAP UI might make sense in very large phased projects. Here, the first phase of the MDM deployment might be a hybrid hub for harmonization purposes and for simplifying the distribution of master data to pure master data consuming systems. An example would be the publication of master data through the GDSN to make it accessible for retailers. In the second phase of the MDM deployment, the MDM System becomes a true hub system by switching from SAP UI to the MDM UI for authoring and maintaining master data. Thus, the direction of the flow of master data is reversed, so that now the changes move from the MDM System to the SAP application systems.

  The same or similar techniques, considerations, and conclusions could be applied to other application systems from other vendors. Therefore, we believe an MDM UI directly invoking the MDM services interface is the best possible way to create and maintain master data.

Conclusion

After providing an overview across various MDM Solution Blueprints for various industries, and MDM Integration Blueprints for solving specific integration issues, we hope you now have a fairly good understanding of individual MDM Blueprints. Proven MDM Blueprints relate business and technology, establishing a clear value proposition. Using them provides guidance for IT Architects designing the detailed solution architecture, reducing the risks for the MDM deployment.

The Integration Blueprints were derived from the MDM Reference Architecture described in Chapter 3. Another input for the MDM Integration Blueprints were the architecture patterns described in Chapter 5. We highlighted how the architecture patterns were leveraged. As with the patterns shown in Chapter 5, you can assemble more comprehensive Blueprints by composition of basic ones presented in Chapters 6, 7, and 8. For an end-to-end MDM Solution Blueprint, for example, for banking and insurance combining the Cross- and Up-sell and the Fraud and Theft Solution Blueprint with the Integration Blueprint for DW and MDM System integration may deliver the desired solution.

References

1. Inmon, W. H. 2005. *Building the Data Warehouse*. New York: John Wiley & Sons.
2. Koncilia, C., and Wrembel, R. 2006. *Data Warehouses and OLAP: Concepts, Architectures and Solutions*. Location: IGI Global.
3. Codd, E. F. 1970. A Relational Model of Data for Large Shared Data Banks. *Communications of the ACM* 13(6): 377–387.
4. Kent, William. 1983. A Simple Guide to Five Normal Forms in Relational Database Theory. *Communications of the ACM* 26(2): 120–125.
5. Codd, E. F. 1974. Recent Investigations into Relational Data Base Systems. *IBM Research Report RJ1385*.
6. Heuer, A., and Saake, G. 2000. *Datenbanken: Konzepte und Sprachen*. 2nd ed. Landsberg, Germany: dpunkt.
7. Gray, J., and Reuter, A. 1993. *Transaction Processing: concepts and techniques*. San Mateo, CA: Morgan Kaufmann.
8. Inmon, W. H. 1999. *Building the Operational Data Store*. New York: John Wiley & Sons.
9. Portal architecture patterns: http://www.ibm.com/developerworks/patterns/portal/.
10. Edling, J., Galic, M., Hisler, C., et al. 2001. *Access Integration Pattern using IBM WebSphere Portal Server*. IBM Redbook™: http://www.redbooks.ibm.com/abstracts/SG246267.html.

Chapter 9

Master Data Management and Data Governance

One of the keys to successfully deploying master data management is effectively using people, processes, and technology to leverage the master data as an enterprise asset. Collectively, this approach is known as **data governance**. This chapter will explore the critical nature of data governance in master data management, and the direct and indirect roles that the MDM architecture plays in enabling data governance.

9.1   Governance

Governance is the way we make and act on decisions about managing a shared resource for the common good. Governance includes:

- Defining the scope and aspects of the shared resource that will be managed to the benefit of the organization based on defined business goals and regulatory requirements
- Deciding *who* (both the roles and the people filling those roles) makes the decisions for the resource, how the governing bodies are *organized,* and the *processes* they will follow
- Distributing the decisions (in the forms of *laws* and *edicts* in a political government, *policies* and *procedures* in other organizations) about what will be done, what will not be done, what will be encouraged, and what will be discouraged when using the shared resource
- Assigning responsibilities for implementing the different parts of the processes, policies, and procedures to the shared resource
- Monitoring the use of the shared resource and the shared resource itself, in order to enforce business and regulatory policies, and to assess the effectiveness of those policies

This is a very broad definition of governance—to place the need for governance in a more practical fashion (in particular, in the context of MDM), let's take a look at a blinded case study of a company looking at deploying an MDM project and some of the concerns that can only be addressed through governance.

9.1.1 Case Study: JK Enterprises

JK Enterprises (JKE) is a large financial services (banking, mutual funds, credit cards, loans, annuities, etc.), mortgage provider, and insurance provider in North America with annual revenues of $20 billion dollars US. Much of JKE's recent growth has come from acquisitions; however, regulations regarding monopolization are limiting future growth via acquisitions— so the company is looking to grow organically. Traditionally, the financial, mortgage, and insurance parts of JKE have been run as independent lines of business, each with its own call centers and IT systems for customer information. This method of operation has led to a number of internal operational problems as well as external customer satisfaction and retention problems, which are typical of the ones described in Chapter 1:

- Redundant data across the enterprise
- Questionable data quality and integrity
- Redundant business processes
- Uncoordinated Customer Data Management initiatives throughout the enterprise
- Nonsystematic recognition of real-time selling and retention opportunities across and within businesses

JKE's lack of integration and consistency in customer data and its effect on growth, customer satisfaction, and retention manifested itself clearly in the interaction with one customer— the Higday family. Matthew Higday and his wife, Carla Watson, and their two college age children, Scott and Jessica, are JKE customers who have had a number of particularly unhappy interactions with JKE:

- Matthew Higday and Carla Watson (who kept her surname from her first marriage) have a mortgage through JKE Mortgage Services. However, the names on all correspondence from the mortgage company are Matthew and Carla *Watson*. Repeated attempts to change this have failed.
- Carla was the original account holder with JKE for insurance, banking, and credit cards. Matthew got his own credit card from JKE after they married. The online system at JKE Financial only allows Carla to view and update her credit card—the householding system does not recognize Matthew as an independent consumer.
- Scott has recently moved out to go to college, and he notified the company of his new address. His insurance notifications are still coming to his parents' house, while his credit card bills are being sent to his new address. Furthermore, although Scott is now renting a new apartment, JKE has not sent him any solicitations for renter's insurance, which would represent a new opportunity for business.

Because of problems like this, senior management has long expressed an interest in developing a consistent view of JKE customers across the enterprise, and it has commissioned a study to quantify the new business and customer retention/satisfaction opportunities related to creating a shared business view of JKE's customers. The analysis revealed a potential of *$70 million US* in potential opportunities across JKE using three initiatives:

- Cross-selling of financial products to insurance customers: $33M–$41M
- Retention benefits associated with increasing share of wallet: $5.6M–$8.5M
- Improved customer information to call center operations: $15M–$19M

JKE recognizes that it has a problem with master data. Previous initiatives for customer data integration have failed, in part due to the fact that these integration efforts were still within the individual lines of businesses and in part because the overall business and overview processes did not change accordingly. For JKE, the success factor for master data is in adding in the *management* aspect of master data management—and recognizing that business change and governance are key parts of that management aspect. In particular, before JKE can roll out an MDM System, they need to find the right people to address the following challenges:

- Coming up with an agreed-upon common definition of a customer that will be accepted across the different lines of businesses, and coming up with a plan to merge and link the master data across those same lines of businesses. Complicating this process (and others) is that certain data (such as the name of a policy holder) cannot be altered even if it is wrong (because the policy is a legal document).
- Deciding how to implement mechanisms to address the master data quality issues they know they have with existing master data, how they will reduce quality problems with new master data as it comes in, and how they will measure the progress of their initiatives in this space.
- Agreeing to and enforcing a set of security rules for who can see and update the master data. For example, legal restrictions require that information about a JKE prospect (a person who is not yet a customer) can be seen only by the agent who is working with that prospect.

As we can see with this case study, an MDM journey initiates a transformational change into how an enterprise creates, manages, owns, cleanses, consumes, shares, reacts to, protects, monitors, and analyzes master data. Before packing for this journey, you must understand the following things:

- First, your enterprise must reach a collective understanding that master data in an enterprise is a common asset, and that it is not being effectively used to the greatest benefit of the organization.
- Second, addressing the problem requires the ongoing collaboration and commitment of a broad spectrum of business and IT people across the organization—starting with executive sponsorship and including the CIO and staff, Line of Business owners, executive data stewards, operational data stewards, data integrators, application developers, data architects, and others.
- Third, you must understand that this is a journey—there will be several intermediate steps along the way that represent specific projects, each with its own distinct business and governance needs. Each stop on this journey should bring your organization closer to its target maturity level for master data governance.

In general, how the group of people identified in the second item just presented manages data for the benefit of the entire organization is *data governance*, and when the scope of the managed data is master data, this is known as **master data governance**. Before we look at master data governance, we first need to explore the topic of governance in some related disciplines.

9.1.2 Governance in Related Disciplines

9.1.2.1 Governance in Information Technology

Enterprise Architects should be quite familiar with the reality of governance as it applies to enterprise architecture. Mature IT organizations have a set of processes, policies, and procedures related to IT architecture, including:

- Defining architectural components, behaviors, interfaces, and integration
- Getting approval of the architecture
- Ensuring that the IT infrastructure and applications align with architecture standards
- Requesting changes to the components to accommodate new application requirements or emerging technologies
- Granting variances to application architects and owners for all or part of the architectural requirements

For all of the items presented, IT organizations typically have a formal process in place to govern each phase of an IT architecture project. Typically, these processes involve architecture review boards and participation of architects in projects that consume and deliver common infrastructure and services across the enterprise. For enterprise architecture, the goal of governance is to work towards a common vision of the IT and business landscape with a focus on reducing overall costs by integrating and reusing technology and increasing flexibility for future growth and change.

Two types of governance that are directly relevant to IT Architects are **IT Governance** and **SOA Governance**.

9.1.2.2 IT Governance—COBIT

IT Governance is the discipline of managing IT as a service to the business and aligning IT objectives with business goals. There are a number of standards related to IT Governance; however, the one most often referenced for regulatory compliance is the COBIT (Control **OBj**ectives for **I**nformation and related **T**echnology) standard [1] from the IT Governance Institute. According to COBIT, IT Governance is a framework that covers the lifecycle of IT deliverables, as shown in Figure 9.1.

COBIT defines four major domains of IT lifecycle activities that we now introduce and discuss in more detail in the upcoming sections:

- **Planning and Organizing:** This domain covers how the IT organization functions in general, including general planning, staffing, architecture, project management, risk management, and quality management.
- **Acquisition and Implementation:** This domain focuses on the selection and preparation for rollout of IT technology to satisfy business requirements.

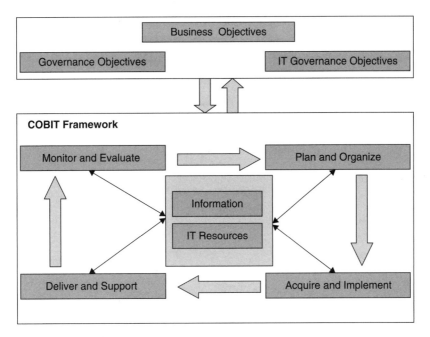

Figure 9.1 Overview of COBIT.

- **Delivery and Support:** This domain specifies how IT resources are made available to the business in a managed, secure, and reliable fashion.
- **Monitor and Evaluate:** This domain is the control domain for the other three, ensuring that appropriate governance activities are being carried out.

Within each of the domains, COBIT defines a set of governance control objectives to help guide the IT organization in making appropriate decisions for each domain. One data-specific governance objective is defined by COBIT: **DS 11 Manage Data.** This objective has controls regarding backup and retention of data, which are primary IT activities.

9.1.2.3 SOA Governance

Chapter 2 describes Information Service Governance—information service governance is a subset of SOA Governance. SOA governance can be considered as all of the activities surrounding the lifecycle and control of reusable business and IT services. Some of these activities are:

- Determining which services are made available by service providers
- Defining the interface and semantics of the services
- Specifying how services are secured and who has access to them
- Deciding if a service is available only to internal consumers or to consumers outside the enterprise
- Controlling how new services are introduced and existing services either retired or revamped

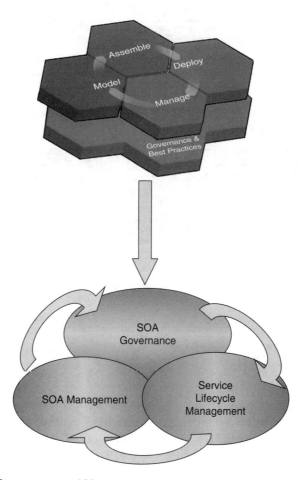

Figure 9.2 SOA Governance and Management.

Figure 9.2 depicts the interaction of SOA governance and SOA lifecycle management.

9.1.3 Data Governance

IT Governance is a long-standing discipline, and SOA Governance is a logical outgrowth of service-orientation. Both disciplines have some data-related governance points. IT Governance has mechanisms to manage aspects of the availability and security of information as well as some aspects of the data lifecycle. SOA Governance (in particular, Information Service Governance) can specify the lifecycle and nature of information services exposed to applications. The notion that data also needs to be governed manifested itself in early efforts, such as the Zachman Framework, and also in the Industry Models, which emphasize governance of the underlying data model and the link between business and technology, including the data and processes needed to manage the data.

What is Data Governance?

*Data Governance is the political process of changing organizational behavior to enhance
and protect data as a strategic enterprise asset*

*Implementing Data Governance is a fundamental change to the methods & rigor both
Business and Information Technology use to define, manage, and use data*

> **The core objectives of a governance program are:**
> - Guide information management decision-making
> - Ensure information is consistently defined and well understood
> - Increase the use and trust of data as an enterprise asset
> - Improve consistency of projects across an enterprise

Figure 9.3 Defining Data Governance and Data Governance Objectives (courtesy of the IBM
Data Governance Council).

However, it has been the explosion over the past few years in the amount of data (and
redundant data) held by organizations that has recently captured the attention of the industry and led to a consistent focus on data as a shared asset and the need to govern it accordingly. At the forefront in this area of data governance is the **IBM Data Governance Council**,
founded in 2004. What makes the IBM Data Governance Council unique is that the Council
is composed of a cross section of business and IT data experts from data-rich enterprises,
vendors, and IBM, giving it a special insight into a broader view of data and its value and
challenges. The IBM Data Governance Council produced three key intellectual work products on data governance (see [2] for details):

1. A standard definition of data governance
2. An architectural blueprint and ontology for discussing the different focus areas of
   data governance
3. A maturity model for assessing where an organization is along a data governance journey

We explore each of these three perspectives on data governance now.

9.1.3.1 Data Governance Defined

As defined by the IBM Data Governance Council, data governance is *"the political process of
changing organizational behavior to enhance and protect data as a strategic enterprise asset."*
Furthermore, as shown in Figure 9.3, the core objectives for data governance are completely
aligned with the benefits of MDM that were described in Chapter 1, which are:

- Provide a consistent understanding and trust of master data entities
- Consistent use of master data across the organization
- Accommodate and manage change (dynamic)

One of the key differentiators of data governance, as opposed to IT and SOA governance, is the importance and involvement in data governance of the business itself in taking on more responsibility when governing data. Data is fundamentally owned by the business—IT manages the repository of the data and provides the architecture, tools, and technologies to enable effective business ownership, stewardship, and use of the data across the organization. As a result, data governance overlaps with IT and SOA governance (specifically, with regard to managing the technology underpinnings of the data, and in providing the service window into the master data), but data governance has many process and people aspects that are separate from these other governance regimes. One of the fundamental tenets of *master* data governance is that the overall responsibility for collective master data is across multiple lines of business, because the data is shared across multiple business units and business processes (however, a particular person or role may be given ownership duties of particular master data for stewardship and legal reasons).

The "people" part of "changing organizational behavior" in master data governance is the key success factor for master data governance—ultimately, it is people who define, create, correct, interpret, and consume master data. Indeed, one entire section of this book (Appendix A) is devoted to describing the various roles of people who participate in master data governance. In an environment where master data is well governed, it is of paramount importance to have business people fulfilling the following roles:

- **Executive Sponsors** that have overall responsibility for master data initiatives. At an enterprise level, these senior managers are usually the true owners of the master data.
- **Business Data Stewards** who are management delegates given direct responsibility for master data, perhaps organized by data domain. Usually business data stewards take the lead in bringing together the key IT staff (IT Architects, Data Architects, Data Integrators, IT Management) and the key business people (stewards, consumers, application owners) to pull together a master data initiative.
- **Operational Data Stewards** are responsible for day-to-day oversight of the content and quality of master data. Operational stewards are typically organized by data domain, such as **Demographic Data Stewards** (for Party data) and **Item/Category Specialists** (for Product data). These stewards may be further specialized within the domains to control the span of master data that individual stewards can manage, based on business and security policies.
- **Business Analysts (or Subject Matter Experts)** with deep domain knowledge with regard to the domains of master data, especially about specific data elements (their formats and meanings) across the enterprise. These business users are critical resources when a project is undertaken to define master data and sources of master data, and to adapt new and existing business processes to consume master data from the central services.

The process aspect of master data governance is how the business and IT users successfully collaborate to *"enhance and protect data as a strategic enterprise asset."* Processes must be put in place to:

- Assess the current state of the information assets (and business processes relating to them) that are targeted for a master data management project.
- Propose an initial scope and goals for the MDM project.

- Establish a project plan for implementing the project.
- Deal with ongoing management of quality and accommodate changes to the master data infrastructure and configuration.

All of these processes need to be integrated with the people and organizational culture of the enterprise.

The technology pieces of master data management were the focus of Chapter 3, following presentation of the relevant definitions of MDM in Chapter 1. From a master data governance perspective, the technology needs to go beyond services and repositories for creating, updating, securing, and deleting master data. The technology needs to support stewardship operations, enforce and report on data quality, provenance, security and privacy, and integrate with change control and lifecycle mechanisms for business rules, security and privacy policies, data models, data classifications, and metadata.

9.1.3.2 Data Governance Maturity Model

The IBM Data Governance Council's Data Governance Maturity Model (DGMM), like many maturity models, follows the format of the Software Engineering Institute's (SEI) Capability Maturity Model Integration (CMMI) model. The DGMM has two major features:

- A set of 11 categories that represent components of a data governance program, as shown in Table 9.1. Each category also includes a set of key indicators representing critical processes or technologies for that category (this is not shown in the figure).
- A hierarchy of maturity levels that can be assessed for each of the elements of the model.

As shown in Table 9.1, the governance components run from the high-level layers such as organizational structures or risk management to the lower-level technology components such as data architecture and metadata. We use these components to guide our discussion of master data governance later in the chapter.

Table 9.1 Major Components of the Data Governance Maturity Model, Courtesy of the IBM Data Governance Council

Category	Description
Organizational Structures and Awareness	Describes the level of mutual responsibility between business and IT for data governance, and recognition of the fiduciary responsibility to govern data at different levels of management.
Stewardship	Stewardship is a quality-control discipline designed to ensure custodial care of data for asset enhancement, risk mitigation, and organizational control.
Policy	Policy is the written articulation of desired organizational behavior.

(continued)

Table 9.1   Major Components of the Data Governance Maturity Model, Courtesy of the IBM Data Governance Council (continued)

Category	Description
Value Creation	The process by which data assets are qualified and quantified to enable the business to maximize the value created by the data assets.
Data Risk Management and Compliance	The methodology by which risks are identified, qualified, quantified, avoided, accepted, mitigated, or transferred out.
Information Security and Privacy	Describes the policies, practices, and controls used by an organization to mitigate risk and protect data assets.
Data Architecture	The architectural design of structured and unstructured data systems and applications that enable data availability and distribution to appropriate users.
Data Quality Management	The methods used to measure, improve, and certify the quality and integrity of product, test, and archival data.
Classification and Metadata	The methods and tools used to create common semantic definitions for business and IT terms, data models, types, and repositories. Metadata is information that bridges human and computer understanding.
Information Lifecycle Management	A systematic, policy-based approach to information collection, use, retention, and deletion.
Audit, Logging, and Reporting	The organizational processes for monitoring the data value, risks, and efficacy of governance.

As illustrated in Figure 9.4, the maturity of an organization's data governance program can be placed at five different levels across the different data governance components.

Unfortunately, far too many organizations start out at level 1, which is where JKE started in our case study. From a data governance perspective, level 1 is characterized by:

- IT is given ownership of data and data quality on a project basis, even within lines of business.
- Lack of integration of data across the silos.
- Inconsistent organizational policies for risk management and compliance with respect to the data, and lack of institutional controls to implement and monitor those policies.
- Little to no reporting on data quality or on overall data metrics beyond the needs of a given project.

- Knowledge of the data, from a semantic and syntactic point of view, is maintained solely by individuals on different teams and is not captured in any tooling.
- Along those lines, responsibility for managing the risks to the data is also vested in the hands of individuals rather than under an organizational process, and their efforts to ensure data integrity are often heroic as part of a response to an immediate crisis.
- Data integration is ad hoc across a few projects, and the quality and consistency of the data is not well understood.

Level 3 (*Defined*) of the maturity model is the initial target level of maturity for master data management projects. Level 3 is characterized by:

- Enterprise ownership of the data, with responsibilities delegated to funded data stewards for ensuring the quality and security of the data.
- Well-defined data models and data integration models across critical enterprise business processes.
- Standard reporting on the governed data, the quality of data, and risks to the data. These reports are communicated across lines of business and up to management.
- A funded internal data governance group responsible for the data used across critical enterprise business processes, with focused governance groups on either particular projects or on master data domains.

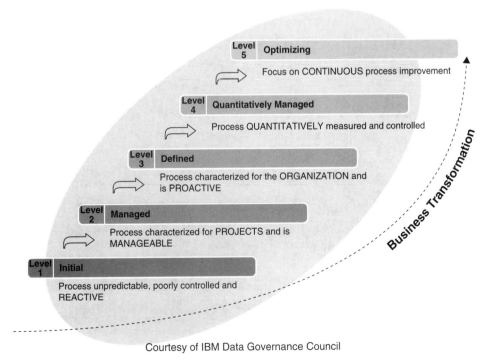

Courtesy of IBM Data Governance Council

Figure 9.4 Levels of maturity for data governance.

The model also includes a set of questions that can be used as part of an assessment process for data governance. An assessment is one of the first steps of instituting a master data governance process—the organization needs a basic understanding of its maturity and capabilities before going forward with a plan to improve the maturity. Note that organizations should not automatically set a goal of achieving the highest level of maturity across all categories. You need to assess your requirements in a given area based on your industry, your business and regulatory requirements, and your organizational culture.

9.1.3.3   MDM Intersection with Data Governance Maturity Blueprint

The IBM Data Governance Council has also organized the 11 categories of data governance into an architectural hierarchy that reflects the value chain for governance—this is shown in Figure 9.5.

At the top of the value chain are the **outcomes**—the expected business value from a successful master data governance program. Below that are the **enablers**, the organizational structures, policies, and processes required to provide value at the business layer. The **core disciplines** are the IT technologies that are consumed by the enablement layers—these core disciplines also rely on the base processes and technologies found in the **supporting disciplines.**

As described in Chapter 1, there are essentially two high-level goals that are supported by data governance: **value creation** (and its sibling, **cost reduction/operational efficiency**) and **data risk management and compliance.** Value creation is a core capability of MDM—delivering clean master data to enable new business opportunities like cross-sell/up-sell,

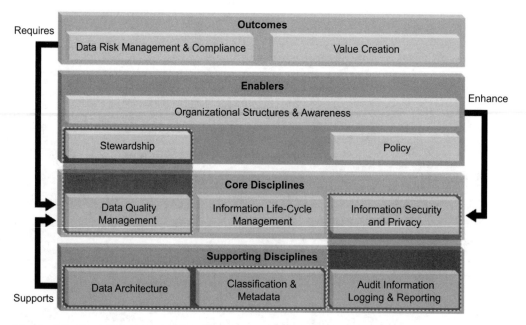

Figure 9.5 Disciplines of Effective Data Governance (Courtesy of the IBM Data Governance Council).

Table 9.2   Data Governance Disciplines in Previous Chapters

Data Governance Disciplines	Covered in ...
Value Creation	Chapter 1—Introduction to MDM Chapter 6—PIM-MDM Solution Blueprints Chapter 7—CDI-MDM Solution Blueprints Chapter 8—MDM Integration Blueprints
Data Risk Management and Compliance	Chapter 1—Introduction to MDM Chapter 4—MDM Security and Privacy
Policy	Chapter 1—Introduction to MDM
Information Lifecycle Management	Chapter 4—MDM Security and Privacy
Security and Reporting	Chapter 4—MDM Security and Privacy
Data Architecture	Chapter 2—MDM as an SOA Enabler Chapter 3—MDM Reference Architecture
Classification and Metadata	Chapter 1—Introduction to MDM

householding and campaign management, and to improve the efficiency and time-to-market of new and existing initiatives.

Most of the 11 disciplines of data governance are covered elsewhere in the book. A brief summary of that coverage is provided in Table 9.2.

In the next sections, we look at the lifecycle of an MDM project and show how that dovetails with two particular elements of the Data Governance Maturity Model:

- Organizational Awareness and Structure (which we extend to discuss the phases of MDM projects and the structures and processes needed to support them)
- Data Stewardship (where we look at how people manage the data to the benefit of the organization)

We also take a close look at the general nature of Data Quality and how quality and stewardship are supported by the MDM Data Quality Services.

9.2   MDM Project Lifecycle and Data Governance

Now that we have introduced what Data Governance is and how Data Governance is related to SOA Governance, we now show how Data Governance applies to master data management. As you will see, establishing strong Data Governance procedures is a key success factor for any MDM implementation.

9.2.1   Assessment and Planning

The first phase of any MDM project is the assessment and planning phase. As shown in Figure 9.6, this consists of the *project drivers, stakeholder management,* and *project scope* activities.

First, you need to understand the current state of your organization and articulate *why* your organization needs a master data management solution. You need to be able to identify the key business and technical drivers for moving to master data management. This initial assessment requires the involvement and financial commitment of major stakeholders across the relevant business and technical areas—these drivers help you determine which initial and ongoing stakeholders are needed (stakeholder management). Next, you need to look at the scope of your MDM project—what your current landscape surrounding master data, business processes, and organizational capabilities is—and what your target for these with regard to an MDM project is. Finally, as you look at a given project, you should consider the solution blueprints provided in Chapters 6 and 7 and see how to customize them for your particular environment.

9.2.1.1   Project Drivers

MDM Solutions are motivated by different reasons and pain points that vary among organizations. There may even be different organizations in an enterprise that initiate the implementation of an MDM project. For example, after a merger of two companies or an acquisition of another company, the driving force for an MDM initiative may be more *business-related* than technology-related. Among many other things, this business change could mean for the different IT organizations that they need to streamline their representation of the joint customer base. In this particular case, the MDM project is most likely initiated by top management and business leaders. A senior management driven project has a strong impact on the overall stakeholder management that accompanies any MDM project implementation. Generally speaking, stakeholder management is an important aspect that

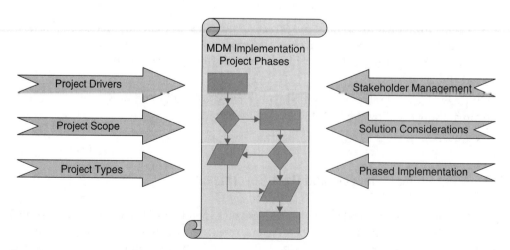

Figure 9.6 MDM Project Phases.

needs to be taken seriously into consideration; we come back to this aspect later in this section. Another example of a business-related driving factor is the improvement of existing business processes or even the need to introduce new business processes for an enterprise, where there is a strong relevance for a certain master data domain or MDM method of use. An example is to streamline the New Product Introduction (NPI) business process, which was discussed in Chapter 6.

There are also driving forces that are more *technical and IT infrastructure-related*, such as master data consolidation requirements that relate to the need to optimize all master data of a certain domain. Having to deal with these technical-related project drivers doesn't necessarily mean that they are detached from any business relevance. Quite the contrary is true; even a highly technically motivated MDM project implementation is grounded and very much embedded in a larger business context. If there weren't going to be any positive impact on the business side—for example, to allow for optimization of a defined set of business processes—the IT organization would most likely not embark on a larger MDM project. Another example of a *technical-related* driving factor is the need to overcome the diverse programming methods required to access master data that is spread across a heterogeneous data management landscape involving multiple repositories.

Other project drivers are related to the ever-increasing need to comply with specific regulations or mandates, as discussed in Chapters 1 and 4. These regulations may be industry-specific (e.g., Basel II Capitol Accord, Solvency II, HIPAA, and Anti-Money Laundering) or generic (e.g., Sarbanes-Oxley Act, PCI-DSS, and data breach laws). One of the more visible drivers might be a data breach—the reputation, legal, and financial costs associated with breaches will get the attention of senior management.

We can take the set of MDM drivers from Chapter 1 and reorganize them around the IBM Data Governance Maturity Model *outcomes* as follows:

Value Creation
- New opportunities with existing customers—cross-sell, up-sell, sales opportunities associated with life events (new child, retirement, etc.), householding and campaign management
- Identification of high- and low-value customers

Operational Efficiencies
- Reduced time to market
  - New product introduction
  - Simplified product bundling
- Reduced IT costs
  - Single container for master data
  - For consumption by business processes and feeding cleaner and timelier master data into data warehouses and data marts
  - Faster reaction and accommodation of business changes related to mergers, acquisitions, and divestitures
- Faster implementation of new business initiatives
- Customer retention
- Improved data quality using MDM improves customer satisfaction

Data Risk Management and Regulatory Compliance

- Using Master Data to implement financial risk management (for credit risk, market risk, and so on)
  - Basel II, Solvency II, and so on.
- Using Master Data for Regulatory Compliance Reporting and Processes
  - Sarbanes-Oxley, Gramm-Leach-Bliley, HIPAA, Anti-Money Laundering, Know Your Customer, SB 1386, and so on.
- Using Master Data Management as a single point to implement data protection (security, privacy, and availability) controls required by regulations and industry mandates
  - Sarbanes-Oxley, PCI-DSS, European Data Protection Law, HIPAA, and so on.

In our JKE case study, the drivers were dealing with both value creation (up-sell and cross-sell) and operational efficiencies (reduced IT costs and customer retention/satisfaction). Underlying all of the drivers are requirements for the key characteristics of master data management: a system of record (or reference) with high-quality master data.

9.2.1.2 Stakeholder Management

After you understand the specific drivers for master data management, you can identify the key initial stakeholders for the MDM project across senior management, lines of business, and information technology based on the drivers. Some of these stakeholders likely participated in the original effort to identify the need for master data management. The stakeholders will make up not only the core oversight for the MDM project but will serve as the nucleus for an Executive Data Governance Board. A recommended list for initial stakeholders includes:

Executive Sponsors

- Chief Information Officer or representative
- Chief Information Security/Privacy/Compliance Officer or representative (especially critical for operational efficiencies and compliance projects)
- Lines of Business Executive Sponsors

IT Architecture and Operations

- Strategist
- Data Architects
- Solution Architect(s)

Business

- Line of Business Resource Owners
- Business Data Stewards
- Business Analysts

Immature organizations (at level 1 or even level 2 of data governance maturity) may not have explicitly defined business data stewards, so you need to look for people who have a solid grounding in the business side of the proposed master data who also can work with the IT staff to ensure the technology can match the business needs. At this point, you may also consider other staff, such as data integrators (who understand how to pull in potential sources of master data) and operational data stewards (who understand and own existing islands of master data).

9.2.1.3   Project Scope

The Executive MDM Team will commission an MDM project group to create a roadmap for the MDM deployment. As part of creating the group, the executive team needs to set up a management and decision-making structure in the project group. There is no single right method for how to structure the group—the best structure is one that can be effective in the culture of the organization. Usually, the initial MDM project group will be seeded with representatives from the Executive MDM Team, with the addition of a project manager. The team will also include at least one executive sponsor.

After the group structure, memberships, and dynamics have been established, the project team will start on defining the scope and governance characteristics of the MDM project. From a governance perspective, the critical questions that need to be answered are:

- What enterprise data will be moved into the master data management system? The proposed candidates for master data will be tied back to the project drivers—however, from a project management perspective, it may be necessary to limit the initial set of master data domains. For example, in a healthcare environment, an organization with HIPAA concerns might first target patient information (for a master patient index) as its first managed master data, and defer moving insurance providers into the master data management system to a later project (or a later phase of the initial project.)
- What are the current business processes, applications, and repositories that consume and store master data, and what are their potential roles in the MDM project? Existing repositories will be the sources for the MDM System, so the project team needs to catalog these systems and understand:
  - What pieces of master data does each repository hold? MDM should have the single, consistent, accurate, and complete view of a master data object, but in the current enterprise environment, different (and overlapping) parts of the master data are held by disjointed repositories and managed by disjointed applications. Developing a consolidated map of the different systems and the parts of the master data they hold should be one of the outputs of the scoping phase.
  - What is the quality of the master data of each repository? Each potential source of master data needs to be profiled for quality (see Section 9.3) to give the project team an assessment of whether or not a particular repository is suitable to feed master data into the MDM System and how much data cleansing and reconciliation needs to take place on an initial and ongoing basis.
  - Existing applications and business processes need to be cataloged and examined to see if they should be repurposed to use the forthcoming Master Data Repository, be retired in favor of other applications and business processes, or be operated as they are right now (potentially with the master data being sourced from the new Master Data Repository using the Coexistence Style).
  - The metadata associated with the current systems should also be captured (or at least noted). This metadata includes quality rules, workflows, event notifications, security controls, and data models. These artifacts can all be mined as intellectual capital in constructing the rules, architecture, and metadata for the proposed MDM domain.

- What are the common definitions for the semantics, structure, and services for the proposed master data domains? The business analysts, data stewards, architects, and data integrators all need to come together to determine how they will answer this question. The catalog of existing master data definitions collected earlier can serve as an initial basis for the semantics and structure of the proposed master data objects and elements, but the team will have to resolve conflicts and discrepancies between the existing repositories. Other factors that should be considered include:

  - Industry Models for representing master data, such as those discussed in Table 1.1 (IFW, IAA, etc.)
  - Regulatory and Compliance requirements that explicitly describe sensitive data. PCI-DSS, for example, mandates a set of controls for credit card information, so it may be important to identify and classify the credit card data, separate it into its own object or attribute group, and provide explicit services to access that sensitive data. This fine grained approach to the data allows the specification of authorization and auditing controls on the regulated master data.
  - It may be prudent to split the process of resolving the semantic, structural, and behavioral aspects of the master data across the different lines of business that "own" different portions of the master data. For example, in the New Product Introduction Business Pattern described in Section 6.3 in Chapter 6, different business users are responsible for creating different parts of the master data: category and item specialists for the product data, marketing and pricing specialists for their data, and so on. The executive data steward and project manager should assist in getting all of the expertise needed to get a complete definition of the master data. But the overall decisions have to be reviewed by representatives of multiple lines of business—master data is not owned by a single entity and should not be controlled or defined by just one Line of Business. This work should also include an initial definition of the data quality rules and the data quality metrics that should be applied to the managed master data (we discuss data quality in more detail in Section 9.4.) The rules will be designed to ensure the MDM System can truly deliver cleansed and accurate master data.

- What are the initial and ongoing sources for master data? After the domains of master data and their structure and semantics have been decided on, the project and governance team needs to decide how to populate the managed master data. Information from the earlier assessments should be used to make that decision. At this point, the data integration team will also look at how to establish the quality rules and mechanisms for taking the initial disjoint data from myriad applications and turning that data into cleansed master data, with cross-references between the different sources so that data from multiple sources can be joined correctly. The governance committee needs to decide who will be responsible for resolving problems that are found in the feeds in the master data and how they will be notified of problems.

9.2.2 Initial Rollout and Ongoing Support

At this point, the project activities segue into *solution considerations* and *phased implementation*, and then they move into ongoing support for the stewardship and use by business processes of the master data. The key questions to be answered at this phase of the project are:

- Who can access the master data, either in part or in whole, and what actions can they perform against the master data? What are the risks to your master data and how are you addressing them?
  - Chapter 4 (MDM Security and Privacy) describes the security and privacy model related to integrating MDM with enterprise security services and enterprise security management. Prior to the rollout of the MDM System, the data stewards and business analysts need to work with the security administrator to map the existing enterprise security roles against the roles needed for MDM Solutions. The solution and integration blueprints in Chapters 6 through 8 can provide some guidance. Additionally, the MDM governance team will need to define a set of data-driven authorization rules (for example, "Only the assigned agent for a Party can update the address for the Party") that go beyond simple role assignment. Chapter 4 also provides guidance on what some of the risks are to MDM Systems. The governance board needs to participate in the overall risk process to determine which risks will be mitigated, which will be transferred, and which will be accepted.
- How will the organization deal with ongoing measurement and management of quality?
  - Reporting on overall master data quality and assessing the return on investment of MDM is a role typically delegated from the MDM Data Governance board to a business data steward. Quality and duplication issues related to specific instances of master data (or even domains) would be handled by the operational data stewards.
- How will the organization accommodate changes to the master data environment?
  - The master data ecosystem will evolve naturally over time. New domains of master data will be added; the elements of the master data will change to enable new business processes, business opportunities, and regulations; and more applications will start consuming the master data. Over time, the implementation style used for master data may change as well, moving away from Coexistence and Registry Styles to Transactional. The MDM Data Governance board has the responsibility for the data side of these changes, and for interacting with the other governance groups to ensure the changes are handled smoothly. The DG Board needs to set up review, approval, test, and deployment processes to handle changes to the MDM environment. Because master data is an enterprise resource, master data governance representing multiple lines of business is a necessity for mitigation of the risk that poorly considered changes get implemented and disrupt key business functions.

9.3   Data Stewardship

One of the tenets of master data governance is that master data is an enterprise asset, as opposed to an asset of a particular business function. As a result, *ownership* of the master data is given to senior management at a high level in the enterprise. Accountability for the master data is a responsibility delegated to *Business Data Stewards*. The business data stewards are chartered to oversee the lifecycle of master data that we covered in Section 9.2: defining the structure and rules relating to the master data, ensuring the master data is properly secured and controlled for regulatory purposes, enhancing the quality of the master data, and promoting the effective use of master data across the business.

Data stewardship functions at two levels—*Business Data Stewards* deal with the higher-level metadata and governance concerns, while *Operational Data Stewards* focus primarily on the instances of master data in the enterprise. The types of operational data stewards vary across master data domains and subsets of master data, business processes, and even location of the stewards. In the CDI space, *Demographic Data Stewards* fix quality and duplicate problems with Party data. *Item Specialists and Category Specialists* act as operational data stewards in the PIM space. Creators of reference data and hierarchies can also be considered data stewards.

9.4   Data Quality

For master data, data quality is of utmost concern. If a customer cannot be identified unambiguously due to poor data quality or if the bill is sent consistently to the wrong address, this is something that might turn customers away. In the upcoming sections, we explain key aspects of data quality.

9.4.1   Introduction to Data Quality

Having a single source of master data that is consumed across multiple business applications fulfills a good portion of the promise of a master data initiative. However, if that master data is simplify a centralized collection of existing enterprise data taken from application silos, the end result will be the viral propagation of bad data to a larger number of data consumers. Governance of master data must support business and technical controls to ensure that master data is (as defined in the DGMM and discussed in Chapter 1) **"timely, relevant, complete, valid, accurate, and consistent"** (for details, see [3]). Master data must possess these characteristics to truly be a trusted authoritative system of record.

Timely master data means that as master data is created, updated, or removed in the enterprise, those changes are quickly reflected in the Master Data Repository. Timeliness is generally not a problem with the registry and transactional hub implementation styles of master data management, because changes to the master data should immediately be made available to all consumers. However, the external reference and coexistence styles can present some challenges in ensuring that updated master data is quickly available to data consumers.

Relevant master data ensures that sufficient business objects are stored in the master data to satisfy the needs of the data consumers. For example, master data for products may have initially come from an application that displayed product catalogs on the Web—however, a regulatory compliance application may need safety certification data about all products that the organization sells. Because this data was not required on the catalog Web site, it may not have been included in the initial definition of the product master data, and thus relevant data is not available to the compliance application. This aspect of quality is usually dealt with during the definition and requirements phase of a master data management project.

Complete master data extends relevant master data to ensure that all of the necessary master data elements for a master business object are present in the master data. In the product domain, this could mean that the dimension data for a product should have length, height, depth, and weight elements. As with relevancy, completeness must span all of the business processes that consume the master data.

Valid master data ensures that the data elements (and their definitions) that make up the master data are correctly represented. This representation covers data typing (a Social Security Number in the United States is a string of 9 digits), ranges of data (the only correct value for the color attribute of a Lenovo laptop is black), and composition of data based on rules (book numbers represented by ISBN-10 have a check digit that represents the remainder of adding the first 9 digits together and dividing by 11).

Accurate master data is correct data—the data must not only be syntactically and semantically valid, but also have the correct values. For example, if a customer record for Judith Hall contains a valid address, but Judith does not live at that address, written communications to that customer will be returned, incurring a high cost to the organization. Accuracy has an interesting correlation with timeliness—certain data may have been accurate at one time (a mailing address) but is no longer valid because the customer moved. Data that is more volatile (location, product attributes, vendor contact, number of dependents, and so on) is subject to **data decay**—as the real-world information changes over time, those elements of master data may become stale and need updating (perhaps through integration with external data sources.)

Consistent master data is data that is complete (all the data that should be there is there, that is, there are no missing values—this also implies that required fields are identified), data that represents the same value for data in the same way in all records (sometimes called **standardization**), and data whose references between data elements match (for example, if Judith Hall's Party data says she has two dependents, there should be records for those two dependents in the master data). Consistent data also means that for most domains of master data, duplicate records should be eliminated from the master data, either by merging them with a gold record or deleting the duplicates after the records have been positively identified as duplicates. As you will see, finding duplicates can be quite complex and involved.

9.4.2 Measuring Data Quality

Tracking data quality, both initially, as part of *profiling* for an assessment, and on an ongoing basis, is one of the cornerstones of a master data governance program. The metrics for quality should be based on:

- The characteristics of data quality described in Section 9.5.3.
- Key business objects and elements in those objects based on domain of master data.
- Sources of master data. These sources include information sources that are used for initial load (across all styles of master data usage) and ongoing synchronization of master data (primarily as part of the Consolidation style of MDM usage).
- Applications that create and update master data via MDM services in the Transactional usage style of MDM.
- Master data that is stored in external registries and referenced using the Registry style of MDM usage.
- Data that is used to enrich master data from external sources.
- Effectiveness of MDM and external data quality services in detecting and correcting quality problems.

Data quality should be applied and monitored across the following points in the *lifecycle* of the MDM project.

- Initial measurement and analysis of the data quality of the data sources as part of the MDM project start-up.
- As the data is initially loaded into the MDM System via ETL. Any quality errors that are found should be corrected in both the source and the MDM System.
- As master data is created/updated, either directly through transactions or loaded in as a delta from source systems.
- Periodically over time (sometimes called *"evergreening"*). Data quality rules evolve over the lifetime of the project—master data that passed a set of quality rules early in the project might not pass when a newer set of rules is applied. Thus, the master data needs to be combed periodically to ensure all data can pass the latest quality checks.

9.4.3 Data Quality Services

Data quality should be driven by the business side—the business has the domain knowledge of the form and semantics of the master data as well as the stewards to manage the master data—but the architecture and implementation needs to provide tools and technology to automatically enforce quality on incoming data, to report on quality issues with master data, and to allow operational data stewards (and other authorized users) to fix quality problems within the master data. In Section 3.6.7, a set of data quality services were described for master data in the context of Figure 3.7, which we do not repeat here.

There are three types of Data Quality Management Services:

- Data Validation and Cleansing Services. These services are usually invoked by the master data access services to ensure relevance, validity, accuracy, and consistency of the master data.

- Reconciliation Services. These services are aimed at helping cleanse the master data of duplicates as part of consistency.
- Cross-Reference Services. These services help with matching master data across multiple systems. These services will not be discussed in detail in this chapter.

9.4.3.1 Data Validation and Cleansing Services

Data validation and cleansing services must support the following data quality mechanisms in the context of master data management:

- Validation of received data
- Standardization of data
- External validation
- Enrichment
- Error Processing

We discuss each of these data quality services in turn in the following subsections.

9.4.3.1.1 Validation

As the master data is created or updated, the validation services can enforce rules for field level correctness. At the field level, the validation service should be able to confirm that:

- A required field is present (no missing fields).
- A required field has a value.
- If the value is specified, that the value is in an acceptable range.
- The value is of the right type.
- The value is composed correctly.
- Cross-field.

9.4.3.1.2 Standardization

A master data element may have a number of different values that are correct at the field level but should resolve to the same value. For example, the business name IBM might be represented as "International Business Machines," "Int'l Bus Mach," or "IBM" across different systems. While these names are all logically representing the same entity, simple searches or matches would not find all valid representations of IBM. So a standardization mechanism would take the names and convert them to a single, consistent value ("IBM"). Standardization is absolutely critical to matching. Issues related to standardization include different representations for the same thing, such as:

> **Abbreviations:** For example, with person names, this could be "Junior" instead of "Jr.". For organizational names, this could be "IBM" versus "International Business Machines." In the location domain, we can contrast "Street," "Drive," and "Boulevard" with "ST," "St.," "DR," "Dr," and "Blvd."
>
> **Nicknames:** People refer to each other by shortened names or aliases on a regular basis. Examples would be "Dan" as a short name for "Daniel", or "Jack" as a nickname for "Jonathan." In the location domain, roads may have multiple names, often allowing the different names to be used simultaneously. In Austin, Texas, for

example, one road is known as "State Highway 183," "Research Boulevard," and "Ed Bluestein Boulevard."

Misspellings: For example, with family names "Smyth" instead of "Smith," or "Millman" instead of "Milman." These small errors can result in reams of duplicate data.

Name changes: People, products, and organizations undergo name changes, usually driven by some external event, making names surprisingly subject to data decay. Name changes can be seen across the different domains as follows:

Person Names

- **Marriage:** The most common name changing event is marriage. People can change their names when they get married—this can take the form of:
  - Changing ones spouse's name to match the spouse's family name.
  - Changing both spouses' names to a common name (for example, having Matthew Higday and Carla Watson, our spouses in the JKE example, both adopt a surname of Watson-Higday).
  - Women often replace their middle name with their maiden (unmarried) name. One example of this is Hillary Rodham Clinton, where Rodham is her maiden name—her other given name at birth was Diane.
- **Personal Preference:** In addition to nicknames, people can change their names to primarily use a second given name, perhaps to differentiate themselves from a relative ("George Robert Boller, Jr." might go by "Bob Boller" to avoid confusion with "George Robert Boller, Sr.")
- **Organization and Product Names:** Organizations change names as they grow (mergers and acquisitions), shrink (divestitures), and try to change their image ("Kentucky Fried Chicken" becomes "KFC"). Products typically change names because of branding ("IBM SecureWay Directory" was rebranded as "IBM Tivoli Directory Server"), or because of legal issues (a name may already be trademarked by a competitor).
- **Locations:** Location information may change as current roads and streets are given honorary names ("1st Street" became "Cesar Chavez Blvd" in Austin Texas). Also, geopolitical boundaries can change—small cities can be absorbed by or spin off from larger cities, and countries can join or split (like Czechoslovakia becoming Czech Republic and Slovakia.)
- **Cultural Representations:** Names may be represented differently across cultures and language variations ("Abraham" vs. "Avraham"). Different countries may add honorifics ("hajj") under different circumstances.

9.4.3.1.3 External Data Validation

Even though the master data may be controlled in a master data management environment, there are circumstances where it makes sense to use external systems to validate incoming and changed master data:

- The IT and business organization have agreed on a common set of data validation tools across the enterprise. From a governance perspective, this common tool is the single consistent mechanism in the enterprise to specify and enforce data quality rules, and master data would naturally consume this service.

- External systems may have timely, consistent, and accurate information that can be matched against the master data. A national name and address data service could be used to validate Party information, for example.

External data services can also be used for standardization (like in the name and address service referenced earlier).

9.4.3.1.4   Enrichment
The master data created inside the enterprise can be enriched by going to a trusted external service for additional information, much like an external system can be used for validation. Some typical examples would be adding a postal code to a location based on information from a GIS system, or adding credit information from a credit scoring system. In the financial industry, Dun and Bradstreet provide services for financial data about organizations (keyed off a DUNS number) that can be used to enrich organizational data.

9.4.3.1.5   Exception Processing
These services allow the MDM System to control how to handle data quality errors. As noted in Chapter 4, an error in data quality may not be a reason to reject the entire update to the master data.

9.4.3.2   Reconciliation Services: Matching and De-duplication
When bringing together master data from disparate services, either for an initial or delta load from enterprise data sources, or updating master data via transactional applications, a major concern is eliminating duplicate data so that the master data only holds the single, complete, accurate golden record for a given item. Failure to eliminate duplicates leads to a host of problems, including:

- Inefficiency in storage and processing. Redundant, duplicate records take up quite a bit of time and space. It is not uncommon for over 90% of the records initially loaded into a master data system to be duplicates—and with large volumes of master data, this quickly becomes a serious problem.
- Unhappy parties. When your customers have to repeatedly give you the same information because multiple inconsistent copies of their data are in the master data, it is pretty natural for customer satisfaction to measurably decline.
- Missed opportunities. When customers are not properly identified, the business may miss the chance to offer those customers new or improved products. For example, failure to recognize a **household** (where multiple customers at the same address should be recognized as a single group).
- Regulatory compliance. Many regulations, such as Sarbanes-Oxley (SOX), require senior management to attest to the correctness of the financial information presented to investors and regulatory bodies. If the data is of poor quality, the resulting reports against the master data will not be accurate—and may inflate revenues, which is a potential legal problem for an enterprise.
- Poor vendor negotiation. When vendors are not properly identified, an enterprise may unknowingly negotiate multiple purchasing agreements with a particular

vendor. The terms and conditions may not be favorable to the enterprise because it doesn't realize the full extent of the business relationships it has with the vendor.

This is not just a problem in the Party domain—duplicate product instances cause serious issues with sales, marketing, and fulfillment. Figure 9.7 shows an example of two duplicate product records, and how they can be merged to form a single master data record.

9.4.3.2.1 Determining Potential Matches

There are three parts to examining data to find potential matches and duplicates in the master data:

- Selecting the Match Criteria and Weights
- Standardizing the master data that is being matched
- Running the master data through matching algorithms to identify potential matches

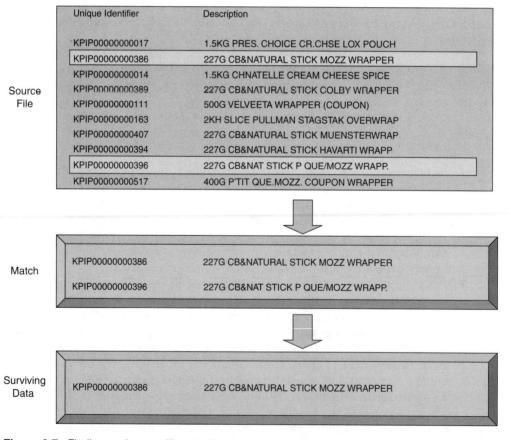

Figure 9.7 Finding and reconciling duplicate master product records.

For each specific domain, the business analysts, data integrators, data stewards, and data administrators need to analyze the master data business object classes and their data elements to select which objects need matching, which elements should be used to determine a match, and how to apply a *weight* to each element used for matching. The result of the weighting (not necessarily a sum of the weights) is used to calculate the strength of a potential match between two records. After the analysis, identification, and weighing of the selected master data object types, elements, and weights, the Data Quality Rule Specification services are invoked to configure the MDM System to enforce the matching rules. Most MDM Systems are pre-configured with a default set of matching objects, elements, and weights.

The data used in matching is known as the *critical* data. In the Party domain, a potential set of critical data to use for matching includes:

- Party name (both family and given names)
- Social Security Number (or tax identifier)
- Date of Birth
- Location (Address)
- Gender
- Location of Birth
- Party ID with internal systems

In the Organizational Party domain, a potential set of critical data to use for matching includes:

- Organization Name
- Corporate Tax ID
- DUNS number
- Location

In the Product domain, the potential set of critical data to use for matching includes:

- Manufacturer Name
- Manufacturer ID
- GTIN or ISBN
- SKU
- Part Number
- Part Type
- Part Description

After the business objects and critical data elements have been selected, weights need to be assigned at the element level. Assignment of weights should be based on the profiling of the master data and the expert domain knowledge of the MDM data governance team. The criteria for selecting weights should look at:

- Which elements are more likely to be discriminators than others. For example, the gender of a person by itself is not as strong a match as Party name.
- Degree of decay of data elements. Non-decaying attributes (like Social Security Number) will have a higher weight for a match than an Address. Although gender is a non-decaying attribute, gender is not usually given as high a weight because the range of values is small.

Table 9.3   Table Matching Map for Party

Critical Data Element	Match Score	Non-Match Score
First Name	1	1
Last Name	2	2
Birth Date	4	4
Address	8	8
SSN	16	16
Gender	32	32
Location of Birth	64	64

The type of weights assigned is based on the mechanics of the algorithms used (and multiple algorithms can be used for matching.) There are these different types of weights:

- Summation of weights: Each element is assigned a weight, with the total of the weights adding to 100. You can also have negative weights for critical data that don't match.
- Table mapping of weights: Each matching and non-matching element is assigned a number in a bitmap, and then a table lookup is done to determine the degree of match. An example of a Party matching table is shown in Table 9.3. After the match relevancy score has been computed, a lookup is done to determine the overall match score (for example, 11 on match indicates that first name, last name, and address match, and 4 indicates that birth date does not match).

In most cases, prior to running the matching algorithm, you must ensure that the data you are checking (new and existing) has been standardized (i.e., Texas vs. TX) or some matching algorithms that use exact comparisons (at a byte level) will not perform correctly. Some matching algorithms can do some standardization inline or use pattern matching to compensate for data that hasn't been standardized. There are two types of algorithms that are used in data matching:

- **Deterministic** algorithms strictly use match criteria and weighting to determine the results. Each field is compared, and either results in:
  - Exact match
  - No match
  - Unknown or Missing, where the field is not present across the match
- **Probabilistic** (sometimes known as frequency-based) algorithms use statistical models to adjust the matching based on the frequency of values found in the data. In the Party domain, certain family names occur more often than others ("Smith," "Johnson," "Williams," "Jones," "Brown" are the most common family names in the United States, according to the 1990 United States Census), and so a match on

Are these two records a match?

```
WILLIAM J      KAZANGIAN  128 MAIN  ST  02111 12/8/62

WILLAIM JOHN   KAZANGIAN  128 MAINE AVE 02110 12/8/62


  B      B      A          A    B    D   B    A  = BBAABDBA


 +5     +2     +20        +3   +4      -1  +7  +9 = +49
```

Deterministic Decisions Tables:
- Fields are compared
- Letter grade assigned
- Combined letter grades are compared to a match configuration file
- Result: Match; Suspect; Clerical; Non-match

Probabilistic Record Linkage:
- Fields are evaluated for degree-of-match
- Weight assigned: represents the **"information content"** by value
- Weights are summed to derived a total score
- Result: Statistical probability of a match

Figure 9.8   Deterministic and Probabilistic Matching.

a frequently occurring family name would carry less weight. For probabilistic matching, a frequency distribution of the critical data has to be created during the assessment phase and used as input to the probabilistic matching.

An example of probabilistic versus deterministic matching is shown in Figure 9.8.

Rather than rely on a single matching algorithm, different ones can be chained together for the best results. Figure 9.9 shows an example of this chaining during a transactional operation on the master data.

In this example, the list of potential matches is scoped based on an initial blocking key, limiting the records that are run through the matching algorithms. Next, the first algorithm is run, and the ordered and ranked results can then either be returned to the caller or run through a second matching service.

With matching, the emphasis from an architectural and governance perspective should be on support for choosing and chaining multiple matching services, configuring match variables, match performance, and determining how and when matching is invoked.

9.4.3.2.2   *Survivorship*

After matching is done, the list of potential matches (also called *suspects*) can be broken down into four categories:

- **Master:** Depending on the context, this is either the record that is being searched for or the best fit record across multiple similar records.
- **Duplicates:** These records are the business objects that are deemed to be matches based on the thresholds set as part of the matching algorithm configurations.

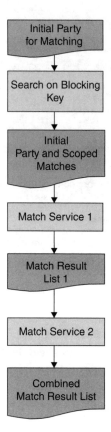

Figure 9.9 Invoking a Matching Service.

- **Clericals:** These records have something in common, but not enough to be considered a full match. However, a data steward may want to look at these records and change the match results based on a better understanding of the data.
- **Non-duplicates:** These are records that don't match and are only returned if asked for explicitly (they may have been part of the blocking record search).

The services can either attempt to automatically resolve the masters and duplicates into a single record or return the list to a data steward for handling. With automation, the data stewards and business analysts would create a set of rules to determine how the fields get merged between the masters and duplicates. At a field level, some typical rules are:

- Use the longest field that is present across the set.
- Valid values take precedence over invalid and missing values.
- Use the most recently updated record.
- Merge fields together (such as descriptions) into a single field.

During automated resolution, if no rules can be applied, the data in the master record is used. After the rules are applied, the merged record is created and the duplicates are deleted (and may be marked as deleted due to a survivorship rule, for auditing and governance).

If manual intervention is used, the resulting match set (including clericals) is sent out to an operational data steward, and the steward manually decides how to merge (or not to merge) the records. The records are marked as master, duplicate, clerical, and so on (pointing back to the match set and the master), and an event (e-mail or workflow) is generated to notify the steward that some records requiring resolution have been detected.

Conclusion

Data Governance plays a crucial role in turning master data into managed master data. There are other types of governance associated with an MDM System: IT Governance for the underlying software and hardware, and SOA Governance for the Information Services. Data Governance goes beyond those governance schemes to manage how the master data is effectively used as a business asset in the enterprise. Data Governance starts at the onset of the MDM project and continues with a governance board and data stewards during the active part of the MDM lifecycle. One of the prime concerns with Master Data Governance is data quality—this is one of the foundations of trust in the master data management system. The MDM architecture provides a number of services to validate, enrich, and reconcile master data to enable the delivery of high-value master data to the enterprise.

References

1. COBIT 4.1 Executive Summary and Framework, http://www.isaca.org/AMTemplate.cfm? Section= Downloads&Template=/ContentManagement/ContentDisplay.cfm&ContentID=34172.
2. IBM Data Governance Maturity Model, http://www-306.ibm.com/software/tivoli/governance/ servicemanagement/data-governance.html.
3. Olson, J. E. 2003. *Data Quality—The Accuracy Dimension*. San Mateo, CA: Morgan Kaufmann.

MDM User Roles

B efore we get started, we have to introduce some typographical conventions. The name of a user role is used with an uppercase letter for each word that is part of the user role name. Thus, the role "solution architect" will appear as Solution Architect throughout this appendix to mark the identifier of a role consistently. Furthermore, in each role description, the first appearance of a user role will appear in bold, so when introducing the user role Solution Architect, the first occurrence will appear as **Solution Architect**, and all subsequent occurrences will appear in normal print as Solution Architect.

Having the right skills and the right people for an IT project is a critical success factor. Therefore, this appendix introduces MDM user roles. Some are domain-specific (such as an Item Specialist for the product information domain), and others are domain independent (such as the Solution Architect); both are, we believe, crucial for successfully implementing MDM Solutions. Note that the scope of MDM user roles is not limited to the implementation phase of MDM Systems. We also present MDM user roles that are critical to operating an MDM System; an example would be the Operational Data Steward, who is required for successfully operating CDI solutions. As you will notice while reading, we exclude user roles such as Integration Hub Architect or Integration Hub Developer, which are not directly involved in building the MDM System (knowing that these roles are needed in the broader scope of an MDM Solution deployment to connect the MDM System to the operational system landscape). We would also like to comment on the fact that, as you will see, some user roles have certain relations or overlaps with other user roles. For example, the aspect of database high availability can be either covered by a Resilience Engineer (described in Section A.3.8) or by the Database Administrator (described in Subsection A.3.9.2). It will depend on your company and the MDM Solution deployed whether or not you will need a person for each MDM user role described. Maybe certain user roles can be combined for execution by a single person. In the example here, if you do not have a dedicated Resilience Engineer, the tasks of this user role might be covered and added to the people performing the IT Administrator and Database Administrator user roles.

If an enterprise decides to look into master data management solutions and later on decides to actually implement one, users with different user roles[1] will have to collaborate in order to make such a project a success. Before looking at the individual user roles, let's take a minute and think about the corresponding attributes. On a high level, a user performing in a certain user role has a range of responsibilities that need to be fulfilled in order to meet external expectations. In order for a person to successfully meet expectations, a user role needs to:

- Define a skill or a set of skills that describes what needs to be understood and mastered by an individual intending to perform in that user role.
- Define a goal or set of goals that can be measured regarding success and identify any optional target deliverables as well.

A person performing in a certain user role uses the skill set applicable for achieving the goals, thus fulfilling the assigned project responsibilities. For example, a Developer would use the skill set of expected programming skills to develop and deliver software artifacts assigned to that person. On the highest level, a Master Data Management project can be divided into three major phases:

- Solution evaluation
- Solution development
- Solution administration and operation

The user roles are grouped along these three major categories, so in Subsection A.1, the roles related to solution evaluation are described. In Subsection A.2, solution development-related roles are described, and in Subsection A.3, solution administration and operation-related roles are introduced. Finally, in Section A.4, the solution user, typically a Line of Business user, is presented.

You might wonder why we did not group the user roles into CDI- and PIM-related user roles. We believe there is group of user roles that is applicable for all master data domains. Therefore, a grouping by master data domain would have caused a lot of redundancy. We do agree, though, that during the project lifecycle of CDI or PIM projects there is a small set of user roles specific to these domains and so these user roles will be marked as such. Finally, we believe it's safe to assume that all user roles in IT have requirements for basic computer skills—such as using e-mail or the Internet, about which we will not elaborate further.

A.1   User Roles for Solution Evaluation

Before any IT solution is bought and deployed by a customer, someone needs to perform a solution evaluation from a business and technical perspective to come up with an assessment of the quality and benefits a solution might deliver. Looking at the user role of the

---

1. Use case modeling often differentiates between human and non-human actors or roles. In this subsection, we will only focus on user roles associated with humans, and we intentionally leave out user roles that are represented by IT systems or their architectural components. We believe the IT system roles and their tasks were described in sufficient detail in previous chapters, thus justifying this narrowed-down scope.

Strategist, you will learn about a key player in this early phase, which potentially leads to an MDM deployment project.

A.1.1 The Strategist

An individual performing in the user role of **Strategist** provides strategic guidance on business and technical matters. The goal of this user role is to have a business strategy in place that aligns the IT projects with this strategic direction. A feasible strategy should be complete, creditable, practical, and affordable. Unless a strategy meets these criteria, a Strategist has failed to put a new strategy in place. Therefore, a Strategist should always check a strategy against these criteria to ensure eventual success—which means that the new strategy will meet the requirements.

The skill set a Strategist must have is strategy management, consisting of the ability to develop, plan, and execute a strategy. On a high level, this requires the skills of thinking and planning strategically and appropriate negotiation skills. For example, since an enterprise-wide rollout of MDM might require a series of implementation projects in a large enterprise spanning a few years of implementation time, it is crucial that the first project creates a "starburst" effect for the executive board. This first project must demonstrate that there is a significant return on investment, thus assuring continuous backing by the decision makers. The strategic insight identifying the spot within the enterprise where this "starburst" effect can be achieved with maximum effect is thus demonstrating the skill to think and plan strategically applied by a Strategist. On a lower level, the skill set can be further divided into project management and executive management. In the area of project management, the Strategist must be able to manage a project successfully, which requires project planning and tracking abilities. In the area of executive management, substantial general executive leadership skills are mandatory. The four most important ones are decision making, investment planning, critical thinking, and change management. The last one is mandatory, for example, to manage the change within a company if an enterprise wide data governance board is established. The key deliverables expected from a strategist are:

- Defining the evaluation criteria for determining how a master data management solution contributes to business improvements and success
- Obtaining executive commitment for deploying MDM using negotiation skills
- Establishing the vision and the right order of the overall implementation project series
- Change management caused by the introduction of a data governance board

Obviously, a Strategist is very relevant in the earliest phases of a master data management project. Individuals performing in this role can be either from an enterprise planning team responsible for deploying MDM or from a system integrator providing consulting expertise to that enterprise.

A.2 User Roles for Solution Development

Solution development covers business and technical aspects for the initial deployment as well as subsequent extensions and enhancements. Thus, we have in this section three different groups of user roles related to business (see Subsection A.2.1), IT platform implementation (see Subsections A.2.2 to A.2.4), and creation of master data (see Section A.2.5). The last set of user roles for the creation of master data are related to the PIM solution space.

A.2.1 The Business Analyst

A person performing in the user role of **Business Analyst** defines, analyzes, and optimizes business processes. As you know by now through the discussion of MDM Solution Blueprints in Chapters 6, 7, and 8, the motivation for deploying Master Data Management Solutions is always driven by desired changes in business for the improvement of business results. Not surprisingly, the goal of the Business Analyst is to ensure that all business processes are running continuously and optimally. The skill set used for achieving this goal has two major areas, namely, requirements engineering and business analysis. Requirements engineering means the ability to capture business and technical solution requirements, appropriately employing skills like use case definition and business process and user modeling. Modeling of use case definitions today usually assumes the ability to express them using the *Unified Modeling Language*[2] to create the model artifacts. UML is used to model the use cases, components, and classes in object-oriented programming activities. The other skill set of business analysis helps the Business Analyst to understand and apply relevant business performance metrics to analyze the current business performance. Insight into current business performance is the foundation for refinements made for business optimization by users acting in this role.

The Business Analyst for an MDM project should have at least five years of work experience in the user role of Business Analyst.

A.2.2 The Solution Architect

The responsibility of the **Solution Architect** is to define the end-to-end architecture for the solution. A Solution Architect has the goal of specifying the component and operational structure as well as the externals for the solution. Two additional goals for the Solution Architect are the cost estimation for defining the solution architecture as well as the cost estimation for the solution implementation.

The basic skill set for the Solution Architect is the ability to author relevant artifacts in UML such as components, classes, activities, and use cases. Requirements engineering and meta-data modeling require knowledge of the UML foundational skills. Requirements engineering is a skill set to capture use case definitions, user roles, business processes, and nonfunctional requirements. For example, nonfunctional requirements include hours of operation, availability, security, performance, and fault tolerance. When a Solution Architect uses meta-data modeling, constraint and stereotype definitions are defined. These objects represent the need for advanced skills in leveraging UML through the end-to-end design process.

The Solution Architect must be skilled in the area of developing software architecture because it is expected that a Solution Architect will create and review software architectures

---

2. The Unified Modeling Language is abbreviated as UML. For details see [1].

with the project team. More specifically, applying these skills leads to the definition of the solution boundaries and software components as well as to the selection of the appropriate architecture patterns. Software architecture skills are based, on one hand, on the ability to use UML, and on the other hand, on the ability to develop software components by applying software engineering practices using the skill set of software component modeling. The ability to select from different component types and recommended patterns, the ability to design appropriate software module structures, and the ability to use the right software platform fulfilling relevant requirements all belong to the group of skills of software component modeling.

Software engineering is the skill set providing the foundation for IT architecture and data architecture. But before we look at the latter, let's start with the first. The objective of software engineering is the definition of high-quality software using proven methodologies and best practices. Functional decomposition, abstraction, cohesion, modularity, and pattern languages are key characteristics of effectively engineered software. The IT architecture skill set leverages skills from the software engineering group of skills to create the operational architecture for the solution. Operational modeling of IT systems topologies in combination with product knowledge belong to the expected skills of the Solution Architect in this area. Certainly, the design process is not complete for any operational architecture unless scalability and performance requirements are reflected, as well as using applicable patterns.

Any business process deals with data to a certain degree. Master Data Management Solutions are focusing on the efficient management of master data. So, not surprisingly, skills related to data architecture belong to the skill set of the Solution Architect for an MDM Solution, too. Data architecture skills will assist in the development of the data models and the definition of the data management capabilities for the solution. Data architecture skills also are necessary in defining and understanding master data management requirements and capabilities in the areas of data cleansing, data transformation, and data de-duplication so that the MDM Solution can effectively and efficiently manage the quality of master data for the enterprise.

Depending on the size of the MDM implementation, the Solution Architect might lead a team of architects specialized in certain areas such as data architecture, infrastructure architecture, security architecture, and application architecture to name a few. The skill sets mentioned here enable the Solution Architect to conceive the overall enterprise MDM Solution architecture on a logical architectural layer where specialized architects design parts of the operational and runtime architecture in their respective subject domains. The skill set of these specialized architects with regard to UML modeling and requirements gathering are comparable to the skill set of the Solution Architect in these areas. With UML models and requirements documents at their fingertips, the specialized architects and the Solution Architect can efficiently communicate with each other. However, the Solution Architect needs to know a broader set of architectural disciplines, with perhaps less depth in the individual architectural domains, whereas the specialized architects need to have highly developed skills in their relevant subject matter areas and a narrower knowledge of other architectural disciplines. As an example, just think about the complexity in designing an appropriate master data integration process if master data from a dozen different source systems need to be cleansed, transformed, and loaded into the MDM System. If, in addition, the MDM System has to feed master data in real time into several invoice, order entry, and billing systems consistently, a data architect might be necessary to take care of the architectural details for this while the Solution Architect focuses on the overall solution picture. Because architects in specialized areas such as data architecture and application architecture perform in architect job roles as well, we believe the user role of the Solution Architect gives an overview of the required skill sets and we omit the more specialized architecture skill sets for the others here.

The Solution Architect for a mission-critical solution such as an MDM Solution should have at least five years of solution architecture experience.

A.2.3 The Developer

The **Developer** implements the solution according to the architecture model, creating the necessary artifacts, such as software components and unit test components. The business application and services are the outcome of the work by users performing in the role of a Developer. The goal for a Developer is to design, implement, and accomplish unit tests for solution artifacts. The performance of the Developer is measured against key performance indicators such as completion time and number of defects.

A Developer requires a set of skills that span software component modeling, software engineering, software programming, and the ability to develop solution artifacts. We will take a quick look at these before digging deeper, and we start with software programming. In this skill set, a Developer should have best practices on writing program code using knowledge on syntax, patterns, style, and in-depth knowledge of development tools. The skills in the software component model skill set are the foundation for the development of software components and thus include knowledge about component types, recommended patterns, modularized structure, and software platform requirements. Some of the skills in the software component model depend on skills in the area of software engineering, which we explain now. Software engineering describes the ability to design and define quality software following best practices. Therefore, skills and knowledge covering abstraction and modeling, functional decomposition, modularity, and cohesion of software components and pattern languages are crucial. Solution artifact development covers design, implementation, and unit tests of software artifacts, leveraging insight into structure and content of the individual IT artifacts.

Software programming skills need to leverage abilities of a skill group named software unit testing. Obviously, in order to obtain good performance metrics regarding the number of defects, which should be as small as possible, a Developer needs the ability to verify each path through the source code, verifying that the software component works according to the design specifications. Not surprisingly, software unit testing skills are debugging and implementing of unit test cases, the latter preferably fully automated as part of build or nightly regression runs.

The MDM user roles A.2.4.1 to A.2.4.3 are specialized Developer roles, creating artifacts needed for building and running an MDM System, which are not necessarily code artifacts in the sense the Developer role creates them.

A.2.3.1   The Business Customizer

A **Business Customizer** uses sophisticated tools to change and adapt business applications and processes in such a way that business users can perform their tasks. The key goal for a Business Customizer is to define and test simple solution artifacts. Performing to achieve this goal, a Business Customizer is measured against completion time (should be as short as possible) and number of defects (should be as low as possible). The skill set the Business Customizer applies is called Form-Based Development. It describes the ability to use structured forms to develop simple solution artifacts using analytical thinking and knowledge on the business domain.

A.2.3.2   The Data Integrator

The **Data Integrator** is responsible for designing and implementing complex data integration and cleansing applications and for granting other users access to a potentially very large number of different data sources. This user role acts in several mission-critical aspects of MDM deployments. In CDI projects, for example, the Data Integrator needs to work with the Operational Data Steward (see A.3.2) to agree on matching algorithms and survivorship rules regarding the collapse operation of one or multiple customer records, removing duplicates from the overall data set. The objective of this user role is to design, implement, and unit test data integration artifacts using tools and products[3] for data integration. The key performance indicators for this user role are development time (as short as possible) and number of defects (preferably none).

The top-level skill set used for achieving this goal is the data integration development skill set, which is built upon software programming and software unit testing (both described in Section A.2.3 for the Developer role and not repeated here to avoid redundancy). In essence, transformation and cleansing routines are the output of the data integration development skill group. Not surprisingly, the ability to develop ETL routines and cleansing definitions are the cornerstones here. However, we believe this user role gets more and more affected by the paradigm shift towards SOA implementations in IT landscapes. This means that many functions performed by this user have to be exposed as services (technology bindings such as EJB, JMS, or Web service using SOAP/HTTP are secondary considerations). Address standardization and verification routines used for improving customer master data quality before loading it into the MDM Hub is often part of the Master Data Integration phase. These routines could (and should) be reused in the business services of the SOA landscape that creates new customers, thus avoiding low-quality data in the IT landscape in the future. Therefore, familiarity with the Information as a Service concept is crucial, because a Data Integrator should consider which other spots in the IT landscape could benefit from it also. Thus, when implementing cleansing and transformation routines, focusing on reusability using this concept is important. Exposing the right cleansing and transformation services allows easy integration in business services in SOA, enriching them and providing, for example, TCO reduction (less work when loading data into the data warehouse).

---

3.   A list of available products can be found in Appendix B.

A.2.3.3 The Information Developer

The responsibility of the **Information Developer** is to create information artifacts for the business and user community, enabling them to work with the software solution. The goal of the Information Developer is the creation of documentation assisting users when working with the solution. Minimizing the time to develop and number of defects are measurements used to judge the work efficiency of the Information Developer. Achieving this goal is possible through the skill set of information development. Design and authoring using appropriate writing and grammar skills are key qualifications in scope of the information development skill set. Occasionally, pictures for the information artifacts have to be generated using graphic design abilities. Because typewriters are history, basic computer skills are imperative. For many corporations, the specialized user role of **Translator** provides information artifacts in foreign languages to users. In the product master data domain, while authoring master data, the user roles of Category Manager, Item Manager, Category Specialist, and Item Specialist (see Subsections A.2.5.1 to A.2.5.4) often collaborate with Translators. Imagine, for example, a company that intends to introduce a new product in all the countries of Europe. The Translators would need to translate a subset or all product attributes into more than a dozen languages.

A.2.4 The Test Engineer

The **Test Engineer** is the link between Developers (see Subsection A.2.4) and Solution Users (see Section A.4.1). The goal for this user is to ensure the software matches all functional and nonfunctional requirements according to specification. Thus, using test cases based on the functional defects should be found and reported to the Developers, and special care should be applied to the areas that are of paramount importance for the Solution Users (might not always be visible from technical specifications), which can be obtained from the Solution Users if the Test Engineers speak with them. The performance is often measured through test coverage and number of tests passed.

The skill sets used are software programming and software unit testing—both explained in Section A.2.4, describing the Developer role. Furthermore, the Test Engineer needs the software testing skill set. With the skills from this group, a Test Engineer designs, implements, and executes tests to prove software works as designed. This skill set leverages the software programming skill set.

A.2.5 Master Data Development

Master Data Management Solutions are designed to be adaptable so that the data model and the master data services can evolve with the needs of the business and with legislative requirements. The driving force of this evolutionary aspect, however, is not the IT department; it is the business. New business requirements drive changes in the master data model and services creating or maintaining master data. Examples could be the creation of a new brand or product category in order to expand by selling a whole new group of products, requiring a new data model and appropriate processes on the product master data. Therefore, all users in this section are Line of Business (LOB) users rather than user roles in the IT department. Before diving into the user roles themselves, we will give you some background about why we believe many of the user roles described hereafter are particularly relevant for the PIM space.

Authoring master data in the customer domain is often done by a single person such as a bank clerk creating a new customer who intends to open an account, or a call center representative in a logistics company adding a new customer record for a person who wants a package shipped from one location to another. In contrast to this, authoring master data in the product domain is usually a process where multiple people in different job roles need to collaborate to get a single record done. For example, the technical designers would author the values for technical attributes, whereas pricing specialists would provide pricing information, marketing managers would assign certain attributes related to sales channels representing routes to market, brand managers create attributes applicable for a certain brand category, and so forth. The tasks for authoring master data representing products can be divided into creating values for the individual product attributes and the classification tasks for assigning a product into one or multiple categories in one or multiple hierarchies. For example, a product can be classified into a supplier hierarchy (once classified, this represents a "supplied by-" relation), into a vendor hierarchy (once classified, this represents a "sold by-" relation), a location hierarchy of stores (once classified, this represents a "sold at-" relation), or any other hierarchy your business requires. Assigning products into categories of hierarchies is a task performed by individuals in the user role of **Category Specialist.** The tasks related to creating values for product attributes is performed by **Item Specialists.** The four upcoming roles appear usually only when PIM solutions are deployed. Unless the PIM system is outsourced, the user roles have to be staffed with employees from the company running the PIM system. Whether or not you need a person for each user role depends on the number of products and categories, the number of attributes describing them, the average number of changes per day in the product data, and a couple of other factors. We have, for example, a customer with about 15,000 products expecting 400 new products per year and about 1000 changes in existing records per year. This means on average two new records and five changes per workday, assuming a five-day work week. In such a scenario, having two persons performing in the user roles Category Specialist and Item Specialist simultaneously might be enough to give sufficient coverage, even if one of them is on vacation or ill. On the other end, a customer we worked with had significantly more than 3 million products in the PIM system, with several thousand changes per day, requiring a much larger staff.

The first two roles (A.2.5.1 and A.2.5.2) are manager roles that usually have people-management responsibilities, whereas the last two roles (A.2.5.3 and A.2.5.4) are subject matter expert roles. Generally speaking, a subject matter expert provides a thorough understanding of the nature of the organization's needs in a given area and of the products and solutions that provide value in solving those problems.

A.2.5.1   The Category Manager

A **Category Manager** has two responsibilities. First, this user role manages people, projects, and assets (such as data or physical assets). Second, this user role is responsible for one or more product categories and the selection of products therein. The goal for the first responsibility is to retain a happy team that has the right skills available at the right time to achieve, through best use of team members, the best possible business results. Furthermore, assets should be used effectively and efficiently. The people managed by the Category Manager are Category Specialists, are described in Section A.2.5.3. The objective for the second responsibility is to have the right product selection, meeting the business needs.

For achieving the first goal, the Category Manager needs the skill sets of the people management and project domains. People management means the ability to manage a team of people to mutual advantage. Knowledge of team skills, skill requirements for a task, and team member availability (not on vacation, etc.) is one foundation. The capability of coaching and mentoring people is required, too. Project Management includes the skills to plan and execute a project on time and within a budget. For this, project planning and project tracking abilities are needed. Complying with the second objective requires the ability to be responsible for products in a product category to meet business needs. This requires strategy, market knowledge, advertisement ability, and contract management. An example for a Category Manager would be a brand manager.

A.2.5.2 The Item Specialist Manager

The **Item Specialist Manager** manages a team of Item Specialists (see A.2.5.4). Therefore, this role requires the people management and the project management skill sets outlined in Section A.2.5.3 for the description of the Category Manager and are not repeated here. Item Specialist Managers have no responsibility for managing product categories, so no additional skill sets are required for this role.

A.2.5.3 The Category Specialist

The **Category Specialist** is a subject matter expert for an organization who assigns products in multiple product categories and ensures product information consistency within a category. The goals for a Category Specialist are to ensure the right products are in the appropriate product categories and that each product has only valid and accurate attribute values. The skill set for this task is product category management, which means the ability to manage product information in one or multiple product categories. This requires knowledge on legal requirements for product categories (e.g., through which channels what type of medicine can be sold) and knowledge about the local guidelines for describing products.

A.2.5.4 The Item Specialist

The **Item Specialist** is a subject matter expert for an organization in a particular aspect of product information management. This might be for a group of attributes (pricing, technical, marketing) across all products or all products in certain product categories. In this case, a group of Item Specialists with expertise in different subject matter areas, such as product technical attributes, pricing attributes, and so forth, would collaborate in a workflow to fully describe the attributes of a product. The Item Specialist could also be the responsible owner of the attributes of all products in specific product categories.

The goal of this user is to ensure that for all attributes for which responsibility exists, accurate values are there at all times.

The skill set required is product information development. It means the ability to define product attributes for a specific product domain. Thus, it requires domain knowledge and knowledge on local guidelines describing product attributes.

The Item Specialist reports to the Item Specialist Manager, described in Section A.2.5.2.

A.3   User Roles for Solution Administration and Operation

After an MDM System is deployed and the implementation team is gone, a client needs to run the MDM Solution. We believe that running and maintaining an MDM Solution need to be considered as part of an overall MDM implementation strategy. Part of this end-to-end perspective about an implementation strategy is the consideration of required user roles to administrate and operate an MDM Solution. The user roles described in this and subsequent sections are a testament to this comprehensive perspective.

A.3.1   The Business Operations Manager

An MDM Solution is deployed due to business justifications. In other words, there are business processes running smoother and more efficiently with an MDM Solution in place. These business processes will change due to changing business requirements. Consequently, there has to be someone implementing the business process changes on the business process level. This is the responsibility of the **Business Operations Manager.** It is the Business Operations Manager who identifies and implements small changes to the business processes, rules, and related definitions to match the changing needs of the business.

The ultimate goal of the business operations manager is to remove all inhibitors for efficient operations.

To reach this goal, a user performing in this role requires project management skills and business operations management skills to manage an organization's operations. The skill set is comprised of the knowledge of the business goals and strategies and the ability to use operational and administrative systems.

A.3.2   The Operational Data Steward

No matter how advanced the matching and survivor algorithms for finding and collapsing duplicates are, there is always a remainder that requires that a person looks at a suspect list of duplicates and decides whether or not they represent duplicates. For this task, which is particularly relevant in the customer master data domain, the user role of the **Operational Data Steward** exists. At least one person needs to perform in this user role as long as the MDM System exists. The responsibilities of this user role are to provide de-duplication when needed, data cleansing, and data enhancements, depending on circumstances. On a high level, the Operational Data Stewards constantly works toward ensuring that customer data is consistent, complete, and accurate. More specifically, the detailed goals are:

- Each customer record is consistent regarding attribute values and represented as such across all IT systems dealing with customer information.
- The relationships between customer records are accurate.

- The customer records are up-to-date at all times.
- There is only one customer record reflecting a customer entity, performing de-duplication if needed.
- Each product record is consistent regarding attribute values and is represented as such across all IT systems dealing with product information.
- The relationships between product records are accurate and up-to-date at all times.
- There is only one product record reflecting a product entity, performing de-duplication if needed.

Similar goals exist for other master data domains such as account or location as well.

We believe that it is mandatory for individuals performing in the Operational Data Steward role to have a thorough and complete understanding of the master data model, code tables, and the semantics of the values in attribute fields. Intimate knowledge of procedures for identifying and correcting anomalies in master information are also essential. Furthermore, we believe the following three-layered sets of skills are necessary, with a top-down dependency upon the layering of the skill groups:

- Electronic data stewardship skills (top layer)
- Electronic record maintenance skills (middle layer)
- Electronic record lookup skills (bottom layer)

The skill set of electronic data stewardship aims for appropriate management of electronic master data records. The basic skill in this group is to define data integrity rules for de-duplication, data cleansing, and standardization, which are enforced by the MDM System as described in Chapter 4, Section 4.6.3 and Section 4.6.9. Simple examples could be that a certain attribute can only be within a certain range or cannot be empty. De-duplication requires the ability to analyze how to uniquely identify a master data entity and determine whether to use deterministic or probabilistic matching logic to avoid duplicate entries of master data entities in the MDM System. Understanding the matching mechanisms used and applying them accordingly is the skill of data screening, with the objective being to find suspects representing potential duplicates. When the suspects are found, the ability to merge[4] and thus de-duplicate data records with a sound understanding of survivorship rules is the next skill. Note that before a collapse operation is done, sometimes, for example, the customers in the suspect list are called by the user performing in this role to obtain additional fields in order to find out if two or more records actually belong to the same real-world person. Sometimes, an Operational Data Steward needs to reverse a former collapse of two data records into one by applying the skill to split data records. Changing data records means the Operational Data Steward applies skills from the second skill set, named electronic record maintenance, which is located in the middle layer. In this set are three skills: record validation, record update, and change of administrative records, which we believe are self-explanatory, so we can immediately move on to the last skill set of this user role,

---

4. Merging data records is also known as collapsing data records. We use these terms interchangeably.

namely, the electronic record lookup, which is on the bottom layer of the aforementioned three-layer skill set stack. This layer consists of the following skills:

- Ability to find and use electronic records
- Search/Query specification
- Selection of a record from result set potentially containing more than one record
- Ability to navigate to individual fields of the record

Unless the IT infrastructure of a company deploying an MDM Solution is outsourced, this user role should be staffed with employees from the company installing the MDM System. Depending on the number of records, the Operational Data Steward user role needs to remain consistent, and one or multiple users performing in this role may be required. We advise that if there is a team of Operational Data Stewards, the team lead should have at least three years of experience with ETL processing and a very deep understanding of the data model used for the MDM System, in addition to the social skills for leading a group of people. Furthermore, for the team lead of the Operational Data Steward team, some analytical background from business intelligence or business warehousing is a plus. The reason for this is the fact that if the amount of master data records is so large that a team of Operational Data Stewards is required, analysis and reporting on how many records required data steward attention per day, per week, or per month allows the identification of trends with respect to master data quality, in other words, if the master data quality degrades or increases over time.

A.3.3   The Data Administrator

For an enterprise, the **Data Administrator** interacts with the MDM System to perform all administrative tasks required to generate reports, issuing queries or submitting updates on the master data records. In many organizations, this user role is specific to the CDI domain, with a particular focus on organization management, in other words, when the Party is a company or an organization instead of a person. If a company decides to do business with another company in a strategic partnership, the companies might work together across multiple departments in various lines of business (marketing, manufacturing, sales, etc.). The initial creation of an organization such as a company with its respective hierarchies, contacts, and relationships between contacts should be performed by someone at the enterprise level. Creating an organization master data entity is a more complex task than creating a new customer record for a person opening a savings account. The Data Administrator might need to work with several Line of Business users to obtain accurate information on contracts, legal considerations, hierarchy structures, privacy settings, shipping addresses, contact information, and so on until all attributes of a new organization can be entered into the MDM System.

The objective for this user is to have no updates and other administrative requests pending. Constraints on this objective are the need to perform them accurately and in such a way that all aspects of Party data reflect reality (e.g., relationship information is current and accurate).

Achieving the goal, the Data Administrator leverages administration skills that include skill at record maintenance. This skill set is built on a skill set named electronic record maintenance,[5] which contains the following abilities: record validation, record update, record lookup through query specification, and navigation through result of query.

A.3.4 The Resource Owner

If MDM is deployed, there are resources of the MDM Solution that are owned by someone, the **Resource Owner.** This user role has the responsibility of ensuring that MDM resources are managed and used appropriately, including the decision about which users might or might not have access to certain MDM resources. The technical implementation of these policies with respect to user access, for example, is done by the IT Security Administrator (see A.3.9.3). Thus, these two user roles have to collaborate.

The goal of this user role is to ensure that only authorized users[6] for the owned MDM resources have access to them. This goal can be further broken down into having appropriate users in access control lists and periodically reviewing them. Obviously, completeness and accuracy of the access control lists is a prerequisite for achieving this goal.

The skill set used for this responsibility is resource security policies that enable the management of access to resources. Granting appropriate levels of access requires consideration of access levels and access control lists as well as user and group accounts. This information is stored and maintained in electronic systems, thus requiring the skill set of electronic record maintenance, described in Section A.3.2.

A.3.5 The Auditor

Recalling that MDM Systems provide access to the most critical information a business owns, someone needs to check whether or not there were attempts at unauthorized access. For complying with certain regulations, someone needs to assess audit trails to determine whether or not only authorized users worked with authorized master data pieces. These responsibilities belong to the core tasks of the **Auditor** user role.

The goal for an Auditor is to find violations and propose remedies to avoid them in the future. Someone performing in this role is interested in the number of undetected violations found and the number of unresolved issues, which should be small.

The skill set of interest for an Auditor is the auditing skill set. This skill set includes the ability to plan an audit, knowledge of regulations and policies, and the ability to negotiate. Since audit-relevant information is stored in IT systems, the electronic record maintenance skill set (see A.3.2 for details) is required as well, because the auditing skill set is based on it.

---

5. We do not further decompose this skill set in more basic skill sets, even though in a fully detailed discussion on the skill sets for this user role, this would be needed.

6. Please note, as outlined in Chapter 4, the security mechanisms might be more complex than described here. We knowingly combine authentication and authorization into a single consideration here to keep the discussion feasibly short. Also, since many of the technical details are part of the IT Security Administrator role, we believe the idea is still clear enough without spending too much in technical detail here.

A.3.6 The Deployer

After the Developers and Test Engineers have completed their work, someone needs to deploy the solution components to the production runtime. This has to be done for the initial release of the MDM Solution as well as for any subsequent enhancements. The person for this job is the **Deployer**. The goal of the Deployer is to assemble and deploy the runtime software components of the solution to the production environment with minimal costs and preferably with minimal or no disruption to the production environment. To achieve this goal, the Deployer must develop and test a broad set of deployment use cases.

The skill set used to reach this goal is the solution deployment skill set, which is based on other skill sets we explore later. With the solution deployment skill set, a Deployer can assemble solution components that are deployed onto a runtime infrastructure of the MDM Solution. Knowledge-wise, the Deployer needs to know the file locations for the involved solution components. Required abilities cover the definition of application platform resources, the load of application and reference data, and configuration of software control properties. The solution deployment skill set is based on the release management skill set (can be in the scope of ITIL[7]) and the solution artifact deployment skill set, which depends on the basic operating system usage skill set. The release management skill set consists mainly of procedures to manage software releases appropriately. A foundation for this is to have an authoritative repository of approved versions and builds for software, often referred to as *Definitive Software Library (DSL)*. The solution artifact deployment skill set means the ability to add a software artifact to a runtime, defining appropriate profiles and putting it into the right file locations. For this ability, the basic operating system skill set is needed, which enables a user to perform tasks on an operating system. It starts with the ability to log on and log off to the system on an operating system level and continues with knowledge of commands to start and stop programs, create, copy, and move files, and so on.

A.3.7 The IT Operator

When the MDM Solution is installed, someone needs to monitor it to see if all components work from a functional and from a performance perspective. This is the responsibility of the **IT Operator.** If a result of monitoring indicates a problem, the IT Operator needs to inform the Problem Analyst (see A.3.10), who has to drill down into the problem to find the cause. Here these two users collaborate.

The goal of the IT Operator is simple: To ensure that all systems provide the expected service from a functional and performance perspective to the service users.

---

7. ITIL is an abbreviation for Information Technology Infrastructure Library, a group of concepts and technologies for managing IT infrastructure. The names ITIL and IT Infrastructure Library are both registered trademarks of the United Kingdom's Office of Government Commerce (OGC); for further details, please see [2] and [3]. With mentioning ITIL here, we intend to make the reader aware of frameworks for managing IT infrastructure, without saying that ITIL is the silver bullet for it. More specifically, someone working in the context of IT infrastructure deployment, administration, or management needs to align any available framework within the overall policies and procedures an enterprise has. Thus, we will keep the description on these tasks very brief because there are many books available on these topics.

On the highest level, a user in this role has two skill sets: the operational procedure skill set and the software system resource operation skill set. The software system resource operation skill set represents the abilities to operate a software resource and to perform the identification, analysis, and reporting of incidents. The operational procedure skill set characterizes the ability to define and execute IT operational procedures. This requires knowledge about best practices for operational procedures and how to apply those to their environment. Software system resource operation is based on two basic skill groups, monitoring and incident reporting. Without monitoring ability to see the state of a software resource, an IT Operator cannot control it. Thus, reading system diagnostics about functional and performance aspects through alert management, locating diagnostic messages, and creating and interpreting diagnostic reports is fundamental. The skill set of incident reporting means the ability to apply incident reporting procedures, using knowledge about lifecycle and use of incident records. The operational procedure skills are based on the basic operating system usage skill set, the change management skill set, and the configuration management skill set. The change management skill set means the ability to conform to a change management procedure. Knowledge about lifecycle and use of Request for Change (RFC) records provide the basics here. For the configuration management skill set, using configuration change management procedures based on the definition and maintenance of Configuration Item (CI) structures is important.

A.3.8   The Resilience Engineer

Enterprise-wide deployments of an MDM Solution should be designed to not create a single point of failure. For example, if LOB systems are dependent upon the MDM System to complete a business transaction and the MDM System were to fail, the entire enterprise could come to a sudden halt. For this reason, state-of-the-art continuous availability functions and tested, proven disaster recovery procedures executed by trained, highly skilled staff are mandatory to ensure continuous business operations. The responsibility for the business resiliency belongs to the **Resilience Engineer,** who is responsible for appropriate capacity of the IT infrastructure, its availability, and the continuity of all IT services, including disaster cases. In the context of MDM deployments, we recommend assigning this task only to skilled Resilience Engineers with five years or more experience in such a role. Furthermore, periodic training of disaster recovery procedures and continuous education for them is very important. It will be to them that your company turns in case of a disaster affecting the entire enterprise, thus justifying this investment.

A user performing in this role has two goals:

- The IT infrastructure has sufficient capacity for the number of users and the given performance service-level agreements (SLA).
- The IT infrastructure is resilient (measured through indicators such as last backup time, disaster recovery time, or average down time, which should be as small as possible).

The skill sets for this user role are disaster recovery, meaning all abilities to plan and execute disaster recovery plans and capacity planning. Capacity planning is the ability to understand and ensure that the IT infrastructure has sufficient capacity based on certain service-level agreements (SLA).

Note that a Resilience Engineer should closely collaborate with a Database Administrator (see A.3.9.2) to ensure the high availability of the database where the master data is stored as well as disaster recovery procedures for this database.

A.3.9   The Administrator

An **Administrator** in a broad sense is responsible for performing all operational processes and procedures to ensure that all IT services are operational and meet specified operational targets. It is also expected that all configurations (as well as updates) for the IT infrastructure are appropriately recorded. In the following three subsections, we describe three specialized roles for Administrators. Depending on your company size and the MDM project, you might need only one person doing all of the items for all three specialized roles or you may need multiple people performing in each role if your company is quite large and the MDM Solution deployment is a project reflecting this size.

A.3.9.1   The IT Administrator

Someone needs to ensure availability and performance of all operational processes and procedures supported by the IT systems. This is the core task of the **IT Administrator.** The goal for this user role is to have the IT systems operational and available and to have them complying with all specified service-level agreements.

The skill sets on a top level are IT system administration and IT system management. IT system management skills consist of the ability to plan and execute IT system management functions according to and within the boundaries of procedures, processes, and legal requirements. The skill set of IT system administration is composed of the skills necessary to configure and tune an IT system. Efficiency to do this means the ability to monitor the systems getting the data for tuning and the automation of repeating tasks. Inventory management with audit support is another area of required skills. Finally, problem and change management are mandatory as well. The skills in the IT system administration group are based on four other skill sets:

- Basic hardware setup skill set: This skill set means the abilities to unpack and assemble hardware or change devices or components as needed.
- Software stack management: Based on the basic operating system usage skill set described in Section A.3.7, the skills of this group enable the IT Administrator to install and uninstall appropriate levels of all software components involved.
- Software system resource configuration: This skill set contains skills to define and maintain software configurations for most efficient usage of all software running in the IT landscape.
- Diagnostics management: With skills from this group, IT administrators configure software resources to obtain diagnostics. This is done by defining alerts, diagnostic reports, and profiles.

As an example, the IT Administrator would assemble the hardware for the IT systems running the components of the MDM software. The IT Administrator would install the operating systems and the MDM software, for example, and configure them appropriately.

A.3.9.2   The Database Administrator

Making data available to users and at the same time complying with security constraints is the goal of the user role **Database Administrator.** Because end users expect to have access to data with certain guaranteed response times, the way information access is made available by the Database Administrator needs to be in a range of agreed upon service-level agreements.

The skill set of the Database Administrators enables installation, configuration, and tuning of database systems. Expected skills span the following topics:

- Physical layout of tables, transactional logs, and table spaces on hard disks
- Database security
- Performance tuning
- Backup
- Continuous availability including disaster recovery
- Problem determination

It is particularly important that the Database Administrator takes special care regarding high availability, continuous operations, failover, and disaster recovery for the database. The database component of the MDM System is one of the components that can bring down the entire MDM System if there is a database system failure. It is therefore the responsibility of the Database Administrator to mitigate this risk as much as possible by configuring appropriate high-availability measures and testing disaster recovery strategies for any efficiency weakness. Regarding this aspect, the Database Administrator collaborates with the Resilience Engineer (see Subsection A.3.8).

The other crucial factor relevant to a MDM System is security, as described in Chapter 3. The database of the MDM System likely contains the most valuable information a company has: the customers and the products. It cannot be over-emphasized that the security of this database should be paramount to the Database Administrator. Close collaboration with the Security Administrator, as described in the next section, could help to determine the overall security measures needed to implement the relevant subset for a secure database system.

A.3.9.3 The Security Administrator

The user in the role of **Security Administrator** is responsible for end-to-end security of the master data solution. The goal for the Security Administrator is the protection of all IT systems from external intruders and the implementation of mechanisms that ensure that internal users can access only information they are entitled to. The security areas a Security Administrator needs to address are described in full detail in Chapter 3. Measuring how effectively the Security Administrator achieved this goal, compliance with legal requirements and security-related service-level agreements is considered. Furthermore, the number of security incidents, and the implementation of auditable procedures for business controls, are part of the job performance metrics for the Security Administrator.

The top-level skill set is solution-wide security administration, which in essence represents the configuration of an end-to-end security model. This group of skills is based on the skill sets of solution security design and solution security implementation.

If a user has the solution security design skill set, the user is able to work out how to secure an MDM Solution. First, the Security Administrator needs to understand the enterprise security architecture and the security vulnerabilities of the MDM Solution. Based on this insight, the enterprise security architecture is then mapped to the MDM Solution, and business roles are mapped to security roles. As a final step, the security implementation is planned.

The solution security implementation group of skills enables the Security Administrator to configure all security components. This includes installation and configuration of all security-related software components. A Security Administrator is also able to define session control mechanisms and user registries. A person in this role can also configure data security and collaborates in this area with the Database Administrator (see A.3.9.2). Finally, the ability to set up keys and audit controls belongs to this skill group. The solution security implementation skill set is based on the skill group of user security management, enabling a user in this role to control user access to IT systems through the management of users and user groups. The User security management skills further depend on user access management skills. Applying user access management skills is required to configure access control lists appropriately in order to set up access for users to a system resource.

A.3.10 The Problem Analyst

If an IT Operator finds a problem or a Solution User encounters something that does not work as designed, both encountered an incident, and both need someone to turn to—which is the Problem Analyst. A user in this role does an initial problem analysis for an incident and has a sharp focus to enable a Solution User to continue to work as soon as possible again. Afterwards, the Problem Analyst does an incident drill-down to find the root of the problem and performs appropriate reporting. In short, the job of a Problem Analyst is to determine the cause and a cure for the IT system's problem. The cure has to be implemented usually by another role such as IT Operator, IT Administrator, Database Administrator, or Security Administrator, thus this user often collaborates with them. We recommend that users in this role have several years of IT experience, because they need to be able to track down a problem potentially through a variety of platforms and operating systems, applications, and middleware components to find the cause. The ultimate goal of a Problem Analyst is to have no unresolved incident or problem.

The top-level skill set for a user in this role is incident and problem management, combined usually with other skills for appropriate solutions of IT problems. A user in this role should also have strong customer relationship management skills, because the customers in this case are the business users of the IT department infrastructure where the MDM Solution is operated—which are all business departments and users therein needing access to master data (in other words, almost all departments of an enterprise).

Decomposing this skill set further, we find the three skill sets:

- IT problem determination skill set: Skills to locate the root cause of an IT problem or incident belong in this group, such as using diagnostic tools, analytical thinking, and performance analysis.
- IT problem management skill set: Using appropriate problem management procedures based on lifecycle considerations, as well as the use of problem records and previous error records, represent the core abilities in this group.
- IT incident management skill set: The characteristics of skills in this group are the appropriate usage of incident management procedures, considering lifecycle and use of incident records.

Even though some of these skill sets could be decomposed further, we think this user role has been described in sufficient detail with regard to the tasks a user in this role needs to perform in the context of an MDM Solution.

A.3.11 The IT Manager

Someone has to be in charge of IT development and IT operations, making decisions and take business ownership of the IT department. This is the **IT Manager.** On a high level, the IT Manager strives to obtain appreciation of the IT assets by the business owners; in short, the IT Manager wants recognition that IT assets are valuable business assets. Thus, IT assets must provide a return on investment, and the associated risks with their operation require appropriate risk management (from a financial, security, and compliance perspective, for example). This high-level goal can be divided into two lower-level objectives:

- The IT systems support current business use: This goal in essence says that IT supports today's business based on service-level agreements, completeness of function, and a business efficiency perspective for users.
- The IT systems can adapt to future business use: This goal is a bit more challenging because it requires the foresight of what the IT systems need to be able to deliver to the business in the future. Because MDM Solutions by design have to be evolutionary in nature to adapt to changing business processes, this objective has to be of paramount importance as well. The IT Manager needs to predict required capacity and enhancements in line with the overall IT strategy.

From the required skill set perspective, the IT Manager requires the people and project management skill set described earlier and basic knowledge of IT infrastructure terminology and management.

A.4 The Solution User

The **Solution Users** are Line of Business (LOB) users working with the MDM Solution knowingly or unknowingly, depending on the way the MDM System is integrated into the application landscape. For example: A Solution User can be a bank clerk using a new portal interface that uses MDM services to create new customers and open accounts. Another example could be a product designer defining product attributes with the existing application, not knowing that behind the scenes the existing application works now with an MDM System with regard to all functions related to product master data. The key point is that if the MDM Solution deployment changes, the Solution Users should not have to become familiar with a new user interface and require training. If an application user interface does require modifications to support integration with the MDM System, we strongly believe that these users be involved in the earliest phases of the design process and accompany the whole implementation through periodic checkpoints. They should be involved in the user acceptance test (UAT) as well in order to avoid surprises when the solution is handed over to them.

Finally, we believe that as the MDM market matures, this user role might further differentiate, requiring updates and a potential split into multiple specialized roles.

A.5 Relations between User Roles

Table A.1 shows which MDM user roles are typically needed in which phase of an MDM project over the entire lifecycle, reaching from strategy to running an MDM System in operational mode.

Table A.1   Job Roles by MDM Project Phase

Job Role	Fine-Grained Job Role	Strategy	Planning	Implementation	Test	Operation
Strategist		X				
Business Analyst			X			
Solution Architect			X			
Developer						
	Business Customizer		X	X		
	Data Integrator		X	X	X	
	Information Developer			X	X	
	Translator			X	X	
Test Engineer				X	X	
Manager				X	X	X
	Category Manager (PIM)			X	X	X
	Item Specialist Manager (PIM)			X	X	X
Specialist				X	X	X
	Category Specialist (PIM)			X	X	X
	Item Specialist (PIM)			X	X	X
Business Operation Manager						X

(continued)

Table A.1   Job Roles by MDM Project Phase (continued)

Job Role	Fine-Grained Job Role	Strategy	Planning	Implementation	Test	Operation
Operational Data Steward				X	X	X
Data Administrator			X	X	X	X
Resource Owner				X		X
Auditor				X		X
Deployer				X	X	X
IT Operator			X	X	X	X
Resilience Engineer			X			X
Administrator				X	X	X
	IT Administrator			X	X	X
	Database Administrator			X	X	X
	Security Administrator			X	X	X
Problem Analyst					X	X
IT Manager			X			X
Solution User					X	X

Table A.2 shows options for staffing MDM user roles from client resources (client in the sense of being a customer of the software vendor selling the MDM software), software vendor resources, and system integrator resources. The table is based on two assumptions. The first assumption is that the IT department is not completely outsourced. The second assumption

Table A.2 Staffing Options

Job Role	Fine-Grained Job role	Client	Software Vendor	System Integrator
Strategist		X	X	X
Business Analyst		X		X
Solution Architect		X	X	X
Developer		X	X	X
	Business Customizer	X		X
	Data Integrator	X	X	X
	Information Developer	X		X
	Translator	X		X
Test Engineer		X	X	X
Manager		X		
	Category Manager (PIM)	X		
	Item Specialist Manager (PIM)	X		
Specialist		X		
	Category Specialist (PIM)	X		
	Item Specialist (PIM)	X		

(*continued*)

is that, since the roles were also presented in the context of running the solution after deployment, certain roles are staffed by the client; we assume this because after implementation, these user roles need to be there to operate the MDM Solution. So it is feasible that some of the MDM user roles shown in the table in the client column for implementing the MDM Solution are staffed with resources from a software vendor or a system integrator; at the end of the implementation, users performing these roles need to be trained on the client side to successfully operate the MDM Solution afterwards.

Table A.2 Staffing Options (continued)

Job Role	Fine-Grained Job role	Client	Software Vendor	System Integrator
Business Operation Manager		X		
Operational Data Steward		X		
Data Administrator		X		
Resource Owner		X		
Auditor		X		
Deployer		X		
IT Operator		X		
Resilience Engineer		X		
Administrator		X		
	IT Administrator	X		
	Database Administrator	X		
	Security Administrator	X		
Problem Analyst		X		
IT Manager		X	X	X
Solution User		X		

References

1. Unified Modeling Language: http://www.uml.org
2. United Kingdom's Office of Government Commerce (OGC): http://www.ogc.gov.uk/, March 2008.
3. Information Technology Infrastructure Library: http://www.itil.org.uk/, March 2008.

Software and Solution Offerings for MDM Deployments

The purpose of this appendix is to provide IT Architects with a sample of software products from relevant software vendors that may be useful for implementing master data solutions. Because information regarding features of software products is volatile in nature and changes frequently with each new release, we limit ourselves to providing the name of the software vendor and the product name. The interested reader can find market and maturity rankings for many of the listed products in reports from Gartner,[1] Forrester, and other market analysts. We also narrow down the scope to software offerings in the master data integration,[2] master data management, and master data solution areas, which enrich or complement core MDM products. The grouping of products is according to the MDM logical reference architecture as outlined in Chapter 3. There are only two exceptions. First, IT security, where we list products for securing MDM deployments due to the high importance of security in such solution scenarios. Second, Enterprise Service Bus products, because as far as we can see, almost all MDM deployments use this type of technology to a certain degree. The listings are by topic, and within a topic, in alphabetical order by software vendor.

---

1. Some Gartner Group and Forrester reports relevant to the product areas covered are:

   The Forrester Wave. Enterprise Database Auditing And Real-Time Protection, written by Noel Yuhanna, October 26, 2007.
   Magic Quadrant for Data Quality Tools by Gartner Group, G00149359, written by Ted Friedman, Andreas Bitterer, June 29, 2007.
   Magic Quadrant for Product Information Management by Gartner Group, G00148303, written by Andrew White, June 21, 2007.
   Magic Quadrant for Customer Data Integration Hubs by Gartner Group, G00147231, written by John Radcliffe, June 29, 2007.
2. ETL tools will be found in Section B.4.

After the product listing, you will find a list of links to the company and product homepages sorted alphabetically by company name. We decided to keep the links out of the listing for readability reasons and listed them separately.

B.1   Analytic Services

The products in this section support analytical use cases of MDM. For example, the product from Endeca offers powerful search capabilities. The Entity Analytics Solution from IBM helps to determine hidden relationships and is particularly useful for CDI deployments of MDM.

- Endeca: Endeca Information Access Platform (IAP) for Guided Navigation
- Exeros: Exeros Discovery
- Fortent: Fortent KYC and Fortent AML
- Memex: Memex Series VI
- IBM: Entity Analytics Solutions, IBM Industry Models and Global Name Recognition
- Norkom: Solution provider for AML, CDD, and Claims Fraud scenarios

B.2   Enterprise Application Integration Using ESB

Products in this section provide capabilities for implementing the ESB concept of a service-oriented architecture. Messaging infrastructure is a key component of these products.

- BEA: BEA AquaLogic Service Bus
- IBM: IBM WebSphere Enterprise Service Bus and IBM WebSphere Message Broker
- SonicSoftware: Progress Sonic Enterprise Service Bus
- Tibco: TIBCO Business Works

B.3   External Data Providers

In this section, we list two types of resources. The first are watch lists such as the OFAC list and the e-CTFSL list. The other products represent external data source providers such as Dun and Bradstreet.

- Acxiom: Product suite, e.g., AbiliTec and AdressAbility
- Dun and Bradstreet: Product suite, e.g., Business Information Report, Comprehensive Report European Union: Electronic-Consolidated Targeted Financial Sanctions List (e-CTFSL), a watch list
- LexisNexis: LexisNexis offers authoritative legal news, public records, and business information
- Experian: Truvue
- U.S. Department of the Treasury: The Office of Foreign Assets Control (OFAC), a watch list

B.4 Information Integration Services

The products listed in this section provide powerful capabilities to analyze, cleanse, standardize, transform, and load data. These products are particularly useful for the master data integration phase. Standardization capabilities are also useful for the operational phase of a MDM System in the lifecycle after the MDM hub has been built.

- BusinessObjects: Data Insight XI, Data Quality XI
- DataFlux: DataFlux Standard Integration Server and DataFlux Enterprise Integration Server
- Fuzzy! Informatik: Various products such as FUZZY! Analyzer or FUZZY! Post
- Group 1 Software: Address Now and CODE-1 Plus suite
- Human Inference: Various products; bundle available as HIquality Product Suite
- IBM: IBM Information Server as Information Integration Platform suite with key product components such as Information Analyzer, QualityStage, DataStage, Business Glossary and MetaData Server
- Informatica: Informatica Data Quality Suite
- Innovative Systems: i/Lytics Suite
- Netrics: Real World Matching Platform
- Trillium Software: TS Discovery and TS Quality

B.5 Master Data Management Services

The products listed in this section represent software for master data management. Many MDM Systems in production are built with one of these products.

- IBM: Global Data Synchronization
- IBM: IBM InfoSphere MDM Server
- IBM: WebSphere Product Center
- Initiate Systems, Inc.: Several tailored solutions for Master Data Management
- Oracle: Oracle Customer Hub, and Siebel UCM Oracle Product Hub
- SAP: Netweaver Master Data Management
- Siperian: Siperian MDM Hub
- Tibco: Collaborative Information Manager

B.6 Security

In this section, we cover security technologies for various security aspects and thus group them by function.

XML Gateway technologies:

- IBM: IBM WebSphere Data Power
- Layer 7: Various product bundles

Secure Proxy technologies:

- Computer Associates: eTrust SiteMinder Secure Proxy Server
- IBM: IBM Tivoli Access Manager for eBusiness
- RSA Security Inc.: RSA Access Manager

SOA Security technologies:

- Single Sign On technologies:
  - Computer Associates: eTrust SiteMinder Secure Proxy Server
  - Evidian: PortalXpert
  - IBM: IBM Tivoli Federated Identity Manager
  - RSA Security Inc.: RSA Access Manager
- User provisioning technologies:
  - Computer Associates: Identity Manager
  - IBM: IBM Tivoli Identity Manager
  - SUN: Sun Java System Identity Manager and Sun Java System Directory Server Enterprise Edition
- Audit technologies:
  - Guardium: AuditGuard and Database Compliance Accelerators
  - IBM: IBM Tivoli Consul
  - Lumigent Technologies: Lumigent Audit DB
  - Tizor: Mantra

B.7   Track and Trace Solutions

The products listed in this section are useful to implement Track and Trace solutions requiring support for ePedigree.

- Axway: Synchrone ePedigree
- IBM: RFID Information Center and IBM Premises Server
- rfXcel: Active ePedigree Management
- Supplyscape: Security-ePedigree product

B.8   Links to Relevant Homepages

With the list in this final section of this appendix, we intend to provide the IT Architect with the link to the company or public institution webpage of the products and watch lists mentioned in previous sections of this appendix. This should allow a fast check of the latest information on the products in order to make an informed decision when selecting the products as part of writing the physical IT architecture document deliverable.

Axway: http://www.axway.com/solutions/healthcare/epedigree.php
Acxiom: http://www.acxiom.com/
BEA: http://www.bea.com/framework.jsp?CNT=homepage_main.jsp&FP=/content
BusinessObjects (taken over by SAP): http://www.businessobjects.com/

Computer Associates: http://ca.com/us/
DataFlux: http://www.dataflux.com/
Dun and Bradstreet: http://www.dnb.com/us/
Endeca: http://endeca.com/
Evidian: http://www.evidian.com/
European Union: http://ec.europa.eu/external_relations/cfsp/sanctions/list/consollist.htm
Exeros: http://www.exeros.com/
Experian: http://www.experiangroup.com/
Fortent: http://www.fortent.com/
Fuzzy! Informatik: http://www.fazi.de/international.php
Group 1 Software: http://www.g1.com/Products/Data-Integration/
Guardium: http://www.guardium.com/
Human Inference: http://www.humaninference.com/
IBM: http://www.ibm.com/us/
Informatica: http://www.informatica.com/
Initiate Systems, Inc.: http://www.initiatesystems.com/Pages/default.aspx
Innovative Systems: http://www.innovativesystems.com/
Layer 7: http://www.layer7tech.com/products/page.html?id=2
LexisNexis: http://www.lexisnexis.com/gov/
Lumigent Technologies: http://www.lumigent.com/
Memex: http://www.memex.co.uk/
Netrics: http://www.netrics.com/index.psp
Norkom: http://www.norkom.com/
Oracle: http://www.oracle.com/index.html
rfXel: http://rfxcel.com/index.htm
RSA Security Inc.: http://www.rsa.com/
SAP: http://www.sap.com/
Siperian: http://www.siperian.com/
SonicSoftware: http://www.sonicsoftware.com/index.ssp
Supplyscape: http://www.supplyscape.com/
SUN: http://www.sun.com/
Tibco: http://www.tibco.com/
Tizor: http://www.tizor.com/
Trillium Software: http://www.trilliumsoftware.com/home/index.aspx
U.S. Department of the Treasury: http://www.treasury.gov/offices/enforcement/ofac/

Appendix C

Master Data Management and Regulations

C.1 Introduction

Throughout this book, we have mentioned a number of regulations that can influence how you configure, manage, and protect a master data management environment. To help understand the relevant regulations and their scope, we have collected some information on each regulation, including:

- **Name of the Regulation (and country where regulation applies):** Note that regulations in one country may apply to organizations based in another one if the organization does business in the regulated country or has customers in the regulated country.
- **Industries Affected:** Many regulations apply to either a broad base of organizations (like Sarbanes-Oxley) or are targeted to a specific industry (like HIPAA, which is a US privacy regulation for the healthcare industry).
- **Master Data Domain:** This lists the different master data domains that are affected by the regulation. The Party domain is present in most of the regulations; however, there may be a specific type of Party (e.g., Patient) affected by the regulation, rather than all types of parties (e.g., Vendor).
- **Notes:** A brief overview of the regulation, including a link to more information about the regulation.

The list of regulations in this appendix is just a snapshot in time of key regulations. Over time, more regulations will be created that are relevant to master data and existing ones will be amended to cover new or different industries and master data domains. As we mentioned in Chapter 4, the architectural emphasis in MDM is to ensure that the architecture is not focused on any single regulation and that it is flexible enough to accommodate a broad range of compliance regulations. Finally, don't construe any of the notes on the regulations as binding legal advice. For a more in-depth discussion of compliance regulations, we would recommend [1] or [2].

C.2   Regulations

Regulation	Industry	Master Data Domain	Notes
17 CFR Part 210, US	Publicly held companies in the US	Customer, Account, Contract, Vendor, Supplier	17 CFR Part 210 covers financial statements for publicly held companies, including format and content of the statements, independence of auditors and independent reviews, and retention of records used in the production of the financial reports. http://ecfr.gpoaccess.gov/cgi/t/text/text-idx?c=ecfr&tpl=/ecfrbrowse/Title17/17cfr210_ main_02.tpl
21 CFR 11 (US Food and Drug Administration)	Healthcare (Pharmaceutical)	Product	21 CFR 11 centers on how pharmaceutical manufacturers submit electronic records to the Food and Drug Administration (FDA) in lieu of or in addition to paper records. Under this regulation, when submitting an electronic record, a digital signature must be affixed. Additionally, guidance for 21 CFR 11 describes a number of operational concerns on systems used to interact with the FDA, including limiting who can access the systems and other policies and controls over the systems. http://www.fda.gov/cder/guidance/5667fnl.htm
Bank Secrecy Act of 1970 (BSA or Currency and Foreign Transactions Reporting Act), USA	Financial, Retail	Customer, Organization, Account	The first law to fight money laundering in the US. The BSA requires businesses to keep records and file reports that are determined to have a high degree of usefulness in criminal, tax, and regulatory matters, such as cash transactions of $10,000 or more. This law has been extended to cover retail organizations as well. http://www.fincen.gov/reg_main.html

Regulation	Industry	Master Data Domain	Notes
Basel II (2004), International	Financial	Product, Account, Contract, Customer	Basel II enhances the previous Basel Accord to strengthen the measures used to assess the minimum amount of capital a financial institution must hold to mitigate against risk (market, credit, and operational), the steps that are used to control, manage, and monitor risk, and the transparency of public reports issued by the institutions (these are considered the three pillars of Basel II).
			Operational risk was added to Basel II. Calculations for credit and market risk require master data on customers, accounts, and contracts.
			The second pillar, Supervisory Review, specifies internal controls similar to those found in Sarbanes-Oxley sections 302 and 404 (specifically section 744 of Basel II).
			The third pillar, Market Discipline, provides guidance on the type of events and financial disclosures that should be provided by regulated companies to give insight into the financial state of the company.
			http://www.bis.org/publ/bcbs128.htm
Bundesdaten-schutz-Gesetz (BDSG or Germany's Federal Data Protection Act)	Government, Companies in Germany	Customer, Account, Contract	One of the oldest European data protection laws (passed in 1977), BDSG mandates strong controls over the collection and dissemination of personally identifiable information by government and businesses. These controls include how the information must be protected (both access control and encryption), and also requires a data privacy officer. BDSG provides a strong statement about the rights of data

(continued)

Regulation	Industry	Master Data Domain	Notes
			subjects and how and when organizations should be allowed to collect and use personal information.
			In 2005, BDSG was amended to reflect the privacy controls specified by EU Data Protection Directive 95/46/EC.
			http://www.privacy.de/recht/de/bdsg/bdsg01_eng.htm
			http://books.google.com/books?id=qulwlMLtwMQC&pg=PA14&lpg=PA14&dq=bdsg+germany&source=web&ots=8zhvsOOMw3&sig=vsSpP5vilBYLaFyiuNm5H29DwsU#PPA9,M1
California Security Breach Information Act (SB 1386), California, US, 2002	Government, Business, and any person that has computerized personally identifiable information on California residents	Party, Account, Contract	SB 1386 requires timely notifications to residents of California affected when a data breach occurs. A data breach is considered to have occurred when unencrypted personal information has been acquired or can reasonably believed to have been acquired by an unauthorized person or organization. Under SB 1386, personal information is a person's name, combined with one of the following: • Social security number • Driver's license number or California Identification Card number • Account number, credit or debit card number, along with any codes or passwords that enable access to an individual's account. SB 1386 is the first law in the US for data breach disclosures and is considered a model for similar laws in other states. http://info.sen.ca.gov/pub/01-02/bill/sen/sb_1351-1400/sb_1386_bill_20020926_chaptered.html

Regulation	Industry	Master Data Domain	Notes
California's ePedigree law (US)	Pharmaceutical Industry	Product, Vendor	Effective in January 2009, the California ePedigree law requires pharmaceutical manufacturers to create unique identifiers for drug information, track each product's pedigree (the change of possession of the product), and maintain electronic supply chain records. In addition to the law, wholesalers expect to receive serialized (i.e., items tagged with a serial number) products in July 2008. http://www.businesswire.com/portal/site/google/index.jsp?ndmViewId=news_view&newsId=20071009005843&newsLang=en and http://law.onecle.com/california/business/4034.html
Data Protection Act of 1984, United Kingdom (Amended 1998)	All industries and businesses that maintain information on data subjects in the UK	Party (Customer), Account, Contract	This law is the major piece of legislation with respect to personal privacy in the UK, and is aligned very closely with EU Directive 95/46 (also covered in this appendix.) The Act describes the rights of individuals to determine what information is being collected on them and how it is used, and also prescribes the following eight principles that organizations must follow in handling personal information: • Fair and lawful processing (not collected under false pretenses) • Processing only for specific, limited purposes • Limited only to information needed for the specific process • Maintaining accurate information (including keeping information up to date)

(continued)

Regulation	Industry	Master Data Domain	Notes
			• Storing personal information for a limited time • Respects the rights of data subjects • Secure handling • Not transferred beyond the EU unless the rights of the data subject can be assured http://www.opsi.gov.uk/acts/acts1998/ukpga_19980029_en_1 and http://www.ico.gov.uk/Home/what_we_cover/data_protection.aspx
European Health Insurance Card (decision 189, decision 190 and decision 191, 18th of June 2003)	Healthcare industry	Customer	On 7 February 2003, the Commission adopted a Communication concerning the introduction of a European health insurance card. • Decision No 189 introduced the European Health Insurance Card and established the principle of gradual replacement of the various paper forms, enabling health care to be obtained during a temporary stay in a Member State other than that in which the claimant is insured by the European Health Insurance Card. It specified the legal implications for the social security institutions in the Member State of temporary stay. Finally, it defined the sole data to be included on the European Health Insurance Card and on the provisional replacement certificate to be used when the European Health Insurance Card was not available.

Regulation	Industry	Master Data Domain	Notes
			• Decision No 190 concerned the European Health Insurance Card's technical characteristics. It established a common model and the specific details for both the European Health Insurance Card and the provisional certificate used instead of the European Health Insurance Card. • Decision No 191 laid down the practical arrangements for replacing forms E111 and 111B by the European health insurance card with effect from 1 June 2004 and provided for the possibility of introducing the European Health Insurance Card gradually and for transitional periods up to 31 December 2005. The outcome: The adoption of this body of law enabled a standard format European health insurance card with eye-readable data concerning the holder to be introduced as of 1 June 2004. The data on the European Health Insurance Card were rationalized and were simpler than those on the E111 form. A major step forward was that only the code of the insured's sickness insurance institution was indicated rather than the full name. A database of these codes has been compiled and can be accessed via the Internet. http://ec.europa.eu/employment_social/healthcard/coinexpert_en.htm

(continued)

Regulation	Industry	Master Data Domain	Notes
European Union (EU) Directive 95/46/EC on the Protection of Personal Data	Cross-Industry	Party, Customer, Citizen, Contract, Account	This directive states that anyone processing personal data must comply with three enforceable principles of good practice. The three principles are: • Transparency—The person whose sensitive personal data is being collected must be notified of the collection and processing. • Legitimate Purpose—The data collected must be used only for valid reasons, such as legal and contractual obligations, or other requests that have been agreed to by the data subject. • Proportionality—The amount and type of data collected should be minimized to only that which is needed for the particular purpose, should be maintained only as long as needed, and should be checked to make sure that the data is valid and accurate. Data subjects are also given the right to view data collected on them, and to object to the use of private data by a particular entity. The directive also states that the personal information must be protected from destruction, loss, and unauthorized disclosure and modification. The protection includes data as it as transmitted and while it is at rest. http://ec.europa.eu/justice_home/fsj/privacy/index_en.htm
EuroSox (EU)	Publicly held companies in the EU	Vendor, Customer, Supplier, Contract, Account	EuroSox is the nickname for a collection of legislation enacted between 2002 and 2006 targeted at improving transparency in corporate governance and increasing public confidence in

Regulation	Industry	Master Data Domain	Notes
			European companies. Some of the focus areas of the legislation are: • Strong internal controls (and assessment of those controls) on data used for financial reporting • Stricter corporate governance and reporting • Risk Management • Independence and liabilities of auditors Some of the EuroSox legislation with respect to financial data and controls are: • The European Union Financial Services Action Plan (FSAP) • The 4th Directive on Annual Accounts of Specific Type of Companies • The 7th Directive on Consolidated accounts • The 8th Company Law Directive on Statutory Audit • The 8th Company Law Directive and Corporate Governance (this directive ties into MiFID) • The 8th Company Law Directive: Committees and Interpretations
Fair and Accurate Credit Transactions Act (FACT), US	Finance	Customer, Organization, Location, Account	This is known as the Red Flag regulation (presumably because the account would be annotated with a red flag indicating a potential problem with the account). FACT requires business processes to detect and mitigate against identity theft, such as using information from consumer reporting agencies, identifying suspicious documents and potentially suspicious use of personally identifiable

(*continued*)

Regulation	Industry	Master Data Domain	Notes
			information, and handling problems reported with change of address requests. There are 26 specific directives in the guidance to financial institutions.
			http://www.ftc.gov/os/2006/07/R611019 IdentityTheftRedFlagsJointNotice%20 of%20ProposedRulemakingFRNotice FRFormat.pdf
Financial Instruments and Exchange Law of 2006 (sometimes known as J-SOX), Japan	Financial	Customer, Product, Account, Contract	FIEL revises and extends the Security and Exchange Law in Japan to provide stricter controls and governance over a larger set of financial instruments and institutions, with a stated goal of stronger investor protection. FIEL requires a greater amount of transparency (via public disclosures, governance, and codification of ethical practices and separation of concerns) and a larger emphasis on financial risk management of the newly regulated businesses.
			http://papers.ssrn.com/sol3/Delivery. cfm/SSRN_ID920303_code565713.pdf? abstractid=920303&mirid=5
Florida's Drug and Cosmetic Act, Chapter 499, F.S., Florida, US, 2005	Pharmaceutical Industry	Product Supplier	The purpose of the Drug and Cosmetic Act is to protect the public from health hazards relating to supplier or manufacture deception (including false advertising) involving drugs, medical devices, and cosmetics.
			This Act was modified in 2006 to require a pedigree to trace the history of a dispensed drug across the supply chain (but does not require a serial number for the drug.)
			http://www.cga.ct.gov/2005/rpt/ 2005-R-0580.htm and

Regulation	Industry	Master Data Domain	Notes
			http://www.leg.state.fl.us/statutes/index.cfm?App_mode=Display_Statute&Search_String=&URL=Ch0499/PART01.HTM
Gramm-Leach-Bliley Act (GLBA), formally known as The Financial Modernization Act of 1999, US	Financial, Insurance	Party (Customer), Product, Account, Contract	GLBA introduced three rules to safeguard personal information held by the financial industry—a Financial Privacy Rule, a Safeguards Rule, and a Pretexting Rule. The Financial Privacy Rule focuses on the notification to customers about how the organization collects, uses, protects and shares non-public data about the customer. Organizations are obliged to send out a yearly privacy notice to customers clearly stating how they handle sensitive financial data, and are further obligated to give customers a reasonable opportunity to "opt-out" of having their information shared with non-affiliated companies (and in some cases, even with affiliated companies like subsidiaries), with some exceptions (such as service providers for billings and mailouts). The Safeguards Rule (also known as 16 CFR Part 314) requires affected organizations to establish procedures and controls for safeguarding the privacy and security of sensitive financial information, including protection from readily anticipated threats to the information, and from unauthorized access and misuse that could cause harm to a customer. The Pretexting Rule is designed to protect the customer from the disclosure of their personal financial information under false pretenses

(continued)

Regulation	Industry	Master Data Domain	Notes
			(such as someone impersonating the customer). It also makes it illegal to solicit others to obtain such information by pretexting. http://www.ftc.gov/privacy/ privacyinitiatives/glbact.html
Health Insurance Portability and Accountability Act (HIPAA) of 1996, US	Healthcare Providers (including prescription drugs), Insurance, Healthcare Clearing Houses, Federal Agencies dealing with patient information	Patient (Party), Account	HIPAA mandates the use of standards for the electronic exchange of medical records, and regulations that protect health information (known as the Privacy Rule), including: • Ensuring the confidentiality, integrity, and availability of Electronic Person Health Information (EPHI) received, created, or transmitted • Defending against any reasonably anticipated threats and risks to the security or integrity of EPHI • Requiring providers to create privacy policies and notify patients of those policies. This gives patients control over the use and disclosure over their health information • Protecting against uses or disclosures of EPHI that are not approved by the privacy rules and policies http://www.hhs.gov/ocr/hipaa/
Homeland Security Information Sharing Act (HSISA, H.R. 4598), US	Public Sector	All domains	HSISA mandates that sensitive information deemed critical to the protection of the US be shared and maintained in a secure fashion (e.g., only made available to those who have a need to know) using a well-defined set of procedures. http://fas.org/sgp/congress/2002/ hr3825.html

Regulation	Industry	Master Data Domain	Notes
International Financial Reporting Standard (IFRS), International Accounting Standards Board	Cross Industry	Customer, Account, Product, Contract, Vendor, Supplier	IFRS defines the reporting measures used in the financial statements required for many major financial regulatory reports (in particular Basel II). http://www.iasb.org/IFRS+Summaries/ Technical+Summaries+of+International +Financial+Reporting+Standards.htm
Markets in Financial Instruments Directive (MiFID), EU	Financial Industry	Customer, Account, Contract	MiFID is a major part of the Euro-Sox collection of regulations. The primary purpose of MiFID is to fight financial crimes in financial markets, especially dealing with best execution (stockbrokers making sure they strive to get the best possible results for their clients). Tracking best execution requires storing significant amounts of data about trades. MiFID also requires that critical information is disclosed to investors, and that conflicts of interests be avoided. http://www.fsa.gov.uk/Pages/About/ What/International/EU/fsap/mifid/ index.shtml
New York State Insurance Regulation 173 (also known as 11 NYCRR 421), New York, US	Financial Industry	Customer, Account, Contract	This regulation defines a set of security standards in New York State to implement the security and privacy requirements of GLBA. http://www.ins.state.ny.us/r_finala/ 2002/pdf/r173ftxt.pdf

(continued)

Regulation	Industry	Master Data Domain	Notes
Office of Foreign Assets Control (OFAC) of the US Department of the Treasury— Specially Designated Nationals (SDN) List, US	Cross-Industry, Public Sector	Customer, Citizen, Account	The Office of Foreign Assets Control enforces economic and trade sanctions based on US foreign policy and national security goals against targeted foreign countries, terrorists, international narcotics traffickers, and those engaged in activities related to the proliferation of weapons of mass destruction. The SDN is related to aspects of KYC to verify that the customer is not on lists of known fraudsters, terrorists, or money launderers. OFAC publishes, updates, and maintains an integrated and comprehensive list of designated parties with whom US persons are prohibited from providing services or conducting transactions and whose assets are blocked. http://www.ustreas.gov/offices/enforcement/ofac/
Part 7 of the Proceeds of Crime Act 2002, United Kingdom	Financial Industry	Customer, Account, Product	Part 7 of this regulation defines crimes around money laundering and lists the disclosures required by financial entities when dealing with cash or security transfers http://www.opsi.gov.uk/acts/acts2002/ukpga_20020029_en_22#pt7
Payment Card Industry—Data Security Standard (PCI-DSS)	Any organization that handles credit card data	Party, Account	PCI-DSS is a standard for securing credit card information. Initially, the standard was created by Visa International and MasterCard. In September 2006, these two companies, along with American Express, Discover Financial Services, and JCB, formed the PCI Security Standards Council.

Regulation	Industry	Master Data Domain	Notes
			PCI-DSS has 12 rules around controlling the lifecycle of sensitive credit card information, specifically if a primary account number on a credit card is stored. These rules are: **Build and Maintain a Secure Network** **Requirement 1:** Install and maintain a firewall configuration to protect cardholder data. **Requirement 2:** Do not use vendor-supplied defaults for system passwords and other security parameters. **Protect Cardholder Data** **Requirement 3:** Protect stored cardholder data. **Requirement 4:** Encrypt transmission of cardholder data across open public networks. **Maintain a Vulnerability Management Program** **Requirement 5:** Use and regularly update antivirus software. **Requirement 6:** Develop and maintain secure systems and applications. **Implement Strong Access Control Measures** **Requirement 7:** Restrict access to cardholder data by business need-to-know. **Requirement 8:** Assign a unique ID to each person with computer access. **Requirement 9:** Restrict physical access to cardholder data

(continued)

Regulation	Industry	Master Data Domain	Notes
			Regularly Monitor and Test Networks **Requirement 10:** Track and monitor all access to network resources and cardholder data. **Requirement 11:** Regularly test security systems and processes. **Maintain an Information Security Policy** **Requirement 12:** Maintain a policy that addresses information security. https://www.pcisecuritystandards.org/pdfs/pci_dss_v1-1.pdf
Personal Information Protection Law (PIPL) of 2003, Japan			PIPL is very similar in nature to other data protection laws (such as the UK Data Protection Act and the EU Directive 95/46). PIPL regulates the collection and handling of personal information by businesses, mandating specific controls with respect to: • Using personal information only for clearly disclosed purposes (Article 15) • Acquiring personal information in a lawful fashion • Ensuring that information is accurate and up to date (Article 19) • Protecting the security of the personal information (Articles 21 through 22) • Restricting distribution of personal information to third parties (Article 23) • Enabling individuals' access to personal information collected by businesses (Article 24) http://www.freshfields.com/publications/pdfs/places/11704.pdf

Regulation	Industry	Master Data Domain	Notes
Personal Information Protection and Electronic Documents Act (PIPEDA) of 2000, Canada	Cross-Industry (Canadian businesses, including foreign companies with operations in Canada)	Customer, Citizen	PIPEDA governs the use, collection, and disclosure of personal information that is held by the entity or transferred to a third party. Like other privacy laws, it establishes a core set of principles and rules related to notification, transparency, accuracy, consent, and individual access to collected personal information. http://www.privcom.gc.ca/legislation/02_06_01_01_e.asp
Prescription Drug Marketing Act (PDMA) of 1988, US	Pharmaceutical Industry	Product, Location, Supplier	PDMA is designed to protect consumers from counterfeit, adulterated, mislabeled, subpotent, or expired medications. PDMA requires licensing of wholesale drug distributors, and requires that drug wholesalers that are not manufacturers or authorized distributors of a drug provide a pedigree for every prescription drug they distribute. http://www.fda.gov/opacom/laws/pdma.html
Sarbanes-Oxley Act (SOX or Public Company Accounting Reform and Investor Protection Act) of 2002, US	US Publicly Traded Companies	Product, Account, Contract, Customer, Vendor	Sarbanes-Oxley was passed in 2002 in response to a number of financial scandals (such as Enron and WorldCom) in the US. The goals of SOX are to improve internal compliance and controls, and to provide greater and more reliable transparency into publicly reported corporate financial information.

(*continued*)

Regulation	Industry	Master Data Domain	Notes
			Of the many components of SOX, the ones that have received the most attention in the IT community are: • Section 404, which states that management is responsible for establishing adequate internal controls and processes for financial reporting, and that an independent assessment must be produced yearly of those controls (along with Section 302, which requires company officers to certify the correctness of financial reports). The SEC guidance on Section 404 is derived from the COSO framework on internal controls. • Section 401, which requires companies to list off-balance sheet arrangements (such as leases, long-term purchase agreements, long-term debt obligations, and so on) that have a material effect on the financial health of the company. • Section 409, which requires real-time disclosure of material changes in the course of business that may significantly affect the health of the business. The SEC interpreted this section as adding eleven new events (such as new or terminated significant material agreements, off-balance sheet obligations, and so on) to the nine existing events that would trigger a disclosure. http://frwebgate.access.gpo.gov/cgi-bin/getdoc.cgi?dbname=107_cong_bills&docid=f:h3763enr.tst.pdf

Regulation	Industry	Master Data Domain	Notes
Solvency II, European Union	Insurance	Product, Account, Contract, Customer	Solvency II is often considered as the equivalent to Basel II for the insurance industry. Solvency II derives from the Financial Services Action Plan (FSAP) discussed in the EuroSox section. Like Basel II, Solvency II has three pillars representing risk assessment and capital reserves, proactive risk management, and accurate disclosure of relevant financial information. http://ec.europa.eu/internal_market/insurance/solvency/index_en.htm
The Do-Not-Call Implementation Act of 2003, US	Cross-Industry, Telecommunication Industry, Public Sector	Citizen, Customer	The Federal Trade Commission maintains a list of citizens who have requested to be removed from calling lists of telemarketers. Telemarketers are required by law to subscribe to the National Do Not Call list, and abide by citizen requests, including updating their lists every 31 days. There are exceptions in the cases of preestablished relationships or calls from political organizations, charities, or telephone survey researchers. http://www.ftc.gov/bcp/edu/microsites/donotcall/index.html
The Third European Money Laundering Directive (3 MLD), EU	Financial, Legal, Gaming	Customer	This directive was passed in 2005 in the wake of the September 11, 2001 terrorist attacks on the US, and is focused on discovering money-laundering before the money is used to finance a terrorist operation. It enhances the due diligence ("Know Your Customer") required of the affected industries and increases the number of affected industries. http://www.hm-treasury.gov.uk/media/D/5/200509RIA1.pdf

(continued)

Regulation	Industry	Master Data Domain	Notes
Uniting and Strengthening America by Providing Appropriate Tools Required to Intercept and Obstruct Terrorism (USA PATRIOT ACT) Act of 2001, US	Finance, Telecommunications, Others	Customer, Organization, Account	The PATRIOT Act is an omnibus piece of legislation aimed at enhancing the ability of the US government to detect and prevent terrorism. With respect to the financial industry, the Act enhances existing US regulations on businesses with regard to Anti-Money Laundering (AML), Know Your Customer (KYC), and Customer Due Diligence (CDD). Among other requirements, financial institutions must keep stricter records on transactions, must increase their efforts to identify the true (beneficial) owners of accounts, keep track of political figures associated with accounts where there is a strong possibility of corruption, and limit or deny certain types of activities if the account owner is a foreign bank or target of an investigation. Stronger requirements were also introduced for tracking and reporting suspected money laundering activities (including adding Money Service Bureaus to the list of businesses that have to perform AML activities). The PATRIOT Act also includes new types of wiretapping and other forms of requests for information on individuals. http://thomas.loc.gov/cgi-bin/bdquery/z?d107:h.r.03162:

References

1. Tarantino, A. 2006. *Manager's Guide To Compliance*. New York: John Wiley & Sons.
2. Shackleford, D. 2007. *Regulations and Standards: Where Encryption Applies*. White Paper, http://www.sans.org/reading_room/analysts_program/encryption_Nov07.pdf.

Standards
and Specifications

Note: Most of the comments in this appendix are taken from the websites provided in the table.

Standard	Acronym	Link	Comment
1SYNC	1SYNC	http://www.1sync.org/ or: http://www.gs1.org/	1SYNC, a subsidiary of GS1 US, is a Global Data Synchronization Network (GDSN)-certified Data Pool that offers a range of data synchronization services.
Advanced Encryption Standard	AES	http://www.csrc.nist.gov/publications/fips/fips197/fips-197.pdf	Block cipher encryption algorithm adopted as a standard by the National Institute of Standards and Technology (NIST) in 2002. 128,192 or 256-bit key length. Originally developed by two Belgian cryptographers under the name "Rijndael." To this date, this algorithm has not been cracked.
Application Level Events Standard	ALE	http://www.epcglobalinc.org/standards/ale/ale_1_0-standard-20050915.pdf	The ALE standard defines an interface through which clients can obtain events regarding Electronic Product Codes (EPC).

(continued)

Standard	Acronym	Link	Comment
Association for Cooperative Operations Research and Development	ACORD	http://www.acord.org	ACORD is a non-profit association whose mission is to facilitate the development and use of standards for the insurance, reinsurance, and related financial services industries.
Association for Retail Technology Standards	ARTS	http://www.nrf-arts.org/	ARTS is an international membership organization dedicated to reducing the costs of retail technology through standards.
Audit Trail and Node Authentication	ATNA	http://wiki.ihe.net/index.php?title=Audit_Trail_and_Node_Authentication	Describes certificate-based security for an individual system for use as part of the security and privacy environment for a healthcare enterprise.
Business Process Execution Language	BPEL	http://docs.oasis-open.org/wsbpel/2.0/wsbpcl-v2.0.pdf	WS-BPEL (or BPEL for short) provides a language for the spccification of Exccutablc and Abstract business processes. By doing so, it extends the Web Services interaction model and enables it to support business transactions. WS-BPEL defines an interoperable integration model that should facilitate the expansion of automated process integration in both the intra-corporate and the business-to-business spaces.
Data Encryption Standard	DES	http://csrc.nist.gov/publications/fips/fips46-3/fips46-3.pdf	Block cipher encryption algorithm adopted as a standard by the National Institute of Standards and Technology (NIST) in 1976. Based on IBM's Lucifer algorithm. 56-bit key length. Currently considered insecure for most applications.

Standard	Acronym	Link	Comment
Document Model ePedigree		http://www.epcglobalinc.org/standards/pedigree/	The Document Model ePedigree Standard is the level 0 pedigree implementation standard. It specifies an architecture for the maintenance and exchange of electronic pedigree documents for use by pharmaceutical supply chain participants. The architecture is targeted for use in complying with document-based pedigree laws.
Domain Name System (Also Domain Name Service or Server)	DNS	http://www.ietf.org/rfc/rfc1035.txt	A DNS associates human-readable domain names into IP addresses.
Drug Pedigree Messaging Standard	DPMS	http://www.epcglobalinc.org/standards/pedigree	DPMS specifies an architecture for the maintenance and exchange of electronic pedigree documents for use by pharmaceutical supply chain participants. The architecture is targeted for use in complying with document-based pedigree laws.
European Article Numbering—Uniform Code Council standards	EAN.UCC Standards	http://www.gs1.org/services/gsmp/kc/ or: http://www.gci-net.org	The group of EAN.UCC standards is maintained by the GS1 organization and supported by the Global Commerce Initiative (GCI).
Electronic Data Interchange	EDI	http://en.wikipedia.org/wiki/Electronic_Data_Interchange	EDI is a set of standard messaging formats for business documents to formalize electronic commerce between companies. It pre-dates the Internet but is still used very widely.

(continued)

Standard	Acronym	Link	Comment
Electronic Product Codes	EPC	http://www.gs1.org/productssolutions/epcglobal/ or: http://www.discover rfid.org/your-questions/faq-on-epc-and-rfid.html	The Electronic Product Code (EPC) is a set of identification coding or numbering standards sometimes referred to as the successor for the bar code. Unlike the bar code, the EPC can identify an individual item of a specific kind by its unique ID number.
EPC Radio Frequency Identification Protocol		http://www.epcglobal inc.org/standards/uhfc 1g2/uhfc1g2_1_1_0-standard-20071017.pdf	EPC Radio Frequency Identification Protocol is a UHF RFID Protocol for communication at 860 MHz–960 MHz. This specification defines the physical and logical requirements for passive-backscatter, Interrogator-Talk-First (ITF) RFID. The system is comprised of Readers and Tags.
EPCglobal standards	EPCGlobal	http://www.epcglobal inc.org/standards	EPCglobal defines relevant standards for RFID and Track & Trace solutions. One example is UHF Gen2 Standard for the data carrier layer.
eXtensible Access Control Markup Language	XACML	http://www.oasis-open.org/committees/download.php/2713/Brief_Introduction_to_XACML.html	XACML is an OASIS standard that describes both a policy language and an access control decision request/response language (both written in XML). The policy language is used to describe general access control requirements, and has standard extension points for defining new functions, data types, combining logic, etc. The request/response language lets you form a query to ask whether or not

Standard	Acronym	Link	Comment
			a given action should be allowed, and interpret the result. The response always includes an answer about whether the request should be allowed using one of four values: Permit, Deny, Indeterminate (an error occurred or some required value was missing, so a decision cannot be made), or Not Applicable (the request can't be answered by this service).
eXtensible Markup Language	XML	http://www.w3.org/XML/	XML is a simple, very flexible text format derived from SGML (ISO 8879). Originally designed to meet the challenges of large-scale electronic publishing, XML is also playing an increasingly important role in the exchange of a wide variety of data on the Web and elsewhere.
File Transfer Protocol	FTP	http://tools.ietf.org/html/rfc959	FTP is a network protocol to transfer data from one computer to another over a network.
Global Data Dictionary	GDD	http://gdd.gs1.org/GDD/public/default.asp	The development of new e-business standards by GS1 has created a critical need to store, reuse, and share precise core component and business definitions and their equivalent representations in targeted standards such as EDI, XML, and AIDC. The storage for this data is the GS1 Global Data Dictionary (GDD). This repository is developed to fully support the GS1 Business Message Standards and GS1 XML Standard Schemas.

(continued)

Standard	Acronym	Link	Comment
Global Data Synchronization	GDS	http://www.gs1.org/services/gsmp/kc/gdsn/	GDS helps keep trading partners in sync by ensuring product data, such as the category and description stored by one company, matches the data stored by their trading partners. Organizations submit their product data in a specified format to data pools around the globe for validation against a global registry, allowing changes to be flagged immediately to all connected retailers and manufacturers. Companies that subscribe to the GDS initiative and publish their product information to the data pools will need to make sure that the data is in the set format and is of the required quality to exchange with any third party.
Global Data Synchronization Network	GDSN	http://www.gs1.org/productssolutions/gdsn/	The GS1 GDSN is an automated standards-based global environment that enables secure and continuous data synchronization, allowing all partners to have consistent item data in their systems at the same time.
Global Location Number	GLN	http://www.gs1.org/glnrules/	GLN provides the global supply chain solution for the identification, using a 13 digit number, of physical locations and legal entities.
Global Product Classification	GPC	http://www.gs1.org/productssolutions/gdsn/gpc/	The Global Product Classification (GPC) is part of the GS1 System and a key enabler for the Global Data Synchronization Network (GDSN) and category management.

Standard	Acronym	Link	Comment
Global Trade Identification Number	GTIN	http://www.gs1.org/gtinrules/	GTIN provides the global supply chain solution for the identification of any item that is traded (priced, ordered, and invoiced). There is a standard for allocating GTIN numbers in order to achieve unique GTINs numbers for GDSN.
GS1	GS1	http://www.gs1.org/	GS1 is a leading global organization dedicated to the design and implementation of global standards and solutions to improve the efficiency and visibility of supply and demand chains globally and across sectors. The GS1 system of standards is the most widely used supply chain standards system in the world.
Health Level Seven	HL7	http://www.hl7.org/	HL7 is one of several ANSI-accredited Standards Developing Organizations (SDOs) operating in the healthcare arena. Most SDOs produce standards (sometimes called specifications or protocols) for a particular healthcare domain such as pharmacy, medical devices, imaging, or insurance (claims processing) transactions.
HyperText Transfer Protocol	HTTP	http://www.w3.org/Protocols/rfc2616/rfc2616.html	The Hypertext Transfer Protocol is an application-level protocol for distributed information systems. It is a generic stateless protocol. A feature of HTTP is the typing and negotiation of data representation, allowing systems to be built independently of the data being transferred. HTTP has existed since the 1990s and is broadly used in the Internet.
HyperText Transfer Protocol Secured over Secure Sockets Layer (SSL)	HTTPS	http://www.ietf.org/rfc/rfc2818.txt	HTTPS is a URI scheme used to indicate a secure HTTP connection. HTTPS is a Web protocol developed by Netscape using SSL as a sublayer to HTTP.

(*continued*)

Standard	Acronym	Link	Comment
IEEE Std 1471-2000	IEEE	http://standards.ieee.org/reading/ieee/std_public/description/se/1471-2000_desc.html	IEEE Recommended Practice for Architectural Description of Software-Intensive Systems—Description.
Integrating the Healthcare Enterprise	IHE	http://www.ihe.net/	IHE is an initiative by healthcare professionals and industry to improve the way computer systems in healthcare share information.
Interactive Financial eXchange	IFX	http://www.ifxforum.org/	The IFX Forum was formed in 1997 to create a messaging standard for financial services that would address the challenges faced with the advent of network-based computing models.
ISO 3166	ISO	http://www.iso.org/iso/country_codes/background_on_iso_3166/what_is_iso_3166.htm	This ISO standard defines the country code representation for countries or regions and their abbreviations as they are established by the United Nations. This means that the standard does not define the names of countries itself, just their representation for processing by computing systems.
Java 2 Platform, Enterprise Edition	J2EE	http://java.sun.com/j2ee/overview.html	The Java 2 Platform, Enterprise Edition (J2EE) defines the standard for developing multi-tier enterprise applications using the Java programming language developed by Sun Microsystems.
Java Message Service	JMS	http://java.sun.com/products/jms/	The Java Message Service (JMS) API is a messaging standard that allows application components based on the Java 2 Platform, Enterprise Edition (J2EE) to create, send, receive, and read messages. It enables distributed

Standard	Acronym	Link	Comment
			communication that is loosely coupled, reliable, and asynchronous.
JSR 168 Portlet specification and JSR 286 Portlet Container specification	JSR	http://jcp.org/about Java/communi typrocess/final/jsr168/ and http://jcp.org/about Java/communi typrocess/edr/jsr286/	JSR 168 is a standard defining how to write portlets for the Java 2 Enterprise Edition (J2EE) Platform. JSR 286 is a standard defining the portlet container runtime for the Java 2 Enterprise Edition (J2EE) Platform.
Kerberos— The Kerberos Network Authentication Service		http://gost.isi.edu/ publications/ kerberos-neuman-tso.html	Kerberos is a distributed authentication service that allows a process (a client) running on behalf of a principal (a user) to prove its identity to a verifier (an application server, or just a server) without sending data across the network that might allow an attacker or the verifier to subsequently impersonate the principal.
Logical Observation Identifiers, Names and Codes	LOINC	http://www. regenstrief.org/ medinformatics/loinc/	LOINC is a database and universal standard for the exchange and pooling of results, such as blood hemoglobin, serum potassium, or vital signs, for clinical care, outcomes management, and research. It was developed and is maintained by the Regenstrief Institute.
Minimal Lower Level Protocol	MLLP	http://en.wiktionary. org/wiki/MLLP	MLLP is a minimalistic OSI-session layer framing protocol that provides an interface between HL7 and the network based on socket communication.
Object Naming Service	ONS	http://www.epcglob alinc.org/standards/ ons/ons_1_0-standard-20051004.pdf	This standard specifies how the Domain Name System is used to locate authoritative metadata and services associated with the serialized GTIN portion of a given Electronic Product Code (EPC).

(continued)

Standard	Acronym	Link	Comment
Open Healthcare Framework	OHF	http://www.eclipse.org/ohf/	The Eclipse Open Healthcare Framework (OHF) is a project within Eclipse formed for the purpose of expediting healthcare informatics technology. The project is composed of extensible frameworks and tools that emphasize the use of existing and emerging standards in order to encourage interoperable open source infrastructure, thereby lowering integration barriers.
Open Standards		http://www.open standards.net/view OSnet2C.jsp?show ModuleName= Organizations	Industry-accepted open computing standards define interoperability specifications that promote the transfer of information between different computing environments and improve accessibility.
Protected Health Information	PHI	http://www.hhs.gov/ocr/hipaa/FinalEnfo rcementRule06.pdf	PHI under HIPAA includes any individually identifiable health information. Identifiable refers not only to data that is explicitly linked to a particular individual (that is, identified information). It also includes health information with data items that reasonably could be expected to allow individual identification.
Radio Frequency Identification	RFID	http://www.rfid.org	A method of identifying unique items using radio waves. Typically, a reader communicates with a tag, which holds digital information in a microchip. But there are chip-less forms of RFID tags that use material to reflect back a portion of the radio waves beamed at them.

Standard	Acronym	Link	Comment
Really Simple Syndication	RSS	http://developer. mozilla.org/en/docs/ RSS:Getting_Started: What_is_RSS	The most popular versions of RSS are XML-based markup languages used for syndication. Common uses of RSS syndication are for the syndication of news websites, of blogs, of Internet Radio, and of Internet Television. RSS makes it possible for people to keep up with websites in an automated manner that is easier than checking them manually.
Representational State Transfer	REST	http://www.ics.uci. edu/~fielding/pubs/ dissertation/top.htm	REST is a style of software architecture for distributed hypermedia systems such as the World Wide Web. The term is often used to describe any simple interface that transmits domain-specific data over HTTP without an additional messaging layer such as SOAP or session tracking via HTTP cookies.
Secure Socket Layer	SSL	http://tools.ietf.org/ html/rfc2246	Transport Layer Security (TLS) protocol and its predecessor SSL are cryptographic protocols to provide communications privacy over the Internet. The protocol allows applications such as Web browsing, e-mail, and FTP to communicate in a way that is designed to prevent eavesdropping, tampering, or message forgery. There are slight differences between SSL and TLS, but the protocol remains substantially the same.
Security Assertion Markup Language	SAML	http://www.oasis-open.org/committees/ tc_home.php?wg_ abbrev=security	SAML, developed by the Security Services Technical Committee of OASIS, is an XML-based framework for communicating user authentication, entitlement, and attribute information. SAML allows business entities to make

(continued)

Standard	Acronym	Link	Comment
			assertions regarding the identity, attributes, and entitlements of a subject (an entity that is often a human user) to other entities, such as a partner company or another enterprise application.
Shared Information/ Data Model	SID	http://www. ifxforum.org/	Provides an information/data reference model and a common information/data vocabulary from a business as well as a systems perspective for the telecommunications industry as part of the NGOSS (the Generation Operation System and Software).
Simple Object Access Protocol	SOAP	http://www.w3.org/ TR/SOAP	SOAP is a lightweight protocol for exchange of information in a decentralized, distributed environment. It is an XML-based protocol that consists of three parts: an envelope that defines a framework for describing what is in a message and how to process it, a set of encoding rules for expressing instances of application-defined data types, and a convention for representing remote procedure calls and responses.
Society for Worldwide Interbank Financial Telecommunication	SWIFT	http://www.swift.com/	SWIFT enables its customers to automate and standardize financial transactions, thereby lowering their costs, reducing their operational risk, and eliminating inefficiencies from their business operations.
Systematized Nomenclature of Medicine	SNOMED	http://www. ihtsdo.org/our_ standards	SNOMED is a clinical terminology, the Systematized Nomenclature of Medicine. It is a common computerized language to facilitate communications between healthcare professionals in clear and unambiguous terms.

Standard	Acronym	Link	Comment
Two-phase commit protocol	2PC	http://ei.cs.vt.edu/ ~cs5204/sp99/distri butedDBMS/duckett/ tpcp.html	The two-phase commit protocol is a distributed algorithm that lets all sites in a distributed system agree to commit a transaction. The protocol results in either all nodes committing the transaction or aborting, even in the case of site failures and message losses.
United Nations Standard Products and Services Code	UNSPSC	http://www. unspsc.org/	This open standard defines a cross-industry classification of products and services for use throughout the global e-Commerce marketplace efficiently and accurately.
Web Service Description Language	WSDL	http://www.w3.org/ TR/wsdl	WSDL is an XML-based language for describing Web services.
Web Services Addressing	WS-Addressing	http://www.w3.org/ 2002/ws/addr/	WS-Addressing provides transport-neutral mechanisms to address Web services and messages. WS-Addressing defines a set of abstract properties and an XML representation thereof to reference Web services and to facilitate end-to-end addressing of endpoints in messages. This specification enables messaging systems to support message transmission through networks that include processing nodes such as endpoint managers, firewalls, and gateways in a transport-neutral manner.
Web Services Choreography Definition Language	WS-CDL	http://www.w3.org/ TR/ws-cdl-10/	WS-CDL is an XML-based language that describes peer-to-peer collaborations of Web Services participants.

(continued)

Standard	Acronym	Link	Comment
Web Services for Remote Portals	WSRP	http://www.oasis-open.org/committees/tc_home.php?wg_abbrev=wsrp	WSRP defines a set of interfaces and related semantics that standardize interactions with portlet components providing user-facing markup, including the processing of user interactions with that markup. This allows applications to consume such components as providing a portion of the overall user application without having to write unique code for interacting with each component.
Web Services Policy	WS-Policy	http://www.w3.org/TR/ws-policy-primer/	WS-Policy is a machine-readable language for representing the capabilities and requirements of a Web service. These are called "policies." Web Services Policy offers mechanisms to represent consistent combinations of capabilities and requirements, to determine the compatibility of policies, to name and reference policies, and to associate policies with Web service metadata constructs such as service, endpoint, and operation.
Web Services Security Policy Language	WS-Security Policy	http://specs.xmlsoap.org/ws/2005/07/securitypolicy/ws-securitypolicy.pdf	WS-SecurityPolicy is a Web Services specification that deals with defining "policy assertions" that are utilized by the WS-Security, WS-Trust, and WS-SecureConversation specifications.
Web Services Security SOAP Message Security	WS-Security	http://www.oasis-open.org/committees/download.php/6367/oasis-200401-wss-soap-message-security-1.0.pdf	The WS-Security SOAP Message Security specification describes enhancements to SOAP messaging to provide message integrity and confidentiality. The specified mechanisms can be used to

Standard	Acronym	Link	Comment
			accommodate a wide variety of security models and encryption technologies. This specification also provides a general-purpose mechanism for associating security tokens with message content.
Web Services Trust	WS-Trust	http://docs.oasis-open.org/ws-sx/ws-trust/200512/ws-trust-1.3-os.html	WS-Trust is an OASIS standard that provides extensions to WS-Security. It provides methods for issuing, renewing, and validating security tokens, as well as ways to establish, assess the presence of, and broker trust relationships between participants in a secure message exchange.
WS-Management	WS-Management	http://www.dmtf.org/standards/wbem/wsman	WS-Management from the Distributed Management Task Force (DMTF) addresses the cost and complexity of IT management by providing a common way for systems to access and exchange management information across the entire IT infrastructure.
XA compliance	XA	https://www.opengroup.org/online-pubs?DOC=969890 9699&FORM=PDF	XA Compliance indicates that a transactional system adheres to the X/Open XA standard for distributed transaction processing as defined by the Open Group. The XA standard describes an interface between the global transaction manager and the local resource manager. (See also two-phase commit).
XML Schema Definition	XSD	http://www.w3.org/XML/Schema	XSD specifies how to formally describe the elements in an XML document. This description can be used to verify that each item of content in a document adheres to the description of the element in which the content is to be placed.

Appendix E

Glossary & Terms

1SYNC: See Appendix D.

2PC (Two-phase commit protocol): The two-phase commit protocol is a distributed algorithm that lets all sites in a distributed system agree to commit a transaction. The protocol results in either all nodes committing the transaction or aborting, even in the case of site failures and message losses.

3 MLD (The Third European Money Laundering Directive): See Appendix C.

ABAP (Advanced Business Application Programming): A high-level programming language created by the German software company SAP.

Absolute Consistency of Data: In a distributed system with multiple replicas of information, absolute consistency means that information will be identical among all replicas at all times that the systems are available. In a distributed environment, we typically achieve absolute consistency by following a two-phase commit transaction protocol that is provided in most distributed databases, messaging systems, and transaction systems.

ACORD (Association for Cooperative Operations Research and Development): See Appendix D.

ADT (Admission Demographic Transaction): A portion of the HL7 (healthcare) communications standard (see Appendix D for more information).

AES (Advanced Encryption Standard): See Appendix D.

ALE (Application Level Event): See Appendix D.

AML (Anti-Money Laundering): See Appendix C.

Analytical MDM: Analytical MDM is about the intersection between Business Intelligence (BI) and master data management. BI is a broad field that includes business reporting, data warehouses, data marts, data mining, scoring, and many other fields.

API: Application Programming Interface.

Application Patterns: Patterns provide a proven solution to a repeating problem in a given context. With application patterns, we are applying these concepts to the domain of applications and application building blocks. An application pattern characterizes the coarse-grained structure of the application—the main application components, the allocation of processing functions and the interactions between them, the degree of integration between them, and the placement of the data relative to the applications.

Architectural Framework: According to The Open Group (TOG), an architecture framework is a "set of methods and tools for developing a broad range of different IT architectures. It enables IT users to design, evaluate, and build the right architecture for their organization, and reduces the costs of planning, designing, and implementing architectures based on open systems solutions."

Architecture: According to ANSI/IEEE Std 1471-2000, architecture is defined as "the fundamental organization of a system, embodied in its components, their relationships to each other and the environment, and the principles governing its design and evolution." While this ANSI/IEEE definition concentrates on design and evolution, the authors believe there are other aspects and characteristics that need to be considered by IT software architectures as well, such as guidelines and principles for implementation, operations, administration, and maintenance.

Architecture Blueprint: Is based on a composition and customization of relevant architectural patterns (meaning to use only a subset from the available architecture pattern portfolio in an appropriate way). Architecture blueprints can be cross-industry or very industry-specific. This composition and customization exercise will yield an architecture blueprint that serves as the architectural underpinning for a solution blueprint. In essence, an architecture blueprint captures the key architectural characteristics from a solution.

Architecture Patterns: Patterns provide a proven solution to a repeating problem in a given context. With architecture patterns, we are applying these concepts to the domain of architecture and architectural building blocks. Considering solution architecture, we start to notice that in a given context for a specific problem, the same architectural building blocks—representing architecture patterns—are used.

Architecture Principles: Architecture principles, policies, and guidelines define the underlying general rules and guidance that an organization will use to deploy business and IT resources and assets across the enterprise.

ARTS (Association for Retail Technology Standards): See Appendix D.

AS2 (Applicability Statement 2): A specification describing how to transport data securely and reliably over the Internet. Security is achieved by using digital certificates and encryption.

ATF (Anti-Terrorist Financing): The abbreviation ATF for Anti-Terrorist Financing is frequently used in the context of Anti-Money Laundering (AML).

ATM: Automatic Teller Machine.

ATNA (Audit Trail and Node Authentication): See Appendix D.

Audit Services: Include maintaining detailed, secure logs of critical activities in a business environment. Such critical activities could be related to security, content management, business transactions, and so on.

Authentication: Provides capabilities to authenticate users. These services may support multiple authentication mechanisms, such as user name/password, hardware token-based, biometric-based, and others.

Authoritative Source: Refers to a trusted source of master data (or information in general). An authoritative source may be an acknowledged system of record or a system of reference.

Authorization: Authorization follows authentication: After a user or system has been authenticated, it is then possible to perform authorization. Authorization means making a decision about whether an authenticated identity is allowed to access a resource.

B2B: Business-to-Business.

B2C: Business-to-Consumer.

BADI (Business Add-In): An interface that was specified by SAP to allow other software vendors to provide modules for address standardization and address de-duplication.

BAPI (Business Application Programming Interfaces): A set of interfaces to object-oriented programming methods that enable a programmer to integrate third-party software into the proprietary R/3 product from SAP.

Basel II: See Appendix C.

BDSG (Bundesdatenschutz-Gesetz or Germany's Federal Data Protection Act): See Appendix C.

Best Practices: A technique or methodology that, through past experience and research, has proven to reliably lead to a desired result. A commitment to using the best practices in any field (for example, in the domain of IT Architecture) ensures leveraging past experience and all of the knowledge and technology at one's disposal to ensure success.

BI (Business Intelligence): At a very high level, a process for increasing the competitive advantage of a business by intelligent use of available data in decision making. BI is a broad field that includes business reporting, data warehouses, data marts, data mining, scoring, and many other fields.

BPEL (Business Process Execution Language): See Appendix D.

BSA (Bank Secrecy Act): See Appendix C.

BSC (Business Service Choreography): In general terms, business service choreography is about the development and execution of business process flow logic, which is abstracted from applications.

Business Patterns: Patterns provide a proven solution to a repeating problem in a given context. With business patterns, we are applying these concepts to the domain of business and business building blocks. Business patterns identify the primary business actors and describe the interactions between them in terms of different archetypal business interactions such as service, collaboration, information aggregation, and so forth.

Business Security Services: These are the security aspects of the business that need to be defined for successful and secure operation of an enterprise. These are based on a number of influencing factors specific to the industry, such as governing laws, competition, and so on.

Business Service Management: Helps you understand how the performance and availability of IT resources affect the applications, processes, and services that power your business. Business service management helps you prioritize your IT systems around processes that carry the highest business values.

BW (Business Warehouse): Mostly used in the context of a SAP BW.

CAGE (Commercial And Government Entity): The CAGE Code is a unique identifier assigned to suppliers (to various government or defense agencies) as well as to government agencies themselves and also various other organizations. CAGE codes provide a standardized method of identifying a given facility at a specific location.

California's ePedigree Law: See Appendix C.

California Security Breach Information Act (SB 1386): See Appendix C.

California Senate Bill 1386: See Appendix C.

CDD (Customer Due Diligence): See Appendix C.

CDI (Customer Data Integration): MDM Systems that focus exclusively on managing information about customers are often called CDI systems.

CERT: Computer Emergency Response Team.

CICS (Customer Information Control System): CICS from IBM is a family of application servers and connectors that provides industrial-strength, online transaction management and connectivity for mission-critical applications.

CMDB (Configuration Management Database): A CMDB is a repository of information describing the configuration of an information system.

COBIT (Control OBjectives for Information and related Technology): COBIT is a set of standards from the IT Governance Institute relating to IT Governance. It defines a set of governance control objectives to help guide the IT organization in making appropriate decisions for each domain.

Coexistence Hub Pattern: The Coexistence Hub pattern belongs to the MDM Hub patterns, and corresponds to the coexistence implementation style.

Coexistence Implementation Style: An MDM implementation in which the MDM system is synchronized with the existing sources of master data and may contain additional information not managed by existing systems.

Collaborative Authoring: An MDM pattern in which the MDM System coordinates a group of users and systems to reach agreement on a set of master data. Collaborative authoring of master data includes the creation, definition, augmentation, and approval of master data.

Collaborative MDM: Deals with the processes supporting collaborative authoring of master data including the creation, definition, augmentation, and approval of master data.

Componentization: Componentization has to do with the isolation of functions and concerns. The individual components will consist of a set of functions that have a certain affinity to each other. This is very much related to composability.

Composability: Composability is a system design principle that deals with assembling multiple self-contained components into new combinations. A system is highly composable if components can be selected and assembled in various combinations that yield new valid systems to satisfy specific user requirements.

Composite Application Management: Provides support for securing the SOA environment, flow content analysis, end-user response time monitoring for service requests, service problem diagnosis, and application trace information that you can then pass back to your development environment.

Composite Patterns: Previously identified combinations and selections of business, architecture, integration, or other patterns for previously identified situations such as electronic commerce solutions, (public) enterprise portals or enterprise intranet portals, or MDM Solutions.

Consistency: Describes whether or not master data is defined and used across all IT systems in a consistent manner. For example, do all systems have the same Customer address?

Continuous Availability: The combination of high availability and continuous operations, thus addressing all categories of outages.

Continuous Operations: Addresses the need to allow for scheduled maintenance tasks to be performed without any disruption to the overall IT systems operation.

Convergent Consistency of Data: In a distributed system with multiple replicas of information, convergent consistency means that all systems will converge to the same set of values when new changes stop. A variety of techniques exist to capture and propagate changes to achieve convergent consistency.

COTS (Custom-off-the-Shelf): A term used to describe vendor software products that can be configured and enhanced to provide application software functionality to support the automation of business requirements.

CPOE: Computer-based Provider Order Entry.

CRUD (Create, Read, Update, and Delete): Often used to describe common operations on a persistent information repository.

CRM: Customer Relationship Management.

CTF: Counter Terrorist Financing.

CTO: Chief Technology Officer.

Data Architecture: Data architecture is one of the pillars of enterprise architecture and correlates with its peer pillars of business architecture, application architecture, and integration architecture. Data Architecture is the design of data for use in defining the target state and the subsequent planning needed to hit the target state. Data architecture includes topics such as database design, information integration, metadata management, business semantics, data modeling, metadata workflow management, and archiving.

Data Currency: Data currency is a measure for the maximum elapsed time between the point in time when data is presented to an application or an end user and the point in time when this data has been changed. (For example, in traditional DW environments, where nightly batch uploads are processed, data currency requirements are rather low.)

Data Governance: The orchestration of people, processes, and tools to leverage data as an enterprise asset.

Data Lineage: This is also called data provenance. It deals with the origin of data; it is all about documenting where data is, how it has been derived, and how it flows so you can manage and secure it appropriately as it is further processed by applications.

Data Mart: A data mart is a specialized database containing a subset of data from a data warehouse that is needed for a particular business purpose. A data mart is used for reporting and analysis of business data.

Data Matching: Data-matching involves bringing together data from disparate services or sources, comparing it, and eliminating duplicate data. There are two types of algorithms that are used in data matching: (1) deterministic algorithms, which strictly use match criteria and weighting to determine the results, and (2) probabilistic algorithms, which use statistical models to adjust the matching based on the frequency of values found in the data.

Data Protection: Deals with issues such as data security, privacy, and availability. Data protection controls are required by regulations and industry mandates such as Sarbanes-Oxley, European Data Protection Law, and others.

Data Protection Act of 1984, United Kingdom: See Appendix C.

Data Provenance: See "data lineage."

Data Quality: Deals with data validation and cleansing services (to ensure relevance, validity, accuracy, and consistency of the master data), reconciliation services (aimed at helping cleanse the master data of duplicates as part of consistency), and cross-reference services (to help with matching master data across multiple systems).

Data Reconciliation: Fine-grained validation and matching of data elements.

Data Replication: A set of techniques and technologies to make and then maintain a copy of data from a source database. Different approaches support different synchronization and performance requirements.

Data Standardization: Normalizes data values to meet format and semantic definitions. For example, data standardization of address information may ensure that an address includes all of the required pieces of information and normalize abbreviations (for example Ave. for Avenue).

Data Stewardship: Deals with the ownership and accountability of data, and how people manage the data to the benefit of the organization. Data stewardship functions at two levels— Business Data Stewards deal with the higher-level metadata and governance concerns, while Operational Data Stewards focus primarily on the instances of master data in the enterprise.

Data Survivorship: After matching is done, the list of potential matches (also called suspects) need to be further processed to create a single 'consolidated' record for retaining the best information. This process is called data survivorship.

Data Validation: The process of ensuring that the values of data conform to specified formats and/or values.

DBMS: Database Management Systems.

Definition Master Data: Definition Master Data describes the attributes, relationships, and hierarchies that are relevant to one or more master data domains.

Degrees of Separation: Degrees of separation refers to the links that can be established between entities in a network, such as people. For example, if person A can be linked to person B, and person B can be linked to person C, then a relationship can be established between person A and person C. This would be referred to as two degrees of separation.

DES (Data Encryption Standard): See Appendix D.

DGMM: IBM Data Governance Council's Data Governance Maturity Model.

Disaster Recovery: A process that is required after a major business disruption caused by the occurrence of a disaster. Typical examples would be flooding, fire, or earthquake.

Disclosure Control: In the context of information and business information privacy (including master data), the disclosure control capability helps reduce privacy compliance costs by automating manual procedures.

DMZ (Demilitarized Zone): The Demilitarized Zone represents the security layer in an architecture that traditionally restricts access from anything outside the control of an organization to the restricted zone, where access is restricted and controlled. The restricted zone is where only authorized users and applications gain access and there is no direct communication with external sources.

DNS (Domain Name System): See Appendix D.

Document Model ePedigree: See Appendix D.

DoDAAC: Department of Defense Activity Address Code.

DPMS (Drug Pedigree Messaging Standard): See Appendix D.

DSL (Digital Subscriber Line): DSL is a technology for bringing high-bandwidth information to homes and small businesses over ordinary copper telephone lines.

DW (Data Warehouse): Also abbreviated as DWH.

e-Business: e-Business is derived from such terms as "e-mail" and "e-commerce." It is the conduct of business on the Internet: buying, selling, and also servicing customers and collaborating with business partners. IBM was one of the first to use the term, in October 1997, when it launched a thematic campaign built around the term.

e-CTFSL (electronic-Consolidated Targeted Financial Sanctions List): The e-CTFSL list enables banks and other EU businesses to integrate the content of the database (of persons, groups, and entities subject to EU financial sanctions) into their IT systems, thereby rendering the freezing of bank accounts and other funds and assets more effective and permitting faster processing of information published in the *Official Journal of the European Union.*

eTOM (enhanced Telecom Operations Map): eTOM is the most widely used and accepted standard for business process in the telecom industry.

EAI: Enterprise Application Integration.

EAN (International Article Number, former European Article Number): EAN is the European bar code format similar to UPC (Universal Product Code).

EAN.UCC (International Article Numbering.Uniform Code Council): See Appendix D.

EDI (Electronic Data Interchange): See Appendix D.

EDW: Enterprise Data Warehouse.

EHIC: European Health Insurance Card.

EII (Enterprise Information Integration): Enterprise Information Integration provides the ability to access, combine, and deliver data from disparate data sources. EII Services enable applications to access and integrate diverse data and content sources as if they were a single resource.

Enterprise System Deployment Pattern: Enterprise system deployment patterns are composite architecture patterns that collectively focus on the deployment of an MDM System and in particular the integration of the MDM System with various application systems such as data warehouse (DWH), CRM, or ERP systems.

EPC (Electronic Product Codes): See Appendix D.

EPCGlobal (EPCglobal standards): See Appendix D.

EPCIS: Electronic Product Codes Information Service.

ERP: Enterprise Resource Planning.

ESB: Enterprise Service Bus.

ETL (Extract, Transform, Load): ETL services support the initial and incremental extract, transform, and load of data from one or more source systems to meet the needs of one or more targets, such as a Data Warehouse and MDM System.

EU: European Union.

European Health Insurance Card: See Appendix C.

European Union (EU) Directive 95/46/EC on the Protection of Personal Data: See Appendix C.

EuroSox (EU): See Appendix C.

FACT (Fair and Accurate Credit Transactions) Act: See Appendix C.

Fault Tolerance: Fault Tolerance is the ability of an IT system to continue to function as designed even though a fault has occurred.

FDA (Food and Drug Administration): See Appendix C.

Federated Query: Queries accessing data on heterogeneous remote relational or non-relational data sources, possibly combining them with tables stored in the federated DBMS server (federation server). Their execution is typically divided between the federation server and the remote data sources.

Federation: Enables applications to access and integrate diverse data and content sources as if they were a single resource (regardless of where the information resides) while retaining the autonomy and integrity of the heterogeneous data and content sources.

Financial Instruments and Exchange Law of 2006: See Appendix C.

Florida's Drug and Cosmetic Act: See Appendix C.

FSA: Financial Service Authority.

FTC: US Federal Trade Commission.

FTDS: Fraud and Theft Detection Services.

FTP: (File Transfer Protocol): See Appendix D.

GCI: Global Commerce Initiative.

GDD (Global Data Dictionary): See Appendix D.

GDS (Global Data Synchronization): See Appendix D.

GDSN (Global Data Synchronization Network): See Appendix D.

GLBA (Gramm-Leach-Bliley Act): See Appendix C.

GLN (Global Location Number): See Appendix D.

Global Transaction: Global transactions are distributed transactions where a unit of work is coordinated across multiple resource managers (such as a database) to either completely succeed (commit) or be rolled back.

Governance: The way we make and act on decisions about managing a shared resource for the common good. Resources can be people, processes, and technology.

GPC (Global Product Classification): See Appendix D.

GS1 Global Registry: See Appendix D.

GSMP: Global Standard Management Process.

GTIN (Global Trade Item Number): See Appendix D.

HADR (High Availability and Disaster Recovery): See the individual terms "high availability" and "disaster recovery."

Hash Algorithm: A hashing algorithm takes a variable length of for instance a data message and creates a fixed-size message digest (the output of a hashing algorithm). When a one-way hashing algorithm is used to generate the message digest, the input cannot be determined from the output.

High Availability: A measure of an IT system of its readiness for production use. Highly available systems continue to operate even after a failure occurs.

HIPAA (Health Insurance Portability and Accountability) Act: See Appendix C.

HL7 (Health Level 7): See Appendix D.

HSISA (Homeland Security Information Sharing Act): See Appendix C.

HTML: Hypertext Markup Language.

HTTP (Hypertext Transfer Protocol): See Appendix D.

HTTP/S (Hypertext Transfer Protocol Secured over Secure Sockets Layer (SSL)): See Appendix D.

IAA: IBM Insurance Application Architecture.

IaaS (Information as a Service): A key concept of IBM's comprehensive vision on Information On Demand. It is an entry point to service-oriented architecture (SOA) that offers information access to complex, heterogeneous data sources within your company as reusable services. These services may be available both within the enterprise and across your value chain.

IAS (International Accounting Standards): See Appendix C.

IBM Data Governance Council: Founded in 2004 and is composed of a cross section of business and IT data experts from data-rich enterprises, vendors, and IBM.

IBM Patterns for e-business: A group of reusable assets that can help speed the process of developing Web-based applications. The Patterns leverage the experience of IBM architects to create solutions quickly, whether for a small local business or a large multinational enterprise.

IDE: Integrated Development Environment.

Identity Analytics: A component that resides within the Analysis and Discovery Services architecture building block. Identity Analytics provide identity resolution capability for the unique identification of a person and the capability to discover obvious and non-obvious relationships between people and organizations.

IDOC (Intermediate Document): A standard data structure for electronic data interchange (EDI) between application programs written for the SAP business system or between an SAP application and an external program.

IEEE (IEEE Std 1471-2000): See Appendix D.

IFRS (International Financial Reporting Standard): See Appendix C.

IFW: IBM Information FrameWork.

IFX (Interactive Financial eXchange): See Appendix D.

IHE (Integrating the Healthcare Enterprise): See Appendix D.

Information Aggregation: Brings data from multiple sources together and presents the result across multiple channels. This is very much related to information integration techniques.

Information Focused Application Integration Pattern: This is one out of four types of architecture patterns for MDM. They are concerned about topics such as the initial load of the MDM hub and information synchronization patterns. This includes profiling, ETL, federation, caching, and information synchronization. These patterns apply to the build as well as the operational phase of the entire life cycle of the MDM hub.

Information Integration Services: In the context of MDM, information integration services encompass important services that are used to build the MDM hub and to operate the MDM System. For example, to build the MDM hub requires services to extract relevant data from legacy systems, to cleanse and transform the data, and to load the data into the MDM hub. Operating the MDM System requires ongoing information integration services such as information synchronization services.

Information Risk Management: A major component of an overall information security program that focuses on mitigating the risks to your information assets. It is the set of ongoing processes that identify and analyze the risks to your information assets, assess the costs and benefits of different approaches to mitigate the risks, and then implement (and monitor) the controls that mitigate the risks.

Information Services: Through information services, information can be reused easily across processes and maintained independently to make the business more flexible. The information services are maintained by the people who know and understand the information best, allowing the process developers to focus their efforts, knowing they have the best available information. Examples of information services are data validation services, data cleansing services, data transformation services, partner data integration services, operational data services, analytical data services, unstructured data (content) services, and master data services.

Information Synchronization Patterns: These patterns address the need to synchronize master data from the MDM hub "down" to the legacy systems and vice versa, "up" to the MDM hub. This is especially vital for MDM Solutions, where either the Coexistence Hub pattern or the Transaction Hub pattern is deployed. The Information Synchronization patterns have a strong relationship with the information integration patterns (for example, data replication and data federation).

Instance Master Data: Instance Master Data is the actual master data attribute values for the core business entities, such as information about a Supplier, Location, Person, Organization, and Agreement. Instance Master Data would contain the actual master data values, relationships, and hierarchies.

ISO (ISO 3166): See Appendix D.

IT: Information Technology.

IT Governance: The discipline of managing IT as a service to the business, aligning IT objectives with business goals.

Initial Load Pattern: This pattern includes important topics such as profiling, ETL, federation, and caching. The purpose of the pattern is to address initial loading of the MDM hub with master data that is derived from a disparate system and data environment.

Integration Patterns: Patterns provide a proven solution to a repeating problem in a given context. With integration patterns, we are applying these concepts to the domain of integration. Integration patterns provide the "glue" to combine business patterns to form solutions. They characterize the business problem, business processes/rules, and existing environment to determine whether front-end or back-end integration is required.

Integrity Services: Integrity is the security service for detecting unauthorized modification of data due to errors or malicious attack. Integrity Services commonly rely on cryptographic techniques such as message integrity codes, message authentication codes, and digital signatures.

Intrusion Protection: An intrusion detection service may be deployed on the Application Server to protect the server from malware and intrusion. Intrusion detection (host and network) is concerned with detecting anomalies in the use of the operating systems or the network. This might be used, for example, to detect external or internal intrusions to these systems.

ISO: International Organization for Standardization.

ISV: Independent Software Vendor.

IT Security Services: The building blocks to provide security functions as services. IT Security Services thus address how to accomplish the definitions put forward by the Business Security Services.

IVR: Interactive Voice Response.

J2EE (Java 2 Platform, Enterprise Edition): See Appendix D.

JMS (Java Message Service): See Appendix D.

J-SOX, Japan: See Appendix C.

JSR (JSR 168 Portlet specification and JSR 286 Portlet Container specification): See Appendix D.

Kerberos (The Kerberos Network Authentication Service): See Appendix D.

Key Management: This includes the generation, exchange, storage, safeguarding, and replacement of cryptographic keys.

KPI: Key Performance Indicators.

KYC (Know Your Customer): Refers to the due diligence that financial institutions and other regulated companies must perform to identify their clients. Typically, KYC is a policy implemented to conform to a customer identification program mandated under well-known regulations such as the Bank Secrecy Act and the USA Patriot Act.

Latency of Information: Latency is a time delay between the moment something is initiated and the moment one of its effects begins or becomes detectable. Latency of information applies this concept to changes, updates, and deletes of information.

LDAP: Lightweight Directory Access Protocol.

Lineage: See "data lineage."

LOB: Line of Business.

LOINC (Logical Observation Identifiers, Names, and Codes): See Appendix D.

M&A: Mergers and Acquisitions.

Malware Protection: Malware is software designed to damage or infiltrate a computer system. Examples are worms, trojan horses, spyware, viruses, and adware. Malware protection is used in a network to protect against these threats.

Master Data: Master data is the core information for an enterprise, such as information about customers or products, accounts or locations, and the relationships between them. In many companies, this master data is unmanaged and can be found in many, overlapping systems and is often of unknown quality.

Master Data Domains: The different categories of master data, such as the customers, suppliers, products, and accounts. Each of these domains of master data represents information that is needed across different business processes, across organizational units, and between operational systems and decision support systems.

Master Data Governance: In general, governance is the way we make and act on decisions about managing a shared resource for the common good. How data is managed for the benefit of the entire organization is data governance, and when the scope of the managed data is master data, this is known as master data governance.

Master Data Harmonization: A term used to refer to the capabilities that support the integration of business systems with the MDM System and the distribution of master data across the enterprise using application-to-application and data integration techniques.

Master Data Integration: The process used to build and initially populate an MDM System with the source data set.

Master Data Lifecycle Management: Supports the definition, creation, access, and management of master data. Master data must be managed and leveraged effectively throughout its entire lifecycle.

Master Data Repository: Master Data Repository refers to the storage of Instance Master Data, Definition Master Data, Reference Data, History Data, and Metadata.

Master Data Services: The services provide integration of master data, accessing of master data, governance of master data, and managing of master data. Master data services are one kind of information service.

Master Data Store: Repository to store master data.

MDI (Master Data Integration): See "Master Data Integration."

MDM (Master Data Management): Through a combination of architecture, technology, and business processes, MDM provides an approach to incrementally reducing the amount of redundantly managed information and providing information consumers throughout an enterprise with authoritative master data.

MDM Architecture Blueprints: An MDM Architecture Blueprint can serve as the architectural underpinning for an MDM Solution. They can be narrowly applicable to a single industry and use case or can be more generally applicable across multiple industries and use cases.

MDM Architecture Patterns: A collection of architecture patterns that facilitate reuse of MDM implementation experiences to simplify and speed the development of MDM solutions.

MDM Base Services: Provide a set of common services used by the MDM services architecture building block. They are further decomposed into four components: (1) security and privacy services, (2) audit logging services, (3) workflow services, and (4) search services.

MDM Business Blueprints: Similar to architecture blueprints, the MDM Business Blueprints are composed of MDM Business Patterns. They can be cross-industry or very industry-specific. They could also be limited to a specific master data domain or MDM method of use.

MDM Business Patterns: Business patterns describe the actors in a business use case and the interactions between them. MDM Business Patterns apply this idea to the MDM domain.

MDM Coexistence Hub Pattern: This MDM hub pattern corresponds to the coexistence implementation style. An MDM System built with this pattern is a system of reference type MDM hub. The master data is materialized in the Master Data Repository, but changes to master data may still occur—at least to some degree—at the legacy systems.

MDM Component Model: The MDM Component Model refers to the set of technical architecture diagrams and associated descriptions that provide lower-level specifications about the MDM Reference Architecture.

MDM Conceptual Architecture: A description of the key concepts and capabilities of an MDM system and a description of how they interrelate.

MDM Data Model: Logical and physical data models for a given collection of MDM domains.

MDM Event Management Services: A set of services that can be used to detect relevant conditions in the MDM context and take a corresponding action.

MDM Hub: An MDM System built and implemented with a certain MDM hub pattern will be called an MDM hub.

MDM Hub Patterns: The MDM Hub patterns are one out of four types of MDM architecture patterns. They bring together the method of use, implementation style, and the system type.

MDM Hierarchy and Relationship Management Services: MDM Hierarchy and Relationship Management Services establish and manage master data relationships, organize master data entities into hierarchies and groupings, and create multiple views of master data hierarchies.

MDM Implementation Styles: Different combinations of implementation and usage requirements have led to the evolution of a number of MDM implementation styles. In essence, there are four implementation styles: Consolidation, Registry, Coexistence, and the Transactional Hub.

MDM Interface Services: The MDM Interface Services component provides a consistent entry point for requesting MDM Services and for MDM Services to interact with external IT components within the overall MDM Solution architecture. MDM Interface Services support multiple integration techniques to request a MDM Lifecycle Management Service, such as to create or access master data.

MDM Lifecycle Management Services: MDM Lifecycle Management Services provide business and information services by master data domain to create, access, and manage master data held within the MDM Master Data Repository.

MDM Logical Architecture: The MDM Logical Architecture is a decomposition of the MDM Conceptual Architecture into a more detailed representation for IT and business users.

MDM Master Data Repository: MDM Master Data Repository refers to the Instance Master Data, Definition Master Data, Reference Data, History Data, and Metadata that reside in the Master Data management services architecture building block.

MDM Method of Use: The three key patterns or methods for using an MDM system are operational, collaborative, and analytical. These methods often reflect the primary consumers of the master data.

MDM Operational Model: An MDM Operational Model represents a physical description of an MDM Solution architecture, identifying the physical components and their connectivity, the network topology, and software placement, including versions of software and key software components.

MDM Privacy: Privacy is focused on the appropriate use of personal data based on regulation and the explicit consent of the Party. MDM Systems that have Party data (customer or patient) are quite sensitive to privacy concerns and regulations.

MDM RA (Reference Architecture): The MDM RA is an industry-agnostic reference architecture that supports implementing the multiple methods of use for Master Data Management and multiple implementation styles, and enables the ability to design business solutions incorporating MDM capabilities.

MDM Registry Hub Pattern: This MDM hub pattern corresponds to the registry implementation style. This pattern represents a system of reference for master data. Usually, only the critical attributes need to be materialized so that uniqueness of master data records can be enforced.

MDM Security: Security in MDM is focused on controlling access to master data. There are multiple security enforcement points within an MDM environment; these are business security services, security policy management, and IT security services.

MDM Solution: An MDM Solution addresses the MDM-related problems and challenges that exist in a specific customer situation; it is comprised of those MDM components that need to be complemented mainly with an MDM strategy, a set of architectures, products and technologies, and best practices.

MDM Solution Blueprint: An MDM Solution Blueprint is composed of one or multiple MDM Architecture Blueprint(s) as well as the corresponding MDM Business Blueprint(s). That is, an MDM Solution Blueprint has an architectural as well as a business representation or facet. This synergistic correspondence between the business and the IT domains is an underlying premise that drives deployments of any MDM Solution.

MDM System: The collection of MDM Services defined within the Master Data Management Services architecture building block that deliver MDM functionality.

MDM System of Record: The most current and accurate source of MDM data, which serves as a point of distribution and usage for authoritative master data.

MDM System of Reference: An authoritative source of master data that is synchronized with a system of record. A system of reference contains high-quality data that may not be as current as that in a system of record.

MDM Transaction Hub Pattern: This MDM hub pattern corresponds to the transaction implementation style. It is the only means to build a system of record-type MDM hub. The master data is fully materialized.

MDM Workflow Services: MDM Workflow Services are contained within the MDM Base Services component. These services provide the ability to model and manage a workflow for the associated user and system activities that support the authoring of master data, a business process, or a data governance process. These services may also delegate work to external providers.

Metadata: In general terms, we will use the term metadata for descriptive information that is useful for people or systems to understand something. Common examples include a database catalog or an XML schema, both of which describe the structure of data.

MiFID (Markets in Financial Instruments Directive): See Appendix C.

MLLP (Minimal Lower Level Protocol): See Appendix D.

MMD (Managed Master Data): Refers to the active management of master data in an enterprise. Without managed master data, it is very difficult to get a complete view of such a customer or product and determine its value to the enterprise.

MPI: Master Patient Index.

MTBF: Mean Time Between Failure.

MTTF: Mean Time To Failure.

MTTR: Mean Time To Recovery.

Multiform MDM: Master Data Management systems that enable multiple domains of master data and that support multiple implementation styles and methods of use are sometimes also called Multiform MDM Systems.

NAT: Network Address Translation.

NDC: National Drug Code.

New York State Insurance Regulation: See Appendix C.

NGOSS: New Generation Operations System and Software.

Non-Repudiation Services: These services protect the requestor and provider from false denials that data has been sent or received. They aim to prevent parties in a communication from falsely denying having taken part in that communication.

NPI: New Product Introduction.

OASIS: Organization for the Advancement of Structured Information.

ODS: Operational Data Store

OFAC: Office of Foreign Assets Control): See Appendix C.

OHF (Open Healthcare Framework): See Appendix D.

OLAP: Online Analytical Processing.

OLTP: Online Transaction Processing.

ONS (Object Naming Service): See Appendix D.

OOD & OOP: Object Oriented Design and Programming.

Open Standards: See Appendix D.

Operational MDM: In the Operational style of MDM, the MDM server acts as an Online-Transaction Processing (OLTP) system, responding to requests from multiple applications and users.

OSI: Open Systems Interconnection.

Part 8 of the Proceeds of Crime Act 2002, United Kingdom: See Appendix C.

Patterns: Patterns provide a proven solution to a repeating problem in a given context. In other words, patterns should be considered as a way to put artifacts into context and to describe a reusable solution to a recurring problem. These artifacts can be best practices, guidelines, services, blueprints, source code skeletons, and frameworks.

PCI-DSS (Payment Card Industry—Data Security Standard): See Appendix C.

PDA: Personal Digital Assistant.

PDMA (Prescription Drug Marketing Act) of 1988, United States: See Appendix C.

PDP (Policy Decision Point): Administrators will update security policies through the resource managers, or administer policies through appropriate PDPs. Policy Enforcement Points rely on PDPs to make decisions. These PDPs contain the security policies defined in the infrastructure.

PDQ: Patient Demographic Query.

PEP (Policy Enforcement Point): Access to a resource is controlled by an appropriate resource manager, which is the logical PEP corresponding to that resource. In a typical deployment, you can find several enforcement points.

PHI (Protected Health Information): See Appendix D.

PII: Personally Identifiable Information.

PIPEDA (Personal Information Protection and Electronic Documents Act) of 2000, Canada: See Appendix C.

PIPL (Personal Information Protection Law) of 2003, Japan: See Appendix C.

PIM (Product Information Management): MDM Systems that focus exclusively on managing the descriptions of products are also call PIM systems.

PIX: Patient Index Cross-Referencing.

Policy Management: A mechanism to create policies based on business drivers and influencing factors (like trust and identity) and distribute them in a consistent manner to all of the relevant components within a logical deployment architecture. Policy management is fundamental to the success of enterprise security architecture. There are three aspects to policy: the abstraction level of policies, lifecycle management of policies, and the domains that policies can be applied to.

Privacy: Privacy is concerned with the appropriate use of personal data based on regulation and the explicit consent of the party.

Process-Focused Application Integration Pattern: This is one out of four types of architecture patterns for MDM. This is a wide range of architecture patterns that describe how to integrate application systems with a focus on the process and workflow capabilities. One of the most important sub-patterns in this category of MDM architecture patterns is the transaction interception pattern.

Profiling: Data profiling (and analysis services) provides functionality to understand the quality, structure, and relationships of data across enterprise systems, from which data cleansing and standardization rules can be determined for improving the overall data quality and consistency.

Provenance: See "data lineage."

Public Data Pools: Data pools such as 1SYNC.

Public-Key Cryptography: Also known as asymmetric cryptography, a form of cryptography in which a user has a pair of cryptographic keys—a public key and a private key. The private key is kept secret, while the public key may be widely distributed. The keys are related mathematically, but the private key cannot be practically derived from the public key. A message encrypted with the public key can be decrypted only with the corresponding private key.

QoS: Quality of Service.

R&C: Risk & Compliance.

RACF: Resource Access Control Facility.

RAID: Redundant Array of Independent Drives.

Reference Data: Reference data is focused on defining and distributing collections of common values to support accurate and efficient processing of operational and analytical activities.

Registry Hub Pattern: The Registry Hub pattern belongs to the MDM Hub patterns, and corresponds to the registry implementation style.

Registry Implementation Style: The registry implementation style can be useful for providing a read-only source of master data as a reference to downstream systems. It holds the minimum amount of information required to uniquely identify a master data record; it also cross-references to detailed information that is managed within other systems and databases.

Regulatory Compliance: See "R&C."

REST (Representational State Transfer): See Appendix D.

RFC: Remote Function Call.

RFID (Radio Frequency Identification): See Appendix D.

RMI: Remote Method Invocation.

RP (Reverse Proxy): The RP is a module in the component relationship diagram of the MDM Reference Architecture. The RP component provides management of IP traffic, leveraging caching and security functionality and encrypted connections to the Presentation Services components.

RPC: Remote Procedure Call.

RSA (Rivest, Shamir, Adleman) Cryptography: RSA is a public-key cryptosystem for both encryption and authentication; it was invented in 1977 by Ron Rivest, Adi Shamir, and Leonard Adleman.

RSS (Really Simple Syndication): See Appendix D.

Runtime Patterns: Application patterns can be implemented by runtime patterns that demonstrate nonfunctional, service-level characteristics such as performance, capacity, scalability, and availability. Runtime patterns describe key resource constraints and best practices.

SAML (Security Assertions Markup Language): See Appendix D.

Sarbanes-Oxley (SOX) Act of 2002, United States: See Appendix C.

SCM: Supply Chain Management.

Security Policy Management: Effective management of security policies requires a holistic approach that manages security policies throughout the lifecycle of applications. Security policy management begins with authoring business policies that are refined to service specific policies such as security, performance indicators, metrics, trust policies, and so on.

SEI CMMI (Software Engineering Institute Capability Maturity Model Integration): The CMMI is a process capability maturity model that aids in the definition and understanding of an organization's processes. These models are not processes or process descriptions, but they provide guidance to use when developing processes.

SEIM (Security Event and Incident Management): SEIM is related to intrusion detection and prevention; it involves processing of incoming events from various sources to detect security penetration attempts.

SGTIN (Serialized Global Trade Identification Number): The SGTIN is an extension of the GS1 Global Trade Item Number (GTIN) that assigns company prefixes and item references for use in identifying a particular class of object.

SID (Shared Information/Data Model): See Appendix D.

SLA: Service Level Agreement.

SME: Subject Matter Expert.

SMTP: Simple Mail Transfer Protocol.

SNOMED (Systematized Nomenclature of Medicine): See Appendix D.

SOA: Service Oriented Architecture.

SOA Governance: SOA governance is the set of activities related to the lifecycle and control of reusable business services, where information service governance is a subset of SOA Governance.

SOA Management: The execution of the underlying infrastructure that supports service life-cycle management.

SOA Management Layers: In the context of an SOA Architecture, there are three SOA management layers: business service management, composite application management, and resource management.

SOAP (Simple Object Access Protocol): See Appendix D.

SOAP/HTTP: SOAP over HTTP.

SOE: Service Oriented Enterprise.

Solvency II, European Union: See Appendix C.

SOX (Sarbanes-Oxley Act): See Appendix C.

SP: Stored Procedure.

SPML: Service Provisioning Markup Language.

SPNEGO: Simple and Protected GSS-API Negotiation.

SRR: Service Registry and Repository.

SSL (Secure Sockets Layer): See Appendix D.

SSN: Social Security Number.

SSO: Single Sign-On.

Staleness of Data: Data staleness reflects the propagation delay from when a change occurs to when that change is reflected by other systems.

Star Schema: Star schemas or snowflake schemas are the common data models for data warehouses to represent the relationship between the facts to be analyzed and the dimensions by which the analysis is done.

STS: Security Token Service.

SWIFT (Society for Worldwide Interbank Financial Telecommunication): See Appendix D.

Symmetric-Key Cryptography: Describes algorithms that use trivially related, often identical, cryptographic keys for both decryption and encryption.

TCO: Total Cost of Ownership

The Do-Not-Call Implementation Act of 2003, United States: See Appendix C.

TLS: Transport Layer Security.

TOG: The Open Group.

Transaction Hub Pattern: The Transaction Hub pattern belongs to the MDM Hub patterns, and corresponds to the transaction implementation style.

Transaction Implementation Style: A transactional implementation style is a centralized, complete set of master data for one or more domains. It is a system of record, serving as the single version of truth for the master data it manages. A transactional hub is part of the operational fabric of an IT environment, receiving and responding to requests in a timely manner.

Transaction Interception Pattern: This application integration pattern describes how existing business transactions can be intercepted to capture and forward master data changes.

Trust Management: Addresses trusted relationships between entities like organizations, enterprises, identities, security domains, and systems. These relationships can be system-to-system, business-to-business, and so on. Trust Management addresses both business and technology.

TTM: Time To Market.

UCC: Uniform Code Council.

UCCNet: Standards organization

UDEX (Universal Descriptor Exchange): A product classification that will be aligned with the GPC classification so that information between the two can be more freely and easily exchanged.

UDF: User Defined Function.

UI: User Interface.

ULAC (Use, Lose, Abuse, and Confuse) Method: Allows for a qualitative approach to looking and estimating the value and risks associated with master data.

UMD (Unmanaged Master Data): Master data within environments that have multiple, often inconsistent, repositories of master data.

UMTS: Universal Mobile Telecommunications System.

UNSPSC (United Nations Standard Products and Services Code): See Appendix D.

UPC (Universal Product Code): A specific type of barcode that is widely used in the United States and Canada for tracking trade items in stores.

URI: Unique Resource Identifier.

URL: Unique Resource Locator.

USA Patriot Act of 2001, United States: See Appendix C.

VAT: Value Added Tax.

VIN: Vehicle Identification Number.

Virtual Record: A construct that results from the dynamic aggregation of structured and unstructured content about a master data entity.

VPN: Virtual Private Network.

WHO: World Health Organization.

WIP: Work In Progress visibility solution.

WS-Addressing (Web Services Addressing): See Appendix D.

WS-CDL (Web Services Choreography Definition Language): See Appendix D.

WSDL (Web Service Description Language): See Appendix D.

Web Services Management (WS-Management): See Appendix D.

WS-Policy (Web Services Policy): See Appendix D.

WSRP (Web Services for Remote Portals): See Appendix D.

WS-Security (Web Services Security SOAP Message Security): See Appendix D.

WS-SecurityPolicy (Web Services Security Policy Language): See Appendix D.

WS-Trust (Web Services Trust): See Appendix D.

XACML (eXtensible Access Control Markup Language): See Appendix D.

XA Transaction Manager: See Appendix D.

XML (eXtensible Markup Language): See Appendix D.

XSD (XML Schema Definition): See Appendix D.

Index

M

Security Administrator role, 526–527
Security Assertions Markup Language (SAML), 569
Security considerations in MDM
  access management, 183
  audit, 180, 185–186
  audit trail, definition, 180
  authenticated identity, 182
  authentication, definition, 179–180
  Authentication Services, 183
  authorization, 180,183–185
  confidentiality, definition, 179
  data protection, 186–187
  identity, definition, 179
  identity management, 183
  identity mapping, 180, 182–183
  identity propagation, 180, 182–183
  identity provisioning, 180, 182–183
  Identity Services, 183
  identity token, 180
  integrity, definition, 179
  MDM Reference Architecture, 180–181
  PDP (Policy Decision Point), 180
  PEP (Policy Enforcement Point), 180
  policies, definition, 179
  Policy Management, 183
  reverse proxy, 180
  sign-on, 180
  trust management, 183
  user registry, 180
Security enablers
  CMDB (Configuration Management Database), 195
  cryptographic hardware, 195
  cryptographic key management, 195
  cryptography, 195
  Directory Server, 195
  firewalls, 196
  hardware key storage, 195
  intrusion detection, 196
  intrusion prevention, 196
  isolation, 196
  key management, 195
  malware protection, 196
  registries and repositories, 195
  SEIM (Security Event and Incident Management), 196
  service registry, 195
  time, 196
Security policy management
  monitoring and reporting, 199
  overview, 197
  PDP (Policy Decision Point), 198–199
  PEP (Policy Enforcement Point), 198–199
  policy administration, 197–198
  policy decision and enforcement, 198–199
  policy distribution and transformation, 198
Security Token Service (STS), 205–206
SEIM (Security Event and Incident Management), 196
Self-Service Website Solution Blueprint for Telco
  advantages, 437
  alternatives, 437

  billing plans, 425–426
  Blueprint overview, 432–437
  business context, 425-429
  business patterns *versus* architecture patterns, 431–432
  business patterns, 431
  components, 432
  customer creation, 433–435
  customer, 425–427, 427–429
  diagram, 433
  eTOM (enhanced Telecom Operations Map), 432
  extensions, 437
  homezone areas, 425
  integration with external systems, 436–437
  location, 425–427, 427–429
  master data model, 425–429
  network assets, 427–429
  NGOSS (New Generation Operations System and Software), 432
  on-demand services, 428
  overview, 424–425
  ports, 426
  product ordering process, 435–436
  product, 425–427, 427–429
  self-service, customer perspective, 429–430
  self-service, provider perspective, 430–431
  subscribed services, 428
  workflows, 433–437
Serialization
  open standard, 346
  pharmaceutical products, 346
Serialized product movement, 346
Service brokers, 59
Service components
  MDM Logical Architecture, 117
  SOA enterprise architecture, 62
Service consumers, 59, 207–208
Service contracts, 59
Service definitions, 59
Service description, 59
Service granularity
  business mapping, 69, 70–71
  management and governance, 70, 72
  overview, 69
  performance, 69–70, 71
  transaction scope, 70, 71–72
Service identification and categorization, 79–80
Service innovation, 49
Service patterns, 223
Service providers, 59
Service Registry and Repository (SRR), 34, 195
Service Registry component, 141
Service representative call
  Cross- and Up-Sell Solution Blueprint for Banking & Insurance, 401–402
Service reuse, 65–67
Service-Oriented Architecture (SOA). *See* SOA (Service-Oriented Architecture).
Service-oriented design, 113
Service-oriented enterprise (SOE), 57

Safari®

BOOKS ONLINE

ENABLED

THIS BOOK IS SAFARI ENABLED

INCLUDES FREE 45-DAY ACCESS TO THE ONLINE EDITION

The Safari® Enabled icon on the cover of your favorite technology book means the book is available through Safari Bookshelf. When you buy this book, you get free access to the online edition for 45 days.

Safari Bookshelf is an electronic reference library that lets you easily search thousands of technical books, find code samples, download chapters, and access technical information whenever and wherever you need it.

TO GAIN 45-DAY SAFARI ENABLED ACCESS TO THIS BOOK:

- Go to **informit.com/safarienabled**

- Complete the brief registration form

- Enter the coupon code found in the front of this book on the "Copyright" page

If you have difficulty registering on Safari Bookshelf or accessing the online edition, please e-mail customer-service@safaribooksonline.com.